Cultural Anthropology

A Reader for a Global Age

Kenneth J. Guest

Baruch College
The City University of New York

W. W. Norton & Company
New York • London

W. W. Norton & Company has been independent since its founding in 1923, when William Warder Norton and Mary D. Herter Norton first published lectures delivered at the People's Institute, the adult education division of New York City's Cooper Union. The firm soon expanded its program beyond the Institute, publishing books by celebrated academics from America and abroad. By midcentury, the two major pillars of Norton's publishing program—trade books and college texts—were firmly established. In the 1950s, the Norton family transferred control of the company to its employees, and today—with a staff of four hundred and a comparable number of trade, college, and professional titles published each year—W. W. Norton & Company stands as the largest and oldest publishing house owned wholly by its employees.

Editor: Peter Lesser
Associate Editor: Samantha Held
Project Editor: Caitlin Moran
Editorial Assistant: Anna Olcott
Managing Editor, College: Marian Johnson
Managing Editor, College Digital Media: Kim Yi
Production Managers: Ashley Horna and Lisa Kraege
Media Editor: Eileen Connell
Associate Media Editor: Mary Williams
Media Editorial Assistant: Grace Tuttle
Marketing Manager, Cultural Anthropology: Erin Brown
Associate Design Director: Hope Miller Goodell
Designer: Juan Paolo Francisco
Permissions Manager: Megan Schindel
Permissions Associate: Elizabeth Trammell
Composition: Jouve
Manufacturing: Sheridan Books

Permission to use copyrighted material is included on p. A-21.

ISBN 978-1-324-00077-8

W. W. Norton & Company, Inc., 500 Fifth Avenue, New York, NY 10110
wwnorton.com

W. W. Norton & Company Ltd., 15 Carlisle Street, London W1D 3BS
1 2 3 4 5 6 7 8 9 0

About
the Author

Kenneth J. Guest is Professor of Anthropology at Baruch College, CUNY, and author of *God in Chinatown: Religion and Survival in New York's Evolving Immigrant Community*. His research focuses on immigration, religion, globalization, ethnicity, and entrepreneurialism.

Professor Guest's ethnographic research in China and the United States traces the immigration journey of recent Chinese immigrants from Fuzhou, southeast China, who, drawn by restaurant, garment shop, and construction jobs and facilitated by a vast human smuggling network, have revitalized New York's Chinatown. His writing explores the role of Fuzhounese religious communities in China and the United States; the religious revival sweeping coastal China; the Fuzhounese role in the rapidly expanding U.S. network of all-you-can-eat buffets and take-out restaurants; the higher education experiences of the Fuzhounese second generation; and the contestation over Chinatown's future in the face of Manhattan's rapid gentrification.

A native of Florida, Professor Guest studied Chinese at Beijing University and Middlebury College. He received his B.A. from Columbia University (East Asian Languages and Cultures), an M.A. from Union Theological Seminary (Religious Studies), and the M.A., M.Phil., and Ph.D. from The City University of New York Graduate Center (Anthropology).

Contents

key:
- vocab terms
- Important Info
- Names & dates

Part 2: Unmasking the Systems of Power

Preface

Cultural Anthropology: A Reader for a Global Age is designed to introduce students to the voices of anthropologists and the lives of the people they study by exploring ethnography—anthropologists' unique approach to writing about the world.

Ethnographic writing lies at the heart of anthropology. Through ethnography, anthropologists convey our unique research strategies, our deep commitment to cross-cultural understanding and engagement, and our attempts to analyze and make sense of the local challenges and global forces that are reshaping our communities and our planet.

Cultural Anthropology: A Reader for a Global Age introduces 37 ethnographic studies, chosen for their diverse voices, engaging writing, accessibility to undergraduate students, and significance to the core concerns of anthropology today. They represent both new, cutting-edge research and studies that have become classics. It is my hope that through these writings, the rich work of anthropologists will come alive for students over the course of the semester and, in the process, tell the story of the field of anthropology as it is emerging in the twenty-first century.

In the following ethnographies you will learn about the ways anthropologists conduct fieldwork—the unique strategy that anthropologists, particularly cultural anthropologists, have developed to put people first as we analyze how human societies work. And you will meet firsthand people from around the world as they live their lives in the context of enormous local and global change. Fieldwork involves living and working in local communities over an extended period of time as we seek to understand people's everyday lives, to see what they do and to understand why. Through fieldwork we look beyond the taken-for-granted experience of daily life to discover the complex systems of power and meaning that people construct to shape their existence. And we try to see how local lives compare to others and fit into larger human patterns and global contexts. Through the deep relationships developed during intensive cross-cultural fieldwork, the anthropologist—our self-understanding, our empathy for others, and our worldviews—may also be transformed. Through ethnographic writing we hope to share what we have learned and experienced with others and to bring into the public imagination the voices and realities of the people with whom we have lived, worked, and studied.

I hope the stories in this reader will challenge, enlighten, and inspire you as you continue your own journey through this global age.

WHY A NEW READER

The world has changed dramatically in the past 40 years and so has the field of anthropology. *Cultural Anthropology: A Reader for a Global Age* presents anthropology as it is developing in the twenty-first century. By introducing the key thinkers, cutting-edge issues, and foundational theory central to our field today, this reader provides students with insights about how anthropologists are approaching the crucial challenges and questions of our times.

Anthropology for the Twenty-first Century. In this contemporary period of rapid globalization, the movement, connection, and interrelatedness that have always been a part of human reality have intensified and become more explicit. There are no peripheries to humanity. We are all connected. And this reminds us that our actions have consequences for the whole world, not just for our own lives and those of our families and friends. Donna Haraway's cutting-edge work (Chapter 9) challenges us to re-imagine kinship in expansive and multi-species ways as we seek to survive this fraught period of human interaction with the planet.

This focus on connection, interaction, and exchange in a global age is central to the framing of this reader, as is its attention to analyzing cultural systems of power and patterns of inequality. The selections in this reader emphasize contemporary theoretical and methodological approaches, in sharp contrast with existing readers built on earlier theoretical formulations, disciplinary debates, and key figures.

The three readings in the first chapter explicitly introduce students to this book's framework. Jason De León and his students confront the stark realities of migrants crossing the desert between Mexico and the United States. Edith Turner accompanies indigenous Alaskan villagers as they seek redress for the U.S. military nuclear dump causing cancer in their community. And Nancy Scheper-Hughes investigates the global trafficking in human organs from Brazil to India to South Africa. The world anthropologists engage today is shaped by movement and encounters, flows, and frictions.

New Voices and Contemporary Classics. *Cultural Anthropology: A Reader for a Global Age* reflects the field of anthropology as it is developing in the twenty-first century. Classic readings in the field have been included, like Horace Miner's "Body Ritual among the Nacirema," Laura Bohannan's "Shakespeare in the Bush," George Gmelch's "Baseball Magic," and Margaret Mead's "Warfare Is Only an Invention—Not a Biological Necessity." But the core of this reader is the pairing of more contemporary classics from Paul Farmer, Nancy Scheper-Hughes, Lila Abu-Lughod, Emily Martin, and Philippe Bourgois that have transformed the theory and practice of anthropology over the last 30 years with emerging new voices such as Jason De León, Yarimar Bonilla, Jonathan Rosa, Audra Simpson, and Dána-Ain Davis, who are pushing the boundaries and exploring the future of anthropology today. Through these pairings, this reader seeks to give students a sense of the dynamism of anthropology today, the theoretical debates that are shaping the field, and anthropology's relevance to thinking about and engaging the crucial issues of our times.

Innovations for Teaching. *Cultural Anthropology: A Reader for a Global Age* is designed to be used either in tandem with *Cultural Anthropology: A Toolkit for a Global Age* or *Essentials of Cultural Anthropology: A Toolkit for a Global Age* or to stand on its own. The chapter structure of the reader parallels that of the other two books. Readings in each chapter emphasize corresponding key concepts in the textbooks. And extensive headnotes and chapter openers are also aligned. The readings offer students direct access to dynamic ethnographic writing that can help the textbooks come alive.

Instructors considering using the reader on its own will find a strong pedagogical framework for support. Three part-openers introduce major frames of analysis, namely anthropology in the twenty-first century, unmasking systems of power, and change in the modern world. Fifteen chapter openers introduce key concepts and terms crucial to understanding the readings that follow. Each reading is preceded by a headnote providing the student with context and orientation and followed by a set of "Engaging the Text, Engaging the World" questions that challenge students to more deeply explore key concepts in the reading and which can be used effectively as classroom discussion starters, essay topics, or quiz and exam questions.

Relevance. Scientist Neil deGrasse Tyson offered a concise yet profound commencement message this past spring to the graduating class of Baruch College, where I teach. The world is a mess—climate change, inequality, racial injustice—and the speakers up on this stage have failed to fix it. We need you, the next generation, to step up. Trying will not be enough. You will need to succeed.

What does anthropology offer to this generation of students who are preparing to take on the challenges of our time? The stories collected here have inspired me to think more deeply and challenged me to more carefully consider my own commitments to the people and other creatures with whom we share this planet. I hope that you will be inspired and challenged by these voices as well.

ACKNOWLEDGMENTS

Selecting thirty-seven readings from among the thousands of fascinating anthropological books and articles has been a daunting task but made immeasurably easier by the insights and wisdom of many colleagues. I am particularly grateful to Angelique Haugerud, who served as an inspiring interlocutor at the earliest stages of this project, providing ideas and suggestions that helped frame this reader. Carole McGranahan, Hugh Gusterson, Carol Greenhouse, Susan Falls, Dána-Ain Davis, Pat Antoniello, Dillon Mahoney and his graduate seminar at the University of South Florida, Glenn Petersen, Robin Root, Carla Bellamy, Andrew Hernandez, Alessandro Angelini, and especially Chris Baum each made significant contributions along the way, identifying readings and influencing the book's direction. Nancy Aries and John Pelosi offered sage and timely professional advice. The board members of the American Ethnological Society, through meetings, conferences, and conversations, have continued my anthropological education in profound ways.

In the course of assembling this reader, I have benefitted from the advice of many keen reviewers, including:

Julie Adkins, University of Texas, Arlington

Mary Altair, Erie Community College

Matthew Amster, Gettysburg College

Deborah Augsburger, University of Wisconsin-Superior

Jennifer Basquiat, College of Southern Nevada

Laura Bathurst, University of the Pacific

AnnMarie Beasley, American River College

Leslie Berry, De Anza College

Michael Blitz, John Jay College

Jessica Bodoh-Creed, California State University, Los Angeles

Stephanie Borios, Eastern New Mexico University

Julian Brash, Montclair State University

Angela Bratton, Augusta University

Charlanne Burke, York College

Noah Butler, Loyola University

Walter Calgaro, Prairie State College

Karol Chandler-Ezell, Stephen F. Austin State University

Tamara Cheshire, Sacramento City College

Mackenzie Crouse, University of New England

JoAnn D'Alisera, University of Arkansas

Marcus Dean, Houghton College

Jeffrey Debies-Carl, University of New Haven

Michael A. Di Giovine, West Chester University of Pennsylvania

Lindsay Donaldson, Saddleback College

Antoinette Egitto, Metropolitan Community College-Penn Valley

Ryan Ellsworth, Webster University

Oscar Escudero, College of Southern Nevada

Tracy Evans, Fullerton College

Douglas A. Feldman, The College at Brockport, State University of New York

Pamela Ford, Mt. San Jacinto College

Jay Gabriel, Rowan University

Sue-Je Gage, Ithaca College

Ismael Garcia-Colon, College of Staten Island

Shasta Gaughen, California State University, San Marcos

Jonathan Gibson, South Dakota School of Mines and Technology

Katie Gillogly, University of Wisconsin-Parkside

Mario J. Gonzales, New Mexico Highlands University

Tom Gordon, Monroe College

Alexis Gray, Norco College

Paul Hanson, Cuyahoga Community College

Walter Harper, Bridgewater State University

Lori Harrington, Butte College

Jean Hatcherson, Western Connecticut State University

Marc Healy, Elgin Community College

Sherri Hilgeman, Indiana University-Southeast

Servando Z. Hinojosa, University of Texas, Rio Grande Valley

Riley Holt, Tri-County Technical College

Rachel Horner Brackett, Black Hawk College

Aimee Hosemann, University of Texas, Austin

Katharine Hunt, Bellevue College

Brittany Hutton, Nevada State University

Jason James, University of Mary Washington

Ben Junge, State University of New York, New Paltz

Michael Kimball, University of Northern Colorado

Anna Konstantatos, Adelphi University

Adrie Kusserow, St. Michael's College

Patrick Lathrop, Marist College

Lisa Lauria, The College of New Jersey

Linda Light, California State University, Long Beach

Emily Lower, Utah Valley University

Ruth Maher, Seton Hall University

Dillon Mahoney, University of South Florida

Kathe Managan, Louisiana State University

Carole McGranahan, University of Colorado

April Mejia, Norco College

Susan Meswick, Queens College

Sharon Methvin, Mt. Hood Community College

Barbara J. Michael, University of North Carolina, Wilmington

Mark Miller, East Texas Baptist University

Smoki Musaraj, Ohio University

Carol A. Nickolai, Rowan University

Kirsten Olson, Chabot College

Karthik Panchanathan, University of Missouri

Amanda Paskey, Cosumnes River College

Heather Paxson, Massachusetts Institute of Technology

Rakhmiel Peltz, Drexel University

Donald Pollock, State University of New York, Buffalo

Christina Pomianek, Lindenwood University

Amanda Poole, Indiana University of Pennsylvania

Charles Porter, North Central University

Sharon J. Rachele, California State Polytechnic University, Pomona

Margaret Rance, Grossmont College

Eric Rayner, Utah Valley University

Amanda Reinke, University of Tennessee

Audrey Ricke, Indiana University–Purdue University Indianapolis

Bruce Roberts, Minnesota State University Morehead

Robin Root, Baruch College

Vicki Root-Wajda, College of DuPage

Daniel Rosenberg, Earlham College

Patricia Ryan, Indiana University Kokomo

Maureen Salsitz, Cypress College

Lindsay Smith, University of New Mexico

Jennie Smith-Pariola, North Central College

Mary Sundal, Washburn University

Rebecca Todd, Hillsborough Community College

Jaime Ullinger, Quinnipiac University

Bernardo Vallejo, University of Houston Downtown

Julie Vazquez, College of the Canyons

Salena Wakim, Mt. San Jacinto College

Stephen Watters, Los Rios Community College District

Adam Wetsman, Rio Hondo College

I would also like to thank the editors and staff at W. W. Norton for their ongoing commitment to advancing the way anthropology is learned and taught. Pete Lesser, my editor, has guided the development of this reader from its conception, helping to weave it into the fabric of my other books, *Cultural Anthropology: A Toolkit for a Global Age*, *Essentials of Cultural Anthropology*, and *Cultural Anthropology Fieldwork Journal*, and encouraging me to continue to find my own voice in the process. Associate editor Samantha Held has brought a keen eye and a generous spirit to the many tasks that required both imagination and craftsmanship in the creation of this reader. Project editor Caitlin Moran and production managers Ashley Horna and Lisa Kraege facilitated the production process with good humor, efficiency, and critical attention to detail.

None of my writing projects, beginning in graduate school, would have been possible without the support and encouragement of an amazing group of friends and family, including the hospitality of the guys at the Metro Diner—Nick, Marco, and Antonio— and my heroes: Douglas, Marybeth, Julia, Charlene, K, Maria, Dayna, Vicki, Shari, Frances-Helen, and TL.

Finally, I would like to thank my students at Baruch College, City University of New York, who every class ask to be introduced to an anthropology that is relevant to their daily lives, that tackles significant contemporary issues, and that provides them the tools of analysis and empowerment to live awake, conscious, and engaged. This book is dedicated to you and your potential to make the world a better place.

Reading Ethnography

As you read the ethnographies in this book, use the following questions as a guide for thinking more deeply about the lives of the people in each community and the strategies anthropologists use in their research and writing.

1. Anthropologists begin their research with a focus on people in local communities. Who are the key people in the ethnography, and what did you learn about them?

2. Anthropologists are committed to letting local people speak for themselves in their writing. How do local people's voices come through in the ethnography?

3. Anthropology has developed a unique set of research tools and strategies. What tools and research strategies has the anthropologist used?

4. Key to successful research is building relationships of trust. How was rapport established and trust gained between the anthropologist and people in the local community?

5. Communities are not static or fixed in time. What kinds of changes, drama, and conflict do you see described in the ethnography?

6. All human relationships involve power dynamics, and all groups have systems of power that shape access to resources, privileges, and opportunities. What are the systems of power at work in the local community?

7. No communities are isolated. All are connected to increasingly dense networks of globalization. How does the local community described in the ethnography connect to global forces and processes?

8. Anthropologists seek to write narratives that reveal what's really going on in a community and why it matters. When did you feel most engaged in your reading? Why?

9. Ethnographic writing styles allow anthropologists to include themselves in their narratives. What have you learned about the anthropologist in this ethnography?

10. Ethnographies draw readers not only into the life of the community but also into the fieldwork process of the anthropologist. What would you want to ask the ethnographer? What would you want to ask the people in the community?

11. In an era of globalization, anthropologists are increasingly sensitive to the reality that their ethnographic writings will be read by those whose lives are being represented. How do you think the people in this community would respond to this ethnography?

12. Anthropologists conduct research to address an important problem or question. What is the author's main research question? How does the author answer the research question?

13. Anthropology's code of ethics require the researcher to consider the study's impact on the local community and at the very least to do no harm. What do you think the purpose of this research was? Is it benefitting the people in this community?

PART 1
Anthropology in the 21st Century

Anthropology is the study of the full scope of human diversity, past and present, and the application of that knowledge to help people of different backgrounds better understand one another. The roots of anthropology lie in the European economic and colonial expansion of the eighteenth and nineteenth centuries, which increased Europeans' contact with people worldwide. But today, in the twenty-first century, **globalization** is creating an unprecedented level of interaction among people, ideas, and systems that is intensifying at a breathtaking pace. These processes are transforming the cultures and communities anthropologists study and the strategies we use to do our work.

Wherever you may live or go to school, you are probably experiencing a deepening encounter with the world's diversity in your classroom, family, religious community, or workplace. Anthropology today provides a toolkit for understanding this rich diversity of human life and seeing the connections between our particular life experiences and those of others. In the process, anthropology offers us the possibility to see the breadth and scope of what it means to be human and so imagine more fully our own human potential.

Cultural anthropology, the study of people's everyday lives and their communities, provides a unique set of tools for understanding our rapidly changing, globalizing world. In the following pages you will meet firsthand anthropologists practicing their craft, conducting **ethnographic fieldwork** among people around the world. You will hear the voices of anthropologists and the people they study. You will consider communities and events near and far. As you will also see in the following readings, we as anthropologists start our research in local communities: we are committed to understanding the local, everyday lives of the people we study. We then look to see how particular cultures are connected with the rest of humanity. Anthropologists constantly work to bring often-ignored voices into the global conversation. As a result, the field has a history of focusing on the cultures and struggles of non-Western and nonelite people. Today, however, anthropology is truly global in scope, with increasing attention paid to urban communities and developed nations. As we will clearly see in the stories ahead, anthropologists' work is not constrained by geographical boundaries.

Ethnographic fieldwork is the research strategy at the heart of cultural anthropology. Through **participant observation**—living and working with people on a daily basis, often for a year or more—the cultural anthropologist strives to see the world through the eyes of others. Intensive fieldwork has the power to educate and transform the anthropologist. Over time, in living, working, talking, and playing with people whose life experiences are different than ours, even our most fundamental understandings of humans and the world may be shaken and altered. In the process, what has seemed strange may become familiar. And what has seemed familiar may come to feel very strange.

Through fieldwork, anthropologists also look beyond the taken-for-granted, everyday experiences of life to discover the complex systems of power and meaning that all people construct. These include the many systems we will consider throughout this book: race, ethnicity, gender, sexuality, religion, kinship, class, and economic and political systems.

At its core, anthropology challenges us to move beyond **ethnocentrism**—the strong human tendency to believe that one's own culture or way of life is normal, natural, and superior to the beliefs and practices of others. Instead, the anthropologist's toolkit of research strategies and analytical concepts that you will encounter throughout this book enables us to appreciate, understand, and engage diverse human cultures in an increasingly global age.

Today's period of rapid globalization may be intensifying the interactions among people and the flow of goods, technology, money, and ideas within and across national boundaries, but interaction and connection are not new phenomena—they have been central to human history. Anthropologists believe that all humans share complex biological, cultural, economic, and ecological connections. Clearly, some groups of people are less integrated than others into the global system under construction today, but none are completely isolated. And for some, their seeming isolation may be of recent historical origin. Our increasing connection today reminds us that our actions have consequences, not just for our own lives and those of our family and friends, but for all people and even every species on the planet.

How will the stories you read in the following pages transform your understanding of the world and your place in it? How will they reshape and expand your sense of what it means to be human? And how can the tools, experiences, and stories of anthropologists help you to better understand and engage the world as you move through it and, if you so choose, to apply an anthropological perspective to the challenges confronting us and our neighbors around the world?

1

Anthropology in a Global Age

Cultural anthropology is the study of people's everyday lives and their communities—their behaviors, beliefs, and institutions. As we will see throughout this book, cultural anthropologists explore all aspects of human culture, such as war and violence, love and sexuality, religion and migration. They examine what people do and how they live, work, and play together. They search for patterns of meaning embedded within each culture, and they develop theories about how cultures work. Cultural anthropologists also examine the ways in which local communities interact with global forces.

Today anthropology and globalization are intricately intertwined as the increased movement of money, people, goods, and ideas within and across national borders reshapes the local cultures and communities anthropologists study and the ways we conduct our research. Whether we call it a global village or a world without borders, we in the twenty-first century are experiencing a level of inter-action among people, ideas, and systems that is intensifying like we have never seen before. Communication technologies link people instantaneously across the globe (**time-space compression**). Economic activities challenge national boundaries (**flexible accumulation**). People are on the move within countries and among them (**migration**). Violence and terrorism disrupt lives. Humans have had remarkable success at feeding the growing world population, yet income inequality continues to increase—among nations and also within them (**uneven development**). And increasing human diversity on our doorstep opens possibilities for both deeper understanding and greater misunderstanding. Clearly, the human community in the twenty-first century is being drawn further into a global web of interaction. We will turn to the concepts that drive and define these interactions again in Part 3 of this book.

The three readings in this chapter make clear that today it is impossible to study a local community without considering the global forces that affect it, as well as the ways local communities in turn contest and reshape globalization.

Jason De León's study of migrant crossings and death along the United States–Mexico border, Edith Turner's study of indigenous Alaskans' fight against nuclear waste dumping, and Nancy Scheper-Hughes's study of the global trade in human organs all show the ways anthropologists today are engaging in multi-sited ethnographies that trace the movement of ideas, things, power, and people within and between communities on a global scale. And all three readings reveal the dynamic and creative strategies that local communities adopt to reshape the effects of globalization.

The selections in this chapter also provide examples of what anthropologists are increasingly calling engaged anthropology. **Engaged anthropology** seeks to apply the research strategies and analytical perspectives of the discipline to address the concrete challenges facing local communities and the world at large. In this way engaged anthropology challenges the assumptions that anthropology, as a science, should focus solely on producing objective, unbiased, neutral accounts of human behavior and that anthropologists should work as disengaged observers while conducting research. Engaged anthropologists instead argue that in a world of conflict and inequality, social scientists must become active, politically committed, and morally engaged with the communities they study.

As Turner's article makes clear, as globalization intensifies, it escalates the human impact on both the planet and other people. Modern humans and our ancestors have been adapting to changes for millions of years. In fact, perhaps our most distinctive characteristic as humans is our ability to adapt—to figure out how to survive and thrive in a world that is rapidly changing. But to say that humans adapt to the natural world is only part of the story, for humans are actively shaping the natural world as well. Our activities have caused profound changes in the atmosphere, soil, and oceans. Human impact on the planet is so extensive that scholars in many disciplines have come to refer to the current historical period as the **Anthropocene**—a distinct era in which human activity is reshaping the planet in permanent ways. Whereas our ancestors struggled to adapt to the uncertainties of heat, cold, disease, and natural disasters, today we confront changes and social forces that we ourselves have set in motion. These changes include climate change, water scarcity, overpopulation, extreme poverty, biological weapons, the mass movement of migrants and refugees, and nuclear waste and warheads. These pose the greatest risks to human survival.

These changes are happening incredibly rapidly, and the studies by De León, Turner, and Scheper-Hughes explore the resulting transformations that people experience in their lives and communities. Globalization brings uneven benefits that break down along lines of nationality, ethnicity, class, race, gender, age, and legal status. These inequalities give rise to issues that we will consider in depth throughout this book. These changes also mean that anthropologists must adjust our fieldwork strategies to span our subjects' entire reality, a reality that may itself span rural villages, urban cities, and many people and places in between. Learning to think like an anthropologist will enable you to better understand and analyze these crucial issues and more successfully navigate our increasingly interconnected world.

From *The Land of Open Graves*
Jason De León

Migrant life and death across the Mexico–U.S. border

Anthropological work often aims to bring to light the daily life experiences of people made vulnerable by powerful systems of inequality. Jason De León's work bears witness to the brutal experiences of undocumented people crossing the Mexico-United States border through the Sonoran Desert in Arizona. The U.S. government's Prevention Through Deterrence strategy, he argues, deliberately funnels border crossers away from populated areas into the desert to use nature to enforce the border. Migrant deaths in the harsh desert climate thus become a warning to future border crossers. In the following selection, De León and a group of anthropology students in his Undocumented Migrant Project find the body of a woman who has died attempting to cross the desert. They come face to face with, and must grapple with, the human suffering and death that is largely ignored in debates over immigration policy and anti-immigrant discourse.

Prevention Through Deterrence

Notes From a Crime Scene

Drive out in the late afternoon to one of the many hills on the outskirts of the tiny Arizona town of Arivaca and look west. You will see the golden sun creep behind the Baboquivari Mountains. The vanishing orb makes it look as if the distant peaks and valleys have been cut out of thick black construction paper. It's the stenciled silhouette you see in old western films. For an hour or so, the backlit barren landscape glows as though it's slowly being covered in liquid amber. The beauty of this Sonoran Desert sunset is overwhelming. It can convince you that there is goodness in nature. It will make you briefly forget

From Jason De León. 2015. *The Land of Open Graves: Living and Dying on the Migrant Trail*. Berkeley: University of California Press. Some of the author's notes have been omitted.

how cruel and unforgiving this terrain can be for those caught in it during the height of summer. Right now I'm dreaming about that sunset; visualizing my hand plunging into a watery ice chest full of cold beers. I can feel the touch of the evening breeze on my skin. These are the tricks you play in your head during the dog days of July in the desert.

The Norwegian explorer Carl Lumholtz once wrote that the summer heat in the Sonoran Desert felt like "walking between great fires" (Lumholtz 1990:37). That's putting it nicely. Right now it feels more like walking directly through flames. Despite the protection of my wide-brimmed cowboy hat, the sides of my face are sunburned after only a few minutes of exposure. Tiny water-filled blisters are starting to form on my temples, cheeks, and other places that get exposed to the sun when I lift my head or stare up at the empty blue sky. I try not to look up unless I have to duck under a mesquite tree or the trail makes a hard break left or right. Better to keep your gaze downward to watch for sunbathing rattlesnakes and ankle-twisting cobbles.

Sweat beads up and rolls off my chin, leaving behind a trail of droplets on the ground as I walk. It takes only a few seconds for these splashes to evaporate. My clothes, on the other hand, are soaking wet. I find myself periodically shivering and getting dizzy; my body is working hard to make sense of this inferno. The overpriced backpack I am wearing has started to heat up along with the water bottles it contains. This means that from here on out, every time I try to quench my thirst, it's like drinking soup. It is easily over a 100 degrees and it is only 10 A.M. My sunset and cold beer fantasies are starting to lose their efficacy. Mike Wells and I are climbing through the Tumacácori Mountains with my longtime friend Bob Kee, member of the southern Arizona humanitarian group the Tucson Samaritans. Bob has been haunting these trails for years, leaving food and water for unseen migrants and occasionally giving first aid to abandoned souls he comes across.

It's a rough path full of sharp-angled rocks and angry mesquites whose branches all seem to be aiming for your eyes. We are moving at a fast clip, which is typical for any outing led by Bob. He is almost thirty years our senior, but is running us ragged as we struggle to keep up. * * * I am convinced he seeks out the most arduous routes just to make sure that those he takes into the desert get a sense of how punishing this environment can be for migrants and anyone else who dares to hike this terrain in the middle of a summer day. "We're almost there. I promise," Bob says. I force a smile because in the past when he has told me this, it was a white lie to make me feel better. "Almost there" is one of Bob's euphemisms for "four more miles to go." On this day, however, the tone in his voice is different. He is not his normal jovial self. He hasn't been joking around, which usually includes offering to carry me on his back. It is clear that he is on a mission. We round a bend and stop. Bob calmly says: "This is the spot where I found the person. The sheriff's department came out and took away what we could find, but it was getting dark and we didn't have a lot of time to go over the entire area. It was mostly arm and leg bones and some pieces of clothing. I want to see if we can find the head. That would make it easier to identify the body. I'm sure there are still bones out here."

Just a few weeks earlier Bob had encountered the fragmented and skeletonized remains of a border crosser in this area. It was the second person he had found in under a month. He called the police, who sent two detectives out to remove what bones they could find. Bob says they spent five minutes poking around before they called it quits. It was too damn hot and the cops were unprepared and unmotivated to do a large-scale survey. Besides, searching for the bones of dead "illegals" has never been a top priority for any law enforcement agency out here. The three of us have returned and are now looking for the rest of what was once a living, breathing person.

Bob is right. There are bones that the detectives overlooked, but we have to cover a lot of ground before we find any of them. There are pieces strewn everywhere. We walk downslope and see part of an articulated arm wedged between two rocks. Aside from sinew still holding the bones together, it has been picked clean of skin and muscle by an unknown creature. Further up the trail I notice several white flecks that stand out against the red mountain soil. It looks as if someone dropped a box of blackboard chalk on the ground. I get closer and realize they are splinters of human bone, mostly sun-bleached rib fragments that have been cracked and gnawed by some long-gone animal. Just off the trail I spot a complete tooth lying on top of a rock. This dental find gives us hope that the skull is nearby.

We start a desperate search for this person's head. Rocks are overturned. Subterranean nests are probed. Bleeding hands blindly grope under thick brush in hopes of finding bones that may have been squirreled away by scavengers or deposited by monsoon flood waters. Everyone is moving with great urgency despite the debilitating heat. After forty-five minutes of intensive survey, we give up. There is no skull. There are no other teeth. We do, however, come across a pair of worn-out hiking boots in close proximity to some of the bones. Where the hell is the skull? I start imagining what has happened to it. A montage of laughing vultures rips this person's eyeballs out of the sockets. I hallucinate two coyotes batting the head around like a soccer ball so that they can access brain matter through the foramen magnum. It's a moment when you despise the capacity of the human imagination. People whose loved ones have disappeared in this desert will tell you that it's the not knowing what happened to them coupled with the flashes of grotesque possibility that drive you insane.

Mike starts snapping photographs while Bob collects bones. The gnarled arm fragment goes into a black trash bag. The ribs and tooth fall into a Ziploc. Bob scribbles down the GPS coordinates and will later deliver the remains to the sheriff's office, where he will be scolded for "disturbing a crime scene." The irony of the statement is that the police were already out here once and Bob is simply collecting what they overlooked during their hasty survey. The fact of the matter is that although this is a crime scene, few people actually care or want to know what has happened here. For many Americans, this person—whose remains are so ravaged that his or her sex is unknown—is (was) an "illegal," a noncitizen who broke US law and faced the consequences. Many of these same people tell themselves that if they can keep calling them "illegals," they can avoid speaking their names or imagining their faces. The United States might be a nation founded by immigrants, but that was a long time ago. Countless citizens today suffer historical amnesia and draw stark divisions between the "noble" European immigrants of the past and Latino border crossers of today. How quickly they forget about the violent welcome receptions that America threw for the Irish, Chinese, and many other newly arrived immigrant groups. The benefit of the chronological distance from the pain and suffering of past migrations is that many Americans today have no problem putting nationality before humanity. A cursory glance at the online comment section of a recent article titled "Border Crossing Deaths More Common as Illegal Immigration Declines" (Moreno 2012) provides insight into some of the more extreme anti-immigrant perspectives on migrant death:

> I'm not condoning deaths or anything, and I do think it's cruel to let a human being die in pain, but in a way isn't it better? I mean after all some of these people are risking their lives because there are nothing better [*sic*] back home, and if they die on the way, at least they end their sufferings [*sic*]. (Moreno 2012)

> Since it is a common practice to print indications on everything in the US, and since just printed indications will not . . . [deter] people from entering the US illegaly [*sic*], why not . . . take some of those dried out corpses, hang them at the places where they [migrants] are known to cross with a legend, "This may be you in a couple of days." (Oscar329, 8/18/2012, in Moreno 2012)

When you see such comments, which accompany practically every article about migrant death on the Internet, you think you're mistakenly reading the American Voices column from the satirical newspaper *The Onion*. It should be easy to dismiss responses like these as extreme forms of Internet hate speech, but this disregard for the lives of undocumented people and the idea that dead bodies should act as a form of deterrence to future migrants are fundamental components of the US federal government's current border security strategy.

But that fact doesn't really matter as we survey the ground for more human remains. The desert has already started to erase this person, along with whatever violence and horror she or he experienced. This event will soon be forgotten before it was ever known.

Bone Dust: Rendering Bare Life

Many border researchers turn to Giorgio Agamben's influential work on sovereignty, law, and individual rights to understand the role that the physical space between adjoining nations plays in the construction of citizens, noncitizens, and state power (Agamben 1998, 2005). Agamben's *state of exception*—the process whereby sovereign authorities declare emergencies in order to suspend the legal protections afforded to individuals while simultaneously unleashing the power of the state upon them—is a particularly salient concept for those working on the margins of nation-states. It is here that the tensions of sovereignty and national security are both geolocated and visibly acted out on a daily basis (Jones 2009). Like Agamben's characterization of the concentration camp, the spatial arrangement of borders often allows a space to exist outside the bounds of normal state or moral law. Border zones become *spaces of exception*—physical and political locations where an individual's rights and protections under law can be stripped away upon entrance. Having your body consumed by wild animals is but one of many "exceptional" things that happen in the Sonoran Desert as a result of federal immigration policies.

Roxanne Doty has pointed out that the US-Mexico border forms an exemplary space of exception where those seeking to enter the country without permission are often reduced to *bare life*—individuals whose deaths are of little consequence—by border policies that do not recognize the rights of unauthorized migrants (Doty 2011). At the same time, these policies expose noncitizens to a state-crafted geopolitical terrain designed to deter their movement through suffering and death (Cornelius 2001; Nevins 2005). The perception that the lives of border crossers are insignificant is reflected in both their treatment by federal immigration enforcement agencies and in the pervasive anti-immigrant discourse, including the online comments cited above. Contributing to this dehumanization is the fact that the Sonoran Desert is remote, sparsely populated, and largely out of the American public's view. This space can be policed in ways that would be deemed violent, cruel, or irrational in most other contexts. Just imagine how people would react if the corpses of undocumented Latinos were left to rot on the ninth hole of the local golf course or if their sun-bleached skulls were piled up in the parking lot of the neighborhood McDonald's.

*   *   *

I often think about this particular day, for two reasons. First, we know this death and its physical erasure are by no means a unique event. Between October 2000 and September 2014, the bodies of 2,721 border crossers were recovered in southern Arizona alone.[1] Approximately 800 of these individuals are still unidentified (Reineke 2013). Second, this particular moment in the desert perfectly illustrates the structure, logic, and corporeal impact of current US border enforcement policy. This point was driven home in the spring of 2012 when I visited the Juan Bosco migrant shelter in Nogales. The stucco walls of this nonprofit organization are always decorated with glossy Mexican government fliers that warn about the conditions in the desert, oversized maps produced by the group Humane Borders showing locations of border crosser deaths, and photocopied posters put up by family members of missing migrants. It wasn't until 2012, though, that I noticed for the first time a tiny sign on the wall of the men's bathroom that had been produced by the US Department of Homeland Security. In Spanish the flier warned, "The next time you try to cross the border without documents you could end up a victim of the desert." This line was accompanied by a pathetic cartoon drawing of a saguaro cactus.

---

1. Data from "Deaths on the Border and the Recovered Remains Project," Coalición de Derechos Humanos, http://derechoshumanosaz.net/projects/arizona-recovered-bodies-project/.

I laughed at this crude representation of the desert, but also started thinking about how this was one of the few times I had seen a warning sign produced by the US government in a Mexican shelter. More interesting, however, was that the wording of the pamphlet personified the desert as a perpetrator of violence targeting migrants. Conveniently, this flier contains no mention of the tactical relationship between federal border enforcement policy and this harsh landscape. When put in historical context, however, this public service announcement offers insight into the structure of the Prevention Through Deterrence (PTD) strategy that since the 1990s has deliberately funneled people into the desert. It also illustrates the cunning way that nature has been conscripted by the Border Patrol to act as an enforcer while simultaneously providing this federal agency with plausible deniability regarding blame for any victims the desert may claim. * * *

Connecting the Dots

Since the beginning of PTD, both the number of people who have been apprehended in the remote regions of Arizona and the annual rate of migrant fatalities have risen steeply. * * * Although Prevention Through Deterrence redirected people toward more "hostile" ground, it has not significantly dissuaded would-be crossers, a point recognized as early as 2001 by the GAO: "Although INS has realized its goal of shifting illegal alien traffic away from urban areas, this has been achieved at a cost to . . . illegal aliens. . . . In particular, rather than being deterred from attempting illegal entry, many aliens have instead risked injury and death by trying to cross mountains, deserts, and rivers" (GAO 2001:3). Many have died since the implementation of this policy, and the correlation between the funneling of people toward desolate regions of the border and an upsurge in fatalities is strong (Rubio-Goldsmith et al. 2006; D. Martinez et al. 2013). * * *

A conservative estimate is that 5,596 people died while attempting to migrate between 1998 and 2012 (Anderson 2013: table 1); and between 2000 and September 2014, the bodies of 2,771 people were found in southern Arizona,[2] enough corpses to fill the seats on fifty-four Greyhound buses. These grim figures represent only *known* migrant fatalities. Many people may die in remote areas and their bodies are never recovered. The actual number of people who lose their lives while migrating will forever remain unknown.

*   *   *

Exposure

Left Behind

The trail had been cold for years. I first walked it in 2009 when I made my initial fieldwork trip to Arizona. During that visit, the area was a debris field of Red Bull cans, potato chip bags, dusty blue jeans, and various other items that people fleeing Border

---

2. "Deaths on the Border and the Recovered Remains Project."

Patrol had either intentionally discarded or accidently lost along the way. It was an active landscape then. The fresh footprints of agents and the people they were chasing were clearly visible in the dirt and sand. A mosaic of heavy and imposing military-style boot prints mixed with the light impressions left by sneakers. Sometimes you would see fragments of shirts caught in the trees or freshly broken branches signaling where someone had recently tried to bushwhack. Walking through that part of the desert, you knew you were in the middle of something but couldn't quite see it. Movement was happening, but it was in your blind spot.

One of the first migrant sites that I visited on that trail, later designated BK-3[3], felt fresh and overwhelming. There were mountains of backpacks, arroyos swollen with tangled clothes. The items left behind were shiny and new. Food containers were still sealed or their contents only half eaten. Animals and insects had not had time to finish off the perishables. Bottles still had water in them. It was like entering into some strange village where the sound of the anthropologist's footsteps had sent everyone running mid-meal. During the initial summer we worked on that trail, I was constantly worried that we would accidentally walk up on some unsuspecting group of people resting in the shadows. Although we didn't see anyone out there that year, it was clear we weren't alone.

When I returned in 2010, many of the things left by migrants had been removed by some unknown person or organization. The desert had been decontaminated, its ghosts cleansed. Most of the evidence of hidden human occupation had been picked up and no doubt sent straight to the trash dump. What remained was largely sun bleached, worn, and breaking apart. After only a year, objects that had once seemed alive and vibrant were slowly dying, victims of solar radiation and rain. People assume that plastic water bottles and nylon backpacks will lie intact on the desert surface forever. It's not true. Things out here fall apart. Clothes are reduced to shreds, leaving only the stitching behind. Backpacks evaporate leaving only metal zippers and polyurethane buckles. Water bottles turn brittle, crack into pieces, and blow away. When I visited again in 2011, barely anything was left to signal that people had once existed here. Nothing on the landscape suggested this route was used anymore.

The trail had become well known to law enforcement after a few years of heavy use. Some of the migrant sites in the area that we documented in 2009 were so large that we could see them using Google Earth. If we could do that, Border Patrol could no doubt spot them from the air-conditioned seats in the helicopters that border crossers refer to as *el mosco* (the fly). After many chases and arrests, the spot had become burned. *La migra* [Border Patrol] was smart about it. They started placing underground motion sensors along the trail to alert them anytime someone passed through. Migrants and smugglers are smarter. They simply stopped using the route altogether and moved someplace else. There is always a canyon or mountain trail that *la migra* doesn't know about or that is

---

3. BK stands for "Bob Kee" and represents sites he showed me in the winter and summer of 2009.

too difficult for them to access on foot. Over five years of hiking, we rarely encountered Border Patrol agents on foot. They often lack the fortitude or motivation to head deep into the brush. Better to sit in your vehicle with a can of Skoal Long Cut Wintergreen and listen for ground sensor alerts. Migrants just keep heading deeper and deeper into the wild. Many get so deep that they eventually just disappear.

*   *   *

On the morning of July 2, 2012, I decide on a whim to revisit this old trail to check out a cleaned-up site that we have been studying as part of an ongoing project on desert conservation and its impacts on migrant material culture. We expect to find very little in the way of artifacts and certainly no people. I want to show a group of students what it looks like when the evidence of migration disappears. We park our rented SUV and begin the three-mile hike toward a high clearing near Lobo Peak that once had hundreds of backpacks strewn across its surface. Our caravan starts the long and arduous climb up and down several large rolling hills. We intermittently snake down into washes where the soft sand makes each step more difficult than the last. All we encounter are a few scattered remnants of backpacks and clothes. A weather-stressed shoe. An empty, rusted can of tuna.

Our group drops into a steep ravine after noticing a torn black tarp and a water bottle buried under a large mesquite tree. At one point someone hid here but the material looks old. Olivia Waterhouse, an undergraduate at Barnard College and one of the more precocious students in the group, decides to take a closer look. She wedges herself deep into the underbrush and pulls out a twisted wreckage of muddy clothes and plastic sheeting. The stuff has been there for a while, and it is difficult to determine what the items originally looked like. She keeps digging and, to our surprise, finds a vibrantly colored *serape* (Mexican blanket) buried deep beneath the pile of soiled clothes. The plastic sheeting has somehow protected it from several seasons of rain and mud flow. The blanket's lines of deep blue and red cut a sharp contrast with the brown backdrop of the desert. It could have just come off a loom and is an unexpected find on a day when our goal is to find nothing. We deem the site too deteriorated to warrant filling out a field form. Still, we can't leave the blanket behind. It is so rare to find something that beautiful and out of place in this context. "Take a GPS reading and bag it," I say. Olivia puts it into her pack and we move on.

We come out of the ravine and begin the ascent up a hill toward a site known as BK-5. It's a long, slow climb, the type you feel in your upper thighs and chest. The grade is deceiving and it's not usually until you're midway that you realize how tough the hike is. * * * The student leading our group hurriedly makes his way up the trail while the rest of us try to keep up with his overactive legs. He is far enough ahead that it is difficult to hear him when he starts yelling back at us, "Hey! Hey! There is someone up here! There is someone up here!" I can't see what he is yelling about, but I figure it's a migrant who has been left behind and needs water or first aid. I throw my pack down and begin to run up the trail. By the time I reach him, I can tell from his wide eyes that it is something more than a person with a sprained ankle. When I am finally close enough to see her, there is no mistaking that she is dead.

N31° 44′ 55″, W111° 12′ 24″

The eight of us stand around her in a semicircle. It is obvious that not everyone has seen a corpse before, because someone asks if she is really dead. Most of the students go and sit under a nearby tree while I figure out what to do next. I walk to the top of the hill to try to get cell phone reception. After fifteen minutes I finally get a 911 operator on the line. I tell her that we have found a dead body while hiking. I give her general directions to our location but it is a fairly useless endeavor: "About three miles northeast of Batamote Road near Lobo Peak." She is not familiar with the area, so I give her the GPS coordinates of our location. She is not sure what they mean, so I tell her that we will send someone back to the road to get law enforcement. There is no way they are going to find us with verbal directions. Haeden Stewart, a graduate student from the University of Chicago, agrees to run back to the vehicle to get help. I tell the rest of the group that we will wait for the sheriff to arrive but in the meantime we need to document and photograph the scene. No one seems particularly enthusiastic about this prospect, me included.

At this point there is the realization that unpleasant work has to be done. I remind myself that directing a research project focused on human suffering and death in the desert means we can't ignore certain parts of the social process just because it sickens us or breaks our hearts. This means looking at the body of this unknown woman up close and recording as much information as possible. This means taking photos. The decision to do this will later lead me to being questioned and criticized by some colleagues who don't think we should have taken pictures of the body or used them in any publication. It makes readers and viewers uncomfortable, which is fine because it made (and continues to make) us as researchers uncomfortable. When this type of death starts to feel normal, that's when we should worry. I start taking photos of her because it feels imperative to record what this type of death looks like up close. The objective is to document this moment for those who are not here.

I am well aware, though, that despite our best intentions, dangers and ethical issues can arise from circulating images such as these. * * * I cannot control the life of these pictures or the meanings that viewers will attach to them. My only hope is that these images can stand as undeniable material evidence that a woman died at N31° 44′ 55″, W111° 12′ 24″ and that witnesses saw her corpse in "flesh and blood."[4]

---

4. The coordinates have been modified to protect a memorial shrine that currently marks this death site. Despite its remote location, the shrine has been vandalized numerous times, likely by hikers or hunters. This vandalism included smashing a picture frame that held a photo of Maricela and her family and then ripping the image to pieces.

She is lying face down in the dirt and it appears that she died while attempting to get up the hill. To get to this point, she easily walked more than 40 miles and likely crossed the Tumacácori Mountains. She is wearing generic brown and white running shoes, black stretch pants, and a long-sleeve camouflage shirt. The shirt is something you expect a deer hunter to wear, but over the last several years migrants and drug mules have adopted the fashion. The brown and green design blends in perfectly with the Sonoran backdrop this time of year. Her position lying face down, exposed on the side of a steep hill, suggests that her last moments were a painful crawl. She collapsed mid-hike. To be left on the trail like this likely means that she died alone out here.

Rigor mortis has set in and her fingers have started to curl. Her ankles are swollen to the point that her sneakers seem ready to pop off at any moment. The back of her pants are stained with excrement and are bubbling with copper-colored fluids that were expelled from her body upon death. It is surprisingly hard to look away. Dead only a few days, the body is in what forensic anthropologists term *early decomposition:* "Gray to green discoloration, some flesh relatively fresh ... Bloating ... Brown to black discoloration of arms and legs" (Galloway 1997: table 7). These descriptions don't do justice to what bodies left out in the desert actually look like, smell like, or sound like. Nothing does. Against the quiet backdrop of the desert you can hear the buzzing of flies busily laying eggs on her, in her. There is a steady hissing of intestinal gases escaping from her bloated and distended stomach. It sounds like a slow-leaking tire.

High above, stiff-winged turkey vultures circle her corpse like black paper airplanes effortlessly surveying the scene. I count at least four of them and marvel at how quickly they have arrived. * * * I get close to the body and awkwardly scribble down more field notes: "No backpack or obvious personal possessions ... a bottle of electrolyte fluids tucked under shoulder and face." As I lean in to look at her, the wind whips across her body sending the sweet smell and taste of rotting flesh directly into my nostrils and mouth. It is the taste of *la muerte* [death].

After several days in the boiling summer heat her body has begun to change. Her skin has started to blacken and mummify and the bloating is beginning to obscure some of her physical features. While parts of her are transforming into unfamiliar shapes and colors, her striking jet-black hair and the ponytail holder wrapped around her right wrist hint at the person she once was. I focus on her hair. It is smooth; the color of smoky obsidian. It's possibly the darkest hair I have ever seen, and its texture gives the impression that she is still alive. I think about reaching down to touch her, but I can't. She has been out here too long and I know that her skin will not feel human. I want to see her face but don't dare roll the body over. This is a "crime scene" and I don't want to destroy any evidence. I start thinking about who she might have been in life. Was she a kind person? What did her laugh sound like? What compelled her to enter this desert? Would she be angry that I am taking her picture? Finally I ask Olivia to get out the blanket that we found, and we use it to cover her. It makes those of us still alive feel better.

I go over and sit with the remaining group of students under a tree a short distance from the body. The silence among us is tense and only occasionally broken when a breeze comes through and rustles the branches of nearby mesquite trees. Out of the blue someone starts crying uncontrollably and is immediately consoled by a neighbor's kind embrace. Others sigh deeply and someone angrily walks off into the distance to be alone. We sit quietly for what seems an eternity. Vultures continue to patiently circle overhead. They are simultaneously implicated in and oblivious to the complex human drama playing out below them. All they know is that we have disrupted their lunch plans.

I want to say something to our group that will comfort us or make this death seem peaceful or dignified. It's a ridiculous thought. There is nothing you can say in this scenario that doesn't sound contrived. Months later someone will corner me after a talk and complain that the photos I showed of this woman's body robbed her of her dignity. I will point out that the deaths that migrants experience in the Sonoran Desert are anything but dignified. That is the point. This is what "Prevention Through Deterrence" looks like. These photographs should disturb us, because the disturbing reality is that right now corpses lie rotting on the desert floor and there aren't enough witnesses. This invisibility is a crucial part of both the suffering and the necroviolence that emerge from the hybrid collectif. As [political scientist] Timothy Pachirat notes, we live in a world where "power operates through the creation of distance and concealment and [where] our understandings of 'progress' and 'civilization' are inseparable from, and perhaps even synonymous with, the concealment (but not elimination) of what is increasingly rendered physically and morally repugnant" (Pachirat 2013:14). These photos thus make visible the human impact of a United States border enforcement policy intended to kill people, and they provide compelling evidence that we don't need to go to "exotic" places to get "full frontal views of the dead and dying" (Sontag 2003:70). The dead live in our backyard; they are the human grist for the sovereignty machine. You need only "luck" to catch a glimpse of the dead before they are erased by the hybrid collectif.

Desert border crossings are cruel, brutal affairs in which people often die slowly and painfully from hyperthermia, dehydration, heatstroke, and a variety of other related ailments. To paint these deaths in any other way is both a denial of the harsh desert reality and a disservice to those who have experienced it. Judith Butler reminds us that the American public rarely gets to see these types of photos for fear of causing internal dissent or undermining nationalistic projects: "Certain images do not appear in the media, certain names of the dead are not utterable, certain losses are not avowed as losses, and violence is derealized and diffused . . . . The violence that we inflict on others is only—and always—selectively brought into public view." It is unclear, though, what impact the photos of this woman's body will have on those who flip through the pages of this book. Will the images evoke sadness or disgust? Does looking behind the curtain at the inner workings of US border enforcement elicit responses that get us closer to political action? Can these images pierce the American public's consciousness? Or, as poet Sean Thomas Dougherty writes in reference to Kevin Carter's (in)famous photo of a "starving Sudanese child being stalked by a vulture," will the violence depicted here become nothing more than an "aesthetic" capable only of evoking appreciation (Dougherty 2006:609)?

Sitting there on that dusty afternoon, I finally blurt out, "At least we got to her before the vultures did."

ENGAGING THE TEXT, ENGAGING THE WORLD

- In what ways did De León's selection of detail in describing his own experience trekking through the desert reveal aspects of the border crossing experience that you had previously not been conscious of?

- De León's work focuses attention on the stuff migrants carry and discard, and thus serves as an archaeology of the present. How does this type of work bring the experiences of immigrants to life?

- Agamben (p. 10) argues that physical spaces between countries coupled with declarations of emergency create a "state of exception" in which legal protections normally afforded to individuals are suspended. How are his ideas reflected in De León's description of migrants crossing the Sonoran Desert between Mexico and the United States? What are the consequences of this state of exception?

- De León muses that if his story makes readers feel uncomfortable, it's okay; it made the researchers themselves uncomfortable. This woman's death, he argues, should not be normal, nor should it be concealed. Did you feel uncomfortable reading this passage? Why? Can discomfort like this be productive?

- Would you want to see De León's photographs of the woman who died on the trail? Why or why not?

There Are No Peripheries to Humanity

Edith Turner

Anthropologist Edith Turner's fieldwork in the northern Alaska village of Point Hope originally focused on religious healing practices of the indigenous Iñupiat people. However, she was ultimately drawn to investigate a more pressing problem: Why were so many people dying of cancer? Her ethnographic journey in pursuit of this question involves a secret nuclear waste dump, environmental pollution, the silence and denial of the U.S. government, and the struggle of indigenous people to control their own future. In the process, Turner finds herself "on the Iñupiats' side," an anthropologist working in the global age, accompanying them in the halls of power in Washington, D.C., and the United Nations as they seek redress.

Turner practices an engaged anthropology. Through intensive fieldwork, key informants become friends. Going into "the field" in a distant community becomes "like going home." This deep involvement pushes Turner to reconsider the blurry borders between research and activism. Where does an anthropologist stand when confronted with conditions of violence, conflict, and inequality? Engaged anthropology, like that practiced by Turner, as well as De León, Scheper-Hughes later in this chapter, and many other anthropologists across time, is characterized by a commitment not only to revealing and critiquing systems of power and inequality but also to working with local communities to confront these systems.

Fieldwork in the Era of Globalization

In 1987 I went to Point Hope, Northern Alaska, to study native healing. I knew that the Iñupiat, Yup'ik, and Siberian Yup'ik of St. Lawrence Island had sent troupes of dancers to Washington from time to time. The dancing of "Eskimos" was admired down in the south [the lower 48 United States], and they were chosen for the president's inauguration. This much was global. I knew too that in order to complete the long journey to Point Hope, where I heard many of the healers lived, I would be taking planes, not

From Edith Turner. 1997. "There Are No Peripheries to Humanity: Northern Alaska Nuclear Dumping and the Iñupiat's Search for Redress." *Anthropology and Humanism* 22(1): 95–109. Some of the author's notes have been omitted.

dogsleds. There was modern transportation. In the arctic there was a clinic connected by satellite phone to the far-off hospital. One of the healers in Point Hope worked regularly on a contract basis in the outpatients' clinic in the big village of Kotzebue. The mail came in by air every day. We were well on in the 20th century.

Midcentury histories of Northern Alaska record as a minor point that the region was of importance in the Cold War after World War II. Therefore there were military installations all along the northern Arctic Slope. I vaguely recall how in 1958 the United States Atomic Energy Commission planned to do what in the climate of the day seemed rather exciting. They were going to create a huge crater next to the ocean, using nuclear explosions, so as to make a harbor for sea-going vessels. This was "Project Chariot." But for some reason the project was abandoned.

Be that as it may, in 1987 when I arrived, Point Hope was a small isolated village of 680 people living in one hundred prefabricated houses beside a mostly frozen ocean. Subsistence hunting was their main occupation. I sat with the people, visiting neighbors' homes when a healing was in progress, and going to church when testimony was being given, which was often. I learned a little bit about what it was like to heal. There could be detected in the process a certain level of spirit power that fascinated me.

After several months I began to see this village as the center of the world; time was doing different things to me. The rest of the world's sense of time and its activities began to look unreal. * * * This effect of being lost in the fieldwork also happened to me in Africa. One goes into the field, becomes lost in it, and then one may wake up with a start to find oneself in the modern scene after all.

As it happened, matters in Point Hope were breaking open on a wider arena—because history itself on a worldwide scale had broken into the peace of Point Hope. Just as in the thirties, forties, and fifties the village had been ravaged by deadly measles and tuberculosis from the south (the marks were still on the village), so now my sense of the village quietly riding through time was disturbed—as the people themselves were disturbed—by a threat that had been growing since the sixties, cancer. My landlady Joanna found that her painful shoulder was not healing. The doctors told her it was cancer of the bone. Amos, the prime whaling captain, had something of the same sort wrong with his previously injured leg. I said to myself, "So much has changed with these people. They seem to be at the mercy of modern life. What can be the cause of this trouble?" I went to the Point Hope clinic and leaned over the counter. The health aide and I chatted about poor Joanna and Amos.

"What's the cause of the cancer, do you think? Why is there so much of it here?"

"The figures are nothing out of the ordinary," she said. "They've always been like that."

*   *   *

The cause of sickness in Point Hope remained a mystery. Everyone knew that Project Chariot had been abandoned. No one had exploded any bombs. In fact, as I discovered, the resistance that the village had mounted in the sixties had prevented the fulfillment of the project; and the same spirit of resistance had the effect of engendering Native protection movements up and down the state.

Very slowly I began to take notice. My main study of healing (Turner 1989, 1996) traced a local method that was turning out to be a good one and even helped patients in minor cases of small cancer nodules. But the major cases of cancer defeated the traditional healers. Only fundamentalist Christians hoped for healing in such cases.***

It was not until 1991 that Rex Tuzroyluk, a western-trained Iñupiaq biologist, and I tried to total up the cancer score.[1] Rex said there had been ten cancer deaths in the previous two years. He was puzzled. He pulled out an old clipping about Project Chariot that clearly demonstrated the mentality of the Atomic Energy Commission and the U.S. Army. The project had been invented by Edward Teller, supposedly as a way to "beat swords into plowshares," under his notorious "Plowshares" scheme. When I read the clipping I realized that the site was at the Ogotoruk Creek, Cape Thompson, only 31 miles south, on the best caribou grazing land—and caribou meat was the second staple of the Iñupiat. I thought, "The area for the project was so near the village. Who'd dare to go up to the site and see what they left behind?" Rex said there had also been a U.S. Army base just to the west of the new village site of Point Hope, on land that drained into what had been the drinking pond for the previous village site. Had toxic wastes such as PCB been spilt there, Rex wondered, causing illness over a long term among the inhabitants? There were reports among villagers of having seen army personnel burying canisters. At Rex's suggestion I wrote anxiously to many agencies on the matter, and from the Environmental Protection Agency and the state Department of Environmental Conservation I received the explanation that the illness was caused by the people's bad lifestyle. They meant by this that the people were smoking too much, using drugs, and consuming alcohol and junk food. There were similar responses from the Native Health Service at the North Slope Borough. The Army Corps of Engineers stated outright—what we found afterwards to be a lie—that there was no toxic waste left in the area.

I was puzzled. It was the lifestyle? Why was the lifestyle supposed to be so much worse in Point Hope than among, for example, many of the wild students I knew down below, or in any village in the lower 48 states where the shopping carts are full of junk food and cigarettes? Presumably, if it were a matter of lifestyle the people in the small towns of the lower 48 ought to be dying of cancer at the same rate as in Point Hope. I began to think that sooner or later I would have to find out what the U.S. cancer rates were.

But others in Point Hope were not waiting. During my visit in the summer of 1991 Caroline Nashookpuk, the Point Hope representative to the North Slope Borough on matters of health, told the villagers at the Elders' Conference that she knew something was wrong and was looking into the matter. It should be noted that during that year

---

1. *Iñupiaq* is the singular of the plural word *Iñupiat*.

the Elders' Conference was moderately attended and featured the usual discussions of concern about drugs and drunkenness, education issues, and the like, with the usual unexceptional resolutions at the end.

That summer Rex and his wife Piquk took me outside their house and showed me a seal stretched on the gravel that looked strange. Its hair was not gray but an orange color, wrong-looking. This orange color was not caused by oil contamination: the EPA office in Anchorage informed us that oil contamination results in black discoloration. I took pictures. Connie Oomituck reported to me later that people had been finding tumors in seals and caribou.

By my next visit in June 1992, matters had changed again. What really upset me was seeing how old Barbara Lane, who had been over-quiet last year at the elders' lunch, now sat hardly moving in the corner next to her healthy old husband. She had further fallen in upon herself. She looked yellow and ate little. We learned later it was a brain tumor.

This year the Elders' Conference seemed to have teeth. Irma Oktollik was chairperson. Through this conference, which constituted a town meeting, the people talked repeatedly about the need for immediate action, and there was a determination to unite and hold the line for their village. Caroline was busy trying to coerce the Native Health Service to investigate the pollution that was the cause of the cancer, but the responses of the white-run service were extremely slow.

This was in June 1992. During those summer months a researcher named Dan O'Neill of the University of Alaska at Fairbanks was busy in the archives of the university library conducting an investigation of the old Project Chariot activities of 1958–1963, which everyone knew by now was a project designed to threaten Soviet Russia during the Cold War. While turning over the material he discovered documents describing the illegal experimental dumping of 15,000 pounds of radioactive soil at the Chariot site in 1962, *after* the project had been officially abandoned. The material was brought from the Nevada test sites, specifically for the purpose of experimentation, and secretly positioned in a loose dump without the legally required containers. This was executed under cover of the withdrawal from the Chariot site.

In the middle of August 1992, the nine villages of the North Slope received the information that Dan O'Neill had revealed. Rex Tuzroyluk told me about it on the phone.

"Edie, when the news came out I went around to my mom's and she just sat and wouldn't talk to me." Her daughter, Rex's younger sister Tuzzy—a brilliant university student—had recently died of cancer. When Piquk, who was not well herself, came on the phone, she also sounded in shock. I said to her, "They have to move that dump. But where will they put it, shoot it out into space?"

"Dump it on Washington, D.C.," she said.

Thus began the story, a true account, of events that joined my field community with perhaps the most serious issue of our day, radioactive pollution, and brought some of the villagers to the center of the world, Washington, D.C.

Politics were changing rapidly. In the middle of this whirlwind of news, Jack Schaefer, the village's self-made lawyer, said on the phone, "We've done it, we've designated ourselves, The Native Village of Point Hope.'"

"Great." ("Native Village" was another title for the Indian Reorganization Act [IRA] body, which had the full rights of a Native Reserve and sovereignty under the federal government, not under the politically conservative state of Alaska). * * *

So already fear of the dump was leading the village toward a more secure self-determination. It was a process that had been developing since 1963 in resistance to white encroachment.

*   *   *

Rex Tuzroyluk was immediately appointed as monitor for the Tikigaq Native Corporation because, as he said in his report of September 14, 1992:

> The general public at Point Hope is concerned about the quality of information reaching them. They have been given little information about what radioactivity is, where it comes from, what it does, and how it is detected. They need information about the half-life of the radioactive isotopes that are reported to be in the dump. The initial objective is to determine how far there is immediate danger to people, animals, and the environment from radioactive material on the site and to determine if any surface or subsurface conditions might remain hazardous in the future.
>
> On September 9 a group of investigating officials from the outside walked up the Ogotoruk Creek and investigated all by themselves. They reported that they tested the site on the surface with a scintilla tor [a sensitive Geiger counter] and found no radiation.
>
> On September 11, Rex Tuzroyluk and a group of Iñupiat, plus a white Army Engineer expert on radiation, Willard Ferrell, and two white environmental experts, Scott Holmes and Ron Short, went to the site to investigate the dump mound. We walked to the site carrying three electric rod drivers for making holes. When we arrived at the mound, I measured its dimensions by my stride, which is accurate. It was 42 ft. by 40 ft. and 6 ft. high. The outside men, who judged by eye, said it was 30 ft. by 32 ft.
>
> We drove a hole into the mound with an augur. Ron Short read the Geiger counter reading at the base of the hole. It read 3 at first. We went down 2½ feet. When the Geiger counter was shoved in the hole it read 6.2. We tried again. It flickered once. I saw it, Rex Rock saw it, and Luke saw it [all Iñupiat]. I did not get the number. Willard Ferrell said he got 1.3. But he said, "Let's get out of here." This is what really got us. He said, "This is it. Cover the hole. Let's get out of here." He had no doubt in his mind we did hit something here. That's what he told us.
>
> Willard, after the little flicker, would not go and try the other side of the mound. He would not say this in the public meeting.
>
> It should be noted that there is a pond right next to the mound. In my experience it thaws down to 8 ft. around and at the bottom of a pond. This was the water source closest to the mound and no samples were taken there.
>
> I respect Willard Ferrell but he is not telling us everything.

Their final report to Mayor Ray Koonuk was that they have determined they have to investigate further with proper equipment.

The point is that the Army Corps of Engineers has this information. Yet very little of it comes to Point Hope. If they have been so concerned about persons and the environment why did they not give information about how radiation works and how to detect it? [Tuzroyluk 1992]

*　　*　　*

In January 1993 I received a phone call in the middle of teaching freshmen undergraduates the course "Ritual and Symbol," which included my lugging a heavy drum into the classroom for a performance of girl's initiation. The call was from the Iñupiat village. Jack Schaefer of Point Hope, Jesse Kaleak of Barrow, who was the Mayor of the North Slope Borough at the time, his assistant Johnny Aiken, and other Iñupiat and some friendly lawyers were meeting in New York City with a number of North American Native leaders to put their various cases to the United Nations. Boutros Boutros-Ghali, then secretary-general, had agreed to give an audience to leaders of indigenous minority communities. Jack telephoned and asked me to come. * * *

Jack had arrived from Point Hope fresh from cutting up seal meat. His hands were stained with the indelible dark red blood of seals, and his fingernails were clogged. He had split his leather jacket right down the back. I sewed up his jacket in the hotel room, using the small skin-sewing stitches that Molly Oktollik had taught me the first year I was there. We went off to find the others and had a meeting. Jack, self-taught lawyer that he was, had already armed the others with stacks of very frightening information. For instance, Peggy, the Native Village secretary, had seen *four* other dumps just like the one that O'Neill had reported; experimental medical tablets containing radioactive substances had been given to Anaktuvuk Pass Iñupiat without any explanation; and Army-supply nuclear generators enclosed in a mere one-inch shell had been left abandoned up and down the North Slope when the DEW line (Distant Early Warning) Army posts were closed down. The latter were dangerous objects, at risk of opening in the melting and freezing conditions on the Slope. These were all true horrors. I went about among my Iñupiat friends hunched and ashamed, willing to follow them up the elevator in the huge rectangular building of the United Nations, and sit as inconspicuously as I could in front of Boutros Boutros-Ghali while he listened to Iroquois, Plains Indians, Natives from Nevada, Hawaiians, and ourselves, the Iñupiat, telling of wrongs. We had no pull, no majority vote; we were quite helpless. Even I told Boutros-Ghali of these wrongs. Now I find myself saying "we," for writing which I have been reprimanded in the past. Disobedient as ever, I still say "we." How could I stand over with the whites and say about my friends, "they"?

Here then is what fieldwork can do in the age of globalization—what it simply did to me: it put me on the Iñupiat's side in their venture into the political heart of the world. And the Iñupiat were as formal and eloquent as they ever were in their elders' conferences, and in ages before that, in their *qalgi* (meeting centers), those underground domed sod houses. Afterwards, Boutros-Ghali, looking like an old and selfish turtle, informed the meeting that he was setting up an office of the United Nations at Geneva to be devoted to the interests of indigenous minorities, those without a United Nations vote. This was good! The man belied his looks. (Now, in 1996, it became apparent that Boutros-Ghali designated this whole decade, the 1990s, as "The Decade of the Indigenous Peoples.")

Finally, we all grouped around the secretary-general and had our photographs taken, the anthropologist too.

When this was over. Jack came down with me to my home in Charlottesville, Virginia, to await an appointment with the two Alaskan senators in Washington and with officials at the Department of Energy. He had to wait for five weeks. Here, Jack's presence * * * constituted a case of a personage from the field arriving at the anthropologist's end of the enterprise—creating a reversal. Jack became interested in Charlottesville, and keenly interested in what the University of Virginia had to offer that might help his people in their struggle to make an obdurate government undertake a thorough investigation of all the dumps. He borrowed many books on nuclear pollution and nuclear law on my library card. We made enquiries around the science faculty for those who understood long-term radioactivity problems. Jack gave a talk in my class on these problems, and on the Iñupiat's need for self-determination, and he met many of the anthropology faculty.

* * *

Meanwhile, as I discovered later, in Alaska on February 23, 1993, the state epidemiologist, Dr. John Middaugh, made a statement referring to the Point Hope dump: "There has been no evidence of radiation impact on the health problems of the local residents. . . ."[2] And later in the letter: "The plan to excavate the Cape Thompson site should be abandoned"—that is, the plan to remove the dump. What then had caused all the cancer I had seen among the villagers of Point Hope?

March 17, 1993. At last, after six weeks' delay, the Department of Energy (DOE) made arrangements for the Iñupiat group to do their business at their office. Appointments also came through with the Alaska senators at the Senate building. It was at DOE that I first started suffering from an auto-immune syndrome, with many aches and pains.[3] So my story, even at a personal level, was a dark one.

Again in Washington, the Iñupiat met with their lawyers to set up the DOE inquiry and decide strategy. We were to meet there with one Tom Gerusky, who headed the nuclear problem affairs office. The Atomic Energy Commission had long since ceased to exist, and the Nuclear Regulatory Commission did not take responsibility for the past;

---

2. Letter to Kevin Cabbie, the Department of Energy, Nevada, from Alaska Governor Hickel's office.
3. After three years this trouble, polymyalgia rheumatica, was eventually cured.

it was the Army Corps of Engineers that was responsible in this matter to DOE—so it was to DOE that we would have to go. This department was no longer located in Washington but was out in Maryland, an expensive taxi ride away. I went with Jack—we were late—and I slammed down the 45 dollars and wrote it off later as tax-deductible. Was this research? It was an interesting question.

The small episode of the taxi fare opens up the question of what it is that anthropologists do in the field. If we are not asking questions all the time—and contemporary fieldworkers are learning not to do so—we will have to go about our research by making real, actual friends, and committing ourselves to acts of friendship. Now *is* this research? I would say yes. It is personal, but of course all fieldwork is personal, and such is the case with fieldwork anywhere on the globe. * * * When one is acting in the field one is acting as a real person.

In this matter of radioactivity I had the same intentions as Jack and the delegation when we visited Washington. Thus it can be seen that a major element of fieldwork is that the people *need* you; you will become their representative. There is a very interesting cross-positioning of roles here that happens constantly in our present age of globalization. * * *

To continue the story; DOE is housed in a recently built and manicured large office complex in a field outside Germantown, Maryland. Jack and I found a classic flight of steps around the side, entered, and walked down a long corridor. The place was throttling, tense. Jack and I looked at each other, reading the signs on the walls. Down a long side corridor we found a person who could tell us the way. At last we came to a door, which when opened revealed a semi-dark conference room full of people—Tom Gerusky and his numerous assistants, and there were our friends, Jesse Kaleak, Ray Koonuk, Johnny Aiken, and the others. This "Tom," as he chose to be called, was in the process of scolding the Iñupiat for submitting a requirement that DOE, in addition to the removal of the dump, should mount a much wider investigation into other radioactive dumping. (Gerusky was quite adamant. At this point, I wonder why that was.)

"No," he was saying. "The $1,000,000 is all you'll get. That's for clearing the dump. Don't expect any more investigations." And his assistant lugged out a huge memorandum, 1,000 pages long, he told us, and started reading about how those who were going to take away the dump would wear such and such protective clothing, and so on, interminably.

I broke in, intensely irritated (unlike the outwardly cool Iñupiat). "What's all this about protecting the white men doing the clearing away? What about the *cancer* now existing in the village? You don't seem to be interested in that at all. Of course there has to be more investigation." This caused a certain hiatus in the reading. Slides illustrating the same material as the memo were put on instead. Jack beside me was shifting his feet. "Let's get out of here," he said. "We'll 'walk out.'"

"Okay."

The two of us achieved quite a good "walk-out" effect, stony-faced, with heads erect.

In the corridor, Jack told me how Gerusky had been persistently slithery in his dealings with him. I shuddered. Who was this Gerusky? I now had a terrible headache and my limbs hurt. When I got back to my lodgings I threw up.

Nevertheless we still had two senators to see. Our Iñupiat friends had also left DOE soon after we did, and were equally seething.

Our Alaska senators were hard to locate. At last we found ourselves outside Ted Stevens's office at the secretary's desk. To Jack's easygoing inquiries, he found out that the office had known about the dump from way back. Jack withdrew quietly, much shaken. "Why did he never say anything?" Stevens had sworn he knew nothing about any pollution.

So now the Iñupiat had arrived right at the heart of the government, and were finding lies and subterfuge firsthand. I followed where my friends led. I was finding these things firsthand too.

Stevens's legislative assistant, David Lundquist, was in his office, and I had a word with him about another case of dumping. The government was offering the Mescalero Apache of Arizona millions of dollars for education and other needs if they would accept nuclear waste on their land. I said to Lundquist, "That is immoral."

I remember his riposte. "You're a bleeding heart."

I turned away, both sick and proud. My heart did bleed.

Eventually we followed our guide through a long tunnel to the Senate itself. Three business-suited gentlemen were walking in front of us. "That's Edward Teller," said the guide, pointing to one of them. This Edward Teller, the "Father of the Atom Bomb," was just another fleshy man. Why was he so at home here at the Senate?

We did meet Stevens, and we also met Senator Murkowski. It was hard to choose between them. Each of their private Senate chambers was large, full of luxury and fine portraits, antique chairs, beautiful things. Every now and then the senator concerned would be called to the floor to vote, hurrying into the huge chamber we had glimpsed while walking around the corridor on its periphery. At Senator Stevens's chambers, Jack in his mended jacket and four-days'-worn T-shirt gave his appeal with his educated dignity. He told the senator about the dumps and the sickness, and described what he was also worried about, the two-foot-wide metal pipes the hunters had discovered that reached deep into the ground on the Chariot site, visible to this day, stuffed with a bit of dirt. "They definitely need investigation," Jack told the senator.

"They would never drill so wide," said Stevens, flustered. "It's impossible! Why would they want to do that?" Here was another denial. The constituency of this senator, back in Alaska, was four-fifths white, the rest native. These four-fifths would not want to hear what Jack said. In our own minds, to this day the question repeats itself, "What was the size of the nuclear bombs the Chariot team had intended to place underground at Ogotoruk Creek, then detonate? Have we any information about the plans and how far they went?" * * *

Shortly after the conclusion of these meetings, I was due to fly to Anchorage and give a paper on the dump and the people's reactions to it at the Alaska Anthropological Association annual meetings (April 1993). First I visited Point Hope. The mood there was black. All the authorities were denying that the dump had anything to do with the people's ill health. In any discussion of the dump, the people doubted that the government would actually do what was necessary and move the material. Barbara Lane was dead, and her husband Jacob, who had been an important man as long as his wife was alive, could no longer run a whaleboat and had given up the captaincy to his daughter. He was now unshaven. Many of the men had let their beards grow. There was more trash lying about in the village. None of the villagers seemed to be able to lift up their heads. There had been insult; the government had been found to play them false. These people embodied the oldest village in America—did no one honor even that? No one from outside cared about that, and dumped nuclear waste on them that would kill them. That gray-black mood was something I did not like to see. I myself was unhappy, embroiled in the dreadful results of globalization.

It was obvious that I had to do some real compiling of figures. My friend Connie knew about many of the cases, Piquk also. Everyone was talking about the latest people in trouble: someone new was suffering the familiar pain—another was in for surgery. I quickly came up with 37 cases. Dr. Bowerman of the Native Health Hospital in Barrow was able to trace an excess of 70 deaths from cancer in Point Hope between 1969 to 1993 (the village was smaller in the earlier years). This translated as an average of 57 per thousand per year.[4] The death rate from cancer in 1950, before the dump, was four per thousand—so that the recent rate represented a more than 14-fold increase. Why the difference between those periods? Nearly every agency to which we appealed argued that it was caused by the people's lifestyle.

Nevertheless, a year after the dump had first been discovered, the Department of Energy did remove it, commenting that it was done so that the people of Point Hope would feel better. It would be of psychological benefit.

It was not until 1995 that the government medical authorities came to a new conclusion: the high rate of cancer in Point Hope *was* indisputably caused by the local radioactive pollution. In October 1995, Rex came on the phone to tell me that he and Caroline, Mayor Ray, and the mayor of the North Slope, George Ahmaogak, had been asked to Washington to the White House because President Clinton wished to apologize to Point Hope village representatives for the previous U.S. administrations' illegal acts.

"Wonderful!" I said, and thought, "About time."

I drove up to Washington when the group had finished at the White House to see them and have dinner. I was to meet them at their hotel and we would drive to Union Station, where their lawyers were waiting for us at a restaurant.

In the hotel lobby, there was Caroline, beaming and full of energy as usual. We hugged comprehensively. Rex and all of them were happy. Then for the restaurant. When we got to the door, it was pouring with rain. We bundled into my car and set forth. * * * At dinner, plans were at last made for the hoped-for further investigations. Even compensation was mentioned.

---

4. The death rate from cancer in the whole of the United States in 1980 was 1.8 per thousand.

And so now we find ourselves in 1996, an era of the reflexivity of our friends in the field. When I go into the field now, it is really like going home, where everyone knows you, and they take it for granted you will turn up some time or other. "Hi Edie. Welcome home"—this is in the store at Point Hope, with snow outside. Snow. That is the natural stuff to find lying outside. The squeak of my sneakers in the snow is what I have been missing—the kids wanting me to play, their little faces turned up like cups, a bit unsteady and about to spill in fun, the smell of the doughnuts Molly has just cooked, and she throws one toward me in the time-honored habitual gesture of Iñupiat ritual giving. Her eyebrows are raised and winsome and thoughtful; she is glad to see me. Then she suddenly sighs. It's her son, who committed suicide last year. John, her husband, says "No don't, Molly. Come on, don't." She tries to fight it down, but the sad look is still there. * * *

They keep looking out the window where they can see the south shore. Is there a water cloud hanging above open sea? The weather is warm for the area, and muggy, 26 degrees Fahrenheit, and the wind is from the south, blowing the ice against the shore. There will be no whales, for there is no water for the whale to come through. But wait, next day, what happens?—and it will not happen without the whole village *doing it*. The wind is the trouble, the wind is still wrong, from the south.

What happened was this. After church on Sunday a call came through on the CB, heard at Molly's, that there was going to be a Rogation (prayer service, a dull affair in my experience) in the church at 3:00. I thought I had better go. The voice went on, "Any volunteers to bring a boat into the church?" Aha! I remembered how they brought a boat into the church the first year I was there, and how they blessed it in the hope of catching whales. I remembered the whaling captains all standing in the sanctuary. I left Molly's and wandered outside in the snow to watch. Over a stretch of snow beside Seymour's house, I saw men collecting around a skin boat, which still rested on its high rack. But not for long; they were manhandling it down and onto a sled. I had to run to keep the boat in view as it glided through the streets, pulled by the snowmobile, then to the side of the church. I came up behind panting, and saw again the captains with five of their young sons heaving and blundering the boat off the sled. Then they took the sled and smartly passed it into the church and parked it up the aisle in the sanctuary, and afterward took the boat itself through the church entrance, sideways, with banging and side-slipping, until they could get it through the door and the right way up again, then up the aisle; and sled and boat were set as on ice and on sea, in church—where the altar boy was in the act of changing the colored altar cloth for a white one. Whales like white. The preacher wore white. The paddles were all scoured white and set upright, as when a whale is caught, in the position of the "catch" signal to other boats.

The church was filling quickly. All 22 whaling captains, including the prime one, Henry Nashookpuk (known for his unspoken gifts), stood in two ranks on each side of the boat. The preacher stood at the prow and began. We sang of the good things from the sea, "The whales and all that move in the waters," "The sea is his and he made it," and "When I in awesome wonder consider all the worlds," songs that brought tears to the eyes of many of us, Molly, Emma, myself—and others, so Emma said. Then the captains came forward to the boat and put their hands on the gunwale, all around, and their wives behind them. (It was just a 16-foot boat.) The congregation went up and put their hands on the wives, and so on. Then we all began to pray for whales. The sound arose till my eyes were starting out of my head. I prayed like mad—there were weird cryings from the crowd, with arms whirling on high. The strength rose and rose and rose. Edie, I told myself, you've never been in a religious event like this! I looked over to where Henry's face appeared. It was calm—and faintly happy. I quieted, and soon the hullabaloo was over, and we finished with one more hymn, most of us in a state of cold chill. The congregation started to leave, the men took the boat down and out the door, and I went gingerly over the snowy step myself, to find Molly waiting to walk back with me. As we passed the end of the church and came into the open, there it was. The wind had changed to the north. It blew icy and fresh from far up the village and fell freely on our cheeks and upon the south shore. It would blow the ice away and there would be water. No one said a word.

The next day there was water, and the men went down on the ice to break trail across the ice toward the open water. By Tuesday there were several crews down at the water, watching. Several whales were seen. * * * Piquk phoned me the week after I got home and said Molly had her whale. * * *

So the people's efforts were rewarded by a favorable north wind. Obviously the Iñupiat had regained their powers. The whale was once more the center of their life. * * * The event of "changing the wind" was *caused by* the prayers, while the possibility of the event also *caused* the prayers. One should refer back in time for the roots of this process. The desire and need for the whaling way of life and the relationship with these animals were what motivated the fight for health and recognition (the anti-pollution struggle); the presidential apology and subsequent improved economy won by the villagers gave birth to the strength to make the Christian-shamanic prayer, which gave birth to the whales' arrival. For the villagers, therefore, the possibility of catching a whale engendered the whale—through ordeal. It reinforced the villagers' knowledge of the whale as a spirit animal.

My own interpretation, long since self-weaned from exclusive faith in either positivism or the "one-faith-only" idea, was that this was the old and excellent shamanism. This Christian shamanism had altered the weather. * * *

*   *   *

Globalization has greatly affected not only peripheral peoples but anthropology itself. Shared memories and shared experiences are a serious side of it. The actual, not virtual, participation in cross-traveling possibilities for both sides—not only one way, but both ways—is another. These are not "observers'" social facts, but participant-based, political, life-and-death social facts, and they concern action. We are not writing societies; this time they seem to be bent on writing us, so as to correct the balance and achieve justice for themselves on global terms.

*   *   *

In conclusion, one will have to see my stories as piecemeal affairs, none directly illustrating how globalization affects fieldwork. One cannot tie down Boutros-Ghali's turtle look, the extraordinary coziness of the Union Station restaurant after the rain-bombarded journey, or Rex standing in light snow at Cape Thompson seeing the Geiger counter flicker, to a theory of globalization. *** Fieldworkers know the global feel first-hand, in those absurd particularities. ***

The Iñupiat live far up in the north. Nevertheless it was they who kept the inter-lacing connection going with the center of power in Washington. Circumstances impelled them to connect. Globalization for them did not take the form of the rela-tively harmless effects of world capitalism, but derived from the boiling of a kind of hysterical power (driven by hidden capitalism on both sides) that brought about the Cold War between two mighty states. Here globalization hit an innocent village, and drew its desperate representatives to the capital. These representatives have mandated that the peripheries of the planet will not do for dumping harmful garbage, because people live there.

ENGAGING THE TEXT, ENGAGING THE WORLD

- Why does Turner call her article "There are no peripheries to humanity"?

- How have the lives of the Iñupiat been shaped by globalization? How has Turner's fieldwork experience been shaped by globalization?

- When Turner finds herself in Washington, D.C., accompanying a group of Iñupiat visiting United States government officials, she asks, "Is this research?" What do you think? Can research and activism be combined into engaged anthropology?

- Anthropologists attempt to be both insiders and outsiders in a community—moving inside to understand local beliefs and practices and outside to place local realities in global context. Re-read Turner's final story of the shamanic ritual in the Iñupiat church. Discuss how Turner's skill at moving from insider to outsider shapes her telling of the Iñupiat people's story.

- What challenges will the Iñupiat continue to face in light of climate change?

Min(d)ing the Body: On the Trail of Organ-Stealing Rumors

Nancy Scheper-Hughes

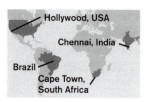

The trajectory of Nancy Scheper-Hughes's career reflects many of the transformations shaping anthropology in a global age, particularly anthropology's attention to the ways local communities around the world are increasingly interconnected by global processes and networks. Her earliest research focused on local life in the impoverished Brazilian shantytown Alto do Cruzeiro where she investigated the meaning of "mother-love" in the face of high, yet seemingly preventable, levels of infant mortality. Today she continues to explore the richness of local life in Brazil but has expanded her scope, tracing rumors of human organ theft from Brazil to countries as far flung as Eastern Europe, South Africa, and India. As told in this selection, Scheper-Hughes's research uncovers a gruesome, illicit global trade in human organs harvested from urban poor people around the world to be used for transplant surgeries primarily available to the world's economic elites. In the process, Scheper-Hughes's work shows how no local community can be viewed as isolated. Instead, anthropologists must consider each local fieldwork site in light of the myriad ways in which local dynamics link to the world beyond. As we will see throughout this book, today anthropological research includes attention to global flows, networks, and processes as anthropologists trace patterns across national and cultural boundaries while keeping one foot grounded in the lives of people in local communities.

For many years I have been documenting the violence of everyday life—the many small wars and invisible genocides—resulting from the structural violence of poverty and the increasing public hostility to the bodies, minds, children, and reproductive capacities of the urban poor. Here I will be addressing an uncanny dimension of the usual story of race and class hatred to which we have become so accustomed. This is the covert violence occurring in the context of a new and thriving global trade in human organs and other body parts for transplant surgery. It is a business that is justified by many—including doctors

From Nancy Scheper-Hughes. 2002. "Min(d)ing the Body: On the Trail of Organ-Stealing Rumors." In *Exotic No More: Anthropology on the Front Lines*, edited by Jeremy MacClancy. Chicago: University of Chicago Press.

and bio-ethicists—as serving "altruistic" ends. But for the poorest and most marginalized populations living on the fringes of the new global dis-order, the scramble for fresh organs for transplant surgery increases the already profound sense of ontological insecurity in a world that values their bodies more dead—as a reservoir of spare parts—than alive.

Descend with me for a few moments into that murky realm of the surreal and the magical, into the maelstrom of bizarre stories, fantastic allegations and a hideous class of rumors that circulate in the world's shantytowns and squatter camps, where this collaborative research project had its origins. The rumors were of kidnapping, mutilation, and dismemberment—the removal of blood and organs—for commercial sale. I want to convey to you the terror and panic that these rumors induce in the nervous and hungry residents of urban shantytowns, tent cities, squatter camps, and other "informal settlements" in the Third World.

I first heard the rumor in the shantytowns of Northeast Brazil in the mid-1980s, when I was completing research for my book, *Death without Weeping*, on maternal thinking and practice in the context of extremely high infant and child morality. The rumors told of the abduction and mutilation of poor children who were eyed greedily as fodder for an international traffic in organs for wealthy transplant patients in the first world. Residents of the ramshackle hillside *favela* of Alto do Cruzeiro, the primary site of my research, reported multiple sightings of large blue and yellow combi-vans (the so-called "gypsy taxis" used by the poor the world over) driven by Americans or Japanese "agents" said to be scouring poor neighborhoods in search of stray youngsters, loose kids and street children, kids that presumably no one would miss. The children would be grabbed and shoved into the van. Later their discarded and eviscerated bodies—minus certain organs—heart, lungs, liver, kidneys, and eyes—would turn up on roadsides, between rows of sugarcane, or in hospital dumpsters. "They are looking for donor organs. You may think this is just nonsense," said my friend and research assistant, "Little Irene" in 1987. "*But we have seen things with our own eyes in the hospitals and the morgues, and we know better.*"

"Nonsense! These are stories of the poor and illiterate," countered another of my friends, Casorte, the skeptical manager of the municipal cemetery of Bom Jesus da Mata. "I have been working here for over a year and never have I seen anything. Where are these bodies?" Yet even as we spoke on the following day, a municipal truck arrived at the gates of the cemetery with the body of a "desconicido," the remains of an unknown, unclaimed man found murdered in an abandoned field not far from town. The eyes and genitals had been removed. "Death squads," whispered Casorte, by way of explanation, and he made the gesture of a throat being slit.

*   *   *

Soon after I began writing articles that interpreted the Brazilian organ-stealing rumors in terms of the normal, accepted, everyday violence practiced against the bodies of the poor and the marginal in public medical clinics, in hospitals, and in police mortuaries, where their ills and afflictions were often treated with scorn, neglect, and general disrespect, I began to hear other variants of the organ-theft stories from anthropologists working in Argentina, Colombia, Peru, Guatemala, Honduras, Mexico, India, and Korea. Though most of the stories came from Central and South America, organ-theft rumors were also surfacing in Poland and Russia, where it was reported that poor children's organs were being sold to rich Arabs for transplant surgery. Luise White recorded blood-sucking/blood-stealing vampire stories from East and Central Africa, and South African anthropologist Isak Niehaus recorded blood- and organ-stealing rumors in the Transvaal collected during fieldwork in 1990-1993. The African variants told of "firemen" or paramedics driving *red* combi-vans looking to capture unsuspecting people to drug and to kill in order to drain their blood or remove their organs and other body parts—genitals and eyes in particular—for magical medicine *(muti)* or for more traditional medical purposes. The Italian variants identified a *black* ambulance as the kidnap vehicle.

The rumors had powerful effects, resulting in a precipitous decline in voluntary organ donation in some countries, including Brazil and Argentina. What does it mean when a lot of people around the world begin to tell variants of the same bizarre and unlikely story? How does an anthropologist go about interpreting the uncanny and the social imaginary of poor, third-world peoples? * * *

To the anthropologist, however, working closely with the urban poor, the rumors spoke to the * * * insecurity of people "to whom almost anything could be done." They reflected everyday threats to bodily security, urban violence, police terror, social anarchy, theft, loss, and fragmentation. Many of the poor imagined, with some reason as it turns out, that autopsies were performed to harvest usable tissues and body parts from those whose bodies had reverted to the state: "Little people like ourselves are worth more dead than alive." At the very least the rumors were (like the scriptures) metaphorically true, operating by means of symbolic substitution. The rumors express the * * * insecurities of poor people living on the margins of the * * * global economies where their labor, their bodies, and their reproductive capacities are treated as spare parts to be bought, bartered, or stolen.

*   *   *

Insofar as the poor of urban shantytowns are rarely called upon to speak before official truth commissions, the body-theft rumors could be seen as a surrogate form of political witnessing. The rumors participated in the spirit of human rights testifying to human suffering on the margins of "the official story." Still, in our "rational," secular world, rumors are one thing, while scientific reports in medical journals are quite another. But in the late 1980s the two distinct narratives began to converge as articles published in *The Lancet, Transplantation Proceedings,* and the *British Medical Journal* began to cite evidence of an illegal global commerce and black market in human organs and other body parts. Indeed, wild rumors, like metaphors, do sometimes harden into ethnographic "facts."

I decided to track down independently the rumors to their most obvious, and yet least studied, source: the routine practices of organ procurement and distribution for transplant surgery. But as soon as I abandoned the more distanced and symbolic analyses of the organ-stealing rumors for anthropological "detective work" to determine whether or not a market in human organs actually existed, my research was both suspect and discredited. "Is this some kind of anthropological detective work?" one anthropological colleague asked. Others charged that I had fallen into the "assumptive world" of my uneducated and gullible informants. Indeed, a great deal is invested in maintaining a social and clinical reality which denies any factual basis for poor people's fears of medical technologies. The transplant community's insistence on the patent absurdity of the organ-stealing rumors offers a remarkably resilient defense and protection against having to respond seriously to allegations of medical abuses in organ procurement, harvesting, and distribution.

*   *   *

Stranger Than Fiction

During the summer of 1998 I was sitting at a sidewalk cafe in downtown São Paulo with Laudiceia da Silva, an attractive, young mother and office receptionist who had agreed to share her bizarre medical story with me. She had just filed a legal complaint with the city government requesting an investigation of the large public hospital where in June 1997, during a routine operation to remove an ovarian cyst, she had "lost" a kidney. The missing kidney was discovered soon after the operation by the young woman's family doctor during a routine follow-up examination. When confronted with the information, the hospital representative told a highly improbable story: that Laudiceia's missing kidney was embedded in the large "mass" that had accumulated around her ovarian cyst. But the hospital refused to produce either their medical records or the evidence—the diseased ovary and the kidney had been "discarded," she was told. When I called on representatives of the São Paulo Medical Council, which investigates allegations of malpractice, they refused to grant an interview. A representative of the council said that there was no reason to distrust the hospital's version of the story, and they had no intention of launching an independent investigation. Laudiceia insists that she will pursue her case legally until the hospital is forced to account for just what happened, whether it was a gross medical error or a criminal case of kidney theft. To make matters worse, Laudiceia's brother had been killed in a random act of urban violence several weeks earlier and the family arrived at the hospital too late to stop organ retrieval based on Brazil's new "presumed consent" law. "Poor people like ourselves are losing our organs to the state, one by one," Laudiceia said angrily.

Across the globe at roughly the same time (summer 1998), [fellow researcher] Lawrence Cohen sat in a one-room flat in a municipal housing-project in a Chennai (Madras) slum in South India talking with five local women, each of whom had sold a kidney for

32,500 rupees (about 1,200 dollars at the time of the sale). Each had undergone their "operation" at the clinic of Dr. K. C. Reddy, India's most outspoken advocate of the individual "right to sell" a kidney. Unlike those who ran the more seedy "organs bazaars" that sprang up a decade ago in Bombay, Dr. Reddy prides himself on running an exemplary clinic; the kidney sellers are fully informed about the implications and potential dangers of the operation. They are carefully followed for two years after the organ removal and receive free health care at his clinic during that period, and he carefully avoids contact with intermediaries and organs brokers. The women Cohen interviewed were primarily low-paid domestic workers with husbands in trouble or in debt. Most said that the kidney sale was preceded by a financial crisis; the family had run out of credit and could not get by. Friends had passed on the word that there was quick money to be had through Dr. Reddy's clinic. Cohen asked if the sale had made a difference in their lives, and was told that it had, for a time, but the money was soon swallowed by the usurious interest charged by the local moneylenders, and the families were all in debt again. Would they do it again? Yes, the women answered; what other choice did they have, with the money gone and the new debts piling up? If only they had three kidneys, with two to spare, then things might be better.

Cohen, who has worked in rural towns in various regions of India over the past decade, reports that in a very brief period the idea of trading "a kidney for a dowry" has caught on and become one strategy for poor parents desperate to arrange a comfortable marriage for an "extra" daughter. In other words, a spare kidney for a spare daughter. A decade ago, when townspeople first heard through newspaper reports of kidney sales occurring in the cities of Bombay and Madras, they responded with predictable alarm. Today, Cohen says, some of these same people now speak matter of factly about when it might be necessary to sell a "spare" organ. Cohen argues that it is not that every townsperson actually knows someone who has been tempted to sell a vital part of the self, but that the idea of the "commodified" kidney has permeated the social imaginary. Today the kidney represents "everyman's" last economic resort; the kidney stands as the marker of one's "ultimate collateral." Some parents say they can no longer complain about the fate of a dowryless daughter. "Haven't you got a spare kidney?" one or another neighbor is likely to respond. With the appearance of new sources of capital, the dowry system is expanding, along with kidney sales, into areas where it had not been a traditional practice.

Several months later, I sat next to Mrs. Rosemary Sitshetshe on a torn black plastic couch in her small but neat concrete slab house in Guguletu township outside Cape Town, South Africa. On her other side sat Rosemary's mother, a powerful woman, who sustained her daughter as she retold the painful story of how the body of her only son, seventeen-year-old Andrew, had been manhandled and mutilated at the police mortuary in Cape Town, his eyes and possibly other body parts removed without consent and given to doctors to transplant into other people's bodies.

Andrew was caught in the crossfire of township gang warfare during the dangerous period just before the end of apartheid. Badly wounded, he was taken to the local police station where Rosemary found him lying on the floor with a bleeding chest wound. By the time the ambulance attendants arrived, late as usual, Andrew was dead (or very nearly so) and the police advised Rosemary to go home until the morning when she could claim her son's body for burial. But the following morning, the officials at the police mortuary turned Rosemary away saying that the body was not yet ready for identification and viewing. Two days later, when the family was finally allowed to view Andrew's body they were shocked at what they saw: the blanket covering the body was bloody and Andrew's head had two deep holes on either side of his forehead "so you could easily see the bone." His face was swollen and there seemed to [be] something wrong with his eyes. "So, I did the unthinkable, I lifted up his eyelids."

But when Rosemary questioned the people in charge, they denied that anything was wrong and treated Rosemary and her estranged husband abusively. Later, accompanied by her own private pathologist paid for by the African National Congress, Mrs. Sitshetshe learned at the morgue that her son's eyes had been removed and that inside his abdominal cavity the organs found there had all been severed and carefully replaced for viewing. "But were those parts his own?" Mrs. Sitshetshe asked me. "I know my son's eyes by color but not his heart or kidneys."

At the local eye bank Rosemary was told that her son's corneas had been "shaved" and given to two "lucky" patients at the nearby academic hospital. The remains of Andrew's eyes were being kept in the refrigerator and the director refused to return them to Andrew's mother for burial. And so, unwilling to argue any further, Andrew Sitshetshe was buried without his eyes. But Rosemary found she could not bury her anger. "Although my son is dead and buried," Mrs. Sitshetshe said, with tears coursing down her cheeks, "Is it good that his flesh is here, there, and everywhere, and that parts of his body are still floating around? Must we be stripped of every comfort? How could the medical doctor know what was most important for us?" Mrs. Sitshetshe has since taken her complaint against the mortuary and eye bank staff to South Africa's Truth and Reconciliation Commission. She wants her case to be treated as but one example of a practice that was widespread in police mortuaries under apartheid and which may have continued out of habit, even in the "new" South Africa.

*   *   *

In September 1999, I sat nursing a cherry Coke in a dilapidated Denny's Restaurant on Sunset Blvd. in Hollywood. Across from me sat a tall, extremely thin, middle-aged man with intensely blue eyes and a nervous, tentative manner. He gulped frequently and seemed ready to flee from our booth at the slightest provocation and put an end to this strange ethnographic interview. Jim Cohan is a notorious "organs broker" who solicits international buyers and sellers from his home office using the telephone, Internet, and fax. No, I could not tape record our conversation, Jim said, though he was willing to be interviewed about his activities on behalf of "matching up people in need."

"There's no reason for anyone to die in this country while waiting for a heart or a kidney to materialize. There are plenty of spare organs to be had in other parts of the world. One can't be choosy. One has to play by my rules and go where I say. And one has to move quickly." Though Jim operates in a gray, nether world, he insists that what he does is not illegal. He deals with doctors, hospitals, and a "soft" commerce in "excess" cadaveric organs. Although he was arrested and jailed in Italy in 1998 for illegally "brokering" organs, the charges were dropped eventually, and Jim maintains his innocence. In fact, he is proud of his newly invented profession. "Don't think of me as an outlaw," he said. "Think of me as a new version of the old-fashioned marriage broker. I locate and match up people in need; people whose suffering can be alleviated on either side."

Following the Bodies: The Traffic in Human Organs

As these few scenarios plucked out of hundreds of transcribed interviews with transplant specialists, transplant patients, organs brokers, organ buyers, and sellers suggest, transplant surgery today is a blend of altruism and commerce; of science and magic; of gifting, barter, and theft; of choice and coercion. We have found that the "organs trade" is real, spectacularly lucrative, and widespread, even though it is illegal in most countries and unethical according to every governing body of medical, professional life. It is therefore covert. In some of the sites we have explored—India, Brazil, South Africa, and the United States—the trade in organs and other body parts links surgeons and technicians from the upper strata of biomedical practice to "body mafia" from the lowest reaches of the criminal world. The transactions involve police, mortuary workers, pathologists, civil servants, ambulance drivers, emergency room workers, eye bank and blood bank managers, biotechnicians, funeral directors, and transplant coordinators.

Together, we are documenting hard and soft forms of organ sales, investigating rumors of body theft, allegations of human rights violations of the nearly dead, and mutilations of pauper cadavers in police mortuaries. We are trying to pierce the secrecy surrounding organ transplantation and to "make public" all practices regarding the harvesting, selling, and distribution of human organs and tissues. These transactions have been protected, even concealed, by a deadly indifference to the population of organ donors, living and dead, most of them poor, and by an unquestioned acceptance in most industrialized nations of transplant surgery as a social and moral good.

But the entry of "free markets" into the business of organ procurement poses a challenge to the social ethics of organ transplant. By their nature, markets are indiscriminate and inclined to reduce everything—including human beings, their labor, and their reproductive capacity—to the status of commodities—things that can be bought, sold, traded, and stolen. And the global economy has stimulated the movement of mortally sick bodies in one direction and detached "healthy" organs—transported for shorter distances by commercial airlines in ordinary Styrofoam beer coolers conveniently stored in the overhead luggage compartment of the economy section—in another direction, creating [an] international trade in surgeries, bodies, and body parts. In general, the flow of organs follows the modern routes of capital: from South to North, from third to first world, from poor to rich, from black and brown to white, and from female to male bodies.

*   *   *

Our initial forays have taken us into alien and, at times, hostile and dangerous territory, where we are exploring some of the backstage scenes of organ transplantation.*** To date, our initial findings reveal the following: (1) race, class, and gender inequalities and injustices in the acquisition, harvesting, and distribution of organs; (2) widespread violation of national laws and international regulations against the sale of organs; (3) the collapse of cultural and religious sanctions against body dismemberment and commercial use in the face of the enormous market pressures in the transplant industry; (4) the appearance of new forms of debt peonage in which the commodified kidney occupies a critical role; (5) the emergence of soft sales in the form of "compensated gifting" of kidneys within extended families along with "coerced" gifts, as vulnerable workers "donate" organs to their employers in exchange for secure work and other entitlements, and prisoners donate them in exchange for reduction in prison sentences; (6) popular resistance to new laws of presumed consent for organ donation; (7) widespread violations of cadavers in public morgues, organs and tissues being removed without any consent for international sale; (8) the disposal and wasting of viable organs in the context of intense competition of public and private hospitals; (9) the critical importance of transplant surgery and commodified organs to the new economics of privatized health care throughout the world; (10) the circulation of narratives of terror concerning the theft and disappearance of bodies and body parts globally, some of which have a basis in reality; (11) the spread of a lucrative transplant tourism in which patients, doctors, and sellers are serviced by rings of organ brokers.

*   *   *

At the heart of this project is an anthropological analysis of postmodern forms of human sacrifice. Though it bears little resemblance to the burnt offerings of the desert Hebrews or to the agony of Christian martyrs thrown to lions at the dawn of the second millennium, human sacrifice is still with us. Organ harvesting carries some trace elements and vestigial images of Aztec hearts ripped—still beating—from the chests of state-appointed, ritual scapegoats. Global capitalism and advanced biotechnology have released new, medically incited "tastes" (a New Age gourmet cannibalism, perhaps) for human bodies, living and dead, for the skin and bones, flesh and blood, tissue, marrow, and genetic material of "the other." Like other forms of human sacrifice, transplant surgery partakes in the really real, the surreal, the magical, and the uncanny. What is different today is that the sacrifice is disguised as a "gift," a donation, and is unrecognized for what it really is. The sacrifice is rendered invisible by its anonymity and hidden within the rhetoric of "life saving" and "gift giving."

*   *   *

In its odd juxtapositions of ethnography, fact-finding, documentation/surveillance, and human rights advocacy, this project blends genres and transgresses cherished distinctions among anthropology, political journalism, scientific report, moral philosophy, and human rights advocacy. These newer ethnographic engagements with everyday violence and human suffering require the anthropologist to penetrate spaces—that is, the "back alleys and police morgues" of this research—where nothing can be taken for granted and where a hermeneutics of suspicion replaces the earlier fieldwork modes of phenomenological bracketing and suspension of disbelief. That these transgressive uses of anthropology make some of my colleagues uneasy or angry is understandable. Neither are my collaborators and I entirely comfortable with what we have taken on. Yet, is any *other* discipline better situated than anthropology to interrogate human values and practices from a position of epistemological "openness" and to offer alternatives to the limited pragmatic utilitarianism and rational-choice models that dominate medical and bio-ethical thinking today?

Rather than views from the armchair, this research reports on views from over, under, and beyond the operating table and mortuary slab. If peering into surgical slop buckets to document the number of "wasted" organs is not ethno-*graphic* research, then I am afraid to consider what *else* it might be. In bridging the normally discrete boundaries between fieldwork in elite medical centers and in shantytowns and back alleys, our orientation holds to the simple dictum—"Follow the bodies!" Problems remain, however, with respect to the incompleteness of the evidence based on innuendo and fragments of conversation, as well as on hundreds of transcribed formal interviews and structured observations in dialysis clinics and operating rooms in each of our multiple research sites. Multisited research runs the risk of being too thinly spread, but the alternatives to this are unclear, given our mandate to investigate rumors, allegations, and scandals of kidnap, body-part sales, and organ theft, many of which prove difficult to verify because of the almost impenetrable secrecy surrounding global practices of organ harvesting and transplant surgery. Our research also demands a sacrifice of the normally leisurely pace of traditional ethnographic work. We have to respond, move, and write quickly. We are learning, and rather quickly, as we go along.

*   *   *

In sum, our goal is to bring broader social and social justice concerns to bear on global practices of organ harvesting and distribution as an alternative to the myopic, case-by-case view of transplant surgeons. While most of our field research to date has taken place in the Third World, we are learning the extent to which these global exchanges involve and implicate the United States and Western Europe. The rapacious demand for organs in one area stimulates the market for brokers and organ sellers or body mafia in other nations. * * *

Organ transplantation depends on a social contract and a social trust. * * * At a very rudimentary level, the ethical practice of organ transplantation requires a reasonably fair and equitable health care system within a reasonably democratic state in which basic human rights are protected and guaranteed. Organ transplantation occurring within the milieu of a police state where political "disappearances" or "dirty wars" are practiced, or where routine police torture and injury and deaths in detention are common, can only generate fears and panics. And organ transplantation occurring within a competitive market economy in which sellers are reduced to "suppliers" of valuable spare parts corrupts the profession of medicine. Under such circumstances, the most vulnerable people will fight back with one of the only resources they have—gossip and rumors which convey, albeit obliquely, the reality of the "situation of emergency" that exists for them.

We are seeking assurances that the social and medical practices around organ transplantation *include attention to* the needs and wishes of organ donors, both living and dead. We are asking transplant surgeons to pay attention to where organs come from and the manner in which they are harvested. We want assurances that organ donation everywhere is voluntary and based on altruistic motives. And we want the bodies of potential donors—living and dead—to be protected and not exploited by those who are charged with their care. We want the risks and benefits of organ transplant surgery to be more equally distributed among and within nations, and among ethnic groups, genders, and social classes. Finally, we want assurances that the so-called "gift of life" never deteriorates into a "theft of life." We hope that this new project will be seen as an attempt to establish a new ethical blueprint for anthropology and for medicine into the twenty-first century.

ENGAGING THE TEXT, ENGAGING THE WORLD

- Describe the strategies Scheper-Hughes uses to conduct her research. How has globalization affected her research strategies?

- What does Scheper-Hughes mean by "structural violence," the violence of everyday life that affects the bodies and minds of the urban poor?

- Where might you see this kind of structural violence even in a wealthy country like the United States?

- Why does Scheper-Hughes suggest that the global trade in human organs is shrouded in secrecy?

- Are you an organ donor? Why or why not? Have you heard rumors like those heard by the urban poor in Scheper-Hughes's study?

- Compare the readings from De León, Turner, and Scheper-Hughes in this chapter. What do they tell you about anthropology in a global age? In particular, what are the impacts of globalization on the local communities and on the research strategies each anthropologist uses?

2
Culture

When people hear the word *culture*, they often think about the material goods or artistic forms produced by distinct groups of people—Chinese food, Middle Eastern music, Indian clothing, Greek architecture, African dances. Sometimes people assume that culture means elite art forms such as those exhibited in museums or performed by operas and ballets. But for anthropologists, culture is much more: It encompasses people's entire way of life.

Culture is a system of knowledge, beliefs, patterns of behavior, artifacts, and institutions that is created, learned, shared, and contested by a group of people. A cultural group may be large or small, and it may have within it significant diversity of region, religion, language, gender, sexuality, class, generation, race, and ethnic identity.

We learn culture throughout our lives from the people and cultural institutions that surround us. We learn certain aspects of culture through formal instruction and other aspects informally and even unconsciously as we absorb culture from family, friends, and the media. Through **enculturation**—the ongoing process of learning culture—members of a group develop a shared body of cultural knowledge and patterns of behavior. Though anthropologists no longer think of culture as a completely separate, unique possession of a specific group of people, most argue that a common cultural core exists, at least among the dominant segments of the group. An anthropologist may consider **norms, values, symbols, and mental maps of reality** in attempting to understand the complex workings of a culture. These elements are not universal; they vary from culture to culture. Even within a group not everyone shares equally in cultural knowledge, nor does everyone agree completely on it. Culture is not static but changes constantly. Aspects of a culture may be debated, negotiated, and contested. But key elements of a culture powerfully frame what its participants consider normal and natural, what they consider appropriate, what they can say, what they can do, and even what they think is possible and impossible.

As globalization intensifies, people all over the world are increasingly confronting the diversity of global cultures. Multicultural encounters are happening closer and closer to home. As we cross cultural boundaries and learn about the cultures of others, our own ethnocentrism may be exposed and we are challenged to see others in a new light. As we will see in Horace Miner's article "Body Ritual among the Nacirema," anthropological approaches to understanding other cultures also offer the possibility of helping us see our own culture more clearly. Anthropologists often refer to this process as making the strange familiar and the familiar strange. Anthropology seeks to broaden our worldview, to enable people to see their own culture as one expression within the context of global cultural diversity, and to recognize that what may seem unusual or unnatural from one cultural perspective may be normal and commonplace from another. To counteract the effects of ethnocentrism on our cross-cultural work anthropologists begin with a research strategy called **cultural relativism**, suspending judgment while attempting to understand another group's beliefs and practices within its own cultural context.

In "Do Muslim Women Need Saving?", Lila Abu-Lughod challenges the ethnocentrism of U.S. culture that assumes Muslim women need to be "saved." Abu-Lughod asks: By whom and for what? She challenges her readers to look more carefully at Muslim women's lives, particularly their varied practices of covering, before making such judgments. What is it about U.S. culture that leads to the assumption that Muslim women need saving? Is it possible to imagine from the perspective of a Muslim woman that Muslim women are fine, and instead that U.S. women might need saving? Abu-Lughod writes that while cultural relativism is far better than colonialism, it may be too late for a cultural relativist approach of non-judgment and non-involvement. After a long history of Western political and military interventions in the lives of people in the Middle East, we are already involved. Our cultures are already intertwined.

Anthropological research reveals that cultures have never been made up of completely isolated or bounded groups of people located in a particular place. As Lucas Bessire shows us in *Behold the Black Caiman,* his book about the lives of the indigenous Ayoreo people of South America, popular cultural myths of isolated and "primitive" groups who have lived on their own, untouched, without contact, fall apart in light of the proven, but less exotic, experiences of encounter, interaction, movement, and exchange that have been much more fundamental aspects of humanity. Cultures have always been influenced by the flow of people, ideas, and goods, whether through migration, trade, or invasion. And as we will see throughout this book, today's flows of globalization are intensifying the exchange and diffusion of people, ideas, and goods, creating even more interaction and engagement.

Body Ritual among the Nacirema

Horace Miner

In this classic article from 1956, anthropologist Horace Miner introduces us to the magical beliefs and practices of the Nacirema. His report of Nacirema medicine men, potions, charms, holy waters, Water Temples, magical powders, gender-specific rituals, and elaborate ritual costumes shines a bright analytical light on this poorly understood culture. Of particular interest to Miner is the Nacirema's fascination—almost obsession—with the human body, its health and appearance, and their unique, mysterious, and elaborate ceremonial practices, rituals, and household shrines. As you read, consider how the Nacirema's rituals are similar to or different from practices you may have experienced in your own life.

The anthropologist has become so familiar with the diversity of ways in which different peoples behave in similar situations that he is not apt to be surprised by even the most exotic customs. In fact, if all of the logically possible combinations of behavior have not been found somewhere in the world, he is apt to suspect that they must be present in some yet undescribed tribe. * * * In this light, the magical beliefs and practices of the Nacirema present such unusual aspects that it seems desirable to describe them as an example of the extremes to which human behavior can go.

Professor Linton first brought the ritual of the Nacirema to the attention of anthropologists twenty years ago (1936:326), but the culture of this people is still very poorly understood. They are a North American group living in the territory between the Canadian Cree, the Yaqui and Tarahumare of Mexico, and the Carib and Arawak of the Antilles. Little is known of their origin, although tradition states that they came from the east. According to Nacirema mythology, their nation was originated by a culture hero, Notgnihsaw, who is otherwise known for two great feats of strength—the throwing of a piece of wampum across the river Pa-To-Mac and the chopping down of a cherry tree in which the Spirit of Truth resided.

Nacirema culture is characterized by a highly developed market economy which has evolved in a rich natural habitat. While much of the people's time is devoted to economic pursuits, a large part of the fruits of these labors and a considerable portion of the day are spent in ritual activity. The focus of this activity is the human body, the appearance and

From Horace Miner. 1956. "Body Ritual among the Nacirema." *American Anthropologist* 58(3): 503–507.

health of which loom as a dominant concern in the ethos of the people. While such a concern is certainly not unusual, its ceremonial aspects and associated philosophy are unique.

The fundamental belief underlying the whole system appears to be that the human body is ugly and that its natural tendency is to debility and disease. Incarcerated in such a body, man's only hope is to avert these characteristics through the use of the powerful influences of ritual and ceremony. Every household has one or more shrines devoted to this purpose. The more powerful individuals in the society have several shrines in their houses and, in fact, the opulence of a house is often referred to in terms of the number of such ritual centers it possesses. Most houses are of wattle and daub construction, but the shrine rooms of the more wealthy are walled with stone. Poorer families imitate the rich by applying pottery plaques to their shrine walls.

While each family has at least one such shrine, the rituals associated with it are not family ceremonies but are private and secret. The rites are normally only discussed with children, and then only during the period when they are being initiated into these mysteries. I was able, however, to establish sufficient rapport with the natives to examine these shrines and to have the rituals described to me.

The focal point of the shrine is a box or chest which is built into the wall. In this chest are kept the many charms and magical potions without which no native believes he could live. These preparations are secured from a variety of specialized practitioners. The most powerful of these are the medicine men, whose assistance must be rewarded with substantial gifts. However, the medicine men do not provide the curative potions for their clients, but decide what the ingredients should be and then write them down in an ancient and secret language. This writing is understood only by the medicine men and by the herbalists who, for another gift, provide the required charm.

The charm is not disposed of after it has served its purpose, but is placed in the charm-box of the household shrine. As these magical materials are specific for certain ills, and the real or imagined maladies of the people are many, the charm-box is usually full to overflowing. The magical packets are so numerous that people forget what their purposes were and fear to use them again. While the natives are very vague on this point, we can only assume that the idea in retaining all the old magical materials is that their presence in the charm-box, before which the body rituals are conducted, will in some way protect the worshipper.

Beneath the charm-box is a small font. Each day every member of the family, in succession, enters the shrine room, bows his head before the charm-box, mingles different sorts of holy water in the font, and proceeds with a brief rite of ablution. The holy waters are secured from the Water Temple of the community, where the priests conduct elaborate ceremonies to make the liquid ritually pure.

In the hierarchy of magical practitioners, and below the medicine men in prestige, are specialists whose designation is best translated "holy-mouth-men." The Nacirema have an almost pathological horror of and fascination with the mouth, the condition of which is believed to have a supernatural influence on all social relationships. Were it not for the rituals of the mouth, they believe that their teeth would fall out, their gums bleed, their jaws shrink, their friends desert them, and their lovers reject them. They also believe that a strong relationship exists between oral and moral characteristics. For example, there is a ritual ablution of the mouth for children which is supposed to improve their moral fiber.

The daily body ritual performed by everyone includes a mouth-rite. Despite the fact that these people are so punctilious about care of the mouth, this rite involves a practice which strikes the uninitiated stranger as revolting. It was reported to me that the ritual consists of inserting a small bundle of hog hairs into the mouth, along with certain magical powders, and then moving the bundle in a highly formalized series of gestures.

In addition to the private mouth-rite, the people seek out a holy-mouth-man once or twice a year. These practitioners have an impressive set of paraphernalia, consisting of a variety of augers, awls, probes, and prods. The use of these objects in the exorcism of the evils of the mouth involves almost unbelievable ritual torture of the client. The holy-mouth-man opens the client's mouth and, using the above mentioned tools, enlarges any holes which decay may have created in the teeth. Magical materials are put into these holes. If there are no naturally occurring holes in the teeth, large sections of one or more teeth are gouged out so that the supernatural substance can be applied. In the client's view, the purpose of these ministrations is to arrest decay and to draw friends. The extremely sacred and traditional character of the rite is evident in the fact that the natives return to the holy-mouth-men year after year, despite the fact that their teeth continue to decay.

It is to be hoped that, when a thorough study of the Nacirema is made, there will be careful inquiry into the personality structure of these people. One has but to watch the gleam in the eye of a holy-mouth-man, as he jabs an awl into an exposed nerve, to suspect that a certain amount of sadism is involved. If this can be established, a very interesting pattern emerges, for most of the population shows definite masochistic tendencies. It was to these that Professor Linton referred in discussing a distinctive part of the daily body ritual which is performed only by men. This part of the rite involves scraping and lacerating the surface of the face with a sharp instrument. Special women's rites are performed only four times during each lunar month, but what they lack in frequency is made up in barbarity. As part of this ceremony, women bake their heads in small ovens for about an hour. The theoretically interesting point is that what seems to be a preponderantly masochistic people have developed sadistic specialists.

The medicine men have an imposing temple, or *latipso*, in every community of any size. The more elaborate ceremonies required to treat very sick patients can only be performed at this temple. These ceremonies involve not only the thaumaturge but a permanent group of vestal maidens who move sedately about the temple chambers in distinctive costume and headdress.

The *latipso* ceremonies are so harsh that it is phenomenal that a fair proportion of the really sick natives who enter the temple ever recover. Small children whose indoctrination is still incomplete have been known to resist attempts to take them to the temple because "that is where you go to die." Despite this fact, sick adults are not only willing but eager to undergo the protracted ritual purification, if they can afford to do so. No matter how ill the supplicant or how grave the emergency, the guardians of many temples will not admit a client if he cannot give a rich gift to the custodian. Even after one has gained admission and survived the ceremonies, the guardians will not permit the neophyte to leave until he makes still another gift.

The supplicant entering the temple is first stripped of all his or her clothes. In everyday life the Nacirema avoids exposure of his body and its natural functions. Bathing and excretory acts are performed only in the secrecy of the household shrine, where they are ritualized as part of the body-rites. Psychological shock results from the fact that body secrecy is suddenly lost upon entry into the *latipso*. A man, whose own wife has never seen him in an excretory act, suddenly finds himself naked and assisted by a vestal maiden while he performs his natural functions into a sacred vessel. This sort of ceremonial treatment is necessitated by the fact that the excreta are used by a diviner to ascertain the course and nature of the client's sickness. Female clients, on the other hand, find their naked bodies are subjected to the scrutiny, manipulation and prodding of the medicine men.

Few supplicants in the temple are well enough to do anything but lie on their hard beds. The daily ceremonies, like the rites of the holy-mouth-men, involve discomfort and torture. With ritual precision, the vestals awaken their miserable charges each dawn and roll them about on their beds of pain while performing ablutions, in the formal movements of which the maidens are highly trained. At other times they insert magic wands in the supplicant's mouth or force him to eat substances which are supposed to be healing. From time to time the medicine men come to their clients and jab magically treated needles into their flesh. The fact that these temple ceremonies may not cure, and may even kill the neophyte, in no way decreases the people's faith in the medicine men.

There remains one other kind of practitioner, known as a "listener." This witch-doctor has the power to exorcise the devils that lodge in the heads of people who have been bewitched. The Nacirema believe that parents bewitch their own children. Mothers are particularly suspected of putting a curse on children while teaching them the secret body rituals. The counter-magic of the witch-doctor is unusual in its lack of ritual. The patient simply tells the "listener" all his troubles and fears, beginning with the earliest difficulties he can remember. The memory displayed by the Nacirema in these exorcism sessions is truly remarkable. It is not uncommon for the patient to bemoan the rejection he felt upon being weaned as a babe, and a few individuals even see their troubles going back to the traumatic effects of their own birth.

In conclusion, mention must be made of certain practices which have their base in native esthetics but which depend upon the pervasive aversion to the natural body and its functions. There are ritual fasts to make fat people thin and ceremonial feasts to make thin people fat. Still other rites are used to make women's breasts larger if they are small, and smaller if they are large. General dissatisfaction with breast shape is symbolized in the fact that the ideal form is virtually outside the range of human variation. A few women afflicted with almost inhuman hypermammary development are so idolized that they make a handsome living by simply going from village to village and permitting the natives to stare at them for a fee.

Reference has already been made to the fact that excretory functions are ritualized, routinized, and relegated to secrecy. Natural reproductive functions are similarly distorted. Intercourse is taboo as a topic and scheduled as an act. Efforts are made to avoid pregnancy by the use of magical materials or by limiting intercourse to certain phases of the moon. Conception is actually very infrequent. When pregnant, women dress so as to hide their condition. Parturition takes place in secret, without friends or relatives to assist, and the majority of women do not nurse their infants.

Our review of the ritual life of the Nacirema has certainly shown them to be a magic-ridden people. It is hard to understand how they have managed to exist so long under the burdens which they have imposed upon themselves. But even such exotic customs as these take on real meaning when they are viewed with the insight provided by [anthropologist Bronislaw] Malinowski when he wrote (1948:70):

> Looking from far and above, from our high places of safety in the developed civilization, it is easy to see all the crudity and irrelevance of magic. But without its power and guidance early man could not have mastered his practical difficulties as he has done, nor could man have advanced to the higher stages of civilization.

ENGAGING THE TEXT, ENGAGING THE WORLD

- Perhaps you have realized that Nacirema is American spelled backward. At what point did you realize this, and how did that change the way you read this selection?

- Consider reading the article again now that you know who the Nacirema are. What new insights do you gain?

- By "flipping the lens," allowing us to see our culture as if from the outside, Miner succeeds in the anthropological project of making the strange familiar and the familiar strange. How has this "outsider's" view of American cultural practices allowed you to see yourself and your culture in a new light?

- What we consider rational, logical, even scientific behavior within our culture may appear irrational, illogical, and full of magical beliefs and practices when seen from the outside. How does Miner's article challenge us to confront our ethnocentrism?

- How would you update this story for the Nacirema culture today?

Do Muslim Women Really Need Saving?

Lila Abu-Lughod

Developing an anthropological approach to cultural "others"

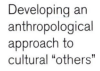

In this 2002 article, Lila Abu-Lughod examines the ways in which the "War on Terror" and the United States's military involvement in Afghanistan have been justified as ways to liberate or "save" Afghan women. Why do so many in the West think Muslim women need saving? Saving from what? And for what? Abu-Lughod explores the dangerous roots of this preoccupation with the situation of Muslim women, using an anthropological approach that offers strategies for thinking more carefully about the veil, the burqa, and the clothing of what she calls "women of cover." Abu-Lughod suggests that we need to fundamentally re-examine and relearn our approach to cultural "others" and cultural differences. Can we move past ethnocentric perspectives that judge others based on our own cultural norms? Abu-Lughod notes that cultural relativism is certainly a better approach to other cultures than ethnocentrism and even colonialism. But is cultural relativism's call for understanding, rather than judgment and interference, enough for today's world? In reality, she contends, it is too late to *not* interfere. There is already a long history of interaction between people throughout the world. And in the case of Afghanistan, Islamic movements continue to be shaped by a long engagement of Western powers in Middle Eastern lives. Abu-Lughod questions the almost obsessive focus on women's lives or religion in popular debates and discussions about the Middle East. She warns of the risks involved in creating an artificially narrow view of a complex cultural reality. Instead she urges attention to issues of power, history, and global connection that are central to contemporary anthropological approaches and essential to engagement with cultural diversity in an increasingly global age.

What are the ethics of the current "War on Terrorism," a war that justifies itself by purporting to liberate, or save, Afghan women? Does anthropology have anything to offer in our search for a viable position to take regarding this rationale for war?

From Lila Abu-Lughod. 2002. "Do Muslim Women Really Need Saving? Anthropological Reflections on Cultural Relativism and its Others." *American Anthropologist* 104(3): 783–790.

I was led to pose the question of my title in part because of the way I personally experienced the response to the U.S. war in Afghanistan. Like many colleagues whose work has focused on women and gender in the Middle East, I was deluged with invitations to speak—not just on news programs but also to various departments at colleges and universities, especially women's studies programs. Why did this not please me, a scholar who has devoted more than 20 years of her life to this subject and who has some complicated personal connection to this identity? Here was an opportunity to spread the word, disseminate my knowledge, and correct misunderstandings. * * *

My discomfort led me to reflect on why, as feminists in or from the West, or simply as people who have concerns about women's lives, we need to be wary of this response to the events and aftermath of September 11, 2001. I want to point out the minefields—a metaphor that is sadly too apt for a country like Afghanistan, with the world's highest number of mines per capita—of this obsession with the plight of Muslim women. I hope to show some way through them using insights from anthropology, the discipline whose charge has been to understand and manage cultural difference. * * *

Cultural Explanations and the Mobilization of Women

It is easier to see why one should be skeptical about the focus on the "Muslim woman" if one begins with the U.S. public response. I will analyze two manifestations of this response: some conversations I had with a reporter from the PBS *NewsHour with Jim Lehrer* and First Lady Laura Bush's radio address to the nation on November 17, 2001. The presenter from the *NewsHour* show first contacted me in October to see if I was willing to give some background for a segment on Women and Islam. I mischievously asked whether she had done segments on the women of Guatemala, Ireland, Palestine, or Bosnia when the show covered wars in those regions; but I finally agreed to look at the questions she was going to pose to panelists. The questions were hopelessly general. Do Muslim women believe "x"? Are Muslim women "y"? Does Islam allow "z" for women? I asked her: If you were to substitute Christian or Jewish wherever you have Muslim, would these questions make sense? I did not imagine she would call me back. But she did, twice, once with an idea for a segment on the meaning of Ramadan and another time on Muslim women in politics. One was in response to the bombing and the other to the speeches by Laura Bush and Cherie Blair, wife of the British Prime Minister.

What is striking about these three ideas for news programs is that there was a consistent resort to the cultural, as if knowing something about women and Islam or the meaning of a religious ritual would help one understand the tragic attack on New York's World Trade Center and the U.S. Pentagon, or how Afghanistan had come to be ruled by the Taliban, or what interests might have fueled U.S. and other interventions in the region over the past 25 years, or what the history of American support for conservative groups funded to undermine the Soviets might have been, or why the caves and bunkers out of which Bin Laden was to be smoked "dead or alive," as President Bush announced on television, were paid for and built by the CIA.

In other words, the question is why knowing about the "culture" of the region, and particularly its religious beliefs and treatment of women, was more urgent than exploring the history of the development of repressive regimes in the region and the U.S. role in this history. Such cultural framing, it seemed to me, prevented the serious exploration of the roots and nature of human suffering in this part of the world. Instead of political and historical explanations, experts were being asked to give religio-cultural ones. Instead of questions that might lead to the exploration of global interconnections, we were offered ones that worked to artificially divide the world into separate spheres—recreating an imaginative geography of West versus East, us versus Muslims, cultures in which First Ladies give speeches versus others where women shuffle around silently in burqas.

Most pressing for me was why the Muslim woman in general, and the Afghan woman in particular, were so crucial to this cultural mode of explanation, which ignored the complex entanglements in which we are all implicated, in sometimes surprising alignments. Why were these female symbols being mobilized in this "War against Terrorism" in a way they were not in other conflicts? Laura Bush's radio address on November 17 reveals the political work such mobilization accomplishes. On the one hand, her address collapsed important distinctions that should have been maintained. There was a constant slippage between the Taliban and the terrorists, so that they became almost one word—a kind of hyphenated monster identity: the Taliban-and-the-terrorists. Then there was the blurring of the very separate causes in Afghanistan of women's continuing malnutrition, poverty, and ill health, and their more recent exclusion under the Taliban from employment, schooling, and the joys of wearing nail polish. On the other hand, her speech reinforced chasmic divides, primarily between the "civilized people throughout the world" whose hearts break for the women and children of Afghanistan and the Taliban-and-the-terrorists, the cultural monsters who want to, as she put it, "impose their world on the rest of us."

Most revealingly, the speech enlisted women to justify American bombing and intervention in Afghanistan and to make a case for the "War on Terrorism" of which it was allegedly a part. As Laura Bush said, "Because of our recent military gains in much of Afghanistan, women are no longer imprisoned in their homes. They can listen to music and teach their daughters without fear of punishment. The fight against terrorism is also a fight for the rights and dignity of women" (U.S. Government 2002).

These words have haunting resonances for anyone who has studied colonial history. Many who have worked on British colonialism in South Asia have noted the use of the woman question in colonial policies where intervention into *sati* (the practice of widows immolating themselves on their husbands' funeral pyres), child marriage, and other practices was used to justify rule. As [Indian literary theorist] Gayatri Chakravorty Spivak (1988) has cynically put it: white men saving brown women from brown men. The historical record is full of similar cases, including in the Middle East. In Turn of the Century Egypt, what [feminist scholar of Islam] Leila Ahmed (1992) has called "colonial feminism" was hard at work. This was a selective concern about the plight of Egyptian women that focused on the veil as a sign of oppression but gave no support to women's education and was professed loudly by the same Englishman, Lord Cromer [British consul-general in Egypt], who opposed women's suffrage back home.

*　　*　　*

Politics of the Veil

I want now to look more closely at those Afghan women Laura Bush claimed were "rejoicing" at their liberation by the Americans. This necessitates a discussion of the veil, or the burqa, because it is so central to contemporary concerns about Muslim women. This will set the stage for a discussion of how anthropologists, feminist anthropologists in particular, contend with the problem of difference in a global world. * * *

It is common popular knowledge that the ultimate sign of the oppression of Afghan women under the Taliban-and-the-terrorists is that they were forced to wear the burqa. Liberals sometimes confess their surprise that even though Afghanistan has been liberated from the Taliban, women do not seem to be throwing off their burqas. Someone who has worked in Muslim regions must ask why this is so surprising. Did we expect that once "free" from the Taliban they would go "back" to belly shirts and blue jeans, or dust off their Chanel suits? We need to be more sensible about the clothing of "women of cover," and so there is perhaps a need to make some basic points about veiling.

First, it should be recalled that the Taliban did not invent the burqa. It was the local form of covering that Pashtun women in one region wore when they went out. The Pashtun are one of several ethnic groups in Afghanistan and the burqa was one of many forms of covering in the subcontinent and Southwest Asia that has developed as a convention for symbolizing women's modesty or respectability. The burqa, like some other forms of "cover" has, in many settings, marked the symbolic separation of men's and women's spheres, as part of the general association of women with family and home, not with public space where strangers mingled.

Twenty years ago the anthropologist Hanna Papanek (1982), who worked in Pakistan, described the burqa as "portable seclusion." She noted that many saw it as a liberating invention because it enabled women to move out of segregated living spaces while still observing the basic moral requirements of separating and protecting women from unrelated men. Ever since I came across her phrase "portable seclusion," I have thought of these enveloping robes as "mobile homes." Everywhere, such veiling signifies belonging to a particular community and participating in a moral way of life in which families are paramount in the organization of communities and the home is associated with the sanctity of women.

The obvious question that follows is this: If this were the case, why would women suddenly become immodest? Why would they suddenly throw off the markers of their respectability, markers, whether burqas or other forms of cover, which were supposed to assure their protection in the public sphere from the harassment of strange men by symbolically signaling to all that they were still in the inviolable space of their homes, even though moving in the public realm? Especially when these are forms of dress that had become so conventional that most women gave little thought to their meaning.

To draw some analogies, none of them perfect, why are we surprised that Afghan women do not throw off their burqas when we know perfectly well that it would not be appropriate to wear shorts to the opera? At the time these discussions of Afghan women's burqas were raging, a friend of mine was chided by her husband for suggesting she wanted to wear a pantsuit to a fancy wedding: "You know you don't wear pants to a WASP [White Anglo-Saxon Protestant] wedding," he reminded her. New Yorkers know that the beautifully coiffed Hasidic [Jewish] women, who look so fashionable next to their dour husbands in black coats and hats, are wearing wigs. This is because religious belief and community standards of propriety require the covering of the hair. They also alter boutique fashions to include high necks and long sleeves. As anthropologists know perfectly well, people wear the appropriate form of dress for their social communities and are guided by socially shared standards, religious beliefs, and moral ideals, unless they deliberately transgress to make a point or are unable to afford proper cover. If we think that U.S. women live in a world of choice regarding clothing, all we need to do is remind ourselves of the expression, "the tyranny of fashion."

What had happened in Afghanistan under the Taliban is that one regional style of covering or veiling, associated with a certain respectable but not elite class, was imposed on everyone as "religiously" appropriate, even though previously there had been many different styles, popular or traditional with different groups and classes—different ways to mark women's propriety, or, in more recent times, religious piety. Although I am not an expert on Afghanistan, I imagine that the majority of women left in Afghanistan by the time the Taliban took control were the rural or less educated, from nonelite families, since they were the only ones who could not emigrate to escape the hardship and violence that has marked Afghanistan's recent history. If liberated from the enforced wearing of burqas, most of these women would choose some other form of modest head-covering, like all those living nearby who were not under the Taliban—their rural Hindu counterparts in the North of India (who cover their heads and veil their faces from affines) or their Muslim sisters in Pakistan.

Even *The New York Times* carried an article about Afghan women refugees in Pakistan that attempted to educate readers about this local variety (Fremson 2001). The article describes and pictures everything from the now-iconic burqa with the embroidered eyeholes, which a Pashtun woman explains is the proper dress for her community, to large scarves they call chadors, to the new Islamic modest dress that wearers refer to as *hijab*. Those in the new Islamic dress are characteristically students heading for professional careers, especially in medicine, just like their counterparts from Egypt to Malaysia. One wearing the large scarf was a school principal; the other was a poor street vendor. The telling quote from the young street vendor is, "If I did [wear the burqa] the refugees would tease me because the burqa is for 'good women' who stay inside the home" (Fremson 2001:14). Here you can see the local status associated with the burqa—it is for good respectable women from strong families who are not forced to make a living selling on the street.

The British newspaper *The Guardian* published an interview in January 2002 with Dr. Suheila Siddiqi, a respected surgeon in Afghanistan who holds the rank of lieutenant general in the Afghan medical corps (Goldenberg 2002). A woman in her sixties, she comes from an elite family and, like her sisters, was educated. Unlike most women of her class, she chose not to go into exile. She is presented in the article as "the woman who stood up to the Taliban" because she refused to wear the burqa. She had made it a condition of returning to her post as head of a major hospital when the Taliban came begging in 1996, just eight months after firing her along with other women. Siddiqi is described as thin, glamorous, and confident. But further into the article it is noted that her graying bouffant hair is covered in a gauzy veil. This is a reminder that though she refused the burqa, she had no question about wearing the chador or scarf.

Finally, I need to make a crucial point about veiling. Not only are there many forms of covering, which themselves have different meanings in the communities in which they are used, but also veiling itself must not be confused with, or made to stand for, lack of agency. As I have argued in my ethnography of a Bedouin community in Egypt in the late 1970s and 1980s (1986), pulling the black head cloth over the face in front of older respected men is considered a voluntary act by women who are deeply committed to being moral and have a sense of honor tied to family. One of the ways they show their standing is by covering their faces in certain contexts. They decide for whom they feel it is appropriate to veil.

*   *   *

Two points emerge from this fairly basic discussion of the meanings of veiling in the contemporary Muslim world. First, we need to work against the reductive interpretation of veiling as the quintessential sign of women's unfreedom, even if we object to state imposition of this form, as in Iran or with the Taliban. (It must be recalled that the modernizing states of Turkey and Iran had earlier in the century banned veiling and required men, except religious clerics, to adopt Western dress.) What does freedom mean if we accept the fundamental premise that humans are social beings, always raised in certain social and historical contexts and belonging to particular communities that shape their desires and understandings of the world? Is it not a gross violation of women's own understandings of what they are doing to simply denounce the burqa as a medieval imposition? Second, we must take care not to reduce the diverse situations and attitudes of millions of Muslim women to a single item of clothing. Perhaps it is time to give up the Western obsession with the veil and focus on some serious issues with which feminists and others should indeed be concerned.

Ultimately, the significant political-ethical problem the burqa raises is how to deal with cultural "others." How are we to deal with difference without accepting the passivity implied by the cultural relativism for which anthropologists are justly famous—a relativism that says it's their culture and it's not my business to judge or interfere, only to try to understand. Cultural relativism is certainly an improvement on ethnocentrism and the racism, cultural imperialism, and imperiousness that underlie it; the problem is that it is too late not to interfere. The forms of lives we find around the world are already products of long histories of interactions.

*　　*　　*

We need to confront two big issues. First is the acceptance of the possibility of difference. Can we only free Afghan women to be like us or might we have to recognize that even after "liberation" from the Taliban, they might want different things than we would want for them? What do we do about that? Second, we need to be vigilant about the rhetoric of saving people because of what it implies about our attitudes.

Again, when I talk about accepting difference, I am not implying that we should resign ourselves to being cultural relativists who respect whatever goes on elsewhere as "just their culture." I have already discussed the dangers of "cultural" explanations; "their" cultures are just as much part of history and an interconnected world as ours are. What I am advocating is the hard work involved in recognizing and respecting differences—precisely as products of different histories, as expressions of different circumstances, and as manifestations of differently structured desires. We may want justice for women, but can we accept that there might be different ideas about justice and that different women might want, or choose, different futures from what we envision as best? We must consider that they might be called to personhood, so to speak, in a different language.

*　　*　　*

My point is to remind us to be aware of differences, respectful of other paths toward social change that might give women better lives. Can there be a liberation that is Islamic? And, beyond this, is liberation even a goal for which all women or people strive? Are emancipation, equality, and rights part of a universal language we must use? * * * In other words, might other desires be more meaningful for different groups of people? Living in close families? Living in a godly way? Living without war? I have done fieldwork in Egypt over more than 20 years and I cannot think of a single woman I know, from the poorest rural to the most educated cosmopolitan, who has ever expressed envy of U.S. women, women they tend to perceive as bereft of community, vulnerable to sexual violence and social anomie, driven by individual success rather than morality, or strangely disrespectful of God.

*　　*　　*

Beyond the Rhetoric of Salvation

Let us return, finally, to my title, "Do Muslim Women Need Saving?" The discussion of culture, veiling, and how one can navigate the shoals of cultural difference should put Laura Bush's self-congratulation about the rejoicing of Afghan women liberated by American troops in a different light. It is deeply problematic to construct the Afghan woman as someone in need of saving. When you save someone, you imply that you are saving her from something. You are also saving her *to* something. What violences are entailed in this transformation, and what presumptions are being made about the superiority of that to which you are saving her? Projects of saving other women depend on and reinforce a sense of superiority by Westerners, a form of arrogance that deserves to be challenged. All one needs to do to appreciate the patronizing quality of the rhetoric of saving women is to imagine using it today in the United States about disadvantaged groups such as African American women or working-class women. We now understand them as suffering from structural violence. We have become politicized about race and class, but not culture.

*   *   *

Could we not leave veils and vocations of saving others behind and instead train our sights on ways to make the world a more just place? The reason respect for difference should not be confused with cultural relativism is that it does not preclude asking how we, living in this privileged and powerful part of the world, might examine our own responsibilities for the situations in which others in distant places have found themselves. We do not stand outside the world, looking out over this sea of poor benighted people, living under the shadow—or veil—of oppressive cultures; we are part of that world. Islamic movements themselves have arisen in a world shaped by the intense engagements of Western powers in Middle Eastern lives.

A more productive approach, it seems to me, is to ask how we might contribute to making the world a more just place. A world not organized around strategic military and economic demands; a place where certain kinds of forces and values that we may still consider important could have an appeal and where there is the peace necessary for discussions, debates, and transformations to occur within communities. We need to ask ourselves what kinds of world conditions we could contribute to making such that popular desires will not be overdetermined by an overwhelming sense of helplessness in the face of forms of global injustice. Where we seek to be active in the affairs of distant places, can we do so in the spirit of support for those within those communities whose goals are to make women's (and men's) lives better[?] *** Can we use a more egalitarian language of alliances, coalitions, and solidarity, instead of salvation?

Even RAWA, the now celebrated Revolutionary Association of the Women of Afghanistan, which was so instrumental in bringing to U.S. women's attention the excesses of the Taliban, has opposed the U.S. bombing from the beginning. They do not see in it Afghan women's salvation but increased hardship and loss. They have long called for disarmament and for peacekeeping forces. Spokespersons point out the dangers of confusing governments with people, the Taliban with innocent Afghans who will be most harmed. They consistently remind audiences to take a close look at the ways policies are being organized around oil interests, the arms industry, and the international drug trade. They are not obsessed with the veil, even though they are the most radical feminists working for a secular democratic Afghanistan. * * * A first step in hearing their wider message is to break with the language of alien cultures, whether to understand or eliminate them. * * * Our task is to critically explore what we might do to help create a world in which those poor Afghan women, for whom "the hearts of those in the civilized world break," can have safety and decent lives.

ENGAGING THE TEXT, ENGAGING THE WORLD

- What did you learn about the clothing of "women of cover," the history of the burqa and other forms of covering, and the moral communities from which they arise?

- What does Abu-Lughod mean when she calls the burqa a liberating invention? Why does she compare them to mobile homes?

- Why does Abu-Lughod reject the use of the word *saving*?

- Why does Abu-Lughod suggest that cultural relativism is not adequate in approaching cultural diversity? What alternative approaches does she suggest?

- Turning the situation around, do you think American women have free choice over what they wear in every situation? What are the norms that apply? How are these norms set through participation in a moral community? How do you think American women's clothing might be perceived by people from other cultures?

- Abu-Lughod urges her readers to become involved in "making the world a more just place." Drawing upon the challenges Abu-Lughod offers in this article, what would this "just" world look like?

Debunking the
myth of isolation
and "the primitive"

From *Behold the Black Caiman*

Lucas Bessire

Bolivia

Paraguay

Gran Chaco

Our popular media is full of images of isolated primitive people: from *National Geographic* specials to the film *Avatar*, from YouTube videos to front page news stories. What is it about isolated cultures and primitive people that so fascinates us? Lucas Bessire's research, including 42 months of fieldwork and film making from 2001–2013, seeks to upend these iconic but stereotypical images of "Stone-Age-primitives" hiding undiscovered in the forest and replace them with the real-world experiences of indigenous people who are relentlessly stalked by bulldozers, trucks, NGOs, missionaries, and world-ending violence. Bessire reports on his time studying the Ayoreo Indians, particularly a confederation of 6,000 indigenous, Ayoreo-speaking people called the Totobiegosode, living in the mission stations and labor camps in the borderlands between Paraguay and Bolivia in South America. Bessire tells us of his encounters with the Areguede'urasade, a small band of 17 Totobiegosode who emerge from the forests in 2004, and his search for two other small bands—the last of the forest-dwelling Ayoreo. But instead of finding these bands of "voluntarily isolated people" and "uncontacted groups" living in "inseparable unity with their habitat" that many humanitarian and development groups have described, Bessire encounters a small group of people living on the edges of industrial agriculture, vast cattle pastures and aggressive forest clearings. Rather than living in harmony with nature, their every effort at concealment is an effort for survival in the face of encroaching disaster and death. Bessire finds a people not isolated but deeply embedded in global politics and economics, agribusiness, cattle ranches, beef exports, hamburgers, and international aid agencies. What is it about our notion of culture that sends us in search of the primitive and isolated when extensive ethnographic evidence reveals instead deep interconnection, encounter, exchange, and movement throughout human history?

From Lucas Bessire. 2014. *Behold the Black Caiman: A Chronicle of Ayoreo Life*. Chicago: University of Chicago Press. Some of the author's notes have been omitted.

This book chronicles my pursuit of the Black Caiman: a shadowy form birthed by the terror of savagery, by the world-ending violence relentlessly stalking certain unruly Indigenous populations and the New Worlds they have tentatively remade. * * * Tracking the Black Caiman through the everyday actualities and precarious lives of a small group of people in South America's Gran Chaco known as the Ayoreo Indians is the aim and method of this account—its beginning and its end.

*   *   *

A New World

I'd like to think that the woman I will call Tié is my friend, even though there is no word in her language for the absent kind of friendship I can offer.[1]

She was one of a small band of Ayoreo-speaking people who emerged from the dwindling forests of northern Paraguay in March 2004, fleeing ranchers' bulldozers and fearing for their lives. These seventeen people called themselves Areguede'urasade ("band of Areguede") and formed part of the Totobiegosode ("People of the Place where the Collared Peccaries Ate Their Gardens"), the southernmost village confederation of the Ayoreode ("Human Beings"). Along with two other small bands that still roam the dense thickets of the Bolivia/Paraguay borderlands, they were the last of the forest-dwelling Ayoreo.

Startling photographs of these brown-skinned people made headlines around the world that spring. Experts jockeyed to declare this one of the final first contacts with isolated Indians. At first everyone wanted in, including me. When the first tremors of the event reached me, I was a second-year anthropology graduate student at New York University. I thought I understood something of Ayoreo people and the Chaco, as I'd already spent fourteen months living among and collaborating with northern Ayoreo-speaking people as a Fulbright scholar in Bolivia three years before. When I heard they'd come out, I couldn't sleep. I rushed through coursework and film training, and by July I was headed south—as if to bear witness.

Reaching the scene of contact meant first passing thousands of other Ayoreo-speaking people struggling to survive in the stark mission stations and makeshift labor camps that lined dirt roads for miles north of the Mennonite colonies. These "ex-primitives," as I started to think of them, were some of the descendants of the nomadic Ayoreo confederacies that had successfully fought off outsiders for centuries. They too had once gained international fame as uncontacted primitives and the über-savages of the Chaco frontier. In 2004, few people cared. * * * The approximately six thousand Ayoreo-speaking people inhabited some thirty-eight settlements on both sides of the Bolivia/Paraguay border.

---

1. Pseudonyms are used throughout this account to protect the identities of people living and deceased.

They were routinely treated as less than human: a labor reserve for sex work or charcoal production, a threat to civic hygiene, a source of myths and dissertations and marketable bodily substances, souls already won by missionaries. * * *

Like many others, I initially mistook the Totobiegosode holdouts as ideal antidotes to such Ayoreo marginality. They were iconic in the region as "Stone-Age primitives" and "the last great hope for Ayoreo cultural revitalization" (Bartolomé 2000). Up close, however, the details of their lives defied any primitivist fantasies I had brought with me. The latest arrivals wore sandals made of tire scrap instead of tapir skin. They tipped their arrows with flattened forks or steak knives and carried water in a plastic grease bucket made in Indiana. * * * They had developed a way of life centered around the practical problem of concealment from the alien beings—trucks, cattle, bulldozers—they thought were relentlessly pursuing them. They inhabited the literal margins of industrial agriculture. They were often forced to camp in the fifteen-meter-wide strips of brush left as windbreaks around vast cattle pastures. They went long periods communicating only with whistled sounds; even the children were whisper quiet. If they saw a boot print or heard a chainsaw, they would flee far and fast, leaving everything behind. They were not the bearers of a vestigial purity but pieced together the means of survival from detritus. It soon became clear to me that they were by no means isolated. Rather, they had structured precarious lives around the daily logistics of eluding starvation, capture, and a death foretold.

Tié was the youngest woman of the group, around seventeen years old, all unruly hair and pale skin and almond-shaped eyes. Two wild parrots followed her out of the forest and slept near her tarp-covered shack. The other Totobiegosode said she was one of the *uitaque* dreamers who could see the future. At the time, I lived in a tent on the margins of the camp. On good days she would invite me to sit with her and her husband. She spoke, in her halting voice, about the time they all called *nanique*, "before." She told me one of the most arresting stories I heard in the Chaco, one I'm still trying to understand. "We saw tracks. *Cojñone*, Strangers. Where? It was hot. We ran far. Faaar. Swollen tongues. We cried. Crawling low. A water tank. It was full. One *Cojñoi*. Fat. A red shirt. Blood in the water. Trembling underneath. We ran."

*   *   *

A Death Foretold

What does it mean to write or read yet another ethnographic account of the seeming destruction of yet another small group of South American Indians? What kind of humanity is possible for anyone once the spectacular upheavals of a twenty-first-century "first contact" supposedly subside?

*   *   *

At first, it was tempting to see traces of decay everywhere I turned. No matter where I went in the Chaco, I found that Ayoreo were disenfranchised as subhuman matter out of place: cursed, subordinated, neither this nor that. On both sides of the Bolivia/Paraguay border, Ayoreo-speaking people were the poorest and most marginalized of any Indigenous people in a region where camps of dispossessed Natives lined the roads and Indians were still held in conditions described as slavery. They confronted a mosaic of violence: enslavement, massacres, murder, and rape were venerable traditions. Many of the girls exchanged sex for money on the peripheries of cities or towns. The pet parrots in one settlement imitated tubercular coughing. People seemed to alternate between nervous motion and opaque waiting. Many sought escape by whatever means were near at hand: prayers, disco music, shoe glue. The violence was unavoidable. * * *

Yet the more time I spent in the Chaco, the more clear it became that death was only part of the story. * * * By the time I left the Areguede'urasade in 2004, I was increasingly convinced that primitivist narratives of culture death were not any kind of answer at all. Rather, they were part of the problem.

*   *   *

When I left the Chaco in November 2004, I was not sure I could ever bear to live among the New People again. My fledgling search for the primitive had come to its abortive—and, in hindsight, inevitable—end. Yet I was haunted by images I could not forget and questions I could not answer. The disquieting sense that I might have gotten everything wrong, that I had misunderstood entirely, compelled me to return in 2006 for long-term fieldwork among the Totobiegosode. Time and again, I wondered what kind of humanity was now possible for the New People, once they transformed from iconic primitives into supposedly degraded ex-primitives whose ties to a legitimating past had become impossible, refused, or suspect. I also wondered what kind of anthropology could take their projects seriously. * * *

What did it mean to abandon the search for primitive society, and stage an ethnographic pursuit of the fractured and dispossessed * * * ex-primitive instead? Where could it begin? And where would it end?

*   *   *

Where the Black Caiman[2] Walks

When I returned in 2006, there were two neighboring Totobiegosode settlements and I split my time between them equally. Whereas my clear sympathies for the New People strained some of my relationships in the place called Chaidi ("the Resting Place"), the people of Arocojnadi took me as one of their own. Yoteuoi, a former *daijnal*, "shaman,"

---

2. [The carnivorous black caiman, of the crocodile family, can grow to more than 16 feet in length and weigh 1,000 pounds.]

asked his wife to adopt me and eventually everyone contributed to my education. It became the place I was most warmly welcomed and I felt most at home.

Arocojnadi translated as The-Place-Where-the-Caiman-Comes-Walking. It was an old name, first given to a nearby campsite long ago. The name referred to the strange appearance of a Caiman—*Arocojnai*—walking over dry land into the encampment. Once common throughout the Chaco, the Caiman was usually associated with permanent rivers and rainy season marshes. It was known to lie hidden under black water, capable of sudden crippling attack. And the migratory Caiman was also said to have an ambivalent spiritual affinity with *jnaropie*, the spirit world of the dead where all color bleeds to gray and where everything is inverted, reversed, upside down. The appearance of one of these large reptiles stalking over parched ground into a camp was a startling event, ripe with portent and menace. In the particular instance referenced by the name of the original place, the walking Caiman was a presage of violence. Enemies massacred most of the inhabitants shortly afterward.

In the stark Totobiegosode settlements of dust and embers, people spent hours, days, weeks apparently doing very little. Sometimes it could seem as if we were all waiting for some nameless event or visitation. When the hunger and heat were particularly acute, my mind wandered. Through fevered hours I imagined those beings that might suddenly appear, walking ribboned paths into the encircled people. As days stretched to months and years, I grew convinced that the walking Caiman had returned in the new ghostly form of world-ending violence relentlessly stalking the New People and their tenuous humanity.

*   *   *

At the time, the sparsely populated Paraguayan Chaco was in the midst of a land rush, and the value of land had increased five hundredfold in the previous ten years. Spurred by the rising price of beef and massive investments by foreign agro-industrial firms, local ranchers turned the slow-growing forest into cattle pastures by bulldozing it bare and burning all matter. Enriched by the ashes, the sandy alkaline earth produced viable grass for a dozen years. On satellite imagery, clear-cut checkerboards exploded around the three Mennonite agro-religious colonies in the center of Paraguay and the soy plantations in southern Bolivia, even as Brazilian agri-capitalists pushed inward from the eastern borders. There were few reliable statistics to quantify the devastation, but it likely outpaced six hundred thousand hectares/year, making it one of the highest local deforestation rates in the world. And this was big business: Paraguay beef exports were a billion-dollar industry in 2010.

Tié and the New People were particularly afraid of the bulldozers used by ranchers to crush the dense forest. The New People hypothesized that the bulldozers were monstrous beings relentlessly following their scent. On several occasions in the 1990s, they attacked bulldozers with arrows and spears but to no avail. The fear of bulldozers was a form of historical consciousness which cited older terrors of genocide. Like all bands of Totobiegosode, the Areguede'urasade were nearly exterminated by Paraguayan soldiers and warriors from hostile Ayoreo groups. Enemy Ayoreo obtained shotguns from missionaries and hunted down the forest bands, which were either killed or brought back to the mission as captives. Such violence dotted the landscape with *dajegeo* places contaminated by human blood, which remained in the soil, capable of inciting future violence. Faced with forest-flattening machines and increasingly surrounded, the former Areguede'urasade began to have visions of group death and a world where no fires would light the darkness.

*   *   *

Meanwhile, the frustrated desires for pure primitives were once again displaced onto the two small bands of Ayoreo-speaking people that remained in the dwindling Chaco forests. Like the Areguede'urasade before them, they gained international prominence as "voluntarily isolated peoples," and three feuding NGOs formed to protect them from sustained relations with outsiders. They legally resembled elements of nature, and were regularly celebrated as existing in a "single, inseparable unity with their habitat." For such NGOs, the only truly legitimate Ayoreo life was that which is "still fully alive among the uncontacted groups" (International Work Group for Indigenous Affairs 2010). While actual Ayoreo-speaking people died from starvation, murder, and disease, a transnational NGO economy was mobilized to preserve the haunting fantasy of an Ayoreo life hidden in a besieged wilderness.

*   *   *

The Politics of Isolation

In northern Paraguay, the few Totobiegosode holdouts hidden in the forest are palpably present. Teenage soldiers warn travelers to take care; the savages are everywhere. "They aren't like you and me," a park ranger near the Bolivian border told me in 2007. "They can be anywhere, we cannot know." During my fieldwork, two ranch hands told me they often went about their work armed. "You never know when a savage Indian might attack you, no?" Pale men in SUVs traveled the backroads inquiring after tracks and sightings. One rancher told me he could always tell when the savages were near, because the dogs acted up like they smelled a wildcat or a storm. The concealed Ayoreo lurked just out of sight, on the edges of wasted pastures, where the dust from the heavy trucks drifted and rolled. The last wild Indians of the Chaco, they assumed the same "nowhere-tangible, all-pervasive, ghostly presence" of the sacrificial violence destroying their homeland (Benjamin 1999 [1921]).

They are just as real as they are fantastic. There are at least two Ayoreo bands and several lone individuals roaming the shrinking forests. One band, of unknown size and origins * * * moves in a great arc across the Bolivia-Paraguay borderlands around Echoi. The second * * * band of eighteen people * * * pursue[s] a life of nomadic conceal-ment. They have structured their lives around the daily logistics of eluding starvation and death from the beings they think are pursuing them. Like the Areguede'urasa-de, they are keenly aware of the invaders pressing in from all directions. This begs the question: how do we make sense of these concealed people and their remarkable way of life? * * *

The Expedition

In November 2010, international attention was briefly focused on their plight. This attention took the form of a controversy over a scientific expedition to the northern Gran Chaco proposed by the London Natural History Museum. The expedition was to be comprised of sixty ecologists, biologists, and other experts on nature, and its aim was to document the biodiversity of the Chaco forest, a region described in a British newspaper article as "one of the most inhospitable, impenetrable and mysterious places on Earth." The expedition would have been the first to quantify the biodiversity of this understudied area.

The British expedition was harshly denounced by Iniciativa Amotocodie, an NGO self-described as the "Isolated Peoples Protection Group" that claimed to be the legal representative of all the concealed Ayoreo-speaking groups in the area. The Cambridge-educated director of this NGO declared that the expedition was equivalent to an act of genocide against the so-called isolated Ayoreo. As he put it during a November 9, 2010, interview on BBC Radio 4, "It would be tantamount to genocide if an involuntary contact actually occurred, which would mean that there could be fatal consequences on both sides and the life-model of these people would break down, would collapse, and also the territory they belong to. This is tantamount to a genocide-like situation." Shaken by such accusations, government and museum officials suspended the expedition less than a week later.

The relation this media event claimed—between the gathering of scientific facts and genocide—rested on the assumption that the concealed Totobiegosode were pure if frag-ile Others who "live in another world" (Glauser 2007). * * * First, their bodies and souls were believed to be inseparable from certain threatened domains of nature. As the NGO director put it in his BBC interview, the Ayoreo "live in complete interdependence with nature . . . in a great extension of completely virgin forest." Second, they were imagined to be the bearers of an uncontaminated culture that has not yet been "eroded" by contact (Glauser 2006). The director described this conflation of pure culture and pure nature as "a principle of life."

Anthropologists and other theorists, of course, have long critiqued the primitivist trope of Indigenous populations that exist beyond "contact," history, or social relations as central to the logics of colonial domination. * * *

Despite exhaustive ethnographic evidence to the contrary, the well-traveled fantasy about a form of cultural life conserved beyond the limits of modern society persists in rising again and again. From blockbuster films like *Avatar* and "first contact" tours in West Papua to recent UN human rights initiatives and best-selling books and the YouTube sensation created by aerial photos of remote Brazilian tribespeople, the figure of the isolated primitive is an increasingly powerful global imaginary. * * *

* * *

Ambiguity of the Hidden

As part of my fieldwork, I spent two years working alongside the first tribal organization of the Totobiegosode, formed in 2005. The name chosen for this institution reflected its futuristic orientation: the Organización Payipie Ichadie Totobiegosode (OPIT), the Organization of New Totobiegosode *Ayipie*. During this time, it was impossible to ignore the real social force that the fantasy of the isolated Indian exerted within and through Ayoreo life. It was a national legal category, a global framework for Indigenous rights, a form of moral reasoning about cause and effect, and a rallying cry for several competing NGOs. Yet it was difficult, if not impossible, for me to recognize this hypervisible "isolated" Ayoreo subject within the realities I encountered on the ground. * * *

Rumors about the forest people blew through the Ayoreo settlements like dust. They were cornered on this ranch or seen over there or shot at near here. "How much money," the leader of a Guidaigosode settlement once asked me, "do you think the NGO would pay if we captured them? Enough for a pickup?" Someone found their tracks and tried to follow. A man heard them whispering at dawn, invisible in the brush near his garden. They must have taken that lost bag of seeds or that one red shirt. They must be close, they must be coming back. People waited for them, but each time they slipped away.

* * *

I remember sitting around the fire one cool evening in Arocojnadi when all at once out of nowhere a shiver seemed to run through the older people like an electric shock or a sudden wind that only they could feel. They flinched in synch as if by collective instinct. As if summoned by a terrible puppeteer that had been waiting all this time. Bodies strange and rigid, they tilted away from the firelight, lurched up, murmured half-words, hushed the children. Everyone grew silent, we listened intently to the darkness. I heard nothing, felt nothing but the nervous tension palpable and building. I looked at Dasua, her finger floating in the air, vaguely pointed northwest, where the edge of the forest loomed black and formless.

After ten or fifteen frozen minutes, she barked at the children to go inside, lie down, and be quiet. In the same curt tones, she told me to go sleep right then in the school building and not to come out until dawn. The next morning everything was back to normal. They later said the forest people were close by that night, although no one would say how exactly they knew.

*   *   *

In my stubbornness, I often tried to argue in favor of leaving [the forest people] alone. Such tentative statements were usually ignored. Finally, Dejai had enough and one evening he turned to me with a steady stare. "Lucas, don't you want to see them too?" I did not respond. With a mocking laugh, he asked, "Wouldn't you like to come and take their pictures?" The others began to taunt me about my prior filmmaking and my concern for the Areguede'urasade. "When the Jotaine'urasade come out, won't you travel from your country to film them too?"

It seemed the concealed people elicited a sense of urgency in us all, but in profoundly ambiguous and different ways that I could never quite comprehend. Why indeed *was* I so concerned about their fate and why in that particular way? * * *

In many ways, the forest bands had already become spirits. Once every two or three months, a story would arrive over the two-way radio that they had been murdered by a rancher. Their bodies buried in a pit, their camp dynamited by an airplane, their water source poisoned. An oil prospector found the corpses of six naked savages lined up head to toe under a tree in Bolivia. A Paraguayan peon confessed that his boss drove him to a massacre site and made him stack the bodies of ten savages in a pile and burn them and he could not forget the smell.

Totobiegosode in both communities took these rumors hard. Three times, I heard women sing the sobbing song of death for their relatives after hearing such news. Another time we made a trip to a place where someone had reportedly found bones. But all we found was dust. The details were always vague, the sources difficult to find. Usually no one pursued the stories; they lingered with others like heat waves.

*   *   *

In November 2006, I participated in the United Nations Regional Seminar on "The Rights of Indigenous Peoples in Voluntary Isolation and Initial Contact in Amazonia and the Gran Chaco," where I witnessed an international political economy of cultural preservation coalescing around the image of isolation. Yet this organizing was premised on the sense that isolation was an empirical reality. * * *

The problem seemed to lie in the particular way that the politics of isolation redefined culture. By definition, the edges of isolated life were rigidly mapped onto the limits set around pure culture. That is, political investments in isolation assigned social force and human substance to the "serious fiction" of culture as a bounded, stable whole: a container for true difference. * * *

The politico-legal category of isolation, then, reiterates an extreme version of what [anthropologist] Eric Wolf [critiqued] as the "pool hall model of the world," in which certain domains of pure culture/nature/life are newly endowed with the qualities of billiard balls: disaggregated, bounded, and brightly colored objects colliding and spinning off one another (Wolf 1982). * * *

The Haunted Forest

Precisely one year after the controversy around the British expedition, I heard that the concealed people had been contacted. Through messages pieced together over radios and cell phones and Facebook, the Totobiegosode leaders told me to pack my bags. They wanted me to come. I wasn't sure why.

I pressed for details but there were no clear answers. Something had happened and no one seemed to know what. As when I first heard about the Areguede'urasade coming out, I stumbled around in a daze with ghostly visions of the Chaco always in my sight. I could barely sleep. When I did, I had terrible dreams of blood and dust and flies, and I woke covered in sweat. Was I really willing to return to a scene I had barely survived the first time? What could motivate such a trip? * * * As I began to sort through such questions, the story itself dissolved.

One person said that twelve naked Indians had been caught on a ranch near Chovoreca. Another said that a group had run away from the bulldozers working by Cerro León and laid down their spears, despondent, at the feet of a rancher. Someone surmised the NGO director had captured the Totobiegosode band. I heard the government sent a delegation. They returned two days later, having found nothing but the strange rectangular tracks of *parode* sandals and stories of naked brown bodies glimpsed at dusk. Within a week, everyone had dropped it completely.

* * *

Yet the forest bands cannot be entirely subsumed into these images of them, at least not yet. One century after Ishi—the Yahi tribesman who gained notoriety as the "last wild Indian in North America"—stumbled into a California corral, the concealed Totobiegosode are facing a similar dilemma. This crisis is only intensified by the sedimented weight and numbing familiarity of the stories we think we know, the sense of an inevitable end foreclosing their futures as surely as the bulldozers.

Like the last Yahi, the forest people have retreated into a life of strenuously maintained concealment. * * *

We know this concealment is unprecedented in Ayoreo history. And we know that this concealment is due to their keen awareness of the beings that they carefully observe and that surround them more completely every passing season. Years have gone by with only the slightest traces of their presence: a glimpse of bare skin by a park ranger, a twig snapping at dusk, a half-hidden track of their *parode* sandals, a scrap of ash or bone.

We know they go to great lengths to conceal their existence from outsiders, waiting hours to cross a road, wiping out their tracks, hiding their fires. We know that they have developed a way to speak with whistles, that even their children are trained to silence. They read the tracks of bicycles and trucks and puzzle over the incredible speed and energy of their *Cojñone* enemies. They run far and fast if they see a bootprint out of place or unexpectedly hear a chainsaw or a tractor. Encounters with bulldozers are catastrophic events, putting the entire group at risk of death from starvation or thirst, each more devastating than the last. They often do not know where they can go or what they can do to escape. We know these people are often enraged and saddened at what they consider an invasion of their ancestral territory, but they rarely wish to risk a confrontation.

Still, they collect the aromatic wild honey and stalk the sharp-tusked peccaries and gather the ancient land tortoises. They bake the starchy roots of the *doidie* in ashes and eat the sweet fruits of *tokode* cacti and the *esode* trees. They make all of their clothing and bags from the leaf fibers of the *dajudie* plant. They meticulously craft bows and spears from *kaunange* and *aidie* hardwoods. They scavenge the roadsides or empty ranch houses for scraps of metal and plastic. They carry a piece of granite from Cerro León to sharpen the metal.

We know they tell *adode* myths and heal one another by sucking out or blowing away sickness with *ujñarone* curing chants. They smoke *sidi* tobacco and *canirojnai* roots to conjure visions of the future before their eyes. When necessary, they ask the spirits for help with *chugu'iji* performances of rage and with the wordless rhythms of the *perane*. They beat on hollow trunks of the *Cukoi* tree to call rain. They carve *tunucujnane* poles with magical designs and leave them as protection in their wake. They sing the same songs as their relatives in Chaidi and Arocojnadi. They are also convinced that death is coming for them, that their world is nearing its end.

Although there is much we do not know, it is clear that this long concealment is no primitive idyll. It is a way of life finely attuned to the daily logistics of concealment from the beings they believe are hunting them down. Their cosmology is partially a response to global political economies; it is a worldview already indistinguishable from the pragmatics of eluding starvation, capture, and death in the face of industrial agribusiness. This is the only kind of primitive society, the only kind of primitive life, that we have permitted to survive anywhere on the face of this earth and even so probably not for much longer. That these small groups of holdouts have been able to endure this long is a testament to their extreme resourcefulness and resolve.

They have managed to achieve a tenuous coexistence despite a permanent state of alarm. Faced with tragic and deteriorating prospects, they still properly care for their children, their sick, their dying, their elderly. When Areguede could no longer walk fast enough to keep up with the group, Siquei carried him in a large bag on his back. Those in the forest, we can presume, do the same. They do not violate the *puyaque* restrictions, and each year they ritually create the world anew. Although they know they cannot escape invasion, war, famine, and intolerance, this has not been enough to make them surrender their compassion, their protagonism, their piety. The end of their world has not forced them to violate the essence of what makes them Ayoreode, Human Beings.

As for the rest of us? It is much less certain what the unfolding tragedy in the Chaco implies about our humanity. What have we surrendered to the feeble magic of isolation and to the allure of the vanishing? What price are we willing to pay for our cheap and unwitting denials, for brightly colored photographs?

Faced with the prospect of the next last first contact in a landscape being destroyed as rapidly as the forces of modern technology will allow, having already jettisoned the few real possibilities to envision any other outcome, we wait . . . for what? I do not know but it is highly likely that the day will dawn when they stumble terrified out of the scraps of forest or choose to take their own lives. Only one thing is certain: when they do, we will not be mourning merely the demise of the last wild Indians.

ENGAGING THE TEXT, ENGAGING THE WORLD

- Reread the myth of the Black Caiman as retold by Bessire. What does the Black Caiman symbolize in the title of the article?

- Bessire argues that the popular way of seeing culture as a bounded, stable, self-contained whole—what Eric Wolf criticized as the "pool hall model" of culture—is central to our misunderstanding of indigenous people and cultures today. What alternative does he suggest?

- What does the hamburger served at your college cafeteria or at the local McDonald's have to do with the plight of the Ayoreo Indians living on the Paraguay/Bolivia borderlands in South America?

- How does our imagination of primitive, isolated, "Stone Age" indigenous people affect our ability to see the global connections that are reality for every group of people today?

- How do you answer Bessire's final questions: What have we surrendered to the feeble magic of isolation and the allure of the vanishing? What price are we willing to pay for our cheap and unwitting denials, for brightly colored photographs?

3

Fieldwork and Ethnography

Ethnographic fieldwork is the unique strategy that anthropologists—particularly cultural anthropologists—have developed to put people first as we analyze how human societies work. Chemists conduct experiments in laboratories. Economists analyze financial trends. Historians pore over records and library archives. Anthropologists start with people and their local communities.

The term fieldwork implies going out in "the field" to do extensive research. Although throughout the history of anthropology this has often meant going a long way from home, as Sienna Craig does in her study of Tibetan *amchi* healers in Nepal, contemporary anthropologists also study human culture and activities in their own countries and local contexts, as Barbara Myerhoff does in her study of elderly Jewish senior citizens in Southern California.

Through fieldwork, often living in a community for a year or more, we try to understand people's everyday lives, to see what they do and to understand why. We participate in their activities (**participant observation**), take careful **field notes**, conduct interviews, take photographs, and record music as we try to see the world through their eyes. We make maps of communities (**mapping**), both of the physical environment and of family (**kinship analysis**) and social relationships (**social network analysis**). Although careful observation of the details of daily life is the first step, through intensive fieldwork anthropologists look beyond the taken-for-granted, everyday experience of life to discover the complex systems of power and meaning that people construct to shape their existence. These include the many systems we will discuss throughout this book: gender, sexuality, race, ethnicity, religion, kinship, and economic and political systems. As we extend our analysis as anthropologists, we try to see how local lives compare to others and fit into larger human patterns and global contexts. All of these research strategies and practical tools become part of what we call our **anthropologist's toolkit**.

Fieldwork experience is considered an essential part of an anthropologist's training. It is the activity through which we learn and hone the basic tools of our trade: careful listening and observation, engagement with strangers, cross-cultural interaction, and deep analysis of human interactions and systems of power and privilege. Through fieldwork we learn empathy for those around us, develop a global consciousness, and uncover our own ethnocentrism. Indeed, fieldwork is a rite of passage, an initiation into our discipline, and a common bond among anthropologists who have been through the experience.

As you read the following passages by Myerhoff and Craig, try to imagine these anthropologists in the field, conducting fieldwork. Both engage in **thick description**, carefully documenting the details of daily life while also examining the deep symbolic meanings and intense systems of power lying just beneath the surface. What challenges and obstacles do they face? What tools and strategies do they employ? How do they go about building rapport—personal relationships of trust—with their **key informants**? In their writing, how do they allow the voices of those they are studying to come through clearly and authoritatively—a process anthropologists refer to as **polyvocality**? How do they engage in **reflexivity**—reflecting on the anthropologist's personal experiences? How do they trace the connections between their local context and global processes? How do the communities in which they are working confront changes internally and externally?

As you might imagine from these readings, the fieldwork experience can become more than a strategy for understanding human culture. Fieldwork has the potential to radically transform the anthropologist. Can you imagine making the same commitments that Craig and Myerhoff do? What preparation would you need before entering the field? What strategies and skills would you need to conduct effective, meaningful fieldwork? How do you imagine your presence might transform the community where you work as well as your own life—a process of **mutual transformation** inevitable in any fieldwork encounter?

Development of the anthropological perspective through fieldwork, in which we investigate the beliefs and practices of other cultures, enables us to perceive our own cultural activities in a new light. Even the most familiar aspects of our own lives may then appear exotic, bizarre, or strange when viewed through the lens of anthropology. Through this cross-cultural training, anthropology offers the opportunity to unlock our ability to imagine, see, and analyze the incredible diversity of human cultures. It also enables us to avoid the tendencies of ethnocentrism, in which we often view our own cultural practices as "normal" and against which we are inclined to judge the cultural beliefs and practices of others.

From *Number Our Days*

Barbara Myerhoff

Barbara Myerhoff's book *Number Our Days* is a classic in anthropological fieldwork and later became an Academy Award–winning documentary film. Her first book, *Peyote Hunt* (1974), traces the religious pilgrimage of the Huichol Indians across the Sierra Madre of Mexico. But in *Number Our Days*, excerpted below, Myerhoff turns her attention closer to home. Her fieldwork focuses on the struggles of older Jewish immigrants in a Southern California community and the Aliyah Senior Citizens' Center. Her rich ethnography brings the neighborhood, the Center, and its members to life. The members' vibrant voices fill the pages. Myerhoff also takes a reflexive approach and becomes a character in her own book, detailing her fieldwork process and reflecting poignantly on her experience as a younger Jewish woman studying a community of older Jews. As she says, "…I would never really be a Huichol Indian. But I would be a little old Jewish lady one day… I consider myself very fortunate in having had, through this work, an opportunity to anticipate, rehearse, and contemplate my own future."

Number Our Days marks a turn in anthropology from the study of the "other" to the study of the self—what Victor Turner calls in his foreword to Myerhoff's book "being thrice-born." The first birth is in our own culture. The second birth immerses the anthropologist in the depths of another culture through fieldwork. Finally, the return home is like a third birth as the anthropologist rediscovers his or her own culture, now strange and unfamiliar in a global context.

"So what do you want from us here?"

> Every morning I wake up in pain. I wiggle my toes. Good. They still obey. I open my eyes. Good. I can see. Everything hurts but I get dressed. I walk down to the ocean. Good. It's still there. Now my day can start. About tomorrow I never know. After all, I'm eighty-nine. I can't live forever.

Death and the ocean are protagonists in Basha's life. They provide points of orientation, comforting in their certitude. One visible, the other invisible, neither hostile nor friendly, they accompany her as she walks down the boardwalk to the Aliyah Senior Citizens' Center.

From Barbara Myerhoff. 1979. *Number Our Days: Culture and Community among Elderly American Jews in an American Ghetto.* New York: Meridian.

Basha wants to remain independent above all. Her life at the beach depends on her ability to perform a minimum number of basic tasks. She must shop and cook, dress herself, care for her body and her one-room apartment, walk, take the bus to the market and the doctor, be able to make a telephone call in case of emergency. Her arthritic hands have a difficult time with the buttons on her dress. Some days her fingers ache and swell so that she cannot fit them into the holes of the telephone dial. Her hands shake as she puts in her eyedrops for glaucoma. Fortunately, she no longer has to give herself injections for her diabetes. Now it is controlled by pills, if she is careful about what she eats. In the neighborhood there are no large markets within walking distance. She must take the bus to shop. The bus steps are very high and sometimes the driver objects when she tries to bring her little wheeled cart aboard. A small boy whom she has befriended and occasionally pays often waits for her at the bus stop to help her up. When she cannot bring her cart onto the bus or isn't helped up the steps, she must walk to the market. Then shopping takes the better part of the day and exhausts her. Her feet, thank God, give her less trouble since she figured out how to cut and sew a pair of cloth shoes so as to leave room for her callouses and bunions.

Basha's daughter calls her once a week and worries about her mother living alone and in a deteriorated neighborhood. "Don't worry about me, darling. This morning I put the garbage in the oven and the bagels in the trash. But I'm feeling fine." Basha enjoys teasing her daughter whose distant concern she finds somewhat embarrassing. "She says to me, 'Mamaleh, you're sweet but you're so *stupid*.' What else could a greenhorn mother expect from a daughter who is a lawyer?" The statement conveys Basha's simultaneous pride and grief in having produced an educated, successful child whose very accomplishments drastically separate her from her mother. The daughter has often invited Basha to come and live with her, but she refuses.

> What would I do with myself there in her big house, alone all day, when the children are at work? No one to talk to. No place to walk. Nobody talks Yiddish. My daughter's husband doesn't like my cooking, so I can't even help with meals. Who needs an old lady around, somebody else for my daughter to take care of? They don't keep the house warm like I like it. When I go to the bathroom at night, I'm afraid to flush, I shouldn't wake anybody up. Here I have lived for thirty-one years. I have my friends. I have the fresh air. Always there are people to talk to on the benches. I can go to the Center whenever I like and always there's something doing there. As long as I can manage for myself, I'll stay here.

Managing means three things: taking care of herself, stretching her monthly pension of three hundred and twenty dollars to cover expenses, and filling her time in ways that have meaning for her. The first two are increasingly hard and she knows that they are battles she will eventually lose. But her free time does not weigh on her. She is never bored and rarely depressed. In many ways, life is not different from before. She has never been well-off, and she never expected things to be easy. When asked if she is happy, she shrugs and laughs. "Happiness by me is a hot cup of tea on a cold day. When you don't get a broken leg, you could call yourself happy."

Basha, like many of the three hundred or so elderly members of the Aliyah Center, was bom and spent much of her childhood in one of the small, predominately Jewish, Yiddish-speaking villages known as *shtetls*, located within the Pale of Settlement of Czarist Russia, an area to which almost half the world's Jewish population was confined in the nineteenth century. Desperately poor, regularly terrorized by outbreaks of anti-Semitism initiated by government officials and surrounding peasants, shtetl life was precarious. Yet a rich, highly developed culture flourished in these encapsulated settlements, based on a shared sacred religious history, common customs and beliefs, and two languages—Hebrew for prayer and Yiddish for daily life. * * * For many, life became unbearable under the increasingly reactionary regime of Czar Alexander II. The pogroms of 1881–1882, accompanied by severe economic and legal restrictions, drove out the more desperate and daring of the Jews. Soon they were leaving the shtetls and the cities in droves. The exodus of Jews from Eastern Europe swelled rapidly until by the turn of the century [1900] hundreds of thousands were emigrating, the majority to seek freedom and opportunity in the New World.

Basha dresses simply but with care. The purchase of each item of clothing is a major decision. It must last, should be modest and appropriate to her age, but gay and up-to-date. And, of course, it can't be too costly. Basha is not quite five feet tall. She is a sturdy boat of a woman—wide, strong of frame, and heavily corseted. She navigates her great monobosom before her, supported by broad hips and thin, severely bowed legs, their shape the heritage of her malnourished childhood. Like most of the people who belong to the Aliyah Center, her early life in Eastern Europe was characterized by relentless poverty.

Basha dresses for the cold, even though she is now living in Southern California, wearing a babushka under a red sun hat, a sweater under her heavy coat. She moves down the boardwalk steadily, paying attention to the placement of her feet. A fall is common and dangerous for the elderly. A fractured hip can mean permanent disability, loss of autonomy, and removal from the community to a convalescent or old age home. Basha seats herself on a bench in front of the Center and waits for friends. Her feet are spread apart, well-planted, as if growing up from the cement. Even sitting quite still, there is an air of determination about her. She will withstand attacks by anti-Semites, Cossacks, Nazis, historical enemies whom she conquers by outliving. She defies time and weather (though it is not cold here). So she might have sat a century ago, before a small pyramid of potatoes or herring in the marketplace of the Polish town where she was born. Patient, resolute, she is a survivor.

Not all the Center women are steady boats like Basha. Some, like Faegl, are leaves, so delicate, dry, and vulnerable that it seems at any moment they might be whisked away by a strong gust. And one day, a sudden wind did knock Faegl to the ground. Others, like Gita, are birds, small and sharp-tongued. Quick, witty, vain, flirtatious, they are very fond of singing and dancing. They once were and will always be pretty girls. This is one of their survival strategies. Boats, leaves, or birds, at first their faces look alike. Individual features are blurred by dentures, heavy bifocals, and webs of wrinkles. The men are not so easy to categorize. As a group, they are quieter, more uniform, less immediately outstanding except for the few who are distinctive individuals, clearly distinguishable as leaders.

As the morning wears on, the benches fill. Benches are attached back to back, one side facing the ocean, one side the boardwalk. The people on the ocean side swivel around to face their friends, the boardwalk, and the Center.

Bench behavior is highly stylized. The half-dozen or so benches immediately to the north and south of the Center are the territory of the members, segregated by sex and conversation topic. The men's benches are devoted to abstract, ideological concerns—philosophical debate, politics, religion, and economics. The women's benches are given more to talk about immediate, personal matters—children, food, health, neighbors, love affairs, scandals, and "managing." Men and women talk about Israel and its welfare, about being a Jew and about Center politics. On the benches, reputations are made and broken, controversies explored, leaders selected, factions formed and dissolved. Here is the outdoor dimension of Center life, like a village plaza, a focus of protracted, intense sociability.

The surrounding scene rarely penetrates the invisible, pulsing membrane of the Center community. The old people are too absorbed in their own talk to attend the setting. Surfers, sunbathers, children, dogs, bicyclists, winos, hippies, voyeurs, photographers, panhandlers, artists, junkies, roller skaters, peddlers, and police are omnipresent all year round. Every social class, age, race, and sexual preference is represented. Jesus cults, Hare Krishna parades, sidewalk preachers jostle steel bands and itinerant musicians. As colorful and flamboyant as the scene is by day, it is as dangerous by night. Muggings, theft, rape, harassment, and occasional murders make it a perilous neighborhood for the old people after dark.

*   *   *

Around thirty years ago, Jews from all over the country began to immigrate to the beach community, particularly those with health problems and newly retired. Seeking a benign climate, fellow Jews, and moderately priced housing, they brought their savings and small pensions and came to live near the ocean. Collective life was and still is especially intense in this community because there is no automobile traffic on the boardwalk. Here is a place where people may meet, gather, talk, and stroll, simple but basic and precious activities that the elderly in particular can enjoy here all year round.

In the late 1950s, an urban development program resulted in the displacement of between four and six thousand of these senior citizens in a very short period. It was a devastating blow to the culture. "A second Holocaust," Sasha called it. "It destroyed our shtetl life all over again." Soon after the urban development project began, a marina was constructed at the southern end of the boardwalk. Property values soared. Older people could not pay taxes and many lost their homes. Rents quadrupled. Old hotels and apartments were torn down, and housing became the single most serious problem for the elderly who desperately wanted to remain in the area. While several thousand have managed to hang on, no new members are moving into the area because of the housing problem. Their Yiddish world, built up over a thirty-year period, is dying and complete extinction is imminent. Perhaps it will last another five or at the most ten years. Whenever a Center member leaves, everyone is acutely aware that there will be no replacements. The sense of cultural doom coincides with awareness of approaching individual death. * * *

As the numbers of such people shrink and the neighborhood changes, the Aliyah Center becomes more and more important to its members. Sponsored by a city-wide philanthropic Jewish organization, it is maintained as a day center that emphasizes "secular Judaism." Officially, about three hundred members pay dues of six dollars a year, but these figures do not reflect the actual importance of the Center to the community. Many more use it than join, and they use it all day, every day. The Center is more halfway house than voluntary association, making it possible for hundreds of people to continue living alone in the open community, despite their physical and economic difficulties. Daily hot meals are provided there, and continuous diverse programs are offered—cultural events, discussions, classes of all kinds, along with social affairs, religious ceremonies, celebrations of life crises, anniversaries, birthdays, memorials, and occasional weddings. The gamut of political and social processes found in larger societies are well-developed in Center life. Here is an entire, though miniature, society, a Blakeian "world in a grain of sand," the setting for an intricate and rich culture, made up of bits and pieces of people's common history.

*   *   *

I sat on the benches outside the Center and thought about how strange it was to be back in the neighborhood where sixteen years before I had lived and for a time had been a social worker with elderly citizens on public relief. Then the area was known as "Oshini Beach." The word *shini* still made me cringe. As a child I had been taunted with it. Like many second-generation Americans, I wasn't sure what being a Jew meant. When I was a child our family had avoided the words *Jew* and *Yid*. We were confused and embarrassed about our background. In public we lowered our voices when referring to "our people" or "one of us." * * * *

I had made no conscious decision to explore my roots or clarify the meaning of my origins. I was one of several anthropologists at the University of Southern California engaged in an examination of Ethnicity and Aging. At first I planned to study elderly Chicanos, since I had previously done fieldwork in Mexico. But in the early 1970s in urban America, ethnic groups were not welcoming curious outsiders, and people I approached kept asking me, "Why work with us? Why don't you study your own kind?" This was a new idea to me. I had not been trained for such a project. Anthropologists conventionally investigate exotic, remote, preliterate societies. But such groups are increasingly unavailable and often inhospitable. As a result, more and more anthropologists are finding themselves working at home these days. * * * There was no way that I could have anticipated the great impact of the study on my life. * * *

Sitting in the sun and contemplating the passing parade on the boardwalk that morning in 1973, I wondered how I should begin this study. At eleven-thirty the benches began to empty as old people entered the Center for a "Hot Kosher Meal—Nutritious—65¢," then a new program provided by state and private funds. * * *

I followed the crowd inside and sat at the back of the warm, noisy room redolent with odors of fish and chicken soup, wondering how to introduce myself. It was decided for me. A woman sat down next to me who I soon learned was Basha. In a leisurely fashion, she appraised me. Uncomfortable, I smiled and said hello.

"You are not hungry?" she asked.

"No, thank you, I'm not," I answered.

"So, what brings you here?"

"I'm from the University of Southern California. I'm looking for a place to study how older Jews live in the city."

At the word *university*, she moved closer and nodded approvingly. "Are you Jewish?" she asked.

"Yes, I am."

"Are you married?" she persisted.

"Yes."

"You got children?"

"Yes, two boys, four and eight," I answered.

"Are you teaching them to be Jews?"

"I'm trying."

"So what do you want with us here?" asked Basha.

"Well, I want to understand your life, find out what it's like to be older and Jewish, what makes Jews different from other older people, if anything. I'm an anthropologist and we usually study people's cultures and societies. I think I would like to learn about this culture."

"And what will you do for us?" she asked me.

"I could teach a class in something people here are interested in—how older people live in other places, perhaps."

"Are you qualified to do this?" Basha shot me a suspicious glance.

"I have a Ph.D. and have taught in the university for a number of years, so I suppose I am qualified."

"You are a professor then? A little bit of a thing like you?" To my relief, she chuckled amiably. Perhaps I had passed my first rite of entrance into the group.

*   *   *

The anthropologist engages in peculiar work. He or she tries to understand a different culture to the point of finding it to be intelligible, regardless of how strange it seems in comparison with one's own background. This is accomplished by attempting to experience the new culture from within, living in it for a time as a member, all the while maintaining sufficient detachment to observe and analyze it with some objectivity. This peculiar posture—being inside and outside at the same time—is called participant-observation. It is a fruitful paradox, one that has allowed anthropologists to find sense and purpose within a society's seemingly illogical and arbitrary customs and beliefs. This assumption of the natives' viewpoint, so to speak, is a means of knowing others through oneself, a professional technique that can be mastered fairly easily in the study of very different peoples. Working with one's own society, and more specifically, those of one's own ethnic and familial heritage, is perilous, and much more difficult. Yet it has a certain validity and value not available in other circumstances. Identifying with the "Other"—Indians, Chicanos, if one is Anglo, blacks if one is white, males if one is female—is an act of imagination, a means for discovering what one is not and will never be. Identifying with what one is now and will be someday is quite a different process.

In working among the elderly—also, I suspect, among the very young—an exceptionally important part of one's information is derived from nonverbal communication and identification, this because the bodily state is such a large determinant of well-being for the growing and declining organism. At various times, I consciously tried to heighten my awareness of the physical feeling state of the elderly by wearing stiff garden gloves to perform ordinary tasks, taking off my glasses and plugging my ears, slowing down my movements and sometimes by wearing the heaviest shoes I could find to the Center. Walking a few blocks to the day-old bakery in this condition became an unimaginably exhilarating achievement. Once by accident I stumbled slightly. The flash of actual terror I experienced was shocking. From the close watching of the elderly it seems I had acquired their assiduous need to avoid falling, though of course, to one my age in good health such a minor accident presents no real danger. This recognition occurred after I had been watching two very old women walk down the alley with great concentration, arms tightly linked, navigating impediments in slow-motion movements that were perfectly coordinated and mutually supportive. So great was their concern with balance they might have been walking a high wire.

The work with the very old people at the Center was not the first time I had employed this imaginative identification as a source of information. Years before, in doing fieldwork with the Huichol Indians of Mexico, I had had similar experiences. However much I learned from that was limited by the fact that I would never really be a Huichol Indian. But I would be a little old Jewish lady one day; thus, it was essential for me to learn what that condition was like, in all its particulars. As a society, we are increasingly cut off from the elderly. We do not have them in the midst of our daily lives, and consequently have no regular access to models of successful old age. How can we then do anything but dread the coming of age? I consider myself very fortunate in having had, through this work, an opportunity to anticipate, rehearse, and contemplate my own future. * * *

What the Center people taught me went beyond knowledge about old age. In addition they provided a model of an alternative lifestyle, built on values in many ways antithetical to those commonly esteemed by contemporary Americans. The usual markers of success were anathema to them—wealth, power, physical beauty, youth, mobility, security, social status—all were out of the question. Lacking hope for change, improvement, without a future, they had devised a counterworld, inventing their own version of what made "the good life." It was built on their veneration for their religious and cultural membership and it was full of meaning, intensity, and consciousness. This they had managed on their own, creating a nearly invisible, run-down, tiny world, containing a major lesson for any who would attend it. It was not the first time that an anthropologist had found in obscure, unworldly folk a message of wide applicability for the larger outside society.

*   *   *

The amount and variety of information accumulated in a field study is overwhelming. There is no definite or correct solution to the problem of what to include, how to cut up the pie of social reality, when precisely to leave or stop. Often there is little clarity as to whom to include as "members," what to talk about with those who are. The deliberate avoidance of preconceptions is likely to result in the best fieldwork, allowing the group or subject to dictate the form the description ultimately takes. But always there is a high degree of arbitrariness involved. Choices must be made and they are extremely difficult, primarily because of what and who must be omitted. In this case, these methodological dilemmas were especially troublesome. Nearly everyone at the Center wanted to be included, feeling so strongly as they did the wish to be recorded and remembered.

In this work I decided to concentrate on the Center, its internal affairs, and its most active members as much as possible. This eliminated the nonjoiners, the marginal individuals, the majority of people living in the neighborhood and, accordingly, limited the generalizations that I could make in the end. I decided not to compare Center elders with others. I felt the Center people and their generation were sufficiently unique to warrant most of my time. The choice favored depth over breadth, tight focus rather than representativeness. * * *

Of the three hundred Center members, I met and talked with about half, though I observed all at one time or another during the years of the study. Of these, I knew eighty personally, and interviewed and spent most of my time with thirty-six. I tape recorded extensive interviews with these, ranging from two to sixteen hours, visited nearly all in their homes, took trips with them from time to time outside the neighborhood—to doctors, social workers, shopping, funerals, visiting their friends in old age homes and hospitals, and often following my subjects to convalescent homes and hospitals; I went to many funerals and memorial services. Apart from these excursions and my interviews with outsiders who knew Center people well—teachers, rabbis, local politicians, volunteers—I concentrated on the Center and its external extensions, the benches, boardwalk, and hotel and apartment lobbies where they congregated.

As often happens, I established a particularly strong and gratifying attachment to one individual, and also as often happens, in addition to being particularly knowledgeable and articulate about the community, this person was also an outsider. "Shmuel the Filo-sofe," he was called, and in a very significant way he was my teacher, critic, and guide. * * * His voice is heard throughout the book. I have included my own voice * * * for it proved impossible to expunge. His statements and retorts did not make sense without that, for he was directing his commentary to me. That is not the only place I have included my words and reactions. For a long time I resisted this. I wanted to focus on the Center, not myself, but it became clear that what was being written was from my eyes, with my per-sonality, biases, history, and sensibility, and it seemed dishonest to exclude that, thereby giving an impression of greater objectivity and authority than I believed in.

As often as possible I have included verbatim materials, heavily edited and selected, inevitably, but sufficient to allow the reader some degree of direct participation. I have tried to allow many individuals to emerge in their fullness and distinctiveness rather than presenting a completely generalized picture of group life without reference to the living breathing people who comprise it, and who are in the end the only reality. In the interest of economy and privacy, I have combined several of the minor characters who appear on these pages, though most would have preferred to have been identified. Wherever possible I have altered identifying biographical features that seemed insignificant. All verbatim statements are presented as they were given, usually taken from tape recordings. Major figures are disguised as much as possible but uncombined. Events reported are actual occurrences, subjectively witnessed and interpreted by me.

The always complex problem of assuring privacy to one's subjects was made more difficult in this study because of the production of a documentary film on which I col-laborated with Lynne Littman toward the end of research. Also called *Number Our Days*, it was based on my fieldwork at the Center. We were not at all sure that the film would cross the ethnic barrier, and were surprised when it was widely viewed and enthusiasti-cally received. To our great satisfaction, it brought the elderly concrete benefits in many forms—unsolicited funds, attention and favors from strangers and friends, and above all, visibility, which they so long for. But it made effective disguise of the Center and its director impossible. Nevertheless, privacy for individuals could be preserved, and so I have changed all names of people and groups mentioned here, this to allow myself freedom to record some of the unflattering things I saw there, as much as possible to prevent the elderly from recognizing themselves and each other, to save them and their children any embarrassment that might accrue. Certainly, I did not want to cause the old people pain that could be avoided, nor did I wish to jeopardize my welcome among them.

*   *   *

The format of this book is designed to meet several purposes. In addition to want-ing to speak within it as a participant, and wishing to preserve particular individuals, I wanted to render the elders' speech. Many verbatim statements are included; the most extensive of these are called "*bobbe-myseh*" or grandmothers' tales, speeches and exchanges between people that occurred in a "Living History" class. * * * The bobbe-myseh were drawn from miles of tape, intended to convey the texture of the speech, people's characteristic thought, and interaction style. It was Shmuel, the critic and philosopher, who dubbed these stories and exchanges "bobbe-myseh." He found them inelegant and rambling. Sometimes they build to a significant point about Center people's beliefs and experiences, but even so, these are much embedded in "trivia." Seldom grand, occasionally self-serving, always vital and original, it was inconceivable to leave them out.

*   *   *

Center people, like so many of the elderly, were very fond of reminiscing and storytelling, eager to be heard from, eager to relate parts of their life history. More afraid of oblivion than pain or death, they always sought opportunities to become visible. * * * They narrated themselves perpetually, in the form of keeping notes, journals, writing poems and reflections spontaneously, and also telling their stories to whoever would listen. Their histories were not devoted to marking their successes or unusual merits. Rather they were efforts at ordering, sorting, explaining—rendering coherent their long life, finding integrating ideas and characteristics that helped them know themselves as the same person over time, despite great ruptures and shifts. * * *

I was eager to respond to Center people's desires to tell me their stories and puzzled as to how to find the means and the time to listen to as many as possible. Abe [the center director] was helpful here, too. He suggested that I offer a class in the Center where people could assemble for recounting their life history. We pondered the subject together and decided it should be called "Living History." * * * People would have an opportunity to bring in their writings, poems, and the like, and read them to the group, an activity they enjoyed greatly and found few opportunities for in the Center's crowded schedule. They might bring in photographs, letters, and any materials they wished to have included. * * * But, I wondered, would people be willing to tell me, a stranger, their life history, and would they be inhibited if I tried to tape record the sessions?

Abe and I sat on a bench talking about the class in the early days of my work. Basha came out of the Center and Abe called to her, "Basha, how would you like to have the professor make a book from your life?" Basha did not hesitate. "You got a pencil? You want to get it down right. I begin with my childhood in Poland. Tell me if I go too fast. Naturally, it's a long story."

The following month, classes began. I was prepared with cookies, tea, coffee, tape recorder, and two-dozen notebooks and pencils for people who would be willing to use them at home. * * * At first a half-dozen people came, but after the word spread that there were no political fights and no insistence on public disclosure of personal matters, more attended. Soon a core of about twenty people had formed and they came faithfully. * * * The longer the classes lasted, the more people had to say. They stimulated one another's memories. * * *

I loved these classes and the style of the exchanges and stories. Shmuel was right to call them grandmothers' tales, for they were the kind of rambling, bubbling, unfocused, running comments that a bobbe might tell her grandchildren without putting down her dough or her sewing. Too busy to stop and shape a tale with grace and art, but too alive to imagination and verbal expression to be silent, so she might weave a kitchen tale that despite its crude surface, came from and went to a deep place. * * *

Hitting on a format that allowed for storytelling was a fortunate accident. When we began the sessions, there was no way I could have anticipated the significance of these exchanges. In time it became clear that storytelling was a passion among these people, absolutely central to their culture. * * *

The Center people who came to the Living History classes were increasingly pleased with the storytelling sessions. Here is Rachel's comment on the class toward the end of our meetings:

> All these speeches we are making reminded me of a picture I have from many years ago, when we were still in Russia. My brother had been gone already two years in America. I can see my mother like it is before me, engraved in my head. A small house she goes out of, in wintertime, going every morning in the snow to the post office, wrapped up in a shawl. Every morning there was nothing. Finally, she found a letter. In that letter was written, "Mamaleh, I didn't write to you before because I didn't have nothing to write about." "So," she says, "why didn't you write and tell me?"
>
> You know this group of ours reminds me of that letter. When I first heard about this group, I thought to myself, "What can I learn? What can I hear that I don't know, about life in the Old Country, of the struggles, the life in the poor towns, in the bigger towns, of the rich people and the poor people? What is there to learn, I'm eighty-eight, that I haven't seen myself?" Then I think, "What can I give to anybody else? I'm not an educated woman. It's a waste of time."
>
> That was my impression. But then I came here and heard all those stories. I knew them, but you know it was laid down deep, deep in your mind, with all those troubles mixed. You know it's there but you don't think of it, because sometimes you don't want to live in your past. Who needs all these foolish stories?
>
> But finally, this group brought out such beautiful memories, not always so beautiful, but still, all the pictures came up. It touched the layers of the kind that it was on those dead people already. It was laying on them like layers, separate layers of earth, and all of a sudden in this class I feel it coming up like lava. It just melted away the earth from all those people. It melted away, and they became alive. And then to me it looked like they were never dead.
>
> Then I felt like the time my mother got that letter. "Why don't you come and tell me?" "Well, I have nothing to say," I think. But I start to say it and I find something. The memories come up in me like lava. So I felt I enriched myself. And I am hoping maybe I enriched somebody else. All this, it's not only for us. It's for the generations.

ENGAGING THE TEXT, ENGAGING THE WORLD

- What did you learn about the experience of being old through Myerhoff's careful description of Basha?

- Why did Myerhoff take off her glasses, plug her ears, and wear heavy shoes and stiff gloves?

- Myerhoff describes her fieldwork experiences in detail. Identify her key fieldwork strategies.

- How would you describe the unique style of ethnographic writing found in Myerhoff's work?

- Why do you think Myerhoff's Living History Classes were so significant for Center members? How did they help Myerhoff's research?

- Describe some of the obstacles and benefits studying her "own kind" created for Myerhoff.

- Myerhoff fully engages the process of reflexivity in her ethnographic writing, reflecting on her own experience in the fieldwork process and becoming a key figure in her own ethnography. How has Myerhoff's commitment to reflexivity shaped the conclusions she draws and insights she offers?

Portrait of a Himalayan Healer
Sienna Craig

Notes on a day
of fieldwork in
Nepal

Sienna Craig's ethnography, set in the rural, isolated mountainous region of Lo Monthang, Nepal, population 14,000, offers a picture of a day in the life of an anthropologist as she studies Tibetan healers and their changing practices. Written like a fieldwork journal, her entries take the reader from an early morning conversation at the home of her friends and colleagues on to a school, a monastery, a royal palace, village health clinics, and farms for cultivating herbs for traditional Tibetan medicine before returning home in the evening. Together she and members of the community walk, climb, make house calls, ride horseback, say prayers, and discuss medicinal herbs and changing funding

From Sienna R. Craig. 2012. *Healing Elements: Efficacy and the Social Ecologies of Tibetan Medicine.* Berkeley: University of California Press. Some of the author's notes have been omitted.

requirements of international agencies. Craig's notes carefully guide you through the hours of the day, marking changing locations, smells, feelings, people, and issues at hand.

Cultures are never static but are constantly changing. Change occurs through internal negotiations and struggles. But in this period of intensifying globalization, communities and their cultures are encountering powerful national, regional, and global forces that are reshaping beliefs and practices of religion, healing, family, gender roles, ethnicity, sexuality, and work. As you read the following passage, pay particular attention to significant changes in the community Craig is studying— changes in religion, economic realities, the intersection of western medical practices and traditional Tibetan healing practices, and even the generational transmission of indigenous knowledge. Also pay attention to the ways these people in apparently isolated, mountainous Nepal are connected to the world beyond their local boundaries through donors, markets, the internet, foreign fundraising trips, and more. Craig's careful fieldnotes, thick description, and thoughtful reflections on these dynamics offer insight into matters anthropologists take into consideration today wherever we conduct fieldwork.

Reading Signs

It is early September 2008. The high-altitude air is tinged with autumn. I walk through the alleys of Lo Monthang, the largest settlement in northern Mustang District, Nepal. This is the time before animals have been let out to graze, before children have gone off to the new local day care, to school, or to help gather dung and tend animals. I pass white-washed homes decorated with protective door hangings above the threshold: colored yarn webs holding sheep skulls, repelling nefarious spirits and gossip. I hear the muffled sounds of cymbals, bells, and the resonant drone of Tibetan Buddhist monks calling forth another day.

*** Mustang lies in the Himalayan rain shadow; it is mostly high-altitude desert, abutting the Tibet Autonomous Region, China. Jomsom, the district's headquarters, is linked to Pokhara, the nearest city, by flights from a small airport and by trails. No all-season motor road connects the district to any urban center, although this reality is changing swiftly. *** Upper Mustang, at the center of which sits Lo Monthang [population 14,000], is home to Tibetan speakers, *tsampa* eaters,[1] and practitioners of Buddhism and Bön, indigenous religious practices of the Tibetan plateau (Snellgrove 1981; Samuel 1993).

*   *   *

On this crisp September morning, I round the corner past Thubchen, a fifteenth-century monastery that has been restored recently (Lo Bue 2011). I walk past a row

---

1. Tsampa is roasted barley flour, a staple among Tibetan communities.

of reliquaries [shrines] and stop before the wood-and-corrugated metal door leading to a school. A window, rimmed in black and red paint, rests above the door. Between window and door hangs a trilingual signboard. There is an arc of English—"Lo-Kunphen Traditional Herbal Medicine Clinic and School"—under which is written an approximation of the same, first in Tibetan and then in Nepali. The Tibetan reads *Lo Kunphen Mentsikhang Lobdra.* The Nepali reads *Lo Kunphen Aamchi Aausbadhyalaya Skul.* My friends and colleagues, Gyatso and Tenzin Bista, run this small institution. * * *

I have passed this sign many times. This morning it stops me short. I realize that, in Nepali, there is nothing *Tibetan* about this place. In Tibetan, centuries of interconnected history between Mustang and centers of Sowa Rigpa in Lhasa, Dharamsala, and beyond are implicit in the choice of names given to this institution. In English, the deceptively simple signifier "traditional herbal medicine" supplants regionally and culturally specific understandings of medicine and heath care. * * *

The only other element on the sign is, in a sense, its heart: a small rendering of Sangye Menla, the Medicine Buddha, his offering bowl brimming with *arura*, the fruit of the myrobalan tree and the "king of medicines." This sign is a mosaic, an assemblage of meaning. To understand only one of these languages is to miss the negotiations of culture and identity wrapped up in my interlocutors' efforts toward increasing the social efficacy of their practice in a new age. To see this sign simply as a handmade entrance to a marginal institution in [a] far away place is to miss the point. Certainly this is a remote locale. But it is a place connected to regimes of value and patterns of social change that stretch out from the Himalaya and Tibetan Plateau, down the Indian subcontinent, across the world, and back again.

Filled with these thoughts about identity and belonging, language and culture, tradition and contemporary life, I walk through the door and enter the courtyard of Lo Kunphen. Several students cluster around a water spigot, brushing their teeth. Older students ready the simple dining hall for breakfast, after prayers and before classes. I greet them and head toward the back door of Lo Kunphen, which lets me out beyond Lo Monthang's city wall, in front of Gyatso and Tenzin's home, the lower floor of which is devoted to an herbarium and small Sowa Rigpa museum. I climb the stairs and call out a greeting. Gyatso's familiar voice answers, inviting me in.

Mantras, IVs, and Morning Tea: 7:30 A.M.

Gyatso is seated on low cushions in the main room, drinking salt-butter tea. The brothers' infirm mother directs morning traffic. Two generations of this family's women perform chores as seamlessly as if playing a symphony. Gyatso's wife loads the stove with sheep and goat dung, blows embers awake, pours water into a kettle, and sets it to boil. She then breaks grassy clumps of brick tea into this tepid water and metes out a pinch of Tibetan salt. Her eldest niece carves a slab of butter from a block with the swiftness of a potter slicing clay. She tosses it into the tea churner. These acts mark a day's beginning here: art, routine, discipline each in its own right. This place would not run without its women.

A stack of notebooks sits on a wooden table in the corner, nestled between divans laid with Tibetan carpets. Some of these books are tea-stained and once or twice soaked through by rain. Their pages contain all manner of notations, written mostly in Tibetan, at times in Nepali, or in approximations of English, sounded out. They bespeak these doctors' networks: prescription notes, names of tourists who might become school sponsors, lists of plants and other raw materials to buy in Etum Bahal or Indra Chowk, old Kathmandu neighborhoods where herb traders hawk and bargain. Beside these notebooks are religious texts wrapped in cloth, a Tibetan-English medical dictionary, and a binder whose plastic sheaves protect stacks of receipts for school expenses. These pieces of paper must be carried to Jomsom in saddlebags, then on to Kathmandu in Chinese-made totes embossed with NGO insignia, gifts from academic conferences and conservation-development workshops these brothers have attended. In Kathmandu these recollections of rupees spent are presented to a Nepali accountant who reconciles the books and sends them to British, German, and U.S. charities that help to support the school. This institution is an experiment in bridging the gaps between Gyatso and Tenzin's father's generation and the worlds their children will inherit.

Tenzin comes into the room carrying a glass bottle of a glucose and saline solution, a splice of IV tubing, and a still sterile hypodermic needle. The glucose is Nepali made, though nearly every other commercial item in this house was manufactured in China: thermoses, blankets, solar panels that charge their satellite telephone. Tenzin moves toward his mother. This woman has been unable to walk for years and has, in a sense, been waiting to die ever since her husband passed away, in 1996. For all her despondency, she is still the center of this home, the voice to which everyone defers.

Tenzin calls his niece, a senior student at Lo Kunphen. They prop up the old woman so she can receive this IV infusion. I ask Tenzin why he has chosen to give this biomedical treatment to his mother. "It gives her strength, since she struggles to eat," he responds. The old woman seems calm until Tenzin produces the needle. Then she wriggles, moans, covers her eyes. The niece struggles to still her grandmother.

Seeing the task will not be easy, Tenzin calls for Gyatso. These sons reassure their mother. Then, deftly, Gyatso pins down her forearm as Tenzin inserts the needle past layers of weathered mountain skin into the river of a bluish vein. Tenzin tapes the needle in place, attaches it to the tubing, and hangs the glass bottle from a hook fitted to the ceiling above the old woman's perch. All the while one of the youngest members of the extended family looks on with fascination, nestled beside her great-grandmother, enfolded in layers of wool.

This simple act—needle into vein and the slow, steady infusion of sugars, salts, and water into this old woman—reminds me there are no easy ways to parse this world of healing. Neither the terms *tradition* and *modernity* nor a presumed ideological divide between Tibetan medicine and biomedicine makes much sense here (Samuel 2006).

These Buddhist *amchi* have given a biomedical anodyne with tenderness to their ailing mother. They do so in great part because empiricism has brought them here. They know it works because their mother's cheeks flush after such infusions. Just the same, a different empiricism instructs them to conduct long-life rituals and wear protection amulets. Ultimately they will face their mother's death as part of sentient existence: one karmic turning of the wheel of life.

Masters of the Gift: 9:00 A.M.

Gyatso, Tenzin, and I move into the school's chapel (*chökhang*) and library. The phrase "someone who wears many hats" works in both English and Tibetan. This is often how I feel about these brothers. In addition to his responsibility as principal of Lo Kunphen, Tenzin is also a senior monk at Chöde Monastery, a *sakya* Tibetan Buddhist institution in Lo Monthang. Yesterday he spent half the day performing a ritual in the household of someone who had recently died. Gyatso, like his father before him, is the householder-priest (*nakpa*) and doctor to the royal family of Lo. Since 2003 he has also been the chairman of the Himalayan Amchi Association.

Yesterday, despite our plans to review clinic records and write a funding proposal, Gyatso was called to the palace to greet officials from across the border in the TAR [Tibet Autonomous Region]. * * *

Yesterday's unexpected visit put off our work on the grant proposal until this morning. Gyatso and Tenzin begin by reiterating to me their need for money. They struggle to raise sufficient funds to maintain this school of thirty to forty students, along with their "factory" and small branch clinics. Our current task is to craft a proposal for a London-based foundation that has normally supported only Tibetan refugees. On occasion it will accept applications from "Tibetan border peoples" such as those from Mustang.

We begin to work. A familiar process of translation ensues. In eloquent Tibetan, Gyatso and Tenzin speak of the decline of Sowa Rigpa across the Himalayas, the role of *amchi* in providing health care to rural populations, the importance of teaching and practicing *amchi* medicine, and then the punch line: the need for funds to develop a more advanced course in Sowa Rigpa in Nepal, to be based in the small city of Pokhara, and the need to expand their clinical practice in Mustang so senior students might have employment to keep them in their rural communities and so that local populations might have access to a complete pharmacy of Tibetan formulas, even those the brothers cannot produce themselves.

*   *   *

Gyatso and Tenzin's search for funding consumes enormous time and energy. * * * Without significant government support for Sowa Rigpa in Nepal—indeed even if such support materializes in the coming years—nongovernmental sponsorship remains paramount. In Tibetan, *jindag* means "master of the gift." These days it is a term used to describe charitable foundations, individual sponsors, private patrons, and NGOs. Gyatso and Tenzin know me as a researcher, a translator, and a friend. But they also know me as a *jindag*. My engagement with Lo Kunphen has included raising money for the clinics and school, in part through an NGO I helped to found (www.drokpa.org). Just because I understand the nuance of an enduring Tibetan form of social relations does not make our allegiance to each other simple, though.

This morning Gyatso echoes a familiar refrain. "*Jindag* are like the wind and the rain," he says. "They come and they go. We cannot predict from which direction. But we need them for these seeds we have planted to ripen." It is an honest assessment, if also an organic metaphor voiced by a person who knows so well this earth of which he speaks.

*   *   *

Gyatso, Tenzin, and I are interrupted by a knock on the chapel door. A mother arrives with her son. He fell off a horse two days ago and appears to have fractured his left forearm. The boy is no more than ten. Rivulets of tears trickle down his dusty cheeks. Gyatso takes the boy's pulse from his ear, as is standard for children, feeling along his shoulder and arm. Tenzin prepares an herbal ointment mixed with rapeseed oil. The boy cringes. Gyatso tells him not to cry. The brothers have established several small clinics in villages surrounding Lo Monthang, but the work of healing still often occurs in their home.

"He was taking care of our sheep and goat," the boy's mother explains. "He shouldn't have been on the horse anyway. He should have been walking, collecting dung. But he never listens!" This mother seems worried and exasperated. You see, she needs his labor. The cost of hiring lowland Nepalis to herd or bring in the barley crop remains prohibitive for this family, like many others in Lo.

"Don't worry," says Gyatso. "The boy will be fine." Tenzin hands his brother the herbal mixture and two *kathag*, white silk offering scarves. Gyatso applies the ointment to the fractured bone and then bandages the boy's arm, creating a sling out of a blessing. Tenzin wraps up some of the powdery herbal mixture in a sheaf of paper. "Mix three spoonfuls of this with rapeseed oil. Change this dressing every day," he instructs. The woman pulls out a money purse that was pinned to the inside of her blouse. She attempts to hand Gyatso several hundred rupees ($2 to $3), but he exits the room, indicating that cash payment is not necessary. Instead the woman leaves a cotton satchel of dried cheese with Gyatso's elder sister, who accepts this gift.

As I watch this exchange, I struggle to square differential regimes of value. How might we reconcile the moral economy of *amchi* work and this in-kind payment of locally produced food with the political economy of becoming self-sustaining and the Excel spreadsheets over which we had just been laboring [to complete the grant application]?

Birth of the Clinic: 1:00 P.M.

After the young boy with the broken arm departs, Gyatso, Tenzin, and I set aside our paperwork. The proposal must wait. Tenzin heads off to teach a lesson from the *Explanatory Tantra*, one of four books that comprise the *Gyüshi*. Gyatso and I saddle two of the family's horses and prepare to visit the clinics north of Monthang. * * * "This," he said, patting the horse's rump, "is Mustang *ambulance*." True enough. Just a few days before, a man from Namdo, a village near the Tibetan border, roused Tenzin from sleep with a message that his wife was severely ill. Tenzin and the husband set off in the predawn darkness. Tenzin treated the woman, left her with medicines, and rode the three hours home, only to see another patient in a nearby settlement later that day.

On this afternoon the horse lives up to its reputation. We fly over chalky paths, past verdant sedges and wildflowers that persist after Mustang's brief, bucolic summer. We arrive midday in the village of Thinker. The clinic sits above the village in a small mud-brick building. * * *

My friend opens the clinic, revealing the rudiments of health care in upper Mustang: a wooden cabinet filled with about fifty small bottles of neatly labeled Tibetan medicines, all produced by Gyatso and Tenzin, with help from senior students; a small table and bench, two chairs; a dusty but well-used clinic logbook in which the name, gender, and age of patients, a shorthand diagnosis, and prescriptions are recorded. This regime of accountability is as new as the clinics themselves, and not unrelated. Gyatso and Tenzin's father never kept such records as he traveled from neighbor to neighbor and received patients in his home. He had no clinic and no need for a written record of these therapeutic encounters. He was not accountable to foreign donors or to a nation-state. Now clinic records render the work of healing legible in new ways to people beyond this immediate social ecology. Reports generated from these logbooks can make the scope of *amchi* medicine visible to government functionaries—the district health officer, the Council on Technical Education and Vocational Training, the Department of Ayurveda at the Ministry of Health—and foreign donors. * * *

This record keeping is also part of Gyatso and Tenzin's hybrid pedagogy: part lineage-based local practice, part formalized institution. Senior students are required to spend time staffing the clinics. Logbooks hold them accountable to their own learning process and to patients because making records requires students to reflect, even briefly, on what they are diagnosing and prescribing. In addition, logbooks are windows onto which medicines are used most, what formulas need to be replenished, and what illnesses are most common in a given season. These rudimentary notes scribbled in Tibetan cursive with whatever writing implement happens to be nearby illustrate how Tibetan medicine is being made "legible" (Scott 1998) to the state and to nonstate actors like NGOs. * * *

Each year since the clinics opened, Gyatso or Tenzin have sent me copies of the logbooks or hand them to me in Kathmandu. With assistance from Lo Kunphen senior students and Dartmouth undergraduates, I have helped Gyatso and Tenzin transform these handwritten records into computer files capable of producing a new kind of authoritative knowledge: statistics. It is helpful to report that these clinics see an average of one thousand patient visits annually during the seven months their doors are open, and that this number has continued to rise each year since the clinics opened in 2004. Or that the median age of patients is forty-two, 46 percent of whom are male. Or that sandalwood and saffron-based medicines are some of the most popularly prescribed, even though neither of these ingredients is local or affordable. Logbook analyses reveal that women suffer more from disorders of the channels (*tsa*) and of wind (*lung*), and that men have more accidents.

*   *   *

There is a knock on the door. Normally this clinic is open only three days a week, staffed by a Lo Kunphen student who is also preparing for his [School Leaving Certificate examinations] at the nearby high school. But word travels quickly when a senior *amchi* is in town. A local woman, middle-aged and moon-faced, stands at the door. She wears a woolen embroidered skullcap typical of upper Mustang's women of an older generation. She complains of sore, swollen knees. She lifts her frock and hitches up her petticoats to reveal fleshy, puckered skin, in marked contrast to her sun- and wind-beaten hands and face. Her knees are visibly inflamed. Gyatso directs the woman inside. She sits on the bench.

Contrary to what one might assume, this medical encounter does not begin with initial questions. Gyatso knows this woman and has treated her for years. Instead much of the therapeutic encounter flows forth from touch. Gyatso places his fingers along the woman's radial arteries, the gold and turquoise ring he inherited from his father glinting in the light. Pulse reading completed, he looks in her eyes and examines her tongue. Gyatso says the woman has a blood-wind disorder along with some infection. From here, stories of suffering spill out. "These keep me awake," she says, pointing at her knees with a look of accusation and annoyance, as if they were a barking dog. The woman asks if the disease is *nyingba*, literally "old," or if it is *drakpo*, a word that approximates "hard" or "recalcitrant." Gyatso reassures her that these pains can be addressed. He gives her two weeks' worth of medications, wrapped in pages torn from an old student notebook.

"Avoid eating too much salt, but poultice your knees with *bultog*," he says, referencing sodium bicarbonate harvested locally. This harsh, demanding place provides at once the grounds for so much suffering and also, bountifully, the possibility of antidote.

Of Sky and Soil: 4:00 P.M.

Our visit to the Thinker clinic complete, Gyatso makes a few house calls before we head back to Lo. Tenzin's horse flies. I balance in the thick steel stirrups, perched above the wooden frame of a saddle, cushioned by carpets. I am bathed in sand, wind, and dust.

We slow to a walk and dismount on the far side of the river that separates the walled city of Lo Monthang from territory beyond. Gyatso leads our sweat-soaked horses across a tawny stretch of land, down the well-worn switchback to the river's edge, where poplars grow. We are tired, horses and humans both. We could have used a rest, but our time together is limited and the day has begun to wane. Instead we head off to Lo Kunphen's medicinal plant cultivation grounds.

The experimental cultivation of high-altitude medicinal plants is a relatively new phenomena in Nepal and has been brought forth by push-pull factors. Some species are being overharvested, in part driven by increasing demand for raw materials to service commercial production of both Ayurvedic and Tibetan formulas ***; this trend has also been linked to increasing market prices for certain ingredients. Yet many such plants require specific soil conditions in which to grow. Some fail to germinate. Sometimes it becomes difficult to reconcile use values and exchange values when considering the lifecycle of a plant.

Interestingly, much of the cultivation of Tibetan medicines—at times combined with species distribution mapping and in-situ conservation—is being carried out by *amchi* on the fringes of the booming Asian medicine industries in China and India, rather than as part of a strategy for growth within these industries themselves. A lot of this work has been funded by conservation NGOs and bilateral research or development organizations. This cultivation project in Mustang is being funded by a grant from the United Nations Global Environmental Facility Small Grants Program, for which I helped the [Himalayan Amchi Association] write the proposal.

As Gyatso and I head toward the cultivation plots, I consider a refrain I have heard from *amchi* in Nepal: "Without plants, we are nothing. Without plants, we have no medicine. And an *amchi* with no medicine is like a bird without wings." This metaphor shifts at times—a car without gas, a teacher without students, a meal without salt, a trader without goods—yet the meaning remains constant. Without these medicinal plants, the future of Sowa Rigpa is jeopardized.

*　　*　　*

Gyatso and I hitch our horses beside the cultivation fields. I follow my friend along the raised perimeters of barley, sweet pea, and buckwheat fields toward a large plot of land rimmed by a wall of adobe brick and stone. ***

"We have 3,000 square meters of farmland and have not used all of it. In the future we could cultivate more," my friend explains. "Water can be a problem, though. And we need to have a path to market. This will get easier when the road really comes to upper Mustang. At present it is difficult to make a profit when the price of transportation to Jomsom remains so high. But in the future, I think there will be opportunities for common people to make money by growing medicinal plants instead of only peas and barley."

*　　*　　*

Gyatso's economics are lucid. As he fiddles with the lock on the gate, he calculates the cost of water rights and labor per square meter of land, the current market price for a kilo of barley versus a kilo of the three species of plants they are now growing and the cost of transport by horseback to the district headquarters in Jomsom, through middlemen, and then on to other markets. The profit margin is there, but barely.

*　　*　　*

Prayers of Aspiration: 8:00 P.M.

We leave the cultivation grounds. Horsetail clouds streak the sky, foretelling a day of rain. Gyatso and I walk slowly, clockwise as is expected, around the perimeter of the wall and back toward Lo Kunphen, horses in tow. We listen to the sounds of early evening in Mustang. Pressure cookers release steam. Donkeys bray. Children play hide-and-seek around rows of *chöten*. Tired-looking men and women return from harvest. Static-filled murmurs from satellite televisions diffuse into the cool air from the dark interiors of Monthang's few taverns.

Horses unsaddled and fed, we collapse on the same divans where we began this day. The room is bustling again. Gyatso's sister is cooking dinner. Tenzin arrives after his day of ritual attendance. Their mother orders her grandniece to give us tea and popcorn. There is not much left to do except to eat and rest, and we dive into both. I reach for more popcorn. Gyatso lets his chin droop to his chest. His eyes close. I watch him sink into sleep, letting the exhaustion of this man's life give way to a certain childlike surrender.

Then Tenzin sits down beside me with his laptop, fully charged. This is the problem of working with brothers. When one is resting, the other is ready to work. We have been discussing plans for Tenzin to visit the United States to fundraise for Lo Kunphen and see relatives in New York. I arranged a similar tour for Gyatso in 2003. The brothers alternate when it comes to foreign excursions; now it is Tenzin's turn. Tenzin's computer boots up. He loads a PowerPoint presentation, a process he has mastered, even though he speaks and reads virtually no English. As I wait for images to appear, I think of all the places these brothers have been: India, China, Bhutan, the United States, Britain, Germany, Japan, France, and Russia, including a stint as the resident doctors at a clinic in Tatarstan. This is difficult to square against the fact that about half of my own fellow U.S. citizens do not own a passport. In this sense "modernity" becomes a way of being in the world that lives within people who, according to stereotype, might seem the epitome of "traditional": a middle-aged monk with dirty robes and dirty hands, here on the edge of the world. In this sense Gyatso and Tenzin's life, and lifework, illustrate [anthropologist] Bruce Knauft's (2001) point that there are many ways of being modern in the world today. To deny the complex local-global realities of people like these *amchi* is to silence key ways that ideologies and socioeconomic influences circulate and shape contemporary life, from the power to buy things to the power to represent oneself on a national or global stage.

"Sienna *la*," Tenzin says, with excitement, "let me show you pictures from England." Tenzin spent some time in the United Kingdom earlier this year and had occasion to lecture on the history of Mustang and the future of *amchi* practice at Oxford's Oriental Institute and the Wellcome Trust for the History of Medicine in London. He had also been blessed by an audience with His Holiness the Dalai Lama. He describes his visit aided by the digital images he took along the way. * * * He advances through a series of images with His Holiness, resting on one of him bowed before the man Tibetans can refer to, profoundly, simply, as "Presence."

I ask him about this gift of time with the Dalai Lama. "I requested his advice about our school. How to move forward, what to do about the problems we face, how to keep working toward our goals," he answers.

"What did His Holiness say?"

Tenzin's reply turns toward prayer. He chants a long, low supplication. Is this Tenzin's answer to my question or His Holiness's answer to Tenzin? Really, both are true. After the prayer Tenzin tells me the advice the Dalai Lama bestowed on him: *Keep working with a pure heart. Keep making connections around the world. Keep finding points of shared interest and collaboration with other amchi. The path forward will reveal itself through this process.* The Dalai Lama then handed Tenzin several packets of *jinden*, ritually consecrated pills made each year in Dharamsala. Medicine from blessing born. This too is efficacious practice.

ENGAGING THE TEXT, ENGAGING THE WORLD

- What questions would you want to ask the brothers Gyatso and Tenzin Bista if you could spend a day with them?

- What effect do you think an ethnography like this might have on them and their community?

- Craig provides a careful, thick description of a stack of notebooks, religious texts, and binders of receipts on a wooden table in the main room of the brothers' home. What insights does her detailed description provide?

- In what ways is the rural, mountainous way of life of the Nepalese shaping and being shaped by global forces beyond their communities?

- How do *amchis* integrate traditional Tibetan healing practices with western biomedical approaches?

- What questions would you ask Sienna Craig about her fieldwork or her ethnographic writing?

4
Language

Language is a system of communication that uses symbols—such as words, sounds, and gestures—organized according to certain rules, to convey information. Today over seven thousand languages are in use in the world. Anthropologists are interested not only in the details of a language's vocabulary, **grammar**, and **syntax**, but also the role of language in people's lives—both as individuals and as communities.

Human language uses an infinite number of forms to communicate a vast array of information. We communicate through poetry, prose, gestures, signs, touch, text messaging, love letters—even anthropology textbooks. Not only can humans communicate content in great detail, but we also have the wondrous capacity to share the content of our imaginations—our anger, fear, joy—and the deepest longings of our souls.

Humans are born with the ability to learn language—not a particular language, but whatever one they are exposed to as they grow up. Exactly what we learn and the context in which we learn it vary widely. Languages are not abstract concepts with ideal forms perfectly displayed in a dictionary or a textbook. Languages are dynamic and alive. Communication is a social act. Words are part of actions. We call a friend, text a classmate, tell a story, say a prayer, ask a favor. As we will see in Laura Bohannan's article, the retelling of Shakespeare's *Hamlet* to the Tiv in a rural west African village involved constant discussion, negotiation and debate among the village elders, and eventually a reinterpretation of the story from their own cultural perspective.

Languages change and grow, constantly adapting to the needs and circumstances of the people who speak them. Culture shapes language, its form and its use. We create language to describe our things, like iPhones and computers, and our activities, like baseball and political elections. But what about the power of language to shape human thought and action? Bohannan's storytelling with the Tiv reveals the remarkable diversity of human language and the role of language in shaping humans' dramatically different ways of perceiving, thinking about, and engaging with the world. Because languages are deeply embedded in culture—

languages *are* culture—they also become arenas where norms and values are created, enforced, and contested, where group identity is negotiated, and where systems of power and status are taught and challenged. **Sociolinguistics** is the study of the ways in which culture shapes language and language shapes culture, particularly the intersection of language with cultural categories and systems of power such as age, race, ethnicity, sexuality, gender, and class. Laura Ahearn's article, for instance, reveals the ways in which kinship, courtship, and marriage norms are being renegotiated in Nepal through the writing of love letters as both young men and women learn new written language skills in literacy programs run by government-sponsored social development programs.

Shakespeare in the Bush
Laura Bohannan

The challenges of cross-cultural communication

In "Shakespeare in the Bush," anthropologist Laura Bohannan explores the challenges that different vocabulary and conceptualizations of the world pose for translation between languages and communication across cultures. In the middle of the rainy season, sitting under a thatched roof on a hillock in rural Nigeria, West Africa, Tiv elders asked Bohannan to tell them a story from her own culture. Trying to pick something she thought had universal themes and so would be universally understandable, she attempts to narrate Shakespeare's classic story of *Hamlet* in the Tiv's local language.

Ultimately the complex plot twists and cultural assumptions woven into this revenge tragedy prove extremely difficult to translate. The King of Denmark has died and his brother Claudius has inherited his throne and married the widowed queen, Gertrude. The king's ghost returns, appearing to night watchmen, the scholar Horatio, and later to the king's son, Prince Hamlet, declaring that he has been poisoned by Claudius. Hamlet vows revenge but drifts into a melancholy madness as he ponders how to execute it. His plans quickly go awry. Hamlet's friends Rosencrantz and Guildenstern help plan a failed attempt to discover

From Laura Bohannan. 1966. "Shakespeare in the Bush." *Natural History* 75: 28–33.

Claudius' guilt. Hamlet then mistakenly kills Claudius's chamberlain Polonius, father of Ophelia, whom Hamlet loves. Overcome by grief, Ophelia drowns herself in the lake. Polonius's son Laertes vows revenge on Hamlet, but in the ensuing confrontation Laertes, Hamlet, Claudius, and Gertrude all die from poisoned blades and drinks.

As Bohannan narrates Shakespeare in the African bush, Tiv elders regularly interrupt her story with questions and statements of disbelief. Their different cultural practices of kinship, marriage, courtship, and proper intergenerational relations and very different beliefs about religion, witchcraft, life after death, and mental illness lead them to interpret *Hamlet* in a dramatically different way. In the end, the elders are pleased that they have helped Bohannan her to understand the true meaning of the story and encourage her to tell them more so that when she returns home, people will know she was not just sitting in the bush but was "among those who know things and who have taught you wisdom."

Just before I left Oxford for the Tiv in West Africa, conversation turned to the season at Stratford. "You Americans," said a friend, "often have difficulty with Shakespeare. He was, after all, a very English poet, and one can easily misinterpret the universal by misunderstanding the particular."

I protested that human nature is pretty much the same the whole world over; at least the general plot and motivation of the greater tragedies would always be clear—everywhere—although some details of custom might have to be explained and difficulties of translation might produce other slight changes. To end an argument we could not conclude, my friend gave me a copy of *Hamlet* to study in the African bush: it would, he hoped, lift my mind above its primitive surroundings, and possibly I might, by prolonged meditation, achieve the grace of correct interpretation.

It was my second field trip to that African tribe, and I thought myself ready to live in one of its remote sections—an area difficult to cross even on foot. I eventually settled on the hillock of a very knowledgeable old man, the head of a homestead of some hundred and forty people, all of whom were either his close relatives or their wives and children. Like the other elders of the vicinity, the old man spent most of his time performing ceremonies seldom seen these days in the more accessible parts of the tribe. I was delighted. Soon there would be three months of enforced isolation and leisure, between the harvest that takes place just before the rising of the swamps and the clearing of new farms when the water goes down. Then, I thought, they would have even more time to perform ceremonies and explain them to me.

I was quite mistaken. Most of the ceremonies demanded the presence of elders from several homesteads. As the swamps rose, the old men found it too difficult to walk from one homestead to the next, and the ceremonies gradually ceased. As the swamps rose even higher, all activities but one came to an end. The women brewed beer from maize and millet. Men, women, and children sat on their hillocks and drank it.

People began to drink at dawn. By midmorning the whole homestead was singing, dancing, and drumming. When it rained, people had to sit inside their huts: there they drank and sang or they drank and told stories. In any case, by noon or before, I either had to join the party or retire to my own hut and my books. "One does not discuss serious matters when there is beer. Come, drink with us." Since I lacked their capacity for the thick native beer, I spent more and more time with *Hamlet*. Before the end of the second month, grace descended on me. I was quite sure that *Hamlet* had only one possible interpretation, and that one universally obvious.

Early every morning, in the hope of having some serious talk before the beer party, I used to call on the old man at his reception hut—a circle of posts supporting a thatched roof above a low mud wall to keep out wind and rain. One day I crawled through the low doorway and found most of the men of the homestead sitting huddled in their ragged cloths on stools, low plank beds, and reclining chairs, warming themselves against the chill of the rain around a smoky fire. In the center were three pots of beer. The party had started.

The old man greeted me cordially. "Sit down and drink." I accepted a large calabash full of beer, poured some into a small drinking gourd, and tossed it down. Then I poured some more into the same gourd for the man second in seniority to my host before I handed my calabash over to a young man for further distribution. Important people shouldn't ladle beer themselves.

"It is better like this," the old man said, looking at me approvingly and plucking at the thatch that had caught in my hair. "You should sit and drink with us more often. Your servants tell me that when you are not with us, you sit inside your hut looking at a paper."

The old man was acquainted with four kinds of "papers": tax receipts, bride price receipts, court fee receipts, and letters. The messenger who brought him letters from the chief used them mainly as a badge of office, for he always knew what was in them and told the old man. Personal letters for the few who had relatives in the government or mission stations were kept until someone went to a large market where there was a letter writer and reader. Since my arrival, letters were brought to me to be read. A few men also brought me bride price receipts, privately, with requests to change the figures to a higher sum. I found moral arguments were of no avail, since in-laws are fair game, and the technical hazards of forgery difficult to explain to an illiterate people. I did not wish them to think me silly enough to look at any such papers for days on end, and I hastily explained that my "paper" was one of the "things of long ago" of my country.

"Ah," said the old man. "Tell us."

I protested that I was not a storyteller. Storytelling is a skilled art among them; their standards are high, and the audiences critical—and vocal in their criticism. I protested in vain. This morning they wanted to hear a story while they drank. They threatened to tell me no more stories until I told them one of mine. Finally, the old man promised that no one would criticize my style "for we know you are struggling with our language." "But," put in one of the elders, "you must explain what we do not understand, as we do when we tell you our stories." Realizing that here was my chance to prove *Hamlet* universally intelligible, I agreed.

The old man handed me some more beer to help me on with my storytelling. Men filled their long wooden pipes and knocked coals from the fire to place in the pipe bowls; then, puffing contentedly, they sat back to listen. I began in the proper style, "Not yesterday, not yesterday, but long ago, a thing occurred. One night three men were keeping watch outside the homestead of the great chief, when suddenly they saw the former chief approach them."

"Why was he no longer their chief?"

"He was dead," I explained. "That is why they were troubled and afraid when they saw him."

"Impossible," began one of the elders, handing his pipe on to his neighbor, who interrupted, "Of course it wasn't the dead chief. It was an omen sent by a witch. Go on."

Slightly shaken, I continued. "One of these three was a man who knew things"—the closest translation for scholar, but unfortunately it also meant witch. The second elder looked triumphantly at the first. "So he spoke to the dead chief saying, 'Tell us what we must do so you may rest in your grave,' but the dead chief did not answer. He vanished, and they could see him no more. Then the man who knew things—his name was Horatio—said this event was the affair of the dead chief's son, Hamlet."

There was a general shaking of heads round the circle. "Had the dead chief no living brothers? Or was this son the chief?"

"No," I replied. "That is, he had one living brother who became the chief when the elder brother died."

The old men muttered: such omens were matters for chiefs and elders, not for youngsters; no good could come of going behind a chiefs back; clearly Horatio was not a man who knew things.

"Yes, he was," I insisted, shooing a chicken away from my beer. "In our country the son is next to the father. The dead chief's younger brother had become the great chief. He had also married his elder brother's widow only about a month after the funeral."

"He did well," the old man beamed and announced to the others, "I told you that if we knew more about Europeans, we would find they really were very like us. In our country also," he added to me, "the younger brother marries the elder brother's widow and becomes the father of his children. Now, if your uncle, who married your widowed mother, is your father's full brother, then he will be a real father to you. Did Hamlet's father and uncle have one mother?"

His question barely penetrated my mind; I was too upset and thrown too far off balance by having one of the most important elements of *Hamlet* knocked straight out of the picture. Rather uncertainly I said that I thought they had the same mother, but I wasn't sure—the story didn't say. The old man told me severely that these genealogical details made all the difference and that when I got home I must ask the elders about it. He shouted out the door to one of his younger wives to bring his goatskin bag.

Determined to save what I could of the mother motif, I took a deep breath and began again. "The son Hamlet was very sad because his mother had married again so quickly. There was no need for her to do so, and it is our custom for a widow not to go to her next husband until she has mourned for two years."

"Two years is too long," objected the wife, who had appeared with the old man's battered goatskin bag. "Who will hoe your farms for you while you have no husband?"

"Hamlet," I retorted without thinking, "was old enough to hoe his mother's farms himself. There was no need for her to remarry." No one looked convinced. I gave up. "His mother and the great chief told Hamlet not to be sad, for the great chief himself would be a father to Hamlet. Furthermore, Hamlet would be the next chief: therefore he must stay to learn the things of a chief. Hamlet agreed to remain, and all the rest went off to drink beer."

While I paused, perplexed at how to render Hamlet's disgusted soliloquy to an audience convinced that Claudius and Gertrude had behaved in the best possible manner, one of the younger men asked me who had married the other wives of the dead chief.

"He had no other wives," I told him.

"But a chief must have many wives! How else can he brew beer and prepare food for all his guests?"

I said firmly that in our country even chiefs had only one wife, that they had servants to do their work, and that they paid them from tax money.

It was better, they returned, for a chief to have many wives and sons who would help him hoe his farms and feed his people; then everyone loved the chief who gave much and took nothing—taxes were a bad thing.

I agreed with the last comment, but for the rest fell back on their favorite way of fobbing off my questions: "That is the way it is done, so that is how we do it."

I decided to skip the soliloquy. Even if Claudius was here thought quite right to marry his brother's widow, there remained the poison motif, and I knew they would disapprove of fratricide. More hopefully I resumed, "That night Hamlet kept watch with the three who had seen his dead father. The dead chief again appeared, and although the others were afraid, Hamlet followed his dead father off to one side. When they were alone, Hamlet's dead father spoke."

"Omens can't talk!" The old man was emphatic.

"Hamlet's dead father wasn't an omen. Seeing him might have been an omen, but he was not." My audience looked as confused as I sounded. "It *was* Hamlet's dead father. It was a thing we call a 'ghost.'" I had to use the English word, for unlike many of the neighboring tribes, these people didn't believe in the survival after death of any individuating part of the personality.

"What is a 'ghost?' An omen?"

"No, a 'ghost' is someone who is dead but who walks around and can talk, and people can hear him and see him but not touch him."

They objected. "One can touch zombis."

"No, no! It was not a dead body the witches had animated to sacrifice and eat. No one else made Hamlet's dead father walk. He did it himself."

"Dead men can't walk," protested my audience as one man.

I was quite willing to compromise. "A 'ghost' is the dead man's shadow."

But again they objected. "Dead men cast no shadows."

"They do in my country," I snapped.

The old man quelled the babble of disbelief that arose immediately and told me with that insincere, but courteous, agreement one extends to the fancies of the young, ignorant, and superstitious, "No doubt in your country the dead can also walk without being zombis." From the depths of his bag he produced a withered fragment of kola nut, bit off one end to show it wasn't poisoned, and handed me the rest as a peace offering.

"Anyhow," I resumed, "Hamlet's dead father said that his own brother, the one who became chief, had poisoned him. He wanted Hamlet to avenge him. Hamlet believed this in his heart, for he did not like his father's brother." I took another swallow of beer. "In the country of the great chief, living in the same homestead, for it was a very large one, was an important elder who was often with the chief to advise and help him. His name was Polonius. Hamlet was courting his daughter, but her father and her brother . . . [I cast hastily about for some tribal analogy] warned her not to let Hamlet visit her when she was alone on her farm, for he would be a great chief and so could not marry her."

"Why not?" asked the wife, who had settled down on the edge of the old man's chair. He frowned at her for asking stupid questions and growled, "They lived in the same homestead."

"That was not the reason," I informed them. "Polonius was a stranger who lived in the homestead because he helped the chief, not because he was a relative."

"Then why couldn't Hamlet marry her?"

"He could have," I explained, "but Polonius didn't think he would. After all, Hamlet was a man of great importance who ought to marry a chief's daughter, for in his country a man could have only one wife. Polonius was afraid that if Hamlet made love to his daughter, then no one else would give a high price for her."

"That might be true," remarked one of the shrewder elders, "but a chief's son would give his mistress's father enough presents and patronage to more than make up the difference. Polonius sounds like a fool to me."

"Many people think he was," I agreed. "Meanwhile Polonius sent his son Laertes off to Paris to learn the things of that country, for it was the homestead of a very great chief indeed. Because he was afraid that Laertes might waste a lot of money on beer and women and gambling, or get into trouble by fighting, he sent one of his servants to Paris secretly, to spy out what Laertes was doing. One day Hamlet came upon Polonius's daughter Ophelia. He behaved so oddly he frightened her. Indeed"—I was fumbling for words to express the dubious quality of Hamlet's madness—"the chief and many others had also noticed that when Hamlet talked one could understand the words but not what they meant. Many people thought that he had become mad." My audience suddenly became much more attentive. "The great chief wanted to know what was wrong with Hamlet, so he sent for two of Hamlet's age mates [school friends would have taken long explanation] to talk to Hamlet and find out what troubled his heart. Hamlet, seeing that they had been bribed by the chief to betray him, told them nothing. Polonius, however, insisted that Hamlet was mad because he had been forbidden to see Ophelia, whom he loved."

"Why," inquired a bewildered voice, "should anyone bewitch Hamlet on that account?"

"Bewitch him?"

"Yes, only witchcraft can make anyone mad, unless, of course, one sees the beings that lurk in the forest."

I stopped being a storyteller, took out my notebook and demanded to be told more about these two causes of madness. Even while they spoke and I jotted notes, I tried to calculate the effect of this new factor on the plot. Hamlet had not been exposed to the beings that lurk in the forests. Only his relatives in the male line could bewitch him. Barring relatives not mentioned by Shakespeare, it had to be Claudius who was attempting to harm him. And, of course, it was.

For the moment I staved off questions by saying that the great chief also refused to believe that Hamlet was mad for the love of Ophelia and nothing else. "He was sure that something much more important was troubling Hamlet's heart."

"Now Hamlet's age mates," I continued, "had brought with them a famous storyteller. Hamlet decided to have this man tell the chief and all his homestead a story about a man who had poisoned his brother because he desired his brother's wife and wished to be chief himself. Hamlet was sure the great chief could not hear the story without making a sign if he was indeed guilty, and then he would discover whether his dead father had told him the truth."

The old man interrupted, with deep cunning, "Why should a father lie to his son?" he asked.

I hedged: "Hamlet wasn't sure that it really was his dead father." It was impossible to say anything, in that language, about devil-inspired visions.

"You mean," he said, "it actually was an omen, and he knew witches sometimes send false ones. Hamlet was a fool not to go to one skilled in reading omens and divining the truth in the first place. A man-who-sees-the-truth could have told him how his father died, if he really had been poisoned, and if there was witchcraft in it; then Hamlet could have called the elders to settle the matter."

The shrewd elder ventured to disagree. "Because his father's brother was a great chief, one-who-sees-the-truth might therefore have been afraid to tell it. I think it was for that reason that a friend of Hamlet's father—a witch and an elder—sent an omen so his friend's son would know. Was the omen true?"

"Yes," I said, abandoning ghosts and the devil; a witch-sent omen it would have to be. "It was true, for when the storyteller was telling his tale before all the homestead, the great chief rose in fear. Afraid that Hamlet knew his secret he planned to have him killed."

The stage set of the next bit presented some difficulties of translation. I began cautiously. "The great chief told Hamlet's mother to find out from her son what he knew. But because a woman's children are always first in her heart, he had the important elder Polonius hide behind a cloth that hung against the wall of Hamlet's mother's sleeping hut. Hamlet started to scold his mother for what she had done."

There was a shocked murmur from everyone. A man should never scold his mother.

"She called out in fear, and Polonius moved behind the cloth. Shouting, 'A rat!' Hamlet took his machete and slashed through the cloth." I paused for dramatic effect. "He had killed Polonius!"

The old men looked at each other in supreme disgust. "That Polonius truly was a fool and a man who knew nothing! What child would not know enough to shout, 'It's me!'" With a pang, I remembered that these people are ardent hunters, always armed with bow, arrow, and machete; at the first rustle in the grass an arrow is aimed and ready, and the hunter shouts "Game!" If no human voice answers immediately, the arrow speeds on its way. Like a good hunter Hamlet had shouted, "A rat!"

I rushed in to save Polonius's reputation. "Polonius did speak. Hamlet heard him. But he thought it was the chief and wished to kill him to avenge his father. He had meant to kill him earlier that evening. . . ." I broke down, unable to describe to these pagans, who had no belief in individual afterlife, the difference between dying at one's prayers and dying "unhousell'd, disappointed, unaneled."

This time I had shocked my audience seriously. "For a man to raise his hand against his father's brother and the one who has become his father—that is a terrible thing. The elders ought to let such a man be bewitched."

I nibbled at my kola nut in some perplexity, then pointed out that after all the man had killed Hamlet's father.

"No," pronounced the old man, speaking less to me than to the young men sitting behind the elders. "If your father's brother has killed your father you must appeal to your father's age mates; *they* may avenge him. No man may use violence against his senior relatives." Another thought struck him. "But if his father's brother had indeed been wicked enough to bewitch Hamlet and make him mad that would be a good story indeed, for it would be his fault that Hamlet, being mad, no longer had any sense and thus was ready to kill his father's brother."

There was a murmur of applause. *Hamlet* was again a good story to them, but it no longer seemed quite the same story to me. As I thought over the coming complications of plot and motive, I lost courage and decided to skim over dangerous ground quickly.

"The great chief," I went on, "was not sorry that Hamlet had killed Polonius. It gave him a reason to send Hamlet away, with his two treacherous age mates, with letters to a chief of a far country, saying that Hamlet should be killed. But Hamlet changed the writing on their papers, so that the chief killed his age mates instead." I encountered a reproachful glare from one of the men whom I had told undetectable forgery was not merely immoral but beyond human skill. I looked the other way.

"Before Hamlet could return, Laertes came back for his father's funeral. The great chief told him Hamlet had killed Polonius. Laertes swore to kill Hamlet because of this, and because his sister Ophelia, hearing her father had been killed by the man she loved, went mad and drowned in the river."

"Have you already forgotten what we told you?" The old man was reproachful. "One cannot take vengeance on a madman; Hamlet killed Polonius in his madness. As for the girl, she not only went mad, she was drowned. Only witches can make people drown. Water itself can't hurt anything. It is merely something one drinks and bathes in."

I began to get cross. "If you don't like the story, I'll stop."

The old man made soothing noises and himself poured me some more beer. "You tell the story well, and we are listening. But it is clear that the elders of your country have never told you what the story really means. No, don't interrupt! We believe you when you say your marriage customs are different, or your clothes and weapons. But people are the same everywhere; therefore, there are always witches and it is we, the elders, who know how witches work. We told you it was the great chief who wished to kill Hamlet, and now your own words have proved us right. Who were Ophelia's male relatives?"

"There were only her father and her brother." Hamlet was clearly out of my hands.

"There must have been many more; this also you must ask of your elders when you get back to your country. From what you tell us, since Polonius was dead, it must have been Laertes who killed Ophelia, although I do not see the reason for it."

We had emptied one pot of beer, and the old men argued the point with slightly tipsy interest. Finally one of them demanded of me, "What did the servant of Polonius say on his return?"

With difficulty I recollected Reynaldo and his mission. "I don't think he did return before Polonius was killed."

"Listen," said the elder, "and I will tell you how it was and how your story will go, then you may tell me if I am right. Polonius knew his son would get into trouble, and so he did. He had many fines to pay for fighting, and debts from gambling. But he had only two ways of getting money quickly. One was to marry off his sister at once, but it is difficult to find a man who will marry a woman desired by the son of a chief. For if the chief's heir commits adultery with your wife, what can you do? Only a fool calls a case against a man who will someday be his judge. Therefore Laertes had to take the second way: he killed his sister by witchcraft, drowning her so he could secretly sell her body to the witches."

I raised an objection. "They found her body and buried it. Indeed Laertes jumped into the grave to see his sister once more—so, you see, the body was truly there. Hamlet, who had just come back, jumped in after him."

"What did I tell you?" The elder appealed to the others. "Laertes was up to no good with his sister's body. Hamlet prevented him, because the chief's heir, like a chief, does not wish any other man to grow rich and powerful. Laertes would be angry, because be would have killed his sister without benefit to himself. In our country he would try to kill Hamlet for that reason. Is this not what happened?"

"More or less," I admitted. "When the great chief found Hamlet was still alive, he encouraged Laertes to try to kill Hamlet and arranged a fight with machetes between them. In the fight both the young men were wounded to death. Hamlet's mother drank the poisoned beer that the chief meant for Hamlet in case he won the fight. When he saw his mother die of poison, Hamlet, dying, managed to kill his father's brother with his machete."

"You see, I was right!" exclaimed the elder.

"That was a very good story," added the old man, "and you told it with very few mistakes. There was just one more error, at the very end. The poison Hamlet's mother drank was obviously meant for the survivor of the fight, whichever it was. If Laertes had won, the great chief would have poisoned him, for no one would know that he arranged Hamlet's death. Then, too, he need not fear Laertes' witchcraft; it takes a strong heart to kill one's only sister by witchcraft.

"Sometime," concluded the old man, gathering his ragged toga about him, "you must tell us some more stories of your country. We, who are elders, will instruct you in their true meaning, so that when you return to your own land your elders will see that you have not been sitting in the bush, but among those who know things and who have taught you wisdom."

ENGAGING THE TEXT, ENGAGING THE WORLD

- In what particular ways did the Tiv's culture and local realities shape their interpretation of this classic English story?

- In what ways did Bohannan's fieldwork experience challenge her initial belief that human nature is pretty much the same the world over?

- If you had been in Bohannan's shoes, what story would you have chosen to tell? In what ways do you think people from another culture might interpret your story differently?

- What do you think the story of retelling Shakespeare in the bush reveals about the nature of language and about its ability to shape the way we think?

- Can you think of any ways that your cultural use of language may limit the way you think about other people in the world? Perhaps refer back to Abu-Lughod's article in Chapter 2, "Do Muslim Women Really Need Saving?"

Literacy, Power, and Agency: Love Letters and Development in Nepal

Laura Ahearn

Love letters,
literacy, and
changing
language use

What can an anthropologist learn from a love letter? Laura Ahearn's study of love letters in Nepal offers insights into the power of literacy to change lives. Literacy is a social act, as individuals learn to read in groups of students and from teachers who shape what is learned, how it is learned, and what it means. In a culture where the power of the written word is revered in social and religious contexts, newly emerging literacy among young people in Nepal, particularly young women, is reshaping local culture, especially in the area of dating, marriage, and kinship. For young women, literacy—and the ability to write and read love letters—has facilitated a shift away from arranged and capture marriages toward elopement. Young people not allowed to date or spend time alone are able to build relationships through correspondence. The ability to correspond, in itself, marks someone as "developed" and not "backward," someone who may be open to the idea of a companionate marriage with a life friend based on romance and love. But Ahearn warns that despite the underlying narrative of development—increasing self-sufficiency, hard work, success, and individual responsibility—literacy does not always lead to women's empowerment, and it may actually reinforce certain cultural notions of gender and undercut cultural practices that have traditionally created avenues of power for women.

There is a common saying in the village of Junigau, Nepal: *bhāvile lekheko, chhālāle chhekeko*, 'It is written by fate but covered by skin'. This adage reflects a belief not only among the Magars who populate Junigau but also among many other Nepali ethnic groups and castes that at birth a person's fate is written underneath the skin of the forehead, making it impossible to ascertain what will happen. According to this view, fate is responsible for events that befall the individual, for it is fate, or, in a different

From Laura M. Ahearn. 2004. "Literacy, Power, and Agency: Love Letters and Development in Nepal." *Language and Education* 18(4): 305–316. Some of the author's notes have been omitted.

translation, God or the gods, who have the power to write. Two other common sayings in Junigau are corollaries to this saying: *dekheko mātrai hunna, lekheko hunu parchha*. 'It is not enough just to see something; it must also be written (i.e. fated)'—and *bhaneko mātrai hunna, lekheko hunu parchha*, 'It is not enough just to say something; it must also be written (i.e. fated)'. Given these connections between fate and the written word, it becomes important to ask what happens when villagers in an incipiently literate community such as Junigau acquire the power to write, and the power to read what others write? How do conceptions of agency, gender, fate, and development shape and reflect new literacy practices? * * *

In this paper, I argue that literacy is both a catalyst for social change and a result of numerous other types of social transformation. * * *

Thus, my approach is to situate emergent literacy practices socially, historically, and, especially for my purposes here, *intertextually* [within actual written texts]. * * * In the case of Junigau, Nepal, in the 1980s and 1990s, female literacy was facilitated by a number of dramatic economic, social, and political changes, and in turn these changes were deepened, challenged, or reconstituted in unexpected (and not always beneficial) ways by the women's literacy practices. * * *

In the analysis that follows, I investigate how villagers have applied their literacy skills to the new courtship practice of love-letter writing in Junigau. I discuss the implications of the emergence of love-letter correspondences for social relations in Nepal and trace out the broader ramifications for conceptions of literacy, gender, love, social change, and agency (which I define as the socioculturally mediated capacity to act). My central argument is that a close examination of love-letter writing in Junigau reveals the microprocesses of social transformation *as it is occurring*. I contend that the new practice of love-letter writing in Junigau has facilitated not only a shift away from arranged and capture marriage towards elopement but also a change in how villagers conceive of their own ability to act and how they attribute responsibility for events—developments with potential ramifications that extend far beyond the realm of marriage and well past the Himalayas.

In addition to offering us valuable insights into the rapidly changing marriage practices in this one community, these love-letter correspondences also provide us with a deeper understanding of the social effects of literacy. * * * The increase in female literacy rates in Junigau in the 1990s made possible the emergence of new courtship practices and facilitated self-initiated marriages, but it also reinforced certain gender ideologies and undercut some avenues to social power, especially for women. Thus, this study reminds us that literacy is not a neutral, unidimensional technology, but rather a set of lived experiences that will differ from community to community.

From Love to Development—and Back Again

In June 1992 Bir Bahadur, a 21-year-old man who at the time often sported flashy jeans, a gold chain, and a winning smile, wrote the following words in his first love letter to

Sarita, whose long black hair, fashionable Punjabi outfits, and demure giggles had caught his eye:

> Sarita, I'm helpless, and I have to make friends of a notebook and pen in order to place this helplessness before you. Love is the sort of thing that anyone can feel— even a great man of the world like Hitler loved Eva, they say. And Napoleon, who with bravery conquered the 'world'; united it, and took it forward, was astounded when he saw one particular widow. Certainly, history's pages are coloured with accounts of such individuals who love each other. In which case, Sarita, I'll let you know by a 'short cut' what I want to say: Love is the agreement of two souls. The 'main' meaning of love is 'life success'. I'm offering you an invitation to love.

At the time this letter was written, Sarita, a 21-year-old woman from the Magar village of Junigau, and Bir Bahadur, who was from another Magar village in western Palpa District, were both studying at the college campus in Tansen, the district centre. They had met only once very briefly two months earlier when he had sought her out to deliver a message about some books she wanted to borrow from a relative. That one brief encounter, however, was enough to prompt each of them to inquire about the other's family, personal qualities, and marriageability. Two months later, Bir Bahadur sent his 'invitation to love', and when Sarita replied, a complex, tumultuous courtship ensued.

Courtships such as this one involving love letters became possible for the first time in the early 1990s as a result of increasing female literacy rates in the village. Since it was still not considered appropriate for young men and women to date or spend time alone together (though many managed to do so occasionally despite close parental supervision), love letters provided them with a way to maintain contact with their sweethearts. Love letters such as Bir Bahadur's above not only kept young people in touch with one another, they also prolonged courtships, enabling the participants to get to know each other better. Moreover, the mere sending and receiving of love letters marked someone as a particular kind of person – a 'developed' (*bikāsi*) as opposed to a 'backward' (*pichhyādi*) individual, someone who was capable of creating a particular kind of companionate marriage with a 'life friend'. Together, the two would try to create a future made brighter by love and by 'life success'.

Although Sarita and Bir Bahadur were among the first young people in their villages to court through love letters, they were not by any means the first to experience romantic love. Indeed, expressions of romantic love in Junigau can be found in old folksongs, poems, and stories, not to mention in villagers' narratives of elopements that occurred decades ago. And yet, Bir Bahadur and Sarita's courtship differed in many respects from those of their parents' generation. The few older Magars in Junigau who eloped rather than taking part in arranged or capture marriages carried on extremely brief courtships, often eloping the day after meeting someone at a songfest or wedding. While these few elopements were frequently triggered by romantic love, and while romantic love sometimes developed between spouses who had had arranged marriages or capture marriages, most Junigau courtships that took place in the 1990s differed significantly from those that occurred in previous decades with regard to how romantic love was conceptualised. Whereas in the past, romantic love was considered an emotion of which to be embarrassed, in the 1990s, love came to be seen as desirable, as it was linked in many young villagers' minds with development and modernity; indeed, desire *itself* came to be viewed as desirable * * * (Ahearn 2003).

Not only did courtships leading to elopements look different in the 1990s; there were also many more of them in Junigau than there had been in earlier periods. The number of elopements rose steadily in the village during the last decades of the twentieth century, whereas the number of arranged marriages and capture marriages declined. More and more emphasis was placed on obtaining the woman's 'consent' (*mañjur*) to the marriage. * * *

Literacy Practices and Development Discourses

For the remainder of this paper, I attempt to situate Junigau love-letter writing in the wider range of literacy practices in which villagers engaged during the 1990s. By doing so, we can begin to discover some of the sources of the villagers' new ideas about love, success, agency, and personhood.

By the 1990s, development discourse was ubiquitous in Junigau: textbooks, magazines and novels, Radio Nepal development programmes and soap operas, Hindi movies in Tansen, love-letter guidebooks, and everyday conversations. * * *

All government schools in Nepal, including Junigau's Sarvodaya High School (grades 1–10), use the same set of textbooks published by the Ministry of Education and Culture. When I taught English and Maths in the Peace Corps in the early 1980s, these were the textbooks I used, and they are the textbooks from which many of Junigau's love-letter writers acquired their literacy skills in their early years of formal schooling. * * * All the messages conveyed in Nepal's national textbooks are important influences on Junigau's constantly shifting structures of feeling. They both reflect and shape villagers' changing notions of personhood, agency, and social hierarchy (cf. Luke 1988, Schieffelin 2000).

Similar themes underlie *Nāyā Goreto* (*New Path*), the textbook used to teach female literacy in Junigau and elsewhere throughout Nepal. The text and images in the female literacy materials through which many Junigau women have learned to read and write differ somewhat from those of the textbooks used for formal education in Nepali schools, yet there are interesting parallels. Like the textbooks used in all government schools in Nepal, *Nāyā Goreto* stresses the need to become 'developed' (*bikāsi*), but while the formal school textbooks emphasise * * * Nepali nationalism and Hinduism and reinforce existing gender and age hierarchies, *New Path* seeks to challenge at least some of those hierarchies. Interestingly, both the textbooks used in Nepali schools and *New Path* are government-sponsored textbooks, which proves that no government is univocal in its publications.

From page one, *New Path* * * * is steeped in development discourse. From the vocabulary words accompanied by full-page illustrations designed to raise students' consciousness to the serialised comic strip stories about villagers and their problems, the textbook clearly presents in unmistakably moral tones a correct—or 'developed'—way to live. Of course, the degree to which literacy students or other villagers who read these materials (for the workbook is in wide circulation in Junigau) accept, resist, or otherwise grapple with this image of the *bikāsi* Nepali varies. The ideology of *New Path* is not absorbed passively or unquestioningly by its Junigau readers. Nor is it by any means the sole source of development discourse in the village. * * *

Where *New Path* has contributed the most to social change in Junigau and to the rhetoric found in love letters, it seems to me, is in its advocacy of the ideological package involving self-sufficiency, hard work, development, success, and individual responsibility. Many of the same messages are being communicated in Sarvodaya School's textbooks and classrooms, albeit within a very different framework that emphasises patriotism, Hinduism, and filial piety. As Junigau residents acquire basic literacy skills, whether through formal schooling or evening literacy classes, they are encouraged to associate the acquisition of all kinds of skills with greater development, capitalist activity, independence, and agency. * * *

Next to the textbooks used in the government school and in female literacy classes, the most popular reading materials in Junigau in the 1990s were magazines. * * * Another type of reading material available to Junigau residents in the 1990s consisted of short stories or novels, but many fewer villagers actually read these materials because of their expense. They also lacked the appeal of magazines, which had more attractive graphics and prose that was easier for villagers to understand. The only work of fiction I saw in the village besides a few collections of folktales was a novel by Prakash Kovid (n.d.) entitled *Love Letters*. Although none of the letter writers with whom I spoke during my research had read the book before they wrote their love letters, other young people in the village had, and the details of the plot were circulated fairly widely, as was the book itself.

Although most Junigau love-letter writers have told me that they write only what is in their hearts/minds (*man*) and have never consulted a guidebook, the examples, rules, and sentiments contained in the love-letter guidebooks that are sporadically available in bookstores in Tansen so closely echo Junigau love letters that I have decided to close with a few examples of these texts here.

When I first heard that 'how to' books were available to Nepalis who wanted to learn how to write love letters, I asked one of the clerks at Shrestha News Agency in Tansen for copies of whatever they had. Sorry, the clerk replied, they were all sold out. I returned a couple of weeks later, but although they had received a new delivery of the guidebooks in the interim, they were again already sold out. By my third trip to the bookseller, the clerk recognised me and gave me an apologetic smile that acknowledged what he must have perceived to be my desperate need to learn how to write love letters. Still no guidebooks. Finally, a few months later, I did manage to obtain a copy of Ara John Movsesian's *How to Write Love Letters and Love Poems* (Movsesian 1993) from Shrestha News Agency, though in all my subsequent trips back to the store they never had any of the popular Hindi [language] guidebooks in stock. I found two more English guidebooks in Kathmandu bookstores, J.S. Bright's *Lively Love Letters* (Bright n.d.) and Manohar's *Love Letters* (Manohar n.d.).

In his guidebook, Movsesian puts forth the same philosophy of love that informs the Junigau love letters. According to this philosophy, love is an eternal centrality of life. At the same time, an evolution is posited that moves away from illiterate 'backwardness' towards 'civilised, refined' expressions of 'Romantic Communication'. The following passages from Movsesian's Preface demonstrate the parallels with the love letters written in Junigau and the ideological assumptions regarding the effects of literacy:

> Verbal language has enabled individuals to personally express their love in a more refined manner than was earlier possible. Written language has provided lover's [sic] a very potent tool which, in turn, has given rise to two forms of Romantic Communication: The Love Letter and Love Poem. Both of these forms have been used by literate people everywhere for centuries to communicate their innermost passions, desires and emotions. Even [English King] Henry VIII and Napoleon wrote love letters to their sweethearts. The most famous legendary writer of love letters was [French novelist and playwright] Cyrano De Berjerac [sic] who wrote countless letters, not for himself, but on behalf of his close friends. (Movsesian 1993: vii)

Similarities are immediately apparent between this passage from Movsesian's guidebook and the first letter Bir Bahadur wrote to Sarita, quoted above, which contains the lines, 'Love is the sort of thing that anyone can feel—even a great man of the world like Hitler loved Eva, they say. And Napoleon, who with bravery conquered the "world", united it, and took it forward, was astounded when he saw one particular widow.' Moreover, the very first letter in Movsesian's book, in the section entitled, 'Love Letters from the Past,' is from Napoleon Bonaparte to Josephine De Beauharnais, written in December 1795. It reads in part:

> I wake filled with thoughts of you. Your portrait and the intoxicating evening which we spent yesterday have left my senses in turmoil. Sweet, incomparable Josephine, what a strange effect you have on my heart! Are you angry? Do I see you looking sad? Are you worried? (Movsesian 1993:7)

These lines are echoed in the many allusions to anger and sadness in the correspondence of Vajra Bahadur and Shila Devi. In the spring of 1990, for instance, Vajra

Bahadur wrote, 'Again, you'll probably get angry reading this letter. Whenever I see you, you're always angry. Why, oh why, when I see you walking, looking angry, does my heart get cut into slices?'

Conclusion

Although it is undeniably true, as [anthropologist Jack] Goody (2000:155) states, that 'Changes in modes of communication do matter and have fundamentally altered the life of mankind [sic]', this statement begs the question of *how* things have changed, for whom, why, and with what results. As [linguistic anthropologist Bambi] Schieffelin (2000: 293) reminds us, 'We know that societies differ significantly in ways of taking up and organising literacy practices (or resisting them), and this relates to cultural as well as historical factors.' In the case of Junigau, it is clear that ideology cannot be separated from literacy, as young villagers in the 1990s acquired literacy skills in the context of certain social forces that emphasised the importance of formal education as part of becoming 'modern' and 'developed'.

Moreover, while some literacy practitioners and scholars might view the increasing rates of female literacy in a place like Junigau as an unmitigatedly positive outcome, as an example of 'the giving of power to the powerless' (Goody 2000: 158), my research indicates that literacy does not always bring with it power (cf. Luke 1996; Street 2001). A Junigau woman who uses her newly acquired literacy skills to write love letters that culminate in elopement with a young man often entirely forfeits the support of her natal family should the marriage turn sour. Having married someone she usually knows only through love letters, she may end up devastated when her husband is less loving in actuality than he sounded in his letters, or when his mother (for couples in Junigau always live with the husband's extended family) is a harsh taskmaster over the new, lowly daughter-in-law— and when no one from her natal family will intervene on her behalf because she eloped rather than having an arranged marriage. That such distressing outcomes have occurred in Junigau belie the simplistic notion of literacy as a neutral skill of empowerment.

Finally, the types of ideological messages conveyed in the texts used in and out of Junigau classrooms, and the unexpected uses to which Junigau young people are putting their newly acquired literacy skills, should open our eyes to the need for a more thoughtful and more culturally specific approach to pedagogy in the context of literacy acquisition. Some might argue that since Junigau women are primarily, or even exclusively, using their literacy skills to conduct love-letter correspondences, perhaps love letters should be brought into female literacy classrooms as texts. Or perhaps the writing of love letters should be made central to the curriculum. And yet, my very strong hunch is that these suggestions would be rejected by the women who attend female literacy classes in Nepal, for they claim that they want a 'real education'—that is, they want to learn to read and write using the same methods of rote memorisation and the same textbooks as their brothers used to acquire their literacy skills. Indeed, female literacy students in the 1980s and 1990s explicitly dismissed the *New Path* text's * * * goals of consciousness raising and social activism as irrelevant to their own goals of becoming 'truly literate'. Despite the fact that these women would be applying their literacy skills to tasks quite different from those of their formally educated brothers, they nevertheless perceived that there was prestige in becoming literate via particular pedagogical methods in particular social contexts. Although the women attending evening female literacy classes were required to use the less prestigious *New Path* textbook and were instructed in ways that could be called more participatory or progressive, they realised that the literacy they were acquiring did not have the same social value as the literacy their brothers had acquired. All means to the end of literacy are *not* created equal.

*   *   *

In conclusion, while I have only managed to scratch the surface of the complexities involved in the Nepali literacy practice of love-letter writing, I hope I have nevertheless provided a glimpse of some of the ways in which these love letters are situated * * * among other commonly read texts in Junigau, all of which are saturated with various development discourses. In addition, by situating the Junigau practice of love-letter writing in its historical, social, and intertextual contexts, I have presented one case study of the sometimes unexpected uses to which newly acquired literacy skills are put, and the many complex meanings and values associated with them. In so doing, I hope to have demonstrated the need for nuanced, fully contextualised analyses of literacy acquisition.

ENGAGING THE TEXT, ENGAGING THE WORLD

- Why has Ahearn chosen love letters as the focus of her study?

- Ahearn refers to literacy as a "technology." How do different kinds of communications technologies—writing, email, texting, speaking on the phone, talking in person—shape linguistic expressions?

- How has literacy enhanced young women's sense of agency—the ability to act in a given cultural context?

- How have the ideas about development presented in the female literacy textbook *New Path* helped reshape Nepalese women's notions of love and marriage?

- What does Ahearn mean when she argues that sometimes literacy does not lead to women's empowerment?

- Have you written a love letter, email, or text recently? How does the content and context of your communication compare to that of the Nepalese young people in the following story? What do they reveal about the sociocultural context in which you live?

PART 2

Unmasking the Systems of Power

Anthropologists in the twenty-first century take seriously the deep interconnections between culture and power. The readings in the following section explore the ways anthropologists work to unmask the dynamics of power embedded in cultures, including systems of power such as race and racism, ethnicity and nationalism, gender, sexuality, class and inequality, and family.

Power is often described as the ability or potential to bring about change through action or influence, either one's own or that of a group or institution. This may include the ability to influence through force, the threat of force, or other forms of persuasion. Power is embedded in many kinds of social relations, from interpersonal relations to institutions to structural frameworks of whole societies. In effect, power is everywhere and individuals participate in systems of power in complex ways.

The anthropologist Eric Wolf (1923–1999) urged anthropologists to see power as an aspect of all human relationships. Consider the relationships in your own life: teacher/student, parent/child, employer/employee, landlord/tenant, lender/borrower, boyfriend/girlfriend. Wolf (1982, 1990, 1999) argued that all such relationships have a power

dynamic. Though cultures are often assumed to be composed of groups of similar people who uniformly share norms and values, in reality people in a given culture are usually diverse and their relationships are complicated.

Power in a culture reflects **stratification**—uneven distribution of resources and privileges—among participants that often persists over generations. Some people are drawn into the center of the culture. Others are ignored, marginalized, or even annihilated. Structures of power such as race and racism, ethnicity and nationalism, and others that we will discuss in this section organize relationships among people and create a framework through which access to cultural resources is distributed. As a result, some people are able to participate more fully in the culture than others. This balance of power is not fixed; it fluctuates over time. By examining the ways in which access to the resources, privileges, and opportunities of a culture are shared unevenly and unequally, we can begin to use culture as a conceptual guide to power and its workings.

One key to understanding the relationship between culture and power is to recognize that a culture is more than a set of ideas or patterns of behavior shared among a collection of individuals. A culture also includes the powerful institutions that these people create to promote and maintain their core values. Ethnographic research considers a wide range of institutions that play central roles in the enculturation process. For example, schools teach a shared history, language, patterns of social interaction, notions of health, and scientific ideas of what exists in the world and how the world works. Religious institutions promote moral and ethical codes of behavior. Various media convey images of what is considered normal, natural, and valued. Other prominent cultural institutions that reflect and shape core norms and values include the family, medicine, government, courts, police, and the military.

These institutions construct and exert two components of power, as described by Italian political philosopher Antonio Gramsci (1891–1937). *Material power*, the first component, includes political, economic, or military power. It exerts itself through coercion or brute force. The second aspect of power involves the ability to create consent and agreement within a population, a condition that Gramsci (1971) called **hegemony**.

Gramsci recognized the tremendous power of culture—particularly the cultural institutions of schools, religion, and media—to shape, often unconsciously, what people think is normal, appropriate, natural, right, wrong, and possible, and thereby directly influence the scope of human action and interaction. In this hegemony of ideas, some thoughts and actions become unthinkable, and group members develop a set of "beliefs" about what is normal and appropriate that come to be seen as natural "truths." The French sociologist Michel Foucault (1926–1984), in *Discipline and Punish* (1977), described this hegemonic aspect of power as the ability to make people discipline their own behavior so that they believe and act in certain "normal" ways— often against their own interests, even without a tangible threat of punishment for misbehavior.

Although hegemony can be very powerful, it does not completely dominate people's thinking. Individuals and groups have the power to contest cultural norms, values, mental maps of reality, symbols, institutions, and structures of power—a potential known as **agency**. Cultural beliefs and practices are not timeless; they change and can be changed. Cultures are not biologically determined; they are created over time by particular groups of people. By examining human agency, we see how culture serves as a realm in which battles over power take place—where people debate, negotiate, contest, and enforce what is considered normal, what people can say, do, and even think.

5

Race and Racism

Anthropologists find no scientific basis for classifications of **race**. Genetically there is only one race—the human race, with all its apparent diversity. Race, instead, is a flawed system of classification, created and recreated over time, that attempts to use certain superficial physical characteristics (such as skin color, hair texture, eye shape, and eye color) to divide the human population into a few supposedly discrete biological groups and attribute to them unique combinations of physical ability, mental capacity, personality traits, cultural patterns, and capacity for civilization (Mullings 2005).

Yet despite consistent efforts over the last century by anthropologists and others to counter the inaccurate belief that races are biologically real, race has remained a powerful framework through which many people see human diversity and through which those in power organize the distribution of privileges and resources. Race—which is scientifically not real—has become culturally real in the pervasive racism found in many parts of the globe, including the United States. Over time, imagined categories of race have shaped our cultural institutions—schools, places of worship, media, political parties, economic practices—and have organized the allocation of wealth, power, and privilege at all levels of society. Race has served to create and justify patterns of power and inequality within cultures worldwide, and many people have learned to see those patterns as normal and reasonable. So anthropologists also examine **racism**: individuals' thoughts and actions, as well as institutional patterns and policies that create or reproduce unequal access to power, privilege, resources, and opportunities based on imagined differences among groups (Omi and Winant 1994).

Race is perhaps the most significant means used to mark difference in U.S. culture. References to it can be found on census forms, school applications, and birth certificates, as well as in the media and casual conversation. Race is also a key framework that shapes the allocation of power, privilege, rewards, and status, and it infuses all of our political, economic, religious, recreational, educational, and cultural institutions (Smedley 1993). Because race is not biologically fixed, we must instead examine the process through which race has been—and still is—constructed in the United States. In the readings that follow, Karen Brodkin Sacks examines just that process as she considers how European immigrants who were marked as racially other, including Jews, became white; Keisha-Khan Perry explores the intersections of race, class, and gender in Brazil as they affect land and water rights; and Yarimar Bonilla and Jonathan Rosa investigate the power of digital activism to create anti-racist movements and communities in the wake of the shooting of Michael Brown in Ferguson, Missouri.

How Did Jews Become White Folks?

Race, immigration, and the changing boundaries of whiteness

Karen Brodkin Sacks

For four centuries, the boundaries of whiteness in the United States have been carefully guarded, and groups' admission to that category has been rare and difficult. When the nation encountered diverse immigration from Asia and eastern and southern Europe beginning in the nineteenth century, debate raged about where the newcomers fit. Were the Irish, Germans, Greeks, Italians, Eastern Europeans, Jews and Catholics really white, or were they biologically distinct from earlier immigrants from England, France, and the Nordic countries? In this article, Karen Brodkin Sacks offers insights into the whitening process of immigrants after World War II. Brodkin Sacks's parents traced the ultimate success of Jewish immigrants to hard work and a high cultural value placed on education. Brodkin Sacks suggests, however, that these factors alone would not have been enough to ensure such large-scale social mobility and the transformation of so many people from "other" to white. Instead she traces the effects of the extensive government-run programs to reintegrate soldiers after the war and finds that they primarily benefited U.S. citizens of European immigrant descent (including Jewish citizens), especially men, through subsidized mortgages,

From Karen Brodkin Sacks. 1994. "How Did Jews Become White Folks?" In *Race*, edited by Steven Gregory and Roger Sanjek. New Brunswick, NJ: Rutgers University Press. Some of the author's notes have been omitted.

educational benefits, and preferential hiring practices, while excluding others. The experience of Jewish immigrants and other European ethnic groups, for instance, stood in stark contrast to that of African Americans in the post–World War II era.

The late nineteenth and early decades of the twentieth centuries saw a steady stream of warnings by scientists, policymakers, and the popular press that "mongrelization" of the Nordic or Anglo-Saxon race—the real Americans—by inferior European races (as well as inferior non-European ones) was destroying the fabric of the nation. I continue to be surprised to read that America did not always regard its immigrant European workers as white, that they thought people from different nations were biologically different. My parents, who are first-generation U.S.-born Eastern European Jews, are not surprised. They expect anti-Semitism to be part of the fabric of daily life, much as I expect racism to be part of it. They came of age in a Jewish world in the 1920s and 1930s at the peak of anti-Semitism in the United States (Gerber 1986). They are proud of their upward mobility and think of themselves as pulling themselves up by their own bootstraps. I grew up during the 1950s in the Euroethnic New York suburb of Valley Stream where Jews were simply one kind of white folks and where ethnicity meant little more to my generation than food and family heritage. Part of my familized ethnic heritage was the belief that Jews were smart and that our success was the result of our own efforts and abilities, reinforced by a culture that valued sticking together, hard work, education, and deferred gratification. Today, this belief in a Jewish version of Horatio Alger has become an entry point for racism by some mainstream Jewish organizations against African Americans especially, and for their opposition to affirmative action for people of color (Gordon 1964; Sowell 1983; Steinberg 1989: chap. 3).

It is certainly true that the United States has a history of anti-Semitism and of beliefs that Jews were members of an inferior race. But Jews were hardly alone. American anti-Semitism was part of a broader pattern of late-nineteenth-century racism against all southern and eastern European immigrants, as well as against Asian immigrants. These views justified all sorts of discriminatory treatment including closing the doors to immigration from Europe and Asia in the 1920s. This picture changed radically after World War II. Suddenly the same folks who promoted nativism and xenophobia were eager to believe that the Euro-origin people whom they had deported, reviled as members of inferior races, and prevented from immigrating only a few years earlier were now model middle-class white suburban citizens.

It was not an educational epiphany that made those in power change their hearts, their minds, and our race. Instead, it was the biggest and best affirmative action program in the history of our nation, and it was for Euromales. There are similarities and differences in the ways each of the European immigrant groups became "whitened." I want to tell the story in a way that links anti-Semitism to other varieties of anti-European racism, because this foregrounds what Jews shared with other Euroimmigrants and shows changing notions of whiteness to be part of America's larger system of institutional racism.

Euroraces

The U.S. "discovery" that Europe had inferior and superior races came in response to the great waves of immigration from southern and eastern Europe in the late nineteenth century. Before that time, European immigrants—including Jews—had been largely assimilated into the white population. The twenty-three million European immigrants who came to work in U.S. cities after 1880 were too many and too concentrated to disperse and blend. Instead, they piled up in the country's most dilapidated urban areas, where they built new kinds of working-class ethnic communities. Since immigrants and their children made up more than 70 percent of the population of most of the country's largest cities, urban America came to take on a distinctly immigrant flavor. The golden age of industrialization in the United States was also the golden age of class struggle between the captains of the new industrial empires and the masses of manual workers whose labor made them rich. As the majority of mining and manufacturing workers, immigrants were visibly major players in these struggles (Higham 1955:226; Steinberg 1989:36).

The [anti-communist] Red Scare of 1919 [in the United States] clearly linked anti-immigrant to anti-working-class sentiment—to the extent that the Seattle general strike of native-born workers was blamed on foreign agitators. The Red Scare was fueled by economic depression, a massive postwar strike wave, the Russian revolution, and a new wave of postwar immigration. Strikers in steel, and the garment and textile workers in New York and New England, were mainly new immigrants. "As part of a fierce counteroffensive, employers inflamed the historic identification of class conflict with immigrant radicalism." Anticommunism and anti-immigrant sentiment came together in the Palmer raids and deportation of immigrant working-class activists. There was real fear of revolution. One of President Wilson's aides feared it was "the first appearance of the soviet in this country" (Higham 1955:226).

Not surprisingly, the belief in European races took root most deeply among the wealthy U.S.-born Protestant elite, who feared a hostile and seemingly unassimilable working class. By the end of the nineteenth century, Senator Henry Cabot Lodge pressed Congress to cut off immigration to the United States; Teddy Roosevelt raised the alarm of "race suicide" and took Anglo-Saxon women to task for allowing "native" stock to be outbred by inferior immigrants. In the twentieth century, these fears gained a great deal of social legitimacy thanks to the efforts of an influential network of aristocrats and scientists who developed theories of eugenics—breeding for a "better" humanity—and scientific racism. Key to these efforts was Madison Grant's influential *Passing of the Great Race*, in which he shared his discovery that there were three or four major European races ranging from the superior Nordics of northwestern Europe to the inferior southern and eastern races of Alpines, Mediterraneans, and, worst of all, Jews, who seemed to be everywhere in his native New York City. Grant's nightmare was race mixing among Europeans. For him, "the cross between any of the three European races and a Jew is a Jew" (qtd. in Higham 1955:156). He didn't have good things to say about Alpine or Mediterranean "races" either. For Grant, race and class were interwoven: the upper class was racially pure Nordic, and the lower classes came from the lower races.

*   *   *

By the 1920s, scientific racism sanctified the notion that real Americans were white and real whites came from northwest Europe. Racism animated laws excluding and expelling Chinese in 1882, and then closing the door to immigration by virtually all Asians and most Europeans in 1924 (Saxton 1971, 1990). Northwestern European ancestry as a requisite for whiteness was set in legal concrete when the Supreme Court denied Bhagat Singh Thind the right to become a naturalized citizen under a 1790 federal law that allowed whites the right to become naturalized citizens. Thind argued that Asian Indians were the real Aryans and Caucasians, and therefore white. The Court countered that the United States only wanted blond Aryans and Caucasians, "that the blond Scandinavian and the brown Hindu have a common ancestor in the dim reaches of antiquity, but the average man knows perfectly well that there are unmistakable and profound differences between them today" (Takaki 1989:298–299). A narrowly defined white, Christian race was also built into the 1705 Virginia "Act concerning servants and slaves." This statute stated "that no negroes, mulattos and Indians or other infidels or jews, Moors, Mahometans or other infidels shall, at any time, purchase any christian servant, nor any other except of their own complexion" (Martyn 1979:111).

The 1930 census added its voice, distinguishing not only immigrant from "native" whites, but also native whites of native white parentage, and native whites of immigrant (or mixed) parentage. In distinguishing immigrant (southern and eastern Europeans) from "native" (northwestern Europeans), the census reflected the racial distinctions of the eugenicist-inspired intelligence tests.

Racism and anti-immigrant sentiment in general and anti-Semitism in particular flourished in higher education. Jews were the first of the Euroimmigrant groups to enter colleges in significant numbers, so it wasn't surprising that they faced the brunt of discrimination there. The Protestant elite complained that Jews were unwashed, uncouth, unrefined, loud, and pushy. * * *

Anti-Semitic patterns set by * * * elite schools influenced standards of other schools, made anti-Semitism acceptable, and "made the aura of exclusivity a desirable commodity for the college-seeking clientele" (Synott 1986:250; and see Karabel 1984; Silberman 1985; Steinberg 1989: chaps. 5, 9).

*   *   *

My parents' conclusion is that Jewish success, like their own, was the result of hard work and of placing a high value on education. They went to Brooklyn College during the Depression. My mother worked days and started school at night, and my father went during the day. Both their families encouraged them. More accurately, their families expected this effort from them. Everyone they knew was in the same boat, and their world was made up of Jews who advanced as they did. The picture of New York—where most Jews lived—seems to back them up. In 1920, Jews made up 80 percent of the students at New York's City College, 90 percent of Hunter College, and before World War I, 40 percent of private Columbia University. By 1934, Jews made up almost 24 percent of all law students nationally, and 56 percent of those in New York City. Still, more Jews became public school teachers, like my parents and their friends, than doctors or lawyers (Steinberg 1989: 137, 227). [Sociologist Stephen] Steinberg has debunked the myth that Jews advanced because of the cultural value placed on education. This is not to say that Jews did not advance. They did. "Jewish success in America was a matter of historical timing.... [T]here was a fortuitous match between the experience and skills of Jewish immigrants, on the one hand, and the manpower needs and opportunity structures, on the other" (1989:103). Jews were the only ones among the southern and eastern European immigrants who came from urban, commercial, craft, and manufacturing backgrounds, not least of which was garment manufacturing. They entered the United States in New York, center of the nation's booming garment industry, soon came to dominate its skilled (male) and "unskilled" (female) jobs, and found it an industry amenable to low-capital entrepreneurship. As a result, Jews were the first of the new European immigrants to create a middle class of small businesspersons early in the twentieth century. Jewish educational advances followed this business success and depended upon it, rather than creating it (see also Bodnar 1985 for a similar argument about mobility).

*   *   *

How we interpret Jewish social mobility in this milieu depends on whom we compare Jews to. Compared with other immigrants, Jews were upwardly mobile. But compared with that of nonimmigrant whites, their mobility was very limited and circumscribed. Anti-immigrant racist and anti-Semitic barriers kept the Jewish middle class confined to a small number of occupations. Jews were excluded from mainstream corporate management and corporately employed professions, except in the garment and movie industries, which they built. Jews were almost totally excluded from university faculties (and the few that made it had powerful patrons). Jews were concentrated in small businesses, and in professions where they served a largely Jewish clientele (Davis 1990:146 n. 25; Silberman 1985:88–117; Sklare 1971:63–67).

*   *   *

My parents' generation believed that Jews overcame anti-Semitic barriers because Jews are special. My belief is that the Jews who were upwardly mobile were special among Jews (and were also well placed to write the story). My generation might well counter our parents' story of pulling themselves up by their own bootstraps with, "But think what you might have been without the racism and with some affirmative action!" And that is precisely what the postwar boom, the decline of systematic, public anti-immigrant racism and anti-Semitism, and governmental affirmative action extended to white males.

*   *   *

Euroethnics into Whites

Like most chicken and egg problems, it's hard to know which came first. Did Jews and other Euroethnics become white because they became middle class? That is, did money whiten? Or did being incorporated in an expanded version of whiteness open up the economic doors to a middle-class status? Clearly, both tendencies were at work. Some of the changes set in motion during the war against fascism led to a more inclusive version of whiteness. Anti-Semitism and anti-European racism lost respectability. The 1940 census no longer distinguished native whites of native parentage from those, like my parents, of immigrant parentage, so that Euroimmigrants and their children were more securely white by submersion in an expanded notion of whiteness. (This census also changed the race of Mexicans to white [U.S. Bureau of the Census, 1940: 4].) Theories of nurture and culture replaced theories of nature and biology. Instead of dirty and dangerous races who would destroy U.S. democracy, immigrants became ethnic groups whose children had successfully assimilated into the mainstream and risen to the middle class. In this new myth, Euroethnic suburbs like mine became the measure of U.S. democracy's victory over racism. Jewish mobility became a new Horatio Alger story. In time and with hard work, every ethnic group would get a piece of the pie, and the United States would be a nation with equal opportunity for all its people to become part of a prosperous middle-class majority. And it seemed that Euroethnic immigrants and their children were delighted to join middle America.

*   *   *

Although changing views on who was white made it easier for Euroethnics to become middle class, it was also the case that economic prosperity played a very powerful role in the whitening process. Economic mobility of Jews and other Euroethnics rested ultimately on U.S. postwar economic prosperity with its enormously expanded need for professional, technical, and managerial labor, and on government assistance in providing it. The United States emerged from the war with the strongest economy in the world. Real wages rose between 1946 and 1960, increasing buying power a hefty 22 percent and giving most Americans some discretionary income (Nash et al. 1986:885–886). U.S. manufacturing, banking, and business services became increasingly dominated by large corporations, and these grew into multinational corporations. Their organizational centers lay in big, new urban headquarters that demanded growing numbers of technical and managerial workers. The postwar period was a historic moment for real class mobility and for the affluence we have erroneously come to believe was the U.S. norm. It was a time when the old white and the newly white masses became middle class.

The GI Bill of Rights, as the 1944 Serviceman's Readjustment Act was known, was arguably the most massive affirmative action program in U.S. history. It was created to develop needed labor-force skills, and to provide those who had them with a lifestyle that reflected their value to the economy. The GI benefits ultimately extended to sixteen million GIs (veterans of the Korean War as well) included priority in jobs—that is, preferential hiring, but no one objected to it then—financial support during the job search; small loans for starting up businesses; and, most important, low-interest home loans and educational benefits, which included tuition and living expenses (Brown 1946; Hurd 1946; Mosch 1975; *Postwar Jobs for Veterans* 1945; Willenz 1983). This legislation was rightly regarded as one of the most revolutionary postwar programs. I call it affirmative action because it was aimed at and disproportionately helped male, Euro-origin GIs.

*   *   *

Education and Occupation

It is important to remember that prior to the war, a college degree was still very much a "mark of the upper class" (Willenz 1983:165). Colleges were largely finishing schools for Protestant elites. Before the postwar boom, schools could not begin to accommodate the American masses. Even in New York City before the 1930s, neither the public schools nor City College had room for more than a tiny fraction of potential immigrant students.

Not so after the war. The almost eight million GIs who took advantage of their educational benefits under the GI bill caused "the greatest wave of college building in American history" (Nash et al. 1986:885). White male GIs were able to take advantage of their educational benefits for college and technical training, so they were particularly well positioned to seize the opportunities provided by the new demands for professional, managerial, and technical labor. "It has been well documented that the GI educational benefits transformed American higher education and raised the educational level of that generation and generations to come. With many provisions for assistance in upgrading their educational attainments veterans pulled ahead of nonveterans in earning capacity. In the long run it was the nonveterans who had fewer opportunities" (Willenz 1983:165).

*   *   *

Postwar expansion made college accessible to the mass of Euromales in general and to Jews in particular. My generation's "Think what you could have been!" answer to our parents became our reality as quotas and old occupational barriers fell and new fields opened up to Jews. The most striking result was a sharp decline in Jewish small businesses and a skyrocketing of Jewish professionals. * * *

Even more significantly, the postwar boom transformed the U.S. class structure—or at least its status structure—so that the middle class expanded to encompass most of the population. Before the war, most Jews, like most other Americans, were working class. Already upwardly mobile before the war relative to other immigrants, Jews floated high on this rising economic tide, and most of them entered the middle class. * * *

Educational and occupational GI benefits really constituted affirmative action programs for white males because they were decidedly not extended to African Americans or to women of any race. White male privilege was shaped against the backdrop of wartime racism and postwar sexism. During and after the war, there was an upsurge in white racist violence against black servicemen in public schools, and in the KKK, which spread to California and New York (Dalfiume 1969:133–134). The number of lynchings rose during the war, and in 1943 there were antiblack race riots in several large northern cities. Although there was a wartime labor shortage, black people were discriminated against in access to well-paid defense industry jobs and in housing. In 1946 there were white riots against African Americans across the South, and in Chicago and Philadelphia as well. Gains made as a result of the wartime Civil Rights movement, especially employment in defense-related industries, were lost with peacetime conversion as black workers were the first fired, often in violation of seniority (Wynn 1976:114, 116). White women were also laid off, ostensibly to make jobs for demobilized servicemen, and in the long run women lost most of the gains they had made in wartime (Kessler-Harris 1982). We now know that women did not leave the labor force in any significant numbers but instead were forced to find inferior jobs, largely nonunion, parttime, and clerical.

Theoretically available to all veterans, in practice women and black veterans did not get anywhere near their share of GI benefits. Because women's units were not treated as part of the military, women in them were not considered veterans and were ineligible for Veterans' Administration (VA) benefits (Willenz 1983:168). The barriers that almost completely shut African-American GIs out of their benefits were more complex. *** Black GIs anticipated starting new lives, just like their white counterparts. Over 43 percent hoped to return to school and most expected to relocate, to find better jobs in new lines of work. The exodus from the South toward the North and far West was particularly large. So it wasn't a question of any lack of ambition on the part of African-American GIs.

Rather, the military, the Veterans' Administration, the U.S. Employment Service, and the Federal Housing Administration (FHA) effectively denied African-American GIs access to their benefits and to the new educational, occupational, and residential opportunities. Black GIs who served in the throughly segregated armed forces during World War II served under white officers, usually southerners (Binkin and Eitelberg 1982; Dalfiume 1969; Foner 1974; Johnson 1967; Nalty and MacGregor 1981). African-American soldiers were disproportionately given dishonorable discharges, which denied them veterans' rights under the GI Bill. Thus between August and November 1946, 21 percent of white soldiers and 39 percent of black soldiers were dishonorably discharged. Those who did get an honorable discharge then faced the Veterans' Administration and the U.S. Employment Service. The latter, which was responsible for job placements, employed very few African Americans, especially in the South. This meant that black veterans did not receive much employment information, and that the offers they did receive were for low-paid and menial jobs. ***

Black GIs faced discrimination in the educational system as well. Despite the end of restrictions on Jews and other Euroethnics, African Americans were not welcome in white colleges. Black colleges were overcrowded, and the combination of segregation and prejudice made for few alternatives. About twenty thousand black veterans attended college by 1947, most in black colleges, but almost as many, fifteen thousand, could not gain entry. Predictably, the disproportionately few African Americans who did gain access to their educational benefits were able, like their white counterparts, to become doctors and engineers, and to enter the black middle class (Walker 1970).

Suburbanization

In 1949, ensconced at Valley Stream, I watched potato farms turn into Levittown and into Idlewild (later Kennedy) Airport. This was a major spectator sport in our first years on suburban Long Island. A typical weekend would bring various aunts, uncles, and cousins out from the city. After a huge meal we would pile in the car—itself a novelty—to look at the bulldozed acres and comment on the matchbox construction. During the week, my mother and I would look at the houses going up within walking distance.

*　　*　　*

At the beginning of World War II, about 33 percent of all U.S. families owned their houses. That percentage doubled in twenty years. * * * The Federal Housing Administration (FHA) was key to buyers and builders alike. Thanks to it, suburbia was open to more than GIs. People like us would never have been in the market for houses without FHA and VA low-down-payment, low-interest, long-term loans to young buyers. * * * Federal highway funding was also important to suburbanization. The National Defense Highway Act of 1941 put the government in the business of funding 90 percent of a national highway system (the other 10 percent came from states), which developed a network of freeways between and around the nation's metropolitan areas, making suburbs and automobile commuting a way of life. * * *

It was here that the federal government's racism reached its high point. * * *

The FHA believed in racial segregation. Throughout its history, it publicly and actively promoted restrictive covenants. Before the war, these forbade sale to Jews and Catholics as well as to African Americans. The deed to my house in Detroit had such a covenant, which theoretically prevented it from being sold to Jews or African Americans. Even after the Supreme Court ended legal enforcement of restrictive covenants in 1948, the FHA continued to encourage builders to write them against African Americans. FHA underwriting manuals openly insisted on racially homogeneous neighborhoods, and their loans were made only in white neighborhoods. I bought my Detroit house in 1972 from Jews who were leaving a largely African-American neighborhood. * * *

With the federal government behind them, virtually all developers refused to sell to African Americans. * * * The result of these policies was that African Americans were totally shut out of the suburban boom. An article in *Harper's* described the housing available to black GIs. "On his way to the base each morning, Sergeant Smith passes an attractive air-conditioned, FHA-financed housing project. It was built for service families. Its rents are little more than the Smiths pay for their shack. And there are half-a-dozen vacancies, but none for Negroes" (qtd. in Foner 1974:195).

*   *   *

The FHA had a one-two punch for African Americans. Segregation kept them out of the suburbs, and redlining made sure they could not buy or repair their homes in the neighborhoods where they were allowed to live. The FHA practiced systematic redlining. This was a system developed by its predecessor, the Home Owners Loan Corporation (HOLC), which in the 1930s developed an elaborate neighborhood rating system that placed the highest (green) value on all-white, middle-class neighborhoods, and the lowest (red) on racially nonwhite or mixed and working-class neighborhoods. High ratings meant high property values. The idea was that low property values in redlined neighborhoods made them bad investments. The FHA was, after all, created by and for banks and the housing industry. Redlining warned banks not to lend there, and the FHA would not insure mortgages in such neighborhoods. Redlining created a self-fulfilling prophecy. "With the assistance of local realtors and banks, it assigned one of the four ratings to every block in every city. The resulting information was then translated into the appropriate color [green, blue, yellow, and red] and duly recorded on secret 'Residential Security Maps' in local HOLC offices." * * *

FHA's and VA's refusal to guarantee loans in redlined neighborhoods made it virtually impossible for African Americans to borrow money for home improvement or purchase. Because these maps and surveys were quite secret, it took the 1960s Civil Rights movement to make these practices and their devastating consequences public. * * *

The record is very clear that instead of seizing the opportunity to end institutionalized racism, the federal government did its best to shut and double seal the postwar window of opportunity in African Americans' faces. It consistently refused to combat segregation in the social institutions that were key for upward mobility: education, housing, and employment. Moreover, federal programs that were themselves designed to assist demobilized GIs and young families systematically discriminated against African Americans. Such programs reinforced white/nonwhite racial distinctions even as intrawhite racialization was falling out of fashion. This other side of the coin, that white men of northwestern and southeastern European ancestry were treated equally in theory and in practice with regard to the benefits they received, was part of the larger postwar whitening of Jews and other eastern and southern Europeans.

The myth that Jews pulled themselves up by their own bootstraps ignores the fact that it took federal programs to create the conditions whereby the abilities of Jews and other European immigrants could be recognized and rewarded rather than denigrated and denied. The GI Bill and FHA and VA mortgages were forms of affirmative action that allowed male Jews and other Euro-American men to become suburban homeowners and to get the training that allowed them—but not women vets or war workers—to become professionals, technicians, salesmen, and managers in a growing economy. Jews' and other white ethnics' upward mobility was the result of programs that allowed us to float on a rising economic tide. To African Americans, the government offered the cement boots of segregation, redlining, urban renewal, and discrimination.

Those racially skewed gains have been passed across the generations, so that racial inequality seems to maintain itself "naturally," even after legal segregation ended. Today, in a shrinking economy where downward mobility is the norm, the children and grandchildren of the postwar beneficiaries of the economic boom have some precious advantages. For example, having parents who own their own homes or who have decent retirement benefits can make a real difference in young people's ability to take on huge college loans or to come up with a down payment for a house. Even this simple inheritance helps perpetuate the gap between whites and nonwhites. Sure Jews needed ability, but ability was not enough to make it.

ENGAGING THE TEXT, ENGAGING THE WORLD

- Why did Teddy Roosevelt raise the alarm of "race suicide" in the early twentieth century?

- Racism is more than an individual prejudice: it can be created, promoted, and sustained by cultural institutions as well. Describe the key institutions that helped reshape the U.S. racial landscape after World War II, as described in this article.

- Describe the GI Bill and its role in creating an expanded notion of whiteness.

- Why does the author call the GI Bill and VA and FHA mortgage programs affirmative action for whites?

- How were African Americans shut out of the postwar suburban building boom and expansion of home ownership? What were the consequences?

- How did the Jews become white folks?

- Discuss what the author means when she says in her conclusion that "Those racially skewed gains have been passed across the generations, so that racial inequality seems to maintain itself 'naturally,' even after legal segregation ended."

"If We Didn't Have Water": Black Women's Struggle for Urban Land Rights in Brazil

Keisha-Khan Perry

Racism is not only expressed through individual thought and action based on racial stereotypes; racism is also a system of power, including institutional patterns and practices that create and reproduce unequal access to power, privilege, resources, and opportunities based on imagined differences among groups. But racism is not natural, fixed, or permanent. In the following article, Keisha-Khan Perry introduces us to the people of Gamboa de Baixo in the city center of Salvador, Bahia, on the northeast coast of Brazil, who are deeply engaged in community-based anti-racism work to undermine and resist patterns of racism. This Brazilian fishing community is undergoing what urban planners refer to as urban revitalization but which residents experience as race-based mass evictions and forced displacement. Perry's research explores a female-led grassroots movement against this land exploitation and highlights the powerful role of spirituality and religion in the resistance movement, particularly as it empowers local women leaders. She also considers the ways gender and class intersect with racism in complex systems of power.

Se não tiver água, se não tiver mata, se não tiver espaço de terra para a gente colocar o pé no chão, na terra, a gente não tem de onde tirar a nossa energia, a nossa força (If we didn't have water, if we didn't have the bush, if we didn't have land for us to put our feet on the ground, on the earth, we wouldn't have where to get our energy, our life force).

—*Makota Valdina Pinto*[1]

In late December 2004, the tsunamis ravished Southeast Asia and Africa, killing more than 140,000 people. In reading about the rescue and recovery efforts, I was struck by

---

From Keisha-Khan Y. Perry. 2009. "If We Didn't Have Water": Black Women's Struggle for Urban Land Rights in Brazil." *Environmental Justice* 2(1): 9–13.

1. Makota Valdina Pinto is a black women environmental rights activist and community and Candomblé religious leader in Salvador, Bahia. This excerpt is from an interview conducted by Afro-Brazilian historian and director of the Palmares Foundation Ubiratan Castro in 1999, published in *Revista Palmares*, vol. 2, (Brasília: Fundação Palmares), 82.

the statement of a Sri Lankan irrigation engineer that, "now people hate the sea, they hate it" (Waldman and Rohde 2005). Although geographically distant, the devastation made me think differently about how Gulf Coast residents, many of whom have long since relocated from coastal cities such as New Orleans, might have viewed the ocean in the aftermath of Hurricane Katrina. Did they develop what [urban geographer] Mike Davis calls, an "ecology of fear" of living on the coast, or, similar to tsunami victims a few months prior, a *hatred* of the sea? (Davis 1998)

These questions about the relationship to coastal landscapes provide a global framing for understanding the Brazilian fishing community and its female-led, grassroots movement against land expulsion that have been the focus of my anthropological work since 1999. Conducting research in Gamboa de Baixo, on the coast of the Bay of All Saints in the city-center of Salvador, Bahia, has challenged me to delve into the way I think about African descendants' simultaneous indictment and celebration of the sea that extends back to slavery. I am reminded of the testimony of abduction by an enslaved African woman, Mrs. Brooks, who recounted to missionaries in nineteenth-century Jamaica: "I was playing by the sea-coast, when a white man offered me sugar-plums, and told me to go with him. I went with him, first into a boat, and then to the ship. Everything seemed strange to me, and I asked him to let me go back, but he would not hear me; and when I went to look for the place where he found me, I could see nothing of land, and I began to cry. There I was for a long time, with a great many more of my own colour, till the ship came to Kingston" (Stewart 2005, 15).

For black people in Brazil, the sea evokes similar memories of the journey and terror of the transatlantic slave trade but also represents a continuous geographic link to Africa that allows them to imagine a psychic return to "full freedom" (Butler 1998). What drives the Gamboa de Baixo struggle for land rights during recent threats of mass eviction and forced displacement as a result of urban revitalization programs, or what neighborhood activists have termed a "wave of black clearance," is partly their love for and spiritual connection to the sea that is the backyard of their urban neighborhood. That collective memory of the blood in the waters between Africa and the Americas has not caused diaspora Africans to hate the sea inspires me whenever I think of the Bahian political context. In this article, I discuss the profound ways in which the sea in African religious traditions shapes everyday black culture and environmental politics in Gamboa de Baixo and in black neighborhoods throughout Salvador.

This privileging of the spiritual in understanding the intricate relationship between black diaspora culture and grassroots politics represents a key aspect of the broader issues with which I grapple in my interdisciplinary research on black women as cultural producers and political agents in Brazil. * * * I highlight how black women in poor urban neighborhoods in Salvador carve out geographic, social, and political spaces for themselves while expanding notions of cultural belonging and citizenship rights at the levels of the city, the nation, and the diaspora (Butler 1998; Harding 2003). It is significant that we see black women's central role in urban social movements as part of a larger diaspora pattern of black women's oppositional politics vested in property rights for both cultural and material gain.

"If we didn't have water . . . "

To begin to comprehend this inseparable connection between black women's religious culture and politics, the words of the late Brazilian literary scholar of Bahian culture, Jorge Amado come to mind: "The ocean is large, the sea is a road without end, waters make up more than half the world, they are three-quarters of it, and all that belongs to Iemanjá." In the African diasporic religion of *candomblé*, practiced by the vast majority of Bahians, Iemanjá is the highly revered *orixá* (goddess) of the sea commonly known as the mother of the waters (*a mãe das águas*). Each year in Salvador, February 2 marks one of the most important days of celebration in *candomblé*, the Festa de Iemanjá, which takes place in the Rio Vermelho coastal neighborhood. With more resources today, particularly government sponsorship, the festival has been transformed from a community practice into a massive cultural project of local interest, as well as national and international tourism. However, the dominant ceremonial presence of black fishermen and *candomblé* religious leaders (most of whom are women) reminds us that * * * black fishing colonies have historically occupied the coastal lands of Salvador and have carried out these traditions since the slavery period. Gamboa de Baixo is now one of the few black urban fishing colonies that exists on the Bahian coast. * * * Like in most fishing communities, local residents pay homage to the goddess of the sea for protecting the fishermen and fisherwomen while they work, and for supplying the sea with sufficient fish, an important natural resource that sustains the local economy and African-inspired culinary traditions. More important, Gamboa de Baixo residents express their gratitude to Iemanjá, who protects their children while they play on the neighborhood's beaches.

Approximately one week after the February 2 festivals, another Iemanjá festival is carried out in Gamboa de Baixo. Preta, a longtime activist and neighborhood association board member, organizes an offering of gifts to the *orixá* Iemanjá, a personalized celebration that has become a local custom. She receives relatives and friends from all over the city and state, as well as her *candomblé* family from Itaparica Island, located in the bay and visible from Gamboa de Baixo. The neighborhood association has been active in preparing Preta's offering each year, from raising funds to creating traditional gifts, many of which are biodegradable after much discussion within the organization about the harmful environmental effects of plastic presents such as dolls and perfumes. When I asked Preta why she joined the community struggle, she first explained that living in proximity to the resources of the city-center, such as schools and hospitals, was very important. Then she explained, chuckling, that few places in the city exist where she can have access to her own beach to carry out her yearly religious obligations to Iemanjá and celebrate with her neighbors. For this right to own and live on these coveted coastal lands, she will continue to fight.

According to black Brazilian feminist scholar and activist Jurema Werneck, female *orixás* have long been a source of black women's political power evident in present-day grassroots movements. From within African religious communities comes a collective imagining of Africa * * * in which women's leadership is recognized as crucial for spiritual and material transformation (Werneck 2007). Rachel Harding has similarly argued that *candomblé* has served as "a collectivizing force through which subjugated peoples," and I would emphasize black women, "organized an alternative meaning of their lives and identities (Harding 2003, 1).***

Local activists assert that not only should the Iemanjá festivals in Gamboa de Baixo be understood within the context of African religious traditions and their reverence for the sea, but also as an aspect of black women's deliberate actions of staking claim to urban land on the Bahian coast. In *terreiros* (*candomblé* houses) throughout the city, not only have black women inherited African religious practices, but they have also inherited the rights to the land on which they practice these traditions. Historically, to speak of these *terreiros* has meant to speak of black women's land. Thus, black women have been uniquely positioned in these communities as having both collective memory and legal documentation of ancestral lands. This memory extends beyond the Bay of All Saints to the practice of women as landowners in Africa, where they served as the primary mediators of family relations within their communities, influencing the distribution of important resources such as land. Signifying more than just the physical space where families live, work, and forge political networks, urban land in contemporary Brazil represents the ability for black women to pass spiritual and material resources from one generation to the next. Land has become one of the greatest social and cultural assets for black people, and particularly for women, who are the most economically marginalized. In essence, the neighborhood fight for land rights has been able to integrate their political demands to legalize collective property rights with demands to preserve the material and the cultural resources the sea provides.

"If we didn't have land . . . "

I am deliberate about not detailing *candomblé* practices nor its specific African-derived cosmologies and mythologies. Rather, the ethnographic examples of the Iemanjá festivals are intended to bring attention to the political formation of a black urban neighborhood located on the geographic and socioeconomic margins of a Brazilian city. The *candomblés* as sociopolitical spaces are understudied, but the political actions of black women in grassroots struggles bridge the relationship between black struggles for self-definition and the freedom of African cultural expression and social movements that make territorial claims to urban space.*** African religious traditions are indissociable from black women's political actions in the local, national, and global black struggle for material resources such as land, employment, and education*** (Alexander 2005, 326). In other words, black women's religious matters are political matters, and black women's collective resistance against the violence of land evictions and displacement are deeply connected to what womanist theologian Dianne M. Stewart also terms the "the liberation motif" of African-centered traditions in black diasporic communities (Stewart 2005). This emphasis shows that black women in Brazil and throughout the black diaspora are cultural producers as well as political agents in their own right with their own African-inspired sensibilities of gendered racial liberation and social transformation in Brazilian cities.

Spirituality, I reaffirm, must acquire a privileged space in the broader understanding of how black women have responded to the barbarous reality of class-based and gendered racism in Brazil and throughout the black diaspora.

Scholars of black social movements have emphasized the importance of culture in antiracism and anticolonialism politics. * * * [Historian] Kim Butler argues that adaptations of *candomblé* have been "rooted in the conscious choice of Afro-Brazilians to use African culture as a mode of support and survival in modern Brazilian society" (Butler 1998, 195). The ethnographic focus on the political mobilization of black urban communities contextualizes black cultural practices within the ongoing processes of gendered racial and economic oppression that mark the black Brazilian experience. The black majority in Bahia and the predominance of African religious traditions does not obscure the lack of black women in positions of political and economic power, such as holding public office, executive positions in financial institutions, or even as store clerks in shopping malls. In many respects, the black population, particularly black women, carry the burden of centuries of enslavement and social marginalization. A legacy of the slave economy, 95 percent of domestic workers are black women who in their majority are underpaid and continue to live in poverty. Serving as spiritual spaces of racial and gender solidarity, the female-centered *terreiros* have been crucial to the maintenance of an African cultural identity and black community formation in the city of Salvador.

From this perspective, we cannot ignore that, historically, the main protagonists, such as Makota Valdina Pinto in Salvador, in antiracist environmental justice movements in Brazilian cities have been black women leaders * * * of *candomblé* communities. Pinto, since her youth, has been a neighborhood activist and one of the city's most outspoken voices against environmental racism, linking the increased lack of public access to unpolluted lands and natural water sources to the widespread neglect of black urban communities. Pinto's actions echo * * * diaspora scholar activists who argue that water and land are two of the greatest natural resources for black people socially, economically, and spiritually, and in Afro-Brazilian communities, gaining access to these resources or protecting them from privatization and destruction has been an ongoing focus of community-based activism. * * *

The leadership of black women in environmental justice movements should also be understood within the larger context of emerging neighborhood movements. Recently, I attended a housing rights forum during which Gamboa de Baixo activist and *candomblé* practitioner Ana Cristina boldly asked the audience, which included activists from other *bairros populares* and urban planning experts: "What kind of city do we live in that prepares architects and engineers to demolish homes and expel local populations in order to implement their urban development projects?" * * * She firmly asserted that "*a terra é do povo* [land belongs to the people]!" The affirmation of collective land ownership alludes to a serious question of why the *povo*, or the masses of blacks who occupy Salvador's poorest neighborhoods, have no legal right to own the land they have lived on and cultivated for generations. In the broadest sense, what does it mean for the likes of Ana Cristina—black women who occupy the racial, gender, and socio-spatial margins of the city—to make claims to it and work for its collective improvement? * * *

The political experiences of Gamboa de Baixo highlight the emergence of black women's militancy at the community-level in struggles to improve the environmental and habitat conditions of Salvador's black neighborhoods. After the outbreak of cholera in Bahia in 1992, which caused several deaths in Gamboa de Baixo, the women organized themselves and founded the Associação Amigos de Gegē dos Moradores da Gamboa de Baixo. They led Gamboa residents to radio stations to bring attention to the cholera outbreak and the contamination of their tap water. They demanded that the state test the natural water sources and the public water pipes in the neighborhood. Testing proved that the victims of cholera had died from contaminated water provided by the city and not from the neighborhood's natural water fountains. After these actions, the community received some social service interventions such as the construction of the *chafariz*, a central water fountain in the area.

*   *   *

"We wouldn't have where to get our energy . . . "

* * * The sea, specifically its relationship to African cosmologies, yields an indispensable source of spiritual, material, and political nourishment in the lives of black women in Bahia. * * * The women of the Gamboa de Baixo neighborhood association illustrate that black political movements imbricate the spiritual with the political (Alexander 2005, 323). In fact, I draw on the insights of the Iemanjá festivals as a way to examine how black women play vital roles in preserving African traditions while creating social networks and politicizing urban communities located on the Bahian coast. The nature of black women's agency in neighborhood-based social movements for land rights in Brazil is interconnected with black women's agency in Bahian *candomblé*. In Gamboa de Baixo, these cultural and political identities merge in the struggle over space, and in particular, the use and control of coastal lands and the sea.

It is not by accident that clean water continues to be a key political demand for neighborhood activists, and that black women lead this fight. As Makota Valdina Pinto suggests in the opening quote, land rights must be considered within the broader quest for water and an overall healthy, clean, urban environment. Politicizing the need for water has been integral to the Gamboa de Baixo's ongoing fight for urban land rights and neighborhood improvement amid state threats of land expulsion. Water, specifically the waters of the Bay of All Saints, has been a spiritual source of black women's political empowerment in Gamboa. Water has been at the center of Gamboa de Baixo's political organizing around issues of land and housing reform since its inception. Poor black women have been key to engendering and racializing political discussions around natural resources, and for broadening black collective claims to citizenship in dignified living conditions. As black feminist anthropologist Faye Harrison reminds us, "racism is an enduring social problem with serious implications for social and economic justice, political conflict, and struggles for *human dignity*" (my emphasis) (Harrison 2005). In Brazil and throughout the diaspora, black women's antiracism activism (as is also evident in post-Katrina New Orleans) is deeply rooted in the politics of the built environment, specifically how to use, protect, restore, and *own* spaces and places.

ENGAGING THE TEXT, ENGAGING THE WORLD

- Perry states that land has become one of the most important social, cultural, and economic resources for black people, particularly for black women in Gamboa de Baixo, who are the most economically marginalized. Describe the role of land in this conflict, including its role in these female-led grassroots movements. How is it a source of both conflict and power?

- What does Perry mean when she describes black women as both cultural producers and political agents? Describe each role.

- What role does religion play in the community and in this social movement?

- How do class and gender intersect with race to reinforce and exacerbate inequality in Gamboa de Baixo?

- Describe the complex understanding of water and the sea in Gamboa de Baixo. Why is this so powerful, both symbolically and materially?

#Ferguson: Digital Protest, Hashtag Ethnography, and the Racial Politics of Social Media in the United States

Yarimar Bonilla and Jonathan Rosa

Anti-racism activism and social media

After a white police officer fatally shot unarmed African American teenager Michael Brown in August 2014, thousands of demonstrators took to the streets of Ferguson, Missouri. Images of daily marches, protests, and confrontations with heavily armed police went viral on social media sites like YouTube, Instagram, and Vine. By the end of the month the hashtag "#Ferguson" had been used more than eight million times on Twitter. In this article Yarimar Bonilla and Jonathan Rosa explore

From Yarimar Bonilla and Jonathan Rosa. 2015. "#Ferguson: Digital protest, hashtag ethnography, and the racial politics of social media in the United States." *American Ethnologist* 42(1): 4–17. Some of the authors' notes have been omitted.

the use of social media in the aftermath of Michael Brown's death and document the ways it has become a powerful platform for social activism. Can a tweet be used to combat racism? Can Twitter accounts and other forms of social media be used to disrupt racialized systems of power? In particular Bonilla and Rosa explore the new possibilities for this digital activism, and in this case "hashtag activism," to create shared political moments across a large and disparate population and to document and challenge police brutality and the misrepresentation of black bodies in the mainstream media.

On Saturday, August 9, 2014, at 12:03 p.m., an unarmed black teenager named Michael Brown was fatally shot by a police officer in Ferguson, Missouri, a small town on the outskirts of St. Louis. Within the hour, a post appeared on the Twitter social media platform stating, "I just saw someone die," followed by a photograph taken from behind the beams of a small wooden balcony overlooking Canfield Drive, where Michael Brown's lifeless body lay uncovered, hands alongside his head, face down on the asphalt. Immediately following the incident, community members assembled to demand an explanation for why this unarmed 18-year-old had been seemingly executed while reportedly holding his hands up in a gesture of surrender, pleading "don't shoot." The impromptu gathering soon turned into a sustained protest marked by daily demonstrations and violent confrontations with highly armed local police—all of which were documented in detail across social media platforms like Twitter, Instagram, YouTube, and Vine.

Occurring on the heels of other highly publicized killings of unarmed black men—such as Eric Garner (who died as a result of an illegal chokehold by New York City police just weeks before the events in Ferguson), Oscar Grant (whose death was emotionally portrayed in the award-winning film *Fruitvale Station* released just one year prior), and 17-year-old Trayvon Martin (whose 2012 killing sparked national outcry and spurred numerous forms of activism)—the death of Michael Brown quickly captured the imagination of thousands across and beyond the United States. Protestors from around the nation flocked to Ferguson to participate in demonstrations calling for the arrest of the officer responsible for the fatal shooting. Television viewers tuned in across the country to watch live news coverage of the violent confrontations between the protestors and the highly armed local police. Images of these confrontations circulated widely in national and international news coverage, and news of these events quickly went "viral" across social media. During the initial week of protests, over 3.6 million posts appeared on Twitter documenting and reflecting on the emerging details surrounding Michael Brown's death; by the end of the month, "#Ferguson" had appeared more than eight million times on the Twitter platform.

These statements are simple facts, but the meaning and consequences of these facts will be occupying social analysts for years to come. Much will be written about Michael Brown: about his portrayal in the media, his treatment by the police, and both the circumstances and consequences of his death. Much will also be written about the protestors who immediately gathered at the site of his killing and about those who remained, under intense police harassment, long after the media spotlight faded. But what are we to make of the eight million tweets? What do they tell us about this event, its place in the social imagination, and about social media itself as a site of both political activism and social analysis?

In 1991, a homemade VHS tape of Los Angeles resident Rodney King being brutally beaten by four police officers sparked outrage across the country and galvanized thousands in what is widely recognized as one of the most influential examples of citizen journalism in the United States (Allan and Thorsen 2009). Today, 56 percent of the U.S. population carries video-enabled smartphones, and the use of mobile technology is particularly high among African Americans.[1] The increased use and availability of these technologies has provided marginalized and racialized populations with new tools for documenting incidents of state-sanctioned violence and contesting media representations of racialized bodies and marginalized communities. In many cases—such as police officers' use of a chokehold in the murder of Eric Garner—the use of mobile technology to record and circulate footage of events has played a key role in prompting public outcry. In the case of Ferguson, video footage of the fatal shooting of Michael Brown has yet to surface, but informal journalism was used to document the scene in the direct aftermath of his murder, to publicize the protests that ensued, and to bring attention to the militarized police confrontations that followed. Through social media, users were able to disseminate these accounts to a broad audience and to forge new mediatized publics that demand anthropological attention. In this essay, we explore how and why platforms like Twitter have become important sites for activism around issues of racial inequality, state violence, and media representations. We examine the possibilities, the stakes, and the necessity of taking these forms of activism seriously while remaining attentive to the limits and possible pitfalls of engaging in what we describe as "hashtag ethnography."

Can a Hashtag Become a Field Site?

In thinking critically about social media as a site of analysis, the first question to ask, for anthropologists in particular, is what kind of field site does a platform like Twitter represent? * * * Is hashtag ethnography the next logical step in an anthropology of the twenty first century[?] * * *

To answer these questions, it is necessary to begin by distinguishing the town of Ferguson, Missouri, from "hashtag Ferguson" and to recognize how each of these contributed to the formation of the larger "event" of Ferguson. As those familiar with Twitter know, the hashtag symbol (#) is often used as a way of marking a conversation within this

---

1. A recent study by the Pew Research Center (Smith 2013) indicates that 53 percent of white Americans, 64 percent of African Americans, and 60 percent of U.S. Latinos/as own smartphones.

platform. The hasthtag serves as an indexing system in both the clerical sense and the semiotic sense. In the clerical sense, it allows the ordering and quick retrieval of information about a specific topic. For example, in the case of Ferguson, as details were emerging about the protests forming at the site of Michael Brown's death, users began tweeting out information with the hashtag #Ferguson. The hashtag in this case provided a quick retrieval system for someone looking for updated news on the unfolding events. But, in addition to providing a filing system, hashtags simultaneously [mark] the intended significance of an utterance. * * * Hashtags allow users to not simply "file" their comments but to performatively frame what these comments are "really about," thereby enabling users to indicate a meaning that might not be otherwise apparent. Hence, someone could write, "Decades of racial tension and increasing suburban poverty boiled to the surface last night" followed by the text "#Ferguson," as a way of creating a particular interpretive frame. * * *

In the case of #Ferguson, patterns emerged in which Twitter became a platform for providing emergent information about the killing of Michael Brown and for commenting on the treatment of the officer who shot him. For example, one user posted, "Prosecutors get real friendly when they have to adjudicate one of their own. But they'll move heaven and earth hunting POC down. #Ferguson."[2] In contrast, other tweets recontextualized the situation in Ferguson as part of global affairs (e.g., "#Egypt #Palestine #Ferguson #Turkey, U.S. made tear gas, sold on the almighty free market represses democracy").

*   *   *

Hashtags * * * serve not just as an indexing system but also as a filter that allows social media users to reduce the noise of Twitter by cutting into one small slice. However, this filtering process also has a distorting effect. Social media create a distorted view of events, such that we only get the perspective of the people who are already in our social network (Garret and Resnick 2011; Pariser 2012; Sunstein 2009). This effect should signal one of the first cautions for anthropologists interested in social media: We must avoid the common slippage made by journalists and others who tend to represent Twitter as an unproblematized "public sphere" without taking into account the complexity of who is on Twitter, as well as how people are on Twitter in different ways.

*   *   *

For example, some have argued that in assessing the importance of Twitter in the Ferguson protests, we must take into account that, despite the enduring digital divide within the United States, the percentage of African Americans who use Twitter (22 percent) is much higher than that of white Americans (16 percent; Bryers 2014). While these simple figures tell us little about the ways and frequency with which these groups use the system and to what ends, the significance of what has been called "Black Twitter"

---

2. POC is an acronym for people of color.

(Florini 2014; Sharma 2013) should not be overlooked. As we discuss below, Twitter affords a unique platform for collectively identifying, articulating, and contesting racial injustices from the in-group perspectives of racialized populations. Whereas in most mainstream media contexts the experiences of racialized populations are overdetermined, stereotyped, or tokenized, social media platforms such as Twitter offer sites for collectively constructing counternarratives and reimagining group identities.

*   *   *

Recognizing that hashtags can only ever offer a limited, partial, and filtered view of a social world does not require abandoning them as sites of analysis. Rather, we must approach them as what they are: entry points into larger and more complex worlds. Hashtags offer a window to peep through, but it is only by stepping through that window and "following" (in both Twitter and non-Twitter terms) individual users that we can begin to place tweets within a broader context. This kind of analysis requires us to stay with those who tweet and follow them after hashtags have fallen out of "trend." Only then can we better understand what brings them to this virtual place and what they take away from their engagement.

The Whole World Is Tweeting

Social movements have long used media and technology to disseminate, escalate, and enlarge the scope of their struggles: Transistor radios allowed Cuban guerrilla fighters to transmit from the Sierra Maestra [from 1956–1958]; television coverage transformed the [1965] riots in Selma, Alabama, into a national event; and e-mail accounts allowed [Mexican rebel] Zapatistas in Chiapas to launch global communiqués [in the 1990s]. #Ferguson did what many of these other tools did: It allowed a message to get out, called global attention to a small corner of the world, and attempted to bring visibility and accountability to repressive forces.

One of the differences between Twitter and these earlier forms of technology, however, is [that] Twitter does not just allow you to peer through a window; it allows you to look through manifold windows at once. On #Ferguson, you could watch six simultaneous live streams. You could read what protestors were tweeting, what journalists were reporting, what the police was announcing, and how observers and analysts interpreted the unfolding events. You could also learn how thousands of users were reacting to the numerous posts. In the era of transistor radios and television sets, one did not necessarily know what listeners or viewers yelled back at their machines, but on Twitter one can get a sense of individual responses to mediatized events.

E-mail, television, radio, and print have long managed to open up windows into the experience of social movements, but * * * Twitter [creates] a unique feeling of direct participation. Twitter allows users who are territorially displaced to feel like they are united across both space and time. For example, during the 2014 World Cup (just a month before the events in Ferguson), the Nigerian American novelist and avid tweeter Teju

Cole encouraged his followers to post pictures of their individual views of the matches and to mark these posts with the hashtag #The time of the game.[3] "We live in different time zones, out of sync but aware of each other," he wrote, "then the game begins and we enter the same time: the time of the game" (Meyer 2014). For Cole, the point was to highlight how a global audience could enter into a shared temporality that he described as "public time" (a counterpart to public space).

#Ferguson and its attendant live streams created a similar feeling of shared temporality—particularly during the protests and confrontations with police. As opposed to someone who might *post about* Ferguson on Facebook, users on Twitter felt like they were *participating in* #Ferguson, as they tweeted in real time about the unfolding events, rallied supporters to join various hashtag campaigns (discussed below), and monitored live streams where they could bear witness to the tear gassing and arrests of journalists and protestors. Engaging in these activities is akin to participating in a protest in the sense that it offers an experience of "real time" engagement, community, and even collective effervescence. Through this form of participation, users can experience the heightened temporality that characterizes all social movements: the way days marked by protest become "eventful," distinguishing them from [ordinary] life. The "eventfulness" of protest-filled days cannot be easily summed up in dated news bulletins; indeed, they often challenge calendrical time itself—thus, not coincidentally, social movement actors often develop their own revolutionary calendars, chronicles, timelines, and alternative forms of marking political time. It was partly because of this heightened temporality that, as others have noted, the news surrounding Michael Brown's death dominated Twitter much more than Facebook. Facebook moved too slowly for the eventfulness of Ferguson. For the denizens of #Ferguson, the posts on Facebook were "yesterday's news"—always already superseded by the latest round of tweets.

Hashtag Activism Versus "Real" Activism?

Many have disparaged hashtag activism as a poor substitute for "real" activism, and, indeed, some suggest that * * * social media can only ever produce fleeting "nanostories" (Wasik 2009) with little lasting impact. However, it is important to examine how and why digital activism has become salient to particular populations. It is surely not coincidental that the groups most likely to experience police brutality, to have their protests disparaged as acts of "rioting" or "looting," and to be misrepresented in the media are precisely those turning to digital activism at the highest rates. Indeed, some of the most important hashtag campaigns emerging out of #Ferguson were targeted at calling attention to both police practices and media representations, suggesting that social media can serve as an important tool for challenging these various forms of racial profiling.

---

3. The collection is viewable at https://twitter.com/tejucole/timelines/486562343044669442, accessed October 15, 2014.

The first of these campaigns was inspired by eyewitness reports that Michael Brown had his hands up in the air as a sign of surrender and had uttered the words *don't shoot* just before he was shot and killed by Officer Darren Wilson. Initial activism around Michael Brown thus revolved around the hashtag #HandsUpDontShoot, often accompanied by photos of individuals or groups of people with their hands up. One of the most widely circulated images from this meme was that of Howard University students with their hands up.

Through this campaign, users sought to call attention to the arbitrary nature of racialized policing, the vulnerability of black bodies, and the problematic ways in which blackness is perceived as a constant threat. Because Michael Brown was allegedly shot while holding his hands up, #HandsUpDontShoot also became a tool for contesting victim-blaming or respectability narratives rooted in the belief that one can control the perception of one's body and the violence inflicted on it. These efforts echoed a previous "meme" that emerged in response to the killing of another unarmed African American teenager, Trayvon Martin, two years earlier. Shortly following Martin's killing, a recording of the 911 call made by George Zimmerman, the killer, describing Martin as someone "suspicious" wearing a "dark hoodie," circulated widely in the press. Fox News commentator Geraldo Rivera suggested that the hoodie was "as much responsible for Trayvon Martin's death as George Zimmerman" (Geraldo Rivera: "Leave the Hoodie at Home" 2012). Rivera argued that hoodies had become emblematic of criminal behavior, given their ubiquitous presence in crime-suspect drawings and surveillance footage of petty theft. This argument elides the role that race plays in structuring the hoodie's alternate status as an innocuous piece of clothing versus a sign of criminality or deviance. That is, hoodies are only signs of criminal behavior when they are contextualized in relation to particular racialized bodies. Many commentators sought to draw attention to this point. In the wake of Trayvon Martin's death, the hoodie became a powerful symbol, with events like the "Million Hoodie March" drawing hundreds of supporters. Online activism at the time included the circulation of images of users wearing hoodies, marked with the hashtags #HoodiesUp and #WeAreTrayvonMartin in a sign of solidarity.

Immediately following Trayvon Martin's killing, many social media users changed their profile pictures to images of themselves wearing hooded sweatshirts with the hoods up. Similarly, in the wake of Michael Brown's death, many posted profile pictures of themselves with their hands up. These instances show how the seemingly vacuous practice of taking "selfies" (i.e., photos of oneself) can become politically meaningful in the context of racialized bodies. These images represent acts of solidarity that seek to humanize the victims of police brutality by suggesting that a similar fate could befall other similarly construed bodies.

Two of the other popular memes that emerged in the wake of #Ferguson also focused on representations of black bodies and, specifically, on media portrayals of Michael Brown. The first of these emerged as a response to the photograph that mainstream media initially circulated in the wake of his death. The image sparked controversy because it showed Michael Brown making a hand gesture that, for some, represented a peace sign and, for others, a gang sign. Like Trayvon Martin's hoodie, the very same hand gesture could be alternately interpreted as a sign of peace or criminality depending on the racialized body with which it is associated. In response, Twitter users began using the hashtag #IfTheyGunnedMeDown to post contrasting pictures of themselves along with various versions of the question "which picture would they use?" For example, 18-year-old Houston native Tyler Atkins (featured in a *New York Times* article about the meme) posted a picture of himself after a jazz concert in his high school, wearing a black tuxedo with his saxophone suspended from a neck strap. This was juxtaposed with a photo taken while filming a rap video with a friend, in which he is wearing a black T-shirt and a blue bandanna tied around his head and his finger is pointed at the camera.

Once again, these images represent an act of solidarity. They suggest that anyone could be represented as either respectable and innocent or violent and criminal—depending on the staging of the photograph. This campaign speaks to larger concerns over privacy in an era when private photos and surveillance footage are routinely leaked, hacked, and repurposed to nefarious ends. More importantly, it also speaks to an acute awareness among young African Americans of how black bodies are particularly vulnerable to misrepresentation by mainstream media (Vega 2014).

The final hashtag campaign we mention here speaks directly to this issue. It emerged in response to a *New York Times* profile of Michael Brown released on the day of his funeral, which described the 18-year-old as "no angel" (Elignon 2014). The piece suggested that Brown "dabbled in drugs and alcohol" and had been involved in "at least one scuffle with a neighbor." Many saw this as a tasteless, unfair portrayal and an extension of the attempted smear campaign carried out by the local police, who had released what they themselves admitted was "unrelated" surveillance video of a purported act of shoplifting at a convenience store. In response, Twitter users began using the hashtag #NoAngel to highlight the mainstream media's inability to acknowledge the possibility of black victimhood or innocence. For example, one person tweeted, "I am #NoAngel, so I guess I deserve to be murdered too. Yep, perfectly acceptable to gun down a person if they aren't a Saint."

The use of hashtags such as #HandsUpDontShoot, #IfTheyGunnedMeDown, and #NoAngel speak to the long history of inaccurate and unfair portrayal of African Americans within mainstream media and to the systematic profiling and victim blaming suffered by racializied bodies. Their use suggests that while social media might seem like a space of disembodied engagement, for many, social media can become an important site in which to foreground the particular ways in which racialized bodies are systematically stereotyped, stigmatized, surveilled, and positioned as targets of state-sanctioned violence. These hashtag campaigns, which seek to identify the insidious nature of contemporary racism, can thus be understood as a powerful response to the "racial paranoia" (Jackson 2008) associated with African Americans' ongoing experiences of abject inequality in an age of alleged colorblindness.

The effort to bring attention to this inequality is powerfully captured by the hashtag #BlackLivesMatter, which emerged in July 2013, after George Zimmerman was acquitted of Trayvon Martin's murder. Many Twitter users also drew on this hashtag in response to the killing of Michael Brown. It is important to understand #BlackLivesMatter not simply as a general statement about the inherent value of black life in the face of state-sanctioned racial violence but also as a reflection of the ways that social media can become a site for the revaluation of black materiality. As illustrated in the memes described above, participants often used photos of themselves to contest the racialized devaluation of their persons. Whereas, in face-to-face interactions, racialized young people like the ones described above might not be able to contest the meanings ascribed to their bodies (or impede the deadly violence exerted on them by the police), through their creative reinterpretations on social media, they are able to rematerialize their bodies in alternative ways. With these creative acts, they seek to document, contest, and ultimately transform their [daily] experiences by simultaneously asserting the fundamental value and the particularity of their embodiment both on- and off-line.

All That Is Tweeted Melts into Air?

It is clear that platforms like Twitter have become essential to contemporary social actors, but the long-lasting effects of digital modes of activism remain hotly debated. For some, these acts represent fleeting moments of awareness, quickly replaced by the customary innocuousness of social media pleasantries. For others, however, participation in forms of digital activism prove transformative in unpredictable ways. *** It is *** important to recognize that the reactions to the death of Michael Brown did not spark in a vacuum; they were fueled by accumulated frustrations over previously mediatized moments of injustice and guided by previous digital campaigns. ***

As Johnetta Elzie, a 25-year-old protestor profiled in the magazine the *Nation*, explained, "We saw it with Trayvon Martin. We saw it with Jordan Davis—but I always felt away from everything. Then I saw Brown's body laying out there, and I said, 'Damn, they did it again!' But now that it happened in my home, I'm not just going to tweet about it from the comfort of my bed. So I went down there" (Hsieh and Rakia 2014). Elzie's words hint at how face-to-face and digital forms of activism work in interrelated and aggregative ways. Although she draws a distinction between tweeting from the comfort of her home and physical presence at an event, her narrative shows how these contexts are interrelated and build on each other—even beyond the confines of one particular historical event or hashtag campaign.

The article goes on to describe how Elzie encountered other activists involved in the protests through their shared use of social media, stating, "They quickly developed a tight-knit community, sustained by their addiction to social media. Together, they live-tweeted, Vined and Instagrammed every protest, through the sweltering days and tumultuous nights, as well as the direct actions taking place elsewhere in the St. Louis area."

The group eventually took on the name Millennial Activists United and shifted their role from "documenting" their actions to "generating" new forms of social community, for instance, through the use of #FergusonFriday to create a space for reflection on the movement, the creation of a daily newsletter *This Is The Movement* to spread news and reflection pieces about unfolding events, and the organization of national "fireside" conference calls during which activists based in Ferguson could speak directly with those following the events from afar. The ways these activists shift seamlessly across spaces and modes of engagement underscore the slippery boundary between analog and digital forms of activism. * * * Anthropologists interested in these social worlds should thus remain attentive to the possibilities of hashtag ethnography while still being prepared to read between and go beyond the digital lines.

Postscript

On November 24, 2014, after a grand jury released its decision not to indict Darren Wilson, Ferguson went viral once again, with over 3.5 million tweets appearing in a matter of hours under the hashtag #FergusonDecision. That evening, and in the days that followed, protestors took to the streets across the nation and beyond to decry the decision, the overall handling of Michael Brown's case by the justice system, and racialized police brutality more broadly. Demonstrators staged "death-ins" at city intersections and shopping malls, they lined suburban sidewalks face down in memory of Michael Brown's lifeless body, and they brought traffic in several cities across the United States to a halt, shutting down multilane highways, bridges, tunnels, and modes of public transportation. Many wore T-shirts proclaiming "I am Mike Brown" and held signs calling for the need to "Indict America." These demonstrations led social media users to claim that "#Ferguson is everywhere," emphasizing the connection between online and offline forms of protest.

The release of the grand jury hearing transcripts also offered a new view of the events as narrated by Darren Wilson, who had until that moment remained silent. His testimony—particularly his description of Michael Brown as "a demon," as a larger-than-life figure, and his use of the pronoun *it* to refer to the 18-year-old—offered further insight into the distorted lens through which black bodies are read by representatives of the state. Michael Brown and Darren Wilson were both 6'4" tall and weighed 290 pounds and 210 pounds, respectively, yet, in his testimony and in television interviews, Wilson said he felt like "a 5-year-old holding on to Hulk Hogan." Wilson's characterization of himself as a child and of Brown as a superhuman monster became part of an exculpatory narrative in which the unarmed teenager was framed as the true threat, not the police officer who shot and killed him. In his testimony, Darren Wilson affirmed that he had done nothing wrong and expressed no remorse for his actions. Describing the moment of Michael Brown's death, he stated that, as the bullets entered the young man's body, "the demeanor on his face went blank, the aggression was gone, it was gone, . . . the threat was stopped." Wilson's reverse logic, sanctioned by the state, presents a narrative in which an unarmed teenager is a terrifying aggressor and an armed police officer is an innocent victim. This inversion underscores the significance of affirming that #BlackLivesMatter in a context where they are disproportionately viewed as threats by state forces and mainstream institutions.

The same week of the Ferguson grand jury decision, news broke of the fatal shooting of 12-year-old Tamir Rice by Cleveland police after a 911 caller reported a "guy" with a gun. The gun was probably fake, the caller had said, and "it" (referring to Rice) was "probably a juvenile," but, still, the mere sight of the boy with a toy gun "is scaring the shit out of me," the caller insisted. Police were dispatched, and they shot the boy dead within two seconds of encountering him. This event made clear once again state agents' distorted views of black Americans, especially teenagers—how their very bodies are perceived as looming, larger-than-life threats and how any objects in their possession (e.g., candies, sodas, toys, articles of clothing) are read as weapons.

Once again, the media focused not on state action but on the worthiness of black bodies. Local news immediately ran profiles of Rice's parents, noting that they both had "violent pasts" (his father had been charged with domestic violence and his mother with drug possession). This history, reporters argued, could help explain why Tamir Rice would be inclined to play with a toy gun in a public place. Under fire for its coverage, the Northeast Ohio Media Group claimed, "One way to stop police from killing any more 12-year-olds might be to understand the forces that lead children to undertake behavior that could put them in the sights of police guns." There was no discussion of a national "gun culture," as there often is in incidents involving youth and guns (though, in this case, the "gun" was a toy), nor was there any discussion of the structural violence that Rice and his family engaged with on a daily basis or of the distorted ways young black bodies are viewed when they end up "in the sights" of police guns.

Within this context, social media participation becomes a key site from which to contest mainstream media silences and the long history of state-sanctioned violence against racialized populations. Upon announcing the Ferguson grand jury decision, St. Louis prosecutor Robert McCulloch claimed that media coverage, and particularly social media, had posed "the most significant challenge" to his investigation. Social media cast a spotlight on this small Missouri township, but more importantly, by propelling Ferguson into a broader, mediatized, virtual space, social media users were able to show that "#Ferguson is everywhere"—not only in the sense of a broad public sphere but also in the sense of the underlying social and political relationships that haunt the nation as a whole.

ENGAGING THE TEXT, ENGAGING THE WORLD

- Social media has been central to social movements both in the United States and internationally. According to Bonilla and Rosa, what is the unique role Twitter can play in social activism and anti-racism work?

- In Ferguson, how did Twitter provide "a unique platform for collectively identifying, articulating, and contesting racial injustices"?

- Bonilla and Rosa argue that Twitter allows a dispersed audience to enter into a shared experience or "public time," like being together in a public space. How would you compare the strengths and weaknesses of digital activism to face-to-face activism?

- How does digital activism, or hashtag activism, create unique opportunities to challenge misperceptions and misrepresentations in the mainstream media?

- Following the events in Ferguson, how has the hashtag activism associated with #BlackLivesMatter provided the foundation for the national Black Lives Matter social movement?

6
Ethnicity and Nationalism

We hear the word **ethnicity** all the time. The press reports on "long-held ethnic conflicts" that shatter the peace in Rwanda, Iraq, India, and the former Yugoslavia. We check boxes on college applications and U.S. census forms to identify our own ethnicity or race. We shop in "ethnic foods" aisles of our super-sized grocery stores. But our use of ethnicity is not particularly consistent or terribly clear.

Ethnicity is one of the most powerful identities that humans develop: it is a sense of connection to a group of people who we believe share a common history, culture, and (sometimes) ancestry, and who we believe are distinct from others outside the group (Jenkins 1996; Ericksen 2010).

Ethnicity can be seen as a more expansive version of kinship—the culturally specific creation of relatives—only including a much larger group and extending further in space and time. Anthropologists see ethnicity as a cultural construction, not as a natural formation based on biology or inherent human nature. Ethnic identity is taught and reinforced in a a number of ways. **Origin myths** and stories—like the American Thanksgiving story—are told and retold to emphasize a shared destiny and shared values. **Ethnic boundary markers** are created to signify who is in the group and who is not: a shared name; shared cultural practices such as food, clothing, and architecture; a belief in a common history and ancestors; association with a particular territory; shared language or religion. But no group is completely homogeneous. Boundaries are usually not clearly fixed or defined. And since we likely will never meet most people in our group, ethnic identification is what Benedict Anderson (1983) called an **imagined community**, primarily perceived, felt, and imagined rather than clearly documentable.

Anthropologists examine the many ways ethnicities and ethnic identities can be invented, performed, and changed over time and according to one's social location. Ethnicity is not only mobilized to rally support in times of conflict but can also be mobilized to create opportunities, including economic opportunities.

For many of the world's people, ethnicity is not a pressing matter in daily life, but it can be activated when power relationships undergo negotiation in a community or a nation. Then people may call on shared ideas of ethnicity to rally others to participate in their causes, whether those causes involve ensuring self-protection, building alliances, constructing economic networks, or establishing a country. As in the case of Rwanda presented by Paul Farmer in this chapter, ethnicity can also be activated by charismatic **identity entrepreneurs**.

Popular discourse often associates ethnic groups with particular nation-states. But this has not always been the case. **States**—regional structures of political, economic, and military rule—have existed for thousands of years, beginning in the regions now known as modern-day Iraq, China, and India. But the nation-state is a relatively new development. The term signifies more than a geographic territory with borders enforced by a central government. **Nation-state** assumes a distinct political entity whose population shares a sense of culture, ancestry, and destiny as a people (Gellner 1983; Hearn 2006; Wolf 2001).

But nation-states are much less stable and self-contained than we have generally been led to believe. Of the nearly two hundred nation-states in the world today, fewer than one-third existed in their current form 40 years ago. And almost none have existed for more than 200 years, certainly not in their present form. Through their colonial conquests over more than 400 years, the emerging nation-states of Europe, and later Japan in Asia, redrew the political borders of much of the world to suit their own economic and political interests, without regard for local ethnic, political, economic, or religious realities. Colonialism had and continues to have a particularly negative impact on indigenous people around the world whose populations and lands were often divided between colonial powers and subsumed under colonial administrations. Audra Simpson's ethnography, *Mohawk Interruptus*, explores the role of Native American identity in relationship to the nation-states of the United States and Canada. In particular, she considers the tensions and conflicts that arise as sovereign indigenous people move across the U.S.–Canadian border. She reflects on her own border crossing experiences as well as strategies of resistance and alternative ethnic, national identity formation.

"Landmine Boy" and Stupid Deaths

Paul Farmer

The construction of ethnicity in Rwanda

In the following article, anthropologist and physician Paul Farmer tells of the dangerous encounter of two young Rwandan boys with a landmine in 2006. While treating them in his rural clinic he begins to investigate the social life of this landmine and in turn reveals the deadly long-term consequences of colonialism, war and violence, the manipulation of ethnic identity, and the global dynamics of local events. Farmer has become well known for applying anthropology's key research strategies and analytical concepts to solve pressing public health problems. Through his work in Rwanda and Haiti, Farmer has argued that the delivery of medicines and medical procedures is not enough to ensure health. What made these people sick in the first place? How could they stay healthy after being treated? These questions expose the underlying conditions leading to illness and disease and the answers require an anthropologist's ethnographic attention to context.

But what does health have to do with ethnicity and nationalism? In his article "'Landmine Boy' and Stupid Deaths," Farmer examines the social construction of ethnicity in Rwanda and its deadly effects in the country's 1994 genocide, during which over 1 million people were killed.

I have been working in Haiti all of my adult life and in Rwanda since 2005. In Rwanda, I work predominantly as a physician rather than as an anthropologist conducting ethnographic fieldwork. Ethnographers of this region know the language, culture, and history of Rwanda far better than I do. If I spoke Kinyarwanda fluently and had spent many years in Rwanda, perhaps I might claim the ethnographer's privilege of systematic knowledge or offer to decipher, as many of my colleagues do, the symbolics or poetics of violence. But work in Haiti and elsewhere in Latin America has given me rough-and-ready interpretive frameworks for understanding violence, both the "event"-centered kind, including war and political violence, and the structural kind, including racism and other forms of social inequalities. In Rwanda, as part of a team reintroducing health and

From Paul Farmer. 2010. "Landmine Boy and Stupid Deaths." In *Partner to the Poor: A Paul Farmer Reader*, edited by Haun Saussy. Berkeley: University of California Press. Some of the author's notes have been omitted.

social services to a rural region devastated by the 1994 genocide, I write as an outsider looking at violence in a place that I am getting to know.

The history of war and genocide in Rwanda will be contested terrain for generations, but some conclusions are inescapable: that European notions of race and ethnicity, some of them inspired by colonial-era eugenics, helped to harden the precolonial social categories of Hutu and Tutsi; that the biased bestowal of colonial-era privileges in a social field of scarcity laid the framework for intergroup violence that began in 1959, at the close of the colonial era; and that control over the state apparatus, and the economic and social privileges associated with proximity to political power, was the chief goal of the government leaders who were the architects of the Rwandan genocide. Equally inescapable, for Rwandans, are the consequences of that damage. * * *

* * * To reflect on the causes and consequences of the Rwandan genocide, we might begin with a series of events that occurred in rural Rwanda on March 22, 2006, when two children picked up a landmine. This incident was just one of many brutal remainders of the genocide, itself the upshot of a complex series of precolonial, colonial, and postcolonial processes that laid the groundwork for what was to happen in 1994.

Event and Structure: Anthropologies of Violence

Violence is a frequent theme in anthropological research nowadays. * * * *Event violence* is ethnographically visible—sometimes spectacularly grisly, as was the case in Rwanda in 1994. There are dozens of journalistic accounts of Africa's most devastating mass violence, which occurred during the course of a hundred days. However, its causes and consequences are complex and too often invisible to those who witness or chronicle violent events. But it is not enough to understand violence done by and to human beings in specific places and times; we must also seek to throw light on *structural violence*, the kind of violence done on a collective and even impersonal scale, topics best analyzed using the complementary frameworks of history and political economy.

*   *   *

Like the genocides of Europe, the Rwandan genocide will one day spawn * * * a literature and, as in the European case, we can expect it to span widely discrepant perspectives and explanatory frameworks. One problem with discrepant accounts—and violence engenders them inevitably—is that it takes time and careful research to weigh their veracity. In the case of genocide, there are victims and there are aggressors, but the victims of genocide are (with rare exceptions) no longer present and are thus unable to offer first-person narratives, even if their relatives can. * * * The necessary sifting and discernment of human perspectives and motives can be usefully complemented by a focus on *things*. Things, at least, don't manipulate their observers—or is that true? Take the case of so commonplace an object (alas) as a landmine. While in graduate school, I read Arjun Appadurai's edited volume *The Social Life of Things* (Appadurai 1986). A focus on the material—on things—need not detract from the everyday business of both physicians and anthropologists, which is a focus on what people say, on what they do, and on the ways they construct meaning. On the contrary, the "materiality of the social" has long been a source of illumination in anthropology (Farmer 2002).

Ever since Bronislaw Malinowski's report on the kula ring, the meanings associated with certain things have been the focus of significant empirical research. Anthropologists agree that things take on meaning through exchange (sale, trade, other transactions), through rituals banal and freighted, and through other processes that confer value on things in the minds of those engaged in their circulation. Landmines and other ordnance, though expendable, are no exception. In the case of Rwanda, they force us to cast our net well beyond the immediate country or culture, since, unlike the cases seen in ritual transactions, the path leading from arms dealers to hapless children and other civilians (and even, at times, to combatants) involves little commonality, but rather a riven diversity, of agency and intent.

Picking up a Landmine

On a Wednesday morning in March 2006, while herding cows, two boys picked up a landmine. In Rwanda, this is an increasingly rare event, as many efforts have been made to find and disarm such weapons. * * * Unfortunately, it is an exceedingly common event elsewhere: in the past decade, it was estimated that there are 110 million landmines in the ground worldwide, and more than twice as many stockpiled. Today, thirteen countries continue to manufacture antipersonnel devices, though as little as fifteen years ago that number was more than fifty countries and almost a hundred private companies, forty-seven of which were based in the United States. Of those who detonate the landmines unintentionally, 80 percent are civilians, one in five of them children; about half die, virtually all the rest are injured, and many of them are permanently maimed.

Both of the Rwandan boys survived. I came to know quite well the one who was injured more seriously, as he spent more time in the hospital and needed physical therapy, home visits, and social assistance. Around the hospital, reopened less than a year earlier, he was termed, affectionately enough, "Landmine Boy," but his real name is Faustin. I met him at ten in the morning on that Wednesday, as I was headed out of the hospital to a clinic a couple of hours away. The hospital had been built and was once owned by a Belgian mining company, which left Rwanda decades ago. After the war and genocide, the facility fell into disuse, essentially abandoned until May of 2005, when we (Partners In Health, the Clinton Foundation, and the Rwandan Ministry of Health) rebuilt and opened it as the sole hospital serving more than two hundred thousand people, most of them resettled refugees, internally displaced persons, with almost all of them living in poverty.

By March 2006, we had cobbled together a medical and nursing staff consisting mostly of Rwandan professionals and a handful of expatriate volunteers. One of my colleagues, a physician from Cameroon, stopped me that morning, saying, "Come quickly to the emergency room. Two children have picked up a grenade." At that moment, I did not think it unlikely that someone in the region would have picked up a grenade and pulled the pin: after all, the boys live (and we practice medicine) in a region hit hard by the war and genocide. The boys said that they merely picked the thing up and threw it toward the cows they were herding; the cows took the full force of the explosion, and two were killed. It was an hour or so after seeing the boys before I began to think about the object itself, what it was, and where it had come from. In the meantime, neither I nor my colleagues were thinking about anything other than trauma care, which is of course precisely what trauma victims need most. In this case, it meant splinting fractures, debriding wounds, and applying dressings. We worked attentively and in near silence.

Of the two boys, one, Grégoire, was not seriously injured. The other, Faustin, sustained multiple fractures, and many fragments had been blown into his skin. I had the privilege of splinting him, pulling the plastic fragments out of him, and preparing him for transport. Although we had just rebuilt the operating room, we did not have an orthopedic surgeon on staff, and Faustin needed to have his fractures set in the operating room with what is called an external fixator.

That was the first hour. The boys, who were alert but very quiet, were not sure of their age. (Faustin was in pain, he allowed, but he complained as little as the other boy.) One way to assess age when children do not know how old they are is to ask, "Were you alive during X or Y or Z?" I learned this in Haiti, where children and adults alike remembered certain political events, such as who was president at the time. In Rwanda, the major defining moment is 1994. I was pretty sure that 1994, or the year before, was when the "grenade" was placed and that 1994 was also about when these boys were born. But during the first hour of attending to these injuries, no one discussed any of this. It was afterward, before the police arrived, that I started to ask whether this really was a grenade. Grenades do not explode when you step on them or touch them; as anyone who watches movies knows, you pull a pin and then it explodes a few seconds later. So another kind of explosive device had to be at issue.

Injured by one thing, an explosive device, Faustin, said to be an orphan, according to one of the Rwandan nurses, needed another thing: a piece of metal to keep his tibia and fibula in place so that the bones would heal in line. It just so happens that this device is readily available in most hospitals in the United States. Such hardware is hard to come by in Rwanda, but the device that would soon be placed in Faustin's leg was actually invented there. It is called a "Byumba fix," named after a town in the northern part of the country, where tens of thousands of landmines, none of them manufactured in Rwanda, were placed in 1993 and 1994. A Rwandan doctor trained in orthopedics in Belgium was finishing his thesis in 1994 when the genocide erupted. Against the advice of his professors, he decided to return to his country to care for the wounded, many of whom needed precisely the sort of services he had been trained to provide. When in 1994 Dr. Innocent Nyaruhirira, who would later become a leading figure in public health, tried to acquire the necessary orthopedic materials from Belgium, he found that the hardware was simply too expensive. So he and colleagues in Byumba decided to manufacture the much-needed external fixators on their own; one of them, a dozen years later, would end up in Faustin's left leg.

Once Faustin was en route to the operating room in Kigali, the capital city, I checked on the other child, Grégoire, who had been admitted to the pediatric ward. I finally had a chance to ask him, "What happened? What was it that you picked up?" "Well, we were herding cattle . . . ," he began, trailing off once again into silence. Herding cattle in the middle of the morning meant that these boys were not in school. I sketched Grégoire a grenade and a landmine on a piece of paper—we looked up these images on the Internet—and he pointed immediately to the latter: "This is what it looked like."

Grégoire did not have much to say about the incident during his brief hospitalization, and Faustin, even in the course of interviews conducted at home, did not wish to add much more. "What I'd most like to do," he said only a few days after surgery, "is to go to school." It turned out that he was not an orphan after all, but that his mother, poor and bereft after the genocide, had struggled for years with mental illness and had finally placed him with another family in 2004. "My mother is not well," he told me later. "She can't take care of me, so she brought me to a relative, and I live here now. I would like to go to school, but [my adoptive family] has no money. So I herd cows every day, make sure they eat, move them to new grass."

When I asked him about the landmine, he was, to my astonishment, apologetic: "I didn't mean to pick up the grenade. I'm sorry I did it. I didn't mean to kill the cows. I'm sorry. It was an accident. We didn't know what we were doing; it was not our intention to kill the cows." Even after I reassured him that it was not his fault and sought to focus on his recovery and return to school, he sounded the same note: "My leg hurts, but I can walk well. I am happy that I can go to school and that they are not angry about the cows. If we had known that it was a grenade, we would not have touched it or thrown it. We didn't mean to throw it at the cows. We didn't know it was a grenade."

Rwanda and the Political Economy of Genocide

Dramatic enough in itself, the event—two boys pick up a landmine on a sunny day in March 2006—demands to be resocialized, linked up to a wider world and a longer period of the calendar. How to do this? We begin by noting that not a single one of these landmines was produced in Rwanda. The cause of the explosion that nearly killed Faustin is to be found in the transnational political economy of armaments, in which there are many willing participants. * * *

About 150,000 landmines were placed in Rwanda, mostly during 1993. Rwanda is a tiny country with a population, before the genocide, of perhaps 8.5 million people. Yet in 1993 it was the third largest importer of arms in all of Africa, coming in behind Egypt and South Africa (still under apartheid). On the Rwandan government's 1993 shopping list were 2,000 plastic MAT-79 antipersonnel mines, copies of an Italian model purchased in bulk. Experts from the United Nations have found thirty-nine types of mines in Rwanda, mostly plastic. Some, it's said, were designed to look like toys. Their provenance: Belgium, the United States, Czechoslovakia, Pakistan, China, and all over the former Soviet Union. It's also known that the *génocidaire* government mined the area around Akagera National Park, which is where we live and work—and where these boys were herding cattle instead of attending school.

Who funded this appetite for arms? Not the local peasant farmers, who would later be the hapless recipients of the shrapnel (as, twelve years earlier, some had been the people who had carried out much of the killing: between 14 and 17 percent of the adult male Hutu population participated in the genocide) (Straus 2006). It was the government of Rwanda that shaped the postcolonial army. France, as the predominant power in the region, also supplied much of the "aid" to Rwanda and influenced other donor nations' priorities in foreign assistance. * * *

The Rwandan genocide resulted in the deaths of up to a million people in a few months and later sparked a war in the Congo. * * * A lot of us remember the machetes; that's the classic impression for anyone who has seen the film *Hotel Rwanda* or read about the genocide in the popular press. But Rwanda's macabre 1993 ranking as the third-largest importer of arms in Africa was not earned by purchase of machetes alone: the government that ordered the genocide had procured surface-to-air missiles, rockets and other large armaments, automatic weapons—and, of course, landmines. * * *

The blast that injured Faustin and Grégoire in 2006 was a long-delayed repercussion of the violence of 1994; that much is hardly controversial. Many know the story of the Hutu and Tutsi, and some understand that 1994 was not, despite quick-release journalistic analyses, either ethnic fratricide or tribal war. Rwanda does not have different tribes, and the categories of ethnicity and race are not really apt, either. The term "ethnicity," to say nothing of "race," did not arrive until long after whichever century saw the evolution of such categories. The ethnic categories are not exactly a "native" product, as historians of the colonial period in Rwanda have argued. * * * We are speaking, rather, about centuries and waves of population movements, unrecorded and largely unknowable. Certainly, there is no evidence of genetic differences, and yet the idea of alien immigration was all too useful, later, to the Belgians and *génocidaires*. When the Batutsi are said to have migrated into what is now Rwanda, the region was already inhabited by people who called themselves Batwa and Bahutu (following convention, I've shortened these terms).

The dates are contested, but for centuries Tutsis and Hutus, both ethnically Banyarwanda, shared a common language, diet, and cultural heritage. Many scholars agree that the so-called tribal categorizations represented, in important ways, social distinctions between those who owned cattle and those who farmed the land—perhaps initially a division of labor between agriculturalists and pastoralists. Intermarriage was common, and a Hutu could become a Tutsi by owning cattle. This is well known—no longer the exclusive affair of specialists—but the myth of tribalism dies hard, probably because it is so convenient for people to attribute the causes of genocide to an alien mode of thought.

*   *   *

Aside from a tiny Tutsi aristocracy, the original difference was largely one of professions, but * * * the Belgians promoted it into something much larger, and fatal. What the colonials focused on when they arrived was the tiny Tutsi aristocracy. * * * The vast majority of Tutsis—like the Hutus, peasants who worked the land—were invisible to them. Most Tutsis were subject to the same taxes and forced labor as the other inhabitants of the colony. The Belgians imagined that Rwanda and Burundi were like European feudal states and then shaped these societies to resemble them. * * * Europeans (first Germans and then Belgians) helped to rigidify these distinctions as part of their obsessions with race and eugenics (Mamdani 2001).

Colonial Rwanda, mountainous and lush, soon became a major producer of tropical commodities, especially coffee and tea. As in the neighboring Congo and in the region surrounding the hospital we have rebuilt, mines were dug; although these would not prove as important as agriculture, the basic thrust of Belgian colonization was, in keeping with tradition, extractive. Who was to do the extracting was a problem, and the Belgians followed, fairly religiously, the divide-and-conquer approach then *à la mode:* they used the Tutsi elite, a minority, to control the "peasant majority," the Hutus. (The Twa, the smallest group in all senses, mostly stayed out of the way.) The enforced *corvée* labor contributions of Hutus originated in precolonial times but, scholars report, were increased significantly—from one day of labor per week to up to three—once Belgian administration was established. But the Belgians seemed to grapple with a problem: who was Tutsi, who was Hutu? The notion that it was possible to answer this question with a glance was just that, a notion. And so the Belgian colonial regime did what colonial regimes often did: it issued ethnic identity cards. Soon, one's ethnic affiliation and social aspirations became a matter of public record and much more immutable.

* * * The 1994 genocide was in essence a political process, and planned to the very last detail. Most Rwandans I know start the countdown to genocide in 1959. The short version: as decolonization swept Africa, the Belgians switched allegiances and began favoring the Hutu majority. Decades of preferential treatment for the Tutsi elites had engendered deep resentment, again in a field of material scarcity and a lack of access to education and other social services. From the moment that it was clear that the Belgians would leave and that Rwanda, like the rest of Africa, would become nominally independent, struggle for control of the state apparatus, the cash cow, began. It was really this—the struggle for control of power and wealth— * * * that laid the foundation for what would come to pass three decades later. "Ethnic" convulsions—unknown before 1959—were registered regularly in the decades that followed (Gourevitch 1998).

France replaced Belgium as the major neocolonial power in Rwanda and had, it would seem, no problem aligning itself with the Hutu military governments that increasingly controlled not only the state but most commerce. The recipe for staying in power was straight from the latter days of colonialism: whip up anti-Tutsi sentiment among the Hutu majority, and count on French support. Most Rwandans relied on radio communications for news and even orders, and this became an instrument for fomenting hatred and violence. Backed by Hutu-Power extremists, proponents of a virulent Hutu-supremacist philosophy used officially sanctioned radio stations to spew forth not only anti-Tutsi (and anti-moderate Hutu) songs but also more explicit directions to the militias, including the *interahamwe* gangs charged with carrying out the genocide, along with the military. These gangs were growing as fast as the ranks of disaffected youth of the country, who faced grim prospects as the Rwandan economy continued to decline.

*　　*　　*

In early August 1993, a year-long process of hammering out a regional peace plan was completed with the signing of the Arusha Accords in Arusha, Tanzania. Eight months later, while en route from Tanzania to Kigali, the French jet of the Rwandan dictator Juvénal Habyarimana was brought down by a missile launched from within the military base near the airport.

The spark that lit the fuse was the downing of that plane in April 1994. The Rwandan government immediately blamed the assassination of Habyarimana on the [Rwandan Patriotic Front (RPF)], an accusation echoed in the French press. More independent observers, however, and much public speculation laid the blame on Hutu extremists—many of them members of the dictator's own entourage—who ardently opposed the Arusha Accords. Within an hour of the plane's destruction, the *interahamwe*, as if waiting for this very signal, swung into action. They clearly had a plan, but confusion reigned among others in Kigali.

*　　*　　*

The genocide was halted when the RPF, growing every day and including more and more Hutus who did not wish to follow orders to kill their neighbors, swept across Rwanda in the summer of 1994. It might be argued that the entire sordid mess was over, but the French had one more card to play: Opération Turquoise became an operation to protect the *génocidaire* government as it fled Rwanda to refugee camps in Goma, Zaïre. From across Lake Kivu, an almost intact *génocidaire* government clearly intended to attack again and again, until their genocidal project was complete. Scores of nongovernmental organizations (NGOs) had materialized to take care of the refugees, most of them probably Hutus chivvied [prodded] along with threats and dire warnings; many had not in fact taken part in the killings. The new administration in Kigali, receiving precious little in the way of any international support, threatened to take out the camps if they could not be controlled by the UN and the NGOs. Then cholera broke out in the camps, and all attention was turned to Goma, and away from Rwanda.

Even though Hutu-generated attacks did come from these camps, the UN claimed that it was powerless to stop them. The genocide ended in 1994, but the violence did not, for the genocide's architects were allowed to flee west (some VIP *génocidaires* made it to France, the United States, and several African nations; warrants for their arrest from the International Criminal Court still exist).

A million or so civilians were in a sense held hostage in the camps by the *interahamwe* and a government in exile. Cross-border attacks continued. In 1996, the Rwandan transitional government did just what it had threatened to do and broke up the camps, encouraging those not involved as architects of the genocide to return. * * * The new government in Kigali was proven right: the camps were being used as military bases from which to attack Rwanda with sophisticated armaments purchased from Russian, European, and U.S. arms merchants. The social life of things can be revealed, it transpires, by airway bills and receipts.

In other words, if Rwandans of the 1990s were struggling with manufactured categories, they were also struggling with manufactured things: armaments, for example, things with a highly active social life. They get around. Italy, the United States, and Russia were the major producers of the antipersonnel and landmine instruments used in Rwanda (ICBL 1999, 2007), while France, Egypt, and apartheid South Africa were the Rwandan government's primary suppliers (Goose and Smyth 1994). In short, a violent event in rural Rwanda in March 2006 reveals links to at least a dozen other countries far from central Africa, links that reach far back in time. This is a lesson that anthropology cannot forget, as Eric Wolf reminded us years ago (Wolf 1997).

What Is to Be Done about "Stupid Deaths"?

*   *   *

When I was a young man, between college and medical school, I had the great good fortune to go to Haiti. A country, rather than a person or a book, became my teacher. Back then, just about everything seemed instructive: interviews, surveys, books, reports, songs, everyday speech, customs, and certainly history, the most important resocializing discipline. But for someone on my trajectory, a physician-anthropologist in training, it may have been inevitable that I would find the most incisive those lessons learned the hard way, by witnessing other people's pain and learning about how they made sense of suffering. The Haitians with whom I lived were world experts on the topic. Everyone had a story, and almost no one, it seemed, was reluctant to share it.

I learned a lot about death, and in particular about a special type that the Haitians termed, simply enough, "stupid deaths." By this, they did not mean deaths by gunshot (there were plenty of these) or in road accidents (as vehicles crammed full went teetering down mountain "roads" with no guardrails). A drowning death in the nearby reservoir was not emblematic of a stupid death, nor was going down in one of the overstuffed wooden boats leaving Haiti for Florida. Rather, these were tragedies and seen by all around me as unfair.

What, then, were examples of stupid deaths in the eyes of those living in central Haiti? Dying in childbirth because obstetric care costs too much was dying a stupid death; worldwide, there are five hundred thousand of these each year. Dying of malaria was stupid, as were deaths from tetanus, rabies, pneumonia. Death from a road accident because of poor medical attention later: stupid. Being hauled out of the nearby reservoir by your kin, only to die two weeks later of pneumonia in a filthy hospital room: stupid.

Fascinated, horrified, with this typology, I developed my own nosology [list or classification] of stupid death and included many others that I knew, from my training in an American medical school, to be tragic and unnecessary: malignancies that could have been cured with timely diagnosis; third-trimester obstetric catastrophes; vaccine-preventable illnesses; and a host of afflictions that our patients would have survived had they been born in a country such as the one in which I was born. Almost all of these deaths occur among the poor.

But the stupidest of all, I thought, was the industrial-strength murder that could come only from bombs, firearms, landmines, and other "modern" ordnance of war, with the casualties occurring disproportionately among civilians, in particular children like Faustin. So, what is to be done to change this state of affairs, in Haiti, in Rwanda, in many other places of today's world?

It is possible to discuss "distal" and "proximal" responses to the sort of violence endured by Faustin and Grégoire. These terms are contested, in part because in anthropology (and in epidemiology and other fields) we use these words in a fashion quite contrary to the way they are used in anatomy and medicine. If you think about an artery, the large end of the vessel is termed "proximal"; the small end, the capillaries, is called "distal." Some colleagues and I recently wrote an essay titled "Structural Violence and Clinical Medicine" and spoke about distal and proximal problems and responses to a number of pressing health issues, from asthma in American cities to AIDS in Africa (Farmer, Nizeye, et al. 2006). Perhaps in part because the meanings of the words are reversed in different fields of inquiry, Nancy Krieger has recently suggested that these terms be banned from discussions of causality (Krieger 2008).

But in the case of Faustin, our distal responses meant debriding the wounds and splinting the fractures; Faustin now walks with the slightest limp. And moving backward, or proximally, our response means getting children in school—Faustin is now regularly attending classes. It means providing basic health care, as we seek to do in rural Rwanda. It means demining all of Rwanda, a process nearly complete, in spite of the misfortune of these boys. Finally, it requires approaches to the big questions, such as how we might prevent people from planting landmines in the first place.

In closing, then, what is to be done? As a doctor, I have to admit that it is not so easy to place an external fixator. A surgeon in the capital city did this for Faustin. But with the right medical equipment, which in this case included orthopedic hardware, it is possible to do a good job in this very distal effort. And that is really what Rwandans ask of us in the event of trauma. They are unlikely to say, "Please, do the ethnography or political economy of brutality; come and study the political economy of landmines." They quite reasonably want action in the present, addressing immediate needs such as food, clean water, shelter, schooling, decent employment, and accessible health care. Retracing the causal links, we are faced with the situation that created Faustin's injury: a countryside once littered with landmines. For that, the remedy is demining. I thought it must be some sophisticated procedure, but the process is rather crude: you sandbag the area around the landmines and then detonate them. These children were demining, in their own way and without the sandbags. Innocently, they mistook a landmine for a toy or a trinket.

*   *   *

There is always going to be distal work, the work of patching up children and anyone else who happens to be injured in this manner. Clinicians should be proud to do this work. But we also need to move closer to the roots of the problem for the sake of prevention, and this will be done only by examining the political economy of brutality. The global health community, which includes physicians, certainly has a very pragmatic role to play in this process. However, anthropology and other resocializing disciplines are uniquely poised to reveal the complexity of these problems and to lay out the challenges faced by all those who seek to lessen the violence that maims and kills so many.

*   *   *

Rwanda will emerge from mass violence by seeking to ensure that social inequalities—in the recent past, Hutu versus Tutsi, and in the present *and* past, the poor versus the nonpoor—are lessened, re-creating a social field in which such distinctions are muted by improving access to the very services that Faustin mentioned repeatedly in his brief commentaries on his own experience. He spoke of school, cows, and medical care. These are things, too—but should they remain commodities only? Should access to school, health care (including, in Faustin's case, orthopedic surgery), and a livelihood be considered mere commodities, to be bought and sold? Or does the framework of basic rights have something to add as postgenocidal Rwanda seeks to lessen the tomorrow of violence?

Elsewhere, I have argued that the framework of social and economic rights—the right to health care, education, and freedom from want—will help us to imagine a future in which poverty alone does not determine who has access to such services. That Faustin was not maimed permanently by poverty and misfortune, not to be confused with accident or happenstance, is the result of his access to modern medical care. By rebuilding a hospital abandoned since the genocide, we were able to take care of him a dozen years after the cessation of "event violence." By insisting that education be a right, rather than a commodity, we were able to alter his trajectory and allow him to participate in a future in which he, a Rwandan citizen, is guaranteed certain rights.

The precise formula by which any of us may participate in a tomorrow with less violence is, granted, uncertain. But asking if basic services might be reimagined as rights rather than commodities is precisely the question we must raise if we seek formulas that will end, or at least lessen, the status quo in which some people are shielded from risk while others, like Faustin, are assured a future in which violence plays a major and determinant role. Stopping "stupid deaths" may play a larger role in lessening the tomorrow of violence than we, shielded from such insults, imagine.

ENGAGING THE TEXT, ENGAGING THE WORLD

- Why did Farmer retell the story of the two boys in his discussion of ethnicity, violence, and stupid deaths?

- How does Farmer's article reveal processes of constructing or inventing ethnicity?

- How does Farmer use a discussion of landmines and the social life of things—how things are created, move, and are used in and across cultures—to advance his analysis of what is happening in Rwanda?

- How does Farmer link the construction of ethnicity in Rwanda, the Rwandan genocide, and the experience of the two Rwandan boys to global causes and dynamics?

- What is Farmer's challenge to anthropologists (and anthropology students) about their role in addressing violence, genocide, and stupid deaths?

- What does Farmer mean by "stupid deaths"?

From *Mohawk Interruptus*
Audra Simpson

Citizenship, nationality, and identity at the border

What happens when members of the Iroquois Confederacy, which predates the settler states of the United States and Canada, attempt to cross the international border now drawn across their territory? All Iroquois communities have moved through and still move through these borders to work, shop, visit family, and enact ceremonial cycles. They are guaranteed this mobility by the Jay Treaty of 1794, but U.S. and Canadian border control agents may not see it that clearly. When Iroquois actually attempt to cross the border, the encounters reveal deep tensions and conflicts between nationality, nation-states, ethnic identity, and the colonial encounter as sovereign people more through settler states.

From Audra Simpson. 2014. *Mohawk Interruptus: Political Life across the Borders of Settler States.* Durham, NC: Duke University Press. Some of the author's notes have been omitted.

While conducting research about life lived across these borders, Audra Simpson began documenting her own encounters at the border—detentions, interrogations, insults, delays—and her anger and resistance to these affronts and aggressions. Her work, *Mohawk Interruptus*, interrupts portraits of timeless, traditional Native Americans, replacing them with the stories of Indigenous border crossers who refuse to recognize the absolute sovereignty of the United States and Canada. Iroquois consider themselves to be legitimate members of their own sovereign nation before, during, and after crossing. In the process, these crossings expose complex power dynamics and moral vulnerabilities too often ignored in contemporary history classes and political debates. Simpson writes that Mohawk mobility is treated as a crime rather than a right. Part of that crime, she argues, is breaking down commonly held notions of fixed places, national borders, and settler states.

The White Man put that there, not us. I don't know why we have to put up with this bullshit.

—*One Mohawk man speaking to another about border issues over dinner at a Red Lobster in Lachine, Quebec, during the late 1990s*

The Iroquois interrupt the portraits of timeless, procedural tradition that have framed scholarly understandings of them. * * * Nowhere is this made clearer than in Iroquois interpretations of the Jay Treaty of 1794 and Iroquois movement across the United States–Canada border, an international border that cuts through their historical and contemporary territory and is, simply, in their space and in their way. It is through their actions and, in particular, their mobility that Indigenous border crossers enact their understandings of history and law, understandings that are then received in particular ways. * * * The border crossers in this chapter interpret and deploy their own sovereignty in ways that refuse the absolute sovereignty of at least two settler states, and in doing so they reveal the fragility and moral turpitude of those states.

* * * If you are born in a place, does that mean that you are of that place? What if you refuse this tacit form of citizenship? And, *how* do you refuse it? *Can* you refuse it and still move? What is the role of *the border* in articulating grounded forms of citizenship outside the space of the state? I work through these questions with contemporary and historical accounts of the legal life of the international boundary line that cuts through Iroquois territory and that all Iroquois communities moved through, and still move through, to enact their ceremonial cycle, to work, to shop, to visit each other. This mobility is sometimes a daily condition of life in the reservation community of Ahkwesáhsne. Ahkwesáhsne means "where the partridge drums" (Morgan [1851] 1996, 474) and is a Mohawk reservation that is bifurcated by the international boundary line between Canada and the United States and is also surrounded by, or lies within, New York State,

Ontario, and Quebec. The community is bound up with the very beginning of settlement, but also the precontact understanding of territory.

Borders

*   *   *

For Iroquois peoples the border acts as a site not of transgression but for the activation and articulation of their *rights* as members of reserve nations, or Haudenosaunee, or Iroquois Confederacy peoples. Thus the people who are crossing borders are reserve members or Iroquois before they cross, they are especially Iroquois *as* they cross, and they are Iroquois when they arrive at the place where they want to be. However, the maintenance of this arc through the day-to-day arenas of recognition * * * can be difficult. Although crossers may perceive of themselves as members of a sovereign nation, the state may not. The criteria for recognition laid out by the state may render the right to exercise the Haudenosaunee right a *claim*, and a claim that is difficult to prove or to maintain without the proper *identification* and *proof*, but still, they *try*.

Consider here what it sounds like to try. The following stories account for this effort— the conversation, where it takes place, and the political labor of the explanation—the moment of articulation between law, history, and the body that constitutes Iroquois peoples' experiences of "crossing."

On Not Passing at the Border

We had disembarked the late bus from Montreal to New York City and were waiting in line to see an agent. People around me looked blanched and tired. While in line, I surveyed the passports around me and tried to guess who was going to get pulled over based on the color of his or her passport. In my years of riding buses across this border, I have noticed that the red passports seem to slow the line down.

I finally got to my agent. She was a white woman, and I heard her speaking French to the person before me. I remember thinking that it was curious for an American border guard, and then I handed her my status card. I was making lists in my head of things I had to do the next day, and I stopped when she asked me where I was going. When I started to answer her, I noticed that she was flipping my card over and over in her hand. I said, "I am going to Brooklyn." She asked why; I said for research. She was staring at my eyes when I spoke and I thought *immediately*, "This is rude." I realized in that moment as well that she was the perfect amalgamation of every person who had aggravated me on a profound level in my life. This was weird, but then I found out why I was struck by this impression— it was anticipatory. She asked me, directly, jarringly, "Are you 100 percent Indian?"

Floored, I said, and without any hesitation, "Yeah." (I lied.) The feeling of "uh, oh" settled in my stomach shortly after I said it. I figured, now this is what *trying to pass* must feel like for those who explore this option daily. But I also figured that the question was so rude and invasive that I was justified in saying whatever I could to end this encounter, fast.

Then she asked me another question, I am not sure what it was: How long will you be in New York, why are you going there? . . . something like that. I responded, "to do research." She asked, "Where will you stay?" "With my parents," I told her. And then she asked, "Are both your parents Indian?"

"My father is." (I told the truth.)

She now had the truth of my lie, and just like a lie that is unacknowledged and public and forced, it propped itself up and sat between us like an indolent and demanding child. We then talked *around* the lie. I was so annoyed with her and with myself and I remember starting to silently and simultaneously demand answers of myself and of her:

Why did I say "yeah" before?

What is my problem?

What is up with this lady?

Why do I, why do *we*, have to answer these questions from strangers and strangers with attitudes!?

Why is she treating me like this?

I had no answers at the time.

She was watching my eyes *again* when I said instead, "Look, I am a status Indian; I belong to a community; this is my card."

She left the lie and my card alone for a moment and then asked me, "Have you thought about applying for a green card while you are in the States?"

She pushed me over the edge of civility and patience. I was having trouble keeping cool because this was taking way too long and she was treating me like *I* had a red passport and was suggesting that I needed a *green* card. So I replied: "I don't need to apply for a green card, I am an Indian!"

At that moment I wanted to say so many things to her, such as "How did she get *her* green card; what is her white quantum[1]; do you have to have a rudeness quantum of over 50 percent to do this job?" But she surely would have detained me if I did so. So I bit my tongue.

"You need to have a green card if you are going to be in the United States longer than x amount of time," she said, to which I replied:

"Look, I was born down there; I don't need a green card; I am not an immigrant; I am part of a *First Nation*, and this is the card that proves it!"

Upon hearing this her posture completely changed, she pushed my card to me, and said, "Well then,

you

are an American."

To which I said,

"*No*, I am not,

I

am a *Mohawk*."

---

1. [*Quantum* refers to a percentage of one's ancestry.]

I walked away from her. But as I was walking toward the door, she yelled across the border house to me,

"You are an American."

And I yelled back,

"I am a Mohawk."

And she yelled,

"No,

You are an American."

At that, I walked out of the din of surveillance and aggravation and onto the bus, sat down, and immediately wrote it all down. Once that was finished, I started a detailed letter to her supervisor and then found that I was too tired to write that one down. I never wrote that letter to her supervisor, but in documenting the interaction, I realized that ethnography in anger can have a historically and politically productive effect. This exchange sits in my "notebook" beside interviews, notes, and the emergent archive of stories of my own experience of the law, which articulates with the people that I was interviewing, observing, hanging out with, and then writing about.

The experience with this woman happened early in my formal fieldwork and remains, so many years later, the most aggressive exchange I have ever had crossing the border. As may be inferred from the moment above, voices were raised; there was palpable "tension." Her complete, summarizing disdain for what I was saying, expressed in *"You are an American,"* registered to the tips of hair that I did not know I had at the nape of my neck. The assertion that I was other than Mohawk, or that this was anything less than a citizenship, was enraging and simultaneously had to be contained. I simply could not flip out. But she was snooty, authoritative, aggressive—everything, historically, politically, to dislike and to dislike with a vigor. When I crossed the following year from Vancouver to Seattle, I was asked similar questions (by another white woman, though less sneering) and instead of entertaining her line of questions, I simply asked her for her immigration papers, then waited for a response. She did not argue with me but sent me to the "room" where many people with red passports were. A white, male customs officer asked me if I "got myself into trouble with her," and I told him I have a right to ask either of them for their papers. Things became jovial; only I was not really joking. Either way, he then printed out the INS regulation 1952 for me to look at. I told him I know about it and our blood quantum is nobody's business, and he told me he went to college with a guy who said he was Indian but was not, and that is why blood quantum is useful. It protects everyone from dishonesty.

The Burden of Proof

Further into my formal fieldwork I encountered this man, with sharp hair and relentless skepticism.

B. J. Riggs wanted to know where the letter was from my tribe stating that I am 50 percent Indian because, as he said while looking at my card in his hand, "these don't mean anything."

I told him that my "tribe" has a 50 percent blood-quantum requirement and that in fact this means that the card does "mean something."

He looked at me like I was an idiot and started flipping my card over and over in his hand. After my previous experience with the French-speaking American woman at the border, I knew that the card flipping was probably a *bad sign.*

"The burden of proof is on you to prove who you are—you know that, don't you? These cards don't mean anything."

He shifted gears, "Where are you going? How long are you staying? Where were you born? Do you have a birth certificate?"

"I was born in Brooklyn, New York. I am staying for a few weeks. Here is my birth certificate."

"This is what I need to see, this other thing here is useless." He pushed it to me across the counter and said, "Next time show me this." He folded up my birth certificate and handed it back to me.

Danny, an interlocutor and friend in his early thirties told me similar stories about being interrogated, being burdened with proving. I asked him very specifically if he had ever had difficulty at the border. His unedited responses follow.

"A Mexican Standoff"

At the JFK Vermont/Quebec border some years ago . . . I was crossing into the states on Christmas Eve. I flash my card to the old dude at the border, who proceeds to ask me my quantum. After giving the double digits, he wants to know if it is on my paternal or maternal side. When I tell him maternal, he informs me that my 50 percent needs to be on my paternal side in order to enjoy free circulation to the states.

He then (like all white people) takes the opportunity to talk about himself for a while and tell me how his grandmother was from "Kan-a-wa-ki" and how he should be entitled to a card, and why can't he have one.

Fucking nuts.

Finally, I hit him with my US citizenship and inform him that I am a US citizen by birth and would like to know under what provision is he denying me reentry into the country.

He concedes and lets me pass, grudgingly.

However, as I'm leaving his vision, he phones ahead to the Vermont state troopers telling them he believes I am smuggling something across the border. About twenty-five minutes later, the Vermont state cops pull me over and pull *everything* out of my car onto the side of the road, going through Xmas presents and everything at 2 AM.

Ultimately, my license was expired, and since the cops had conducted a search of my vehicle against my wishes, we agree to each look the other way and leave each other alone.

A true Mexican standoff.

"Sleepless in Seattle"

It was October 1998, and I was flying from Montreal to Vancouver on my way to Seattle to attend the National Association of Broadcasters annual convention. Traveling with me was my good friend J.D., also from Kahnawàike.

After making the long walk across the Vancouver airport to catch our departing plane, we were ready to make the standard pass through customs to enter in the US. Greeting us was a man in his late thirties, who wore a thick "NASCAR-style" mustache, had hair parted down the middle, and looked to be about twenty to twenty-five pounds overweight. He had the skin tone of somebody who had not worked outside of an office for at least ten years. As per the usual protocol, both J and I handed over our status cards when asked for a form of photo ID.

The customs agent was satisfied with J's and promptly handed it back to him; however, when he received mine, his tone began to change. He then asked me what my blood quantum was, and I responded, "Fifty percent."

"On your mother or your father's side?" he asked.

"My mother's," I responded.

He then took my card and sternly directed both J and I to take a seat. The agent then went into a back office and did not reappear as soon as I had expected.

After about twenty minutes had passed, it was clear that we were about to miss our connecting flight.

When he returned, he called me forward and asked if I had a letter from my "Tribal Council" stating that I was indeed a member of the community.

"I've never had any need for such a letter," I responded.

"Without that letter, I can't let you pass through."

He then went on to say that he was a "Cherokee," and in his "tribe" everyone needs a letter if they want to pass through the border. I told him I am not a Cherokee—I am a Mohawk, and my freedom to pass through the border is guaranteed by the Jay Treaty.

"Yes, I know about your 'Jay Treaty,' but that's only good for your area in New York State."

I was getting pretty upset by this point, realizing that this guy has his own membership issues and is now making very liberal interpretations of our right to free passage.

"Then you would know that nowhere in the Jay Treaty is mention made of our ability to pass exclusively through the eastern corridor" was my answer.

"Be that as it may, unless you show me something else, I can't let you pass through."

Realizing that I still had my CBC [Canadian Broadcasting Corporation] Reporter ID on me, I said, yes I *do* have one more piece of ID and it is issued by the federal government, indicating that I have passed through their security clearance.

I then slid the card across the counter, and he looked puzzled for a split second and swiftly disappeared into the back office again. This time I could see him talking with a supervisor behind venetian blinds.

J.D. just looked up at me from his seat and shook his head in bewilderment. Upon his return, he gave me back my CBC ID and said that his supervisor was satisfied.

As we left the desk though, his last words were "Make sure you get that letter from your chief, or next time it might not be so easy."

Fucking "Cherokees."

Ultimately, we were held for an hour and some change and were able to catch a connecting flight later that afternoon.

These stories join the multitude circulating in Haudenosaunee territories on border experience, border trouble, border nonsense, the "bullshit" that we go through when we cross the border. The ongoing "bullshit" referenced in the epigraph was heightened after 9/11, at the very start of my research, when our rights were constructed, along with those of others, as a threat to national security and our forms of self-identification (and formal identification by the state) became subjected to greater scrutiny. "Status cards" issued by Canada and the United States attesting to our recognition as Indians would no longer suffice; our traditional "red cards" or passports deemed not up to security standard; our bodies, narratives, and arguments then folded into the seemingly newer threat to settler sovereignty and security—the illegal alien, the always-possible terrorist—rendering perhaps all bodies with color as border transgressors with the presumed intent to harm.

These post-9/11 anxieties have a deeper history. The legal underpinnings of these exchanges and the interpretive gymnastics that they entail in day-to-day border crossing will be contextualized throughout the course of this chapter. But suffice it to say for now that both Danny and I were committed to having our Mohawk identity and, by extension, our Jay Treaty rights, upheld from the moment we attempted to cross to the moment we finally did cross the border. This was made difficult by the interpretive spin on the Jay Treaty (as limited to the Northeast, as gendered, and racialized) that was put forth by particular guards.

Why are we so inspected? Why does Danny maintain and continue to assert this form of identification, and the law that confirms it, in the face of such inconvenience? Why would I do the same, and argue—with a stranger no less—loudly, vociferously, in public? Here we move from the textual domain of procedural, fetishized culture in anthropological productions of the Iroquois (as tradition) to another mode of representation. The Iroquois becomes, in the public eye, something else, "Mohawk," and that Mohawk is lawless—perhaps especially so after 9/11. Settler law is one of several keys to this interpretation, which, in these border-crossing stories, Danny invokes and the agents of the settler state ignore.

*** Political subjects are, to some extent, supposed to stay still, or to move with permission, according to one law: settler law that authorizes Canada or the United States to govern. Yet when the settler law actually allows these subjects mobility, then their actions must be curtailed, especially perhaps in states of "exception," in what is presumed to be a time of danger so profound that rights have to be monitored, abridged, and suspended.

The continuity of Indigenous self-descriptions during these times and the defense of this identity as a Mohawk owe to a sense of self and to the history of Mohawk people's recognition *as just those people* in the law.* * * Although Mohawks such as Daniel are border crossers, they are not border *transgressors*, because they have this unique temporal and rights-based relation to the nation-states of the United States and Canada. This relation is temporal because the Haudenosaunee predate both political regimes. Their unique legal and historical arrangements with these regimes reflect the importance of this temporal arrangement.* * * It is also because of this temporal relationship to these settler regimes that the geopolitical boundary of the United States–Canada border actually transgresses *them*.

*   *   *

When I stand at the border guard's counter and present myself in terms that are *not* * * * "spatialized" into settler terrains or colluding easily with one fully recognized citizenship or another, I am pulling up these histories into this critical moment of translation, and possibility. *Will I get to cross, to get where I am going? Can I get through this and have the moral sense of what is right or wrong, upheld? Will I have this political authority that I answer to respected? Will I lose all respect for you? Will I keep cool if I do?* The same applies to countless others who slow down lines, sit in detention rooms; who get sneered at, otherwise inspected, or completely demobilized when they do not proffer up the easy answer. The problem is, an easy answer does not exist in the history that upholds these ethnographic moments, the perception of Mohawk mobility as already a crime, a contravention of the fixity of place, borders, and settled states.

ENGAGING THE TEXT, ENGAGING THE WORLD

- What is the Jay Treaty and why is it important in this conversation about border crossings?

- Simpson and her colleagues frequently encounter detentions, interrogations, inspections, and delays when using their tribal identity passbooks at the border. Why do they "continue to assert this form of identification, and the law that confirms it, in the face of such inconvenience"?

- Why did being encouraged by a border guard to apply for a green card push Simpson "over the edge of civility and patience"?

- Why does Simpson say that conducting ethnography in anger is such a powerful tool?

- The United States and Canada are rarely discussed as colonial states or settler states in contemporary history or politics. Does this reframing push you to rethink the experience of Native peoples in these countries?

- By including her own personal stories in her ethnography, Simpson engages in the anthropological practice of reflexivity—reflecting on how her own experience and position shape her fieldwork. What are the benefits and complications of bringing one's own experience to the foreground in ethnographic writing?

7
Gender

Questions of **gender**—that is, the characteristics associated with being a woman or man in a particular culture and the ways those characteristics intersect with dynamics of power—are central to the practice of anthropology. Over the last forty years, **gender studies**—research into understanding who we are as men and women—has become one of the most significant subfields of anthropology. Indeed, anthropologists consider the ways in which gender is constructed to be a central element in every aspect of human culture, including sexuality, health, family, religion, economics, politics, sports, and individual identity formation.

Much of what we stereotypically consider to be "natural" male or female behavior—driven by biology—turns out, upon more careful inspection, to be imposed by cultural expectations of how men and women should behave. To help explore the relationship between the biological and cultural aspects of being men and women, anthropologists distinguish between sex and gender. **Sex**, from an anthropological viewpoint, refers to the observable physical differences between male and female human beings, especially the biological differences related to human reproduction. Gender is composed of the expectations of thought and behavior that each culture assigns to people of different sexes.

Humans are born with biological sex, but we learn to be women and men. From the moment of birth we begin to learn culture, including how to walk, talk, eat, dress, think, practice religion, raise children, respond to violence, and express our emotions like a man or a woman. We learn what kinds of behavior are perceived as masculine or feminine. Thus, anthropologists refer to the **cultural construction of gender**. Over a lifetime, gender becomes a powerful, and mostly invisible, framework that shapes the way we see ourselves and others. Our relationships with others become an elaborate gendered dance of playing, dating, mating, parenting, and loving that reinforces our learned ideas of masculinity and femininity and establishes differing roles and expectations. Gender is also a potent cultural system through which we organize our collective lives, not necessarily on the basis of merit or skill but on the constructed categories of what it means to be a man or a woman.

Recently, anthropologists have moved from focusing on gender roles toward examining **gender performance**. Gender roles can mistakenly be seen as reflecting stable, fixed identities that fall in one of two opposite extremes—male or female. But anthropologists increasingly see gender as a continuum of behaviors that range between masculine and feminine. Rather than being something fixed in the psyche, gender is an identity that is expressed through action. Indeed, people regularly make choices—conscious and unconscious—about how they will express their gender identity, for whom, and in what context. This is why we say that gender is performed. Evelyn Blackwood's article "Tombois in West Sumatra" explores how gender and sexuality are constructed and performed in an Indonesian community and how they intersect in ways that may be surprising to someone raised in North America.

The emphasis in gender studies on the cultural construction of gender challenges anthropologists to explore the dynamics of specific cultures to understand what processes serve to construct gender in each society. Today anthropologists are asking questions like these: What are the processes that create **gender stratification**—an unequal distribution of power in which gender shapes who has access to a group's resources, opportunities, rights, and privileges? What are the gender stereotypes and gender ideologies that support a gendered system of power?

Gender stereotypes are widely held and powerful, preconceived notions about the attributes of, differences between, and proper roles for women and men in a culture. Men, for instance, may be stereotyped as more aggressive, whereas women might be seen as more nurturing. These stereotypes create influential assumptions about what men and women might expect from one another. **Gender ideology** is a set of cultural ideas—usually stereotypical—about men's and women's essential character, capabilities, and value that consciously or unconsciously promote and justify gender stratification. Gender stereotypes and ideologies vary from culture to culture, though their effects may appear similar when viewed through a global lens. Emily Martin, whose article "The Egg and the Sperm" appears here, has explored the ways in which cultural ideas about gender—that is, gender ideologies—have influenced the way biologists have understood, described, and taught about human reproduction, and consequently how misrepresentative scientific language has reinforced gender inequality.

Tombois in West Sumatra

Evelyn Blackwood

Evelyn Blackwood conducted fieldwork on gender and sexuality among the Minangkabau people of Indonesia. There she found that gender and sexual identities, like other identities in their lives, were fluid, not fixed. She describes an ongoing social process in which individual identities were shaped and reshaped in relationship to and often in resistance to the dominant gender ideologies of the society. Minangkabau are not monolithic.

Hegemony—the way dominant ideas define what is permissible, even thinkable, and the way new meanings and identities emerge—is key to Blackwood's analysis of gender and sexuality. Her intimate research among people identifying as *lesbi* (lesbian) or *tomboi* (tomboy) explores the cultural construction of gender and sexuality and the ways in which *tombois* challenge a hegemonic system in which the only legitimate grounds for gender identity is biological sex. Instead they choose to perform their gender identities in ways that defy expectations, placing themselves in conflict with cultural norms, values, and even mental maps of reality held by many Minangkabau people and Indonesians in general.

During anthropological fieldwork on gender and agricultural development in West Sumatra, Indonesia, in 1989–90, I pursued a secondary research goal of investigating the situation of "lesbians" in the area. I met a small number of "women" who seemed butch in the way that term was used in the United States at the time.[1] In West Sumatra these individuals are called *lesbi* or *tomboi* (derived from the English words *lesbian* and *tomboy*). Although there are similarities, a tomboi in West Sumatra is different from a butch in the United States, not surprisingly, for social constructionists have shown that sexual practices reflect particular historical and cultural contexts (Elliston 1995; Weston 1993). The term *tomboi* is used for a female acting in the manner of men *(gaya laki-laki)*.

From Evelyn Blackwood. 1998. "*Tombois* in West Sumatra: Constructing Masculinity and Erotic Desire." *Cultural Anthropology* 13(4): 491–521. Some of the author's notes have been omitted.

1. I put *women* in quotes to problematize the use of "woman" for individuals who are female bodied but do not identify as women. As I use it, *female* refers to physical sex characteristics, and *woman* refers to a set of social behaviors and characteristics that are culturally constructed and attributed to female bodies. I use "women" in this instance because at the time of first meeting, I assumed these individuals were women.

Through my relationship with a tomboi in West Sumatra, I learned some of the ways in which my concept of "lesbian" was not the same as my partner's, even though we were both, I thought, women-loving women.

This article explores how tombois in West Sumatra both shape their identities from and resist local, national, and transnational narratives of gender and sexuality.* * *

Theories concerning the intersection of genders and sexualities provide considerable insights into, and a variety of labels for, gendered practices cross-culturally (see, for example, Bullough, Bullough, and Elias 1997; Devor 1989; Epstein and Straub 1991; Herdt 1994; Jacobs, Thomas, and Lang 1997; Ramet 1996; Roscoe 1991). In opposition to biological determinism, social constructionists argue that gender is not an essence preceding social expression but an identity that is constructed and fluid.* * * Learning, piecing together, adopting, or shaping identities (such as race, class, gender, or sexuality) is an ongoing social process through which individuals negotiate, produce, and stabilize a sense of who they are. These identities are shaped and redefined in relation to dominant gender ideologies that claim constancy and immutability.

*　　*　　*

Hegemonic or dominant gender ideologies define what is permissible, even thinkable; they serve as the standard against which actions are measured, producing codes, regulations, and laws that perpetuate a particular ideology. Dominant ideologies generate discourses that stabilize, normalize, and naturalize gender (Yanagisako and Delaney 1995); yet within any dominant ideology there are emergent meanings, processes, and identities vying for legitimacy, authority, and recognition (Williams 1977).

*　　*　　*

Misreading Identities

*　　*　　*

West Sumatra is the home of the Minangkabau people, one of the many ethnic groups that have been incorporated into the state of Indonesia. The Minangkabau, with a population over 4 million people, are rural agriculturalists, urban merchants, traders, migrants, and wage laborers. They are also Muslim and matrilineal. Being matrilineal means that, despite the fact that they are devout Muslims, inheritance and property pass from mother to daughter.* * *

Far from being an isolated region, the province is well integrated into global trade networks. Rice and other agricultural products produced in the region are traded well beyond Sumatra. Many Minangkabau men and women work for years in cities outside West Sumatra, providing further connections to the national and international scene. Villages have anywhere from 15 percent to 25 percent of their residents on temporary out-migration. Despite out-migration, many villages maintain a rich cultural life based on kinship ties; most social and economic activities are centered in and organized by matrilineally related groups. Other villages are more urban oriented, particularly where migration has led to reliance on outside sources of income.

I had no trouble locating males in West Sumatra who were *bancis*, a term that is defined in Echols and Shadily's Indonesian-English dictionary (1989) as "effeminate or transvestite homosexual[s]" (see also Oetomo 1991). This definition links bancis' gender identity (effeminate or transvestite) and sexuality (homosexual). In the district capital I met several bancis or *bencong*, as they are referred to in West Sumatra. Bancis are obvious to local people, who comment on their appearance or taunt them when they walk down the street. Although bancis do not carry themselves as men do, they do not carry themselves exactly like women, either; rather, they behave in the exaggerated style of fashion models, a style that in itself is a caricature of femininity, one they have been exposed to through fashion magazines and televised beauty pageants. Their sexual partners are indistinguishable from other men and are generally thought to be bisexual, or *biseks* in local parlance, as these men might also have relationships with women.

My search for "lesbians" was more difficult. I asked some high school–aged acquaintances of mine, who had friends who were bancis, whether they knew any lesbis—the term they used with me—in the area. I was told that there were several but that those women were worried about being found out. I was given the impression that such women were very coarse and tough, more like men than women. After several months in West Sumatra, one of my young friends introduced me to Dayan.[2] S/he, however, did not fit the stereotype.[3] In hir midtwenties, s/he appeared to me to be boyish-looking in hir T-shirt, shorts, and short hair, but s/he did not seem masculine or tough in any way that I could perceive. I consequently felt quite certain that I had met another "lesbian." The term *lesbi* that my friends used also offered familiar footing to an outsider from the United States.

Negotiating our identities was a perplexing process in which we each tried to position the other within different cultural categories: butch-femme and *cowok-cewek. Butch-femme*

---

2. I use fictitious names for the individuals mentioned in this article. Dayan (pronounced "Dai-yon") lived with an older married sister in a small town about an hour from where I lived. I visited Dayan mostly on weekends at the sister's house.

3. Although I have used the pronoun *she* in the past to refer to a tomboi (Blackwood 1995a), at this point in my thinking "she" and "her/him" seem inadequate to represent the complexity of the tomboi identity, particularly because of the connotations an English-speaking reader brings to them. The Indonesian language provides no guidance in this matter because its pronouns are gender neutral. The third-person pronoun for both women and men is *dia*. I have chosen to use the pronominal constructions *s/he* (for "she/he"), *hir* (for "her/his" and "her/him"), and *hirself* (for "herself/himself"). These pronouns are gaining currency within the transgender movement in the United States (see Wilchins 1997). By doing so, I am not making any claims about the "gender" of tombois. These terms should not be read as suggesting that the tomboi is a transgendered person or some combination of masculine/feminine or not-masculine/not-feminine. Rather, by using these terms I want to unsettle the reader's assumptions about gender and gender binaries.

is an American term that refers to a masculine-acting woman and her feminine partner.[4] *Cowok-cewek* are Indonesian words that mean "man" and "woman" but have the connotation of "guy" and "girl." It is the practice of female couples to refer to a tomboi and hir feminine partner as cowok and cewek. (Most Indonesians are unfamiliar with this use of the two terms.) In both the United States and West Sumatra, female couples rely on and draw from dominant cultural images of masculinity and femininity to make sense of their relationships. These similarities were enough to cause both my partner and myself to assume that we fell within each other's cultural model, an assumption I was forced to give up.

Dayan operated under the assumption that I was cewek, despite the inconsistencies of my behavior, because that fit with hir understanding of hirself in relation to hir lovers, who had all been cewek. For instance, my failure to cook for hir or organize hir birthday party were quite disappointing to Dayan. On another occasion, when I visited an American friend of mine at his hotel, s/he accused me of sleeping with him. In hir experience, ceweks are attracted to men and also like sex better with men. Yet, as the one with the cash in the relationship, I was allowed to pay for things despite it not being proper cewek behavior. In rural Minangkabau households, men are expected to give their wives their cash earnings. * * * Perhaps Dayan justified my actions on the grounds that I was an American with considerably more income than s/he. Certainly s/he was willing to entertain the possibility of my difference from hir understanding of ceweks.

One day I overheard the following exchange between Dayan and a tomboi friend. Dayan's friend asked if I was cewek, to which Dayan replied, "Of course."

"Can she cook?"

"Well, not really."

The friend exclaimed, "How can that be, a woman who can't cook? What are you going to do?"

I was surprised to find that my gender identity was so critical to this (macho) tomboi. The fact that I had a relationship with Dayan said very little to me about what kind of woman I was. I interpreted my relationship with Dayan as reflective of my sexual identity (a desire for other women).

For my part, I assumed that Dayan was a butch, more or less in congruence with the way I understood butches to be in the United States in the 1980s, that is, as masculine-acting women who desired feminine partners. S/he always dressed in jeans or shorts and T- or polo shirts, a style that was not at odds with the casual wear of many lesbians in the United States. One day, however, I heard a friend call hir "co," short for cowok. I knew what *cowok* meant in that context; it meant s/he was seen as a "guy" by hir close friends, which did not fit my notion of butch. I heard another female couple use the terms *mami* (mom) and *papi* (pop) for each other, so I started calling Dayan papi in private, which

---

4. Nestle describes butches more eloquently as follows: "a butch lesbian wearing men's clothes in the 1950s was not a man wearing men's clothes; she was a woman creating an original style to signal to other women what she was capable of doing—taking erotic responsibility" (1992:141).

made hir very pleased. But when I told Dayan s/he was pretty, s/he looked hurt. Then I realized my mistake: "pretty" *(cantik)* is what a woman is called, not a man. Dayan wanted to be called "handsome" *(gagah)*, as befits a masculine self.

Dayan's personal history underscored hir feelings that s/he was a man. S/he said s/he felt extremely isolated and "deviant" when s/he was growing up and acted more like a boy. People in hir town called hir *bujang gadis*, an Indonesian term meaning boy-girl (*bujang* means bachelor or unmarried young man, and *gadis* means unmarried young woman) that used to refer to an effeminate male or a masculine female (although not much in use currently). As a teenager, s/he only had desire for girls. S/he bound hir breasts because s/he did not want them to be noticeable. They did not fit with hir self-image. As a young adult, s/he hung out with young men, smoking and drinking with them. S/he said s/he felt like a man and wanted to be one. I finally had to admit to myself that tombois were not the Indonesian version of butches. They were men.

Cowok-Cewek

I met two other tombois in West Sumatra, Agus and Bujang, who were both friends of Dayan. The first time I met Agus, s/he was wearing a big khaki shirt and jeans; even I could not mistake the masculine attitude s/he projected. S/he wore short hair that was swept back on the sides. S/he carried herself like a "man," smoked cigarettes all the time, played cards, and made crude jokes. S/he struck me as coarse and tough like cowoks were said to be. Dayan admired Agus and thought hir the more handsome of the two.

Dayan told me that Agus, who was approximately thirty years old, had only been with women, never with a man. S/he had had several lovers, all beautiful and very feminine, according to Dayan. One former lover married and had two children, but Dayan thought Agus probably still saw her occasionally. Agus spent much of hir time with hir lover, Yul, who lived in a large house only a few minutes by bus outside of Payakumbuh. Yul, who was in her early fifties, was a widow with grown children, some of whom were still living at home. After Agus started living with her, Yul wanted her children to call Agus papi. She said she did not care if her children disapproved of her relationship. If her children did not act respectfully toward Agus, Yul would get angry with them and not give them spending money when they asked for it. But one of Yul's daughters argued that because Agus is not married to her mother, s/he should not be part of the family and be treated better than her own father had been. The frequent squabbling and lack of privacy at Yul's house was too much for Agus, who spent less and less time with Yul and finally moved back to hir sister's house nearby.

The other tomboi I met, Bujang, was at that time living at hir mother's in a rural village. Bujang seemed quiet and somber. Boyish features and oversized clothes that hid hir breasts made it impossible for me to tell if s/he was male or female. We talked very little because hir mother was there. Later Dayan told me Bujang's story. Hir mother had forced hir to marry; s/he had had a son but then left hir husband. S/he had a lover (who, Dayan said, was feminine) and moved with her to Jakarta, where they lived for some time to avoid the prying eyes of relatives. Under continued pressure from hir family, however, and lacking adequate income, Bujang finally returned home with hir son, leaving hir lover temporarily in hopes of finding a better way to support hir family. Hir cewek lover, however, eventually married a man.

Partners of tombois fit within the norms of femininity and maintain a "feminine" gender identity. Their sexual relationships with tombois do not mark them as different; their gender is not in question.[5] Like an earlier generation of femmes in the United States, tombois' partners are nearly invisible (see Nestle 1992). Yul, Agus's lover, was feminine in appearance. She had shoulder-length permed hair, wore makeup and lipstick, and had long fingernails. Yul had never been with a tomboi before she met Agus. She had not even thought about sleeping with one before. Although she sometimes wore slacks and smoked, even hung out at the local coffee shop with Agus to play cards, she was called *ibu* (mother) by men and mami by Agus. No one would think she was a tomboi just because she was partners with one; she was cewek. As a cewek, she adhered to the hegemonic standards of femininity in her appearance and behavior.

Although the fact that they sleep with tombois makes them "bad" women in the eyes of local people, for premarital sex and adultery are disapproved of for women, ceweks are still women. Even tombois expect ceweks to have greater desire for men because that is seen as natural for their sex. Dayan once said, "Unfortunately, they will leave you for a man if one comes along they like. It's our fate that we love women who leave us." No one seems to consider a cewek's desire for tombois problematic; she remains a woman who desires men.

Performing Masculinity

Tombois model masculinity in their behavior, attitudes, interests, and desires. Dayan often spoke of being *berani* (brave), a trait commonly associated with men, as an important part of who s/he was. S/he attributed the ability to be a tomboi to being berani; it meant, among other things, that one could withstand family pressures to get married. S/he said the ones that are berani become cowok. In talking about Agus's situation with hir lover Yul, Dayan commented that Agus was not brave enough to sleep at Yul's house anymore. S/he thought that Agus should not let Yul's children force hir to move out. Agus was not being as brave as Dayan thought a person should be in order to live up to the cowok identity.

Tombois pride themselves on doing things like men. They know how to play *koa*, a card game like poker, which is thought to be a men's game. They smoke as men do; rural women rarely take up smoking. They go out alone, especially at night, which is a prerogative of men. Like men, they drive motorcycles; women ride behind (women do

---

5. This practice is similar to one found in some Latin American cultures in which men who take the dominant (insertor) role in sex with another man are not marked as different because of their sexual behavior. They are seen as normatively masculine (see Carrier 1995; Parker 1986).

drive motorcycles, but in mixed couples men always drive). Dayan arrived at my house on a motorcycle one time with a man friend riding behind. Like Minangkabau husbands, they move into and out of their partners' houses. Dayan said s/he often gets taken for a man if someone only sees hir walking from behind. Sometimes in public spaces, particularly in urban areas, s/he is called *mas*, a contemporary Indonesian term of address for a man. The thought that a tomboi might marry a man or bear a child like a woman seemed unconscionable to Dayan. S/he had little sympathy for Bujang, who was forced to marry, saying, "This person is cowok! How could s/he have done that, especially having a baby. That's wrong."

The taunting and joking between Agus and Dayan reflect one way in which their masculinity is negotiated. Agus's teasing questions to Dayan about whether I was a proper cewek is one example. Another incident occurred one evening when we were hanging out with Agus at a coffee shop. S/he had been playing cards (koa) with some men for awhile and it was getting late. Dayan told Agus s/he wanted to leave. Agus said tauntingly, "You're a guy *[laki-laki]!* How come you're afraid of the night?" * * *

The sparring and comparing of masculine selves reveal one of the ways tombois create, confirm, and naturalize their identities as men. The teasing helps to reinforce and interrogate the masculine code of behavior. Their actions suggest that being cowok is an identity one can be better or worse at, more or less of; it is something that must be practiced and claimed—which is not to say that it is inauthentic, for no gender identity is more or less authentic than another, but, rather, is more or less an approximation of the hegemonic ideological domain accorded to that gender (see Butler 1991). As any man does, they are negotiating their culture's ideology of masculinity.

Tombois construct their desire for and relationships with women on the model of masculinity. The oft-repeated statement that their lovers are all feminine underscores their position as men who attract the "opposite sex." Because I was Dayan's partner, hir friend assumed that I was a particular gender, in this case the feminine woman. Their use of gendered terms of endearment, *mami* and *papi*, and the terms *cowok* and *cewek* reflect tombois' understanding of themselves as situated within the category "men" (laki-laki). Tombois' adherence to the model of masculinity and their insistence on replicating the heterosexuality of a man-woman couple point to the dominance of the normative model of gender and heterosexuality.

*   *   *

Minangkabau Ideology and Oppositional Genders

Although the Minangkabau people are considered a single ethnic group, there are many Minangkabaus—many "fantasies" of Minangkabau ethnic identity* * *. Minangkabau people are urban, rural, educated, and devout; they are civil servants, migrants, and farmers. Their identities vary according to their exposure to media, state ideology, Western-oriented education, and religious fundamentalism. The multiplicity of identities attests to the complex processes at work in contemporary Indonesia as individuals and ethnic groups situate themselves within the postcolonial state.

The construction of gender in West Sumatra is equally complex.* * *

How does [the Minangkabau] sex/gender system induce the tomboi to claim a masculine identity? Why is (or was) this the form that transgression took? * * * To answer these questions, one needs to look at the way tombois are treated within the dominant culture. Tombois imagine themselves masculine, and as such are tolerated to a certain extent, but there is a contradiction between the way tombois define themselves and the way others define them. Tombois are under great pressure to carry out family obligations, to marry a man and be reproductive. Dayan said that every time s/he saw hir mother, she asked when s/he was getting married. Hir mother worried that a woman could not support herself alone; she needs a husband. Hir mother's statement was a clear refusal of Dayan's self-definition as a man, a refusal that typifies the attitude of others within the local community.

The constant pressure to get married and the threat of forcible marriage reveal the way a person's body determines a person's gender. In this system the hegemonic, legitimate gender is based on one's sex; gender is not considered an "identity," performed or otherwise. In many ways this ideological rendering is similar to the dominant sex/gender paradigm in European and U.S. societies: gender is believed to derive naturally from physiological sex; a "real" woman possesses female genitalia, desires men, bears children, and acts like a woman. A tomboi, according to the Minangkabau sex/gender system, is a "woman" even though s/he enacts a masculine gender, hence the refusal to legitimate that enactment and the insistence on the fulfillment of hir reproductive duties. Denying the female body is impermissible. Although tombois insist on being treated as men by their partners, their masculinity lacks cultural validation. Society insists on the priority of the body in determining gender.

Dayan said s/he played too rough and enjoyed boys' activities when s/he was little, so people called hir bujang gadis, a label that meant others perceived hir as masculine. At that time s/he had no other recourse but to assume s/he was a boy. Without other options available, and seeing that hir behavior falls outside the bounds of proper femininity, the tomboi denies hir female body, binding hir breasts so that the physical evidence will not betray hir. S/he produces the only other gender recognizable in the sex/gender system, the masculine gender. That interpretation would accord with the hegemonic cultural ideology, in which masculinity is male—with a twist, a twist that s/he continually has to substantiate and rectify in hir own mind and to others. Dominant ideologies, as noted by Poole, are "enshrined in prominent, powerful and pervasive stereotypes . . . and deployed in centrally institutionalized or otherwise significantly marked arenas of social action" (1996: 198). The hegemonic persuasiveness of such ideologies means that other forms of identity are unimaginable. Consequently, some masculine females appropriate the masculine gender because it is the most persuasive model available.

*   *   *

Plural Identities

I want to pull together the various threads of my argument to reveal how one particular tomboi is situated within these narratives of gender, sexuality, and culture.* * *

* * * A product of the postcolonial Indonesian school system, [Dayan] graduated from a technical high school with ambitions for a career. But, like many others in the working class, s/he struggles to find work. S/he is a member of hir mother's lineage but lives with hir older sister on their deceased father's land in a community that is only 15 minutes from the district capital, where some of hir brothers work.* * *

Dayan's location on the fringes of urban culture helps to explain hir rejection of Minangkabau womanhood. Raised in a family with little matrilineal money or land and thus dependent on the father's family to provide land and house, s/he, hir mother, and hir sister have lost some of the crucial connections that authorize women's power. Further, because not all daughters benefit equally or are treated favorably by their mothers, some, like Dayan, may never attain the power of a senior woman. * * *

Like many youth growing up, Dayan has been influenced by divergent ideologies of womanhood. Educated in the "modern" school system, Minangkabau youth have received little state validation for the importance of Minangkabau women. Recent local efforts to provide more education about Minangkabau culture have only highlighted the role of men as "traditional" leaders (see Blackwood 1995b). Schoolgirls learn "proper" gender roles and are indoctrinated in the importance of becoming wives who serve their husbands' needs. They are inundated through media with representations of urban, middle-class, docile women. Yet with the increased availability of education, civil service, and other wage-labor jobs in the last 30 years, young women now have the right to choose their spouses or to pursue higher education and careers in urban areas. * * * To these young women, the Minangkabau world of powerful elite women, wrapped up in * * * ritual ceremonies and hard work in the rice fields, seems distant and old-fashioned. Thus, the images of womanhood with which Dayan is familiar underscore the burden of privilege—of marriage, children, and lineage priorities—and the fear of dependence—of being a wife under the husband's control. * * *

The masculinities that tombois construct reflect their different locations in the global market as well as the local community. Hegemonic masculinity is represented and enacted differently in the village, in urban areas, and on movie screens. It also is a hybrid of local, national, and transnational representations. In rural villages a young man may smoke, drink, gamble, and use coarse language, but he is also admonished to be strong, industrious, respectful of his elders, and responsible to his lineage and his wife's family. The bravado and coarseness of young urban (poor, working-class) men in Indonesia is far from the politeness and respectfulness of rural men. While Dayan's masculinity reflects more of the village, Agus's interpretation reflects a combination of the coarse masculinity and male privilege of urban areas. Dayan told me that when Agus is at Yul's house, "s/he expects to be served and won't do anything for hir wife except give her money." This interpretation of a man's role could be drawn from middle-class Indonesian images of manhood but also seems to selectively draw on older representations of high-ranking Minangkabau husbands who, as guests in their wives' houses (male duolocal residence), were served by their wives. Agus's "macho" behavior, like the banci's performance of a fashion model persona, presents an extreme style of masculinity, one that is easily read as masculine by others.

Dayan's experience of lesbian and gay discourse creates another distinction between hirself and Agus. Dayan described Agus as an old-fashioned tomboi, one who "is like a man and won't be any other way." Hir statement implies that s/he sees Agus as holding onto certain normative ideas of gender that contemporary Indonesian lesbians no longer find satisfying. S/he said further that "Agus has never been out of the *kampung* [village]," implying that had s/he been, Agus might see other models of lesbian relations and quit trying to be so much like a man.

In the past few years, Dayan has lived in Jakarta for one to two years at a time. Both at home and in Jakarta hir friends are cowok-cewek, but these friends also know about the Euro-American model of lesbian identity. * * * As with the proliferation of transgendered identities in the United States (Bolin 1994; Cromwell in press), tomboi identity is constantly being negotiated and redefined in response to local, national, and transnational processes.

Conclusion

Identity for tombois in West Sumatra at this point in time is * * * a mix of local, national, and transnational identities. If their identity growing up was shaped by local cultural forces that emphasized oppositional genders, their movement between cities and rural areas means that they have been exposed to other models of sexuality and gender identity that they have used to construct a new sense of themselves. The complexities of their gender identity make it impossible to align tombois with any one category, whether "woman," "lesbian," or "transgendered person."

*   *   *

At the national level the tomboi can be read * * * in much the same manner as European and North American lesbians, gay men, and transgendered people are said to resist dominant gender ideology. Although the Indonesian state enforces heterosexuality, wage labor and capitalism create a space for the tomboi to live as a single female. The discourse of modernity—the importance of education, careers, and middle-class status—legitimates models other than motherhood and femininity for females. Though the tomboi remains a deviant, s/he is also finding more room to negotiate a future.

At the same time, other models of sexuality and gender are becoming visible in a globalized world. * * * Where sexuality was embedded in the ideology of oppositional genders (man-woman, cowok-cewek, banci–*laki asli* [real man]), sexual "identity" and the possibility of sexuality between two women or two men are emergent cultural practices. Desiring women is being rewritten for some as a product of the variability of human sexuality rather than the "natural" urge of the male body and the prerogative of "men."

ENGAGING THE TEXT, ENGAGING THE WORLD

- How has the economic activity of some Minangkabau people, particularly out-migration to urban areas, affected local ideas of gender and sexuality?

- Why does Blackwood use the pronouns "s/he" and "hir" rather than he or she, his or her?

- Compare the differences between *cowok–cewek* and *Butch–femme*. How did these different cultural understandings of sexuality and its relationship to gender create misunderstandings between Blackwood and her partner, Dayan?

- Have you had an experience in which you felt you had tested your culture's norms of masculinity or femininity? How did it go? How did you feel?

- How do *tombois* reinforce and challenge Minangkabau expectations of masculine behavior?

- Debates have erupted over gender identity and bathroom usage in the United States. Do you see parallels in the Indonesian situation, particularly in the ways cultural hegemony about gender identity are promoted and challenged?

- Anthropologists rarely discuss romantic relations in the field. Were you surprised to learn that Blackwood had a romantic partner while conducting fieldwork? How did her relationship shape her understanding of gender and sexuality among the Minangkabau people?

- Blackwood's "coming out" in the field reveals the complex experience of real people meeting across cultures trying to understand one another in the fullness of their humanity. How did Blackwood's revelation shape the way you read the text?

The Egg and the Sperm
Emily Martin

Gender myths and metaphors in human reproduction

In this article, Emily Martin discusses what she calls the fairy tale of the egg and the sperm. By examining the college biology textbooks most widely used at the time of her research, Martin found that the distinct roles of eggs and sperm were described in stereotypically gendered ways, even when those

From Emily Martin. 1991. "The Egg and the Sperm: How Science Has Constructed a Romance Based on Stereotypical Male-Female Roles." *Signs* 16(3): 485–501.

descriptions did not match up with scientific findings. Images of the egg and sperm were instead based on cultural stereotypes of male and female. Moreover, the scientific language of biology has promoted these gender stereotypes. Martin warns that by reading stereotypical feminine and masculine behavior into our accounts of eggs and sperm, we enshrine these gender roles in nature—we make them seem natural. When this narrative becomes a common description of nature, it reinforces culturally constructed gender patterns, roles, and hierarchies. It becomes part of a gender ideology that rationalizes inequality by claiming its roots in biology.

As an anthropologist, I am intrigued by the possibility that culture shapes how biological scientists describe what they discover about the natural world. If this were so, we would be learning about more than the natural world in high school biology class; we would be learning about cultural beliefs and practices as if they were part of nature. In the course of my research I realized that the picture of egg and sperm drawn in popular as well as scientific accounts of reproductive biology relies on stereotypes central to our cultural definitions of male and female. The stereotypes imply not only that female biological processes are less worthy than their male counterparts but also that women are less worthy than men. Part of my goal in writing this article is to shine a bright light on the gender stereotypes hidden within the scientific language of biology. Exposed in such a light, I hope they will lose much of their power to harm us.

Egg and Sperm: A Scientific Fairy Tale

At a fundamental level, all major scientific textbooks depict male and female reproductive organs as systems for the production of valuable substances, such as eggs and sperm.[1] In the case of women, the monthly cycle is described as being designed to produce eggs and prepare a suitable place for them to be fertilized and grown—all to the end of making babies. But the enthusiasm ends there. By extolling the female cycle as a productive enterprise, menstruation must necessarily be viewed as a failure. Medical texts describe menstruation as the "debris" of the uterine lining, the result of necrosis, or death of tissue. The descriptions imply that a system has gone awry, making products of no use, not to specification, unsalable, wasted, scrap. An illustration in a widely used medical text shows menstruation as a chaotic disintegration of form, complementing the many texts that describe it as "ceasing," "dying," "losing," "denuding," "expelling" (Guyton 1984, 624).

---

1. The textbooks I consulted are the main ones used in classes for undergraduate premedical students or medical students (or those held on reserve in the library for these classes) during the past few years at Johns Hopkins University. These texts are widely used at other universities in the country as well.

Male reproductive physiology is evaluated quite differently. One of the texts that sees menstruation as failed production employs a sort of breathless prose when it describes the maturation of sperm: "The mechanisms which guide the remarkable cellular transformation from spermatid to mature sperm remain uncertain.... Perhaps the most amazing characteristic of spermatogenesis is its sheer magnitude: the normal human male may manufacture several hundred million sperm per day" (Vander, Sherman, and Luciano 1980, 483–84). In the classic text *Medical Physiology*, edited by Vernon Mountcastle, the male/female, productive/destructive comparison is more explicit: "Whereas the female *sheds* only a single gamete each month, the seminiferous tubules *produce* hundreds of millions of sperm each day" (emphasis mine) (Mountcastle 1980, 2:1624). The female author of another text marvels at the length of the microscopic seminiferous tubules, which, if uncoiled and placed end to end, "would span almost one-third of a mile!" She writes, "In an adult male these structures produce millions of sperm cells each day." Later she asks, "How is this feat accomplished?" (Solomon 1983, 678). None of these texts expresses such intense enthusiasm for any female processes. It is surely no accident that the "remarkable" process of making sperm involves precisely what, in the medical view, menstruation does not: production of something deemed valuable.[2]

One could argue that menstruation and spermatogenesis are not analogous processes and, therefore, should not be expected to elicit the same kind of response. The proper female analogy to spermatogenesis, biologically, is ovulation. Yet ovulation does not merit enthusiasm in these texts either. Textbook descriptions stress that all of the ovarian follicles containing ova are already present at birth. Far from being *produced*, as sperm are, they merely sit on the shelf, slowly degenerating and aging like overstocked inventory: "At birth, normal human ovaries contain an estimated one million follicles [each], and no new ones appear after birth. Thus, in marked contrast to the male, the newborn female already has all the germ cells she will ever have. Only a few, perhaps 400, are destined to reach full maturity during her active productive life. All the others degenerate at some point in their development so that few, if any, remain by the time she reaches menopause at approximately 50 years of age" (Vander, Sherman, and Luciano 1980, 568). Note the "marked contrast" that this description sets up between male and female: the male, who continuously produces fresh germ cells, and the female, who has stockpiled germ cells by birth and is faced with their degeneration.

Nor are the female organs spared such vivid descriptions. One scientist writes in a newspaper article that a woman's ovaries become old and worn out from ripening eggs every month, even though the woman herself is still relatively young: "When you look through a laparoscope ... at an ovary that has been through hundreds of cycles, even in a superbly healthy American female, you see a scarred, battered organ" (Konner 1987, 22–23).

To avoid the negative connotations that some people associate with the female reproductive system, scientists could begin to describe male and female processes as

---

2. For elaboration, see Martin 1987, 27–53.

homologous. They might credit females with "producing" mature ova one at a time, as they're needed each month, and describe males as having to face problems of degenerating germ cells. This degeneration would occur throughout life among spermatogonia, the undifferentiated germ cells in the testes that are the long-lived, dormant precursors of sperm.

But the texts have an almost dogged insistence on casting female processes in a negative light. The texts celebrate sperm production because it is continuous from puberty to senescence, while they portray egg production as inferior because it is finished at birth. This makes the female seem unproductive, but some texts will also insist that it is she who is wasteful. In a section heading for *Molecular Biology of the Cell*, a best-selling text, we are told that "Oogenesis is wasteful." The text goes on to emphasize that of the seven million oogonia, or egg germ cells, in the female embryo, most degenerate in the ovary. Of those that do go on to become oocytes, or eggs, many also degenerate, so that at birth only two million eggs remain in the ovaries. Degeneration continues throughout a woman's life: by puberty 300,000 eggs remain, and only a few are present by menopause. "During the 40 or so years of a woman's reproductive life, only 400 to 500 eggs will have been released," the authors write. "All the rest will have degenerated. It is still a mystery why so many eggs are formed only to die in the ovaries" (Alberts et al. 1983, 795).

The real mystery is why the male's vast production of sperm is not seen as wasteful. Assuming that a man "produces" 100 million (10^8) sperm per day (a conservative estimate) during an average reproductive life of sixty years, he would produce well over two trillion sperm in his lifetime. Assuming that a woman "ripens" one egg per lunar month, or thirteen per year, over the course of her forty-year reproductive life, she would total five hundred eggs in her lifetime. But the word "waste" implies an excess, too much produced. Assuming two or three offspring, for every baby a woman produces, she wastes only around two hundred eggs. For every baby a man produces, he wastes more than one trillion (10^{12}) sperm.

How is it that positive images are denied to the bodies of women? A look at language—in this case, scientific language—provides the first clue. Take the egg and the sperm. It is remarkable how "femininely" the egg behaves and how "masculinely" the sperm. The egg is seen as large and passive. It does not *move* or *journey*, but passively "is transported," "is swept," (Guyton 1984, 619; Mountcastle 1980, 1609) or even "drifts" (Miller and Pelham 1984, 5) along the fallopian tube. In utter contrast, sperm are small, "streamlined," (Alberts et al. 1983, 796) and invariably active. They "deliver" their genes to the egg, "activate the developmental program of the egg," and have a "velocity" that is often remarked upon (Alberts et al. 1983, 796; Ganong 1975, 322). Their tails are "strong" and efficiently powered (Alberts et al. 1983, 796). Together with the forces of ejaculation, they can "propel the semen into the deepest recesses of the vagina" (Guyton 1984, 615). For this they need "energy," "fuel," (Solomon 1983, 683) so that with a "whip-lashlike motion and strong lurches" (Vander, Sherman, and Luciano 1985, 580) they can "burrow through the egg coat" (Alberts et al. 1983, 796) and "penetrate" it.[3]

---

3. All biology texts quoted above use the word "penetrate."

At its extreme, the age-old relationship of the egg and the sperm takes on a royal or religious patina. The egg coat, its protective barrier, is sometimes called its "vestments," a term usually reserved for sacred, religious dress. The egg is said to have a "corona," (Solomon 1983, 700) a crown, and to be accompanied by "attendant cells" (Beldecos et al. 1988). It is holy, set apart and above, the queen to the sperm's king. The egg is also passive, which means it must depend on sperm for rescue. Gerald Schatten and Helen Schatten liken the egg's role to that of Sleeping Beauty: "a dormant bride awaiting her mate's magic kiss," which instills the spirit that brings her to life" (Schatten and Schatten 1984). Sperm, by contrast, have a "mission," (Alberts et al. 1983, 796) which is to "move through the female genital tract in quest of the ovum" (Guyton 1984, 613). One popular account has it that the sperm carry out a "perilous journey" into the "warm darkness," where some fall away "exhausted." "Survivors" "assault" the egg, the successful candidates "surrounding the prize" (Miller and Pelham 1984, 7). Part of the urgency of this journey, in more scientific terms, is that "once released from the supportive environment of the ovary, an egg will die within hours unless rescued by a sperm" (Alberts et al. 1983, 804). The wording stresses the fragility and dependency of the egg, even though the same text acknowledges elsewhere that sperm also live for only a few hours (Alberts et al. 1983, 801).

* * *

Bringing out another aspect of the sperm's autonomy, an article in the journal *Cell* has the sperm making an "existential decision" to penetrate the egg: "Sperm are cells with a limited behavioral repertoire, one that is directed toward fertilizing eggs. To execute the decision to abandon the haploid state, sperm swim to an egg and there acquire the ability to effect membrane fusion" (Shapiro 1987). Is this a corporate manager's version of the sperm's activities—"executing decisions" while fraught with dismay over difficult options that bring with them very high risk?

* * *

One depiction of sperm as weak and timid, instead of strong and powerful—the only such representation in western civilization, so far as I know—occurs in Woody Allen's movie *Everything You Always Wanted To Know About Sex** (*BUT WERE AFRAID TO ASK). Allen, playing the part of an apprehensive sperm inside a man's testicles, is scared of the man's approaching orgasm. He is reluctant to launch himself into the darkness, afraid of contraceptive devices, afraid of winding up on the ceiling if the man masturbates.

The more common picture—egg as damsel in distress, shielded only by her sacred garments; sperm as heroic warrior to the rescue—cannot be proved to be dictated by the biology of these events. While the "facts" of biology may not *always* be constructed in cultural terms, I would argue that in this case they are. The degree of metaphorical content in these descriptions, the extent to which differences between egg and sperm are emphasized, and the parallels between cultural stereotypes of male and female behavior and the character of egg and sperm all point to this conclusion.

New Research, Old Imagery

As new understandings of egg and sperm emerge, textbook gender imagery is being revised. But the new research, far from escaping the stereotypical representations of egg and sperm, simply replicates elements of textbook gender imagery in a different form. * * *

In all of the texts quoted above, sperm are described as penetrating the egg, and specific substances on a sperm's head are described as binding to the egg. Recently, this description of events was rewritten in a biophysics lab at Johns Hopkins University—transforming the egg from the passive to the active party.[4]

Prior to this research, it was thought that the zona, the inner vestments of the egg, formed an impenetrable barrier. Sperm overcame the barrier by mechanically burrowing through, thrashing their tails and slowly working their way along. Later research showed that the sperm released digestive enzymes that chemically broke down the zona; thus, scientists presumed that the sperm used mechanical *and* chemical means to get through to the egg.

In this recent investigation, the researchers began to ask questions about the mechanical force of the sperm's tail. (The lab's goal was to develop a contraceptive that worked topically on sperm.) They discovered, to their great surprise, that the forward thrust of sperm is extremely weak, which contradicts the assumption that sperm are forceful penetrators. Rather than thrusting forward, the sperm's head was now seen to move mostly back and forth. The sideways motion of the sperm's tail makes the head move sideways with a force that is ten times stronger than its forward movement. So even if the overall force of the sperm were strong enough to mechanically break the zona, most of its force would be directed sideways rather than forward. In fact, its strongest tendency, by tenfold, is to escape by attempting to pry itself off the egg. Sperm, then, must be exceptionally efficient at *escaping* from any cell surface they contact. And the surface of the egg must be designed to trap the sperm and prevent their escape. Otherwise, few if any sperm would reach the egg.

The researchers at Johns Hopkins concluded that the sperm and egg stick together because of adhesive molecules on the surfaces of each. The egg traps the sperm and adheres to it so tightly that the sperm's head is forced to lie flat against the surface of the zona, a little bit, they told me, "like Br'er Rabbit getting more and more stuck to tar baby the more he wriggles." The trapped sperm continues to wiggle ineffectually side to side. The mechanical force of its tail is so weak that a sperm cannot break even one chemical bond. This is where the digestive enzymes released by the sperm come in. If they start to soften the zona just at the tip of the sperm and the sides remain stuck, then the weak, flailing sperm can get oriented in the right direction and make it through the zona—provided that its bonds to the zona dissolve as it moves in.

---

4. Jay M. Baltz carried out the research I describe when he was a graduate student in the Thomas C. Jenkins Department of Biophysics at Johns Hopkins University.

Although this new version of the saga of the egg and the sperm broke through cultural expectations, the researchers who made the discovery continued to write papers and abstracts as if the sperm were the active party who attacks, binds, penetrates, and enters the egg. The only difference was that sperm were now seen as performing these actions weakly (Baltz and Cone 1985; 1986). Not until August 1987, more than three years after the findings described above, did these researchers reconceptualize the process to give the egg a more active role. They began to describe the zona as an aggressive sperm catcher, covered with adhesive molecules that can capture a sperm with a single bond and clasp it to the zona's surface (Baltz, Katz, and Cone 1988). In the words of their published account: "The innermost vestment, the *zona pellucida*, is a glycoprotein shell, which captures and tethers the sperm before they penetrate it . . . . The sperm is captured at the initial contact between the sperm tip and the *zona* . . . . Since the thrust [of the sperm] is much smaller than the force needed to break a single affinity bond, the first bond made upon the tip-first meeting of the sperm and *zona* can result in the capture of the sperm" (Baltz, Katz, and Cone 1988, 643, 650).

Experiments in another lab reveal similar patterns of data interpretation. Gerald Schatten and Helen Schatten set out to show that, contrary to conventional wisdom, the "egg is not merely a large, yolk-filled sphere into which the sperm burrows to endow new life. Rather, recent research suggests the almost heretical view that sperm and egg are mutually active partners" (Schatten and Schatten 1984, 51). This sounds like a departure from the stereotypical textbook view, but further reading reveals Schatten and Schatten's conformity to the aggressive-sperm metaphor. They describe how "the sperm and egg first touch when, from the tip of the sperm's triangular head, a long, thin filament shoots out and harpoons the egg." Then we learn that "remarkably, the harpoon is not so much fired as assembled at great speed, molecule by molecule, from a pool of protein stored in a specialized region called the acrosome. The filament may grow as much as twenty times longer than the sperm head itself before its tip reaches the egg and sticks" (Schatten and Schatten 1984, 52). Why not call this "making a bridge" or "throwing out a line" rather than firing a harpoon? Harpoons pierce prey and injure or kill them, while this filament only sticks. And why not focus, as the Hopkins lab did, on the stickiness of the egg, rather than the stickiness of the sperm? Later in the article, the Schattens replicate the common view of the sperm's perilous journey into the warm darkness of the vagina, this time for the purpose of explaining its journey into the egg itself: "[The sperm] still has an arduous journey ahead. It must penetrate farther into the egg's huge sphere of cytoplasm and somehow locate the nucleus, so that the two cells' chromosomes can fuse. The sperm dives down into the cytoplasm, its tail beating. But it is soon interrupted by the sudden and swift migration of the egg nucleus, which rushes toward the sperm with a velocity triple that of the movement of chromosomes during cell division, crossing the entire egg in about a minute" (Schatten and Schatten 1984, 53).

Like Schatten and Schatten and the biophysicists at Johns Hopkins, another researcher has recently made discoveries that seem to point to a more interactive view of the relationship of egg and sperm. This work, which Paul Wassarman conducted on the sperm and eggs of mice, focuses on identifying the specific molecules in the egg coat (the zona pellucida) that are involved in egg-sperm interaction. At first glance, his descriptions seem to fit the model of an egalitarian relationship. Male and female gametes "recognize one another," and "interactions . . . take place between sperm and egg" (Wassarman 1988). But the article in *Scientific American* in which those descriptions appear begins with a vignette that presages the dominant motif of their presentation: "It has been more than a century since Hermann Fol, a Swiss zoologist, peered into his microscope and became the first person to see a sperm penetrate an egg, fertilize it and form the first cell of a new embryo" (Wassarman 1988, 78). This portrayal of the sperm as the active party—the one that *penetrates* and *fertilizes* the egg and *produces* the embryo— is not cited as an example of an earlier, now outmoded view. In fact, the author reiterates the point later in the article: "Many sperm can bind to and penetrate the zona pellucida, or outer coat, of an unfertilized mouse egg, but only one sperm will eventually fuse with the thin plasma membrane surrounding the egg proper (*inner sphere*), fertilizing the egg and giving rise to a new embryo" (Wassarman 1988, 79).

The imagery of sperm as aggressor is particularly startling in this case: the main discovery being reported is isolation of a particular molecule *on the egg coat* that plays an important role in fertilization! Wassarman's choice of language sustains the picture. He calls the molecule that has been isolated, ZP3, a "sperm receptor." By allocating the passive, waiting role to the egg, Wassarman can continue to describe the sperm as the actor, the one that makes it all happen: "The basic process begins when many sperm first attach loosely and then bind tenaciously to receptors on the surface of the egg's thick outer coat, the zona pellucida. Each sperm, which has a large number of egg-binding proteins on its surface, binds to many sperm receptors on the egg. More specifically, a site on each of the egg-binding proteins fits a complementary site on a sperm receptor, much as a key fits a lock" (Wassarman 1988, 78). With the sperm designated as the "key" and the egg the "lock" it is obvious which one acts and which one is acted upon. Could this imagery not be reversed, letting the sperm (the lock) wait until the egg produces the key? Or could we speak of two halves of a locket matching, and regard the matching itself as the action that initiates the fertilization?

It is as if Wassarman were determined to make the egg the receiving partner. * * *

Wassarman does credit the egg coat with having more functions than those of a sperm receptor. While he notes that "the zona pellucida has at times been viewed by investigators as a nuisance, a barrier to sperm and hence an impediment to fertilization," his new research reveals that the egg coat "serves as a sophisticated biological security system that screens incoming sperm, selects only those compatible with fertilization and development, prepares sperm for fusion with the egg and later protects the resulting embryo from polyspermy [a lethal condition caused by fusion of more than one sperm with a single egg]" (Wassarman 1988, 70–77). Although this description gives the egg an active role, that role is drawn in stereotypically feminine terms. The egg *selects* an appropriate mate, *prepares* him for fusion, and then *protects* the resulting offspring from harm. This is courtship and mating behavior as seen through the eyes of a sociobiologist: woman as the hard-to-get prize, who, following union with the chosen one, becomes woman as servant and mother.

And Wassarman does not quit there. In a review article for *Science*, he outlines the "chronology of fertilization" (Wassarman 1987). Near the end of the article are two subject headings. One is "Sperm Penetration," in which Wassarman describes how the chemical dissolving of the zona pellucida combines with the "substantial propulsive force generated by sperm." The next heading is "Sperm-Egg Fusion." This section details what happens inside the zona after a sperm "penetrates" it. Sperm "can make contact with, adhere to, and fuse with (that is, fertilize) an egg" (Wassarman 1987, 557). Wassarman's word choice, again, is astonishingly skewed in favor of the sperm's activity, for in the next breath he says that sperm *lose* all motility upon fusion with the egg's surface. * * * The section called "Sperm Penetration" more logically would be followed by a section called "The Egg Envelops," rather than "Sperm-Egg Fusion." This would give a parallel—and more accurate—sense that both the egg and the sperm initiate action.

*   *   *

Social Implications: Thinking Beyond

All three of these revisionist accounts of egg and sperm cannot seem to escape the hierarchical imagery of older accounts. Even though each new account gives the egg a larger and more active role, taken together they bring into play another cultural stereotype: woman as a dangerous and aggressive threat. In the Johns Hopkins lab's revised model, the egg ends up as the female aggressor who "captures and tethers" the sperm with her sticky zona, rather like a spider lying in wait in her web (Baltz, Katz, and Cone 1988, 643, 650). The Schatten lab has the egg's nucleus "interrupt" the sperm's dive with a "sudden and swift" rush by which she "clasps the sperm and guides its nucleus to the center" (Schatten and Schatten 1984, 53). Wassarman's description of the surface of the egg "covered with thousands of plasma membrane-bound projections, called microvilli" that reach out and clasp the sperm adds to the spiderlike imagery (Wassarman 1987, 557).

These images grant the egg an active role but at the cost of appearing disturbingly aggressive. Images of woman as dangerous and aggressive, the femme fatale who victimizes men, are widespread in Western literature and culture (Ellman 1968, 140; Auerbach 1982, 186). More specific is the connection of spider imagery with the idea of an engulfing, devouring mother (Adams 1981). New data did not lead scientists to eliminate gender stereotypes in their descriptions of egg and sperm. Instead, scientists simply began to describe egg and sperm in different, but no less damaging, terms.

Can we envision a less stereotypical view? Biology itself provides another model that could be applied to the egg and the sperm. The cybernetic model—with its feedback loops, flexible adaptation to change, coordination of the parts within a whole, evolution over time, and changing response to the environment—is common in genetics, endocrinology, and ecology and has a growing influence in medicine in general (Arney and Bergen 1984). This model has the potential to shift our imagery from the negative, in which the female reproductive system is castigated both for not producing eggs after birth and for producing (and thus wasting) too many eggs overall, to something more positive. The female reproductive system could be seen as responding to the environment (pregnancy or menopause), adjusting to monthly changes (menstruation), and flexibly changing from reproductivity after puberty to nonreproductivity later in life. The sperm and egg's interaction could also be described in cybernetic terms. J. F. Hartman's research in reproductive biology demonstrated fifteen years ago that if an egg is killed by being pricked with a needle, live sperm cannot get through the zona (Hartman, Gwatkin, and Hutchison 1972). Clearly, this evidence shows that the egg and sperm *do* interact on more mutual terms, making biology's refusal to portray them that way all the more disturbing.

*   *   *

The models that biologists use to describe their data can have important social effects. During the nineteenth century, the social and natural sciences strongly influenced each other: the social ideas of [philosopher Thomas] Malthus about how to avoid the natural increase of the poor inspired [naturalist Charles] Darwin's *Origin of Species* (Hubbard 1983). Once the *Origin* stood as a description of the natural world, complete with competition and market struggles, it could be reimported into social science as social Darwinism, in order to justify the social order of the time. What we are seeing now is similar: the importation of cultural ideas about passive females and heroic males into the "personalities" of gametes. This amounts to the "implanting of social imagery on representations of nature so as to lay a firm basis for reimporting exactly that same imagery as natural explanations of social phenomena" (David Harvey, personal communication, November 1989).

Further research would show us exactly what social effects are being wrought from the biological imagery of egg and sperm. At the very least, the imagery keeps alive some of the hoariest old stereotypes about weak damsels in distress and their strong male rescuers. That these stereotypes are now being written in at the level of the *cell* constitutes a powerful move to make them seem so natural as to be beyond alteration.

The stereotypical imagery might also encourage people to imagine that what results from the interaction of egg and sperm—a fertilized egg—is the result of deliberate "human" action at the cellular level. Whatever the intentions of the human couple, in this microscopic "culture" a cellular "bride" (or femme fatale) and a cellular "groom" (her victim) make a cellular baby. Rosalind Petchesky points out that through visual representations such as sonograms, we are given "*images* of younger and younger, and tinier and tinier, fetuses being 'saved'?" This leads to "the point of visibility being 'pushed back' *indefinitely*" (Petchesky 1987). Endowing egg and sperm with intentional action, a key aspect of personhood in our culture, lays the foundation for the point of viability being pushed back to the moment of fertilization. This will likely lead to greater acceptance of technological developments and new forms of scrutiny and manipulation, for the benefit of these inner "persons": court-ordered restrictions on a pregnant woman's activities in order to protect her fetus, fetal surgery, amniocentesis, and rescinding of abortion rights, to name but a few examples (Arditti, Klein, and Minden 1984; Goodman 1987; Lewin 1987; Irwin and Jordan 1987).

Even if we succeed in substituting more egalitarian, interactive metaphors to describe the activities of egg and sperm, and manage to avoid the pitfalls of cybernetic models, we would still be guilty of endowing cellular entities with personhood. More crucial, then, that what *kinds* of personalities we bestow on cells is the very fact that we are doing it at all. This process could ultimately have the most disturbing social consequences.

One clear feminist challenge is to wake up sleeping metaphors in science, particularly those involved in descriptions of the egg and the sperm. Although the literary convention is to call such metaphors "dead," they are not so much dead as sleeping, hidden within the scientific content of texts—and all the more powerful for it. Waking up such metaphors, by becoming aware of when we are projecting cultural imagery onto what we study, will improve our ability to investigate and understand nature. Waking up such metaphors, by becoming aware of their implications, will rob them of their power to naturalize our social conventions about gender.

ENGAGING THE TEXT, ENGAGING THE WORLD

- Growing up, what story did you learn about the egg and sperm? Describe the character of each and their interaction.

- How does the story you learned differ from the one presented by Martin in this article?

- What terms does Martin find in medical texts that place the female reproductive process in a negative light? And vice versa for men?

- How do these misrepresentations of the biological activities of the egg and sperm provide an ideological basis and rationale for gender stereotypes and inequality? Why do these myths persist, even though the science has been revised?

- How do imaginations of character, personality, and intention of eggs and sperm contribute to the current social debates around women's health choices, from amniocentesis to abortion to fetal surgeries?

- What does Martin mean by "waking up sleeping metaphors in science"? Why do you think anthropologists might be uniquely positioned to take on that task?

- Do you think it matters how we describe the reproductive process? Why or why not?

8

Sexuality

Sexuality is a profound aspect of human life, one that stirs intense emotions, deep anxieties, and rigorous debate. The U.S. population holds widely varying views of where sexuality originates, what constitutes appropriate expressions of sexuality, and what its fundamental purpose is. It is fair to say that our cultural norms and mental maps of reality are in great flux, and have been for several generations, in response to theological shifts, medical advances, and powerful social movements promoting the equality of women and gay, lesbian, bisexual, transgender, and queer individuals.

Sexuality involves more than personal choices about who our sexual partners are and what we do with them. It is also a cultural arena within which our desires are expressed, socialized, and even thwarted. And it is an arena in which people debate ideas of what is moral, appropriate, and natural, and use those ideas to create unequal access to society's power, privileges, and resources. Indeed, conflict about sexuality often reveals the intersections of multiple systems of power, including those based on gender, religion, race, class, and kinship.

Since the mid-1980s, sexuality has reemerged as a key concern in anthropology, paralleling a rise of interest in the wider academic community spurred by the successes of the U.S. women's movement and the emergence of gay and lesbian studies in the 1980s and queer theory in the 1990s. Recently, anthropological scholarship has more intensely considered the diverse expressions of sexuality in cultures worldwide, including Western cultures, and the way those expressions are being shaped by the intersection of local practices and globalization.

A look at human sexuality over time and across cultures reveals significant diversity in (1) how, where, when, and with whom humans have sex; and (2) what certain sexual behaviors mean. As we considered in Evelyn Blackwood's article "Tombois in West Sumatra" in the previous chapter, this diversity challenges Western culture-bound notions and suggests alternatives for reinterpreting assumed cultural categories of sexuality. Indeed, mapping the global scope of human sexual beliefs and behaviors suggests that dominant Western models of limited, fixed sexual categories do not represent the diverse, complex, and fluid array of human sexual desires and behaviors. And as Bobby Benedicto suggests in *Under Bright Lights: Gay Manila and the Global Scene*, increasing globalization is adding further complexity to local expressions of sexuality.

Sexuality is more than an expression of individual desires and identities. It is also a highly contested arena in which appropriate behavior is defined and relations of power are worked out. As we see in Deborah Gould's article about the AIDS activist group ACT UP, sexuality is also an arena for resistance to dominant narratives and deeply entrenched patterns of inequality and discrimination.

Despite the prominence of sexuality in academic and popular conversations today, especially in the media, Americans often struggle to find a common language with which to discuss it (whether in their personal lives, their families, their religious communities, the political arena, or the classroom) and often lack the theoretical and analytical frameworks to add depth to emotionally heated conversations. Anthropology can provide you with a broader understanding of the vast diversity of human sexuality across cultures, prepare you to discuss sexuality in your culture, and help you to better understand the role of sexuality in your own life and in your relations with others.

From *Under Bright Lights: Gay Manila and the Global Scene*
Bobby Benedicto

Mobility, class, and queer sexualities

Manila, capital of the Philippines, is a sprawling, dense city of 1.8 million people, full of extremes of rich and poor, elites and the marginalized, where the powerful cannot help but pass by street children begging for food. In this selection, Bobby Benedicto explores the construction of gay life in Manila, particularly a gay "bright lights scene," in which movement and mobility—namely driving—through the city is both a key process and a powerful symbol of desire. In a city where gay men, lesbians, and queer folk are marginalized by the dominant culture, Benedicto reflects

From Bobby Benedicto. 2014. *Under Bright Lights: Gay Manila and the Global Scene.* Minneapolis, MN: University of Minnesota Press. Some of the author's notes have been omitted.

on the ways that the construction of gay, queer identity, in the search for upward mobility and global connection, replicates rather than resists dominant systems of race, gender, and class.

Making a Scene

If I were to map gay Manila as I recall it, it would appear not as an enclave but as a series of privileged sites pieced together, vaguely cast against the noise and squalor of the third-world city. This map would include not only the gay clubs where my informants and I spent many weekend nights and the homes where private parties were occasionally held but also bars, clubs, and commercial developments that were not identified as "gay" and yet served as routine destinations for gay men. The lines that link these places and that we ourselves traced whenever we drove through the city late at night reveal that shape of an urban world in the making, a scene that can be imagined only as a flow of movements, a shuttling back and forth between and among places similarly invested in the dream of a fast life unencumbered by Manila's disorder.

*   *   *

This book is not about a discrete, containable space defined by dimensions that can be exhaustively explained but about a world that resists straightforward mapping and that I refer to as the "bright lights scene" or, simply, the "scene." This is a world enmeshed in increasingly global processes such as the incorporation of gay men into consumer markets, the emergence of hybridized gay identities in globalization, the spread of "mainstream" gay representations, the legitimation of LGBT politics in "multicultural" democracies, and gay tourisms and migrations. At the same time, however, this is a world bound up in the local cultural politics of a city caught in the throes of global modernity and of the neoliberal order that sets its rules. * * * The story of the scene's emergence is, as I tell it, the story of the fabulation of a lifeworld, folded into larger narratives about mobility, aspiration, and the fashioning of a "global-metropolitan milieu" out of the "noisy matter" of urban life in a megapolitan environment (Tadiar 2009, 148).

Under Bright Lights is * * * an investigation of how the world-making practices of gay men reproduce the cultures of domination that govern present-day Manila and that are predicated on categories such as gender, race, and especially class. * * * Here, the story of struggle, injury, and resistance that stands as the abbreviated account of gay life in Manila, and in other de-centered places around the world, is reread with one eye trained on the convivial relations that exist between gay men and the forces that keep the wheels of the prevailing order of things turning.

Though this book draws attention to lived experiences of gay male privilege, the unfinished world it refers to remains a space on the margins, not only because it is made by and for sexual others, but precisely because it takes form in a "third-world city"— Manila—imagined and narrativized by those within and those without as a city that stands on the beaten end of the present geopolitical order and that has grown accustomed to the feelings of futility and failure that accompany modernization.[1] * * *

What I am calling the bright lights scene * * * does not refer to an anthropological place that exists, somewhere, fixed, a destination waiting to be arrived at and represented through a list of abstracted traits, but to a tangle of potential connections, an assemblage that comes together when links are anxiously traced, felt, and made between spaces, forms, bodies, objects, dreams, trajectories, images, signs, styles, and other forceful and affecting elements (Stewart 2008, 72). This is an assemblage that is, at once, a part of the city and apart from it. It takes form as "real" spaces like bars and clubs that materialize the scene as a distinctively urban experience. It bursts into imagination when event organizers assert that the transformations in local club culture mark the entrance of Manila into a global network made up of cities such as New York, London, San Francisco, and Sydney, among others. It is made by bodies that inhabit Manila and that are, at the same time, plugged into tele-technologies that allow distant sites and virtual worlds to be glimpsed. It is in publications sitting on local newsstands; in pirated DVDs bought and sold in the basements of run-down shopping malls; and in parties and events set in gated villages, high-rise apartments, and rented venues. The bright lights scene is a world dense with circulating expressive forms that effect transnational belonging and a world textured by local historical forces such as unchecked urbanization, hardened class relations, received meanings, and the surges of modernization and technologization that have punctuated life in Manila over the past few decades.

A scene such as this is necessarily difficult, if not impossible, to represent. It has no clear beginning or end and becomes apparent only partially and fleetingly, during instances when "collective sensibilities seem to pulse in plain sight" and in moments one suddenly feels immersed in "something that feels like something" (Stewart 2008, 74). Some of these moments take on the status of events like the night in 2003 when Manila's first gay dance club opened its doors, the emergence in 2004 of the city's first glossy gay magazine and of a rival club in another part of the city, the introduction of circuit parties in 2005, or the arrival of celebrity DJs and the birth of Internet portals during those same years. More often, the scene becomes apparent in ordinary moments. It takes form during nights when people drive around and seem to know exactly where to go, not because they have set plans but because they are able to sense the energy in the air and know how to follow it to places where "things are happening." It takes shape when looks are exchanged between strangers who recognize each other purely because they seem to always be in the same places at the same time. In moments such as these, something happens that produces the quality of being in a scene. * * *

---

1. Though the term *third world* has fallen out of fashion in both academic and popular writing, I use it here to retain the material and visceral experience of poverty and global marginality it evokes and that is largely lost in euphemisms such as *developing, underdeveloped*, and *global South*.

Moments such as these speak to how, in spite of the elusiveness of its dimensions, the scene is nonetheless palpable as a thing; how it can be named and recognized even though its relationship to territory cannot be easily defined. * * *

At first glance, one could say that what animates the borders of the bright lights scene is sexual identification, that at the heart * * * lies the universalized, commercialized, and mediatized sign of "gay." Indeed, sexual identity—taken as a property of both subjects and spaces—plays a critical part in the * * * scene, as evidenced, for instance, in the near total absence of women from the sites I describe in these pages. Still, gay identity, even in its most fluid formulation, cannot evoke all the logics involved in the production of the scene's charged borders. The scene fragments in gay bars, where layers upon layers of codes allow otherness to be quickly read in outward appearances and where whispers, jokes, glances, and untranslatable pejoratives establish the fault lines of belonging. The borders of the scene are, in other words, more than the slash that splits the homosexual/heterosexual divide. They are the invisible lines that emerge on the streets outside the gay clubs, the intangible cordon that surrounds a group of gay men as they stand on the road, talking * * * while a beggar hovers around them with her hand stretched out. They operate in modes of attachment to particular places in the city, in the routes taken when driving from one pocket of privilege to another, and in the interplay of desire and disgust that turn the strip clubs in destitute districts into symbols of danger and a time gone by.

The borders of the bright lights scene, in other words, point to the varied ways gay men are implicated in emplaced hierarchies and to the way those hierarchies are redeployed and reconfigured in practices of mobility. It is, in turn, this interplay between movement and boundary-making that serves as the recurring theme. * * * I examine a particular form of mobility, beginning with systems such as automobility that operate within the city and leading up to practices such as gay tourism that involve travels out of the city and into the world. * * *

This book also stands as a critique of the idealization of movement in the study of nonnormative sexualities. Indeed, the focus on transgression and resistance that I am breaking away from here and that is inscribed in the very term *queer* has long been hinged on [ideas] of mobility. As Eve Sedgwick once noted, *queer* itself means *across*; it comes from the Indo-European root *twerkw*, from which other terms such as the German quer (transverse), the Latin *torquere* (to twist), and the English *athwart* also derive. "Queer" in "queer theory" thus comes to stand for "a continuing moment, movement, motive—recurrent, eddying, troublant" (Sedgwick 1993, viii). It has sought, by definition, to indicate "unpredictable mobilities of bodies, desires, and practices" (Wiegman 2001, 382) and to name "cultures" that have "no locale" (Warner 1993, xvii). In turn, much attention has been given to the way dominant orders are challenged by "queer" mobility practices, from movements into and within cities that enable the founding of places where "counterhegemonic" norms prevail, to the oscillation of individuals between "fluid" identity categories, to the traversal of cyberspace and the creation of queer virtual worlds, and to other "queer" movements. Taken as a practice engaged in by queers, mobility has emerged as an integral part of the arsenal of strategies that can be employed to resist normative systems that are understood as mechanisms of stricture, constraint, and discipline—that is, as barriers to movement or forces of immobilization. In this book, stories of mobility are brought together, not as examples of a primarily resistant queer culture, nor as authoritative representations of an organized cultural real but as inroads to an investigation of the yearning trajectory that directs gay life in Manila outward toward the global, forward toward modernity, and upward toward higher states of class privilege.

*　　*　　*

Automobility and the Gay Cityscape

Metro Manila has no gay village, no neighborhood or individual street seen and identified as gay. * * * Indeed, when I recall Manila's gay sites, I think of movement rather than districts. My memories of gay Manila are of driving and being driven to and from houses, high-rise apartments, sleek clubs, bars, and restaurants. These were satellites built for the upper strata: trendy havens cordoned off from the disorder of older quarters and joined by inadequate, pothole-ridden roads that betrayed their immersion in Manila's urban squalor. My memories also include the faces and bodies of strangers, people I did not know but knew of and whom I recognized from those pockets of privilege where we sat drinking cocktails under clouds of cigarette smoke and watched each other pose against dim violet backlighting. On certain nights, those familiar strangers and I appeared at the same places at the same time. We passed one another without a word or even a single raised eyebrow, though we were utterly aware, as Manileños always were, of each other's recurring presence. On those nights, more than on any other, I could see us driving around in our darkened cars, tracing the same routes past the same soot-stained infrastructure. I imagine that we were all similarly thankful that so much of our lives were conducted late at night, when Manila's normally dense arteries slackened and we were able to speed through blinking stoplights, unmindful of the unruly streets of the postcolonial metropolis.

Nowhere do the streets of Manila feature less than in my memories of driving to Manila's gay clubs, which, as a consequence of the common desire to arrive after everyone else, came to life even later than the rest of the city's nightspots. I have many memories of such journeys, densely clustered in little time frames from the years I spent as a casual inhabitant of the clubs to my various returns as a researcher investigating those very sites where I might have been considered an insider. Recalling those journeys now, I am struck by how little they resemble the more obvious images of Manila: the ones that might feature a car stuck in standstill traffic slowly forcing its way into a treacherous shortcut dominated by garbage piling on street corners, gnarled wires and cables, remnants of posters from elections past, iron shantytowns, and packs of dogs and groups of street children only to exit at another road where the traffic was worse and cars were as immobile as the dilapidated buildings that surrounded them. * * *

At night, however, there was little time or reason to consider the city. Its edifices flew past windows, were blurred and disappeared like the buses that retired soon after rush hour and the smog that became indiscernible in the absence of daylight. To reach the clubs, I often passed Epifanio delos Santos Avenue (EDSA), Manila's main thoroughfare. During the day, EDSA was the site of epic gridlocks, an experience made worse in those instances when you were caught between buses or next to a wet market and had no choice but to hold your breath or inhale the smoke and the stench of raw meat, which seeped through the windows and mingled with the odor of air-conditioning. My memories of EDSA at night, however, are clear of such intrusions. I remember seeing only large billboards featuring Eurasian models in their underwear and a smattering of video advertisements. In a city as poorly lit as Manila, these billboards and screens served as central guideposts and, on nights when I drove alone, the figures they contained were my only companions. Indeed, at night, the cityscape seemed to evaporate under the cover of darkness and the aesthetic of speed. The frustration and introspection of daytime traffic were replaced by the thrill of the freedom to accelerate and the anticipation of the destination. I was a member of my class and took pleasure in all these disappearances.

*　　*　　*

On Nearness

* * * During the mid-2000s, I lived in a high-rise apartment in San Juan, roughly midpoint between what were the twin centers of the gay club scene: Government, located at the fringes of the Makati CBD [Central Business District], and a club called Bed, located in the district of Malate. The fact that I was a short drive away from Malate was a late discovery. Whenever I went there I took a circuitous route: exiting at EDSA and then driving down Buendia Avenue all the way to the coastal road of Roxas Boulevard, which brought me to the intersection of Nakpil and Orosa, touted as the "X" that marks the spot of gayness by travel guides that insist on locating a single center. This was a reasonable route from the gated village where I grew up, but from my apartment in San Juan, it was almost comical; and yet, no one I drove with knew better, or perhaps they all took comfort in the unadventurous straight lines of the path I was used to taking. One night I found myself with someone who knew another path and I let him steer me westward, through roads I had never seen, dirtier roads crammed with more jeepneys and people. It was a more treacherous drive, but in a matter of minutes we were crossing the rusted old rail tracks that I regarded as an informal entrance to the old City of Manila. After that crossing, the roads became visibly narrower, the buildings older, more colonial,

and the street lamps more garish. * * * Then the traffic became heavier, restaurants began appearing on the sides of the road, and then there it was: Malate—a dense cluster of small bars converted from two-story apartments, a smattering of street vendors, and young people walking in packs. During the late nineties, I could walk the streets of Malate. * * * Everything was familiar, the places were known to me by name, the faces on the street recognizable. Then the winds changed and one by one the places I knew died under the weight of whispers that Malate was passé and were replaced by new venues that catered to what many saw as an underclass. The exodus that followed was quick. Many fled to Makati, gentry under siege, and I was wholly unsurprised when I heard someone say, condescendingly, that Malate had become a democracy.

In some ways, Bed survived this small revolution, and it was there where we were headed that night that I discovered the shorter route to Malate. Bed was larger than Government, but the two were cut from the same cloth. They shared a modern aesthetic, common prices, and indistinct lights and music. Even the bodies that inhabited them were similar: mostly hardened by hours in the gym and sporting the same uniform of tight T-shirts and jeans. During the years I was in Manila for fieldwork, however, Government acquired a reputation as more exclusive, more *sosyal*. Many of the men I knew, including almost all my informants, preferred Government. Bed was sleazier, they said. It was dirtier. One informant said that the boys there looked like they stank. Still, such distinctions struck me as somewhat exaggerated. The crowds at both clubs were more mixed in terms of class than people implied, and it was only by calling on a lifetime of privilege that my eyes were able to see through the strobe lights and split the hairs of class distinction, spot the stylistic differences, and catch the threads that connected persons to the right networks. There were, however, more bodies at Bed that bravely bore the markers that signaled class difference: perhaps a little tail of hair at the back of their necks or the dead giveaway of poor English. *Jologs*, Tristan and Carl would call them, and their presence, even if it was not overwhelming, was enough to drive many away. We knew, after all, what their presence meant; we saw them (or figures callously likened to them) arriving in the days, weeks, and months before the deaths of other establishments in Malate and of hundreds of other bars, clubs, restaurants, even entire malls scattered across the city. In Bed, they appeared like signs that the streets were about to pour in. Thus the prudent ones became nothing more than occasional visitors and found safety in Makati, rallying around a center far away from the rest of what passes for a circle.

Government's very distance from the cluster of gay spaces in Malate was thus, iron-ically, the source of its cachet. There was nothing around Government; it stood alone on the northern end of Makati Avenue, flanked only by a bank and a midpriced hotel. A couple of blocks away, there was a branch of the fast food chain Wendy's, then a 7-Eleven, then a twenty-four-hour Chinese restaurant. There were no people on the streets other than those coming to and from the club. There were only cars speeding down Makati Avenue. (Makati Avenue, a major thoroughfare: this was the site of Government, not a village or a neighborhood, but a pathway.) * * * Still, no one ever spoke of that part of the city as dead. In fact, Government became the site of the after-parties for the large circuit events, the fêtes thrown by glossy magazines, and the destination of DJs from overseas. For many, Malate became a distant, other world, home to a different set of gay men and to those who clung to the dream of gentrification. No such pretense hung over Government. It stood alone, proud of its isolation, comfortable sitting alongside an ATM machine, a temporary abode, a fast food chain—the symbols of quick, ephemeral commerce. I, too, was comfortable in those surroundings and knew all the routes to get there, even the obscure one that cut through the Mandaluyong rotunda and jumped over the murky waters of the Pasig River. Once, during an interview with a group of men who were regulars at Bed, I was asked why I was at Government more often. It was a mine-field of a question and all I could do was shrug sheepishly and say that it was "nearer."

Other(ed) Places

Still, it would be too simple to assert that the scene was moved only by the logic of distance, for even in the midst of struggles to rise above, elude, and speed through the contradictions that surrounded us, there existed a secret, perverse desire to see the very things we avoided, to come close to them, touch them, smell them. I am thinking now not even of Malate, which in its erstwhile separation still remained recognizable and unexotic, but of the darker, older, poorer recesses of gay life in Manila: the world of strip clubs and *callboys*—not tourist sites like in other Asian cities but somber places frequented mostly by older queers. There were nights when we were seized by a sudden urge to visit these other(ed) places.[2] We journeyed to them like schoolchildren on fieldtrips, eager to break the rhythm of our overprivileged boredom.

I once went with a small band of young gay men to one of the largest strip clubs in Quezon City. I remember that none of us knew its exact location and that we had to drive slowly, staring out of the car windows in order to read the neon signs that dotted the wide, sparse stretch of Timog Avenue. We found the club at the tail end of the road, marked by a modest pink sign and a lit canopy. We parked half a block away and rushed to the entrance, keeping our heads bowed between the collars of our jackets and chuckling about the embarrassing possibility of being seen in that part of town. Inside, the club was large and pitch-dark. The only lights shone on a wide catwalk in the center, where strippers came out one by one in identical denim cutoffs and motorcycle boots, dancing in slow motion to ballads that radio stations had retired long ago. It was a peculiar sight and not at all what we expected. We laughed under our breaths and earned irked looks from the lonely figures that occupied the surrounding tables. * * *

*   *   *

---

2. In Manila, *callboy* is used to refer to all male prostitutes.

There were times when our desire to wade in darker waters took us farther than we intended. During those instances, even the car offered little security: I was in a suite in a four-star hotel in Ortigas, sitting in front of large windows that overlooked the city. It was September, a Sunday afternoon, and though in theory it was the time for rains and storms, the sun was streaming hard into the hotel room. It shone on the wreckage of a party—sheets were scattered about; empty glasses and bottles cluttered the coffee table, the nightstands, the desk; and ashtrays overflowed with cigarette butts and matchsticks. Across from me sat Bernard, dressed only in a thick white bathrobe, his legs crossed. A cigarette, his breakfast, was dangling from his right hand. Bernard was only twenty, but he looked older as he recounted the events of the previous two nights under the harsh glare of sunlight.

He and a few friends had gotten bored at the clubs and decided that they wanted to see a live sex show, but they only knew of one place that offered them and another friend had denounced it as unremarkable, full of ugly boys that could only get half hard. So they decided to create their own show and hire callboys from a prostitution block called Gold Loop, located a few minutes from the hotel we were at and also, ironically, from a university run by the [Catholic organization] Opus Dei. They drove in separate cars from the clubs and split up in Ortigas, with some going ahead to the hotel to book a suite while Bernard and a few others drove around Gold Loop in search of callboys to pick up. The Loop itself was a small square block in a neighborhood dominated by moderately expensive condominium buildings. It was an unlikely site for prostitution and only gay men seemed to know that late at night, johns and callboys moved in like ghosts.

Bernard was driving and driving slowly. None of them had picked up callboys before, and they were all nervous, unsure of the protocol and wary of the authorities. They drove several times around the block, spotting a few stray figures standing in corners or walking under the shadows of trees, away from the few, scattered street lamps. There was a patrol car on one of the streets, but it looked abandoned and uninterested. Bernard and the others ignored it and kept driving around in circles. It might have been over half an hour before they slowed down in the darkest part of the block and turned off their headlights. One of the other boys quickly opened his door and got out, rushing off to talk to a dark figure in a tank top standing next to a telephone pole. Bernard wanted to tell him to get back in the car, but he had gotten out in a flash, emboldened and deafened by alcohol, and was making the transaction that Bernard and the others were too sober to attempt. Inside, Bernard was getting more anxious. He turned to look behind the car and saw that suddenly there were callboys coming out of all directions, walking slowly toward them. They were hovering around his car. It was, he told me, just like [the zombie horror film] *Night of the Living Dead*. Finally, the one who stepped out returned and squeezed into the backseat with the callboy he was talking to. By then, they were all too worked up to find another callboy to hire and decided to speed back to the hotel.

*   *   *

Beached

*** When we drove through the less-familiar streets of Manila in search of cheap thrills in strip clubs that were, invariably, less sordid than we had hoped or imagined, we relished the descent; it was a dip, a glance, a fall couched by romance and by the wealth that bought private rooms and safe passage back to loftier sites. This was modern spectatorship as lived in the third-world city by those who benefited from the privilege of class—an economy of heights and distances traversed and ruled by the multiply mobile.

There were, however, places where the distance between the sky and the earth did not need to be bridged, where they blended together and became indistinguishable naturally like the horizon viewed from a beach. There was an island off the coast of Luzon where every summer gay men from Manila flocked to escape the tremendous heat in the city. ***

We tried to escape once on a hot night in June, the end of summer in Manila. I remember sitting on the hood of my car, drinking beers with two gay men I had known for several years. We thought of hitting the bars and clubs, but the stickiness of the air seemed to strip the city of its capacity to enchant. "Let's go to the beach," someone suggested, "someplace empty." We drove for hours, past the hazards of EDSA and then through the long stretch of the South Luzon Expressway. We sped through Makati City, Pasay City, and Parañaque City, until we crossed the waterparks and amusement parks and the only thing in sight were rice paddies. Our destination was not the port where boats left for that famous island frequented by gay men but the quieter beaches behind the mountains of Batangas. It was morning by the time we arrived, and we spent that first day on the rocky beaches where divers and fishermen parked their boats, content to be bathing in the breeze blowing with no discernible direction. The next morning, however, that beach was no longer enough, and we longed for someplace with purer sands and fewer people. We hired a fisherman to take us to a nearby island. There, we baked in the sun and were completely alone. ***

We left later that same day. The trip went by fast (home was always near), and we found ourselves back in the thick of the city right in the middle of rush hour. By then I was too tired to be bothered by the traffic and found myself half asleep in the passenger seat watching the orange skeins streaked across the sky disappear from behind the quasi-opaque windows of the car. The heat was no longer coming from the city but bouncing off the sunburned skin on my knees and shoulders. It was a quiet drive until we got caught at a standstill along Ortigas Avenue. There, a boy about ten years old started knocking on the driver's side window begging for change. We ignored him, and after a few seconds he backed off and walked in front of the car. Midway, he turned to look at us. There was sudden recognition in his eyes. He smiled, a nasty smile, and yelled, "*Bakla!* [Fags!]"

He ran off, leaving us sitting there with our mouths open, paralyzed as much by the traffic as by the shock of being called *bakla*, a word that bound us to the older queers lurking in the shadows of the strip bars, the cross-dressers who ran the low-end beauty salons scattered all over the city, the classed figures for whom the term *bakla* was often reserved and whose lives took place (in our minds, at least) outside the world of bars and clubs and privilege that we called our own. At that moment, the traffic-clogged roads and the street child who took advantage of them seemed to hold us in a state of arrest. Named, recognized, and held in *place*, our ties to the city seemed suddenly visible, as though the walls we built through speed and wealth had, in an instant, become transparent. For a moment, I was stunned. I did not know whether to scream or yell something back, how to react to this grave insult from a child. Then the moment of shock passed, and the three of us in the car looked at each other and burst out laughing: "Fucking kid," said my friend who was driving. "If the traffic wasn't so bad, I'd run him over."

Detours

In writing movement, there is always the risk of getting lost.

I wanted to write about gay men in Manila, to zoom in on a scene, only to find that I had to keep stepping out into the city. Stepping out—not stepping back or zooming out—for Manila makes no sense when viewed as a panorama, even less when viewed from above. It is only on the streets that one can get a feel for the stark contradictions of the third-world city, the relentless crumpling together of privilege and marginality. In some ways, the bright lights scene is the perfect site of contradiction, for there the sexually abject are also aligned with the interests and hierarchies of capital. It is in light of such an alignment that I have begun to weave together memories and anecdotes, stories that foreground complicity rather than resistance. These stories have invariably been about driving through and inhabiting space. I chose them in part because I can only remember Manila as a combination of nodes and travels but also because that combination is precisely what allows for the mastery of the contradictions etched onto the city streets. It is what allows us to see and hear some things more than others, to erect imagined borders and perceptual limits, to be sunk but flying, beasts and angels. Flyovers, hotel suites, VIP rooms, clubs, intersections, caves, standstills, and traffic jams: these are not only mundane sites but also the means for a play of heights, of density and emptiness, of speed and slowness, the very shifts that disturb and sustain the dreams of mobility that underpin life under the bright lights.

ENGAGING THE TEXT, ENGAGING THE WORLD

- Why does Benedicto use the word "scene" in his ethnographic description rather than a specific place or community?

- Benedicto's "scene" cannot be mapped as a discrete geographic place. What are the key sites of the bright lights landscape he describes?

- Can you apply Benedicto's notion of a "scene" to other connections, networks, or worlds you know of or have experienced that may not be defined by discrete, containable spaces?

- Why is driving through the city such a key metaphor in Benedicto's reflections on gay life in Manila?

- What is the role of movement and mobility in shaping emerging gay identity in this global city?

- Why does Benedicto say that the bright lights scene is complicit in replicating Manila's social, economic, and political order? How does it reproduce cultures of domination along lines of race, gender, and class?

- What connection does Benedicto make between movement and queer sexuality in Manila? Movement toward what?

Life During Wartime: Emotions and the Development of ACT UP

AIDS activism and queer identities

Deborah Gould

In the 1980s and 1990s, the AIDS epidemic took a terrible toll on gay men in the United States. Deborah Gould documents the emergence of ACT UP (AIDS Coalition To Unleash Power) as a leading player in the social movement that emerged to combat this disease. AIDS, or Acquired Immune Deficiency Syndrome, as the U.S. Centers for Disease Control first named it in 1983, is caused by the Human Immunodeficiency Virus, or HIV. By 1990 the World Health Organization estimated that 8–10 million people were living with HIV worldwide. While early AIDS activism focused primarily on caretaking, service provision, and lobbying, the rise of ACT UP marked a dramatic shift to militant, in-your-face street activism in an attempt to force people and institutions to address the epidemic. Gould, whose 2009 book, *Moving Politics*, won the Association for Queer Anthropology's Ruth Benedict Prize, suggests that the success of the ACT UP movement relied on emotion work—cultivating the emotions needed to build and sustain a militant movement. Shifting the paradigm

From Deborah B. Gould. 2002. "Life During Wartime: Emotions and the Development of ACT UP." *Mobilization: An International Journal* 7(2): 177–200. Some of the author's notes have been omitted.

from shame to anger was key. So was the emergence of a new queer identity among lesbians, gay men, and other sexual and gender outlaws that remapped gender and sexual social worlds and imaginations.

ACT UP's Context

Gay men, lesbians, and other sexual and gender outlaws began to engage in militant street AIDS activism in mid-1986. After the October 1987 March on Washington for Lesbian and Gay Rights, the militant AIDS activist movement took off. Dozens of ACT UP chapters sprouted up across the United States. Thousands of lesbians, gay men, and other sexual and gender outlaws embraced the new militance and joined the movement. Many other lesbian and gay individuals and institutions, even those that were more establishment-oriented, articulated support for ACT UP and its brand of militant street activism; lesbian and gay politicians, directors of AIDS service organizations (ASOs), traditional lesbian and gay activists, newspaper editors praised the new militance, and many even joined in the action (Gould 2000: ch.5). ACT UP was of course sometimes challenged by other lesbians and gay men; still, the national militant AIDS activist movement flourished through the late 1980s and into the early 1990s. In this article, I ask why and how ACT UP was able to garner and maintain widespread support from individuals and from many segments of mainstream lesbian and gay communities and thereby sustain itself.

The question of movement sustainability is particularly pertinent in the case of ACT UP. The turn to angry, militant street activism was in striking contrast to earlier AIDS activism that had focused primarily on care taking and service provision along with lobbying. ACT UP greatly extended the repertoire by engaging in angry protests, disruptions, civil disobedience, die-ins, and other confrontational actions designed to force the government, scientific-medical establishment, pharmaceutical corporations, media, and society at large to address the AIDS epidemic. This new embrace of angry, oppositional, militant street activism was remarkable for a number of reasons. As is true for other U.S. social movements, ACT UP confronted a mainstream emotion culture (Gordon 1989) that typically disparages angry people, seeing anger as chaotic, impulsive, and irrational, and thus "something which a mature person ideally can or should transcend" (Lutz 1986: 180). Anger takes on an especially negative cast when expressed by large numbers of people who are purposefully taking to the streets and breaking the law in order to disrupt "business as usual," particularly when those people are marked as "other" by mainstream society. ACT UP also confronted an American ideology of democracy that locates legitimate political activity in the voting booth and in the halls of legislatures and maligns street activism as unnecessary and extreme, as well as a threat to social order. ACT UP also existed in a moment when other militant movements had disappeared or were in quick decline. Given this context, ACT UP had to make angry street activism a normative and legitimate route for lesbians and gay men.

ACT UP's task was complicated even further by the existence of what I call *ambivalence* among lesbians and gay men about their homosexuality and about dominant U.S. society. This contradictory constellation of emotions—simultaneous self-love and self-doubt, along with attraction toward and repulsion from dominant society—affects lesbian and gay politics. How do you confront a society when you want to be part of it but you simultaneously reject it? How do you make demands of state and society when you simultaneously feel proud *and* ashamed of your homosexual identity and practices? That pervasive ambivalence and attempts to resolve it affected earlier lesbian and gay responses to AIDS, often encouraging lesbian and gay activists to embrace a politics of respectability. To be sure, in the earliest years, uncertainty, confusion, and fear reigned, and lesbian and gay communities were utterly overwhelmed by AIDS; there was little time for anything more than care-taking. In the face of government inaction and with the hope of preserving their besieged communities, early AIDS activists engaged in the vital work of creating the earliest ASOs to care for their loved ones. But AIDS greatly magnified the stigma of homosexuality, intensifying lesbians' and gay men's shame about their sexual practices and anxieties about social rejection, and those emotions also helped to shape lesbian and gay responses to AIDS in the first years of the epidemic.

*   *   *

Most lesbian and gay rights activists had spurned militance by the mid-1970s. As occurred with other radical movements in the increasingly conservative 1970s, gay rights activists decisively shifted the movement's agenda away from liberation, which encompassed a vision of broad social transformation, and instead sought "gay inclusion into the system as it stood, with only the adjustments necessary to ensure equal treatment" for gay men and lesbians (D'Emilio 1992: 247). ACT UP, then, marked a return to and extension of gay liberation tactics and politics that had been rejected by gay rights activists in the mid-1970s. Given the unfavorable emotional and political norms that have historically prevailed both within mainstream U.S. society and in lesbian and gay communities, how was ACT UP able to attract so many participants and to garner wide support within lesbian and gay communities for its angry, militant street activism?

*   *   *

ACT UP and a New Emotional Common Sense

*   *   *

The first national AIDS protest occurred on June 1, 1987 in Washington, D.C. ACT UP and other lesbian and gay groups and individuals (including elected officials and directors of community organizations) targeted the Reagan administration for its failure to address the AIDS crisis. ACT UP/NY's flier advertising the protest action buttressed a newly emerging emotional common sense, expressing emotions that differed markedly from those that had previously prevailed in lesbian and gay communities. Text in bold declared,

WE ARE ANGRY:

- At the Government's policy of malignant neglect
- At the irresponsible inaction of this president
- At the shameful indifference of our elected representatives
- At the criminal hoarding of appropriated funds by government agencies

They Waste Our Money, Our Time, Our Lives! TAKE ONE DAY OFF FROM WORK . . . TURN RAGE INTO ACTION!

—ACT UP/New York 1987, emphases in original

Facts and demands on the leaflet laid bare the realities of the AIDS crisis and explicated the government's role in the deaths of tens of thousands of people. Overall, the leaflet was an angry condemnation of the government and an invitation to lesbians and gay men to turn what was deemed to be their understandable and appropriate "rage" into "action."

*   *   *

As this (and almost every other) ACT UP leaflet reveals, part of the work of a social movement is emotional. To attract and retain participants and to pursue the movement's agenda, activists continually need to mobilize emotions that readily articulate with the movement's political tactics and objectives, and suppress those that counter the movement's emotional and political common sense. Although terms like "mobilize," "counter," and "emotion work" might suggest conscious, purposive behavior, I want to emphasize that much of a movement's emotion work is non-strategic and unpremeditated. Where other tasks of a movement like mobilizing resources and organizing actions are deliberate and consciously undertaken, emotion work is often a less-than-fully conscious component of a movement's various activities. That is, the mobilization of emotions is often an *effect* of a movement's activities, but not necessarily the *intention* lying behind them.

Grief into Anger

ACT UP's response to the enormous grief pervading lesbian and gay communities provides a useful entry point to explore the question of the movement's ability to buttress and expand the emerging emotional common sense and its concomitant politics among lesbians, gay men, and other sexual and gender outlaws. Grief has been a constant presence throughout the AIDS epidemic. Beginning in 1983, lesbians and gay men began to hold candlelight memorial vigils to honor those who had died from AIDS-related complications. The vigils were typically somber affairs that provided a space for public expression of the intense grief that was wracking lesbian and gay communities across the country as the death toll continued to mount. The Names Project Memorial Quilt—containing thousands of three feet by six feet patches that commemorate people who have died from AIDS-related complications—has afforded lesbians and gay men a similar opportunity. ACT UP offered an alternative route for grief: militant AIDS activism.

*   *   *

ACT UP's emotion work succeeded because it effectively altered how lesbians, gay men, and other queers were actually feeling. Like other feelings, grief is a complicated constellation of emotions that includes sadness, loss, depression, fear, anger, and probably a host of other emotions. ACT UP's repeated emotional expressions elevated one of these emotions—anger—and submerged the others; reiterated over time and in the context of the growing AIDS crisis and government inaction, ACT UP's grief/anger/action nexus became commonsensical to many queers. * * *

* * * ACT UP/Chicago member Frank Sieple recalled that ACT UP did not really grieve the deaths of its members, but instead turned that grief into angry activism.

> It's almost like we didn't have time to grieve, you know, turning that grieving into like, the energy to move on ... One way of ... grieving was taking that energy that I would use on grieving and putting it into [activism] to ... make their deaths not seem in vain, you know? ... I think a lot of people did that (Sieple 1999).

* * * In the early 1990s, ACT UP/Chicago initiated a ritual that elevated anger over sadness and loss. Rejecting one member's proposal that ACT UP start its meetings with a moment of silence to commemorate its dead, the group voted instead to remember its dead by beginning meetings with a "moment of rage" in the form of a loud chant.

ACT UP effectively altered the meaning of grief by renaming and enacting as "anger" that complicated constellation of emotions. By this process, sadness, despondency, and loss were suppressed, eclipsed by the now-elevated anger. Lesbians and gay men could then re-experience grief as an outward-directed, action-oriented anger. Repeated articulations of phrases like "turn your grief into anger" transformed feelings of grief into anger. * * *

* * * Activists' framings of the hostile political environment that queers faced during the late 1980s and early 1990s (the Reagan/Bush years) were important components affecting lesbians' and gay men's positive responses to AIDS activists' mobilizations of anger and call to militant action. Militant AIDS activists repeatedly pointed to the

government's failure to address the crisis. From their perspective, little positive was being done, and even more ominously, calls for quarantine and other repressive measures were being seriously considered. AIDS activists repeatedly labeled the government's actions "genocidal," and such an extreme characterization consistently made sense to lesbians and gay men who were paying close attention to the government's negligent and punitive response to the epidemic. The perception that potential political opportunities—access to power or to influential elites for example—were tightly closed to them, made recourse to routine political channels an unacceptable option and made street activism, particularly amidst a holocaust, seem imperative. ACT UP's interpretations and framing of the political context and of an appropriate political course of action animated and helped to sustain participation in the movement.

*   *   *

The Rhetoric of Death

The rhetoric of death played a particularly potent role in the emotional dynamics of ACT UP's framing of the AIDS crisis. [Sociologist] Josh Gamson has argued that ACT UP gave AIDS deaths a new meaning by redefining the cause of death (1989: 361). Whereas earlier gay rhetoric had frequently blamed a virus, and even gay male sexuality, for AIDS, militant AIDS activists laid the blame for the epidemic squarely on the homophobic government and other institutions of society, including regimes of normalization that categorized sexual "deviants" and made them expendable. Along with the reclaiming of the deviant label as a source of pride, militant AIDS activists repeatedly offered an interpretation of AIDS that shifted attention from death by virus to murder by government neglect. * * * At the 1988 national demonstration targeting the Food and Drug Administration, members of ACT UP's national PISD caucus (People with Immune System Disorders) carried a banner that foregrounded the government's role in the epidemic by offering a more appropriate name for the FDA: "Federal Death Administration" (Wockner 1988: 13). Similarly, posters at ACT UP demonstrations often were in the shape of gravestones with the names of people who had died and the epitaph, "Killed by Government Neglect."

These shifts in the meaning of death had an emotional component to them. Where an understanding of death as the result of deviant sexual practices typically evoked shame and an understanding of death as the result of a virus evoked terror and despair, an understanding of death as produced by government neglect—that is, of AIDS deaths as *murder*—evoked anger. ACT UP's alterations in the meaning of death nourished and justified already existing feelings and inspired a renewed anger. They also helped to counter mainstream society's emotional and political norms: angry, militant street activism was certainly rational and reasonable in the face of murder.

*   *   *

ACT UP's Transmutations of Pride, Responsibility, and Shame

ACT UP had to authorize anger and militant activism, and another way it did so was by making angry, militant activism the object of lesbian and gay pride. Since the Stonewall Rebellion in 1969 that launched the modern lesbian and gay movement, pride has been a dominant trope, a response both to attempts by mainstream society to shame queers for their sexual difference and to lesbians' and gay men's internalization of those homophobic discourses. During the mid-1980s, lesbian and gay leaders and institutions repeatedly articulated and elicited pride about the community's commendable and responsible efforts to fight the AIDS epidemic in the face of little outside help (Gould 2000). Sometimes the pride seemed to revolve around respectability. A *New York Native* column from 1985 about AIDS volunteer work being done by gay men in San Francisco was typical. "Not surprisingly, the AIDS struggle has given San Franciscans new cause for civic pride, pride of a deeper sort than the pride we felt when we were the gay party capital of the world." The writer approvingly quoted a friend: "'We have a chance to prove something now, to show the world that we aren't the giddy, irresponsible queens it often takes us to be. Sure, AIDS has changed things here, but not necessarily for the worse'" (Hippler 1985: 31). Lesbians and gay men were encouraged to feel proud that their responsible efforts to address the crisis had earned them new respect from a society that previously had either misunderstood them, or perhaps had been correct in its negative assessment. ACT UP dramatically altered the object of pride, dislodging it from its place within a politics of respectability and linking it instead to militant AIDS activism. Repeated articulations and evocations of this street activism-oriented pride had a number of important, if not always intended, effects: * * * the new pride fortified ACT UP members' commitment to their activism and encouraged others to support, and even join, ACT UP.

* * *

Related to militant AIDS activists' alterations in both the object of pride and in the connotations of the term "responsibility," ACT UP also transformed the subject and object of shame. Earlier mainstream and lesbian/gay discourses that blamed gay men for AIDS elicited shame among many gay men about their sexual practices, on top of an already-existing shame among lesbians and gay men about their homosexuality (Gould 2000). ACT UP inverted gay shame by asserting that the (in)actions of the government and other institutions responsible for the AIDS crisis were shameful. A frequent mantra at ACT UP demonstrations was "shame, shame, shame," chanted while pointing to a specific target. The alteration of shame was connected to ACT UP's other emotions: lesbians and gay men angrily fighting back were righteous and, rather than feeling ashamed, they should feel proud of both their sexual practices and their militant activism.

* * *

The (Re-)Birth of Queer

As an oppositional, anger driven, militant AIDS activist organization, ACT UP not only inaugurated a new era in AIDS and lesbian and gay politics, it also gave birth to a new queer identity that was embraced by lesbians, gay men, and other sexual and gender outlaws across the country. This new identity—weaving together anger, oppositional politics, and sex-radicalism—helped to generate broad appeal for militant AIDS activism. Largely as a result of its emotional effects, it was a vital force sustaining ACT UP into the early 1990s.

Queer: Anger, Political Oppositionality, Sex-Radicalism

By 1990, to be queer was to be righteously angry about homophobia and the AIDS crisis, politically militant, free of shame about non-normative sexualities, and unconcerned about social acceptance. Apparently stirred by ACT UP's emotion work around anger, pride, and shame, the new queer generation proudly and joyously embraced both sexual non-conformity and a politics of confrontation, shaking up social norms (including emotional norms) in straight and gay society. "Queerness connoted a provocative politics of difference—an assertion that those who embraced the identity did not 'fit in' to the dominant culture *or* the mainstream gay and lesbian culture and had no interest in doing so" (Epstein 1999: 61, emphasis his). Anger—about the erotophobia [fear of erotic desires] and homophobia (and for some, about the racism and sexism as well) that propelled the dominant responses to AIDS and allowed AIDS to become an epidemic—became normative.

ACT UP queers re-eroticized sex and catapulted their proud sexual difference into the public realm. In doing so, they fought the AIDS-era equation of sex with death, and they also made a clear link between militant AIDS politics and liberatory sexual politics. ACT UP/Chicago's speech at the 1992 Lesbian and Gay Pride Parade drew the connection in these terms:

> Fighting the AIDS epidemic must go hand-in-hand with fighting for queer liberation . . . We need to celebrate our sexuality, our erotic innovations created out of this epidemic, our fantasies and fetishes, our particular ways of fucking, sucking, and licking. It is our queer love that has made us capable of fighting the insurance industry, the drug companies, the government, the bureaucracies, the gay-bashers, the right-wing zealots, the AIDS crisis (ACT UP/Chicago 1992: 5).

ACT UP/Chicago member Mary Patten extolled ACT UP's conjoining of sex and politics:

> ACT UP combined the red fists of radical 1970s feminism and the New Left with the flaming lips of neo-punk, postmodern, pro-sex queer politics . . . [R]ed now stood for lips, bodies, and lust as well as anger and rebellion; fists connoted not only street militancy, but sex acts (Patten 1998: 389).

The sex radicalism was infectious. Jeanne Kracher recalled that gay men's openness about their sexuality had a strong influence on her own sexuality.

> There was a way that these guys were so . . . expressive about their sexuality. There was something about being in that crowd . . . that was very freeing, about being a lesbian, about being gay, . . . that this was about sex . . . on a very deep level. These guys . . . would take their shirts off at the first possible moment at a demonstration and . . . [they] would have like, a million nipple rings, and [they] were making out whenever they could possibly incorporate that into anything. And there was a way that that was very freeing (Kracher 2000).

Fred Eggan credits lesbians for the movement's embrace of queer sexuality:

> I think that one of the reasons why ACT UP and the AIDS movement in general became a movement about . . . gender and sexuality was because of lesbians and all the advanced work that [they] had been doing during the '80s, like *On Our Backs* [a lesbian sex magazine] (Eggan 1999).

Challenging the recent attacks on queer sexuality, gay men brought their highly developed (and much maligned) sexual cultures to the movement while lesbians brought their expertise from the feminist sex wars and the recent renaissance in lesbian sexual experimentation. United, at least temporarily, by their confrontational street activism, emotions and emotional sensibility, and sex radicalism, lesbians and gay men in ACT UP turned to each other as political allies and friends, embracing and even trying on each other's identities. Men in ACT UP/Chicago wore the Women's Caucus "Power Breakfast" t-shirt which pictured two women engaged in oral sex. Across the country, dykes wore "Big Fag" t-shirts and fags wore "Big Dyke" t-shirts. Queers embraced gender and sexual fluidity; some queer dykes and fags started having sex with one another (Black 1996). "Queer" enveloped sexual and gender outlaws of all stripes, particularly those who were outcasts in the mainstream lesbian and gay community—leather dykes, drag queens and kings, trannies, S&M practitioners, butches and femmes, bisexuals, public sex lovers, sluts, dykes donning dildos. The new queer attitudes about sexuality, society, and politics affected lesbian and gay identities and practices, and while they took shape in the intense, emotional atmosphere of ACT UP meetings and actions, they quickly spread to queers not directly involved in the movement.

The Emotions of "Queer"

Knitting together militant politics, sex-radicalism, and a new emotional common sense, "queer" offered a potent and alluring response to lesbian and gay ambivalence. The AIDS epidemic had ravaged lesbians', and more strongly gay men's, already conflicted psyches; the new queer identity offered a new attitude that included a changed orientation both to self and to dominant society. Jasper has noted that "a collective identity is not simply the drawing of a cognitive boundary; most of all, it is an emotion, a positive affect toward other group members on the grounds of that common membership. Defining oneself through a collective label entails an affective as well as cognitive mapping of the social world" (1998: 415). The new queer identity valorized anger, defiant politics, and sexual non-conformity, and disavowed gay shame, self-doubt, fear of rejection, and the desire for social acceptance.

This new queer identity that flowered in ACT UP and that the movement in many ways represented did not eradicate lesbian and gay ambivalence. As a provocation to both gay and straight establishments, ACT UP was challenged by lesbians and gay men who disputed ACT UP's representation (in both senses of the word) of the lesbian and gay movement and community. Still, ACT UP's world view, tactics, and queer identity momentarily overturned the gay status quo, effecting sweeping changes in many lesbians' and gay men's, in many queers', political, sexual, and emotional subjectivities and practices.

This new queer identity—an identity that initially was conceptually inseparable from ACT UP, its site of origin—helped to sustain the militant AIDS activist movement. Specifically, the emotional dynamics of reclaiming the term "queer" were crucially important to the success of ACT UP. The joining of sexual, political, and emotional identities under the banner "queer" effectively displaced gay shame and elevated pride in an identity that was grounded in a celebration of sexual difference, anti-assimilationism, and angry, militant political activism. These emotional effects of "queer" were perhaps what most attracted lesbians and gay men to embrace the identity as well as the movement from which it grew.

*   *   *

In short, the new queer identity—born within ACT UP and championed by the movement—offered an emotionally compelling response to lesbian and gay ambivalence about self and society. Additionally, as a collective identity category that embraced oppositionality and an outsider status, "queer" appealed to those who historically had been marginalized by the mainstream lesbian and gay movement and community. It validated those who held radical politics, those who refused assimilation, and those who celebrated sexual difference; eliciting and fortifying a strong pride in difference, "queer" commanded a strong pull that enticed many to adopt the label and to support the politics out of which "queer" emerged. For all these reasons, the birth of "queer" helped to generate and maintain support for ACT UP.

ENGAGING THE TEXT, ENGAGING THE WORLD

- What does Gould mean when she says ACT UP had to challenge both the American ideology of democracy and the mainstream emotion culture? Define each set of norms and how ACT UP worked to destabilize them.

- Gould states that emotion is key to sustaining social movements. What was the emotional shift Gould documents that sustained ACT UP?

- How does Gould describe "queer"? How did queer sexuality and politics challenge the politics of respectability and in the process transform ACT UP and the fight against the AIDS epidemic?

- Compare the strategies of ACT UP with that of the Names Project Memorial Quilt. What are the advantages and disadvantages of each?

9

Kinship, Family, and Marriage

Humans live in groups. As a species, we rarely live alone or in isolation. The relationships we sometimes call family and that anthropologists have explored under the category of kinship are perhaps the most effective strategy humans have developed to form stable, reliable, separate, and deeply interconnected groups that can last over time and through generations.

What is kinship? Anthropologists define **kinship** as the system of meaning and power created to determine who is related to whom and to define their mutual expectations, rights, and responsibilities. Of course, humans also form groups through work, religion, education, and politics. But none compare to the power of families and kinship networks to provide support and nurture, ensure reproduction of the next generation, protect group assets, and influence social, economic, and political systems.

Kinship groups are often assumed by many in Western cultures to have a biological basis and to arise around the **nuclear family** of mother, father, and children. But as we will see in Melvyn Goldstein's article "When Brothers Share a Wife," when we examine these assumptions in a cross-cultural context, they show themselves to be a Euro-American ideal that not even those cultures have realized. Kinship groups come in a variety of shapes and sizes. We trace our connections through biological ancestors. We create kinship relations through **marriage** and remarriage. We adopt. We foster. We choose families of people who care about us. Sometimes we even imagine everyone in our nation to be part of one big, related, kinship community. Perhaps, as Donna Haraway challenges us to imagine in the following selection from *Staying with the Trouble: Making Kin in the Chthulucene*, in this era of globalization our concept of kinship may even need to expand to include all living species on the planet.

In the twenty-first century, we are vividly aware of new forms of family life as kinship relations shift, closing off familiar patterns and opening up new ones. The image of the family with mother, father, and two kids gathered around the dining room table every evening for a home-cooked meal and conversation may be familiar as a cultural icon, but for many people the experience of family is more complicated as families are made, taken apart, reconstructed, and blended. Gay and lesbian couples and their families are achieving increased acceptance and official recognition. New reproductive technologies, including artificial insemination, in vitro fertilization, and surrogacy, continue to stretch our ideas of kinship and families by showing how human culture, through science and technology, is shaping biological relationships. And as Dána-Ain Davis shows us in her article "The Troubling Case of Nadya Suleman," these changes often expose complex intersections of kinship, race, class, power, and inequality.

Although the term *kinship* may be unfamiliar to you, the subject material is not. Through kinship studies, anthropologists examine the deepest and most complicated aspects of our everyday lives—our relationships with people closest to us, including our mothers, fathers, brothers, sisters, grandparents, cousins, husbands, wives, partners, and children. These are the people we live with, eat with, count on for support, and promise to take care of when they are in need. We pour our emotions, creative energy, hopes, and dreams into these relationships. Many of the most emotionally vibrant moments of our lives—from joy and love to anger and pain—occur at the intersection of individual and family life: birthdays, holiday celebrations, shared meals, weddings, illnesses, and funerals. Through kinship, we see our lives as part of a continuum. We look back to see the history of the people we come from, and we look ahead to imagine the relatives and families yet to be. And in this era when human activity is so radically transforming and destabilizing the habitats of humans and all other creatures, our sense of connection, kinship, family, and responsibility increasingly is intertwined with every creature on this small planet called Earth.

Marriage and polyandry in Nepal

When Brothers Share a Wife
Melvyn Goldstein

Humans have a variety of ways of organizing kinship relationships. Some groups construct kinship along lines of genealogical descent, what U.S. culture refers to as "blood" relatives. Others form kinship groups through marriage, which builds ties between people who are (usually) not immediate biological kin. Something like marriage exists in every culture, but its exact form and characteristics vary widely. Marriages may be based on attraction and the romantic idea of love (companionate marriage) or they may be arranged by others. They may involve two people in a monogamous relationship. They may involve multiple people in a polygamous relationship.

In "When Brothers Share a Wife," Melvyn Goldstein tells the story of three Tibetan brothers—Dorje, Pema, and Sonam—in northwest Nepal, who participate in fraternal polyandry, the rarest form of marriage in the world, but one quite common in Tibetan culture. In the process Goldstein brings his anthropological skills to bear on the question of why three men would marry one woman. Pushing past the ethnocentric judgment and mistaken assumptions of many observers, Goldstein interviews the brothers and wife and conducts long-term fieldwork in their community to understand the economic, political, and social context of this kinship and marriage practice. Ultimately he brings to light the community's internal logic—why this makes sense to them—and challenges us to rethink our expectations of the role of marriage and the forms it can take. Does fraternal polyandry seem unfamiliar or uncomfortable to you? Goldstein's research exemplifies how the practice of anthropology pushes us to keep our own ethnocentrism in check, to understand cultural practices in their local context, to evaluate their strengths and weaknesses, and in the process to reevaluate our own cultural patterns and expectations in light of the diversity of human behavior.

Eager to reach home, Dorje drives his yaks hard over the 17,000-foot mountain pass, stopping only once to rest. He and his two older brothers, Pema and Sonam, are jointly marrying a woman from the next village in a few weeks, and he has to help with the preparations.

Dorje, Pema, and Sonam are Tibetans living in Limi, a 200-square-mile area in the northwest corner of Nepal, across the border from Tibet. The form of marriage they are about to enter—fraternal polyandry in anthropological parlance—is one of the world's rarest forms of marriage but is not uncommon in Tibetan society, where it has been practiced from time immemorial. For many Tibetan social strata, it traditionally represented the ideal form of marriage and family.

The mechanics of fraternal polyandry are simple. Two, three, four, or more brothers jointly take a wife, who leaves her home to come and live with them. Traditionally, marriage was arranged by parents, with children, particularly females, having little or no say. This is changing somewhat nowadays, but it is still unusual for children to marry without their parents' consent. Marriage ceremonies vary by income and region and range from all the brothers sitting together as grooms to only the eldest one formally doing so. The age of the brothers plays an important role in determining this: very young brothers

From Melvyn Goldstein. 1987. "When Brothers Share a Wife." *Natural History* 96: 39–48.

almost never participate in actual marriage ceremonies, although they typically join the marriage when they reach their midteens.

The eldest brother is normally dominant in terms of authority, that is, in managing the household, but all the brothers share the work and participate as sexual partners. Tibetan males and females do not find the sexual aspect of sharing a spouse the least bit unusual, repulsive, or scandalous, and the norm is for the wife to treat all the brothers the same.

Offspring are treated similarly. There is no attempt to link children biologically to particular brothers, and a brother shows no favoritism toward his child even if he knows he is the real father because, for example, his other brothers were away at the time the wife became pregnant. The children, in turn, consider all of the brothers as their fathers and treat them equally, even if they also know who is their real father. In some regions children use the term "father" for the eldest brother and "father's brother" for the others, while in other areas they call all the brothers by one term, modifying this by the use of "elder" and "younger."

Unlike our own society, where monogamy is the only form of marriage permitted, Tibetan society allows a variety of marriage types, including monogamy, fraternal polyandry, and polyandry. Fraternal polyandry and monogamy are the most common form of marriage, while polygyny typically occurs in cases where the first wife is barren. The widespread practice of fraternal polyandry, therefore, is not the outcome of a law requiring brothers to marry jointly. There is choice, and in fact, divorce traditionally was relatively simple in Tibetan society. If a brother in a polyandrous marriage became dissatisfied and wanted to separate, he simply left the main house and set up his own household. In such cases, all the children stayed in the main household with the remaining brother(s), even if the departing brother was known to be the real father of one or more of the children.

The Tibetans' own explanation for choosing fraternal polyandry is materialistic. For example, when I asked Dorje why he decided to marry with his two brothers rather than take his own wife, he thought for a moment, then said it prevented the division of his family's farm (and animals) and thus facilitated all of them achieving a higher standard of living. And when I later asked Dorje's bride whether it wasn't difficult for her to cope with three brothers as husbands, she laughed and echoed the rationale of avoiding fragmentation of the family and land, adding that she expected to be better off economically, since she would have three husbands working for her and her children.

Exotic as it may seem to Westerners, Tibetan fraternal polyandry is thus in many ways analogous to the way primogeniture functioned in nineteenth-century England. Primogeniture dictated that the eldest son inherited the family estate, while younger sons had to leave home and seek their own employment—for example, in the military or the clergy. Primogeniture maintained family estates intact over generations by permitting only one heir per generation. Fraternal polyandry also accomplishes this but does so by keeping all the brothers together with just one wife so that there is only one *set* of heirs per generation.

While Tibetans believe that in this way fraternal polyandry reduces the risk of family fission, monogamous marriages among brothers need not necessarily precipitate the division of the family estate: brothers could continue to live together, and the family land could continue to be worked jointly. When I asked Tibetans about this, however, they invariably responded that such joint families are unstable because each wife is primarily oriented to her own children and interested in their success and well-being over that of the children of the other wives. For example, if the youngest brother's wife had three sons while the eldest brother's wife had only one daughter, the wife of the youngest brother might begin to demand more resources for her children since, as males, they represent the future of the family. Thus, the children from different wives in the same generation are competing sets of heirs, and this makes such families inherently unstable. Tibetans perceive that conflict will spread from the wives to their husbands and consider this likely to cause family fission. Consequently, it is almost never done.

Although Tibetans see an economic advantage to fraternal polyandry, they do not value the sharing of a wife as an end in itself. On the contrary, they articulate a number of problems inherent in the practice. For example, because authority is customarily exercised by the eldest brother, his younger male siblings have to subordinate themselves with little hope of changing their status within the family. When these younger brothers are aggressive and individualistic, tensions and difficulties often occur despite there being only one set of heirs.

In addition, tension and conflict may arise in polyandrous families because of sexual favoritism. The bride normally sleeps with the eldest brother, and the two have the responsibility to see to it that the other males have opportunities for sexual access. Since the Tibetan subsistence economy requires males to travel a lot, the temporary absence of one or more brothers facilitates this, but there are also other rotation practices. The cultural ideal unambiguously calls for the wife to show equal affection and sexuality to each of the brothers (and vice versa), but deviations from this ideal occur, especially when there is a sizable difference in age between the partners in the marriage.

Dorje's family represents just such a potential situation. He is fifteen years old and his two older brothers are twenty-five and twenty-two years old. The new bride is twenty-three years old, eight years Dorje's senior. Sometimes such a bride finds the youngest husband immature and adolescent and does not treat him with equal affection; alternatively, she may find his youth attractive and lavish special attention on him. Apart from that consideration, when a younger male like Dorje grows up, he may consider his wife "ancient" and prefer the company of a woman his own age or younger. Consequently, although men and women do not find the idea of sharing a bride or a bridegroom repulsive, individual likes and dislikes can cause familial discord.

Two reasons have commonly been offered for the perpetuation of fraternal polyandry in Tibet: that Tibetans practice female infanticide and therefore have to marry polyandrously, owing to a shortage of females; and that Tibet, lying at extremely high altitudes, is so barren and bleak that Tibetans would starve without resort to this mechanism. A Jesuit who lived in Tibet during the eighteenth century articulated this second view: "One reason for this most odious custom is the sterility of the soil, and the small amount of land that can be cultivated owing to the lack of water. The crops may suffice if the brothers all live together, but if they form separate families they would be reduced to beggary."

Both explanations are wrong, however. Not only has there never been institution-alized female infanticide in Tibet, but Tibetan society gives females considerable rights, including inheriting the family estate in the absence of brothers. In such cases, the woman takes a bridegroom who comes to live in her family and adopts her family's name and identity. Moreover, there is no demographic evidence of a shortage of females. In Limi, for example, there were (in 1974) sixty females and fifty-three males in the fifteen-to thirty-five-year age category, and many adult females were unmarried.

The second reason is also incorrect. The climate in Tibet is extremely harsh, and eco-logical factors do play a major role perpetuating polyandry, but polyandry is not a means of preventing starvation. It is characteristic, not of the poorest segments of the society, but rather of the peasant landowning families.

In the old society, the landless poor could not realistically aspire to prosperity, but they did not fear starvation. There was a persistent labor shortage throughout Tibet, and very poor families with little or no land and few animals could subsist through agricul-tural labor, tenant farming, craft occupations such as carpentry, or by working as servants. Although the per person family income could increase somewhat if brothers married polyandrously and pooled their wages, in the absence of inheritable land, the advantage of fraternal polyandry was not generally sufficient to prevent them from setting up their own households. A more skilled or energetic younger brother could do as well or better alone, since he would completely control his income and would not have to share it with his siblings. Consequently, while there was and is some polyandry among the poor, it is much less frequent and more prone to result in divorce and family fission.

An alternative reason for the persistence of fraternal polyandry is that it reduces pop-ulation growth (and thereby reduces the pressure on resources) by relegating some females to lifetime spinsterhood. Fraternal polyandrous marriages in Limi (in 1974) averaged 2.35 men per woman, and not surprisingly, 31 percent of the females of child-bearing age (twenty to forty-nine) were unmarried. These spinsters either continued to live at home, set up their own households, or worked as servants for other families. They could also become Buddhist nuns. Being unmarried is not synonomous with exclusion from the reproductive pool. Discreet extramarital relationships are tolerated, and actually half of the adult unmar-ried women in Limi had one or more children. They raised these children as single mothers, working for wages or weaving cloth and blankets for sale. As a group, however, the unmar-ried woman had far fewer offspring than the married women, averaging only 0.7 children per woman, compared with 3.3 for married women, whether polyandrous, monogamous, or polygynous. While polyandry helps regulate population, this function of polyandry is not consciously perceived by Tibetans and is not the reason they consistently choose it.

If neither a shortage of females nor the fear of starvation perpetuates fraternal poly-andry, what motivates brothers, particularly younger brothers, to opt for this system of marriage? From the perspective of the younger brother in a landholding family, the main incentive is the attainment or maintenance of the good life. With polyandry, he can expect a more secure and higher standard of living, with access not only to his family's land and animals but also to its inherited collection of clothes, jewelry, rugs, saddles, and horses. In addition, he will experience less work pressure and much greater security because all responsibility does not fall on one "father." For Tibetan brothers, the question is whether to trade off the greater personal freedom inherent in monogamy for the real or potential economic security, affluence, and social prestige associated with life in a larger, labor-rich polyandrous family.

A brother thinking of separating from his polyandrous marriage and taking his own wife would face various disadvantages. Although in the majority of Tibetan regions all brothers theoretically have rights to their family's estate, in reality Tibetans are reluctant to divide their land into small fragments. Generally, a younger brother who insists on leaving the family will receive only a small plot of land, if that. Because of its power and wealth, the rest of the family usually can block any attempt of the younger brother to increase his share of land through litigation. Moreover, a younger brother may not even get a house and cannot expect to receive much above the minimum in terms of movable possessions, such as furniture, pots, and pans. Thus, a brother contemplating going it on his own must plan on achieving economic security and the good life not through inheritance but through his own work.

The obvious solution for younger brothers—creating new fields from virgin land—is generally not a feasible option. Most Tibetan populations live at high altitudes (above 12,000 feet), where arable land is extremely scarce. For example, in Dorje's village, agriculture ranges only from about 12,900 feet, the lowest point in the area, to 13,300 feet. Above that altitude, early frost and snow destroy the staple barley crop. Furthermore, because of the low rainfall caused by the Himalayan rain shadow, many areas in Tibet and northern Nepal that are within the appropriate altitude range for agriculture have no reliable sources of irrigation. In the end, although there is plenty of unused land in such areas, most of it is either too high or too arid.

Even where unused land capable of being farmed exists, clearing the land and building the substantial terraces necessary for irrigation constitute a great undertaking. Each plot has to be completely dug out to a depth of two to two and a half feet so that the large rocks and boulders can be removed. At best, a man might be able to bring a few new fields under cultivation in the first years after separating from his brothers, but he could not expect to acquire substantial amounts of arable land this way.

In addition, because of the limited farmland, the Tibetan subsistence economy characteristically includes a strong emphasis on animal husbandry. Tibetan farmers regularly maintain cattle, yaks, goats, and sheep, grazing them in the areas too high for agriculture. These herds produce wool, milk, cheese, butter, meat, and skins. To obtain these resources, however, shepherds must accompany the animals on a daily basis. When first setting up a monogamous household, a younger brother like Dorje would find it difficult to both farm and manage animals.

In traditional Tibetan society, there was an even more critical factor that operated to perpetuate fraternal polyandry—a form of hereditary servitude somewhat analogous to serfdom in Europe. Peasants were tied to large estates held by aristocrats, monasteries, and the Lhasa government. They were allowed the use of some farmland to produce their own subsistence but were required to provide taxes in kind and corvée (free labor) to their lords. The corvée was a substantial hardship, since a peasant household was in many cases required to furnish the lord with one laborer daily for most of the year and more on specific occasions such as the harvest. This enforced labor, along with the lack of new land and the ecological pressure to pursue both agriculture and animal husbandry, made polyandrous families particularly beneficial. The polyandrous family allowed an internal division of adult labor, maximizing economic advantage. For example, while the wife worked the family fields, one brother could perform the lord's corvée, another could look after the animals, and a third could engage in trade.

Although social scientists often discount other people's explanations of why they do things, in the case of Tibetan fraternal polyandry, such explanations are very close to the truth. The custom, however, is very sensitive to changes in its political and economic milieu and, not surprisingly, is in decline in most Tibetan areas. Made less important by the elimination of the traditional serf-based economy, it is disparaged by the dominant non-Tibetan leaders of India, China, and Nepal. New opportunities for economic and social mobility in these countries, such as the tourist trade and government employment, are also eroding the rationale for polyandry, and so it may vanish within the next generation.

ENGAGING THE TEXT, ENGAGING THE WORLD

- What is the Tibetan rationale for fraternal polyandry, according to Dorje and Dorje's bride?

- Goldstein critiques two common assumptions about the rationale for fraternal polyandry. What are they and how do they compare to Goldstein's ethnographic findings?

- Humans construct a vast array of kinship groups. Did you find that your own cultural assumptions about marriage made it difficult to think openmindedly about fraternal polyandry?

- Part of the anthropological project is to see one's own culture more clearly by seeing the global diversity of human behavior. How has considering another culture's marriage practices changed your perception of your own cultural norms and practices, underlying values, or practical concerns?

- What are your own culture's marriage practices, ideal and real, and how do you think a Tibetan anthropologist might analyze them? How are they shaped by your specific economic, political, religious, and social context?

- How might Tibetan marriage practices be sensitive to changes brought about by globalization, economic development, migration, or political shifts? Consider the differences between Goldstein's article and Laura Ahearn's article on Nepalese love letters in Chapter 4, written 20 years later.

The Troubling Case of Nadya Suleman

Dána-Ain Davis

Intersectionality, artificial reproductive technology, and reproductive justice

What rules and mechanisms does a society put in place to define and enforce the norms and values of kinship? In "The Troubling Case of Nadya Suleman," Dána-Ain Davis explores the implications of the construction of kinship in American culture through the media events surrounding the birth of octuplets to Nadya Suleman in 2009. Big families are not unfamiliar in American pop culture. The reality television show *Jon and Kate plus Eight* featured a large family created through artificial reproductive technologies (ART). Religious beliefs about reproduction were central to the show *Eighteen and Counting*. But when Nadya Suleman had octuplets, a different narrative emerged. The birth of her eight children, assisted by ART, became a source of media speculation and frenzy. When it was discovered she already had six children at home, talk show hosts called for her to be criminalized and the children taken away. Medical experts questioned the safety and wisdom of her use of ART. Bloggers raised unrelated and often incorrect questions about her race, class, marital status, and legal status.

In examining the case of Nadya Suleman, Davis raises important questions about the complicated ways race and class intersect with cultural norms and values of reproductive rights and kinship practices. She identifies deeply held stereotypes that emerge in the course of conversations and debates that surround these practices. And she challenges the effectiveness of largely white reproductive rights organizations to champion the rights of poor women of color. In conclusion, she argues for the need to expand the cultural debate around kinship beyond a narrow focus on reproductive choice to include a far broader concern for reproductive justice.

The USA's first set of octuplets was born in Houston, Texas, in December 1998 to Nkem and Iyke Chukwu. The Nigerian-born couple, who were US citizens, had used fertility drugs to achieve the pregnancy, and all but one of the children survived (Lyman, 1998). Just as with the Chukwu octuplets, the global media trumpeted the arrival of another

From Dána-Ain Davis. 2009. "The Politics of Reproduction: The Troubling Case of Nadya Suleman and Assisted Reproductive Technology." *Transforming Anthropology* 17(2): 105–116. Some of the author's notes have been omitted.

high-order multiple birth on January 26, 2009, when Nadya Suleman gave birth to the nation's second set of octuplets in Bellflower, California, at Kaiser Permanente Hospital. Following the delivery the mother and the children were doing well—despite the infants being two and a half months premature. Initially the story possessed all the elements of a mediagenic success. * * *

The blogging public viewed the event as a joyous miracle. Simultaneously, [however] medical and bioethical professionals' appearance on news programs tempered the public's elation by conjecturing how Suleman became pregnant. Embryologists thought it unlikely that the octuplets were the result of natural conception, but rather the product of assisted reproductive technology (ART). The range of ART options that might have been used included in vitro fertilization (IVF) or intrauterine insemination (IUI), with partner or donor sperm. As answers to various questions unfolded, there was a rising tide of sentiment against Suleman, and as the din of chastisement grew louder, I began to wonder why so few mainstream reproductive rights groups weighed in on the discussions. My interest was piqued since Suleman's utilization of ART quite clearly reflects the reproductive rights movement's goals of access and choice. But there was more to this story than meets the eye. * * *

My goal is to make sense of the messy representation of Nadya Suleman in thinking about issues of race, class, marital status, family formation, and the idea of choice within the realm of reproductive politics. * * * I uncover subtle systems of racialization and classism in the biased representations of Ms. Suleman and her reproductive choice. * * * I use Suleman's story to [explore] the implications of her choice [for] the broader reproductive concerns of women of color, low-income women, and others whose reproduction is organized hierarchically in relation to White heterosexual women and those who can afford to pay for health services. * * *

The Landscape of ART

* * * From the low-tech strategies of artificial insemination (using turkey basters) to surrogate mothers as the solution for mostly White middle-class infertility, reproductive technologies [have proliferated] over the last 30 years. The technologies hold both promise and challenge, and their implications are being critiqued in global and domestic contexts. * * * Domestically, analysis of ART encompasses, among other issues, ethics, health-related concerns, equitable access, and regulatory matters. * * *

Among the health-related concerns [is the effect] on the neurocognitive development of children born of these technologies. Another is the uncertain consequences of multiple and high-order multiple births (more than two) on women since health risks may include increased cardiovascular risks and challenges on the respiratory system. With regard to equity issues a major question that ART raises is its inaccessibility to all women given the often-high costs that can run into and beyond tens of thousands of dollars. And finally, there are regulatory issues. Europe regulates ART to a far greater degree than the USA. For example surrogacy is illegal in most of Europe. IVF is limited to the implantation of two embryos. While ART guidelines have been developed by the fertility industry in the USA, it is not illegal to not follow the standards. Some have called this lack of regulatory oversight the "Wild West" of assisted reproduction (Spar 2009).

Not surprisingly the phrase *Wild West* in many ways illustrates the startlingly biased representations of Ms. Suleman that circulated. The media, blogging public, and fertility professionals used Ms. Suleman to police reproductive boundaries similarly to how marginalized women have been scrutinized, at almost every stage of their reproductive lives. The ways in which Suleman was cast, as unfit, and the possible policies that may be implemented as a consequence reflect a striking resemblance to the racial and class discourses controlling the "untamed" reproduction of marginalized or unqualified women in the past.* * *

Nadya Suleman's story cannot and should not be separated from interrogating ART and the reproductive rights movement, since Ms. Suleman ostensibly actualized the movements' stated goals of choice. What is of concern though is the apparent silence of mainstream reproductive rights groups [in] public debates about Suleman. Their omission or self-imposed exile from commenting on the issue left it to the media, fertility specialists, and the blogging public to shape Suleman's denigration. My critique of their absence is influenced by my participation with reproductive issues since 1974 as an activist, as Coordinator of the Reproductive Rights Education Project at Hunter College, working with the National Network of Abortion Funds (The Network), and as the former co-Chair of NARAL Pro-Choice New York. I left NARAL somewhat jaded because there seemed to be resistance to embracing a broad reproductive justice approach in favor of a reproductive choice perspective. While the latter centers on legal protections for women to obtain abortions, the former includes addressing housing and employment, among other issues. A reproductive justice approach emphasizes reproductive health, as well as the social, economic, and political power to make healthy decisions about one's body, sexuality, and reproduction. Thus, the lens through which I consider Suleman's representation is based on familiarity with the distinction between mainstream reproductive rights and reproductive justice.

Let me make clear from the outset that I refer to this story to neither justify nor condemn Ms. Suleman's use of ART, nor to speculate on the logic of her maternal impulses. However, Suleman's scathing public treatment elucidates some of the broader implications of who ART is intended for, as well as the meaning of choice, which is inflected with race and class reproductive normativity.

Stratified Reproduction

On the day the octuplets were born, the *LA Times* reported in an update that the "event" was unbelievably rare. One medical professional claimed that the arrival of the eight infants, if it had been achieved by ART, was not a medical triumph but rather a serious complication. While the first blog responses on January 26 were positive, by 10:54 am on January 27—just one day after the birth—suspicions surfaced regarding the mother's intentions. Questions arose about why she would want so many children. By the 28th, bloggers inquired if the woman had plotted to have that many children for monetary gain—a la Angelina Jolie or Jennifer Lopez; suggesting that she may have wanted to be paid for magazine exclusives which come with substantial compensation.* * *

Then on January 29, the mother, Nadya, was "outed"—she already had six children at home being cared for by her mother while she was at the hospital. Upon this revelation, one blogger wrote: "Who know who the *dads* are?" [of the other six]. Another wrote, "Now she brings a liter [litter] of eight kids into an already over populated world. Those babies will cost taxpayers millions. I think this is criminal" (Posted by Joe 1/29/09 6:13 pm—*LA Times* Blog). But still there was too little information about who the parents were, allowing Ms. Suleman to escape the full denunciation based on her martial status. On February 9 Suleman's mother Angela confirmed that her daughter had undergone IVF. Professionals asked such questions as: Had she been appropriately counseled regarding reductive abortion of some of the fetuses since she already had six children? Which doctor might have assisted her? Medical professionals' concerns about the conception process and the medical risks continued to center on the questionable ethics of any fertility clinic that did not follow industry standards which limit implantation to two embryos. However, this discussion only lasted as long as it was assumed Suleman was married; an assumption based on the imagined social script that ART is only for people in sanctioned heterosexual relationships. When it was discovered Suleman was a single mother (although previously married) criticism against her crystallized. Initially, the fact that Suleman had a large number of children did not necessarily define her as an imperfect mother in the eyes of medical professionals. But the trajectory of their questions revealed a sea change. It was only after Suleman's non-normative statuses came to light that her childbearing decisions constituted bad judgment and bad mothering. In thinking about the children's birth and health, the potential cause of harm was redirected away from the ethics of the fertility clinic and directed toward Ms. Suleman for her irresponsibility and moral ineptitude.

As for some members of the blogging public "the miracle" turned into disgust, which seemed to be fueled in part by an inability to "profile" the woman who gave birth. On February 5, for example, in a *Good Morning America* interview Suleman's newly hired publicist Joanne Killeen was asked by Diane Sawyer "Who is this woman? We know nothing about her." Since no pictures of Suleman had been released, newscasters had no idea what she looked like, making it difficult to use visual cues to determine class status, educational achievements and race or ethnic categories. Seemingly, her unknown identity frustrated attempts to establish the legitimacy of both her maternal aspirations and her use of ART.

[For] bloggers, the missing information about Suleman's class and race resulted in indexing her citizenship status and then her race. It was her fertility that became the marker identifying Suleman as an illegal alien evidenced by this blog entry "Does anyone know if the mother is 'Legal'? I still remember the last story the *Los Angeles Times* ran about the illegal alien mom who used fertility drugs and ended up with 10 kids, all at California [T]axpayer expense" (Posted by Skip 1/27/09 at 11:29 am). Shortly thereafter another blogger claimed that Suleman was African American. Cumulatively the inferences were that "illegal" and African American women are hyperreproductive. Another blogger hoped that the Superbowl would overshadow the "welfare baby momma" news. From there it did not take long for an ideological default to be asserted: she was on welfare. In fact, Ms. Suleman received $460 a month in food stamps and disability payments for two of her six children. It should be pointed out that welfare includes government programs that provide benefits and economic supports to no and low-income people. But the negative shroud of welfare, erroneously associated as it is with people of color and single mothers who presumably take advantage of the system by having more children, overrode any possibility that Suleman might have just wanted to be a mother. By using the welfare card to justify denigrating Suleman's decision to have children using IVF, * * * the right to use ART was inextricably linked to White middle-class * * * family making.

Oddly neither Ms. Suleman's race/ethnicity nor her citizenship status was remarked upon on the news programs except a passing mention that her father is Iraqi. Once it became clear that she had been a stay-at-home mom with an unknown source of income, Suleman "achieved" a level of toxicity replicating a decades old stereotype that single and low-income or poor women are bad mothers. This logic led to the view that she should be punished, and Suleman even received death threats. Thus it was no surprise when bloggers and media personalities such as Bill O'Reilly and radio host Dr. Carole Lieberman demanded either Suleman's arrest or that she have her children removed based on the argument that although having 14 children was not abuse, there is bound to be some form of neglect in the future.

Suleman, vis-à-vis her childbearing, was vilified in much the same way that low-income and women of color have been in the past for their reproductive acts. As is so often the case, assessments of women's childbearing are related to race and class. For example, in a response to a Salon.com inquiry about Suleman, Lynn Paltrow, Executive Director of National Advocates for Pregnant Women, remarked that when a pregnant woman is not brown or black and the drugs/technologies are provided by big pharmaceuticals the discussion (of reproduction) focuses on questions of ethics. She went on to say that when drugs/technologies are related to low income [women] and women of color and their reproduction, the focus is on punishment through the criminal justice or child welfare system. Take as one example the rising arrests of pregnant women who test positive for drugs and are then charged with child abuse (reinterpreted as fetal abuse) for delivering drugs to a minor either through the umbilical cord or breast milk. In some cases women are charged with homicide if the baby is stillborn or is born and then dies. Yet there is differential treatment of mothers at the intersection of race and the drugs used. Campbell (2000) concludes that the type of drugs White women use (such as methamphetamine) does not register the same portrayal or castigation as mothers of color who use such drugs as crack. Legal scholar Dorothy Roberts (1997) also points out that most of the women arrested while pregnant and criminally charged are poor and Black. These observations are clearly congruent with the reproductive control, stigmatization and criminalization of what I call "particular others" — those who are valued differentially based on race, ethnicity, citizenship, class, nationality, sexuality and gender (Silliman et al. 2004:4).

Backlash against "particular other" women and their reproductive desires [is] evident in the representational and linguistic repertoires often used to describe them. One example is when they are referenced in nonhuman terms such as "brood mare" (Lister 2004). A similar repertoire was directed at Suleman, whose moniker "octo-mom" can be used interchangeably to describe the fact that she had eight children and to summon up an image of the notorious invertebrate with eight arms. Deploying the term *octo-mom* generated images of Suleman's supposedly questionable subhuman qualities, making it easier to condemn her reproductive decisions. * * *

Technologies associated with infertility, according to [medical anthropologist Seline Szkupinski] Quiroga (2007), are often directed to creating families that reproduce the heteropatriarchal norm. Many feminist scholars have critiqued how ART has been used toward this end, but much less attention has been paid to the ways in which race operates in the delivery and utilization of ART. One notable exception is [legal scholar Dorothy] Roberts (1997) who argues that keeping whiteness pure is one goal of American law and social convention related to genetics, racial classification, and reproduction. Ms. Suleman's Iraqi–Latvian background, although identified later during the media blitz, came too late to rescue her from being maligned relative to the dominant racial privilege associated with ART. She had already been "marked," if you will, as a "particular other" despite her ethnicity.* * *

One might even argue that her marital status, the number of children she had, and her Middle Eastern/Eastern European parentage conspired to "primitivize" her [in contrast to] the celebrated White middle-class standard of motherhood, making her culturally ineligible for IVF.

Further, in terms of kinship, Ms. Suleman as a single woman was not viewed as having a "real" family, and there was broad acceptance that her transgression reflected the ways in which family formation and kinship are believed to be immutably normative. Nadya Suleman may be seen as a casualty of stratified reproduction, whereby her right to reproduce and nurture was denounced because she was single, had no verifiable source of income, and was an inadequate representative of whiteness. This, despite Ms. Suleman's constant claim of wanting a large family and saying that all she wanted in life was to be a mother (Garrison and Yoshino 2009). In the court of public, medical professional, and elite media opinion, Suleman violated the stratified privileges associated with ART and maternalism, leading to calls for measures to circumscribe the choice she made.

*   *   *

Touted as an open market accessible to all, ART is in fact highly restricted both economically and geographically. Here again, Ms. Suleman's story is instructive. She took advantage of a reproductive option using a portion of a $165,000 settlement received after a work-related injury to pay to have six embryos implanted—two of which split. Ironically, while she complied with two constructed ideologies, that of maternalism and consumption, some saw Ms. Suleman's choice to participate in the reproductive market-place to actualize her maternalist impulse * * * as an abomination of science and morality.

* * *

Ms. Suleman's choice and her access to ART generated ire which was fueled by questioning her judgment and denaturalizing her, a project in which her mother and to a lesser degree her father participated. Her mother commented that instead of "becoming a kindergarten teacher or something, she started having them, but not the normal way" (Associated Press 2009). There were further insinuations that Ms. Suleman had mental health issues, and some television broadcasters made provocative comments saying that Suleman would not be able to love 14 children; she has an Angelina Jolie fetish; and that her priorities were mixed up because she got her nails done after the delivery and release from the hospital.* * *

Are questions about using ART and the possibility of having to raise large families being asked of married White middle-class women? Evidently race, marital status, and class results in varying degrees of acceptance with regard to having large families especially when they are formed through reproductive technology. We see this in the more positive depiction bestowed upon two large families, the first being Jon and Kate Gosselin, a married couple with eight children and the stars of their own TLC show *Jon and Kate Plus Eight*. Kate underwent fertility treatments, first having twins, followed by more treatments which resulted in the birth of sextuplets. For several years the public has watched this reality TV show with great interest, and although the tides of public support have turned somewhat against the Gosselins due to infidelity and other issues, questions about their rights to have used ART have not been as virulent as against Suleman (see Stelter 2009). A second example of a circumstance in which large families are deemed acceptable, even valorized, rests with Michelle and Jim Bob Duggar who have 18 children and are also the subjects of a TLC program, *18 and Counting*. In the Duggars' case, their religious beliefs justify the number of children they have. At the same time their source of income, primarily from rental property, helps solidify the construction of White heteronormative families achieved through marital and class status.

* * *

The Reproductive Choice Conundrum

The Suleman case exemplifies what a politics of reproduction can descend into when reproductive justice is not front and center in framing issues—issues centered on the complete physical, mental, spiritual, political, social, environmental, and economic well-being of women and girls based on the full achievement of women's human rights. In the context of the broad themes that emerged from Nadya Suleman's story, it is curious that no mainstream reproductive rights organization participated in the debates. * * * The silence rendered despite how the story was represented in the media and on blogs is disturbing because the conclusions that circulated in the public sphere included Suleman being marginalized, symbolically criminalized, and castigated for her maternalism and her reproductive decisions and process.

These conclusions speak to some of the ideological and political incongruencies surrounding the politics of reproduction. As Andrea Smith (2005) argues much of that politics depends on the language of "choice" narrowing the broad focus of reproductive justice politics. This is the case because "choice" can be conditional. It is "choice" that is of concern to the mainstream reproductive rights organizations, and the problem is that the lure of "choice" obscures the legitimate needs and concerns of women who do not have any. * * * In other words "choice" rests on the availability of resources and sanctioned status; without resources and status some women are unable to actualize "choice" in the same way that others might.* * *

Further the "choice" framework rests on consumerist ideas of free choice that operate neatly with the neoliberal stance of individualism. In the Suleman case, it was her right not as a citizen but as a consumer of goods and services that was challenged. Challenging her decision to use IVF and then to carry all of the implanted eggs to term illustrates one problem of neoliberalism. It creates a hierarchy among women based on who is capable of making "legitimate" choices. In the marketplace of reproductive services, then, "choice" serves in the interest of those with access and the privilege of legitimacy, trumping the "choices" of those in need. Because choices can be reined in, it is consistent to withdraw reproductive options from any number of categorically marginalized women including poor women who, for example, have experienced the consequences of restrictive reproductive policy in the form of the Hyde Amendment, which eliminated federal funding for abortion (Smith 2005:128).

This is where reproductive justice is more efficacious because it is concerned with rights that are accessible regardless of the woman's resources. The justice approach is organized around the particular understanding that women of color have of their reproductive needs and operates within a political agenda that seeks to make linkages between all women's oppression, their agency, and reproductive rights. For example, asking what are the reproductive implications for Asian women being exploited through sweatshop labor policies and then organizing around labor issues is what reproductive justice work can entail. Reproductive justice is certainly concerned with pointing out stereotypes that circumscribe women's reproductive options, such as those stereotypes leveled against Suleman. Moreover, reproductive justice workers can speak to developing policy and organizing efforts that ensure comprehensive treatment of women's reproductive circumstances (Silliman et al. 2004). A reproductive justice approach does not condemn Suleman for her choice but asks what supports does she have a right to as a person raising 14 children?

In the absence of principles and politics guided by reproductive justice, few mainstream groups opposed Suleman's public condemnation, and few challenged the harmful discourse, which was the very same discourse that has dominated marginalized women's reproductive rights. This left an awkward opening to undermine political projects seeking to secure the full articulation of rights to information, birth control, economic resources, and the multitude of supports needed to control fertility, activate fertility, raise children, select birthing options, and live in fundamentally good housing, among other concerns. With too few critiques of the call for state regulatory agencies to investigate and remove Suleman's children, other women—poor and low-income, women of color, disabled women and lesbians—were put at risk for being subjected to similar punitive demands. By not challenging the media's obsession on the "failure" of one woman to make good choices, the possibility of creating panics that result in marking others as having made bad choices, was reinvigorated. * * *

[The] troubling Nadya Suleman story demonstrates the fragility of the choice framework and complicates the implications of ART, where race, class, marital status, and family formation intersect. * * * Suleman was portrayed as a "bad" mother. In contradistinction to Suleman, a "good" mother would not choose to have a child if she were poor or low-income, and/or single. * * * Using this logic, poor, low-income, single and non-White women should not seek to have children.

Suleman's case also reveals two crises, both imagined. One is that White middle-class women have fertility problems that should be addressed. The other is that women of color, or women marked as being of color, poor or low-income women, and single women, do not have fertility problems that should be addressed. While arguing for the "choice" to use ART by deserving White middle-class women, this construct simultaneously limits the understanding of reproductive justice issues for "particular other" women as one of having to control their reproduction in terms of preventing conception or birth. But also the fact remains that illegible women * * * neither possess legitimate claims to the choice to have children through ART nor legitimate claims to not have children (specifically abortions). This is the story that was so spectacularly erased in the troubling case of Nadya Suleman.

ENGAGING THE TEXT, ENGAGING THE WORLD

- Why do you think the public and media were so interested in Suleman's race, class, marital status, and legal status?

- Compare the media's assumptions about Suleman to her actual identity. How did cultural stereotypes about race and class play into those assumptions?

- Which elements of Suleman's story surprised you as Davis revealed them over the course of the article? How did they challenge your own preconceived notions of Suleman and her family?

- How did the public, media, and medical expert responses reveal assumptions about reproductive privileges stratified along lines of race and class?

- Why was the reproductive rights movement largely silent in the case of Nadya Suleman, according to Davis?

- What does Davis mean by "reproductive justice"?

- Why does Davis argue that, especially for poor women of color, reproductive rights are inadequate and reproductive justice is needed instead?

Anthropocene, multispecies ethnography, and expanding ideas of kinship

From *Staying with the Trouble: Making Kin in the Chthulucene*
Donna Haraway

 Donna Haraway challenges us to radically expand our notion of kinship to include all creatures on Earth. Thinking about multi-species kinship, she argues, is central to our survival and the survival of all those we share the planet with. This change in thinking requires a shift from the Anthropocene to a new era—what Haraway inventively calls the "Chthulucene." In the Anthropocene, people are changing the planet. Rooted in the eighteenth-century invention of the steam engine and discovery of fossil fuels, today globalization of these forces has driven the warming of the planet, acidification of oceans, and mass extinctions of species. As a result, today the world is full of refugees, and not just human refugees.

In this selection Haraway challenges us to "stay with the trouble," to not look away but to stir up new ways of thinking and acting, and make kin—community, relatives—of all species in a new era: the Chthulucene. Can humans stop dithering during this crisis and move past individualism to a new collective sense of danger and responsibility? Haraway's inventive use of words and images is designed to make you read more carefully, to spark closer attention, and to inspire deeper thinking. Who are our kin? Who are we responsible for? And what is our collective strategy for surviving into a new era?

Trouble is an interesting word. It derives from a thirteenth-century French verb meaning "to stir up," "to make cloudy," "to disturb." We—all of us on Terra [Earth]—live in

---

From Donna Haraway. 2016. *Staying with the Trouble: Making Kin in the Chthulucene*. Durham, NC: Duke University Press. Some of the author's notes have been omitted.

disturbing times, mixed-up times, troubling and turbid times. The task is to become capable, with each other in all of our bumptious kinds, of response. Mixed-up times are overflowing with both pain and joy—with vastly unjust patterns of pain and joy, with unnecessary killing of ongoingness but also with necessary resurgence. The task is to make kin in lines of inventive connection as a practice of learning to live and die well with each other in a thick present. Our task is to make trouble, to stir up potent response to devastating events, as well as to settle troubled waters and rebuild quiet places. In urgent times, many of us are tempted to address trouble in terms of making an imagined future safe, of stopping something from happening that looms in the future, of clearing away the present and the past in order to make futures for coming generations. Staying with the trouble does not require such a relationship to times called the future. In fact, staying with the trouble requires learning to be truly present, not as a vanishing pivot between awful or edenic pasts and apocalyptic or salvific futures, but as mortal critters entwined in myriad unfinished configurations of places, times, matters, meanings.[1]

Chthulucene is a simple word. It is a compound of two Greek roots (*Khthôn* and *Kainos*) that together name a kind of timeplace for learning to stay with the trouble of living and dying in response-ability on a damaged earth. *Kainos* means now, a time of beginnings, a time for ongoing, for freshness. Nothing in *Kainos* must mean conventional pasts, presents, or futures. There is nothing in times of beginnings that insists on wiping out what has come before, or, indeed, wiping out what comes after. *Kainos* can be full of inheritances, of remembering, and full of comings, of nurturing what might still be. * * *

Chthonic ones are beings of the earth, both ancient and up-to-the-minute. I imagine chthonic ones as replete with tentacles, feelers, digits, cords, whiptails, spider legs, and very unruly hair. Chthonic ones romp in multicritter humus but have no truck with sky-gazing Homo [humans]. Chthonic ones are monsters in the best sense; they demonstrate and perform the material meaningfulness of earth processes and critters. They also demonstrate and perform consequences. Chthonic ones are not safe; they have no truck with ideologues; they belong to no one; they writhe and luxuriate in manifold forms and manifold names in all the airs, waters, and places of earth. They make and unmake; they are made and unmade. They are who are. No wonder the world's great monotheisms in both religious and secular guises have tried again and again to exterminate the chthonic ones. The scandals of times called the Anthropocene and the Capitalocene[2] are the latest and most dangerous of these exterminating forces. Living-with and dying-with each other potently in the Chthulucene can be a fierce reply to the dictates of both Anthropos and Capital.

---

1. *Critters* is an American everyday idiom for varmints of all sorts. Scientists talk of their "critters" all the time; and so do ordinary people all over the U.S., but perhaps especially in the South. * * * [Here,] "critters" refers promiscuously to microbes, plants, animals, humans and nonhumans, and sometimes even to machines.
2. [A distinct historical era in which all of nature, including humankind, is transformed by a focus on the accumulation and movement of capital.]

Kin is a wild category that all sorts of people do their best to domesticate. Making kin as oddkin rather than, or at least in addition to, godkin and genealogical and biogenetic family troubles important matters, like to whom one is actually responsible. Who lives and who dies, and how, in this kinship rather than that one? What shape is this kinship, where and whom do its lines connect and disconnect, and so what? What must be cut and what must be tied if multispecies flourishing on earth, including human and other-than-human beings in kinship, are to have a chance?

*   *   *

[This work] and the idea of "staying with the trouble" are especially impatient with two responses that I hear all too frequently to the horrors of the Anthropocene and the Capitalocene. The first is easy to describe and, I think, dismiss, namely, a comic faith in technofixes, whether secular or religious: technology will somehow come to the rescue of its naughty but very clever children, or what amounts to the same thing, God will come to the rescue of his disobedient but ever hopeful children. In the face of such touching silliness about technofixes (or techno-apocalypses), sometimes it is hard to remember that it remains important to embrace situated technical projects and their people. They are not the enemy; they can do many important things for staying with the trouble and for making generative oddkin.

The second response, harder to dismiss, is probably even more destructive: namely, a position that the game is over, it's too late, there's no sense trying to make anything any better, or at least no sense having any active trust in each other in working and playing for a resurgent world. Some scientists I know express this kind of bitter cynicism, even as they actually work very hard to make a positive difference for both people and other critters. * * * Sometimes scientists and others who think, read, study, agitate, and care know too much, and it is too heavy. Or, at least we think we know enough to reach the conclusion that life on earth that includes human people in any tolerable way really is over, that the apocalypse really is nigh.

That attitude makes a great deal of sense in the midst of the earth's sixth great extinction event and in the midst of engulfing wars, extractions, and immiserations of billions of people and other critters for something called "profit" or "power"—or, for that matter, called "God." A game-over attitude imposes itself in the gale-force winds of feeling, not just knowing, that human numbers are almost certain to reach more than 11 billion people by 2100. This figure represents a 9-billion-person increase over 150 years from 1950 to 2100, with vastly unequal consequences for the poor and the rich—not to mention vastly unequal burdens imposed on the earth by the rich compared to the poor—and even worse consequences for nonhumans almost everywhere. * * * There is a fine line between acknowledging the extent and seriousness of the troubles and succumbing to [their] affects of sublime despair and [their] politics of sublime indifference.

This [work] argues and tries to perform that * * * staying with the trouble is both more serious and more lively. Staying with the trouble requires making oddkin; that is, we require each other in unexpected collaborations and combinations, in hot compost piles.

We become-with each other or not at all. * * * Alone, in our separate kinds of expertise and experience, we know both too much and too little, and so we succumb to despair or to hope, and neither is a sensible attitude. Neither despair nor hope is tuned to the senses, to mindful matter, to material semiotics, to mortal earthlings in thick copresence. * * *

Anthropocene

*   *   *

It is past time to turn directly to the time-space-global thing called Anthropocene. The term seems to have been coined in the early 1980s by University of Michigan ecologist Eugene Stoermer. * * * He introduced the term to refer to growing evidence for the transformative effects of human activities on the earth. The name Anthropocene made a dramatic star appearance in globalizing discourses in 2000 when the Dutch Nobel Prize–winning atmospheric chemist Paul Crutzen joined Stoermer to propose that human activities had been of such a kind and magnitude as to merit the use of a new geological term for a new epoch, superseding the Holocene, which dated from the end of the last ice age, or the end of the Pleistocene, about twelve thousand years ago. Anthropogenic changes signaled by the mid-eighteenth-century steam engine and the planet-changing exploding use of coal were evident in the airs, waters, and rocks. Evidence was mounting that the acidification and warming of the oceans are rapidly decomposing coral reef ecosystems, resulting in huge ghostly white skeletons of bleached and dead or dying coral. * * *

The Anthropocene obtained purchase in popular and scientific discourse in the context of ubiquitous urgent efforts to find ways of talking about, theorizing, modeling, and managing a Big Thing called Globalization. * * * By 2008, many scientists around the world had adopted the not-yet-official but increasingly indispensable term, * * * for facing both accelerating extinctions across all biological taxa and also multispecies, including human, immiseration across the expanse of Terra. Fossil-burning human beings seem intent on making as many new fossils as possible as fast as possible. They will be read in the strata of the rocks on the land and under the waters by the geologists of the very near future, if not already. * * *

A complex systems engineer named Brad Werner addressed a session at the meetings of the American Geophysical Union in San Francisco in 2012. His point was quite simple: scientifically speaking, global capitalism "has made the depletion of resources so rapid, convenient and barrier-free that 'earth-human systems' are becoming dangerously unstable in response." Therefore, he argued, the only scientific thing to do is revolt! Movements, not just individuals, are critical. What is required is action and thinking that do not fit within the dominant capitalist culture. * * * The reporter who covered this session summed up Werner's address: "He is saying that his research shows that our entire economic paradigm is a threat to ecological stability" (Klein 2008; 2013). * * *

*   *   *

Making Kin

There is no question that anthropogenic processes have had planetary effects, in inter/intra-action with other processes and species, for as long as our species can be identified (a few tens of thousand years); and agriculture has been huge (a few thousand years).* * *

People joined the bumptious fray early and dynamically, even before they/we were critters who were later named *Homo sapiens.* But I think the issues about naming relevant to the Anthropocene * * * or Capitalocene have to do with scale, rate/speed, synchronicity, and complexity.* * *

World-Ecology Research Network coordinator Jason Moore [argues] that cheap nature is at an end; cheapening nature cannot work much longer to sustain extraction and production in and of the contemporary world because most of the reserves of the earth have been drained, burned, depleted, poisoned, exterminated, and otherwise exhausted (Moore 2015). Vast investments and hugely creative and destructive technology can drive back the reckoning, but cheap nature really is over. [Anthropologist] Anna Tsing argues that the Holocene was the long period when refugia, places of refuge, still existed, even abounded, to sustain reworlding in rich cultural and biological diversity. Perhaps the outrage meriting a name like Anthropocene is about the destruction of places and times of refuge for people and other critters. I along with others think the Anthropocene is more a boundary event than an epoch. * * * The Anthropocene marks severe discontinuities; what comes after will not be like what came before. I think our job is to make the Anthropocene as short/thin as possible and to cultivate with each other in every way imaginable epochs to come that can replenish refuge.

Right now, the earth is full of refugees, human and not, without refuge.

So I think a big new name, actually more than one name, is warranted.* * *Maybe, but only maybe, and only with intense commitment and collaborative work and play with other terrans, flourishing for rich multispecies assemblages that include people will be possible. I am calling all this the Chthulucene—past, present, and to come. * * *

One way to live and die well as mortal critters in the Chthulucene is to join forces to reconstitute refuges, to make possible partial and robust biological-cultural-political-technological recuperation and recomposition, which must include mourning irreversible losses. * * * The boundary that is the Anthropocene/Capitalocene means many things, including that immense irreversible destruction is really in train, not only for the 11 billion or so people who will be on earth near the end of the twenty-first century, but for myriads of other critters too. (The incomprehensible but sober number of around 11 billion will only hold if current worldwide birth rates of human babies remain low; if they rise again, all bets are off.) The edge of extinction is not just a metaphor; system collapse is not a thriller. Ask any refugee of any species.

*   *   *

We, human people everywhere, must address intense, systemic urgencies; yet so far, * * * we are living in times of "The Dithering," * * * a "state of indecisive agitation"

(Robinson 2012). Perhaps the Dithering is a more apt name than either the Anthropocene or Capitalocene! The Dithering will be written into earth's rocky strata, indeed already is written into earth's mineralized layers.***

My purpose is to make "kin" mean something other/more than entities tied by ancestry or genealogy.*** Kin making is making persons, not necessarily as individuals or as humans. I was moved in college by Shakespeare's punning between *kin* and *kind*—the kindest were not necessarily kin as family; making kin and making kind*** stretch the imagination and can change the story.***

I think that the stretch and recomposition of kin are allowed by the fact that all earthlings are kin in the deepest sense, and it is past time to practice better care of kinds-as-assemblages (not species one at a time). *Kin* is an assembling sort of word. All critters share a common "flesh."*** Ancestors turn out to be very interesting strangers; kin are unfamiliar (outside what we thought was family), uncanny, haunting, active.

*   *   *

Neither the critters nor the people could have existed or could endure without each other in ongoing, curious practices. Attached to ongoing pasts, they bring each other forward in thick presents and still possible futures; they stay with the trouble in speculative fabulation.

ENGAGING THE TEXT, ENGAGING THE WORLD

- How does Haraway define the Anthropocene? What is the Capitalocene and how are the two related?

- What does Haraway mean when she says the era of cheap nature is over?

- Why does Haraway begin with the world *trouble*? What is the trouble? How should we make trouble?

- How would you explain Haraway's idea of a multi-species kinship?

- Haraway suggests the Anthropocene and Capitalocene are transitions and boundaries rather than full eras. What is Haraway's imagination of the new Chthulucene era she is calling on us to help create?

- How did Haraway's writing style and inventive language use challenge you to think in new ways?

- How does Haraway's perspective on multi-species kinship help you think differently about your role as our planet confronts problems of overpopulation, climate change, and resource scarcity?

10

Class and Inequality

Of all the systems of stratification and power, class may be the most difficult to see clearly and discuss openly. When we talk about **class**, we refer to a system of power based on wealth, income, and status that creates an unequal distribution of a society's resources—usually moving wealth steadily upward into the hands of an elite. Systems of class stratify individuals' life chances and affect their possibilities for upward social mobility. Each society develops its own patterns of stratification based on race, ethnicity, gender, sexuality, or other factors that differentiate people into groups or classes. Such categories serve as the basis for unequal access to wealth, power, resources, privileges, and status. In addition, systems of social class create and sustain patterns of inequality, structuring the relationships between rich and poor, and between the privileged and the less well-off.

In recent years anthropologists have increasingly analyzed the deep connections among class, race, gender, and sexuality—an approach we call **intersectionality**. Building on the field's long history of holistic ethnographic studies of local communities, like the study by Philippe Bourgois that follows, anthropologists argue that class cannot be studied in isolation but, instead, must be considered together with other interlocking systems of power.

The United States's national myth tells of a classless society with open access to upward **social mobility** for those who are hard-working and talented, including the potential to rise from rags to riches in a single generation. This is the cultural story we tell, but is it reality? In fact, in the United States one's **life chances** are heavily influenced by the class position of one's family—the financial and cultural resources passed from generation to generation. In addition to accumulated wealth and earned income, anthropologists look to **cultural capital** as another key to the social reproduction of class. We define cultural capital as the knowledge, habits, and tastes learned from parents and family that individuals can use to gain access to scarce and valuable resources of society. Children with opportunities to travel abroad, learn multiple languages, go to concerts and museums, and have enriching summer experiences acquire a kind of cultural capital—the social skills, networks, and sense of power and confidence that are essential for shaping and maintaining class position and identity in stratified societies.

Globalization has produced unprecedented opportunities for the creation of wealth, but it has also produced widespread poverty. This **uneven development**, as seen in Karen Tranberg Hansen's article on the second-hand clothing trade, is a central characteristic of global capitalism. How do we understand growing economic inequality on a global scale? Why do so many people live in poverty? Some theorists trace ongoing poverty to personal failings of the individual, family, or community. Such theories—which most anthropologists reject—see these failings as stemming from a combination of dysfunctional behaviors, attitudes, and values that make and keep poor people poor. Many anthropologists have critiqued this "culture of poverty theory" and have proposed instead that poverty is a structural economic problem. If there are no jobs, inadequate education and healthcare, and systematic failure to invest in the infrastructure of impoverished neighborhoods and communities, poverty cannot be changed by changing attitudes and values. What are often considered to be characteristics of a culture of poverty are actually characteristics of poverty itself; they have nothing to do with the attitudes, values, and life choices of those forced to live in poverty.

Growing global inequality affects the life chances of the world's population on many fronts—including hunger and malnutrition, health, education, vulnerability to climate change, and access to technology—as well as individuals' possibility for social mobility. Despite the centrality of class-based stratification in the dynamics of globalization, class arguably remains the most overlooked of the systems of power we have considered in this book. How will the ethnographic research and case studies presented in this chapter position you to more fully engage issues of income and wealth inequality as you participate in a rapidly globalizing world?

From Jíbaro to Crack Dealer: Confronting the Restructuring of Capitalism in El Barrio

Philippe Bourgois

Philippe Bourgois conducted five years of fieldwork on street culture and the "crack economy" during the late 1980s and early 1990s in El Barrio, otherwise known as East Harlem, New York, living with his family in the neighborhood for much of that time. His work on this visibly impoverished community in the heart of the richest city on Earth has become a classic of anthropological efforts to understand the intersections of class, race, gender, immigration, and global economic restructuring. In "From Jíbaro to Crack Dealer," Bourgois follows the lives of 25 young Puerto Rican men who live and work on the blocks around his apartment. Through them he traces the effects of New York's dramatic shift from working-class manufacturing jobs to service sector employment in culturally white settings, the scaling back of social services, and the impact of a new wave of even poorer immigrants from Mexico. His immersion into their jobs as crack dealers, their struggles to sustain service sector jobs, and their search for respect reveals an intimate portrait of lives lived in an economic environment not of their making, filled with unnecessary human suffering. In the process Bourgois challenges the tendency to blame the victim when looking for the roots of poverty. Even for anthropologists, he warns, it is difficult to look beyond personal suffering to see the historical patterns and structures of power beyond any one individual's control.

Following his year and a half of fieldwork in a rural coffee-growing county in the central highlands of Puerto Rico from 1948 through 1949, Eric R. Wolf warned that even the small farmers and coffee pickers in the most isolated and traditional rural barrio that he was studying "in the future will supply many hundreds of hands to the coast, to the towns, and to the United States" (Wolf 1956, 231). Macroeconomic and political forces proved Wolf's warning to be an understatement. * * * The * * * exodus over the next three

---

From Philippe Bourgois. 1995. "From Jíbaro to Crack Dealer: Confronting the Restructuring of Capitalism in El Barrio." In *Articulating Hidden Histories: Exploring the Influence of Eric R. Wolf*, edited by Jane Schneider and Rayna Rapp. Berkeley: University of California Press. Some of the author's notes have been omitted.

and a half decades of almost a third of Puerto Rico's total population resulted proportionally in one of the larger labor migrations in modern history.

Structural Constraints of the Nuyorican Experience

The majority of the immigrants found employment in New York City's most vulnerable subsector of light manufacturing. * * *

Over the past three or four generations, the Puerto Rican people—especially those living in New York—have passed * * * (1) from small landowning semisubsistence peasantry or hacienda peons; (2) to export agricultural laborers on foreign-owned, capital-intensive plantations; (3) to factory workers in urban shantytowns; (4) to sweatshop workers in ghetto tenements; (5) to service sector employees in high-rise inner-city housing projects; (6) to underground economy entrepreneurs homeless on the street.

This marathon sprint through economic history onto New York City's streets has been compounded ideologically by an overtly racist "cultural assault." Literally overnight the new immigrants—many of whom were enveloped in a *jíbaro* (hillbilly)-dominated culture emphasizing interpersonal webs of patriarchal *respeto* [respect]—found themselves transformed into "racially" inferior cultural pariahs. Ever since their arrival they have been despised and humiliated with that virulence so characteristic of America's history of polarized race relations in the context of massive labor migrations. Even though the Puerto Rican experience is extreme, it is by no means unique. * * *

The historic structural transformations imposed upon the Puerto Rican jíbaro translate statistically into a tragic profile of unemployment, substance abuse, broken families, and devastated health in U.S. inner cities. No other ethnic group except perhaps Native Americans fares more poorly in the official statistics than do mainland U.S. Puerto Ricans. This is most pronounced for the majority cohort living in New York City. * * *

The Ethnographic Setting

These contemporary expressions of historical dislocation formed the backdrop for my five years of participant-observation fieldwork on street culture in the "crack economy" during the late 1980s and early 1990s. For a total of approximately three and a half years I lived with my wife and young son in an irregularly heated, rat-filled tenement in East Harlem, better known locally as EI Barrio or Spanish Harlem. This two hundred-square-block neighborhood is visibly impoverished yet it is located in the heart of the richest city in the western hemisphere. Its vacant lots and crumbling abandoned tenements are literally a stone's throw from multimillion-dollar condominiums. Although one in three families survives on public assistance, the majority of EI Barrio's 130,000 Puerto Rican and African-American residents comprise the ranks of the "working poor." They eke out an uneasy subsistence in entry-level service and manufacturing jobs in a city with one of the highest costs of living in the world.

In my ethnographic research, I explored the ideologies (i.e., the powercharged belief systems) that organize "common sense" on the street—what I call "street culture." Consequently, over the years, I interacted with and befriended the addicts, thieves, dealers, and con artists who comprise a minority proportion of El Barrio residents but who exercise hegemony over its public space. Specifically, I focused on a network of some twenty-five street-level crack dealers who operated on and around my block.

On the one hand, such an intensive examination of street participants risks exoticizing the neighborhood and may be interpreted as reinforcing violent stereotypes against Puerto Ricans. On the other hand, case studies of the "worthy poor" risk "normalizing" the experience of class and racial segregation and can mask the depths of human suffering that accompanies rapid economic restructuring. Furthermore, the legally employed majority of El Barrio residents has lost control of the streets and has retreated from daily life in the neighborhood. To understand the experience of living in the community, the ideologies of violence, opposition, and material pursuit which have established hegemony over street life—much to the dismay of most residents—have to be addressed systematically. Furthermore, on a subtle theoretical level, the "caricatural" responses to poverty and marginalization that the dealers and addicts represent provide privileged insight into processes that may be experienced in one form or another by major sectors of any vulnerable working-class population experiencing rapid structural change anywhere in the world and at any point in history. Once again, there is nothing structurally exceptional about the Puerto Rican experience except that the human costs involved are more clearly visible given the extent and rapidity with which Puerto Rican society has been absorbed by the United States and the particularly persistent virulence of American ideologies around "race" and culture.

My central concern is the relationship of the street dealers to the worlds of work—that is, the legal and illegal labor markets—that employ them and give meaning to their lives. The long-term structural transformation of New York from a manufacturing to a service economy is crucial to understanding this experience. * * *

Through my ethnographic data I hope to show the local-level implications of the global-level restructuring of capital and, in the process, give voice to some unrepentant victims. In a nutshell, I am arguing that the transformation from manufacturing to service employment—especially in the professional office work setting—is much more culturally disruptive than the already revealing statistics on reductions in income, employment, unionization, and worker's benefits would indicate. Low-level service sector employment engenders a humiliating ideological—or cultural—confrontation between a powerful corps of white office executives and their assistants versus a mass of poorly educated, alienated, "colored" workers.

Shattered Working-Class Dreams

All the crack dealers and addicts whom I have interviewed worked at one or more legal jobs in their early youth. In fact, most entered the labor market at a younger age than the typical American. Before they were twelve years old they were bagging groceries at the supermarket for tips, stocking beer off-the-books in local *bodegas* [delis], or shining shoes. For example, Julio, the night manager at a video games arcade that sells five-dollar vials of crack on the block where I lived, pursed a traditional working-class dream in his early adolescence. With the support of his extended kin who were all immersed in a working-class "common sense," he dropped out of junior high school to work in a local garment factory:

> I was like fourteen or fifteen playing hooky and pressing dresses and whatever they were making on the steamer. They was cheap, cheap clothes.
>
> My mother's sister was working there first and then her son, my cousin Hector—the one who's in jail now—was the one they hired first, because his mother agreed: "If you don't want to go school, you gotta work."
>
> So I started hanging out with him. I wasn't planning on working in the factory. I was supposed to be in school; but it just sort of happened.

Ironically, little Julio actually became the agent who physically moved the factory out of the inner city. In the process, he became merely one more of the 445,900 manufacturing workers in New York City to lose their jobs as factory employment dropped 50 percent from 1963 to 1983 (Romo and Schwartz 1993). Of course, instead of understanding himself as the victim of a structural transformation, Julio remembers with pleasure and even pride the extra income he earned for clearing the machines out of the factory space:

> Them people had money, man. Because we helped them move out of the neighborhood. It took us two days—only me and my cousin, Hector. Wow! It was work. They gave us seventy bucks each.

Almost all the crack dealers had similar tales of former factory jobs. For poor adolescents, the decision to drop out of school and become a marginal factory worker is attractive. It provides the employed youth with access to the childhood "necessities"—sneakers, basketballs, store-bought snacks—that sixteen-year-olds who stay in school cannot afford. In the descriptions of their first forays into legal factory-based employment, one hears clearly the extent to which they and their families subscribed to mainstream working-class ideologies about the dignity of engaging in "hard work" versus education.

Had these enterprising, early-adolescent workers from El Barrio not been confined to the weakest sector of manufacturing in a period of rapid job loss their teenage working-class dream might have stabilized. Instead, upon reaching their mid-twenties they discovered themselves to be unemployable high school dropouts. This painful realization of social marginalization expresses itself generationally. * * * They are constantly accused of slothfulness by their mothers and even by friends who have managed to maintain legal jobs. They do not have a regional perspective on the dearth of adequate entry-level jobs available to "functional illiterates" in New York City and they begin to suspect that they might indeed be "vago bons" (lazy bums) who do not *want* to work hard and help themselves. Confused, they take refuge in an alternate search for career, meaning, and ecstasy in substance abuse.

Formerly, when most entry-level jobs were found in factories the contradiction between an oppositional street culture and traditional working-class, shop-floor culture was less pronounced—especially when the worksite was protected by a union. Factories are inevitably rife with confrontational hierarchies; nevertheless, on the shop floor, surrounded by older union workers, high school dropouts who are well versed in the latest and toughest street-culture styles function effectively. In the factory, being tough and violently macho has high cultural value; a certain degree of opposition to the foreman and the "bossman" is expected and is considered appropriately masculine.

In contrast, this same oppositional street identity is nonfunctional in the service sector that has burgeoned in New York's finance-driven economy because it does not allow for the humble, obedient, social interaction—often across gender lines—that professional office workers impose on their subordinates. * * * Workers in a mailroom or behind a photocopy machine cannot publicly maintain their cultural autonomy. * * * Instead they are besieged by supervisors and bosses from an alien, hostile, and obviously dominant culture. When these office managers are not intimidated by street culture, they ridicule it. Workers like * * * Julio appear inarticulate to their professional supervisors when they try to imitate the language of power in the workplace and instead stumble pathetically over the enunciation of unfamiliar words. * * * When they attempt to improvise or show initiative they fail miserably and instead appear inefficient—or even hostile—for failing to follow "clearly specified" instructions.

Their "social skills" are even more inadequate than their limited professional capacities. They do not know how to look at their fellow co-service workers—let alone their supervisors—without intimidating them. They cannot walk down the hallway to the water fountain without unconsciously swaying their shoulders aggressively as if patrolling their home turf. Gender barriers are an even more culturally charged realm. They are repeatedly reprimanded for harassing female co-workers.

The cultural clash between white "yuppie" power and inner-city "scrambling jive" in the service sector is much more than a difference of style. Service workers who are incapable of obeying the rules of interpersonal interaction dictated by professional office culture will never be upwardly mobile. * * *

"Gettin' Dissed"

On the street, the trauma of experiencing a threat to one's personal dignity has been frozen linguistically in the commonly used phrase "to diss" which is short for "to disrespect." * * *

Puerto Rican street dealers do not find "respect" in the entry-level service sector jobs that have increased twofold in New York's economy since the 1950s. On the contrary, they "get dissed" in their new jobs. Julio, for example, remembers the humiliation of his former work experiences as an "office boy," and he speaks of them in a race- and gender-charged idiom:

> I had a prejudiced boss. She was a fucking "ho'," Gloria. She was white. Her name was Christian. No, not Christian, Kirschman. I don't know if she was Jewish or not. When she was talking to people she would say, "He's illiterate."
>
> So what I did one day was, I just looked up the word, "illiterate," in the dictionary and I saw that she's saying to her associates that I'm stupid or something!
>
> Well, I am illiterate anyway.

The most profound dimension of Julio's humiliation was being obliged to look up in the dictionary the word used to insult him. In contrast, in the underground economy, he is sheltered from this kind of threat:

> Big Pete [the crack house franchise owner] he would never disrespect me that way. He wouldn't tell me that because he's illiterate too. Plus I've got more education than him. I got a GED.

To succeed at Gloria Kirschman's magazine publishing company, Julio would have had to submit wholeheartedly to her professional cultural style but he was unwilling to compromise his street identity. He refused to accept her insults and he was unable to imitate her culture; hence, he was doomed to a marginal position behind a photocopy machine or at the mail meter. The job requirements in the service sector are largely cultural—that is, having a "good attitude"—therefore they conjugate powerfully with racism:

> I wouldn't have mind that she said I was illiterate. What bothered me was that when she called on the telephone, she wouldn't want me to answer even if my supervisor who was the receptionist was not there. [Note how Julio is so low in the office hierarchy that his immediate supervisor is a receptionist.]
>
> When she hears my voice it sounds like she's going to get a heart attack. She'd go, "Why are you answering the phones?"
>
> That bitch just didn't like my Puerto Rican accent.

Julio's manner of resisting this insult to his cultural dignity exacerbated his marginal position in the labor hierarchy:

> And then, when I did pick up the phone, I used to just sound Porta'rrrican on purpose.

*   *   *

One alternative for surviving at a workplace that does not tolerate a street-based cultural identity is to become bicultural: to play politely by "the white woman's" rules downtown only to come home and revert to street culture within the safety of one's tenement or housing project at night. Tens of thousands of East Harlem residents manage this tightrope, but it often engenders accusations of betrayal and internalized racism on the part of neighbors and childhood friends who do not have—or do not want—these bicultural skills.

This is the case, for example, of Ray, a rival crack dealer whose black skin and tough street demeanor disqualify him from legal office work. He quit a "nickel-and-dime messenger job downtown" to sell crack full-time in his project stairway shortly after a white woman fled from him shrieking down the hallway of a high-rise office building. Ray and the terrified woman had ridden the elevator together and coincidentally Ray had stepped off on the same floor as her to make a delivery. Worse yet, Ray had been trying to act like a "debonair male" and suspected the contradiction between his inadequate appearance and his "chivalric" intentions was responsible for the woman's terror:

> You know how you let a woman go off the elevator first? Well that's what I did to her but I may have looked a little shabby on the ends. Sometime my hair not combed. You know. So I could look a little sloppy to her maybe when I let her off first.

What Ray did not quite admit until I probed further is that he too had been intimidated by the lone white woman. He had been so disoriented by her tabooed, unsupervised proximity that he had forgotten to press the elevator button when he originally stepped on after her:

> She went in the elevator first but then she just waits there to see what floor I press. She's playing like she don't know what floor she wants to go to because she wants to wait for me to press my floor. And I'm standing there and I forgot to press the button. I'm thinking about something else—I don't know what was the matter with me. And she's thinking like, "He's not pressing the button; I guess he's following me!"

As a crack dealer, Ray no longer has to confront this kind of confusing humiliation. Instead, he can righteously condemn his "successful" neighbors who work downtown for being ashamed of who they were born to be:

> When you see someone go downtown and get a good job, if they be Puerto Rican, you see them fix up their hair and put some contact lens in their eyes. Then they fit in. And they do it! I seen it.
>
> They turnovers. They people who want to be white. Man, if you call them in Spanish, it wind up a problem.
>
> When they get nice jobs like that, all of a sudden, you know, they start talking proper.

Self-Destructive Resistance

*   *   *

At the same time that young men like Julio * * * and Ray recognize how little power they have in the legal labor market, they do not accept their domination passively. They are resisting exploitation from positions of subordination.* * *

Unfortunately, for people like Julio * * * the traditional modes of powerless resistance—footdragging, disgruntlement, petty theft, and so forth—which might be appropriate in traditional peasant or even proletarian settings (Scott 1985) contradict the fundamental "technological" requirement for enthusiastic "initiative" and "flexibility" that New York's finance-driven service sector demands. * * *

In the service sector, however, there is no neutral way to express cultural nonconformity. Scowling on the way to brewing coffee for a supervisor results in an unsatisfactory end-of-year performance evaluation. Stealing on the job is just cause for instant job termination. Indeed, petty theft is the avenue for "powerless revenge" most favored by Julio. * * * [He was] skilled at manipulating the Pitney-Bowes postage meter machines and at falsifying stationery inventory to skim "chump change."

*   *   *

Julio's victories over his employer, Gloria, were Pyrrhic [costly and shortlived]. In the cross-cultural confrontation taking place in the corridors of high-rise office buildings there is no ambiguity over who wields power. This unequal hierarchy is constantly reasserted through the mechanisms of cultural capital so foreign to participants in street culture. For example, when someone like Julio * * * or Ray is "terminated" for suspicion of theft, the personnel report registers an insulting notation: "lack of initiative," "inarticulate," or "no understanding of the purpose of the company." Julio correctly translates this information into street-English: "She's saying to her associates that I'm stupid!"

*   *   *

Surprisingly, in his accounts of being laid off Julio publicly admitted defeat and vulnerability. On repeated occasions I had seen Julio brave violence on the streets and in the crack house. I knew him capable of deliberate cruelty, such as refusing to pay for his fifteen-year-old girlfriend's abortion or of slowly breaking the wrist of an adolescent who had played a prank on him. Downtown, however, behind the computer terminal where he had held his last job "in printing," he had been crushed psychologically by the personnel officers who fired him. Ironically, I registered on my tape recorder his tale of frustration, humiliation, and self-blame for losing his last legal job as a printer only a week after recording with him a bravado-laced account of how he mugged a drunken Mexican immigrant in a nearby housing project:

> I was with Rico and his girl, Daisy. We saw this Mexican. . . . He was just probably drunk. I grabbed him by the back of the neck, and put my 007 [knife] in

his back [making the motion of holding someone in a choke hold from behind]. Right here [pointing to his own lower back]. And I was jigging him *HARD* [grinning for emphasis at me and his girlfriend, who was listening, rapt with attention]!

I said: *"No te mueve cabron o te voy a picar como un pernil* [Don't move mother-fucker or I'll stick you like a roast pork]." [More loud chuckles from Julio's girl-friend.] Yeah, yeah, like how you stab a pork shoulder when you want to put all the flavoring in the holes.

*   *   *

As a knife-wielding mugger on the street, Julio could not contrast more dramatically with the panic-stricken employee begging for a second chance that legal employment had reduced him to:

I was more or less expecting it. But still, when I found out, I wanted to cry, man. My throat got dry, I was like . . . [waves his hands, and gasps as if struck by a panic attack].

They called me to the office, I was like, "Oh *shit!*"

I couldn't get through to them. I even told them, "I'll let you put me back to messenger; I will take less pay; just keep me employed. I need the money; I need to work. I got a family."

But they said, "Nope, nope, nope." I left.

I just stood right outside the building; I was fucked, man. All choked up. *Me jodieron* [They jerked me].

The New Immigrant Alternative

The flooding of cocaine and then crack onto America's streets during the 1980s infused new energy into the underground economy, making drug dealing the most vibrant equal opportunity employer for Harlem youths. Normally, in order to fill jobs adequately in the expanding service sector, New York's legal economy should have to compete for the hearts and minds of the growing proportion of the inner city's "best and bright-est" who are choosing to pursue more remunerative and culturally compatible careers in the underground economy. A wave of cheaper, more docile and disciplined new immi-grant workers, however, is altering this labor power balance. These immigrants—largely undocumented—are key agents in New York's latest structural economic adjustment. Their presence allows low-wage employment to expand while social services retrench. * * * The breakdown of the inner city's public sector is no longer an economic threat to the expan-sion of New York's economy because the labor force that these public subsidies maintain is increasingly irrelevant.

* * * Many of New York's newest immigrants are from remote rural communities or squalid shantytowns where meat is eaten only once a week, and where there is no running water or electricity. In downtown Manhattan many of these new immigrants are Chinese, but in East Harlem the vast majority are Mexicans from the rural states of Puebla and Guerrero. To them, New York's streets are still "paved in gold" if one works hard enough.

Half a century ago Julio's mother fled precisely the same living conditions these new immigrants are only just struggling to escape. Her reminiscences about childhood in her natal village reveal the trajectory of improved material conditions, cultural dislocation, and crushed working-class dreams that is propelling her second-generation son into a destructive street culture:

> I loved that life in Puerto Rico, because it was a healthy, healthy, healthy life. We always ate because my father always had work, and in those days the custom was to have a garden in your patio to grow food and everything that you ate.
>
> We only ate meat on Sundays because everything was cultivated on the same little parcel of land. * * * But thanks to God, we never felt hunger. My mother made a lot of cornflour.
>
> Some people have done better by coming here, but many people haven't. Even people from my barrio, who came trying to find a better life [*buen ambiente*] just found disaster. * * *
>
> In those days in Puerto Rico, when we were in poverty, life was better. Everyone will tell you life was healthier and you could trust people. Now you can't trust anybody.
>
> What I like best was that we kept all our traditions ... our feasts. In my village, everyone was either an Uncle or an Aunt. And when you walked by someone older, you had to ask for their blessing. It was respect. There was a lot of respect in those days. [Original in Spanish]

Ironically, at sixty, Julio's monolingual Spanish-speaking mother is the only one of her family who can still compete effectively with the new immigrants who are increasingly filling Manhattan's entry-level labor market. She ekes out a living on welfare in her high-rise housing-project apartment by taking in sewing from undocumented garment industry subcontractors.

Rather than bemoaning the structural adjustment which is destroying their capacity to survive on legal wages, street-bound Puerto Rican youths celebrate their "decision" to bank on the underground economy and to cultivate their street identities. Willie and Julio repeatedly assert their pride in their street careers. For example, one Saturday night after they finished their midnight shift at the crack house, I accompanied them on their way to purchase "El Sapo Verde" (The Green Toad), a twenty-dollar bag of powder cocaine, sold by a reputable outfit three blocks away. While waiting for Julio and Willie to be "served" by the coke seller, I engaged three undocumented Mexican men drinking beer on a neighboring stoop in a conversation about finding work in New York. One of the new immigrants was already earning five hundred dollars a week fixing deep-fat-fry machines. He had a straightforward racist explanation for why Willie—who was standing next to me—was "unemployed":

> OK, OK I'll explain it to you in one word: Because the Puerto Ricans are brutes! [pointing at Willie] Brutes! Do you understand?
>
> Puerto Ricans like to make easy money. They like to leech off of other people. But not us Mexicans! No way! We like to work for our money. We don't steal. We came here to work and that's all. [Original in Spanish]

Instead of physically assaulting the employed immigrant for insulting him, Willie turned the racist tirade into the basis for a new, generational-based, "American-born," urban cultural pride. In fact, in his response, he ridiculed what he interpreted to be the hillbilly naivete of the Mexicans who still believe in the "American Dream." He spoke slowly in street-English as if to mark sarcastically the contrast between his "savvy" Nuyorican identity versus the limited English proficiency of his detractor:

> That's right, m'a man! We is real vermin lunatics that sell drugs. We don't want no part of society. "Fight the Power!"
>
> What do we wanna be working for? We rather live off the system. Gain weight, lay women.
>
> When we was younger, we used to break our asses too. [Gesturing toward the Mexican men who were straining to understand his English] I had all kinds of stupid jobs too . . . advertising agencies . . . computers.
>
> But not no more! Now we're in a rebellious stage. We rather evade taxes, make quick money and just survive. But we're not satisfied with that either. Ha!

Conclusion: Ethnography and Oppression

America was built on racial hierarchy and on blame-the-victim justifications for the existence of poverty and class distinctions. This makes it difficult to present ethnographic data from inner-city streets without falling prey to a "pornography of violence" or a racist voyeurism. The public "common sense" is not persuaded by a structural economic understanding of Willie's and Julio's "self-destruction." Even the victims themselves psychologize their unsatisfactory lives. Most concretely, political will and public policy ignore the fundamental structural economic facts of marginalization in America.* * *

Engulfed in an overwhelming whirlpool of personal suffering it is often difficult for ethnographers to see the larger relationships structuring the jumble of human interaction around them. Structures of power and history cannot be touched or talked to.

Empirically this makes it difficult to identify the urgent political economy relationships shaping everyday survival—whether they be public sector breakdown or economic restructuring. For my own part, in the heat of daily life on the street in El Barrio, I often experienced a confusing anger with the victims, the victimizers, and the wealthy industrialized society that generated such a record toll of unnecessary human suffering. For example, when confronted with a pregnant friend frantically smoking crack—and condemning her fetus to a postpartum life of shattered emotions and dulled brain cells—it was impossible for me to remember the history of her people's colonial terror and humiliation or to contextualize her position in New York's changing economy. Living the inferno of what America calls its "underclass," I—like my neighbors around me and like the pregnant crack addicts themselves—often blamed the victim. To overcome such a partial perspective when researching painful human contexts it is especially important to develop a sensitive political economy analysis that "articulates the hidden histories" of the peoples raking themselves over the coals of the latest forms of capitalism.

ENGAGING THE TEXT, ENGAGING THE WORLD

- Describe the economic conditions of El Barrio. How are they changing over the course of Bourgois's study?

- What does Bourgois mean by the "informal, underground economy"?

- From the 1970s to the 1990s, New York's economy was restructured away from manufacturing to service sector jobs. What does Bourgois mean when he suggests that service sector job requirements are largely cultural, requiring a certain type of cultural capital? How does this affect the job prospects and life chances of the young people in this study?

- Some have criticized Bourgois's ethnography of the violence of the inner-city for engaging in a "pornography of violence." What is his argument about the importance of conducting this kind of study?

- Bourgois warns that we have been enculturated to assign the blame for poverty and suffering to the victims. What are the larger structural forces at work beyond the control of the individuals that Bourgois identifies in this study and encourages us to look to instead?

- Would you have been willing to conduct this kind of ethnographic fieldwork in order to explore this complex situation?

Helping or Hindering? Controversies around the International Second-Hand Clothing Trade

Karen Tranberg Hansen

In the following article, Karen Tranberg Hansen explores the social life of second-hand clothes as they journey across continents and class divides. The movement of clothing, its production, consumption, redistribution, and reuse reveal how an international market in second-hand clothes is shaping local economies and patterns of inequality in communities all along the economic spectrum.

How did that shirt you donated to Goodwill or the Salvation Army end up in Africa? Clothing donations are usually associated with "giving and helping." You may be surprised to find out that as much as 75 percent of donated clothing is resold by not-for-profit organizations to textile recyclers and grading companies for export and resale. The United States is the world's largest exporter of second-hand clothes. The countries of sub-Saharan Africa are the largest destination, followed by Asia and the Middle East. U.S. clothing recyclers sort garments by type, fabric, and quality. Stylish garments are retained for the U.S. vintage clothing market. Worn or damaged garments are shredded and turned into rags and fibers for industrial use. The rest are shipped abroad for resale.

What is the impact of these vast quantities of second-hand clothes moving through the global economy into local communities of developing countries? How do they affect local consumers and local economies? Hansen explores these global flows and their local impacts, building on her years of research in Zambia, southern Africa. Her conclusions are fascinating and surprising.

From Karen Tranberg Hansen. 2004. "Helping or Hindering? Controversies around the International Second-Hand Clothing Trade." *Anthropology Today* 20(4): 3–9.

The international second-hand clothing trade has a long history, yet it is only very recently that its changing cultural and economic nexus has become the focus of substantive work, at the point of either collection or consumption (see, for example, Haggblade 1990, Hansen 1994, Milgram 2004, Norris 2003). Although second-hand clothes have been around in much of Africa since the early colonial period, I found almost no social science scholarship on this trade when I began examining it in relationship to Zambia in the early 1990s. Were it not for articles in news media from the last two decades, I would never have been able to trace recent shifts in this trade, both at its source in the West and its end-point in Zambia (Hansen 2000).

The international second-hand clothing trade is a commodity trade subject to the fluctuations of supply and demand in domestic and foreign markets. Yet the news stories about this trade that I came across rarely changed. Shrouding the export of second-hand clothing in a rhetoric of giving and helping, news accounts hide the economic process—including the cultural construction of demand—from view. Above all, the news story tends to hand down moral judgment about everyone involved: people in the West who donate clothing to charitable groups, the not-for-profit organizations which resell the major part of their huge donated clothing stock, and the commercial textile recyclers, graders, exporters and importers who earn their living from marketing clothing that was initially donated. And at the receiving end, ordinary people in poor countries like Zambia are chided for buying imported second-hand clothing instead of supporting domestic textile and garment industries.

International and local concerns about second-hand clothing imports to the Third World cannot be ignored. They matter, but perhaps not in the way that has been most vocally argued. * * *

The Second-Hand Clothing Trade

In the West today, the second-hand clothing trade in both domestic and foreign markets is dominated by not-for-profit organizations and textile recycling/grading firms. Charitable organizations are the largest single source of the garments that fuel the international trade in second-hand clothing, through sales of a large proportion—between 40 and 75 per cent, depending on whom you talk to—of their clothing donations. The textile recyclers and graders purchase used clothing in bulk from the enormous volumes gathered by the charitable organizations, and they also buy surplus clothing from resale stores.

The bulk of this clothing is destined for a new life in the second-hand clothing export market. Poor-quality, worn and damaged garments are processed into fibres or wiping rags for industrial use. At their warehouses and sorting plants, the clothing recyclers sort clothing by garment type, fabric and quality. Special period clothing is set aside to be purchased by domestic and foreign buyers on the lookout for stylish garments for the changing vintage market. The remainder is usually compressed into standard 50-kg bales, although some firms compress bales of much greater weight, usually containing unsorted clothing. The lowest-quality clothing goes to Africa and medium-quality to Latin America, while Japan receives a large proportion of top-quality items.

The economic power and global scope of the second-hand clothing trade have increased enormously since the early 1990s. * * * Between 1980 and 2001 the world-wide trade grew more than sevenfold (from a value of US$207 million to $1,498 million [United Nations 1996, 2003]).[1] The United States is the world's largest exporter in terms of both volume and value,[2] followed in 2001 by Germany, the United Kingdom, Belgium-Luxembourg and the Netherlands (United Nations 2003). * * *

The countries of sub-Saharan Africa form the world's largest second-hand clothing destination, receiving close to 30 per cent of total world exports in 2001 * * * (United Nations 1996, 2003). Almost 25 per cent of world exports in 2001 went to Asia, where Malaysia, Singapore, Pakistan and Hong Kong are large net importers (United Nations 2003). Other major importers include Syria and Jordan in the Middle East, and a number of countries in Latin America. The export trade is not exclusively targeted at the Third World: sizeable exports go to Japan, Belgium-Luxembourg and the Netherlands, which all import and reexport this commodity. In fact Europe, including Eastern Europe and the former USSR, imports about 31 per cent, slightly more than Africa's share of world totals (United Nations 2003).

Many large importers of second-hand clothing in South and Southeast Asia, such as Pakistan and Hong Kong, are also textile and garment exporters, putting an interesting spin on arguments about the negative effects of used clothing imports on domestic textile and garment industries. This is also the case with some African countries, for example Kenya and Uganda, which are large importers of second-hand clothing but also have textile and garment manufacturing firms that export to the United States under the duty-/quota-free provisions of the African Growth and Opportunity Act.[3]

Second-Hand Clothing in the News

Ministries of trade and commerce, customs departments, textile and garment workers' unions and manufacturers' associations from Poland through Pakistan to the Philippines take issue with second-hand clothing imports. * * *

---

1. The chief source, United Nations commodity trade statistics on used clothing based on reports from individual countries, is incomplete and must be approached with caution. There is a widespread tendency to underestimate used clothing consignments in terms of both volume and value. Country-specific statistics on imports are not very accurate because of illegal practices, including cross-border smuggling. While there are no United Nations statistics on used clothing donated for charitable export in international crisis situations, a proportion of these clothes is sold on arrival in commercial markets.
2. A specialist from the U.S. Commerce Department suggested that the official figure for second-hand clothing exports represents only what is shipped in compressed bales, and that the total export, including garments used as filler or smuggled, is twice as large (Hansen 2000).
3. The African Growth and Opportunity Act (AGOA) came into effect in 2000 to cover an eight year period. AGOA imports accounted for half of all US imports from sub-Saharan Africa in 2002, three-quarters of which were petroleum products. Textiles and clothing accounted for less than one per cent of AGOA exports, a tiny percentage of overall garment imports into the US (Feldman 2003).

By far the most frequently raised issue is the adverse effect of used clothing imports on domestic textile and garment industries. Second-hand clothing imports are banned in Indonesia because of the threat they pose to local garment production (Indonesian National News Agency 2002). Poland's growing demand for, and re-export of, second-hand clothes to the former Soviet republics led clothing manufacturers to attribute their industry's decline to this trade (*Warsaw Voice* 2002). Second-hand clothing disrupts the retail, clothing and garment industry according to the Clothing and Allied Workers Union in Lesotho (*Africa News* 15 May 2002), where many Southeast Asian–owned factories manufacture garments for export, several of them under AGOA provisions. Philippine law forbids the import of used clothing that the ministry of industry and trade views as a threat to textile industries (*Business World*, 19 March 2003).

Most strikingly, allegations about the dumping effects of imported used clothing demonstrate widespread ignorance about the economic dynamics of the trade. * * * I heard many poorly informed economic arguments about this trade in Zambia during the time when second-hand clothing imports were growing rapidly in the early 1990s. One clothing manufacturer, for instance, complained that the import was 'killing local industry'. Like many others, he pleaded with the government to 'create a level playing field', either by banning or increasing tariffs on a commodity entering the country as 'donated' clothing (Hansen 2000: 235). A union representative from Lesotho expressed a similar misconception when he explained that 'in most cases, this clothing leaves its overseas destinies [*sic*] to be donated to the poor and destitute in the developing countries, but end up in market stalls' (*Africa News* 15 May 2002).

Many countries forbid the import of second-hand clothing, while others restrict the volume or limit it to charitable purposes rather than resale. Regardless of import rules, and because borders are porous, smuggling and other illegal practices accompany the trade. Illegal imports of second-hand clothing and shoes into the Philippines are alleged to hide drugs (*Business World* 7 September 2001). In Pakistan, where used clothing imports are legal, under-invoicing and imports of new clothes from Southeast Asia make it impossible for local garment manufacturers to complete, as brand-new goods enter the country with customs declarations as second-hand clothes (Pakistan Newswire 2001). * * *

A recent study questioned the claim that imported second-hand garments flood the clothing markets in developing countries, highlighting the very small proportion of total world trade in textiles and garments made up by second-hand clothing, and pointing out that, as we noted above, imports are not targeted solely at the Third World (Bigsten and Wicks 1996). Such observations do not by themselves tell us much, but they do invite closer investigation at continental, regional and national levels. * * *

Rwanda in the 1980s, before the civil wars, * * * was the world's fifth largest net importer by value of second-hand clothing, and the largest in sub-Saharan Africa (Haggblade 1990). Rwanda is a special case, as it had no textile and garment manufacturing industry. The 88 per cent employment loss in informal-sector tailoring was compensated by better paid work in distributing second-hand clothing. The second-hand clothing trade created jobs in handling, cleaning, repairing and restyling.

Value-added comparisons suggested that the used clothing trade increased national income, providing higher returns to labour than tailoring. The trade also generated government revenue from import tariffs and market fees. Last but not least, low-income rural and urban consumers were able to buy not only more, but better-quality clothes. These observations, according to Haggblade, provide 'grounds for cautious optimism that used clothing imports [in countries in Sub-Saharan Africa without large domestic textile industries] may offer a modest but rare policy lever for directly increasing not only national income but also incomes of the rural poor' (1990: 517). While income growth in the Third World over the long term might reduce the demand for second-hand clothing, in the short term these imports might constitute an important element of clothing markets in situations marked by skewed income distributions and economic decline. * * *

*   *   *

The Philippines forbid the import of second-hand clothing, yet the trade has grown in the wake of the shift to democratic government in 1986. Second-hand clothing from North America, Europe, Australia and Japan is shipped in containers to Manila and Cebu, where the bales are retailed illegally. * * *

The number of second-hand clothing stores in northern Luzon grew dramatically between the mid-and late 1990s * * * as both a small-scale business enterprise for women and a source of trendy clothing. As a collection and distribution hub, Baguio City in northern Luzon is an important retail centre. The second-hand clothing trade is largely in women's hands, and * * * it provides women with new opportunities for self-employment. The traders organize their enterprises through personalized relations, often based on kin, social networks and associations that they draw on locally, and similarly personalized contacts with wholesalers and importers. The women's active work, harnessing economic capital from this international trade to support the household, offers a stark contrast to the image of the powerless Filipina woman as foreign contract worker in domestic service across Southeast Asia and beyond, her overseas employment a major source of revenue for the Philippines' declining economy.

Controlling an important part of the dress market, women traders in second-hand clothing offer customers an attractive alternative to new factory-produced garments. Combining second-hand garments into dress styles that display knowledge of wider clothing practice or alter their meanings, traders and consumers refashion this imported commodity to express their personal and community identities. * * *

India forbids the import of second-hand clothing—yet it permits the import of wool fibres, including 'mutilated hosiery', a trade term for woollen garments shredded by machine in the West prior to export. * * *

The raw material of imported and domestic second-hand clothing gets a new life through recycling and a variety of processes that create employment at many levels of the Indian economy. By establishing links between specific global economic domains and clothing recycling in India, Norris's work casts an illuminating light on the growth of an informal economy that turns used garments into industrial rags, reassembles fabrics for interior decoration and manufactures 'Indian' fashions for tourists. In the process, an export supply chain has emerged, formalizing what had begun as an informal trade (Norris 2003). The work of both Milgram and Norris shifts the debate from asserting straightforward causal connections between second-hand clothing imports and the decline of the local textile and garment industry to address broader questions about how local traders and consumers create a place for themselves in today's interconnected global economy.

'Killing' Local Industry in Zambia?

In recent media accounts about Zambia, second-hand clothing imports are used as an example of the negative effects of the neo-liberal market, alleged to be killing the local textile and garment industry (*Washington Post* 2002), or as a metaphor for the adverse effects of the policies of the World Bank, the International Monetary Fund and 'America' on the lives of the country's many poor people (Bloemen 2001). *** Such accounts fail to take into account local perceptions about the availability of second-hand clothing as an improvement of livelihoods. A real exception to such accounts from small-town Zambia highlights local views on second-hand clothing: because 'no two items look alike', it enables people to dress smartly (*Guardian* 2004).

Zambia has permitted the import of second-hand clothing since the mid- to late 1980s, when the centrally controlled economy began to open up. The term *salaula* (meaning, in the Bemba language, to select from a pile in the manner of rummaging) came into use at that time. Imports grew rapidly in the early 1990s, and came to form the largest share of both urban and rural markets. According to a clothing consumption survey I conducted in 1995 in the capital, Lusaka, three-quarters of the urban population bought the vast majority of garments for their households from second-hand clothing markets (Hansen 2000).

It is easy to blame *salaula* for the dismal performance of Zambia's textile and clothing industry. Numerous textile and garment manufacturers closed down in the early 1990s, not because of *salaula* imports but because they were already moribund. When government protection gave way to free-market principles in the transition to multi-party politics in 1991, the industry was in a precarious state. Its heavy dependence on imported raw materials, its capital intensity, inappropriate technology, poor management and lack of skilled labour, especially in textile printing, resulted in gross under-utilization of capacity. The new government was slow to improve circumstances for the industry. High interest rates, lack of domestic credit and high import tariffs on new machinery and raw materials such as dyes, chemicals and artificial fibres made it difficult for the industry to rehabilitate its outmoded equipment and manufacture goods at a price consumers could afford—not to mention of a quality and style they were willing to purchase. The firms that survived rationalized production towards niche markets such as industrial clothing and protective wear. On the verge of collapse, the two major textile plants were taken over by Chinese investors in the late 1990s.

* * * While the growing import of *salaula* in the first half of the 1990s served as an easy scapegoat for the decline of Zambia's textile and garment factories, the experience of other industries in recent years reveals general problems facing the manufacturing sector in the era of economic liberalization.

Zambia is one of the world's least developed countries, in United Nations terms. Development economists would be inclined to view the growth of the second-hand clothing market in Zambia as a response to economic decline. While this observation is accurate, there is much more involved here than cheap clothing. Such an account fails to do justice to the opportunities this vast import trade offers for income generation in distribution, retail and associated activities, as well as for consumers to construct identity through dress.

My research in Lusaka's large markets, in some provincial towns and at rural sites where people are wage-employed clearly demonstrates the economic importance of *salaula* retailing in Zambia's declining economy (Hansen 2000). The reduction in public- and private-sector employment and the decline in manufacturing jobs have drawn old and young job-seekers of both sexes to second-hand clothing distribution and allied activities. Urban *salaula* traders employ workers or pay for the upkeep of young relatives to help them run their business. When constructing market stalls, they purchase timber and plastic sheeting from other traders. They buy metal clothes hangers from small-scale entrepreneurs, and snacks, water and beverages from itinerant vendors. Young men carrying *salaula* bales on their heads or hauling them in 'Zam-cabs' (wheelbarrows) move goods from wholesale outlets to markets or bus stations for transport to peri-urban township and more distant locations.

The displacement of employment from tailoring to second-hand clothing distribution that Haggblade observed in Rwanda has not occurred in the same way in Zambia. While *salaula* has put some small-scale tailors out of work, it has kept many others busy with repairs and alterations, including the transformation of *salaula* into differently styled garments. Above all, the growth of the *salaula* market has challenged tailors to move into specialized production of garments and styles not readily found in *salaula*: women's *chitenge* cloth ensembles, two-piece office outfits, large sizes, inexpensive trousers, girls party dresses, and many more—styles that they find it easy to produce because of the ready availability of a wide range of fabrics whose import was restricted in the days of the centralized economy.

When I completed this research in 1998, the *salaula* trade appeared to have settled in Zambia. Imports had stabilized, no longer increasing from year to year. Government efforts to create a level playing field for industry had led to increased import tariffs rather than prohibition. The textile plants began to print *chitenge* cloth again. Efforts were being made to improve the collection of daily stall fees in established markets, including from *salaula* traders who comprise the single largest market segment across the country. *Salaula* was rarely a subject of debate in the local media.

Conducting research in Lusaka on an unrelated subject every year since 2000, I still take time to follow developments in the second-hand clothing trade. In retailing and distribution in 2003, stallholders at Soweto market, Lusaka's largest, employed proportionately more workers than in the 1990s. In a snap survey of every tenth stallholder, my assistant and I found workers and helpers everywhere, with some traders employing several workers. Some stallholders, especially men, have consolidated, combining numerous stalls where they sell different types of garments, displayed in the manner of a department store floor. And while Zambian consumers today have access to many more imported garments, especially inexpensive new clothes from Southeast Asia, than when I began my study in 1992, they all go to *salaula* markets for value for money, everyday fashions and more. In the view of consumers, garments from *salaula* are 'incomparable' and 'not common'.

Clearly, much more is involved in the growth of second-hand clothing imports in a country like Zambia, and probably elsewhere, than the purchase of inexpensive garments to cover basic clothing needs. Clothing is central to the sense of well-being among all sectors of the population. Zambia's rural areas, where basic necessities were scarce throughout the 1980s, were described in 1992 with some enthusiasm: 'there is even *salaula* now' (Hansen 1994: 521). People in Zambia approach second-hand clothing as a highly desirable consumer good, and incorporate the garments they carefully select into their dress universe on the basis of local norms of judgment and style. In short, second-hand clothing practices involve clothing-conscious consumers in efforts to change their lives for the better.

Where Are the Consumers?

While the transition from a centrally controlled to an open economy was shaped by Zambia's particular political, economic and cultural background, that country's experience with second-hand clothing imports highlights issues that are pertinent elsewhere. At the level of production, we see a moribund textile and garment industry unable to compete with clothing imports, including *salaula* and low-priced garments from Asia. When the industry upgrades to target the export market * * * the end consumer is non-local. * * * The revision to the popular media's account of the dangers used clothing imports pose to local industries that I offer here suggests that, by and large, domestic textile and garment manufacturing firms and second-hand clothing imports do not target the same consumers.

The single most striking point about accounts of the negative effects of the second-hand clothing trade appearing in local and Western news media is their lack of curiosity about the clothes themselves and how consumers deal with them. In effect, in these accounts the clothes are entirely incidental. Aside from their utilitarian value for money, what in fact accounts for the attractions of imported second-hand clothing? The points of view of local consumers command our attention, if we are to understand why clothing, in particular, is central to discussions about democratization and liberalization.

ENGAGING THE TEXT, ENGAGING THE WORLD

- The social life of second-hand clothing intersects with communities all along the economic spectrum. Describe the global journey of second-hand clothes from donation to final purchase.

- How does the movement of second-hand clothing bring to light class divisions within the global economy?

- What are some of the common criticisms of the second-hand clothing trade and how does Hansen complicate that picture?

- What are some of the negative impacts of the trade on local, domestic textile industries?

- Rather than second-hand clothes, what does Hansen suggest was the cause of the collapse of Zambia's textile industry?

- What is *salaula* in Zambia and how does it benefit local consumers and economies?

- What did you learn from this reading that surprised you about class and inequality in the global economy?

PART 3
Change in the Modern World

Today globalization is driving rapid change in human activities and in the physical world. Although change has been a constant in human history and globalization is not an entirely new phenomenon, the pace of change in the modern era is unlike anything humans experienced in the past. Our institutions and practices today, including economics, migration, politics, religion, health, and art, would be nearly unrecognizable to people living even 200 years ago.

The term *globalization* refers to the worldwide intensification of interactions and the increased movement of money, people, goods, and ideas within and across national borders. Growing integration of the global economy has driven the intense globalization of the past 40 years. Corporations are relocating factories halfway around the world. People are crossing borders legally and illegally in search of work. Goods, services, and ideas are flowing along high-speed transportation and communication networks. People, organizations, and nations are being drawn into closer connection.

Globalization and anthropology are intricately intertwined, both in history and in the contemporary world. The field of anthropology emerged in the mid-nineteenth century during a time of intense globalization. At that time, technological innovations in transportation and communication were consolidating colonial encounter, the slave trade, and the emerging capitalist economic system and were enabling deeper interactions of people across cultures. Today another era of even more intense globalization is transforming the lives of the people anthropologists study in every part of the world, and, as we have seen throughout this book, it is also transforming the ways anthropologists conduct research and communicate their findings.

Globalization today is characterized by several key dynamics: time-space compression, flexible accumulation, increasing migration, and uneven development, all of which are happening at an increasingly rapid pace.

Time-space compression refers to the rapid innovation of communication and transportation technologies that have transformed the way we think about space (distances) and time. Jet travel, supertankers, superhighways, high-speed railways, telephones, computers, the Internet, digital cameras, and cell phones have condensed time and space, changing our sense of how long it takes to do something and how far away someplace or someone is. The world is no longer as big as it used to be.

Flexible accumulation refers to the way that advances in transportation and communication have enabled companies to move their production facilities and activities around the world in search of cheaper labor, lower taxes, and fewer environmental regulations—in other words, to be increasingly flexible about the ways they accumulate profits. Global corporations increasingly move their factories to developing countries (offshoring) and shift work to employees in other countries (outsourcing). Flexible accumulation allows corporations to maximize profits, while time-space compression enables the efficient management of global networks and distribution systems.

Globalization is accelerating the movement of people both within countries and between countries. In fact, recent globalization has spurred international **migration** of more than 232 million people, 46 million of them to the United States alone. An estimated 700 million more are internal migrants within their own countries, usually moving from rural to urban areas in search of work. This movement of people within and across national borders is stretching out human relationships and interactions across space and time. Immigrants send money home (remittances), call and email friends and family, and sometimes even travel back and forth. Political movements take on international dimensions. Religious practices, practitioners, and even gods cross previous boundaries. Local health practices are adopted by other cultures. Art flows into global art markets. Migration is building connections between distant parts of the world, replacing face-to-face interactions with more remote encounters and potentially reducing the hold of the local environment on people's lives and imaginations.

Globalization is also characterized by **uneven development**. Although many people associate globalization with rapid economic development and progress, globalization has not brought equal benefits to the world's people. Some travel the globe for business or pleasure; others are limited to more local forms of transportation. Although 3.2 billion people now have Internet access, the distribution is uneven. In developing countries two-thirds of the population—4 billion people—remain off-line. Although the global economy is creating extreme wealth, it is also creating extreme poverty. Excluding China (which has experienced rapid economic growth), global poverty has increased over the past 20 years. Forty percent of the world's population lives in poverty, defined as having an income of less than two dollars per day. And nearly 1 billion people live in extreme poverty, surviving on less than $1.25 each day. Anthropologists consider the possibility that the rapid growth seen in globalization actually depends on uneven development—as resources are extracted from some to fuel the success of others.

The readings in this section explore the rapid change occurring in the modern world as a result of globalization. Globalization is transforming the global economy, migration, political systems, religion, health, the arts, and the ways anthropologists study these systems. As you will see in the following readings, anthropologists, along with key informants, friends, and colleagues in local communities, are deeply engaged in addressing the challenges facing the contemporary world, including those created by intensifying globalization. How will you choose to engage the challenges of our rapidly changing modern world?

11

The Global Economy

Today's global economy integrates all of the world's peoples to one extent or another into a global system of exchange. Although images from *National Geographic* magazine or Discovery Channel programs often imply that human history is a story of isolated tribes with little or no outside contact or exchange, anthropological research tells a different story (Wolf 1982; Bessire 2014). It is one of connection and encounter, not isolation. Economic anthropology—the study of human economic activity and relations—views the world through the lens of movement and exchange rather than through the perspective of fixed and discrete groups.

At the most basic level, an **economy** is a system of production, distribution, and consumption developed to meet the needs of a human group in a particular environment. Most humans who have ever lived have been food foragers, hunting and gathering for their livelihood. In recent centuries hunting and gathering, small-scale horticulture, and pastoralism have been transformed into industrial agriculture and factory farms. Long-distance mercantile trade has been replaced by rapid industrialization and most recently by a dramatic shift to financial exchange and management as the dominant driver of the global economy.

Many scholars regard Christopher Columbus's 1492 voyage to the Americas as the symbolic beginning of the modern world economic system. His journey certainly launched the encounter between Europe and the Americas and a centuries long colonial system. But his search for spices, silver, and gold was a response to world economic activity already dominated by China and India. Over the next 400 years, European powers redrew the map of the world and fundamentally reorganized the political and economic balance of power on a global scale. European colonialism played a pivotal role in establishing the framework for today's global economic system.

By the late 1960s and 1970s, however, the industrial expansion of the capitalist economy that dominated the nineteenth and twentieth centuries began to shift toward what geographer David Harvey (1990) has called "strategies of flexible accumulation." Faced with increased global competition, a 1973 oil crisis, and global recession, corporations began to use increasingly flexible strategies to accumulate profits. In particular, they relocated factories and jobs from former **core countries** to **periphery countries** to find lower taxes, cheaper labor, and fewer environmental restrictions.

Transportation and communication technologies (resulting in time-space compression) have facilitated flows of capital, goods, and services associated with flexible accumulation. Powerful international financial institutions and international and regional trade agreements, drawing on an economic philosophy called **neoliberalism**, have promoted an even deeper integration of nations and local communities into one free market with minimal barriers. Neoliberalism views the free market—not the state—as the main mechanism for ensuring economic growth. Neoliberal policies promote free trade on a global scale, reducing trade barriers, taxes, tariffs, and most government intervention in the economy; the privatization of public assets (industries, utilities, and transportation systems); and a reduction or privatization of government spending on health, education, and welfare. The ethnography that follows by Elizabeth Dunn describes the practical implications of a shift from Fordist industrial production to flexible accumulation as she traces the effects of privatization and other policies associated with neoliberalism on a factory and its workers in post-socialist Poland.

Most recently the global economy has undergone another dramatic shift from the industrial production associated with Fordism and flexible accumulation to a period of rapid financialization. Anthropologists of finance suggest that circulation of capital has displaced manufacturing to become the principal means of generating global profits and the driving force behind the global expansion of capitalism in the twenty-first century. Accumulated global capital reserves have increasingly been moving away from manufacturing and toward the creation of financial products and the construction of new infrastructures to facilitate their circulation. As a result, while the total gross domestic product for goods and services in the global economy was estimated to be $77 trillion in 2014, the face value of derivatives circulating through the global financial markets is now estimated to be between 700 trillion and 1 quadrillion dollars (Bank for International Settlements 2016).

The U.S. financial collapse of 2008 and its subsequent impact on other countries brought this shift into sharp relief. Gillian Tett, in the selection in this chapter from her book *Fool's Gold*, explores the roots of the 2008 financial crisis and the need for the involvement of more anthropologists and cultural translators in our increasingly specialized global economy in order to avoid future collapses.

Today's global economy has also accelerated the movement of people within and across national borders, extending human relationships and small-scale, personal financial interactions across space and time. Immigrants not only move. They also send money home, call, text, email and Facetime friends and family, and engage in political, economic, social, and religious activities in both their receiving and sending countries. As we will see in Julie Chu's article, "The Attraction of Numbers: Accounting for Ritual Expenditures in Fuzhou, China", immigrants are creating deep transnational connections between local and global economies that are reshaping people's lives and cultural activities in local communities around the world.

From *Privatizing Poland: Baby Food, Big Business, and the Remaking of Labor*

Economic globalization and local workers

Elizabeth Dunn

In *Privatizing Poland*, Elizabeth Dunn considers a local example of the shift from Fordism to flexible accumulation that, on a large scale, has been central to the process of globalization today. In 1992 Gerber Products Company, the U.S. maker of baby foods, purchased the Alima Fruit and Vegetable Process- ing Company of Rzeszów, Poland. With declining birthrates and market saturation in the United States, Gerber decided, like many other U.S. cor- porations, to expand into other countries to reinvigorate sales. To the surprise of Gerber officials, however, apparent similarities in landscape and community structure between the United States and Poland masked vast differences in worker culture. The company struggled to implement its production processes in

From Elizabeth Dunn. 2004. *Privatizing Poland: Baby Food, Big Business, and the Remaking of Labor.* Ithaca, NY: Cornell University Press. Some of the author's notes have been omitted.

this newly post-socialist Eastern European country. Dunn's ethnography traces the company's attempts to replace a socialist, Fordist production model with one based around principles of flexible accumulation, including attempts to reshape the factory workers' thinking and behavior. In the process, Dunn reflects on the question of human nature in relationship to work and the role of the workplace in shaping our notions of human identity and personhood. She also notes the distinct historical and cultural differences that positioned Polish workers to resist privatization in ways U.S. workers could not.

Gerber Products Company, the baby food company, is headquartered in the tiny town of Fremont, Michigan, population four thousand. It is an hour away by car from the nearest airport, in Grand Rapids. Gerber is a major player—some might say it was *the* major player—in the jarred baby food industry, which Dan Gerber and the Fremont Canning Company pioneered in 1901. Gerber dominates the U.S. baby food market. Every year, across America, it sells more than four hundred jars of baby food per baby.

Despite its American dominance, declining birthrates and market saturation have forced Gerber to seek markets outside the United States. In 1992, soon after the fall of the Berlin Wall and the end of state socialism in Eastern Europe, Gerber bought the Alima Fruit and Vegetable Processing Company of Rzeszów, Poland, and formed the new Alima-Gerber S.A. baby food company. Alima, Gerber officials imagined, could follow the same developmental trajectory that transformed Dan Gerber's small Fremont Canning Company into the multinational baby care firm, Gerber Products, and reinvigorate the mature parent firm back in Michigan.

Driving from Grand Rapids to Fremont, one easily sees why Gerber officials were struck with the similarity of Alima and Gerber, since their settings look so much the same. Like Rzeszów, Fremont is a fairly small town surrounded by other small towns and villages. The rural landscape is one of rolling hills, fields, and brown scrubby brush punctuated with evergreen trees. The road from Grand Rapids to Fremont is lined with small farmhouses with peeling faded paint, grain silos, and small apple orchards. * * *

The road to Rzeszów from Warsaw is much the same. The November climate has the same gray skies and chilly air. The brown scrub, the vegetable fields, and the small villages, one after the other, are like those in Michigan. There are small roadside cafés and small farmhouses with peeling paint similar to those near Fremont. Small shrines punctuating rural roads are marks of everyday religious sentiment * * *. The road to Rzeszów has fewer gas stations and fewer McDonald's than the road from Grand Rapids to Fremont. Rzeszów has more factories, more people (a population of 250,000), and the occasional horse-drawn wagon to hold up traffic. Nonetheless, the road to Rzeszów *feels* a lot like the road to Fremont. These are two communities shaped by a common industry, surrounded by apple orchards, and full of small farmers who love the outdoors.

The two factories are also quite similar. Each depends on produce from farms around the plant that is cooked and canned by local people working inside the factory. The most important products in each factory are the same: apples and carrots, the major ingredients for the baby food and juice. Like socialist-era Alima, Gerber was—and, to some extent, still is—a local company with close ties to the surrounding agricultural community. Generations of workers from the same family, both in Fremont and in Rzeszów, have supplied the fruit, vegetables, and labor to make baby food. * * *

Given how similar the two firms and their settings look, it is no wonder that Gerber executives believed they could duplicate their firm's phenomenal rise in the new Polish setting. They assumed that Poland was a case of arrested development and that somehow both the firm and the country were developing along the same lines Gerber followed in the early twentieth century. * * * Seeing the firm and the nation as similar also led Gerber executives to assume that Polish rural entrepreneurs, factory workers, and consumers were like the ones they had come to know in Fremont. Since they believed the people were similar and the places were similar (except that Poland was somehow ninety years behind Fremont), Gerber managers believed Alima could follow Gerber's road to capitalist success.

This, in microcosm, was the same set of assumptions governing the privatization and economic transformation process in Poland at the national level. The designers of postsocialist economic reform believed the people of Poland were essentially the same as people in Western capitalist countries. If only the constraints of communism could be removed, natural tendencies toward capitalist economic rationality, profit maximization, entrepreneurship, work ethics, and consumption patterns would ensure that a market economy would develop spontaneously. According to neoliberal reformers like Leszek Balcerowicz, Poland's first post-Communist minister of finance and the architect of Poland's "shock therapy" plan for economic reform, privatization in all its forms would allow those natural tendencies in persons to be expressed in economic behavior. In the best liberal tradition, the designers of economic reform assumed that the aggregate of these natural human behaviors would create a market economy. * * *

Balcerowicz and other post-Solidarity neoliberal reformers believed that once fundamentals of capitalism such as private property were established, the Polish economy would resume its place on the path to capitalist development. They assumed that this path was the same one followed by the Western market economies, which Central Europe left in 1945 (and Russia much earlier). According to this ideology, Eastern Europe may have been "backward in time," but with the advent of privatization, it would be back on the road to a capitalism identical to that found in the West. * * *

But Poland is not the United States, and Rzeszów is not Fremont. The apartment blocks, the smokestacks of the town's airplane engine factory, and the huge concrete monument to the "heroes" who helped the Russians invade the city during World War II are all reminders that Rzeszów's people experienced more than forty years of socialism. While their apple orchards and rural roads may look the same, the two towns were part of systems with vastly different social relationships that gave those orchards and roads widely differing meanings. Rzeszovians and Fremonters might both grind carrots, pack baby food, go to church, and go fishing, but they do not experience the world in the same way. This discovery came as a surprise to Gerber's managers. * * * When Gerber discovered that Alima employees and Rzeszów area farmers were not the same as the people of Fremont, the company began to try to *make* the people it deals with in Poland into the kind of people it is familiar with. Because Gerber believed Alima was *like* the Gerber of the 1920s, it applied the same kinds of management techniques to Alima that it had used upon itself in recent decades to transform itself into a "new," "global," and more "flexible" corporation. Whether by applying Western management techniques like audit, niche marketing, and standardization to its employees, by reorganizing the relationships between the farmers and the firm and actively changing their farming practices, or by advertising to Polish mothers in order to change the way they feed their babies, Gerber actively sought to reproduce the system of relationships between the firm, its suppliers, and the customers that it had in the United States in the 1990s. In a sense, the underlying assumption of Gerber's Polish venture, like that of many American companies in Eastern Europe, is that to make the kinds of products it knows, the company first has to make the kinds of people it knows: shop floor workers, managers, salespeople, and consumers like those in the United States.

But why pay attention to the management strategies of a small, not-very-important factory in an out-of-the-way Polish town? What do Alima's experiences have to say about larger, more widespread issues? * * *

[It] became obvious even to supporters of radical economic liberalization that privatization was a necessary but not sufficient condition for economic restructuring (McDonald 1993; Kozminski 1992; Johnson and Loveman 1995, 32). A "culture change" was called for, or so it was thought (Fogel and Etcheverry 1994, 4; Tadikamalla et al. 1994, 216). Some argued that "the socialist mentality is basically at odds with the spirit of capitalism" (Sztompka 1992, 19–20; see also Kozminski 1993). * * *

Alima-Gerber's attempts to reeducate and reconstruct its managers, employees, and customers thus illustrate one of the most fundamental aspects of the "transition" from socialism. They show that the successful creation of a market economy requires changing the very foundations of what it means to be a person. The case of Alima-Gerber highlights how important workplaces are in transforming economies. Firms not only change patterns of production and investment, but also instill new ideas about different kinds of people and what they like, transform notions about what kinds of actions people of different ages, classes, and genders supposedly can do, and change the ways that people regulate their economic behavior.

A close study of Alima also shows that the transformation of state socialist societies is not merely a question of changing political parties, building democratic institutions, or even shifting property regimes, as difficult as all those tasks may be. Rather, the "transition" is a fundamental change in the nature of power in Eastern Europe. Observing new forms of management and the inculcation of new forms of personhood shows that *governmentality* [how a state exercises control over, or governs, its populace] in Poland has undergone a sea change in the years since 1989. * * *

The postsocialist transformation is a conscious effort to make the systems of governmentality in the former Soviet Bloc and the capitalist "First World" alike—that is, to put Eastern Europe back on the "road to capitalism" by making its steering mechanisms the same as those in Western Europe or the United States. Poland's transformation is not just a transition to ideal-typical capitalism but part of a much larger process of globalization that entails the adoption of many of the same systems of governmentality and regulation used in countries like Germany, the United States, or Japan. Just as in these countries, politicians and managers in Poland are trying to make the leap to a more flexible, "post-Fordist," or neoliberal form of capitalism. It comes as no surprise, then, to discover that many of the ideas and techniques for transforming people and economies in Poland are based on techniques developed in Japan, Western Europe, and the United States.

Just as in Poland, changes in labor discipline have been a key technology for changing the economies of the First World. Techniques like niche marketing, accounting, audit, and quality control have been used in firms throughout Western Europe and the United States, including at Gerber. These techniques are used to make people into flexible, agile, self-regulating workers who help their firms respond to ever more rapidly changing market conditions. * * *

For many American and Western European workers, it is difficult to critique the new "flexible management" or even to criticize the "flexible economy" that threatens their job security whenever there is an economic downturn. Fundamental tenets about what it means to be a person—an individual, "accountable," responsible, self-managing person—mean that many workers blame themselves, not their firms or the national economy, when they are unhappy about discipline at work or when they become unemployed (Newman 1999). Polish workers, however, have a stronger standpoint from which to criticize these changes in management and in personhood. * * * Polish workers spent more than forty years under socialism, which organized both production and personhood in very different ways. While Poles accept many of the changes that global capitalism brings—and eagerly welcome some of them—their historical experience of socialism and the cultural system built and sustained in those decades also allow them to contest, modify, and reinterpret many initiatives of multinational corporations. Certainly, their sense of themselves as persons has been drastically altered by their contact with the ongoing dramatic changes in world capitalism. However, their history, religious background, concepts of gender and kinship, and ideas about social relationships all ensure that their sense of themselves as parts of a capitalist system is not the same as that found in the United States.

How, then, do Polish workers respond to attempts to make them into the new, "flexible" workers of late capitalism? How do Polish workers, managers, and consumers contest and rework the categories of persons imported by American management, and how might those contestations form the basis of a critique of contemporary capitalism? * * *

Alima in Global Context, or, Why Rzeszów and Fremont Are Nowhere Near the Same Place

*　　*　　*

The idea that Eastern European socialism and American capitalism shared specific ways of organizing industrial work comes from a peculiar historical conjuncture. Ironically, given that the early Soviets were trying to create a society antithetical to capitalism, it was the innovations of Henry Ford, a pathbreaking American capitalist, which inspired early models of Soviet production systems. Planners argued that the utopian values of efficiency, rationality, and industrialization would lift Russia out of backwardness, and they grouped those values under buzzwords like *Amerikanizatsiya* (Americanization). *Fordizatsiya* became a metaphor for the speedy industrial tempo, high growth, and productiveness that characterized the Soviets' ideal modernity (Stites 1989, 149). Ford's memoir, *My Life*, appeared in eight translated editions in the USSR in the 1920s, and peasants went so far as to name both their tractors and their children after Henry Ford (Stites 1989, 148).

The cult of Henry Ford that emerged in 1920s Russia went beyond metaphor and imagery. Ford not only shaped the Soviet imagination, but he also exercised a profound influence on the organization of state socialist industry. Between 1920 and 1926, the Soviet regime ordered more than twenty-four thousand Fordson tractors, as well as Ford motorcars (Stites 1989, 148). Fascinated by the technology, both Lenin and Stalin became great admirers of Henry Ford's River Rouge plant in Michigan, which at that time was the largest industrial enterprise in the world. Seeking to emulate the assembly line, which he saw as the centerpiece of capitalist economic power, Stalin invited Henry Ford himself to design the Gorkovskiy Automotive Plant and arranged for American engineers and skilled American workers to train the Soviets in the proper administration of production (Dyakanov 2002).

* * * In the early 1960s, Polish planners began reorganizing the Alima factory along Fordist lines as part of a plan to rationalize the food system. Although Alima had been built as a candy and jam factory before World War II, socialist planners in the 1960s ordered Alima to specialize in the production of a standardized range of baby foods. * * * Alima became a part of a socialist corporation * * * which was run directly by the Ministry of Food and Agricultural Industries as if it were one vast, vertically integrated enterprise. With vertical integration and with assembly-line technology imported from Western Europe, socialist Alima modeled itself on the basic Fordist model as much as capitalist Gerber did.

Large enterprises organized along Ford's assembly-line model—whether state socialist or capitalist—demanded a distinctive form of labor discipline. In the United States, Ford's River Rouge plant and Gerber's Fremont Canning Company, like other enterprises of the 1920s, used a form of discipline known as "Scientific Management" and organized their shop floors along the lines sketched out by efficiency expert Frederick Winslow Taylor. Fordist firms used Taylor's methods to separate mental and manual labor, to wrest control of the production process out of the hands of skilled craftsmen and to centralize control of the production process in the hands of managers. Managers using the Taylor method applied engineering principles to workers to improve their efficiency. Since Ford's assembly line had already broken the production process down into simple, repetitive jobs that each worker did over and over, Taylorist industrial engineers focused on breaking those jobs down even further. They hovered over workers with stopwatches, timing each worker's tiniest movements, and then tried to recombine those movements to increase the amount of output per shift. The Taylor system aimed at making workers into parts of the machines they controlled: passive objects performing the same motion over and over, in a rhythmic and efficient fashion. To spur workers to produce more and to goad them into accepting the dictates of the industrial engineers, Fordist firms paid employees on the shop floor by the piece rather than by the hour. * * *

Workers in Taylorized plants often rose up against the system, demanding that managers put away their stopwatches and give workers back their abilities to decide how best to accomplish their tasks. The Taylor system of labor discipline was never implemented in its entirety anywhere in the United States (Aitken 1960; Van Atta 1986, 330). However, elements of scientific management found their ways into Fordist factories in the United States and around the world, where they shaped factory life for decades. * * *

*   *   *

State socialist factories attempted to use similar disciplinary techniques. * * * As new, vertically integrated megafactories were being built across Eastern Europe, managers attempted to install Taylorist labor practices in order to discipline the peasants who were becoming urban workers. Labor discipline was a particularly important element in the socialist drive to industrialize, because the Eastern Bloc countries were largely impoverished. Without the resources to invest in the technology that was state of the art in the capitalist world, the socialist countries tried to drive development by producing a highly disciplined and efficient workforce. Man-as-machine became a dominant metaphor, as Communist Party leaders and industrial managers held up the Taylorized worker as the image of the New Socialist Man (Stites 1989). * * *

Like factory workers in the capitalist world, state socialist workers struggled against a form of discipline that promised to rob them of control over their labor and the performance of their jobs (cf. Braverman 1974, 116). Yet, there was one element * * * which made the physical experience of industrial labor dramatically different in capitalist and socialist factories: *the Plan*. The Plan—the key element in the socialist economy—so fundamentally changed Eastern European economies that it made the daily experience of factory work into something distinct both from the Fordist/Taylorist vision and from the actual realities of factory work inside capitalist firms.

In basic terms, the difference has to do with the scale at which power was central-ized. In a Fordist factory, the power to organize the labor process was taken away from the workers and centralized in the hands of management. In a socialist economy, the power to plan production was centralized at the level of the nation-state rather than the firm. * * * It was the central planners, not the enterprise managers, who were supposed to decide what kinds of goods would be produced, how much raw material was needed, and how the material would be transformed into the desired product. * * *

In a vertically integrated Fordist corporation like Gerber, upper-level managers decided what each division would produce and then prepared budgets that detailed how the firm's resources would be allocated among the divisions. Gerber's managers decided whether to invest in making jarred baby food or boxes of cereal. They decided how much to invest in new capping machines, how many jars of strained peas to produce and how many jars of strained apricots, and how much produce to buy from local farmers.

At Alima, by contrast, central planners at the *national* level usually took over this function. In the late 1960s, during a wave of consolidation, planners at the Ministry of Agriculture decided Alima would specialize in baby food. * * * Central planners decided on whether to invest in the company's physical plant and what kind of machinery to buy, set targets for how many jars Alima would produce of what, and decided how many tons of vegetables Alima would receive from local peasants. * * * This meant that while the planning process was similar in capitalism and socialism, the *scale* at which major decisions were made was always different.

Centralizing managerial authority at the level of the national government elimi-nated competition between multiple firms in an open marketplace. But it also elimi-nated the need for an enterprise to make any profit. Unlike capitalist enterprises, state socialist enterprises had *soft budget constraints.* Since the state owned the firms, they did not have to worry about losing money or going bankrupt. There were no penalties for demanding—and using—as many resources as socialist enterprises could convince cen-tral planners to give them (Kornai 1992). In aggregate, however, this constant hunger for more inputs led to extreme shortages. Central planners simply received more requests for inputs than they had goods to allocate (Verdery 1996, 21). Shortage, in turn, led managers to request even more goods, in the hopes that they might be able to stockpile enough resources to produce the amount specified in the plan and perhaps have enough left over to trade with other firms for inputs they could not get from the state. * * *

The shortage-hoarding cycle drove socialist factories away from the classic American Fordist model and made the experience of factory work in them different. Because the dedicated machinery used in assembly-line production was so expensive, Fordist man-agers sought to keep the line running around the clock. This necessitated a steady flow of supplies into the factory (Schoenberger 1997, 35). But under socialism, shortage[s] made a smooth flow of material through the plant impossible. In the early weeks of a planning period, the line might sit idle for days, while managers scrambled to assemble all the inputs needed for production. At Alima, the line would often grind to a halt while wagonloads of fruit and vegetables quietly rotted in the sun, waiting for the arrival of glass bottles or sugar or some other good that was in shortage. Far from being watched at all times or clocked with a stopwatch, or being subjected to endless days of muscle-aching labor, workers often had time to leave the factory and stand in the eternal lines in front of food shops or go home to work in their fields. Toward the end of the planning period, however, the tempo of work changed dramatically. Once all the necessary inputs were assembled, workers "stormed," or labored furiously to meet the Plan's targets before the end of the period. Management's careful specifications about how to do the job, which were supposed to ensure consistent product quality, were discarded as workers worked frantically to produce the quantities the Plan demanded. Socialism did not share the steady machine-rhythm of work that the Taylorist disciplinary grid gave to Fordist enterprises but rather proceeded in fits and starts.

*   *   *

On the shop floor, shortage at least partly undid Taylorism's separation of mental and manual labor. To compensate for the variable quality of inputs, workers often had to circumvent the recipes and instructions provided by management and continually adapt their work procedures. Fruit, for example, would arrive in varying degrees of ripeness, depending on when peasants had been able to marshal the labor needed to pick it and how long it had been sitting outside the factory waiting to be used. Riper fruit was sweeter, which meant that the quantity of sugar, the cooking times, and the temperatures in the official instructions had to be altered. Varying qualities of bottle caps and glass jars meant workers had to change the fill temperature and the torque of the capping machine. And always, aging machines were breaking down. With parts in shortage, workers had to use their ingenuity to improvise solutions and get the freezers, cooking vats, labelers, and palletizers back online. Just as in most state socialist enterprises, Alima's workers and shop-floor supervisors—not upper-level managers—had to deploy craft knowledge in order to make the necessary adjustments in real time and ensure that the line continued to run smoothly (cf. Burawoy and Lukács 1992, 103; Verdery 1996, 23).

Finally, central planning and the economy of shortage gave workers political power that workers in Fordist enterprises could not have marshaled. The Communist Party premised the legitimacy of one-party rule on the notion that through rational planning, it could provide worker-citizens with what they needed, including food, housing, and medical care (Verdery 1996, 63). * * * Unhappy with the state's incapacity to provide basics, like bread and meat, and displeased by the state's continual attempts to wrest power away from the shop floor, workers sometimes coordinated large-scale strikes (such as those under the banner of the Solidarity [labor] movement), which threatened the party's ability to rule society. Even during periods of what seemed like labor peace, workers used the ability to withdraw their labor as a tool against the state and against the managers of state-owned enterprises. Using implicit threats to work to rule or to slow down production, workers parried managers' attempts to impose stringent labor discipline and negotiated the organization of work on the shop floor.

* * * Capitalist Fordism and state socialism may have started out with similar visions and even initially deployed similar disciplinary grids, but the presence of the Plan ensured that by the late 1980s, power was distributed quite differently in socialist workplaces than in capitalist ones. While Fordism and state socialism may have shared the same *modernizing project*, they resulted in two different *modernities*, which led to both radically different experiences of labor and the construction of workers as different types of persons.

Meanwhile, Back at the Ranch: From Fordism to Flexible Accumulation

In the United States and other capitalist countries in the 1970s, the Fordist system was also changing. Capital, which under Fordism largely stayed within the boundaries of a single domestic economy, began to circulate at a greater rate across national boundaries. * * * Goods, too, were circulating across national borders more rapidly and in ever greater numbers. Increasingly, corporations shipped semifinished goods to production plants in different countries and sent finished goods to be sold in foreign markets.

These changes in world capitalism were given a variety of names: flexible accumulation (Harvey 1989), disorganized capitalism (Offe 1985), post-Fordism (Amin 1994), neoliberalism, or simply globalization (Dicken 1992). Whatever name it was given, it was clear that a shift within capitalism had both intensified its processes and opened new spaces—including Eastern Europe—to the penetration of capital. * * *

The shift to "flexible production" did require dismantling many of Fordism's key tenets. Factories struggled to shift from long production runs to making small batches of different products, each tailored to a niche market (Harvey 1989, 155). Product differentiation meant producers had to turn their attention to quality rather than quantity. So they introduced audit-based, quality-control systems like Total Quality Management (TQM) and ISO 9000 (Casper and Hancké 1999). Since rapidly shifting product arrays required an ever-changing list of inputs, vertically integrated corporations broke themselves apart, sold off their subsidiaries, and entered into new, loose networks with geographically dispersed independent suppliers.

Big organizational changes meant substantial changes in labor discipline, as well. Management gurus drew a parallel between Fordist firms, which had been diagnosed as too rigid, and what they believed were the passive bodies of workers disciplined by Taylorism. The attempt to make workers more "flexible"—which often translated to teaching them to tolerate risk and job insecurity—was first done by having them "experience the metaphor" of flexibility in a bodily sense. Experiential education programs took employees to the tops of teetering poles, made them rappel off cliffs, and provoked so much fear in them that some literally soiled their pants (Martin 1994, chap. 11). But transforming employees from the supposedly passive and unthinking bodies of Fordism to active, thinking subjects took more than metaphors and adventure courses. Tools to inculcate and institutionalize flexibility soon appeared in workplaces, from factory floors to university departments.

*   *   *

Most analyses of workplace relations in Western Europe or the United States assume that self-reliance, independence, rights, and decision-making capabilities are innate properties of human beings. Some writers see management reforms relating to empowerment, participation, and so on as liberating these innate qualities of employees from the heavy hand of corporate hierarchy (while, of course, harnessing the productive capacities of these human qualities to serve the interests of the firm). * * * These qualities are assumed to exist prior to the moment an employee enters a firm. What all these perspectives miss—and what the Eastern European experience makes explicit—is that the workplace is one of the most important places in modern society where agency, the ability to choose, and the right of self-determination are produced. * * * Work is one place where identity, * * * including the idea that human beings are endowed with autonomy and rights, are forged (Miller and Rose 1990; Burawoy 1985).

*   *   *

"Government" in market democracies, then, is the art of managing choosing subjects without violating their ability and right to choose. Both democratic governments and industrial managers address this problem not by limiting choice but by altering the field of alternatives and the method of calculating costs and benefits. Particular choices come to be seen as logical and rational (Miller and Rose 1990). Governments, of course, have a wide variety of social policies, tax incentives, interest rates, and so on with which to achieve this aim. So, too, do industrial managers. Armed with hiring procedures and performance evaluations, department audits and management consultants, industrial managers create a system of incentives and costs that make particular forms of behavior the logical and natural choice for employees.

But the choosing self of post-Fordist market democracy is more than a person with an attitude and the right to choose. The "enterprising self," a person who actively seeks to construct him- or herself by actively choosing and assembling the elements of a life, is now as important in the definition of a citizen as it is in the definition of the employee (Miller and Rose 1990, 455). Persons who are "entrepreneurs of themselves" flexibly alter their bundles of skills and manage their careers, but they also become the bearers of risk, thus shifting the burden of risk from the state to the individual (Maurer 1999). In Eastern Europe, transforming persons into choosers and risk-bearers soon became the project at the heart of the postsocialist transition.

*   *   *

If Polish workers in postsocialist, privatized firms are subject to the same disciplinary techniques as workers in other parts of the world, though, they have a unique vantage point from which to criticize new forms of management and person-making. Socialism—of both the "ideal" and "actually existing" varieties—contained radically different notions about work, individuality, choice, production, and power.

*   *   *

As one of the first state-owned socialist enterprises ever to be privatized, AG's struggles and compromises have served as models for other firms, employees, and policymakers. AG's experience is not paradigmatic, but it does have much in common with what firms, employees, and governments throughout the Eastern Bloc and the rest of the world are experiencing. Studying the details of life at AG, then, can help us to understand not only the postsocialist transition and the ways Eastern European workers react to the imposition of market discipline but also the forms of selfhood new managerial techniques impose on workers in capitalist firms across the globe. From the standpoint that Alima workers provide, it is possible to evaluate these new forms of capitalist relations.

ENGAGING THE TEXT, ENGAGING THE WORLD

- Describe some of the assumed natural tendencies of humans that economic planners, including executives at Gerber, believed would be unlocked in a shift from a socialist planned economy to a capitalist market economy. What kind of new worker had to be created? What were some of the obstacles Gerber officials faced?

- Why was Fordism so influential to early socialism?

- How did centralized planning interfere with the implementation of Fordist assembly line production and open the door for greater worker empowerment in Eastern Europe than in the United States and Western Europe?

- Why are experiential education courses that include high ropes courses, rappelling off cliffs, and climbing to the tops of teetering poles considered key to creating the new flexible worker in post-Fordist capitalism?

- The workplace, along with school, the media, and family, is a key location for shaping our ideas about human nature and our human identity. What was Polish workers' unique vantage point from which to criticize new forms of management and person-making?

The Attraction of Numbers: Accounting for Ritual Expenditures in Fuzhou, China

Remittances, religion, and local effects of global migration

Julie Chu

Since the 1980s, large numbers of rural villagers have left the Fuzhou area of southeast China and made their way to the United States, Europe, Japan, the Middle East, and Australia to seek their fortunes in restaurant work, garment trades, construction industries, and nail salons. In turn, these immigrants, many undocumented and indebted to human smuggling networks, have sent millions of dollars of remittances back home to support their families, build homes, and, as Julie Chu shows us, repay their debt to the local gods who have blessed them with this economic success. In this reading, Chu highlights the construction of elaborate temples throughout these rural areas of China, including detailed public displays of donations on the walls of temples and gigantic stone tablets.

Chu's work highlights the transnational integration of the local village economy with the global economy as the global labor market draws immigrant workers across oceans and those workers return vast amounts of money to their hometowns. She uncovers the complexity of the local economy as it revolves not only around money, donations, construction, elaborate public festivals, and rituals but also around ideas of cosmic credit owed to local deities who have the power to influence the life chances of past, current, and future generations. Make the gods happy since they can shape your chances of success. If you are successful, thank the gods, so they know you are grateful. Perhaps they will continue their generosity toward you. As Chu notes, the public listing of donations represents more than one system of accounting, both of which are very real for local villagers and both of which hold great power over economic and karmic success.

From Julie Y. Chu. 2010. "The attraction of numbers: Accounting for ritual expenditures in Fuzhou, China." *Anthropological Theory* 10(1–2): 132–142. Some of the author's notes have been omitted.

Since the Fuzhounese began to leave China en masse via illicit smuggling networks in the mid-1980s, signs of overseas prosperity have commonly manifested first through lists of temple donations publicly displayed on large red poster boards on the walls of temples or more elaborately commemorated through gigantic stone steles built into the very sides of these buildings. Some say one can read the wealth of a village like Longyan, where I did my fieldwork, from the figures on such temple posters and steles. In fact, one local historian had assembled the bulk of his data for a report on the impact of overseas remittances in Fuzhou by literally walking from temple to temple in Longyan while jotting down all the numbers made visible on the walls and in the hallways of each site. "From the stone tablets containing the donors' surnames in front of the temple," he noted in his report, "you can see how much temple renovation is dependent on the power and strength of large numbers of overseas Chinese."

*　　*　　*

Public displays of ritual expenditure in China have commonly been analyzed by scholars as a means for worshippers to gain status or "face" (*mianzi*) in their social world (Basu 1991; Oxfeld 1992; Wong 2004; Yang 2000). Local elites and officials have also explained temple contributions to me in similar terms, albeit with a pejorative emphasis on *mianzi* as "a kind of vanity" rather than on its functionalist implications as social capital. Either way, as meticulous lists of donor names ordered by particular monetary sums and denominations (e.g. Chinese RMB, US Dollar, Japanese Yen, etc.), temple steles and posters certainly lend themselves to readings of the social status of donors, particularly in terms of "the power and strength of . . . the overseas Chinese," as the local historian suggested above. Given the prevalence of foreign contributions, particularly in USD, on temple steles and posters all throughout Longyan, it was also not difficult to read these lists as signs par excellence of the dollarization (and transnationalization) of the village's economy and social life in the era of mass emigration overseas. As the historian argued, steles enabled one to see just how central overseas Chinese and their remittances have been in "vigorously pushing forward the [post-Mao] renewal and development of Fujian's folk religion . . . well beyond ordinary people's imagination." The extra-ordinary here was perhaps even easier to "see" when the various numbers listed discretely in foreign denominations were all converted into Chinese RMB and summed up as single total figures—300,000 RMB for a temple renovation here, 500,000 for another—as the historian did in his final report. Not unlike other local officials and observers of popular religion at the time, this historian personally went on to lament how these displays of monetary numbers, particularly when translated into huge aggregate figures, revealed only so much "vanity" (*xurongxin*) and "superstition" (*mixin*) among the newly wealthy and overseas-connected Fuzhounese. For him, temple steles and posters were no more than accounts of squandered surplus, of money's promise diverted and lost from more worthy and rational investments in things like public schools and public works.

Longyan worshippers themselves were not without their suspicions of the vanity of *some* of the donors inscribed on temple steles and posters. *Mixin* (superstition), too, was a term commonly deployed by villagers to describe the logic of ritual expenditure, though unlike their critics, this was rarely cast as a "problem" of some extra-ordinary belief or faith to be evaluated on the grounds of "rational" knowledge. Typically used in compound form as *zuo mixin* or *gao mixin*—meaning "to do" or "to make superstition"—*mixin* was embraced by villagers instead as a kind of practical activity better judged in terms of its efficacy. In contrast to their critics, however, temple worshippers and caretakers did not read efficacy from temple steles and posters through zero-sum calculations of aggregate gains or losses. For these practitioners of *mixin*, the effects of "doing superstition" could not be made legible simply through arithmetic operations on the numbers of donors and donations from overseas. * * *

It was true that whether inscribed as RMB or USD quantities, most temple donations were understood by local villagers as the fruits of transnational migration to the US. Temple caretakers, for instance, regularly guided me through their ritual spaces by enumerating the specific USD price of every new architectural feature and religious object in their space as well as the transnational status of the contributor responsible for the respective improvement. Pointing to an intricately sculpted altar, an elaborate floral vase and so forth, one elderly overseer repeatedly asked me, "guess how much is this?" during my first visit to the Temple of the Jade Emperor (*Yuhuang Dadi*) in Longyan. His answer in each case inevitably began with an amount in US dollars: "500 US dollars" or "800 US dollars," followed by a short description of its source, "an old overseas Chinese (*lao huaqiao*), lives in New York," or "an 'American guest,' owns a restaurant there." At the Temple of the Monkey King (*Qitian Dasheng*) on the other side of the village, the overseer once took out a large red poster listing the names of all contributors for a Lunar New Year ritual and proceeded to sketch the transnational connections and emigration history of each person listed *and* of that person's family members. Given the prevalence of illicit human smuggling and its known dangers in Longyan, it went without saying how extraordinary overseas ties were in these accounts of temple donations. To connect a particular number to a transnational source implicitly gestured to the miraculous in each case. Despite specificity in the temple caretakers' account, however, their litany of monetary figures, names and overseas location also never failed to overwhelm and render the extra-ordinary mundane after a while, the ever-cascading details and hypnotic rhythms of their descriptions conveying not so much the distinction of particular numbers as the scale of their resonance and depth as a concatenation of sums.

* * * When prompted, no one had trouble summoning ballpark figures of total donations given to this or that temple project. What struck me, however, was how often I had to ask specifically for such information by interrupting the temple caretaker's ongoing litany of donor names and their specific contributions. Issuing totals was just not part of the preferred style of enumeration. Yet not unlike the local historian reading temple steles, it was still hard to "see" the unity of partial quantities strung together on steles without some ultimate summation on the part of the temple overseers. This often came not as some bottom-line pronouncement of monies gained or lost but rather as a general statement of the *ling* or divine efficacy of the gods. As one of the temple caretakers above concluded after guiding me through a list of recent renovations and donations, "You see, the Monkey King is really so *ling*."

* * *

In Longyan, the *ling* of specific deities could be discerned not only by the visible displays of temple contributions but also by the frequency of religious festivities financed through these very contributions and staged for a god in the form of processions, banquets, opera performances and movie screenings. * * * Ritual expenditures, after all, never just involved transfers of money per se but, rather, specific conversions of cash into this-worldly luxuries for gods: spectacular performances and parades, sumptuous banquets, dazzling temple renovations.

* * *

Moreover, like other temple spectacles and visual displays, public commemorations of donations were orchestrated primarily for the god's edification rather than the interest of human spectators (Hansen 1990: 14). If anything, drawing large numbers of onlookers only bolstered a temple's claim to *ling* by demonstrating the magnetic pull of the resident god's powers. As elsewhere in China, ritual celebrations of *ling* were deemed successful in Longyan only insofar as they generated the festive quality of "heat and noise" (*renao*)—a quality best embodied by the very exuberance of crowds mobilized for the occasion (Chau 2006; Hatfield 2009; Weller 1994). Crowds became part of the visual awe of *ling* itself. They, in turn, could sway others to become worshippers and thereby further enhance the god's efficacy for bringing prosperity to all its followers. * * * The circularity of *ling* might be better described here as a kind of centripetal force drawing devotees, divine power and prosperity together through an ever broadening and reinforcing cycle of opulent displays and miraculous manifestations. Numbers attracted more numbers. Large donors drew large crowds to temples. Crowds enhanced the public staging of *ling*. *Ling* brought in more temple devotees and donations. More donations meant more lists of sums crowding temple steles and posters.

Accordingly, one did not need to extrapolate number's mathematical meaning from steles to appreciate the *ling* of the gods. Instead, *ling* could be gleaned simply from number's aesthetics and materiality as so many elaborate and well-crafted engravings spanning a visible stretch of the temple's wall. Numbers did not have to add up to some elegant figure here. Instead, they needed to overflow as public spectacle, unfolding one after another in a recursive and resonating pattern to convey the vast scale and magnetism of divine power.

* * *

For temple donors in Longyan, the key calculation at stake here was not about monetary sums per se but about how one's net balance of otherworldly credit and debt was shaping life spans and life's fortune in this world. As in other Chinese communities engaged with popular religion, a concept of ongoing karmic debt informed Longyan residents in their ritual uses of money (Brokaw 1991; Cole 1998; Eberhard 1967; Hou 1975). This debt was understood both as a result of demerits or wrongdoing against other people accumulated through past and present lives, and also as indebtedness to gods for giving the dead new chances to settle their karmic accounts through reincarnation. While spirits also incurred debt to the parents who conceived them and who must suffer to give birth and raise them, they relied even more on gods who provided them with new bodies and fates in rebirth. In this sense, gods could be seen as the fundamental creditors of debt-ridden spirits, giving them literally a new lease on life and another chance to escape the mortal coil of death and rebirth perpetuated by deep cosmic debt.

This initial line of divine credit made all other accumulations of wealth—money, karmic merit and otherwise—possible for the living and, in this way, anchored the entire mortal sphere of value-production to the more basic and generative logic of an encompassing spiritual economy. So that debt relations with gods not only structured the conditions for life itself but also one's possibilities for living "the good life." New money wealth then could not be taken as merely surplus at the disposal of the living. Rather, it was better understood as the material manifestation of divine credit, as an extended line of good credit, if you will, from gods who could never truly be paid back.

Ultimately, the centrality of cosmic debt was evident in the way worshippers described their temple contributions as repayment rather than as a gift to the resident god. Just as temples produced steles and posters for the god's edification, worshippers also ritually burned temple receipts of their donations so that, as one villager put it, "the gods know how much money you gave." Within a bureaucratically imagined cosmic order, it was underworld deities who regulated life spans and destinies by keeping track of the shifting balance of people's individualized karmic accounts. This was the ultimate sum that mattered and it was only the gods who had the capacity to calculate such numbers. For humans themselves, it was impossible to pinpoint the bottom line of one's cosmic account and, by extension, one's prospects in this world.

* * * The precise amounts of this-worldly money given to gods were always meticulously recorded in temple ledgers, publicly displayed in steles and ritually remitted as receipts to the gods. However, it was also generally acknowledged that for humans themselves, only the vague contour of one's cosmic account (e.g. as either on the upswing or downswing) could ever be gleaned from this-worldly numbers like monetary sums. In contrast, by sending receipts of their ritual expenditures to the spirit world, worshippers hoped that the gods would perform the crucial math to keep their karmic accounts solvent and, by extension, their life's fortune in check.

* * * One could say that the numerical figures inscribed into temple walls, posters and receipts offered a common point of departure, a shared staging ground and gateway, to

different genres of accounting and ways of reading—one based on number's aggregation as total surplus "wasted" on personal vanity and superstition, the other on * * * unfolding of miraculous gains, each sum reverberating with all the others as testament to the joint efficacy of gods and the "doing of superstition." * * *

* * * For one thing, both the local historian and the village worshippers could agree that the figures listed on temple walls largely indexed remittances from overseas and, moreover, that such numbers testified, whether for good or for ill, to something extraordinary in villagers' fortunes. Beyond that, however, they certainly diverged in their methods of accounting for remittance's means and ends, its generative sources and enabling effects, as so many monetary sums gathered and translated into elaborate public inscriptions on stone and on paper.

ENGAGING THE TEXT, ENGAGING THE WORLD

- What do the temple rituals and records in Longyan, China, tell us about today's changing global economy?

- Up to 75 percent of the local population of Chinese villages like the one studied by Chu has migrated out to find work overseas or elsewhere in China. How are immigrant remittances reshaping religious practices in Longyan?

- What is *ling* and how do temple donations and religious festivities make it visible?

- How do local government officials and historians view these temple expenditures?

- Chu states that there are two interlocking systems of accounting present in temple donations and festivities, one monetary, one karmic. Describe both.

- What role do villagers believe the local deities play in economic success and living the good life?

- Why are villagers focused on repaying cosmic debts to the local gods? How does that relate to their concerns about economic success in daily life?

From *Fool's Gold: The Inside Story of J.P. Morgan*

Gillian Tett

Anthropologist Gillian Tett is one of the keenest observers of the global economy today. As a journalist and U.S. managing editor of the *Financial Times*, Tett was one of the few to identify and warn of the unsustainable financial practices that led to the collapse of derivative and mortgage markets in the financial crisis of 2008. For this foresight, she gives credit to her training as an anthropologist. Two years of ethnographic research at J.P. Morgan from 2005–2007, published in *Fool's Gold*, revealed an insular culture that blinded the financial services industry to its own flawed assumptions.

"In today's society," says Tett, "we have this incredible paradox that we live in a world that's more interconnected than ever before. And yet our jobs, our lives, our thinking, and our economic structures encourage a tunnel vision and tribalism—a fragmentation. We end up living in a customized world where we define our information content, our friends, and our identities around ourselves. And the deeper we get trapped in these tunnels, these silos, and this tribalism, the less we understand how the world works and the more vulnerable we become to risks."

Following the U.S. financial collapse—the worst in more than 70 years— $5 trillion of pension money, real estate values, 401(k) retirement plans, savings, and bonds disappeared in the United States alone. Eight million people lost their jobs. Six million people lost their homes to foreclosure. At the center of the crisis was a massive credit bubble created by millions of high-risk mortgages and other complex new financial instruments generally called credit derivatives. Tett's research explores the roots of this financial collapse and the changes that need to be made to avoid the same mistakes in the future, including the insights anthropology can contribute to understanding the contemporary global economy.

Were the bankers mad? Were they evil? Or were they simply grotesquely greedy? To be sure, there have been plenty of booms and busts in history; market crashes are almost as old as the invention of money itself. But this crisis stands out due to its sheer size;

From Gillian Tett. 2009. *Fool's Gold: The Inside Story of J. P. Morgan and How Wall Street Greed Corrupted Its Bold Dream and Created a Financial Catastrophe*. New York: Free Press.

economists estimate that total losses could end up being $2 trillion to $4 trillion. More startling still, this disaster was *self-inflicted.* Unlike many banking crises, this one was not triggered by a war, a widespread recession, or any external economic shock. The financial system collapsed on itself, seemingly out of the blue, as far as many observers were concerned. As consumers, politicians, pundits, and not the least financiers, contemplate the wreckage, the question we must drill into is *why?* Why did the bankers, regulators, and ratings agencies collaborate to build and run a system that was doomed to self-destruct? Did they fail to see the flaws, or did they fail to care?

*   *   *

Back in early 2007, before the credit bubble burst, I hit upon the idea of writing a book about credit derivatives and other forms of complex finance because I thought the public should understand more about the dangers they posed. Back then the world was in the midst of a dizzy credit boom, and there wasn't much scrutiny in the press about complex finance. The area seemed too technical to be of much interest to non-bankers; indeed, the only group of people who seemed to care about the issue were those involved in it, eagerly finding ways to get rich.

No longer. The first edition of my book was published in the spring of 2009, as the financial world was still reeling from the bursting of the credit bubble. It would be quite wrong to claim that the credit derivatives sector—or, indeed, the world of financial innovation in general—was the *only* factor behind this terrible financial crisis, the worst seen for seventy years. Poor mortgage regulation, global savings imbalances, and excessively loose American monetary policy all played critical roles, too. * * * A key issue, however, that exacerbated the credit bubble during the boom—and then vastly complicated the disaster when the bubble burst—was the presence of all those credit derivatives contracts and other complex instruments.

When the insurance giant AIG teetered in the autumn of 2008, for example, it emerged that the company had cut so many credit derivatives contracts with other banks in America and Europe that any collapse of AIG threatened to spark a string of bank collapses. Indeed, this was a fundamental reason why the U.S. government stepped in to prop up AIG, producing for taxpayers a bill that had risen to around $180 billion by the autumn of 2008. And a big reason for that bill was the presence of those credit derivatives contracts.

*   *   *

I first crashed into this world back in early 2005, when I happened to spot—almost by chance—a frenzy of activity occurring in the credit sector that was being under-reported by the mainstream press. Between 2005 and 2007, I tried to penetrate this world, writing a string of articles for the *Financial Times.* * * * As I tried to piece together what the purveyors of derivatives were up to, I was startled by the scale of it. The balance sheet of AIG alone was being stuffed with more than $400 billion worth of credit derivatives deals—which would later turn sour, producing that stupendous taxpayers' bailout bill.

Yet there was barely a whisper of this activity in public view, particularly when compared with the attention being given to the stock market. Indeed, the difference was so stark that I sometimes likened the financial system to an iceberg: a small piece of activity, in particular, the equity markets, poked above the surface, in plain sight, while a vast chunk was submerged from public view. Until, of course, late 2008.

* * * I encourage you to reflect on exactly *why* it took a crisis for those outside the credit derivatives sector to delve deeply into the way derivatives were structured and the risks they carried. Why had there been such a climate of silence? If more people had asked hard questions at an earlier stage about what was happening in the credit derivatives world, there is every reason to think that the worst excesses might never have happened. Debate and scrutiny might have sparked concern and brought about more common sense, not just among the regulators but among the bankers, too. Of course, some journalists and politicians argue that the bankers were deliberately concealing the risks in credit derivatives. Personally, though, I suspect that the problem was more subtle—while at the same time more alarming, in terms of its implications for modern society, both inside and outside the financial world.

When I first started asking questions about credit derivatives back in 2005 and 2006, it was clear that some bankers were consciously obscuring aspects of the business—for example, * * * bankers were usually reluctant to discuss *precisely* how their teams were creating their derivatives. They were also secretive about their profits, the risk models they were using to test the derivatives, and their internal systems for pricing them. Such information was considered to be "proprietary," and thus kept secret not just from journalists but from other bankers, too. I also found, however, that plenty of activity was not regarded as top secret and the bankers would talk about it fairly readily.

When I asked specific questions about new credit derivatives ideas, they were usually willing to talk in some detail. I therefore believe that if any regulator, shareholder, politician, or journalist had asked a few questions about AIG's credit derivatives activity back then, they could have gleaned a rough sense of what the insurance group was up to. It's also true that a fair amount of detail was published in AIG's own accounts. This is why I think we have to look to another reason for the silence.

Many years ago, before I became a journalist, I earned a PhD in social anthropology, and one of the writers I studied who made a big impact on me was Pierre Bourdieu, an anthropologist-cum-sociologist who was part of a wave of creative intellectual thought that emerged in France in the 1970s. In his seminal work *Outline of a Theory of Practice*, Bourdieu observed that the way that elites tend to control a society is not simply by controlling the physical means of production (money and other resources), but also by influencing the cultural discourse, the way the society talks about itself, or its cognitive map. Moreover, when it comes to influencing a cognitive map, what matters is not merely what is publicly discussed, but also what is *not* mentioned in public—because it is deemed impolite, taboo, boring, or simply taken completely for granted. Areas of social silence, in other words, are crucial to supporting a story that a society is telling itself, such as that about the credit boom.

Sometimes such a silence is maintained through overt strategies devised by members of a social group. They can consciously choose to hide facts, as part of a plot. But on many occasions, Bourdieu observed, social silences arise less deliberately, as a result of patterns of social conformity or shared ideology and assumptions—for example, about the ability of the market to regulate itself. And it is at this semiconscious level that the most insidious types of social silence develop, insidious particularly when they serve the interest of one particular group. Or as Bourdieu wrote: "The most successful ideological effects are those which have no need of words, and ask no more than a complicitous silence." In many ways, the tale of the boom and bust of credit is exemplary.

Both inside and outside the banking world, a social silence developed about credit derivatives. This was in part because the topic was thought to be so technical, and therefore generally uninteresting to non-specialists, but also because the lack of scrutiny suited the banking industry so well. Opacity in the world of finance breeds fat margins. Another factor at play was the widely accepted presence of so-called silos—or self-contained realms of activity and knowledge that only the experts in that silo can truly understand. The banking system was producing fat profits as well as a stream of cheap credit for consumers. The boom had a strong allure.

The situation was almost akin to that of the European medieval church: although almost nobody in the congregation really understood the financial Latin in which the service was being conducted, few rebelled, because they were receiving blessings. The congregation was mystified, but it accepted that the priests were the keepers of the faith.

These days, of course, it has become self-evident that this lack of questioning—the excessive laziness-cum-trust on the part of those who should have been probing more trenchantly—was a crucial reason why the banking system was able to spin so badly out of control. The real tragedy of this story, in other words, was that most of the folly was *not* due to a plot; instead, it was hidden in plain sight.

Therein lies a larger lesson of the financial crisis. The modern world is littered with pockets of specialist knowledge. Indeed, these silos are proliferating, for as the pace of innovation speeds up, and spreads farther and farther around the globe, our world is becoming more technologically complex by the day. Just think of the advances being made in genetic engineering, environmental science, telecommunications, and energy, to name but a few. In theory, as these innovations spread, we are all being connected more closely to one another. In practice, though, innovation is causing as much fragmentation as unity. After all, only a tiny pool of people today have the educational training or technological knowledge to truly understand the details of some of these silos; even fewer have the ability to hop between silos.

Alongside the need for technical experts, therefore, we also need generalists who can act as cultural watchdogs and translators. The world is critically short today of these cultural translators. Of course, the media might appear to be charged with this role, but in practical terms, the media's resources are increasingly squeezed, limiting the time reporters have to do the kind of in-depth digging that is required. As for the politicians and regulators who are tasked with oversight, they are too often compromised by conflicts of interest and are at any rate spread dangerously thin.

The good news, in one sense, is that the damage to the financial world from this crisis has been so severe that this problem is now being rectified in some ways. * * * Regulators and politicians have—albeit belatedly—been scrutinizing the innovations that bankers are producing. The new fashion among Western policy makers is so-called macro prudential supervision, or the idea of taking a much more encompassing approach to regulation, leaving no pockets unexamined. The senior management of the major banks and insurance groups are also now frantically trying to devise new methods to keep tabs on their silos—and track the activity of their junior bankers. Politicians have been working on reform ideas as well.

How far these measures will go is a crucial question the public must ask. * * * But the relevance of this tragic story reaches further, to the issue of the many other potentially dangerous silos that are developing in our world. The story of the 2008 financial crisis is not only a story of hubris, greed, and regulatory failure, but one of these deeply troubling problems of social silence and technical silos. If we do not use the crisis as an occasion to seriously tackle these problems, then it is a crisis we may well be doomed to revisit, albeit in an innovative new form.

ENGAGING THE TEXT, ENGAGING THE WORLD

- Why does Tett suggest the 2008 financial crisis was self-inflicted?

- Describe Pierre Bourdieu's ideas of social silences as developed in his work *Outline of a Theory of Practice*, and as summarized by Tett here. What role do they play in shaping a cognitive map of what is and is not possible in a culture?

- What is the key shared assumption or "ideology" that Tett suggests allowed bankers, regulators, ratings agencies, investors, pundits, and politicians alike to miss the warning signs of the market collapse?

- What is Tett's concept of the silo? And how do silos create problems in today's increasingly specialized and technical global economy?

- Are there other silos—areas of specialist knowledge—emerging in the world today that may have detrimental effects on the global economy and political systems?

- What role does Tett see for anthropologists, people trained as cultural watchdogs and translators, in recognizing social silences and combating technical silos?

12
Politics and Power

The Greek philosopher Aristotle spoke of humans as political animals. By this he meant that we organize ourselves with other people in communities through which we strive to achieve the good life—not as hedonists seeking the maximization of individual pleasure, but as a collective partnership seeking happiness, virtue, and beauty through community. The presence of politics and relations of power in the ebb and flow of daily life is a central focus of anthropological study. Although uprisings, demonstrations, and wars may draw attention to the most public, dramatic, and sometimes violent aspects of politics, anthropologists also consider the multiple local forms of politics—the careful political interactions and activities that occupy much of daily life and are essential in making a community a decent place to live.

Throughout this reader we have explored power and its intersections with culture. As anthropologists, we work to unmask the structures of power built on ideologies of race, gender, ethnicity, and sexuality, and institutions of kinship and religion. We also examine the power dynamics of the world economy and class stratification. **Power** is often described as the ability or potential to bring about change through action or influence—either one's own or that of a group or institution. Indeed, power is embedded in all human relationships, whether that power is openly displayed or carefully avoided—from the most mundane aspects of friendships and family relationships to the myriad ways humans organize institutions and the structural frameworks of whole societies.

Over the course of history, humans have organized themselves politically by using flexible strategies to help their groups survive and make their communities a better place to live. Our earliest human ancestors appear to have evolved in small, mobile, egalitarian bands of hunter-gatherers. It is in these types of groups that core human characteristics and cultural patterns emerged. For nearly a century, beginning in the late 1800s, anthropologists studying politics and power focused primarily on small-scale, stateless societies—**bands**, **tribes**, and **chiefdoms**— attempting to understand human political history through the political activities of contemporary hunter-gatherers, pastoralists, and small-scale farmers. But beginning in the 1960s, as **nation-states** emerged to dominate political activity on a global scale, the anthropological gaze shifted significantly to encompass more complex, **state**-oriented societies and the process by which local settings are politically incorporated into a larger global context. The increasing intensity of contemporary globalization only reinforces the need to examine all political actors, whether individuals, organizations, corporations, or nation-states, within a global framework.

The readings in this chapter take just such an approach. In "Warfare Is Only an Invention—Not a Biological Necessity," Margaret Mead, one of our best-known anthropologists, explores the origins of human warfare. By evaluating warfare from a cross-cultural, global perspective, Mead challenges assumptions that war is intrinsic to human nature and challenges us to imagine a world in which conflicts are resolved through new inventions. In the selection from *Shadows of War* that follows, Carolyn Nordstrom employs her ethnographic skills to explore the relationship between personal experiences of violence in local contexts and the global business of warfare that mobilizes political, economic, and even humanitarian interests in an endeavor that appears to support near-perpetual warfare around the globe. Finally, Melissa Checker, in her book *Polluted Promises*, explores how local communities can exercise their **agency** and band together into **social movements** that fundamentally challenge entrenched power structures and political ideologies that create inequality.

Warfare Is Only an Invention— Not a Biological Necessity
Margaret Mead

Warfare, violence, and imagining alternatives

Perhaps no use of power is more troubling and challenging than violence, the "bodily harm that individuals, groups and nations inflict on one another in the course of their conflicts" (Ury 2002, 7). Conflict happens on the playground, in the classroom, in the boardroom, and on the battlefield. As we look globally today, we seem to be experiencing a period during which violent conflict is not sporadic, but permanent—a time of continuous war in one place or another involving extraordinarily sophisticated tools, weaponry, and systems of war-making.

Underlying many discussions and debates about politics, war, and peace is the question of whether humans are naturally violent or peaceful. Is there something in the human evolutionary past that predisposes modern humans to behave in a particular way when confronted with conflict?

Margaret Mead conducted pioneering fieldwork in the 1920s, famously examining teen sexuality in *Coming of Age in Samoa* (1928) and, later, the wide diversity of gender roles in three separate groups in Papua New Guinea (1935). At a time when many in the United States argued that gender roles were biologically determined, Mead's fieldwork testified to the fact that U.S. cultural norms were not found cross-culturally but were culturally specific. Mead's unique blend of fieldwork and dynamic writing provided her with the authority and opportunity to engage a broad public audience and made her a powerful figure in the roiling cultural debates of her generation. Mead explored the difference between the human instinct for violence and the cultural institution of war in her article, "Warfare Is Only an Invention—Not a Biological Necessity," written in 1940 as World War II was building momentum. She presents ethnographic examples of people who do not go to war to settle disputes, thereby undermining the theory of a universal biological imperative for warfare. She also describes the wide variety of reasons people go to war—not only for land and loot but also for prestige and women—that can be satisfied without violence. In the end, Mead comes down firmly on the side of war as a cultural invention and a bad one at that. What then are we to do about this invention?*

Is war a biological necessity, a sociological inevitability or just a bad invention? Those who argue for the first view endow man with such pugnacious instincts that some outlet in aggressive behavior is necessary if man is to reach full human stature. It was this point of view which lay back of William James's famous essay, "The Moral Equivalent of War," in which he tried to retain the warlike virtues and channel them in new directions. A similar point of view has lain back of the Soviet Union's attempt to make competition between groups rather than between individuals. A basic, competitive, aggressive, warring human nature is assumed, and those who wish to outlaw war or outlaw competitiveness merely try to find new and less socially destructive ways in which these biologically given aspects of man's nature can find expression. Then there are those who take the second view: warfare is the inevitable concomitant of the development of the state, the

---

From Margaret Mead. 1940. "Warfare Is Only an Invention—Not a Biological Necessity." *Asia: A Journal of the American Asiatic Association.* August: 402–405.

* Editor's Note: As you read, try to not be distracted by Mead's occasional use of outdated language like "man" rather than "humanity," or references to "low" or "simple" forms of organization or "simple" people.

struggle for land and natural resources of class societies springing, not from the nature of man, but from the nature of history. War is nevertheless inevitable unless we change our social system and outlaw classes, the struggle for power, and possessions; and in the event of our success warfare would disappear, as a symptom vanishes when the disease is cured.

One may hold a sort of compromise position between these two extremes; one may claim that all aggression springs from the frustration of man's biologically determined drives and that, since all forms of culture are frustrating, it is certain each new generation will be aggressive and the aggression will find its natural and inevitable expression in race war, class war, nationalistic war and so on. All three of these positions are very popular today among those who think seriously about the problems of war and its possible prevention, but I wish to urge another point of view, less defeatist perhaps than the first and third, and more accurate than the second: that is, that warfare, by which I mean recognized conflict between two groups *as groups*, in which each group puts an army (even if the army is only fifteen pygmies) into the field to fight and kill, if possible, some of the members of the army of the other group—that warfare of this sort is an invention like any other of the inventions in terms of which we order our lives, such as writing, marriage, cooking our food instead of eating it raw, trial by jury or burial of the dead, and so on. Some of this list any one will grant are inventions: trial by jury is confined to very limited portions of the globe; we know that there are tribes that do not bury their dead but instead expose or cremate them; and we know that only part of the human race has had the knowledge of writing as its cultural inheritance. But, whenever a way of doing things is found universally, such as the use of fire or the practice of some form of marriage, we tend to think at once that it is not an invention at all but an attribute of humanity itself. And yet even such universals as marriage and the use of fire are inventions like the rest, very basic ones, inventions which were perhaps necessary if human history was to take the turn that it has taken, but nevertheless inventions. At some point in his social development man was undoubtedly without the institution of marriage or the knowledge of the use of fire.

The case for warfare is much clearer because there are peoples even today who have no warfare. Of these the Eskimo are perhaps the most conspicuous examples, but the Lepchas of Sikkim described by Geoffrey Gorer in *Himalayan Village* are as good. Neither of these peoples understands war, not even defensive warfare. The idea of warfare is lacking, and this idea is as essential to really carrying on war as an alphabet or a syllabary is to writing. But whereas the Lepchas are a gentle, unquarrelsome people, and the advocates of other points of view might argue that they are not full human beings or that they had never been frustrated and so had no aggression to expand in warfare, the Eskimo case gives no such possibility of interpretation. The Eskimo are not a mild and meek people; many of them are turbulent and troublesome. Fights, theft of wives, murder, cannibalism, occur among them—all outbursts of passionate men goaded by desire or intolerable circumstance. Here are men faced with hunger, men faced with loss of their wives, men faced with the threat of extermination by other men, and here are orphan children, growing up miserably with no one to care for them, mocked and neglected by those about them. The personality necessary for war, the circumstances necessary to goad men to desperation are present, but there is no war. When a traveling Eskimo entered a settlement he might have to fight the strongest man in the settlement to establish his position among them, but this was a test of strength and bravery, not war. The idea of warfare, of one *group* organizing against another *group* to maim and wound and kill them was absent. And without that idea passions might rage but there was no war.

But, it may be argued, isn't this because the Eskimo have such a low and undeveloped form of social organization? They own no land, they move from place to place, camping, it is true, season after season on the same site, but this is not something to fight for as the modern nations of the world fight for land and raw materials. They have no permanent possessions that can be looted, no towns that can be burned. They have no social classes to produce stress and strains within the society which might force it to go to war outside. Doesn't the absence of war among the Eskimo, while disproving the biological necessity of war, just go to confirm the point that it is the state of development of the society which accounts for war, and nothing else?

We find the answer among the pygmy peoples of the Andaman Islands in the Bay of Bengal. The Andamans also represent an exceedingly low level of society; they are a hunting and food-gathering people; they live in tiny hordes without any class stratification; their houses are simpler than the snow houses of the Eskimo. But they knew about warfare. The army might contain only fifteen determined pygmies marching in a straight line, but it was the real thing none the less. Tiny army met tiny army in open battle, blows were exchanged, casualties suffered, and the state of warfare could only be concluded by a peace-making ceremony.

Similarly, among the Australian aborigines, who built no permanent dwellings but wandered from water hole to water hole over their almost desert country, warfare—and rules of "international law"—were highly developed. The student of social evolution will seek in vain for his obvious causes of war, struggle for lands, struggle for power of one group over another, expansion of population, need to divert the minds of a populace restive under tyranny, or even the ambition of a successful leader to enhance his own prestige. All are absent, but warfare as a practice remained, and men engaged in it and killed one another in the course of a war because killing is what is done in wars.

From instances like these it becomes apparent that an inquiry into the causes of war misses the fundamental point as completely as does an insistence upon the biological necessity of war. If a people have an idea of going to war and the idea that war is the way in which certain situations, defined within their society, are to be handled, they will sometimes go to war. If they are a mild and unaggressive people, like the Pueblo Indians, they may limit themselves to defensive warfare; but they will be forced to think in terms of war because there are peoples near them who have warfare as a pattern, and offensive, raiding, pillaging warfare at that. When the pattern of warfare is known, people like the Pueblo Indians will defend themselves, taking advantage of their natural defenses, the *mesa* village site, and people like the Lepchas, having no natural defenses and no idea of warfare, will merely submit to the invader. But the essential point remains the same. There is a way of behaving which is known to a given people and labeled as an appropriate form of behavior; a bold and warlike people like the [Native American] Sioux or the Maori [of New Zealand] may label warfare as desirable as well as possible; a mild people like the Pueblo Indians may label warfare as undesirable; but to the minds of both peoples the possibility of warfare is present. Their thoughts, their hopes, their plans are oriented about this idea, that warfare may be selected as the way to meet some situation.

So simple peoples and civilized peoples, mild peoples and violent, assertive peoples, will all go to war if they have the invention, just as those peoples who have the custom of dueling will have duels and peoples who have the patterns of vendetta will indulge in vendetta. And, conversely, peoples who do not know of dueling will not fight duels, even though their wives are seduced and their daughters ravished; they may on occasion commit murder but they will not fight duels. Cultures which lack the idea of the vendetta will not meet every quarrel in this way. A people can use only the forms it has. So the [Indonesian] Balinese have their special way of dealing with a quarrel between two individuals: if the two feel that the causes of quarrel are heavy they may go and register their quarrel in the temple before the gods, and, making offerings, they may swear never to have anything to do with each other again. Today they register such mutual "not-speaking" with the Dutch government officials. But in other societies, although individuals might feel as full of animosity and as unwilling to have any further contact as do the Balinese, they cannot register their quarrel with the gods and go on quietly about their business because registering quarrels with the gods is not an invention of which they know.

Yet, if it be granted that warfare is after all an invention, it may nevertheless be an invention that lends itself to certain types of personality, to the exigent needs of autocrats, to the expansionist desires of crowded peoples, to the desire for plunder and rape and loot which is engendered by a dull and frustrating life. What, then, can we say of this congruence between warfare and its uses? If it is a form which fits so well, is not this congruence the essential point? But even here the primitive material causes us to wonder, because there are tribes who go to war merely for glory, having no quarrel with the enemy, suffering from no tyrant within their boundaries, anxious neither for land nor loot nor women, but merely anxious to win prestige which within that tribe has been declared obtainable only by war and without which no young man can hope to win his sweetheart's smile of approval. But if, as was the case with the [Maroon] of Dutch Guiana, it is artistic ability which is necessary to win a girl's approval, the same young man would have to be carving rather than going out on a war party.

In many parts of the world, war is a game in which the individual can win counters—counters which bring him prestige in the eyes of his own sex or of the opposite sex; he plays for these counters as he might, in our society, strive for a tennis championship. Warfare is a frame for such prestige-seeking merely because it calls for the display of certain skills and certain virtues; all of these skills—riding straight, shooting straight, dodging the missiles of the enemy and sending one's own straight to the mark—can be equally well exercised in some other framework and, equally, the virtues—endurance, bravery, loyalty, steadfastness—can be displayed in other contexts. The tie-up between proving oneself a man and proving this by a success in organized killing is due to a definition which many societies have made of manliness. And often, even in those societies which counted success in warfare a proof of human worth, strange turns were given to the idea, as when the plains Indians gave their highest awards to the man who touched a live enemy rather than to the man who brought in a scalp—from a dead enemy—because the latter was less risky. Warfare is just an invention known to the majority of human societies by which they permit their young men either to accumulate prestige or avenge their honor or acquire loot or wives or slaves or sago lands or cattle or appease the blood lust of their gods or the restless souls of the recently dead. It is just an invention, older and more widespread than the jury system, but none the less an invention.

But, once we have said this, have we said anything at all? Despite a few instances, dear to the hearts of controversialists, of the loss of the useful arts, once an invention is made which proves congruent with human needs or social forms, it tends to persist. Grant that war is an invention, that it is not a biological necessity nor the outcome of certain special types of social forms, still, once the invention is made, what are we to do about it? The Indian who had been subsisting on the buffalo for generations because with his primitive weapons he could slaughter only a limited number of buffalo did not return to his primitive weapons when he saw that the white man's more efficient weapons were exterminating the buffalo. A desire for the white man's cloth may mortgage the South Sea Islander to the white man's plantation, but he does not return to making bark cloth, which would have left him free. Once an invention is known and accepted, men do not easily relinquish it. The skilled workers may smash the first steam looms which they feel are to be their undoing, but they accept them in the end, and no movement which has insisted upon the mere abandonment of usable inventions has ever had much success. Warfare is here, as part of our thought; the deeds of warriors are immortalized in the words of our poets; the toys of our children are modeled upon the weapons of the soldier; the frame of reference within which our statesmen and our diplomats work always contains war. If we know that it is not inevitable, that it is due to historical accident that warfare is one of the ways in which we think of behaving, are we given any hope by that? What hope is there of persuading nations to abandon war, nations so thoroughly imbued with the idea that resort to war is, if not actually desirable and noble, at least inevitable whenever certain defined circumstances arise?

In answer to this question I think we might turn to the history of other social inventions, and inventions which must once have seemed as firmly entrenched as warfare. Take the methods of trial which preceded the jury system: ordeal and trial by combat. Unfair, capricious, alien as they are to our feeling today, they were once the only methods open to individuals accused of some offense. The invention of trail by jury gradually replaced these methods until only witches, and finally not even witches, had to resort to the ordeal.

And for a long time the jury system seemed the one best and finest method of settling legal disputes, but today new inventions, trial before judges only or before commissions, are replacing the jury system. In each case the old method was replaced by a new social invention; the ordeal did not go out because people thought it unjust or wrong, it went out because a method more congruent with the institutions and feelings of the period was invented. And, if we despair over the way in which war seems such an ingrained habit of most of the human race, we can take comfort from the fact that a poor invention will usually give place to a better invention.

For this, two conditions at least are necessary. The people must recognize the defects of the old invention, and some one must make a new one. Propaganda against warfare, documentation of its terrible cost in human suffering and social waste, these prepare the ground by teaching people to feel that warfare is a defective social institution. There is further needed a belief that social invention is possible and the invention of new methods which will render warfare as out of date as the tractor is making the plow, or the motor car the horse and buggy. A form of behavior becomes out of date only when something else takes its place, and in order to invent forms of behavior which will make war obsolete, it is a first requirement to believe that an invention is possible.

ENGAGING THE TEXT, ENGAGING THE WORLD

- How does Mead define warfare?

- What does she mean when she states that warfare is only an invention?

- Why do people mistakenly assume warfare is inevitable and rooted in human nature, according to Mead?

- What evidence does Mead present to undermine our assumptions about the inevitability of war?

- Why does Mead think people go to war?

- What conditions does Mead suggest are necessary for replacing a poor invention with a better one?

- Do you believe a better invention for resolving human conflicts is possible? Discuss alternatives to war with your classmates and identify your top three options.

From *Shadows of War*

Carolyn Nordstrom

Political anthropologists actively explore the complicated cultural processes through which war is invented, learned, and enacted. Over the past 100 years, war has become far more complex than waging hand-to-hand combat or pulling a trigger at close range—actions that we might associate with aggression driven by hormones. Instead, modern warfare is considerably more premeditated and calculated, relying on computers, satellites, missiles, GPS tracking, and airborne drone strikes. Today warfare has become one of the most visible of all human political institutions, and anthropologists study a highly militarized world in which war seems normalized and permanent.

As we will see in Carolyn Nordstrom's work, warfare can no longer be viewed solely as a local military phenomenon. Indeed, modern warfare is embedded in a global system of war-making. And so anthropologists examine the intersection of multiple factors that play a role in constructing warfare as a reasonable means for resolving conflicts. Nordstrom's work exemplifies contemporary anthropological contributions to this kind of study. She turns the spotlight on the complex web of local and foreign interactions and actors that drive war and make warfare a global phenomenon. At the same time, she focuses on the real, messy, *local* expressions of violence, resistance, survival, and creativity in actual communities where war occurs, not in the comfortable offices and remote institutions of military officials and political leaders.

Nordstrom warns that when war is portrayed only through the prism of weapons, soldiers, territory, and strategic interests won or lost, a more significant reality is ignored: the heroic efforts of people on the front lines to resist and maintain life in the face of violence and death.

These people say that war is a crocodile which is always hungry. It has dishonest eyes and a thrashing tail. It creeps up quietly while you wash at the river, while you pound your corn, while you rock your old mother in her time of dying.

From Carolyn Nordstrom. 2004. *Shadows of War: Violence, Power, and International Profiteering in the Twenty-First Century.* Berkeley: University of California Press. Some of the author's notes have been omitted.

It is with you always, war, waiting to explode your life and throw you down beside a river to die. War wants death, always; war wants to quiet your mother's songs. War wants your sorrow. (Pinnock 2000, 15)

War is one of those impossible words: it refers to war as a soldier in Sudan lives it, as a child in Sri Lanka experiences it, as a torture victim in Argentina's dirty war felt it, as a Greek in Troy died it. A mere three letters covers a sweep of hundreds of thousands of events across several millennia. How do we understand so vast a phenomenon while retaining the vibrancy of the lives that constitute it?

There is an image of war that has stuck in my mind for nearly two decades. It seems to point toward some deep understanding, something that stands just outside of conscious grasp, or maybe beyond intellectual thought to a more profound conception of . . . what? Not just war, but something that tugs at the heart of what it means to be human. And in the curious combination that links devastating disasters with the profoundly mundane, this image involves a watermelon amid some of the worst violence marking recent decades. A Sri Lankan acquaintance and I had traveled to the July 1983 Kataragama religious festival in southeastern Sri Lanka. She is a middle-aged woman from the capital city of Colombo, a mother with a ready laugh and a maternal charm that holds a bit of impishness. We had shared a room, and I remember her unpacking her travel bag the first day; she had a towel, food, and other useful items I had not thought to pack. She laughingly lectured me: "Carry what you will need."

The 1983 riots in which thousands were killed in seven days broke out the last night of the festival. No one knew the violence was about to erupt as they said goodbye to one another and began their journeys home. Almost no one: curiously, the last two evenings of the festival several of the homeless "mentally ill" people spoke at length and with great emotion about the impending violence. One directed his agitated monologue at me, perhaps because I was a foreigner. As a large crowd gathered around us, he launched into an aggressive explanation of the cataclysmic violence that was soon to erupt, the blood that would stain the streets and homes of the country, the screams of pain and anger he could hear, and the ways in which the responsibility for this violence went all the way to my country in cycles of global inequality. The audience around us sought to brush off his belligerent words with a reference to his madness, but a troubling clarity in his speech unsettled all of us.

Just before my traveling companion and I left Kataragama, she found a large watermelon, and bought it to take home to her family. She tried to give me a hug as we parted company to travel to our respective homes and broke out laughing as she juggled her suitcase in one hand and the watermelon in the other.

The bus she took to Colombo arrived at a city overtaken by flames and overrun by mobs. The next time I saw her, she told me of that night:

> We left the Kataragama festival that is meant to put the world together and arrived home to find the world being taken apart. We arrived to a nightmare worse than any the mind could conceive in dream. As we took the bus out of

Kataragama, night began to fall, and we were lulled to sleep by the rocking of the bus, the camaraderie of sharing food, and warm memories of the festival. Sometime after midnight as we began to near Colombo, we opened our eyes to a world gone mad. Entire blocks of buildings were in flames, and people broke out of these buildings aflame themselves. Buses and cars burned in the roads, some with the occupants locked inside. Crowds of people ran in the streets, some shouting and beating people, overturning cars and setting them on fire, attacking homes and businesses . . . others running for safety and for their lives. Nothing made sense. As buses were being stopped, passengers being hauled out and killed, and the vehicles firebombed, our bus driver stopped suddenly and turned all of us passengers out onto the street, and drove away. It was nowhere near the bus terminal, and none of us knew where we were.

*   *   *

I had all my belongings from my trip with me, my handbag, my wrap, my suitcase, and that large watermelon. I just set my feet moving and tried to find my way home. Every street I turned down seemed as unfamiliar as the last. The horror never stopped. Fires, mobs, beatings, murder. I was exhausted, and my mind could not grasp what it saw. Nothing was clear: not who was killing whom, nor why. Not where it might be safe nor how to get there. Not how to respond nor whom to turn to, and no way of finding out.

I walked for hours. I grew painfully tired, and the things I was carrying seemed to weigh more and more. At some point, I stopped and set my handbag down on the sidewalk and left it there. It just seemed too much to carry. A while later I took my wrap and wiped the sweat and soot off my face, and left the wrap there on someone's fence as I picked up my suitcase and that watermelon and trudged off again in search of my home. Somehow in my mind I thought I'd go back and collect my handbag the next day—I really thought it would just be sitting there where I left it. That's how hard it is to think realistically when everything around you is unrealistic. I left all my identification, my money, everything sitting there on the road while I carried off that heavy unwieldy watermelon with me. Sometime later, it might have been hours or days to my mind, the suitcase became unbearably heavy, and I set that down too and left it. But I never let go of that watermelon. To this day, I can't explain it. But I carried that watermelon all night long through all the chaos and horror, and finally arrived home clutching that darned thing, having left everything else on the road.

You know, my handbag had all my necessities in it: my identification, my money and bank cards, my glasses and licenses. My suitcase had my favorite saris, my daily necessities and medicines, and presents and blessed religious relics for my family. I have always been considered the organized and responsible one of the family. And yet I left all these beside the road and carried home a heavy watermelon through some of the worst rioting imaginable. I will always wonder at that, at the will I had to get home, to keep walking through hell, and to carry a watermelon. How it is we all survive the unbearable.

This is the image that sticks with me: what made my friend drop her bags, with their familial associations and useful documents, in fatigue and terror, but hold on to a watermelon? "Carry what you need," she had said in Kataragama. In the seven days of the rioting, I watched thousands of people act and react to the events at hand, each in his or her own unique way; and hundreds of these people's responses made a strong impression on me. Each story, each behavior I observed during the riots, was a piece of the puzzle, a call to follow the question. But what was the puzzle, what was the question? Perhaps this watermelon is why I study war.

*   *   *

I doubt she would want me to use her real name. I was speaking with her half a world away, and nearly two decades after the Sri Lankan riots. But she would understand the story of the watermelon: she lives in a warzone where one-third of the entire population has been forced to flee their homes, and one-twelfth of the population have lost their lives to war in the last ten years. She had made time in a very busy day to sit and talk with me about the impact of the war on daily life. As the conversation came to an end, I thanked her for her time and asked her if there was anything I could do for her, to reciprocate her kindness.

Yes, *she said*, there is. We have tens of thousands of internally displaced people in this area who have lost everything to the war. They do any kind of work to try to make enough to buy food and keep their families alive. This often falls on the women's shoulders: do you know, in most of the camps for the displaced here, the majority of households are headed by a woman? Women and girls scrape together just enough to get some food or goods to sell to make some money to feed their families.

And then you see the police and the military, taking what little these girls and women have. They feel entitled. You see it all the time: a woman will be walking down the street with goods to sell, and the police or the soldiers will just go up and take it.

They have the power, she has nothing now. And she may not make it without that bit to sell—how is she to survive?

What can you do for me? Tell this story. Write about it. Tell the truth of war and what happens to people like these women who stand on the thin line of survival.

For the people standing on that thin line of survival between living and becoming a casualty of war, the impact of these actions is of existential proportions. They may even be cataclysmic. But for most people in the world, these brushes with life, death, and profiteering are largely invisible. They are invisible because militarily, much of war violates human sensibilities; because logistically, the front lines are difficult to document with neutrality; because economically, fortunes are made and lost in less than ethical ways; because politically, power covers its tracks.

The story doesn't end with the women giving up their goods to the police and military. This is just ground zero of the front-line intersections of war and invisible economies that ultimately extend worldwide. Just as these troops demand payment from poor women, so must they pay up the ladder, compensating their commanding officers. And their commanding officers are able to demand far greater goods in their own sphere of work: at the highest levels of power, they may control national concessions over valuable resources, as well as the companies that work the concessions, transport the goods, and oversee the profits. This might be called corruption if it stopped at the national level, but these systems of profit are international. In the shadows, beyond public scrutiny, commanders may partner with international wildcatters who move consumer items, from weapons to cigarettes, into a warzone while moving valuable resources, from diamonds to timber, out to the cosmopolitan centers of the world in less than legal ways. More visibly, they may partner with international state-sponsored vendors to procure expensive weapons and goods—exports that peacetime countries are eager to sell for their own profits, but which rarely match the actual needs of the purchasing country and its war.

Systems of partnership, alliance, coercion, dependency, and outright violation variously mark these transactions, from the poor woman who gives up her only food to the foot soldier all the way to the vast global flows of weapons or resources for hard currency. It is in these intersections that power in its most fundamental sense is forged. In the midst of vast political systems in which riots and wars scar human landscapes and mold global economies, a woman discards her handbags and clutches a watermelon in trying to get home in a city besieged by mobs. This, in total, is the body of war and the hope for peace.

How do we understand, not abstract text-bound definitions of war's violence, but what it lives like, experiences like, tastes, feels, looks, and moves like? Many of the truths of war disappear in unsung deeds and unrecorded acts.[1] "The war tells us: nothing is what it seems. But the war also says: I am the reality, I am the ground under your feet, the certainty that lies beneath all uncertainties" (van de Port 1998, 30). What place do we give to the profound good that beats in the hearts of so many I meet on the front

---

1. War so little matches classic accounts of war that a truism has emerged for me through the years I have studied violence at its epicenters: if you want to prepare yourself for studying violence and peace, assume that what popular wisdom in society—the prefabricated configurations of "truth" that ripple across the fluid bodies of social talk and text—tells you is exactly the opposite.

lines that "conventional wisdom" tells us are populated with Hobbesian brutes? At the broadest level these inquiries merge into the question: "What is war?" Or perhaps more accurately, "Why would humans engage in one of the most profoundly unpleasant activities imaginable—one capable of extinguishing humans themselves?"

> I soon found that there are no theories of war or—depending on what you are willing to accept as a "theory"—far too many of them. Ask a scholar for an explanation of war, and he or she will most likely snicker at your naiveté in expecting that something so large and poorly defined could even be explained. Ask a nonspecialist, however, and you will get any of a dozen explanations, each proffered with utter confidence: it is because of our innate aggressiveness . . . or because of innate male aggressiveness . . . or because of imperialism and greed . . . or overpopulation and a shortage of resources . . . or it is simply a manifestation of unknowable evil . . . Our understanding of war, it occurred to me, is about as confused and uninformed as theories of disease were roughly 200 years ago. (Ehrenreich 1997, 1–2)

* * * Violence is defined both by local realities and histories and by internationally forged norms of militarization: a large and well-developed set of networks stretch across the globe and into the most remote battlefield localities to provide everything required by militaries, from weapons to training manuals, food, medicines, tools, and state-of-the-art computers. If war is powerfully shaped by the intersections of individual acts, national histories, and transnational cultures of militarization and economic gain, so too are the more profound questions that attach to studies of war: What is power? Violence? In/humanity? Resolution?

These observations set in motion a new set of research issues: much of this trade passes across boundaries of il/legality. * * * I found these "extra-state" exchange systems—what I here call "shadow" networks—are fundamental to war, and in a profound irony, are central to processes of development, for good or bad. Simultaneously, my research showed that their centrality in world economic and power systems is accompanied by an almost inverse proportion of information on them. * * * A startlingly large portion of the entire global economy passes through the shadows: 90 percent of Angola's economy; 50 percent of Kenya's, Italy's, and Peru's economies; 40 to 60 percent of Russia's economy; and between 10 and 30 percent of the United States economy enters into extra-state transactions (Greif 1996, 239–65). But a comparable percentage of research and publication does not take place on the non-legal. This of course prompts the question, "Why?"

The repercussions of leaving extra-state realities in the analytical shadows are extensive. Today, trillions of dollars and millions of people circulate around the globe outside of formal legal reckoning. This set of economic and personnel flows ranges from the mundane (the trade in cigarettes and pirated software), through the illicit (gems and timber), to the dangerous (weapons and illegal narcotics).

The trillions generated in these extra-legal financial empires must be laundered to legitimacy, and thus enter global financial markets in uncharted ways. The relative freedom from controls found in warzones and the financial powerhouses found in the cosmopolitan centers of the world combine in ways that tend to merge war and global profiteering.

Complex production, transport, distribution, and consumption systems have emerged to move goods and services through the shadows. Sophisticated banking systems exist to transfer unregulated monies. Highly developed regulatory mechanisms are in place to oversee extra-state trade—from lawyers to conflict resolution specialists. The profits have a substantial impact on the economies of all of the world's countries. And much of this remains invisible to formal state-based accounting systems and theories. We can't, with any accuracy, tell what impact hundreds of billions of dollars worth of illicit weapons gains has on European stock markets; how laundered drug proceeds affect the financial viability of smaller states; how market manipulation of unregulated goods affects interest rates and currency valuations internationally.

Nor, without studying the shadows, can we predict crises such as the Asian market crash in the late 1990s or the September 11, 2001, attack on the USA. The shadows permeate these realms. Extra-state economies are central to the world's power grids.

*   *   *

It may be that in the past we could understand a locale solely by focusing our gaze on it. Perhaps not. But today, clearly, locales are not islands surrounded by the vast and churning waters of fluid geographical space. Today humans feel the tug and pull of societal waves generated in regions far afield; they share the currents, even the riptides, that move across vast global stretches. For example, my experiences in Sri Lanka took on greater meaning when I began to do research in Mozambique. When I saw the same cast of characters selling arms, profiteering, and brokering peace in Mozambique as I had in Sri Lanka, I realized that these international players were not necessarily ideologically linked to the causes defining either South Asia or Southern Africa, nor were they necessarily drawn into a national drama for a specific set of reasons unique to this "locale." They were international players. In following the networks brokering war and peace across all distinctions of legal and illegal, I realized that these represent anthropological flows that span the globe both physically and epistemologically—at once dependent on locales and local cultural knowledges but also linking across them.

What, then, is ethnography?

The answer is not the same for everyone. But for me, and for this particular research, ethnography *must be able to follow the question*. It must be able to capture not only the site, but also the smell, feel, taste, and motion of a locale, of a people that share a common space and intertwined lives. It must be able to grasp at least a fleeting glimpse of the dreams that people carry with them and that carry people to distant places of world and mind; of the creative imaginary through which people give substance to their thoughts and lives. And quite pragmatically, it must be able to delve into why a soldier pulls the trigger against one human and not another; to illuminate how people suffer the ravages of violence and grieving and still craft humanitarian resistance; to chart the realities of how weapons are traded for diamonds and power, and the lives of those who trade them.

Today, such questions can't be encompassed by studying a single site. The gun that fires the bullet in Mozambique was made in the USA, or Bulgaria, or Brazil, or China. It was traded through a vast network of agents, "advisors," and alliances—all of whom have a say in how the weapon should be used: who can legitimately be killed (and who cannot, starting with the arms vendors), and how this is all to be justified. Perhaps the weapon was smuggled through the legal world into the shadows, entering another global set of alliances. The soldier who aims the gun aims along years of training, not only on how to kill, but how to draw divisions, hatred, fears, and justifications—a mix of cultural and military lore that has been fed by everything from local grievances through foreign military advisors to global media and music. All of this intersects to shape the lives of everyone involved in war, from the elite decision makers to the youth-soldiers fighting on shifting and hazy front lines.

*　　*　　*

"We just got a dead Irish Protestant mercenary, you want to see his body?" the fifteen-year-old said as he propped his AK-47 against a tree trunk, sat down next to me, and asked for a cigarette. It was at the height of the war in Mozambique, itself a long way from Europe and the conflicts in Northern Ireland. The boy and I sat in a bombed-out town in the middle of Mozambique, many hundreds of kilometers from the country's capital and cosmopolitan centers. We were, as traditional scholarship would say, in a profoundly "local" setting. "No thanks," I replied, "but how do you know he's a Protestant from Northern Ireland?"

"We looked at his identity papers," the boy said, looking at me as if I were a half-wit. The boy was thin, and dressed only in a pair of tattered shorts and a T-shirt. His gun was strung on an old piece of cloth. He had been press-ganged into joining the military, and had never left his home village region until he walked out as a "soldier" about the time he hit puberty. The boy settled in the sun, and began to talk:

> You know, these white guys are often a whole lot meaner than we are. I mean, we fight and we kill and all, but it's like these white guys think killing is the answer to everything. We have so many white guys, so many foreigners, around; training us, getting mad at us, fighting us, making money from us. Some are OK, I got sent to this training camp far away, and there were some who were friendly, tried to make sure we got enough to eat, and worked to teach us. People from all over. Got a whole lot of strange ideas, stuff that sometimes' useful, but a lot of times just didn't make a lot of sense, like it was a lot of trouble to do things that way, and dangerous too. * * * Truth is, I don't think a lot of these guys care if we win or lose. We all see

them moving on the mines, doing "business." Someone's making a whole lot in this war, and I can tell you, it sure isn't me.

If I were going to understand this war, and this youth's experiences in it, what story would I best follow? I could follow his movements; those of his compatriots and the foreigners he interacted with; the media and movies that shaped his ideas; the war merchants and profiteers from around the world that passed through his life, his country, and its war; the various cultures of militarization that move from warzone to warzone around the world; the vast international systems of economic gain that shape political violence. This "local" youth-soldier was far from "local." The Mozambican war was deeply internationalized. Where does war begin and end?

*   *   *

I'll never know why my friend in Sri Lanka left her handbag, wrap, and suitcase in the roadway, yet carried a watermelon as she struggled to get home through the rioting. She says she doubts she will ever figure it out herself. But we speculated about this for months:

> You know, *she said*, it seems illogical to leave what I might most need in the midst of a life-threatening night. But, when you think of it, it seems illogical to kill people for an identity: are you Tamil, Sinhalese, Hindu, Muslim, Buddhist? It seems illogical to target people on their jobs and associations, voter registration designations, and location of their homes. My handbag was filled with such "identity": my registrations and designations, licenses and addresses. It just occurred to me: these are like licenses to kill. Leaving my glasses, my keys? Perhaps I just didn't want to see what was going on; and what are keys but an illusion of safety shattered by mobs who just break windows and enter houses? What did I care that night if I broke my window to get into my home? If I had to break in, that would be wonderful, it would mean my house had not been attacked. My suitcase? It was heavy, and when your life is on the line, all those pretty saris and comfortable shoes don't mean a whole lot. But I think it was more: all around me people were looting the goods of the maimed and the murdered, of the burning shops and the deserted houses. What have we humans become, I believe I worried that night, that we will feast on the dead for a television or a trinket? When did we begin to value goods above good? My suitcase, filled with my goods, became heavy in more ways than one. I left those behind. I left behind the presents I bought for my family. Somehow I think they seemed to embody the religious strife that was tearing my country to shreds that night. But that watermelon. It was heavy, and unwieldy, and I can't imagine what I looked like, an old mother struggling down burning streets covered in dirt and ash carrying a large watermelon in her arms. But it was something pure of violence; a present for my family that cost no one their life; something that seemed to represent sanity and succor in a world gone mad. A watermelon carries its own seeds for the future. Perhaps that is what I was trying to do.

ENGAGING THE TEXT, ENGAGING THE WORLD

- Following Margaret Mead's argument in the previous reading that war is an invention, and a bad one at that, how do you see war, its motivations, and its mechanisms being invented in the scenarios in Nordstrom's text?

- Compile a list of all the players/actors who make up the global landscape of warfare, as described by Nordstorm.

- What does Nordstrom mean by "shadow networks" and why does she prioritize them in her research?

- Although these shadow networks are global enterprises, where do we see them manifested locally in this selection?

- Why does Nordstrom suggest ethnography is a uniquely effective strategy for examining the complex realities of warfare and violence? What does she mean when she says that ethnography "must be able to follow the question"?

- What is the symbolic meaning of the watermelon carried by Nordstrom's Sri Lankan friend? Why does she think she left everything else behind on the street as she headed home through the violence?

- What can be done in response to such violence and warfare? Nordstrom's friend urged her to "Tell this story. Write about it. Tell the truth of war and what happens to people like these women who stand on the thin line of survival." What can you do?

From *Polluted Promises*
Melissa Checker

Environmental racism and resistance

Systems of power, including the state, are never absolute. Their dominance is never complete. Even when a culture's elite groups and institutions are very powerful in terms of their ability to exercise force or to establish control through hegemony, they do not completely dominate people's lives and thinking. Individuals and groups with less power or no power may still contest established power relationships and structures through political, economic, religious, or military means and challenge and change cultural norms, values, symbols, and institutions. This power is a potential that anthropologists call agency.

From Melissa Checker. 2005. *Polluted Promises: Environmental Racism and the Search for Justice in a Southern Town.* New York: New York University Press. Some of the author's notes have been omitted.

In such displays of human agency, we see the way culture becomes the realm in which battles over power are waged; where people can test, negotiate, and enforce what is considered normal and what people can say, do, and even think. Because of human agency, cultures do not remain rigid and static. They change.

Efforts to change cultural patterns take various forms. Social movements, such as the one explored in this selection from Melissa Checker's book *Polluted Promises*, are collective, group actions in response to uneven development, inequality, and injustice that seek to build institutional networks to transform cultural patterns and government policies. Social movements may engage in contentious politics, usually outside the mainstream political process, to address specific social issues, although they usually do not seek to overthrow the social order.

Checker conducted fieldwork in a poor, rural, predominantly African American community near Augusta, Georgia, that was struggling with the effects of decades of toxic waste dumping by local factories. The toxins were taking a terrible toll on the environment, seeping into people's homes and destroying their health. Checker provides a powerful account of local activism as a community of color painstakingly built a social movement over three decades to challenge the deep and troublesome connections between race and environmental pollution. The stakes for the community were much higher than ridding their neighborhood of chemical contaminants. Organizers also challenged persistent and commonplace forms of racial discrimination that blamed bad health, education, and economic conditions on the victims. Checker's work raises the crucial questions, "Why are the life chances of so many African Americans different than those of white Americans? And what on earth does the environment have to do with it?"

You Can Run, But You Can't Hyde

On the afternoon of his thirty-ninth birthday, Arthur Smith Jr., a tall, handsome African American[1] man with graying hair and an easy smile, rushed into the library of the Clara E. Jenkins Elementary School. It was 3:30 P.M., and Smith was late. His last engagement, one of four community organization meetings or activities he had attended that day, had run over. Although it was only March, in Augusta, Georgia, heat and humidity had already descended, and small beads of sweat stood out on Smith's brow. Catching his breath and assuming one of his trademark grins, Smith strode into the room. Seated around three small tables, twelve African American fourth and fifth graders turned their heads.

---

1. Following the general usage of the people in this book, I use the terms "African American" and "black" interchangeably.

"Mr. Arthur Jr.'s here," exclaimed Frank, a bright fourth grader.[2]

Smith walked to the library's windows and stood before the children. Behind him stretched the school's well-trodden brownish green field, with its rusting jungle gym. Framed on two sides by long ditches, the field marked the beginning of Augusta's Hyde Park neighborhood, home to approximately two hundred African American families. If you followed the ditches, which lined both sides of the neighborhood's seven streets, you would see rows of small, mostly one-story shotgun-style homes surrounded by ample lawns. Some of these houses were freshly whitewashed cottages. Others were covered in peeling paint and leaned on their foundations. Between almost every home and its yard was a porch, usually set up with chairs and often filled with families and neighbors. Some yards bloomed with daisies, chrysanthemums, and lilacs, but since the early 1990s, none included a single patch of vegetables.

Clearing the spring's pollen from his throat, Smith asked, "What's contamination?"

"Pollution," answered Cherise.

Smith nodded and then explained,

> Pollution. That's right. Poison is another word for it. Contamination is poison. What did Dr. King do during the civil rights movement? He marched. Why was he a marcher? Because everybody's an American no matter what race, color, or creed you are. He was marching because the poor in this country are left out. To show the country how to live up to its constitution, "We the people" means everything. Forty years ago, nobody thought that racism in the South could be broken. What is racism?

Fifth grader Shanequa Jones replied, "Somebody don't like the color of your skin."

Smith nodded once again. Having spent most of his life a block from the home of Shanequa's grandmother (where Shanequa spent half the week), Smith had known her since the day she was born. He continued,

> That's right. Somebody don't like you for the color of your skin. See that's what happened in Hyde Park and Aragon Park. Somebody said that we wasn't human. But the God who serves, sits high and looks low. So, things are happening in this area and it's all for you. It's for your college education; it's to make sure that you have a job when you grow up. It's to make sure you get everything you're entitled to.

Pausing for a moment, Smith glanced out of the window. "Has anybody ever noticed the signs that say playing in ditches is hazardous to your health?" he asked.

---

2. Children's names have been changed, although those of many adults have not.

Lorenzo Thomas, a shy fourth grader who lived a few houses away from Smith on Willow Street, answered quietly, "On Willow Street."

Smiling briefly at Lorenzo, Smith continued,

> You know, when I was a little boy we used to catch tadpoles in the ditches and save them and trade them. Yeah, we did all that. But young people, do not go in the ditches out here. Ditches here are highly polluted. Contaminants can get into your feet. Understand you got to take care of you. We need y'all healthy.

Arthur Smith's speech to the children of Jenkins Elementary School that warm spring day traversed subjects from contamination to civil rights to democracy to educational and economic opportunity to childhood memory and back to contamination.[3] The multitude of topics that Smith wrapped into one discussion of his neighborhood's history is no accident. For Smith and his fellow activists in Hyde Park, all these things are inextricably linked to each other and to a history fraught with discrimination and struggle.

Like many Americans, I spent most of my life thinking of the environment as primarily a white middle-class issue. Saving whales, recycling, and preserving forests seemed hardly to affect the lives of poor and minority people, especially since these people tend to live in urban areas. My own activist endeavors centered on housing and other urban social justice concerns. Then, while searching for a research topic on a major issue facing America's cities, I read Robert Bullard's *Dumping in Dixie* (1990), which clearly and explicitly outlined how racist institutions caused people of color to bear a disproportionate burden of our nation's toxic waste. Bullard made me realize that I had been dead wrong in not considering the environment a social justice issue. Rather, it is inextricably linked to our country's history of racism.

I began my research on environmental justice activism in Brooklyn, New York, where I worked with a group of Hasidic, Latino, and African American activists who had come together to fight the installation of a fifty-two-foot incinerator in their neighborhood. Over the course of several months, I sat at community meetings and interviewed activists, listening as they described how many of their children, relatives, and neighbors were sick with strange forms of cancer and other diseases. I marveled at how the New York City government could slate this neighborhood, which already had two highways running through it and a Superfund site on its perimeter, for an incinerator. In this case, local activists eventually won the support of enough politicians to stop the plan. As I further

---

3. Contamination in this case is loosely defined as the presence of contaminants in air, water, or soil, over the permissible standards set by either federal or state government. In the case of Hyde Park, it is certain that contaminants exist in the neighborhood; I therefore use the term without qualification. However, whether or not contaminants pose a health risk to residents is a highly contested issue.

researched environmental justice and searched for a location for a longer research project, I realized that the Brooklyn situation was not uncommon—but the residents' success in fighting it was.

I thus set out to investigate (1) how environmental organizing has both changed and been incorporated into urban African American activism, and (2) what I, as an anthropologist, could do to participate in environmental justice. Hyde Park turned out to be a perfect location for answering both questions: it has been polluted in both an ecological and social sense since its inception as a neighborhood, and its residents have been fighting that pollution equally as long. For not only are Hyde Park's ecological resources (air, water, and soil) contaminated, but its social resources (access to decent jobs, housing, schools, and police protection) are also contaminated due to a history of discrimination against African Americans. The resilience and fortitude that I found among Hyde Park's residents, despite all these experiences, truly enlightened and inspired me. * * *

Welcome to Hyde Park

Just after World War II, Hyde Park's first residents finally said farewell to sharecropping in rural Georgia and used their savings to buy small plots of land in a swampy area, a few miles from the heart of downtown Augusta. For the next twenty-plus years, even as the neighborhood swelled to two hundred families, Hyde Park residents made do without indoor plumbing, running water, or gas stoves. Living on swampland also meant that they struggled through numerous floods, often having to canoe out of the neighborhood to get to work and school. Back then, Hyde Park residents were nearly all employed—many in nearby factories or as domestics. The neighborhood was a vibrant place, with small groceries, churches, barbershops, and even a few bars where residents could take the edge off a long week's work. But for the rest of Augusta, Hyde Park was almost invisible. Surrounded by a junkyard, a railway line, and an industrial ceramics plant on one side, a power plant on another, a brickyard and a second railway on a third, and a highway on the remaining side, Hyde Park essentially formed the hole of an industrial donut. The fact that low-income African American families lived inside that hole made it even less likely to be noticed, especially by Augusta's mostly white politicians.

In the late 1960s, Hyde Park residents, fed up with their lack of county services, caught on to the heels of the national civil rights movement and formed the Hyde and Aragon Park Improvement Committee (HAPIC). After several years of tenacious community agitation, HAPIC activists won water, gas, and sewer lines, streetlights, paved roads, and flood control ditches—infrastructure that most other Augusta neighborhoods had received long before. Throughout the 1970s, as local industries downsized and employment rates declined, they worked hard to improve residents' education, job opportunities, and access to health care. In the 1980s, they added a fight against the selling of drugs and drug-related violence to that agenda, as Hyde Park's streets became a popular local venue for buying and selling crack cocaine.

Some residents also began to fall ill with mysterious or uncommon forms of cancer and skin diseases. Around 1990, they discovered one possible reason for local maladies. In the early part of the 1980s, Southern Wood Piedmont (SWP), a nearby wood-preserving factory, detected soil and groundwater contamination, including dioxins, chlorophenols, and other wood treatment chemicals. On further investigation, SWP found that the groundwater pollution extended off-site along two plumes. The factory closed in 1988 and began to remediate the contamination. Two years later, Virginia Subdivision, a low-income, predominantly white community that backed right onto SWP property, settled a class action lawsuit against SWP and its parent companies, International Telephone and Telegraph Corporation (ITT) and ITT Rayonier. Although the ditches that lined Hyde Park's streets eventually made their way to the edges of SWP's property, residents had never been told about the lawsuit, let alone asked to join it; therefore, they received no compensation. Hyde Park residents believed that this exclusion had much to do with the fact that their neighborhood is 99 percent African American. HAPIC geared up for another community-wide struggle, now making environmental justice its main priority. This time, however, rather than fighting Augusta's city hall, the organization took on an international conglomerate.

Hyde Park residents soon realized that Southern Wood was not the only nearby industry to emit toxins. There were reports that Georgia Power's transformer station, which sits on one side of Dan Bowles Road, just across from a number of homes, had leaked polychlorinated biphenyls (PCBs) (ATSDR 1995, 6). For years, the plume from Thermal Ceramics, an industrial ceramics plant on the neighborhood's edge, had lit the skies at night. Many mornings, people living just down the road found their cars covered in a fine white dust. Chemicals also flowed from Goldberg Brothers scrap metal yard (about a half a block from Georgia Power) into Hyde Park's ditches and yards. Residents (children in particular) suffered from rashes, lupus, respiratory and circulatory problems, and rare forms of cancer.

An array of studies conducted throughout the 1990s found high levels of certain chemicals in the neighborhood's soil and groundwater, but no conclusive evidence could link those chemicals to health problems. * * *

For every study that has shown evidence of significant contamination, there seems to be another that contradicts or mitigates it, leaving residents (and researchers) confused. At least some of the dangerous chemicals just mentioned appeared in nearly every study report, but how intensely they were concentrated, and whether and to what degree they posed a health threat remain very much up for debate. Therefore, residents have won neither a corporate settlement nor government funds to help them clean up or relocate from the neighborhood. At the same time, it became almost impossible for them to sell their homes due to fears of contamination. By the time I came to Hyde Park in 1998 to conduct research with HAPIC, I found that the neighborhood's inhabitants had gotten mired in the (figurative and literal) toxic stew that surrounded them.

Hyde Park residents have thus had the deck stacked against them from the get-go. They grew up under the cruel thumb of Jim Crow and over the years had to fight for neighborhood infrastructure and against the unemployment, drugs, and violence that plagued their community. Then, people in the neighborhood seemed to get sick and to die at an alarming rate. Although high levels of dangerous chemicals had been found in their air, water, and soil, they could not link the two issues according to established scientific standards. What Hyde Park's approximately 250 residents *have* had, however, is a history of successful organizing, as well as a history of being a close-knit, "pull-together" kind of community. They also had a cadre of activists, like Arthur Smith, who managed to hold on to a tremendous amount of faith, energy, and hope, working tirelessly to come up with strategies for improving neighborhood schools, reducing crime and violence, and finding a way out of contamination.

*   *   *

Racial segregation, discrimination, and disparities remain pernicious in today's United States, despite the passing of civil rights legislation, the dismantling of ideas about the biological basis of race, and contemporary celebrations of multiculturalism. Why are the life chances of so many African Americans, especially in urban settings, different than those of white Americans? And what on earth does the environment have to do with it?

Somewhere in the middle to late 1980s in the United States, two important social movements—environmentalism and civil rights—converged in an effort to answer these questions. This convergence is taking place around the globe in rural areas, small towns, and big cities, wherever marginalized people realize that they bear the brunt of housing the world's industrial waste. In the United States, environmental justice seeks not just relief from contamination but also access to a host of resources (such as decent housing, schools, and/or police protection) that are traditionally denied to people of color. For this reason, U.S. environmental justice activities initially dubbed their movement "the civil rights [movement] of the new millennium." For many, a civil rights legacy provides a foundation from which activists think about and struggle with environmental problems.

* * * Environmental racism extends far beyond the straightforward poisoning of air, water, or soil. That Hyde Park residents cannot point a finger at one deliberate polluter is highly typical of environmental justice communities. Their difficulties in meeting established scientific and legal standards to prove their case are also typical, due in large part to the inexactness of environmental science and the biases that it contains. The Hyde Park case is thus emblematic of the complicated and invidious ways in which environmental racism works—how it is embedded in discriminatory institutional practices, policies, and procedures, and how it accumulates over many years.* * *

For example, pernicious assumptions that poor, urban African Americans are "disorganized," "uneducated," and mired in poverty led to the proliferation and the permanence of unwanted industry and land uses in Hyde Park. It appears that local politicians and corporations assumed residents would not care about, or contest, such sites. As recently as the summer of 2001 (long after Hyde Park's toxic problems had attracted numerous local news reports and even federal grants), Augusta's planning department permitted a local company to establish a landfill in the neighborhood. Even more recently, late in 2003, the planning department approved a new recycling facility directly across from the former junkyard. After twenty years of protest, residents had finally received a federal grant that led to that junkyard's cleanup. Despite all the publicity and effort surrounding that cleanup, someone in the planning department seemed to assume that another landfill or another "recycling center" (often this is a euphemism for "junkyard") would go unnoticed and uncontested in a neighborhood like Hyde Park.

As * * * HAPIC's eventual success in stopping the recycling center attest[s], the planning department got it wrong. From the inception of their neighborhood and for more than three decades, Hyde Park residents organized against the racial discrimination they faced. * * *

* * * [One] of my biggest aspirations is that the stories of the people depicted here—their courage, their stamina, and their consistent ability to adapt their strategies to changing circumstances—will inspire readers to engage in some activism of their own.

Race-ing the Environment

For hundreds of communities of color in the United States, what happened in Hyde Park is not an exception but the rule. Race, numerous studies tell us, is the most potent variable in predicting where hazardous waste facilities are located—more powerful than poverty, land values, or homeownership. Three out of every five African Americans and Hispanics and roughly 50 percent of Asian/Pacific Islanders and Native Americans live in communities containing at least one uncontrolled toxic waste site (Commission for Racial Justice 1987).[4] The percentage of African Americans or Latinos in a census tract significantly predicts whether that tract hosts a toxic waste facility (Been and Gupta 1997; Been 1993). African Americans are more than three times more likely than whites to die from asthma, and the hospitalization rate for African Americans with asthma is three times that for whites (American Lung Association 2004, 2002). * * * Such environmental disparities are widespread throughout the United States, but the South has had particularly lax environmental policies. As a result, the region (which houses more than half of the nation's African American citizens) claims eight of the ten states ranked worst in terms of pollution, poor health, and environmental policies. In

---

4. A follow-up study found that these numbers had increased by as much as 8 percent by 1993 (Center for Policy Alternatives 1994).

the EPA's [Environmental Protection Agency's] southeastern region, three out of the four largest hazardous waste landfills in the region sit in majority black areas (Center for Policy Alternatives 1994; Institute for Southern Studies 1992).

*   *   *

Defining the Terms of Debate

"Environmental racism" describes the process that leads to the disproportionate siting of hazardous waste facilities in communities of color. The Reverend Dr. Benjamin F. Chavis Jr., a former executive director of the National Association for the Advancement of Colored People (NAACP), coined the phrase in his foreword to the United Church of Christ Commission on Racial Justice's landmark study, *Toxic Wastes and Race in the United States.* In Chavis's words, environmental racism includes:

> racial discrimination in environmental policy-making, enforcement of regulations and laws, the deliberate targeting of communities of color for toxic waste disposal and the siting of polluting industries. It is racial discrimination in the official sanctioning of the life-threatening presence of poisons and pollutants in communities of color. And, it is racial discrimination in the history of excluding people of color from the mainstream environmental groups, decision-making boards, commission, and regulatory bodies. (Chavis 1993, 3)

Many people, however, argue that * * * siting decisions are based on economics, not race—hazards tend to be located on cheap land, and people of color tend to live around cheap housing. Indeed, I do not suggest that every example of environmental racism means some corporation or local agency deliberately decided to put a landfill in a black neighborhood.

At the same time, middle-income black and Hispanic neighborhoods have higher rates of contamination than low-income white neighborhoods, clearly illustrating that the market is not the only influence. The factors that lead to disproportionate pollution and contamination include a host of sometimes subtle racist practices and procedures. For example, real estate agents steer black families toward areas within or near existing ghettos. Minorities with the same resources and credit records as whites are denied mortgages at twice the rate. Minority neighborhoods are more likely than white neighborhoods to be rezoned (often by all-white planning boards) from residential to commercial or light industrial uses. And the list goes on. Due in part to historical exclusions and negative stereotyping, African Americans hold far fewer seats on city councils and other local governing boards. Housing segregation leads to lower tax bases, which lead to poorer schools. Employment discrimination against African Americans continues to prevail in our society. Lower wages and a lack of access to jobs limit the opportunities of African Americans to leave a contaminated neighborhood (although, even if they did leave, they would likely have little choice but to move to another contaminated neighborhood). Growing up with lead, dioxin, or mercury poisoning makes children miss or perform more poorly in school, further limiting their educational and job opportunities.

*　　*　　*

Environmental justice activists define the environment as "where we live, work, and play." For them, the environment is not just ecological but also includes a host of *social* factors such as housing, schools, neighborhood safety, and employment. The pursuit of environmental justice, then, is "the right of all people to share equally in the benefits of a healthy environment." Put slightly less simply,

> Environmental justice initiatives specifically attempt to redress the disproportionate incidence of environmental contamination in communities of the poor and/or communities of color, to secure for those affected the right to live unthreatened by the risks posed by environmental degradation and contamination, and to afford equal access to natural resources that sustain life and culture. (Adamson, Evans, and Stein 2002, 4)

The environmental justice movement encompasses hundreds of activists around the globe, who fight to protect themselves from unsafe environments. Overseas, environmental justice movements include the Chipko, or "tree-hugging" movement against deforestation in India, the struggles of the Ogoni people in Nigeria to stop oil drilling on their farmlands, and the work of indigenous peoples in Malaysia to stop the destruction of their rain forests. In the United States, environmental justice movements range from the struggles of Chicano women in South Central Los Angeles opposing a hazardous waste facility, to Navajo sheepherders fighting to stop the world's largest open-pit coal mine from encroaching on sacred land, to native Alaskans exposed to radioactive waste, to workers in California's Silicon Valley. Environmental injustice affects women, poor people, people of color, and workers, and the issues it raises are global, human rights issues.

*　　*　　*

No Progress without Struggle

"End it on a positive note," said Arthur Smith when I called him in despair, after staring at my blank computer screen for what seemed like an entire day. I had sat down that morning to write the conclusions to nearly six years of research and writing, not to mention a struggle that is very much ongoing. * * * "Right," I murmured, thinking of all the ways that my account might portray Hyde Park's quest for environmental justice as hopeless, foolhardy, or depressing—Goliath besting David time and again.

Still, I could see Smith's point. On the one hand, thanks to the 1999 EPA Brownfields grant, the Goldberg scrap metal yard had been assessed and cleaned. Gone were the towers of tires that inauspiciously marked Hyde Park's entrance. Gone, too, was the creaky old shed turned office where contractors found buckets, pails, and jars spilling over with elemental mercury (collected by one of the scrap yard's owners). In fact, once they realized the extent of cleanup needed, the EPA asked the Georgia EPD [Environmental Protection Division] for assistance. In an almost unprecedented cooperative effort, the two agencies removed 20,000 tons of surface waste, including 6,770 tons of miscellaneous debris, 12,000 tons of hazardous lead-contaminated soil, and 181 tons of mercury-contaminated debris.

The EPD's contractor also hired and trained three Hyde Park residents to help with the cleanup operations; later, he hired one of them to work on another cleanup nearby. In February 2003, HAPIC won a second Brownfield grant for a site across the road. Even more exciting, this grant would test properties on the sites' perimeters and then install monitoring wells in certain people's yards. The EPA has pronounced the SWP site, as well as the lead-contaminated ditch across from Jenkins Elementary School, "clean." And in the summer of 2004, Hyde Park residents convinced city council members to revoke the permit for the new recycling facility that had set up shop across from the former scrapyard. Mayor Young promised that no more unwanted land uses would be slated for Hyde Park.

On the other hand, it was hard not to think about how the Brownfield project's preliminary investigations had revealed significant levels of arsenic, cadmium, lead, chromium, mercury, PCBs, and petroleum hydrocarbons on the edges of the Goldberg site— a stone's throw from the yards of David Jackson, Hattie Elam, and other residents. I also thought of the metal signs planted throughout the neighborhood warning children not to play in the ditches, some of which are now so faded as to be barely readable. *** Every time I visit the neighborhood, at least one or two people are being "funeralized." Like many people in Hyde Park, I wonder whether these deaths are brought on by decades of exposure to contamination. *** Finally, although HAPIC activists' recent victory against the new recycling center was certainly significant, promises to remove the landfill at the end of Carolina Road (which residents complained smelled of gasoline) had gone unfulfilled. It was difficult not to question how these facilities had gotten through the permitting process in the first place. How many fires would Hyde Park residents need to extinguish as, every few years, local officials conveniently forgot about their situation?

"Well, how do you mean?" I questioned Smith, always encouraged—and intrigued— by his unrelenting optimism. He replied,

> Too often in the struggle, there's no victories. To get people attached to the movement, you've got to celebrate the victories. The Brownfields grant is to me the end

of the rainbow. For a low-income community like ours to know that we are part of the federal government. . . . We've been blessed as a community that so many people—Augusta State University, Paine College, and Clark Atlanta University—understand our pain and our suffering and also want to see relief [for us]. At first, people said that we were on the wrong side of the tracks, that we were gangsters. Who would have thought the federal government, the EPA, and the EPD would be sitting at the table working on a place like Hyde Park? So much pain, so much abuse of a community. But with the impact of all of this [contamination], we still carry on a somewhat normal and decent life.

As usual, Smith's speech hit on many of the subjects central to this study. HAPIC's successes and disappointments alike demonstrate some of the ways that African Americans adapt past legacies to contemporary challenges as they struggle to make democratic ideals match their lived experiences.

*   *   *

For Hyde Park residents, the pursuit of environmental justice entails putting democratic ideals into practice and integrating neighborhood concerns into governmental agendas. In other words, pursuing environmental justice presents a new opportunity to pursue more traditional goals of democracy and inclusion, or to simply become "part of the government."

Martin Luther King Jr. wrote in a Birmingham jail, "The passage of time alone does not bring change." For change to occur in even incremental ways, people must strive every day to push the barriers that confine their opportunities and to alter the status quo. Over a thirty-year period, this has been the goal of one group of neighbors who have worked steadily to improve the conditions in which they live. Developing a greater understanding of those three decades of struggle—the obstacles residents have faced, the strategies they have used to overcome those obstacles, how they conceptualize and articulate the things that have happened to them, and the things that they wish to make happen—tells us how discriminated-against people can work together successfully to make a difference in their lives and the lives of those around them.

ENGAGING THE TEXT, ENGAGING THE WORLD

- Describe the role Arthur Smith plays as a community activist.

- How do environmental justice activists define "environment"? Why is it important that their definition moves beyond the purely ecological?

- How does Checker define environmental racism?

- Checker notes that race is the most potent variable in predicting where hazardous waste facilities are located. Why does Checker think this is true?

- Why does Arthur Smith encourage Checker to "End it on a positive note"?

- Checker chose to become directly involved in the community organizing work in Hyde Park. How did this affect her anthropological research?

- Environmental pollution is a problem for communities across the globe. Are you aware of cases in your local community and efforts to address them?

13
Religion

Religion plays a central role in human life and human culture. Through the study of religion, anthropologists engage some of the deepest, most difficult, and most enduring human questions—about meaning, difference, power, love, sexuality, mortality, morality, human origins, and kinship. Religion offers a rich vein of material for exploring the complexity of human culture, including systems of belief and systems of power. It is perhaps the hottest topic in the world today as globalization brings different traditions, beliefs, and practices into contact. In the United States, immigration over the past five decades has transformed the religious landscape, as we will see in my article about young Chinese immigrants in New York City. Temples, mosques, gurdwaras, and retreat centers now join churches and synagogues in small towns and big cities across the country. College campuses, too, reflect an expanding religious diversity. And while some politicians have called for sweeping bans on Muslim immigrants, as people of different religious traditions encounter one another at the local level, their exchanges create the potential for tension and misunderstanding as well as opportunities for interfaith encounters, learning, and engagement. An anthropological understanding of religion can help you to navigate and engage this changing landscape.

Since the beginning of the discipline, anthropologists have been attempting to create a universal definition that might apply to all religions' manifestations. But the vast global diversity of unique local expressions makes defining religion a difficult task. The unique anthropological approach to religion begins with the everyday religious practices of people in their local communities—**rituals**, beliefs, **magic, pilgrimages**, **rites of passage**, notions of the **sacred** and **profane**. Through fieldwork, anthropologists focus on the real religious worlds in which humans experience religion physically and express it through their actions. We may study a religion's history, theology, scriptures, and major figures, but we do so to understand their meaning and significance in the life of a community of people. Religion is not theoretical in people's daily activities. People make sense of the world, reach decisions, and organize their lives on the basis of their religious beliefs.

Starting from these beginning principles, anthropologists also explore the myriad ways religion intersects with other systems of power, whether economics—as in Daromir Rudnyckyj's article about Islamic banking practices—politics, race, gender, or sexuality.

As a working definition, we might then say that a religion is a set of beliefs and rituals based on a unique vision of how the world ought to be, often focused on a supernatural power and lived out in community. As social scientists, anthropologists have been uninterested in questions of any religion's ultimate truth or falsity. Instead we understand that religious worlds are real, meaningful, and powerful to those who live in them. Our task is to carefully make those worlds come alive for others by capturing their vivid inner life, sense of moral order, dynamic public expressions, and interactions with other systems of meaning and power. George Gmelch's article "Baseball Magic" does just that, explaining the use of magical beliefs and ritual practices among American baseball players while challenging us to see the universality of certain religious expressions, even though they may be practiced in very different contexts.

Baseball Magic
George Gmelch

Magic, ritual, and taboo

Trobriand
Islands   United
              States

Anthropology has a long history of studying cultures where magic is practiced and witches are real. Magic involves the use of spells, incantations, words, and actions in an attempt to compel supernatural forces to act in certain ways, whether for good or for evil. Magic is part of cultural practices in every part of the world. And religion, almost everywhere, contains some components of magic.

In case you think that the Western world relegates belief in magic to children's books and movies like the *Harry Potter* series, anthropologist George Gmelch's classic article "Baseball Magic" provides a surprisingly contemporary exploration of magical beliefs and practices, including rituals, taboos, and fetishes practiced by American baseball players of all ages. A former professional ballplayer himself, Gmelch draws on personal observations and interviews to explore the many ways contemporary baseball players attempt to influence chance and shape their

From George Gmelch. 2017. "Baseball Magic." Some of the author's notes have been omitted.

luck through the practice or avoidance of particular behaviors and the carrying of particular charms. In order to make the strange familiar and the familiar strange, Gmelch compares baseball magic with fishing magic used by the South Sea Trobriand Islanders. For those of us who actively play sports, Gmelch's examples challenge us to be more conscious of the rituals, taboos, and charms we have seen and used. For all of us, perhaps Gmelch's work may ring a bell and awaken us to things we do and magical beliefs we hold in other areas of our lives.

On each pitching day for the first three months of a winning season, Dennis Grossini, a pitcher on a Detroit Tigers [minor league] farm team, arose from bed at exactly 10:00 a.m. At 1:00 p.m. he went to the nearest restaurant for two glasses of iced tea and a tuna fish sandwich. When he got to the ballpark he put on the unwashed sweatshirt and jock he wore during his last winning game; one hour before the game he chewed a wad of Beech-Nut chewing tobacco. On the mound during the game, after each ball Grossini touched the letters on his uniform and straightened his cap. And after every inning in which he gave up a run, he washed his hands.

When I asked which part of his ritual was most important, he said, "You can't really tell what's most important so it all becomes important. I'd be afraid to change anything. As long as I'm winning, I do everything the same." So do many ballplayers.

Trobriand Islanders, according to anthropologist Bronislaw Malinowski, felt the same way about their fishing magic (Malinowski 1948). Trobrianders fished in two different settings: in the *inner lagoon* where fish were plentiful and there was little danger, and on the *open sea* where fishing was dangerous and yields varied widely. Malinowski found that magic was not used in lagoon fishing, where men could rely solely on their knowledge and skill. But when fishing on the open sea, Trobrianders used a great deal of magic to ensure safety and increase their catch.

By magic, anthropologists refer to practices, notably the use of *rituals, taboos,* and *fetishes* (good luck charms), designed to gain control over the supernatural. Baseball, America's national pastime, is an arena in which players behave remarkably like Malinowski's Trobriand fishermen. There are three essential activities of the game—pitching, hitting, and fielding. In the first two, chance can play a surprisingly important role. The pitcher is the player least able to control the outcome of his efforts. He may feel great and have good stuff warming up in the bullpen and then get in the game and get clobbered. He may make a bad pitch and see the batter miss it for a strike or see it hit hard but right into the hands of a fielder for an out. Conversely, his best pitch may be blooped for a base hit. He may limit the opposing team to just a few hits yet lose the game, and he may give up many hits and win. And the good and bad luck doesn't always average out over the course of a season. For instance, [in 2013] Boston Red Sox pitcher John Lackey gave up slightly fewer runs per game (ERA 3.52) than his teammate Jon Lester (ERA 3.75) but only won 43 percent of his games (10–13) while Lester won

65 percent of his games (15–8). Both pitchers, of course, had the same players on the field behind them. Regardless of how well a pitcher performs, the outcome of the game also depends upon the proficiency of his teammates in scoring runs, the ineptitude of the opposition, and luck. In the words of Red Sox pitcher Kyle Snyder, "there is only so much that is within your control and the rest is left up to the so-called baseball gods."

Hitting, which most observers call the single most difficult task in the world of sports, is also full of uncertainty. Unless it's a home run, no matter how hard the batter hits the ball, fate determines whether it will go into a waiting glove or find a gap between the fielders. The uncertainty is compounded by the low success rate of hitting: the average hitter gets only one hit in every four trips to the plate, while the very top hitters average only one hit in every three trips. Fielding, which we will return to later, is the one part of baseball where chance does not play much of a role.

How does the risk and uncertainty in pitching and hitting affect players? How do they try to control the outcomes of their performance? These are questions that I first became interested in many years ago both as a ballplayer and anthropology student. I had devoted much of my youth to baseball, and played professionally as a first base-man in the Detroit Tigers organization in the 1960s. It was shortly after the end of one baseball season that I took an anthropology course called "Magic, Religion, and Witchcraft." As I listened to my professor describe the magical rituals of the Trobri-and Islanders, it occurred to me that what these so-called "primitive" people did wasn't all that different from what my teammates and I did for luck and confidence at the ballpark.

Routines and Rituals

The most common way athletes in all sports attempt to reduce chance and feelings of uncertainty is to develop a routine—that is, a course of action which is regularly followed. * * * Routines are comforting; they bring order into a world in which players have little control. The varied elements in following a routine also produce the tangible benefit of helping one concentrate. Ballplayers know that it is easy to "overthink" as opposed to just reacting, and that following a routine can keep them from thinking too much.

But some of what players do goes beyond mere routine. These actions are what anthropologists define as *ritual*—prescribed behaviors in which there is no connection between the behavior (e.g., tapping home plate three times) and the desired end (e.g., getting a base hit). Because there is no empirical relationship between the two, rituals are not *rational*. In fact, they can be quite irrational, as in kissing a medallion to get a base hit.

Baseball rituals are infinitely varied. Most are personal—performed by individuals rather than by a team or group. Most are done in a casual and unemotional manner with no more fanfare than when a player applies eye-black to his cheeks or pine tar to his bat. A player may deliberately put on the items of his uniform in a particular order.

For outfielder Jim Austin it was always his left sleeve first, then left pants leg, and left shoe before the right. After hitting two home runs in a game ex-Giant infielder Jim Davenport discovered that he had missed a buttonhole while dressing for the game. For the remainder of his career he left the same button undone. For outfielder Brian Hunter the focus is shoes: "I have a pair of high tops and a pair of low tops. Whichever shoes don't get a hit that game, I switch to the other pair." At the time of our interview, he was struggling at the plate and switching shoes almost every day.

A ballplayer may ritualize any activity that he considers important or somehow linked to good performance. Recall the variety of things that Dennis Grossini does, from specific times for waking and eating, to dress. Some players listen to the same songs on their iPods over and over before the start of every game. And that's 162 games a season. Astros infielder Julio Gotay always played with a cheese sandwich in his back pocket. Red Sox Wade Boggs ate chicken before every game during his career, and that was just one of many elements in his pregame ritual, which also included leaving his house for the ballpark at precisely the same time each day (1:47 p.m. for a night game), running wind sprints at 7:17 p.m., and drawing a chai—the Hebrew symbol for life—upon entering the batter's box, despite not being Jewish.

Many hitters have a preparatory ritual before stepping into the batter's box. These include tugging on their caps and batting gloves, touching their uniform letters, crossing themselves, and swinging the bat a prescribed number of times. Boston third baseman Mike Lowell always took four warm-up swings in the on-deck circle. Not five. Not three. He did it in a high school game one day and got four hits and never gave it up. Before each at bat Pablo Sandoval draws a cross behind the plate and thanks God for the opportunity to get another hit, then skips through the box and taps his spikes alternately three times for his grandmother, grandfather, and sister who died together in a car crash. Former Cleveland Indians first baseman Mike Hargrove had so many time-consuming elements in his batting ritual that he was nicknamed "the human rain delay." Like most players, Hargrove believed his batting rituals also helped him regain concentration, or as some players put it, "get locked in."

But some wonder if players like Hargrove and Sandoval have become prisoners to their elaborate superstitions. Players who have too many or particularly bizarre rituals risk being labeled as "flakes," and not just by teammates but by fans and the media as well. Former Mets pitcher Turk Wendell's eccentric rituals, which included chewing black licorice while pitching—only to spit it out, brush his teeth, and reload the candy between innings—and wearing a necklace of teeth from animals he had killed, made him a cover story in the *New York Times Sunday Magazine.*

Baseball fans observe some of this ritual behavior, such as a player tagging a base when leaving and returning to the dugout between innings, or a pitcher smoothing the dirt on the mound after giving up a base hit, never realizing its importance to the player. The one ritual many fans do recognize, largely because it's a favorite of TV cameramen, is the "rally cap"—players in the dugout folding their caps and wearing them bill up in hopes of sparking a rally.

What are the origins of ballplayer rituals? Most grow out of exceptionally good performances. When a player does well, he seldom attributes his success to skill alone; after all, his skills don't vary much from day to day. So, then, what was different about today which can explain his three hits? He makes a correlation. That is, he attributes his good fortune, at least in part, to a food he ate, or not having shaved, or a new shirt he bought, or just about anything out of the ordinary. By repeating that behavior the next day, he hopes to bring more good luck. * * *

Almost anything can become ritualized. Take former Yankee manager Joe Torre, who during one game stood on the dugout steps instead of sitting on the bench when his team was batting. The Yankees scored a few runs, so he decided to keep on doing it. As the Yankees won nine games in a row, Torre kept standing. Torre explained, "As long as we score, I'll be doing the same thing." Similarly, pennant-winning teams seldom change the design of their uniforms or caps the next season, following the principle of "Never mess with success." Conversely teams with losing records (or poor attendance) are far more likely to make changes in the design of their uniforms and hats.

When in a slump, most players make a deliberate effort to change their routines and rituals in an attempt to shake off their bad luck. * * * Some players try sitting in a different place in the dugout, or driving a different route to the ballpark, or putting their clothes on in a different order. Some shave their heads; others let their beards grow. Jason Giambi took to wearing a gold thong. Hector Martinez put his bat in the trash can for a few innings, as if to punish it, threatening to leave it there if it didn't start producing hits. I played for a manager who rattled the bat bin when the team was not hitting well, as if the bats were in a stupor and could be aroused by a good shaking. Diamondbacks left fielder Luis Gonzalez sometimes placed his bats in the room where Baseball Chapel—a Sunday church service—was about to get underway. Gonzales hoped his bats would get some benefit, though he didn't usually attend the service himself.

Taboo

Taboos are the opposite of rituals. These are things that you shouldn't do. The word comes from a Polynesian term meaning prohibition. Among the Trobriand Islanders, for example, Malinowski observed that before they went fishing on the open sea, neither men nor women could adorn their bodies or comb their hair or apply coconut oil to their skin. Breaking a taboo, both Trobrianders and ballplayers believe, can lead to bad luck. Most players observe a few taboos. White Sox outfielder Adam Dunn, for example, will never stand in the on-deck circle, and during my career I would never hold a baseball during the playing of the National Anthem. Many taboos concern behaviors off the field. On the day a pitcher is scheduled to start, he will avoid activities he believes may affect his luck. This can mean not shaving, avoiding certain foods or even not having sex (this notion is probably based on an eighteenth-century belief about preserving vital body fluids, but experts now agree there is no ill effect and there may actually be a small benefit).

Taboos grow out of exceptionally poor performances, which players later attribute to a particular behavior. During my first season of pro ball I ate pancakes before a game in which I struck out three times. A few weeks later I had another terrible game, again after eating pancakes. The result was a pancake taboo: I never again ate pancakes during the season. But for former Orioles pitcher Jim Palmer, a stack of pancakes on the day he was to pitch was a requisite and the source of his nickname: "Cakes."

While most taboos are idiosyncratic, a few are universal to all ballplayers and are unrelated to personal misfortune. These taboos are learned as early as Little League and form part of the wider culture of baseball. Mentioning a no-hitter while one is in progress is a well-known example (this is true for almost any pitching or hitting streak; to bring it to the streaking player's attention may "jinx" him). Another universal taboo is not stepping on the white chalk foul lines. The origins of these shared beliefs are lost in time, though the taboo against stepping on the chalk lines may relate to the children's superstition, "step on a crack, and break your mother's back."

Fetishes

Fetishes are charms—usually small objects believed to embody supernatural power (luck) that can aid or protect the owner. Good-luck charms are standard equipment for some ballplayers. These include a wide assortment of items, from coins, chains, and crucifixes to rabbit's feet or a favorite hat or glove. The fetishized object may be a new possession or something the player found that coincided with the start of a streak and which he believes contributed to his good fortune. Pitcher Sean Burnett carries a poker chip in his back pocket; for Al Holland it's a two-dollar bill; and for Mark LaRosa it's a perfectly round stone. My teammate Doc Olms kept a lucky penny for each win in his plastic athletic supporter cup, whose clanging could be heard when he ran the bases. Nyjer Morgan decided that blue argyle socks might help his Milwaukee Brewers break a slump, and after they did he regularly wore them under his baseball socks.

Some players have fetishes and rituals that overlap with their religious beliefs, such as touching a Saint Christopher's medal, making the sign of the cross before going to bat or the mound, and blowing a kiss to the heavens after some success. Here magic and religion overlap in addressing the universal human need to minimize uncertainty and insecurity.

Some players regard certain uniform numbers as lucky. Often it is a number they wore on a previous team where they had a lot of success. When Ricky Henderson came to the Blue Jays, he paid teammate Turner Ward $25,000 for the right to wear number 24. Don Sutton got off cheaper, convincing teammate Bruce Bochy to give up number 20 in exchange for a new set of golf clubs. Turk Wendell wore number 99 when he was with the Mets, Phillies, and Rockies (and once asked that his new contract be for

$9,999,999.99). Oddly enough, there is no consensus about the effect of wearing number 13. Some players shun it, while a few request it.

Number obsessions can extend beyond the uniform. Former Colorado Rockies' Larry Walker's fixation with the number 3 was well known to baseball fans. Besides wearing 33, he took three, or any multiple of three, practice swings before stepping into the box, showered from the third nozzle, set his alarm for three minutes past the hour and was wed on November 3 at 3:33 p.m. Fans in ballparks all across America rise from their seats for the seventh-inning stretch before the home club comes to bat because the number 7 is lucky, although the actual origin of this tradition is uncertain.

Fetishes and rituals sometimes intersect. During hitting or winning streaks, for example, players may wear the same clothes day after day. My former teammate, Jim Leyland of the Detroit Tigers, wore the same pair of boxers to the ballpark every day until his team's winning streak ended. Manager Art Howe wouldn't wash his socks after his Oakland A's were victorious (he would also write the lineup card with the same pen). Once I changed undershirts midway through the game for seven consecutive nights to keep a hitting streak going. * * *

Losing streaks often produce the opposite effect as players discard and try new attire in hope of breaking the "jinx." Most of the Oakland As went out and bought new street clothes after losing 14 in a row. The Nationals' left fielder Matt Swope, mired in a slump, threw away all his Under Armour and went to Dick's and bought new underwear. That night, he began a 26-game hitting streak. In the words of one veteran, "It all comes down to the philosophy of not messing with success—and deliberately messing with failure."

Baseball's superstitions, like most everything else, change over time. Many of the rituals and beliefs of early baseball are no longer observed. In the 1920s and '30s sportswriters reported that a player who tripped en route to the field would often retrace his steps and carefully walk over the stumbling block for "insurance." A century ago some players spent time on and off the field intently looking for items that would bring them luck. To find a hairpin on the street, for example, was believed to assure a batter of hitting safely in that day's game. A few managers were known to strategically place a hairpin on the ground where a slumping player would be sure to find it. Today few women wear hairpins—a good reason the belief has died out. * * *

One belief that appears to have died out recently is the notion about crossed bats being unlucky, or worse. Several of my Latino teammates in the 1960s took it seriously, and I can still recall Cuban Julio Perez becoming annoyed when during batting practice I tossed my bat from the batting cage and it landed on top of his bat. The brawny outfielder came over and with his foot flicked my bat aside, and asked that I not do it again, explaining that my bat might "steal" hits from his bat. Like Julio, Hall-of-Famer Honus Wagner, who played in the early 1900s, believed that bats contained a finite number of hits, and that when those hits were used up no amount of good swings would produce any more. While I don't know of any players today who still believe this, other superstitions about bats do survive.

*　　*　　*

Uncertainty and Magic

The best evidence that players turn to rituals, taboos, and fetishes to control chance and uncertainty is found in their uneven application. As I have noted above, they are associated mainly with pitching and hitting—the activities with the highest degree of chance—and not with fielding. Unlike hitting and pitching, a fielder has almost complete control over the outcome of his performance. Once a ball has been hit in his direction, no one can intervene and ruin his chances of catching it for an out (except in the unlikely event of a "bad hop"). Compared with the pitcher or the hitter, the fielder has little to worry about. He knows that at least 9.7 times out of 10 he will execute his task flawlessly. With odds like that there is little need for ritual. Clearly, the rituals of American ballplayers are not unlike those of the Trobriand Islanders studied by Malinowski many years ago. In professional baseball, fielding is the equivalent of the inner lagoon, while hitting and pitching are like the open sea.

While Malinowski helps us understand how ballplayers respond to uncertainty, behavioral psychologist B. F. Skinner sheds light on why personal rituals get established in the first place (Skinner 1938; 1953). With a few grains of seed Skinner could get pigeons to do anything he wanted. He merely waited for the desired behavior (e.g., pecking) and then rewarded it with some food. Skinner then decided to see what would happen if pigeons were rewarded with food pellets at fixed intervals, like every fifteen seconds, regardless of what they did. He found that the birds associated the arrival of the food with a particular action, such as walking in clockwise circles. Soon after the arrival of the last pellet, the birds would begin doing whatever they associated with getting food and they would keep doing it until the next pellet arrived. They had learned to link a particular behavior with the reward of being given food.

Ballplayers also associate a reward—wins or base hits—with prior behavior. If a player touches his crucifix and then gets a hit, he may link that gesture to his good fortune and touch his crucifix the next time he comes to the plate. Some psychologists, like Stuart Vyse, offer an evolutionary explanation for such behavior, namely, that humans, like Skinner's pigeons, tend to repeat any behavior that is coincident with success. This tendency, says Vyse, is adaptive: if turning in a circle really does operate the feeder, the pigeon eats and survives another day; if not, little is lost. Likewise for ballplayers. Unlike pigeons, however, most ballplayers are quicker to change their rituals once they no longer seem to work. Skinner found that once a pigeon associated one of its actions with the arrival of food, only sporadic rewards were necessary to keep the ritual going.

One pigeon, believing that hopping from side to side brought pellets into its feeding cup, hopped ten thousand times without a pellet before finally giving up. But, then, didn't Wade Boggs eat chicken before every game, through slumps and good times, for seventeen years?

Obviously the rituals and superstitions of baseball do not make a pitch travel faster or a batted ball find the gaps between the fielders, nor do the Trobriand rituals calm the seas or bring fish. What both do, however, is give their practitioners a sense of control, and with that added confidence.[1] And we all know how important that is. If you really believe eating chicken or carrying a two-dollar bill in your back pocket will make you a better hitter, it probably will.

ENGAGING THE TEXT, ENGAGING THE WORLD

- Watch a baseball game on television or at your local Little League ballpark. What ritual behaviors and magical beliefs do you see on the field?

- Do you have any magical rituals that you perform or any fetishized charms you carry when you take a test, play in a game, or go out on a date?

- What is George Gmelch's goal in comparing Trobriand Islanders' fishing magic with American baseball magic?

- How does Gmelch's article provide a model for the anthropological task of "making the strange familiar and the familiar strange"?

- Define *ritual*, *taboo*, and *fetish* and provide examples of each one for both Trobriand fisherfolk and American baseball players.

- Gmelch does not suggest that magical beliefs and practices can affect chance or create good or bad luck. But what benefits does he see in these practices?

---

1. In an experiment conducted in the psychology department of a German university, L. Damisch and several colleagues [2010] were able to demonstrate that believing in luck could actually make a group of college students perform better. The students were divided into two groups and taken to a putting green and told to make as many putts as they could. One group was given golf balls that were said to be "lucky" and—surprise—they sank significantly more putts than the comparison group where there was no mention of luck.

From Wall Street to
Halal Street

Daromir Rudnyckyj

In the 1970s and 1980s Malaysia developed one of the Asian "tiger economies," attracting foreign investment to its export processing zones where electronics became the country's primary product for the global economy. As export processing declined in the 1990s, Malaysia's government turned to the emerging area of Islamic banking to fuel the country's twenty-first-century economy. Over the past two decades, Malaysia has positioned itself as the key transnational hub of Islamic finance. Particularly in the aftermath of the 2008 global financial crisis, many investors, especially in the Middle East, have grown skeptical of the conventional financial system's ability to regulate itself and maintain stability and so have been looking for alternative strategies for managing the global flow of capital.

In the following article Daromir Rudnyckyj examines the key characteristics of Islamic banking that distinguish it from conventional finance and the key infrastructures that Malaysia has put in place to make it work, from an Islamic stock market to educational institutions to train workers in Islamic finance. The result has been an expansion of an Islamic financial system that has forged strong relations with majority Muslim countries in the Middle East, South Asia, and Central Asia, and become an alternative to the conventional financial system centered in the financial capitals of North America, Europe, and East Asia. Rudnyckyj's article reminds us that religion is not simply a set of beliefs or rituals but is a framework through which people organize their lives and make crucial economic, political, and social choices.

Introduction

Today, in the streets and public spaces of Malaysia's larger cities, the ubiquity of Islamic finance cannot be missed. As much of the rest of the world recoils in the wake of a financial crisis that spread across the United States and Europe, signs, promotions, and

From Daromir Rudnyckyj. 2013. "From Wall Street to *Halal* Street: Malaysia and the Globalization of Islamic Finance." *The Journal of Asian Studies* 72(4): 831–848. Some of the author's notes have been omitted.

new office towers visually attest to the conspicuous growth of Islamic financial services in the country. Along Kuala Lumpur's main arteries, advertisements seek to lure customers with the Bank Islam credit card that provides "free *takaful* [a form of Islamic insurance] coverage, low fees, and no compounding finance charges." Inside the city's massive, ultramodern train station and on the streets outside, eye-catching advertisements for Al-Rajhi Bank, a Saudi Arabian firm that claims to be the world's largest Islamic bank, encourage potential customers to "Get There Fast" with "Al Rajhi Personal Financing." On the other side of the station, a branch of Kuwait Finance House does brisk business. Malaysian ringgit are readily available at the numerous ATMs owned by over twenty Islamic banks operating in the country, and long lines often form at the terminals during peak commute times and prime shopping hours. Banks and other financial firms across the country have readily sought to develop this market, and Islamic financial institutions are aggressively promoting *shariah*-compliant credit cards, home loans, and targeted insurance schemes, among other financial instruments.

In Malaysia, Islamic finance is big business. An Asian "tiger economy," Malaysia is a key site in which to comprehend the dynamics of contemporary Islamic finance. The Malaysian state is seeking to forge an integrated Islamic alternative to the conventional financial system that is centered in the financial capitals of North America, Europe, and East Asia. * * * Malaysia's ambitions to make its capital, Kuala Lumpur, the "New York of the Muslim world" are the outcome of thirty years of state efforts to promote Islamic finance as an economic and political strategy.

Scholars have drawn attention to grassroots efforts to develop transnational connections through Islam in Southeast Asia (Noor 2010; Osman 2010). Rather than focusing on such bottom-up efforts, * * * Malaysia's plans to become a transnational hub for Islamic finance represent an effort to globalize Islam from the top down, by mobilizing religion to create new economic networks. Scholars have previously shown how Islam was invoked within the space of the nation-state to create an environment conductive to growth and development. I argue that today Malaysia is extending that earlier effort by leveraging Islamic practice to make the country a key center for both flows of capital marked as Islamic and the creation of instruments for Islamic banking. * * * Malaysia has sought to make Islamic finance a critical component of its strategy for future economic growth. * * * Efforts to facilitate the investment of surplus capital from wealthy Middle Eastern petrostates into centers of industrial production in East and Southeast Asia illustrate * * * the state's shrewd development strategies in a rapidly changing global economy.

Islamic Finance and the Malaysian Modernity Project

The promotion of Malaysia as a global hub for Islamic finance is part of state strategies to sustain the nation's impressive record of economic development since the early 1970s. * * * Malaysia's current efforts to become a leader in the Islamic world are tied to its colonial and postcolonial history, and reveal the role that Islam has played in * * * Malaysia's "modernity project."

Even prior to colonial occupation, Islam served as a key marker of Malay identity (Shamsul 2001). Later, after Britain began to expand its occupation of the Malayan peninsula, Islam differentiated the Malay population from migrants from elsewhere in Asia, whose numbers grew rapidly during the nineteenth century as the colonial economy expanded and the demand for labor increased. Due to colonial policies that promoted the transnational movement of laborers from the South Asian subcontinent and what is today southern China for work in the colonial economy, Malaysia became a paradigmatic example of * * * "plural societies," consisting of three main groups, labeled by the British as the Indians, Chinese, and Malays. * * * Although the three main racial groups * * * were culturally and linguistically heterogeneous, prior to independence in 1957, they were differently incorporated into the colonial economy. Indian workers were mainly plantation or public works laborers, Chinese pursued industrial and entrepreneurial activities, and the Malays were overwhelmingly rural and engaged in either small-scale agriculture or fishing (Chin 1998, 41). * * *

These divisions * * * bred resentment, as the Chinese were perceived to have benefited more from the colonial economy and enjoyed better economic standing after the end of British sovereignty compared to the majority Malay population. This resentment culminated in the riots of May 13, 1969, which saw violent clashes in cities across Malaysia between Chinese and Malay groups. * * * In the aftermath of the riots, the state introduced the New Economic Policy (NEP) (Jomo 1990–91). The NEP had two fundamental objectives. First, it was meant to eradicate poverty and increase economic opportunity for all groups; second, it was meant to accelerate the "process of restricting Malaysian society to correct economic imbalance, so as to reduce and eventually eliminate the identification of race with economic function." In practice, * * * the NEP was designed to create an "urban, educated, entrepreneurial and shareholding Malay middle class" (Fischer 2008, 33) known as "new Malays" (*Melayu Baru*) (Ong 2006, 35). * * * Today, of Malaysia's population of roughly twenty-nine million, the state identifies roughly 67 percent as *bumiputra* (indigenous or literally "sons of the soil"), 25 percent as Chinese, and 7 percent as Indian (Department of Statistics Malaysia 2010). Most of those classified as *bumiputra* are further identified as ethnically Malay and are granted special rights by the state in virtue of their claims to be the original inhabitants of Malaysia (Ong 1999, 284 n.83). Islam is a central criterion for Malayness, and most (although certainly not all) Malaysians of Indian and Chinese descent are non-Muslim.

Malaysia's initial development success stemmed from its position as a global center for high-tech assembly and offshore industrialization in the 1970s and 1980s. * * * Japanese, American, and European firms set up shop in extensive industrial zones and hired a vast number of new workers to provide the labor for export-oriented growth. * * * In the 1990s, the state embarked on a series of ambitious development projects (Baxstrom

2008), such as the Multimedia Super Corridor (MSC), which was conceived as a hub for the development of information and multimedia technology. The MSC included sites like Cyberjaya, which was intended to become the Silicon Valley of Southeast Asia (Bunnell 2004).

Islam has played a pivotal role in the state's development strategy, as the state has sought to develop industries and services deemed suitable for an increasingly educated and skilled laboring population. * * * Thus, "government policies seek to bring Islam in line with capitalism" by promoting a form of Islam that is fully compatible with the state's development objectives (Ong 1999, 204). The "new Malay" citizen is represented as "self-disciplined, able and wealth accumulating, but in a way that is cast within the precepts of Islam rather than of capitalism." * * *

Today, the state is not only representing Islam as conductive to economic growth, but also cultivating the religion to forge stronger relations with majority Muslim countries in the Middle East, South Asia, and Central Asia. Mahathir Mohamad, who was prime minister during the period in which Malaysia achieved its most impressive economic growth, actively sought to enhance the country's profile in the Muslim world. During Mahathir's tenure (1981–2003), Malaysia assumed an increasingly prominent role in the Organization of the Islamic Conference as well as a range of affiliated institutions and initiatives, such as the Islamic Development Bank, the International Islamic University, and the Islamic Solidarity Fund (Milne and Mauzy 1999, 135).

Recently, rising income levels and the emergence of other, lower-wage sites for industrial assembly in East and Southeast Asia (most notably China, Vietnam, and Indonesia) have called into question the export-oriented economic growth paradigm that fueled Malaysia's initial development success. This has precipitated a turn away from export-oriented production and instead toward the provision of services. Indeed, as income and education levels in Malaysia have risen, the state has sought to develop sectors to which its "knowledge-based" population can add value (Evers 2003). Malaysia hopes to isolate a particular niche in providing services labeled Islamic, including making the country a global *halal* food certification center.[1] The state's most aggressive endeavor in developing a service-oriented sector has been to make the country a global center of Islamic financial services. Thus, the state has sought to construct the infrastructure necessary for Islamic finance to function both domestically and transnationally, promoting research and innovation in Islamic financial instruments and creating some of the premier global institutions for higher education in Islamic finance. This state promotion of Islamic banking furthers its development ambitions, given the changing educational and class composition of the country, which will require new development initiatives to promote ongoing economic growth.

---

1. *Halal* refers to food (and now increasingly other commodities) that are permissible for Muslims to consume.

Delimiting Islamic Finance

Most simply, "Islamic finance" refers to the management of money and the provision of capital in a manner that complies with Islamic prescriptions on economic action (Rosly 2005, 20). However, there is a lack of consensus as to exactly what counts as compliance and exactly what qualifies as economic action that conforms to Islamic prescriptions (Pepinsky, n.d.; Warde 2010, 2). * * *

Islamic finance experts most often refer to the Qur'anic prohibition against the payment of interest, or what is called *riba* in Arabic, as the central difference between Islamic finance and what they call "conventional finance." According to Islamic finance experts, accepting interest is among the most serious sins that are proscribed in the Qur'an and referred to in the hadiths.[2] The collection of interest would therefore severely impact one's possibilities for otherworldly salvation. As one former conventional banker in Kuala Lumpur—who had in his own words "converted" to Islamic banking—said to me with a smile, "the prophet Muhammad stated that collecting interest is a sin worse than committing adultery [*zina*] thirty-six times." This equation was mentioned to me several times by bankers, regulators, and scholars in defining the existential problems confronting those who sought to engage in commerce and simultaneously live according to the prescriptions set forth in key Islamic texts.

In explaining the moral imperative to avoid *riba*, Islamic scholars trained in the classical disciplines of *shariah* (Islamic law) and *fiqh* (Islamic jurisprudence) explain the prohibition on interest by arguing that Islam endorses economic action grounded in "real" (as opposed to speculative) exchanges (Abdul Ghafar 2010). Thus, the morality of economic activity is dependent on whether it involves the production or exchange of actual assets or services. * * * In the wake of the deepest effects of the financial crisis, many Islamic finance experts attributed the better performance of Islamic financial institutions compared to their conventional counterparts to the fact that they did not partake in speculative investments in money itself, such as mortgage-backed securities and to which the economic crisis and the failure of many conventional financial firms have been attributed (Tett 2009).

Restrictions on interest and proclamations that Islam is averse to speculation (*maysir*) and endorses only those exchanges grounded in real production are often invoked to delimit Islamic finance, according to many experts in the field. However, Islamic scholars and Islamic economists have endorsed other practices as constitutive of Islamic finance as well. These include promoting investments that "share risk" rather than transfer it, avoiding uncertainty, and facilitating ethical investments that enhance social well-being.

Proponents of Islamic finance argue that whereas the debt-based contracts that characterize conventional finance involve the transfer of risk, the preferred contracts in

---

2. The hadiths are compilations of the words and deeds of the prophet Muhammad and are interpreted by most Muslims as guides for their own worldly actions.

Islamic finance are based on sharing risk between contracting parties. Thus, partnership contracts like *musharakah* and *mudarabah*, which date to the time of the prophet and are frequently mentioned in classical juristic texts, are most preferred (Udovitch 1970, 170–248). These contracts involve profit-and-loss sharing agreements rather than simple money lending (Warde 2010, 145–49). For example, a *mudarabah* is an equity-based contract in which a *mudarib* and a capital provider enter into a partnership. The *mudarib* typically has expertise and entrepreneurial acumen, but possesses no capital of his or her own. Hence, the entrepreneur forms a partnership along the lines of the venture capital arrangements that have served as key sources of financing for entrepreneurial endeavors in places like Silicon Valley (Çizakça 2011, 249–74). Profits generated by the business venture are split between the parties according to a predetermined ratio. However, the party providing the capital bears all financial losses, while the investment manager bears the opportunity costs associated with managing the venture.

Promoting risk sharing is not only evident in the redesign of contracts dating to the early history of Islam in order to make them commensurable with the demands of modern financing. Indeed, some of the most creative efforts in contemporary Islamic finance have been to redesign modern institutions to realize the emphasis on partnership, mutual benefit, and risk sharing that is constitutive of Islamic economic action. For example, in late January 2010, at a well-attended lecture hall deep in the recesses of Malaysia's sleek but staid Central Bank complex, I watched as Dr. Abbas Mirakhor (a former director at the International Monetary Fund and one of the world's leading authorities on Islamic banking and finance) presented a bold proposal. With most of the country's key Islamic and conventional bankers and regulators in attendance, including the Central Bank's highest official, Governor Dr. Zeti Akhtar Aziz, Dr. Mirakhor argued that the global financial landscape was changing and that the future would present tremendous opportunities for the industry. In a lecture titled "Paradigm Change in Shaping the Future of Islamic Finance," Dr. Mirakhor suggested that "after thirty years of development" the next step in the "necessary evolution of Islamic finance" was the establishment of a central location to trade assets. He proposed an Islamic stock market specifically dedicated to the provision of capital for Islamic firms. Dr. Mirakhor justified the need for such a market by citing the low levels of stock market participation in Muslim Southeast Asia, stating, "Malaysia and Indonesia have the lowest risk-sharing parameters in Southeast Asia, but risk sharing is necessary to make Malaysia a hub [of Islamic finance]." He said that a centralized equities market to "trade assets" would be the next step in the "necessary evolution of Islamic finance." He also noted that a central tenet of Islamic finance was risk sharing, which enables "economic growth and poverty reduction, [and] . . . the best instrument for risk sharing is a stock market."

*   *   *

[Another] constitutive feature of Islamic finance is facilitating ethical investments that enhance social well-being and avoid objects that are not commensurate with expressions of Islamic piety. This ethical dimension of Islamic finance has led some scholars to compare it to corporate social responsibility movements and specifically socially responsible investing (Pitluck 2008). Minimally, it includes efforts to direct investment away from objects explicitly prohibited in the Qur'an, such as pork, alcohol, and gambling. More restrictive versions discourage investment not only in activities explicitly prohibited in Islam but also in any sectors that are contrary to Islamic morality, such as certain weapons, entertainment that might depict illegitimate sexuality, or financial activities that might involve the payment or collection of interest.

From National Development to Global Growth

* * * The Malaysian state has moved from seeking to cultivate Islamic finance nationally to making the country the lynchpin of a globally integrated Islamic financial system. * * *

Islamic Finance and Islamization

By the 1980s, the presumption that development was a secular project underwent a thorough reexamination in Malaysia. In part this was an effect of the 1979 revolution in Iran, which brought Islamists to power in a modern state for the first time (Esposito 1998, 309–10). This event coincided with, and some have argued it gave rise to, a wider resurgence of Islam across Asia and elsewhere in the world (Hefner 2010). * * * Mahathir Mohamad, who became [Malaysia's] prime minister in 1981, initiated a measured rejection of some of the underlying features of modernization and the presumption that the manner in which economic development unfolded in the West was a universal model for developing countries to follow (Beeson 2000). Mahathir invoked Japan as an alternative model of development, embracing so-called "Asian values" and suggesting that Malaysia did not need to abandon its cultural inheritance in pursuing economic growth (Ong 1999, 197). * * *

Mahathir's rejection of "western capitalist blueprints" for modernity (Ong 1999, 73) meant that a major preoccupation of the state's developmentalism was the creation of a viable financial system grounded in Islamic prescriptions for economic action. Indeed, the Islamic revolution in Iran initiated strong interest in Islamic finance across the Muslim world. In addition to Malaysia, Sudan, Iran, and Pakistan also sought to develop Islamic banking systems in the early 1980s (Warde 2010, 114–25). However, unlike those three countries, which sought the wholesale transformation of their banking systems over to full Islamic systems, Malaysia "initiated Islamic banking in parallel with conventional banking on a trial basis" (Venardos 2006, 146). * * *

[Malaysia's] National Steering Committee [on Islamic Banks] had realized that economic action in accordance with Islamic prescriptions would require an integrated, comprehensive financial system consisting of not only banking institutions but also an Islamic money market, Islamic capital markets, and an Islamic insurance system. * * *

Making Islamic Banking National

Islamic finance expanded apace with Malaysia's rapid economic development through the 1980s and early 1990s. Within its first ten years of operation, Bank Islam grew to approximately eighty branches across the country and by 1992 was listed on the main board of the Kuala Lumpur Stock Exchange (Iqbal and Molyneux 2005, 45). After the establishment of the Islamic banking and insurance sectors, the Central Bank's next phase involved establishing an Islamic securities market in conjunction with Malaysia's Securities Commission. Thus, in 1990 an Islamic debt securities market was created to facilitate the creation and exchange of Islamic bonds (*sukuk*), in 1994 an Islamic inter-bank money market was established (facilitating the provision of short-term capital between Islamic banks to enable them to balance their books on a daily basis), and in 1995 an Islamic equity market was formed (Venardos 2006, 153).

To further facilitate the growth of Islamic finance, the Malaysian government sought to build a network of Islamic banking institutions, rather than rely on a single state-supported Islamic bank. The "dual banking system" established in Malaysia "allowed Islamic banking and conventional banking to co-exist side by side" (Venardos 2006, 146). To encourage conventional banks to participate in the Islamic system, in 1993 the Central Bank introduced the Interest-free Banking Scheme. This program offered tax breaks for conventional banks that opened up Islamic "windows" to offer Islamic financial products, such as home mortgages or savings accounts. Thus, conventional banks could use their existing institutions and infrastructure to expand into Islamic banking on a gradual basis and offer conventional and Islamic financing options under the same umbrella. * * *

From Wall Street to *Halal* Street

* * * The Malaysian state established a coordinated effort to aggressively scale up Malaysia's domestic Islamic finance infrastructure to become a transnational hub for Islamic financial services. The state sought to create the institutional infrastructure and regulatory environment to ensure that Malaysia became a central node in the emerging transnational Islamic financial architecture. An explicit goal of these efforts was to provide an alternative to the conventional financial system, which by the end of the first decade of the 2000s was facing its most severe challenge since the 1930s and at times seemed to teeter on the brink of collapse. To become a global hub, the Malaysian state sought

to make a number of key interventions in Islamic finance through regulatory reform and clarity, the reduction of ambiguity in Islamic financial services, enhanced research and education regarding *shariah*, the development of innovative instruments, and the creation of new institutions.

*   *   *

The state has also sought to create new institutions vital to the functioning of transnational Islamic finance. In 2009, at the behest of Malaysia's Central Bank, the country's stock exchange Bursa Malaysia launched Bursa Suq Al-Sila', a commodity trading platform specifically dedicated to facilitating liquidity management in the Islamic banking system. In so doing, it sought to enable Islamic banks around the world to balance their daily accounts through a sale, rather than through interest-based loans. Using Malaysia's most important agricultural commodity, crude palm oil, as an underlying asset, the exchange enables institutions to comply with *shariah* restrictions by avoiding interest-based lending. Under a contract known as a commodity *murabaha*, the exchange enables the circulation of capital through a formal sale of palm oil (Dusuki 2010).

Another step the state has taken to make Kuala Lumpur a global node for Islamic finance has been to locate key institutions in Malaysia. After a successful lobbying initiative by then prime minister Mahathir, the Organization of the Islamic Conference awarded Kuala Lumpur the headquarters of the Islamic Financial Services Board, an international standard-setting body that develops global standards and guiding principles for Islamic finance, including banking, *takaful*, and capital markets. This institution seeks "to coordinate bank supervision, promote Islamic finance, and facilitate the integration of the Islamic sector in mainstream finance" (Warde 2010, 130).

The Malaysian state has also sought to create other institutions to cement its position as a key Islamic finance center, notably those engaged in the production of Islamic financial knowledge. The Central Bank has spent $200 million to create key research and educational institutions intended to address what has been termed a "knowledge gap" in Islamic finance. This has been primarily used on two key bodies: the International Center for Education in Islamic Finance and the International Shariah Research Academy, to which Islamic finance practitioners most often refer by their acronyms INCEIF and ISRA.

Islamic finance experts had long bemoaned the dearth of potential employees with training in Islamic finance and the lack of educational programs to train such professionals. Typically most employees in the industry have been conventional bankers who are then recruited into Islamic financial institutions. This has precipitated critiques by those who allege that such hiring practices threaten the integrity of Islamic banking because such transplants do not always recognize the important differences between the two types of providing credit. * * * To remedy these problems, the Central Bank founded INCEIF in 2006 and designated it the "global university" for education in Islamic finance. The university offers graduate degrees in fields related to Islamic finance and occupies an impressive new campus close to the national university, the University of Malaya. Students at INCEIF come from around the world: while I was studying there I met students from across Asia, Africa, Europe, North America, and Australia. The goal of the university is to cultivate the human resources necessary to create a critical mass of professionals, skilled in both *shariah* and finance, to staff Islamic financial institutions around the world. Another effect of this initiative would be to extend the influence of what practitioners call the "Malaysian model" of Islamic finance. Many faculty members were recruited from the International Islamic University outside Kuala Lumpur but come from across the Muslim world.

Another obstacle to the growth of Islamic finance and the global integration of institutions around the world has been a lack of basic research in the field. To remedy this, ISRA was founded by the Central Bank of Malaysia in 2008 to promote applied research on *shariah* questions in Islamic finance and bridge the gap between critical scholars and more applied bankers and businesspeople. In addition to creating new knowledge, it is also a repository of knowledge for *shariah* decisions (*fatwa*) on Islamic finance and examines debates over *shariah* in the Islamic financial industry both in Malaysia and abroad. A major function undertaken by ISRA is the translation of Arabic documents into English and vice versa, in order to reduce language barriers in the circulation of knowledge in fields pertaining to Islamic finance.

Finally, the state has sought to promote integration of banking institutions and spur growth and innovation by opening its borders to competition from Islamic financial institutions based in the Persian Gulf region. These include Kuwait Finance House; the Saudi-based Al Rajhi Bank; and Asian Finance Bank, which is mostly owned by Qatari investors (Warde 2010, 130). The aggressiveness of these institutions is evident in the bold advertisements that they have posted on prominent thoroughfares. Branches of these banks can be found in major cities across the country. Most recently, the Central Bank has floated plans to create a $1 billion mega Islamic bank, and is actively soliciting foreign capital to fund its operations (Sadiq 2012).

Conclusion

*   *   *

Today the [Malaysian] state is extending its efforts to mobilize Islam for development * * * through creating what one interlocutor referred to as an "Islamic Wall Street." Thus, it is positioning itself as the center of global financial networks that are structured according to Islamic prescriptions for economic action. It is invoking Islam for development, not just as a national project but to cement a role as a key center for the provision of services with transnational value. This draws on the legacy of mobilizing Islam for creating a self-disciplined and wealth-accumulating citizenry and also scales up these efforts by emphasizing Malaysia's common Islamic heritage with countries in the Persian Gulf region. Given Malaysia's shared Islamic tradition with much of the Middle East and its proximity to the world's fastest-growing export economies in Southeast and East Asia, including China, Indonesia, and Vietnam, the country is well-positioned to become a key broker for flows of Islamic capital between these two regions. High energy prices and the resulting vast amount of surplus capital in the oil- and gas-producing countries of the Middle East have led to the emergence of massive sovereign wealth funds in countries like the United Arab Emirates, Saudi Arabia, Kuwait, Qatar, and Libya. By developing the world's most sophisticated Islamic financial system, Malaysia seeks to become the manager for Islamic investment in the expanding economies of Asia and beyond. Indeed, the economic crisis that continues unabated in the United States and Europe and the massive losses that many investors from the Middle East suffered led many to question the reliability of conventional finance. Thus, state planners seek to emphasize Malaysia's advantageous position, both geographically and culturally, between the two most dynamic centers of global growth today, and Islamic finance offers an opportunity to capitalize on that growth.

ENGAGING THE TEXT, ENGAGING THE WORLD

- What key Islamic values are central to Islamic finance?

- What are the key values embedded in Western, free-market-style capitalism? (Think back to Elizabeth Dunn's article in Chapter 11 about opening a Gerber food processing plant in Poland.) Do any of them have religious roots or overtones?

- What key strategies have Malaysian leaders used to transform Kuala Lumpur into a global hub for Islamic banking? How has globalization facilitated its rise? What unique Islamic banking infrastructure have they put in place?

- In what ways do the ethical dimensions of Islamic finance parallel corporate social responsibility markets and socially responsible investing popular in North America and Europe today?

- In what ways does the author suggest that Islamic banking practices may be more economically stable than Western financial models, particularly in light of the 2008 collapse of the U.S. and Western European financial markets? Do you think Western models have anything to learn from their Islamic counterparts?

- In the headnote to this article we discussed how religion is not simply a set of beliefs or rituals but is a framework through which people organize their lives and make crucial economic and political choices. Discuss this in light of the Islamic banking practices described in Rudnyckyj's article.

Liminal Youth Among Fuzhou Chinese Undocumented Workers

Kenneth J. Guest

Anthropologists of religion have paid particular attention to the role of ritual. They are aware that religion is not so much talked about as it is performed in public displays, rites, and rituals. The following article explores the ritual of baptism in an immigrant Chinese church in New York City, and the role the church plays more generally in the lives of marginalized immigrants working in Chinese restaurants, garment shops, construction trades, and nail salons.

French ethnographer and folklorist Arnold van Gennep (1873–1957) first theorized a category of ritual called rites of passage that enacts a change of status from one life stage to another, either for an individual or for a group (van Gennep 1908). Religious rites of passage are life-transition rituals marking moments of intense change, such as birth, coming of age, marriage, and death. Victor Turner (1920–1983) theorized that the power of ritual comes from the drama contained within it, in which the normal structure of social life is symbolically dissolved and reconstituted.

First, the individual experiences separation—physically, psychologically, or symbolically—from the normal, day-to-day activites of the group. This may involve going to a special ritual place, wearing special clothing, or performing certain ritual actions. The second stage, liminality, involves a period of outsiderhood during which the ritual participant is set apart from normal society, existing on the margins of everyday life. From this position the individual can gain a new perspective on the past, the present, or the future, and thereby experience a new relationship to the community. The final stage of ritual returns the individual to everyday life and reintegrates him or her into the ritual community, transformed by the experience of liminality and endowed with a deeper sense of meaning, purpose, and connection to the larger group. See how the Church of Grace and the ritual of baptism provide a rite of passage and an experience of liminality for recent Chinese immigrant young people in the following article.

From Kenneth J. Guest. 2004. "Liminal Youth among Fuzhou Chinese Undocumented Workers."
In *Asian American Religions: The Making and Remaking of Borders and Boundaries*, edited by Tony
Carnes and Fenggang Yang. New York: New York University Press.

A Liminal Space

Entering the Church of Grace is strikingly reminiscent of walking into a church anywhere in rural China, particularly the churches around Fuzhou. The language and narratives change. The clothing changes. Personal kinship and village networks become revitalized. The food changes. Even the smells change. The foyer of the Church of Grace is a liminal space for young Fuzhounese Christian immigrants, a place of transition between one reality and another, a place that removes them, even if temporarily, from their day-to-day reality and affords them a glimpse of something different (Turner 1969). Young immigrants who outside these churches are foreigners in a very strange land are transformed into insiders. Outside the youth cannot speak the dominant U.S. language, English, or even the dominant Chinese dialects of Cantonese and Mandarin spoken in Chinatown. They have little contact with non-Fujianese youth. Inside, their language, Fuzhounese, is predominant. Outside they are seen by earlier Chinese immigrants as "country bumpkins" (*tubaozi*) and derided as uncultured and uncouth youth. Inside, they celebrate a common cultural story of an exploring people.

In subtle ways the Church of Grace and other Fuzhounese religious communities in New York City provide sites for counterhegemonic discourse and community building that are central to young immigrants' ability to create narratives and identities for survival. Outside, the youth are considered poor; inside, they are considered adventurous wage earners supporting a church in New York City and family and community at home in China. Outside, they may be young illegal immigrants, undocumented workers, invisible to the U.S. state or even targets of INS raids and crackdowns. Inside, they are children of God who through the death of Jesus have had their sins forgiven. God's grace is available to all, regardless of age, home village, kin group, debt burden, social position, or legal status.

This religious self-understanding distinguishes the Church of Grace and other emerging Fuzhounese religious communities from other Chinatown social institutions. It demarcates the religious institution from the village or surname association, from the union or political party. People participate and contribute not only because of the familiarity of friendship and village, but also because of the church's ability to convey meaning and religious significance to immigrants whose lives are more regularly filled with disorientation and dislocation. * * *

Liminal Youth and a Rite of Passage

The Church of Grace is jam-packed, even more than usual. It is Easter Sunday and family, friends, and the congregation fill every inch of space with their curiosity. The sanctuary has standing room only. The foyer, the upstairs social hall, the downstairs classrooms are all full. Closed-circuit television beams the service into each room. The crowds spill out of the front doors and into Allen Street where Chinatown's northern border meets the Lower East Side.

Fifty mostly young Fuzhounese, including the recently immigrated Chen Qiang, fill the front rows of the sanctuary at the Church of Grace waiting their turn for immersion into the faith. One by one they file into specially constructed dressing rooms beside the altar where they shed their street clothes and don long white robes. Assisted by members of the Board of Deacons they step into the pool, socks and all.

"I baptize you in the name of the Father, and of the Son, and of the Holy Spirit, Amen!" says Rev. Chen and plunges a young man under the water. He arises gasping, startled, crying from the experience. He steps out of the pool drenched and, braced by church members, staggers back to the dressing room, the water cascading from his soaked robes and hair onto the marble floor of the old bathhouse-turned-church in Manhattan's Chinatown, cleansed spiritually as generations before have been cleansed physically in that space.

This moment marks a dramatic transition in the lives of these young people. Stepping out of the Chinatown street, they leave behind a U.S. society by which they are exploited and from which they are totally marginalized. Through this rite of passage they are invited to join their stories to a rich narrative of a sojourning people seeking freedom and salvation. In a process carefully orchestrated by church volunteers, within forty-five minutes each person will receive an official certificate of baptism, complete with name, date, location, pastor's signature, and color photograph commemorating and documenting the occasion. Some may have very practical uses for these documents, perhaps needing them to support applications for political asylum. But for most they serve a much more metaphoric role, marking a dramatic spiritual, physical, and emotional transition and a reconceptualization of their lives and their system of meaning in the harsh reality of New York City's Chinese immigrant community.

This baptism signifies a ritual welcoming to a safe place between a distant Chinese homeland and the harsh sweatshop conditions of New York City. For the young Fuzhounese the ritual opens a doorway for examining the intersection of changing ideas of community, identity, and meaning.

The Church of Grace is full of young people who have recently emigrated from Fuzhou, the capital of Fujian Province on China's southeast coast. Survey responses show 38 percent of the congregation under thirty years old and 63 percent under age forty. Since the late 1980s tens of thousands of mostly rural young Fuzhounese have flooded into the United States, with New York City's Chinatown serving as their main point of entry. Their numbers have increased so rapidly that today Fuzhounese have supplanted the Cantonese as Chinatown's largest ethnic Chinese community and they are vying for leadership in the area's economics, politics, social life, and even language use. Fueled by this massive migration, the Church of Grace is now one of the two largest Chinese churches in New York City.

Leaving China

Over a bowl of noodles after church a few months later, Chen Qiang talked about his journey to America and the Church of Grace.

> To tell you the truth, I never really thought much about coming to America. I had been going to high school. Then all of a sudden my parents said I was going to America. They said there wasn't much of a future for me in China. No way of making a living. In the beginning I really didn't want to come. I didn't have a very good impression of America. * * * That's the kind of news we got from the TV. But I was being sent to make money.
>
> I didn't know anything about Christians in China. There is a church in my town, but I never went in. My only memory is that my little sister got into a fight with another little girl who was a Christian. But they were just kids. There are a lot of temples in my hometown. My parents visit them to light incense and make offerings to the gods. They don't go regularly, but on holidays—New Years, Autumn Festival. They make offerings for my grandparents. And they visit their graves. But they don't talk about it very much.

Since the early 1980s whole segments of Fuzhounese communities have been uprooted. Most young people between the ages of eighteen and forty have gone abroad, spurred by economic restructuring in both China and the United States, and enabled by a vast and highly organized human smuggling syndicate. Younger teenagers await their opportunity to go. This massive international migration has dislocated people economically, culturally, and legally, and placed them in a receiving country for which they are unprepared and which is unprepared to incorporate them. The undocumented status of many of the new immigrants further complicates the picture.

Their primary destination is Chinatown, New York City, a densely populated Chinese community on Manhattan's Lower East Side where they hope to utilize kinship, village, and faith connections to survive in an unfamiliar environment. * * * These highly transient workers move constantly to fill jobs across the United States in "all-you-can-eat" Chinese buffets, garment sweatshops, or construction sites. New York City's Chinatown is their home base, the place to which they return to recuperate, reconnect with family and friends, and find their next job.

Fuzhounese Youth and Family Economic Strategy

The towns and villages around Fuzhou, previously reliant on farming and fishing, are not wealthy. Nor are they poverty stricken. The steady inflow of remittances from workers already in the United States stabilized the standard of living during the 1990s. Despite recent industrial growth fueled by foreign investment, local opportunities for economic development remain limited. Many Fuzhounese have turned to outmigration as an economic strategy.

Few immigrants make this momentous decision on their own. The journey is too dangerous and too expensive. Most, like Chen Qiang, are sent by their families in the hope of beginning a chain migration—or continuing one already begun—that eventually will extend to the whole kin group. Outmigration is a form of family economic diversification and leaving Fuzhou is usually a family decision.

Chen Qiang's story follows this pattern. To launch his journey, he did not borrow the money himself. Rather, his family made the arrangements, securing a $48,000 loan to pay his smuggling fees to the United States, a relative bargain compared to the standard $60,000–70,000. * * *

While his elder brother had previously attempted to migrate to Japan, Chen Qiang would be the first in his family to go to the United States. So, Chen Qiang began his long elaborate journey, alone in the hands of a vast human smuggling network with the hopes of his family resting heavily on his shoulders.

*   *   *

Lost in the United States: Social and Legal Limbo

Nineteen-year-old Chen Qiang sat quietly in his little room in the old tenement building on Catherine Street, a tenement where countless generations of immigrant workers—Irish, German, Italians, Jews, Chinese—had lived before him. He leaned over a little table, head in his hands. Every once in a while his fingers would run back through his hair, as if trying to squeeze the pressure out of his skull. His room was no more than eight feet by twelve feet. A toilet was packed into one closet, a bathtub in another. There was a small sink in one corner. Most of the room was taken up by a bunkbed that he shared with another Chinese worker. He was fighting back the tears. * * *

With interest accumulating daily, it was essential that he keep working to pay off the debt. Failure to keep up would mean threats of violence against his family back home. To compound the pressure, Chen Qiang had learned the week before that his older brother, who had been smuggled to Japan, had been arrested and would soon be deported to China. This was the third time he had been caught and sent back. Each time he faced higher fines and longer imprisonment in China. Now, these debts too would fall on Chen Qiang.

For the past eight weeks he had been working as a busboy in a Chinese restaurant in New Hampshire, arranged through a Chinatown employment agency. He lived and ate in the restaurant, working seven days a week, fourteen to sixteen hours a day. He made $1,300 a month. It was a long way from New York City, but it was a job, an increasingly scarce commodity in a rapidly shrinking economy.

The previous week he had returned to New York City to attend an immigration court hearing of his application for political asylum. After months of waiting and several postponements, he and his lawyer would argue that his family had been persecuted in China based on the government's one child per family policy and that he feared reprisals from the government if he were sent home. Despite waiting all day, Chen Qiang's case was never heard. The judge's docket was full. The hearing was postponed again for six months. In Chen Qiang's room three days later, his disappointment was palpable and his sense of being in limbo was debilitating. What would he do next? Where could he turn for help? His options were extremely limited.

Catching the Christian Network Lifeline

One place Chen Qiang had successfully sought support was the network of Christian churches and agencies assisting recent immigrants. His first encounter with Christianity came at the Children's Home where he was sent after he came ashore on the United States. He explained, "Since I wasn't eighteen yet they sent me to a children's home in Georgia until we could find a sponsor." Members of local churches would visit each Sunday and take the detainees out to worship services in the nearby city. They provided Chen Qiang's first entry into a Christian network that would play a significant role in his survival of the immigrant experience.

> I didn't know anything about Christianity until after my detention by the INS. I spent a year in the children's home. People came on Sundays to take us to different churches. It was nice to get out. And the services were very interesting. That's the first time I had ever been in a church. It's the first time I had heard about God or Jesus.

The social worker at the children's home in Georgia also contacted a representative of Lutheran Family and Community Services in New York City to enlist her help. * * *

> I wasn't really that worried when I was in the children's home. Life there was pretty good. When I got to New York the social worker at the children's home put me in touch with a social worker from Lutheran Family and Community Services. She checked on me to make sure I had a job and a place to stay. She took me to the Church of Grace the first time. I went to church when I was in town. They kept asking me to be baptized. I really didn't want to.

> *   *   *

> It was only after I was released that I got worried. Find a place to stay. Find a job. Food to eat. How to get through the day. I had to rely on myself. I didn't have any

friends. It was very hard. When I first got to New York, my uncle's friend helped me find a place to stay for a while. I had to find my own work. I went to the employment agencies. I've been working in restaurants, mostly doing deliveries on a bicycle.

* * *

The financial and emotional pressure on young people like Chen Qiang is intense. In the post–September 11 economy, jobs are hard to find. Failure to keep up with debt payments leads to threats and violence against them and their families in China. When family networks prove inadequate, these marginalized yet resourceful immigrants seek to mobilize alternative sources of support. Religious communities like the Church of Grace are primary locations for Fuzhounese youth to supplement both their social capital and their emotional support. * * *

Building an Alternative Community: Supplementing and Transforming Chinese Kinship Networks

* * *

After worship on Sunday the renovated bathhouse that holds the Church of Grace changes from ritual center to community center. Over bowls of noodles served after worship the conversations roar. News of home from new arrivals. News of jobs and places to live. Discussions of recent events in China or in the U.S. media. A member of the Board of Deacons passes along a videotape from his home church outside Fuzhou that describes their building project and solicits funds from overseas compatriots. The president of the Women's Fellowship collects money from members for an emergency relief gift for a middle-aged garment shop seamstress whose husband just died of cancer in a Lower East Side hospital. She collects over $2,000 by the end of the day. A bulletin board lists job openings and beds for rent. The evangelists gather together first-time visitors for a discussion of basic principles of the Christian faith and invite them to join the baptism and membership class that will be starting in a few weeks. A group of college students meets in a corner to discuss their upcoming exams. The decentralized interactions are wide-ranging and have their own style and order.

A bulletin board for job postings and apartment listings has been revived after succumbing several years earlier to complaints that "a church should not be an employment agency." Representatives of a neighborhood women's health program set up a table in the lobby after church to sign up more than thirty women for consultations about services ranging from birth control and AIDS testing to nutrition and prenatal care.

While these developments are not a radical comprehensive organizational response, they do reflect an attempt to supplement the informal networking that has emerged spontaneously among the congregants. The developments suggest a movement from an island of nurturing personal piety toward a civic evangelicalism encompassing the worldly needs of Fuzhounese immigrants as well. The church is gradually establishing itself as a bridge between its largely young membership and the structures of American society.

Marginalization and Meaning: Fuzhounese Youth Convert

Twice a year, at Easter and again in the fall before the weather turns too cold, the Church of Grace conducts a baptism ritual during Sunday worship. Congregation leaders place a tremendous emphasis on this event and persistently recruit potential converts. Over the past few years as many as fifty people have been baptized on each occasion.

Although Chen Qiang had grown quite familiar with the Church of Grace in his early days in New York City, he was not exactly sure what baptism entailed or what it would mean for his life. His family in China was Buddhist. He had never been to a church before coming to the United States. He would be the family's first Christian.

> I haven't told my parents [about possibly converting to Christianity]. I'm too scared to tell them! They wouldn't understand. They don't think very highly of Christianity. My uncle said that I could go to the church to meet nice young girls or to get some help. But I shouldn't get too involved there. No, my family wouldn't understand.

Interaction with clergy and lay members of the Church of Grace launched Chen Qiang on a quest to understand his immigrant journey. In the midst of his turmoil and marginalization, what does his life mean? Chen Qiang recalls wrestling with these questions one particular Sunday.

> I heard a sermon by the minister. He said, "Be careful. Life can be very short. You don't know when your time may come. You don't know when the end of the world will come. You may be walking down the street and be struck by a car. You may only have a few minutes left. Don't delay. Don't wait to accept Jesus. Don't miss your chance to turn your life around. Don't miss your chance for salvation." That really scared me! I was really afraid. What if I die crossing the street? I finally decided to get baptized.

*   *   *

The ritual emphasis placed on baptisms reflects their symbolic importance for this religious community. They are at their core outward and visible signs of inner conversion, a transformation of these individuals in both body and spirit. And they are for many a personal yet public identification of their life journeys with a larger metanarrative, that of the Christian faith and of the United States, which many Chinese immigrants consider to be inextricably linked with Christianity. This is no small shift for Chinese born and raised in an environment infused with non-Christian religious practices, a culture deeply tied to popular religious traditions entwining the individual with family, lineage, and village, and a political discourse which has disparaged and at times harshly repressed all religious belief.

The baptism ritual also has tremendous importance for the congregants observing or administering this sacrament as they recall their own conversion and reflect on their own life journey. At the Church of Grace, the baptism—the washing away of sins, the purification of body and soul, the acceptance of Jesus Christ as personal Lord and Savior, as guiding light and source of life—represents for many of these immigrants a claim to a new life narrative and a search for new frameworks of meaning for their radically changed reality.

*   *   *

The Dream

Even as a nineteen-year-old undocumented worker, burdened by crushing debt and locked into an exploitative ethnic economic network by virtue of his lack of English language skills, Chen Qiang, like other young Fuzhounese, struggles to keep alive a dream of success here in America.

> Someday I hope I can move up from delivery boy to busboy, then waiter, then to reception and then finally to open my own restaurant. Fuzhounese in America all have this hope. They don't speak any English. They have a huge problem with their legal status. So they dream of working their way up and someday owning their own restaurant.
>
> Someday I would really like to fully enter American society. This is an American place. There are not a lot of Chinese in America. But being in this Chinese environment in Chinatown is like being in jail. If you go out you can't speak English. If you want to travel, you don't know where to go. Life here is so much worse than in most of America. Being in Chinatown is just like being in China! So I would like to be able to get out into American society. I need to learn English. If only I had the opportunity! I'd like to go to school. But that's probably unrealistic considering how much money I have to pay back.

But Chen Qiang's dream is not only a dream of economic success. It is also a dream to understand the significance of his immigrant journey.

After his baptism, I asked Chen Qiang what it felt like and why he had decided to become a Christian. He took down from his bunkbed the baptism certificate from the Church of Grace and gently handed it to me to see. It was clear that this simple piece of paper marked a significant transition in his life.

After my baptism I realize that I have something important that they [the rest of his family] don't have—the most important thing. One of the evangelists said that baptism in your life is like the coming of Jesus in the history of the world. Before Jesus, the world didn't know him and strayed from God. Then Jesus came and the world was different. He showed the world a different way. That's the way my life is too. Now I have a way of understanding what's going on in my life, the big changes from my life before to my life now. That's something my parents don't have. That's the most important thing.

Baptism, the outward and visible sign of conversion to Christianity, marked a liminal moment when he could step back from the normative activities of his life and attempt to gain perspective on the larger questions of meaning and existence.

One evening about a year after his baptism Chen Qiang and I took a walk. He hadn't found a job in a few days. His father had just called to ask how much he could pay toward the debt that month. He said he wanted to take his mind off things. We walked around Chinatown for a while, visiting a nighttime fruit vendor, lingering under the statue of the Fujianese patriot Lin Zexu in Chatham Square, and gazing north along the Bowery toward the lights of midtown. I suggested we head downtown, perhaps to a part of the city he hadn't seen. We walked past the courthouses of Foley Square, the African slave memorial, the Brooklyn Bridge, the brightly lit City Hall. Our feet kept leading us south along Broadway, first to the makeshift memorial along the cemetery fence of St. Paul's Church, then to the glaring brilliance of the World Trade Center site itself. The size of the crater spoke of the magnitude of the devastation. The new construction of subway and train lines spoke of New York City's will to move on, making sense of its difficulties by continuing to live. After a long while looking at the pictures on display and gazing down into the construction site we walked slowly back toward the East River and Chinatown. "What are you thinking about?" I asked. "What do you think God is really like?" he asked. After a few moments he continued, "I still don't really know. Sometimes it is very confusing. I better go home now, though. Tomorrow I have to get up early and try to find another job."

Fuzhounese youth in New York, like Chen Qiang, are among the most vulnerable and marginalized members of American society. They lack the language skills to enter the mainstream economy. They lack the background to pursue further education. They are deeply indebted and obligated either to smugglers, their family networks, or both. And many are undocumented, leaving them cut off from the right to fully participate in this society and constantly concerned about being caught and deported.

In the midst of this harsh reality, Fuzhounese youth consistently prove to be resilient, persistent, and sometimes ingenious innovators who sustain themselves and their dependent families against great odds. Over the past fifteen years they have sought out—and at times helped create—religious networks and communities to mobilize the resources needed for surviving their immigrant experience. These religious communities, like the

Church of Grace described in this chapter, serve as locations to access social, financial, and emotional support. They serve as bridges between these isolated youth and the social structures of the Chinese enclave and the broader U.S. society. And they serve as ritual locations where Fuzhounese young people are offered the opportunity to reflect on the meaning of their immigrant journey and the radical transformations that have occurred in their lives between China and the Lower East Side of Manhattan.

ENGAGING THE TEXT, ENGAGING THE WORLD

- Discuss Victor Turner's notion of liminality and the way Fuzhounese immigrants experience liminality as they participate in the Church of Grace.

- Guest describes the Church of Grace as not only a ritual center but a community center. How does the church facilitate the mobilization of social capital?

- In what additional ways does the Church of Grace facilitate the dreams of recent Chinese immigrants?

- What surprised you most about Chen Qiang's story? What would you like to ask Chen Qiang or other members of the Church of Grace?

- Have you had a liminal experience linked to a rite of passage? How does it compare to the experience of Chen Qiang and other members of the Church of Grace?

14
Health, Illness and the Body

Conventional wisdom attributes **health** and longevity to a combination of good genes and good behavioral choices: eating right, not smoking, drinking in moderation, avoiding illegal drugs, exercising, and even flossing. These criteria mesh with certain core American cultural values of individualism, personal responsibility, and the benefits of hard work and clean living. But are these factors sufficient to explain health and longevity—or the lack of it? Getting sick is a part of life. Everyone experiences colds, fevers, cuts and bruises, perhaps a broken bone. But some people get sick more often than others. Death and dying are part of life; but some people suffer more and die sooner, while others are healthier and live longer. Anthropologists are interested in knowing why.

Today anthropologists have a growing interest in health, **illness**, and the body. Although these concerns have deep roots in our discipline, the specialization of medical anthropology has grown immensely since the 1980s as anthropology's key research strategies—intensive fieldwork, extensive participant observation in local communities, and immersion in the daily lives of people and their problems and experiences—have proven profoundly effective in solving pressing public health problems.

Medical anthropologists use a variety of analytical perspectives. We study the spread of **disease** and pathogens through the human population (known as epidemiology) by examining *medical ecology*: the interaction of diseases with the natural environment and human culture. Looking more broadly, medical anthropologists use an *interpretivist approach* to study health systems as systems of meaning: How do humans across cultures make sense of—and how do we think, talk, and feel about—illness, pain, suffering, birth, and mortality? **Critical medical anthropology** explores the impact of inequality on human health in two important ways. First, it considers how economic and political systems, race, class, gender, and sexuality create and perpetuate unequal access to healthcare. Second, it examines how health systems themselves are systems of power that promote disparities in health by defining who is sick, who gets treated, and how the treatment is provided.

Medical anthropology's holistic approach to health and illness—examining epidemiology, meaning, and power—assumes that health and illness are more than a result of bacteria, viruses, individual behavior, and genes. Health is also a product of our environment—our access to adequate nutrition, housing, education, and healthcare, and freedom from poverty, violence, and warfare. The article in this chapter, "Life and Times of Magda A." applies this holistic approach to understanding one woman's health in the context of an HIV and AIDS epidemic, sexual violence, and structural inequalities in South Africa.

Medical anthropologists document healing practices and health systems around the globe and have identified a vast array of cultural ideas about the causes of health and disease and strategies to address pain, treat illness, and promote health. These beliefs and practices are intricately intertwined with the ways in which local cultures imagine the world works and the relationship of an individual's body to his or her surroundings. Early research on **ethnomedicine** focused primarily on non-Western health systems and natural healing remedies such as herbs, teas, massage, religious ritual, and locally trained healers. But today, even Western **biomedicine**, which emphasizes science and technology in healing, is also considered through the lens of ethnomedicine, reflecting a particular system of norms, values, and cultural meanings.

Anthropologists have also taken an interest in different cultural notions of the body. Bodies are perceived, known, and understood in various ways by cultures and medical traditions around the world. Of course we live in our bodies. We are embodied beings. Our bodies mediate all of our experiences of living in and encountering the world. But what exactly is a body, and what does the body signify? Anthropological research has challenged the prevalent Western biomedical notion of the body as an isolated, natural, and universal object. Instead, anthropologists recognize the body as a product of specific environments, cultural experiences, and historical contexts. Culture has shaped the evolution of the human body and shapes individual bodies today. It also shapes our experience of the world around us, including how we feel and how others feel about us. This is particularly evident in the lives of people with disabilities, whose embodied experiences are often shaped not by their physical impairments but by social and material conditions that "disable" them and impair their access to full participation. The selection in this chapter from Michelle Friedner's *Valuing Deaf Worlds in Urban India* explores these issues as they relate to the deaf community in Bangalore, India, and the strategies used by deaf people to build social networks and development opportunities in the context of rapid political and economic change.

Life and Times of Magda A
Didier Fassin, Frédéric Le Marcis, and Todd Lethata

Africa

South Africa

Writing in the late 1800s, Rudolf Virchow, a renowned pathologist considered to be one of the ancestors of medical anthropology, asked why the distribution of health and illness appeared to mirror the distribution of wealth and power. Although anthropology from its inception has focused on concerns of health and illness, in recent years Virchow's question has become central to critical medical anthropology. If the distribution of health and illness cannot be explained solely on the basis of genetic vulnerabilities, individual behaviors, and the random spread of pathogens through a population, then what causes health disparities?

In "Life and Times of Magda A," Didier Fassin, Frédéric Le Marcis, and Todd Lethata explore the story of Magda A and attempt to place her health history in the context of her life and times in South Africa. The biography of this young woman reveals extreme poverty, sexual abuse, and living with HIV, and culminates with Magda A becoming an AIDS activist. How do we make sense of the violence in her life and times: domestic, sexual, physical, and structural?

The authors wrestle with the question of how to write about violence, particularly when the researchers themselves have not experienced the kind of violence central to the experience of those they are studying. They propose a three-part formula that includes story, life, and times. In this way, the authors attempt to create an ethnographic account that places Magda A's life and individual experience within the political and economic context of gender violence, economic inequality, and racial discrimination in South Africa. In the process they work to place her individual experiences of disease and illness within a framework of structural violence.

From Didier Fassin, Frédéric Le Marcis, and Todd Lethata. 2008. "Life & Times of Magda A: Telling a Story of Violence in South Africa." *Current Anthropology* 49(2): 225–246.

On March 30 and 31, 2004, Magda A sat down in an office on the university campus and started her narration. She lived in Alexandra, [South Africa], the oldest [racially segregated] township still existing in Johannesburg, but we had agreed to record her story far from that noisy and overcrowded place. The academic setting seemed more propitious for anonymity and serenity. Although one of us spoke Sotho, which is her language, she had decided to talk in English as she generally did with us. She started abruptly:

> Myself when I was there I was staying with my granny in Lesotho. And then my uncle was raping us every time and my mother come and say to my granny, "I want to take my child and go with her to Natal," and then my grandmother say "Okay, you can take her because there is a problem." And then my mother and my stepfather took me and came with me in Natal. And when we were there my mother go back to her mother's place. And then that man again sleep with us, sleep with me every day. Myself, I say, "What can I do?" But there is nothing I can do because that man he promised he can kill us.

With few interruptions, she continued in her monotonous tone for hours, telling how as a child from a poor rural family she was regularly raped by her uncle and father-in-law, how she later went to town and had sex with men to survive, how she eventually found a boyfriend who loved her but was violent, how they both discovered that they were infected with HIV after the death of their child, and how this revelation changed her life and threw her into activism for the prevention and treatment of AIDS.

We were in fact no strangers to Magda: she had known us for several years; we had come to see her quite often; we had met her former boyfriend and her aging mother; we had gone together to the funerals of young colleagues of hers working in the same nongovernmental organization and victims of the same disease as herself; we had had many conversations about the past and present, about violence and illness, about sex and death; every time we returned to her shack in the township she loudly expressed her joy. Thus many fragments of her life were already familiar to us, but this time we had asked her to put the parts of the puzzle together. * * *

Our aim here is to make sense of the violence in her life and times: domestic and gender violence, physical and structural violence. Although our empirical material comes from hearing Magda's story and sharing parts of her everyday life, we think that it becomes understandable as more than just an individual trajectory * * * only when it is referred to its historical context, both during and after apartheid.[1] * * *

*   *   *

Anthropology is about telling others' stories, but it is also about listening to others' stories (Angel-Ajani 2004). * * * Her story, as we will present it here, is informed by this

---

1. [A system of racial segregation and political and economic discrimination imposed by whites in South Africa between 1948 and 1991.]

mundane knowledge of her life, by the contradictory assertions or facts we have been confronted with, by the documents she gave us and our interviews of her relatives and friends, by the scenes we have witnessed in her home and in the course of her work and her militant activity. * * * It is also part of the larger picture of South African AIDS that we have been putting together for the past six years. In contrast to the usual approaches in the biomedical and even the applied social sciences, * * * our approach attempted to link an ethnography of gender violence, economic inequality, and racial discrimination with the epidemiology of the infection. Magda's life is therefore to be read as an element of this collective investigation of the political economy of the disease. * * *

* * * We [also] assert that by putting together Magda's story as she told it to us, her life, which we shared fragments of, and her inscription in the eventful times of the past three decades, we make of her biography a contribution to the understanding of violence. Insofar as it is obviously problematic—for practical and ethical reasons—to be there when violence is inflicted and thus to develop a direct ethnography of it, the analytical triptych we propose—story, life, and times—offers the possibility of writing about what often remains out of reach of anthropological intelligibility. The story told is not a mere expression of her life; its articulation with what is known of her times gives a sense of what violence was and meant in South Africa at the time. * * *

Childhood: Scenes of Rural Life

Magda was born 33 years ago in Lesotho, the small kingdom landlocked in the centre of South Africa. * * * Her grandmother had been brought up there by a family of migrant workers from Lesotho who had adopted her while they were temporarily residing in the South African mining city ironically called Welkom. Living in a village in Lesotho, she had had five children by different men, and Magda's mother, Anna, was one of them. Anna and her siblings were left with their own grandmother when their mother went to work on the other side of the border, where job opportunities were better. Visiting her mother on the farm where she was working in the Free State, Anna discovered that she had had three other children with a "boyfriend" there.

Anna became pregnant by and married a man from Lesotho when she was 15. Their child was called Magda. Magda's father was absent and abusive. He worked in the province of Gauteng, near Johannesburg, but he did not send money to his wife and daughter. Every time he came home there were violent quarrels. Finally the couple broke up, and Anna left for the Free State in search of work. Magda, who was only a few years old, was left in her grandmother's care. She thus spent her childhood in the large rural homestead where the whole family—Anna's three brothers with their wives and children—was settled. The older brother was married and had four children, two of them being twins. He did not work, stayed at home all day, and drank a lot. One day he decided to sell the twins to a traditional healer who said that he wanted to use their supernatural powers, probably by incorporating parts of their bodies in rituals and treatments (practices that are reported as persisting today). After a violent argument, his wife left the house, taking the twins with her, and he remained alone with his two other children. By that time, Magda was 7 years old. One evening when he was drunk, this uncle raped her, and from then on he abused her constantly. When the girl complained to her grandmother or to her other uncles, they told her that they could not do anything about it: "Everybody knew what happened but they never took action. Nothing. They left the matter as it was." * * *

Magda liked school, but she often missed it because of her work at home. She had to cook and clean the house before going to school, and if she had not finished her grandmother hid her uniform. Back from school, she had to go out and fetch wood and cow dung for the fire. Every other week she was supposed to look after the small cattle. She had no time to play, and she often received physical punishment. But she liked her grandmother:

> It is not nice to grow far away from your mother but I think with my granny it was nice but the problem was they were suffering but it was not bad because my mother she didn't like us. My granny even if the food was less she could leave the food for us saying. "This food is for sharing, we can share this food." My mother even when she came from Natal—maybe you're happy but she can hit you the same time. So sometimes I think my granny was better.

One day, when Magda was 15, her mother, who had learned about the sexual abuse, decided to take her to her home in Natal, where she was married to a Zulu man. But, surprisingly, she warned her: "My mother, she told me that if I tell her that her husband rape me she is going to kill me." For Magda, retrospectively, this threat suggests, on the one hand, that her mother considered her at least partly responsible for having been sexually abused by her uncle and, on the other hand, that she knew perfectly well that her husband was susceptible to having forcible sexual relations with her.

Anna's fears were not unfounded. Very soon, Magda was confronted with her step-father's sexual desire and violence: "When he was from anywhere drinking, when he was drunk, every time, he would sleep with me, same like that. If he want to sleep with us he's not even going to say: 'Friend my friend.' He just say: 'Come, we can sleep.'" Sometimes, though, he gave her a kind of justification: "He said he wanted to do the child with me and then myself I say, 'So how?' and he said my mother is not making the baby, so he wants to make the baby with me." She was afraid of him; he made weapons and had threatened to kill her if she were to say anything. Besides, she had no relatives or friends to confide in. Anna herself pretended to be unaware of what was happening to her daughter. In the evening she often went out to see her boyfriends, leaving Magda with her husband. When she came home she would bring the food and money she had received. This sexual arrangement within the couple had an economic aspect, as they were involved in growing and trading cannabis. Magda herself had to help them plant the herb and harvest it; at some point, she even became their dealer and went around selling the illegal product. After three years in Natal, having finally revealed to her mother that she had been constantly abused by her stepfather, she decided to go to Johannesburg, where one of her mother's younger sisters was living.

Incest has long been ignored in South Africa. * * * In fact, the subject of sexual coercion had remained largely absent from the autobiographical and even—at least until the late 1990s—the sociological literature. Significantly, studies on African women under apartheid mainly emphasized the effects on them of racial oppression and segregation. * * *

Sexual violence became a major issue only after 2000 in the context of AIDS, when series of tragic stories made headlines and numerous reports of forced sex revealed the importance of the problem (Jewkes and Abrahams 2002). * * *

Magda's story allows a different perspective. Forced sex cannot be considered separately from the production and reproduction of poor rural families. The three generations of women from her grandmother to herself seem to be caught in the same political economy of migration and its consequences in terms of family dislocation. * * *

Representations of Lesotho's women as "wicked" describe them as leaving their children with their mothers, founding new households in their new places, developing illicit activities of brewing beer or growing cannabis, and selling domestic and sexual services to men (Epprecht 2000). All these elements—which we actually find in Magda's mother's and grandmother's lives—are not in fact cultural characteristics but structurally linked to labour migration and the consequent necessity of surviving in this context (Bonner 1990). The economic situation of the area explains—as far as we can understand from Magda's narrative and interviews with her mother—why she was raised by her grandmother under the traditional authority of her uncle, her parents having had to cross the border to find work in South Africa.

*   *   *

Although these elements remain in the background of the young woman's story, it is not difficult to see the close relations between economic structures, political norms, gender roles, and sexual abuse. Social inequality, inscribed in local and national history, is embodied in the materiality of lives. Physical and sexual violence cannot easily be separated from "structural violence" (Farmer 2004). Considering it structural avoids psychological evaluation and moral judgement of social agents (the mother, the grandmother, even the uncle and the stepfather) we know little about in any case. This does not mean that we confine our analysis to a sort of social determinism; rather we simply acknowledge the limits of the individual perspective. Magda expresses this in her own way: "When I was young my life was not nice because I was staying with my uncles. They were hitting me the way they want. They told me, 'Your mother jumped the borders, she is gone' and they were telling me a lot of things."

Youth: Scenes of Urban Life

Coming to Egoli, the City of Gold (as Johannesburg is popularly named), in those years of political transition from apartheid to democracy, with their uncertainties about tomorrow and even today, must have been quite an experience for a young woman raised in a rural area. Magda's initiation to urban life was immediate. Two days after her arrival, her aunt—whom she calls "my sister"—gave her the tune:

> When I am there my sister told me: "Okay, this is Joburg, you're going to get nothing if you don't have a boyfriend." "Hey," I said, "What can I do?" She said, "There are a lot of people, you can get a boyfriend, you see, there are other guys there, they are working, choose which one you want." And I said, "I don't want a boyfriend," and she said, "Choose, you are going to get nothing if you don't have a boyfriend."

Magda's aunt was speaking from experience. She took her young protégée to a bar evocatively called Kiss Kiss near the hotel where she was staying. "There we sit and the guys they were wearing nice and she say, 'There's the guys from the hotel, you can choose one.' Me I say, 'I want that one,' and then he buy me beer, dry we drink. We enjoyed that day and then, after that, we go and sleep." Her boyfriend, who worked in the hotel, thus offered her a bed to share in the dormitory on the eleventh floor where all the male employees spent their nights. Each individual space was isolated by curtains to maintain a very limited intimacy. Women were not supposed to stay there, so they sneaked in late in the evening and left early in the morning.

Unfortunately, Magda's boyfriend did not intend to give her more than overnight hospitality. Receiving no money from him, she had to earn her own living. Since she could not find a job, she was dependent on the men she met on the streets where she wandered during the day:

> To eat you can get another boyfriend, so that you can eat, because my sister she can tell me "If you're hungry, you must get yourself a boyfriend, so that you can eat." The guys sometimes if you find them by the street they can say, "Let's go to the room," and you go to the room and get some food there. Sometimes they give you to eat first, sometimes they can give you money, but not money because ten rands is not money or five rands, it's just for cold drinks. And you eat and you go and you do sex and you go. And then next day you come, maybe if you still want that side, when you are hungry you can go to see him again.

After six months of this precarious life Magda finally got a job as a maid in a Coloured [mixed race] family. She worked all day seven days a week cleaning the house, preparing the meals, and looking after the children. She ate leftovers alone in the kitchen and slept on a foam mattress in the dining room when everybody had gone to sleep. She earned 150 rands a month. She went back to her mother's every month and got cannabis that she transported and dealt in town. By that time, her existence was not dependent on the support of a boyfriend anymore. However, she often went to a night club named 702 to meet men, spent the night at their homes, and hurried back to her workplace in the morning. "I was having a lot of boyfriends at that time. First come, first serve." This is how she met Christos, a young man who had recently migrated from Limpopo. * * * They fell in love, but he was jealous of her other boyfriends, drank a lot, and easily became violent.

Magda spent three years working for the Coloured family. Then she quit her job and went to live with Christos, who was sharing a room in a friend's apartment. These years were happy ones, although they were not free from hardship. One day the girls she sometimes went out with took her to a place of prostitution in Hillbrow, the hot spot of the city, where they went regularly to supplement the meagre resources received from their official boyfriends. It was 100 rands a time, and they got several clients during the day, they told her:

> They showed me the building where they were selling. When you enter that place, the guys they are many and they just bump and touch you like this. I screamed, and that lady she said, "Magda, you're supposed to keep quiet." I said, "No, it's better to take me home." It was not nice because you sleep with many boys. Today you find this one. Tomorrow you find that one. That day we left the other one, that girl, by the room, she said, "Hey, that guy, the tall one, me I'm bleeding because of him." And then she said if she want to sleep with that guy she must sleep with the others first, because this one make her lose business. Sometimes they used to say they are using condoms. Sometimes they were just sleeping, those people.

Magda soon left the place and never went back.

With Christos's help she had now found a job in a factory and was earning 150 rands a week. A year later she had saved enough money to buy a shack in Alexandra: a kitchen and a bedroom illegally connected to the public electric system for which she paid 1,000 rands. For the first time, she could consider herself completely autonomous and even started to host members of her family for transitory or permanent stays. Her relationship with Christos started to deteriorate. When he returned to his village, she met a man from Zambia who supported her. She wanted to learn how to sew, and he bought her a machine and gave her material. During several months of this partnership, which she describes as economic and platonic, he maintained a relationship of affectionate protection with her that was interrupted only when his wife arrived from Zambia.

Thus Magda's years in Johannesburg represent a profound change in her life: the young rural girl gradually became a city dweller. *** The demographic transformation of the centre from a "Whites-only" area into a mixed cosmopolitan quarter *** had started in the 1980s with the relaxation of the economically counterproductive apartheid laws and the installation of a growing number of migrants from the neighbouring townships, the rural areas, and the rest of the continent (Morris 1999). It was in this peculiar urban context that Magda obtained her sentimental education. The naïve young woman had to learn quickly. The first lesson was to find a boyfriend. The second was to make sure that he supported her financially. Having understood the first rule but not implemented the second, Magda spent her days searching for men who were willing to have sex with her for the equivalent of a cheap meal.

In her study of violence in the bars of Johannesburg and two of its townships, Janet Maia Wojcicki (2002, 268) analyzes these practices in terms of "survival sex" and observes that other writers also use the term "transactional sex or informal sex work" to "describe similar non-commercial, non-professional sex-for-money exchanges." For Magda, as for many girls recently arrived from rural areas, the word "survival" is more than a mere equivalent of "transactional" or "informal": it must be taken in a strict sense. What "survival sex" means is reduction of the body to merchandise that is, more-over, little valued in the market—the exchange of sex for food. In South Africa as in many other parts of the world, sexual politics may become literally a politics of bare life (Agamben 1998). ***

For Magda integration into urban life was marked by a passage from food to gifts, from the logic of subsistence to the logic of consumption, from mere responding to basic necessity to searching for pleasure and leisure. This passage is symbolically illustrated by her shift from the Kiss Kiss to the 702. In the meantime, she had made her own way in the city.

Contrary to what has been assumed by many experts survival and transactional sex, sex for subsistence and sex for consumption, have, in the local moral economy, very little in common with prostitution. When Magda goes to the brothel in Hillbrow, she is horrified by what she sees (the packed room), feels (the attempts to touch her), hears (the physical trauma of sexual intercourse), and imagines (the uninterrupted succession of men having sex with women). Significantly, she uses two distinct words to designate what her friends do and what she does. "They sell," she says, and the verb needs no explicit direct object, since it obviously refers to the body as commodity. *** In this *** context one recognizes how inadequate and problematic is the notion of "sexual promiscuity" which has served to explain the spread of sexually transmitted diseases in African populations—yesterday syphilis, today AIDS (Butchart 1998). In Magda's experience of the city, promiscuity is primarily physical: sleeping in the overcrowded dormitory of the hotel and having sex for food in shabby rooms, later being totally deprived of intimacy in her patrons' house, then sharing half a room with her boyfriend in someone else's apartment, and finally living in a two-room shack soon overcrowded by relatives who have left impoverished rural areas. Moreover, under these circumstances sexuality is highly determined by economic constraints: chronic underemployment and low wages make the financial support of boyfriends a vital necessity as well as a social norm. * * * Most medical and even anthropological studies have long ignored this political economy of sexuality. Although she also felt the sentimental loss of her boyfriend when Christos went back to Limpopo, Magda dryly commented, "Me I must get another boyfriend so that I can eat again."

Adulthood: Scenes of a Life with AIDS

Magda gave birth to a girl when she was 24. Christos was presumed to be the father. When she was nine months old, their daughter became sick. Christos asked Magda to join him in Limpopo, where he had found a job and was building a house for them. The child got worse and was admitted to a rural hospital, where she was determined to be HIV-positive. They had a serological test themselves and discovered that they were infected too. In the medical ward, they were stigmatized and excluded. * * * As the medical condition of their daughter worsened, Magda and Christos took her to Johannesburg General Hospital, and she died there a few weeks later. At that time, antiretroviral drugs were not yet available in the public health system. The funeral took place in Limpopo, but Christos's family refused to bury the little body in the kitchen of the family house as was traditional, thus adding the humiliation of being rejected and anxiety for the baby's soul to their grief over the loss of their child.

In the following months the couple broke up. Christos had withdrawn his offer to marry Magda and pay the dowry to her family because, he told her, she had lost her economic value. They constantly quarrelled and fought. Christos decided to start a new life with a young woman from his village without telling her his HIV status. Magda went back to her shack, where five relatives were now living with her, and started a new relationship with a man who she discovered was suffering from AIDS too. "I get another boyfriend and I make sleep, but before I tell him I am HIV-positive, he say also he is HIV-positive, and then I say, 'Where did you get it?' He say from his girlfriend, the other one, and she had passed away." After months of depression following the death of her child, her obsession was to have another baby. In spite of the potential risk of reinfection, the couple had decided to have sexual relations without using condoms. "Myself on my mind I used to say, 'I can die, I don't care about dying.' We die, we can die, no problem I will see what is going to happen. And I used to say, 'Hey, the others, they have the babies and me, I don't have the baby, I want the baby.' And then I make that and then I sleep with him until I am pregnant." This time, she benefited from the new national policy of prevention of mother-to-child transmission and got an antiretroviral treatment when she gave birth to her second child, who was not infected.

At that time, her economic resources included the social grants she received for her illness and for her little boy. Compared with many women living alone in Alexandra, hers was a relatively privileged situation. Moreover, she had started working for a non-governmental organization which develops activities in the domain of AIDS, particularly a support group for the ambulatory sick and home-based care for bedridden patients. Soon she was receiving a salary, in compensation for which she had to give up her government grant. Her regular income represented more than twice the minimum wage. This job also sanctioned her new community involvement. In fact, for more than a year she had been active as a volunteer worker, with the promise that she would eventually receive a salary. Although her main reason for getting the job was economic, she thus became an actor on the local AIDS scene. * * *

Much more significant of her social engagement was her participation in the Treatment Action Campaign. This national movement was created in 1998 to demand universal access to antiretroviral drugs. Its demonstrations against the pharmaceutical firms and the government are spectacular, often using elements of the classical anti-apartheid repertory such as toyi-toying [dancing/marching] protests and civil disobedience campaigns. It expresses its solidarity with patients not only by helping them while they are alive but also by attending their funerals, which became occasions for publicizing their fight. This was a completely novel experience in Magda's life. For the first time, she felt respected: here, people with and without HIV shared the same ethical values. For the first time also, she felt important: she was travelling all over to go to marches and being interviewed by journalists, even on television. Being a member of the movement also allowed her to be recruited into a clinical trial * * *. At a time when antiretroviral drugs were not yet available in the public sector, this was the only way for the poor to get treatment. A few weeks after she started taking her medicines, she was physically transformed, had gained weight, and looked radiant. She commented almost enthusiastically: "So what I can say, 'Those who are having HIV, it is not the end of the world.'"

* * *

The tragic situation of the AIDS epidemic in South Africa, where the estimated prevalence of the infection officially reaches 6 million out of a population of 45 million, has provoked an unprecedented social crisis. * * * As was the case with syphilis and tuberculosis in the first half of the twentieth century, the progression of AIDS, which is particularly rapid in the black population, results from the combination of social, economic, and political factors rather than mere cultural ones. Magda herself epitomizes this combination: the migration of her parents in search of work dismantled her family and left her at the mercy of her uncle's incestuous relations; the routinized political and ordinary violence in the homelands exposed her again to sexual abuse, and the pauperization of both rural and urban segregated areas led to the multiplication of male partners in sometimes extremely precarious conditions. The culturalist stereotypes of "wicked . . . women" and "violent . . . men," the essentialized features of female seductiveness and male brutality, cannot be maintained when confronted with this historical evidence. * * *

In a sense, the most recent developments of Magda's story demonstrate how it is * * * possible to resist these attributions and, at least partially, these determinations. Having a regular job and a decent salary, being the owner of a house, taking care of others, and engaging in activism, she has taken over her own life, something that had appeared out of reach for so many years. Ironically, it is her lethal illness that has allowed her to do so. However, it is less through the exploration of the meaning of her disease than through the mediation of institutions: the state from which [she] receives her grants, the non-governmental organization for which she works, the support group in which she meets other patients, and the activist movement in which she discovers the sense of collective action. * * *

Conclusion

A story never speaks for itself. * * * However, taken in its historical and social context, the narrative makes sense. We can understand what Magda tells us because we relate it to a larger picture in which * * * women's experience of migration is a sociological fact, sexuality is inscribed in survival practices in South African cities, and AIDS has introduced new political subjectivities. * * *

Here the shift in Magda's biography, from forced sex during childhood to survival sex during youth opens a possible way of understanding the underlying forms of violence, physical (repetition of rape) and structural (commodification of sex), respectively. * * * Sexual violence cannot be understood outside of the social context and history of its production. No life is outside of its times. It has been too easy to erase decades of depreciation of human lives, human bodies, and human dignity and merely explain the incidence of sexual abuse and the progression of sexual diseases in simple terms of idiosyncratic and irrational conduct * * *. This asocial and ahistorical approach has had a high cost in terms of policy making for the prevention of HIV infection and the care of AIDS patients. * * *

But adopting Magda's point of view on her biography is also trying to understand what it means or, more simply, what it is to live one's life under such circumstances of violence. * * * The question here is not only how to explain violence but how to account for the experience of it. It is not merely to illuminate Magda's life by her times but to describe her life in her times.

ENGAGING THE TEXT, ENGAGING THE WORLD

- What do the authors mean when they say, "No life is outside its times"?

- What do the authors mean by "the political economy of disease," and why do they suggest it is needed to understand health and illness?

- How does the title of this article reflect the three-part strategy the authors suggest for writing about violence when we as researchers rarely see or experience it personally?

- What do the authors mean by "structural violence"? How does structural violence shape individual experiences like Magda A's?

- Why do the authors see the experiences of Magda, her mother, and her grandmother not as cultural characteristics but as structurally linked to the political economy of labor migration?

- The authors argue against reliance on stereotypes of "wicked women" and "violent men" that place blame for illness and disease on "culture" or individual actions. They recommend instead an analysis that draws upon the historical, political, and economic context to make sense of individual stories. Why do they see this as essential for understanding sexuality in South Africa, sexual violence, and the spread of sexually transmitted disease?

From *Valuing Deaf Worlds in Urban India*

Michele Friedner

Disability, sociality, and human development

Anthropology's increasing attention to the body has been accompanied by a recent expansion of work on issues of disability—the embodied experiences of people with impairments as shaped by broader forms of social inequality. Significantly, anthropologists have explored the ways disability is lodged not simply in the body but is socially defined, specifically by the often painful and isolating encounters that "disable" and impair people considered to be atypical in a particular culture. So, for instance, people restricted to wheelchairs experience their impairment—are "disabled"—differently by the presence or absence of accessibility ramps.

Michelle Friedner's work, *Valuing Deaf Worlds in Urban India*, explores the dynamic ways that people in the city of Bangalore work to create alternative social worlds and pursue what they refer to as "deaf development"—opportunities for deaf people to enhance their social and economic life chances and achieve equality,

From Michele Friedner. 2015. *Valuing Deaf Worlds in Urban India*. New Brunswick, NJ: Rutgers University Press. Some of the author's notes have been omitted.

though not sameness, with hearing people. Bangalore, once known as a quiet British colonial outpost, has in recent years become India's Silicon Valley, known for its high-tech industries and call centers. India's neoliberal political-economic policies have attracted global corporate investment in information technology, hospitality, and other sectors that offer people with disabilities new employment opportunities and support for training programs and related NGO work. But changing Indian policies have simultaneously led to fewer social and economic protections, social services, and public sector job opportunities.

Friedner's ethnographic research provides an intimate portrait of Bangalore's deaf community in this rapidly changing node of the global economy, including the unique strategies deaf Indians are developing to resist cultural norms of ability and disability. Friedner describes the emergence of a complex network of deaf-centered, and deaf-run, sign language–centered churches, businesses, NGOs, schools and old-age homes that are enabling deaf people to develop language, educational, economic, and social skills to improve their lives. She explores the centrality of taking "deaf turns"—becoming oriented toward one another in the deaf community—to this success. And she considers what it means for her own research when her friends hope that she herself will make a deaf turn.

Sunday Circulations

It was late morning on a Sunday in June 2009. True Life Bible Fellowship, one of Bangalore's eight deaf churches, had just finished its weekly fellowship. Energized by a particularly spirited discussion of "*question answer,*" or question and answer, in which fellowship attendees discussed their relationships with their normal families and the importance of helping other deaf people, attendees chatted on the lawn of the theological college where the meeting had been held. In addition to sharing news and information, many attendees were deciding what to do that afternoon. The options included a statewide Jehovah's Witness conference where there would be sign language interpreters, a meeting to discuss disability pensions and government certifications sponsored by a Bangalore-based deaf nongovernmental organization (NGO), and an information and recruitment session for a multilevel marketing business with a deaf leader.

Many of those present decided to attend the multilevel marketing business meeting, and so a diverse group of young deaf people—including manual laborers, business process outsourcing employees, and hospitality sector workers from different economic, caste, religious, and geographic backgrounds—boarded a bus to go to the meeting location. The deaf business leader had strategically rented the courtyard of the sole college in Bangalore that provided sign language interpreters, and as a result many of Bangalore's deaf people knew where the meeting was to be held. On the bus, I sat with Zahra, a young woman who worked as a barista (or "silent brewmaster") at Café Coffee Day, one of Bangalore's new coffee chains. As we traveled through the city, we chatted about Zahra's job, the many deaf churches and deaf-focused NGOs in Bangalore, and the fact that we had attended other churches and multilevel marketing business recruitment sessions together. Along the way, the bus stopped at a major transit connection point and two deaf women climbed on.

I knew one of the women from a basic computer course at the Disabled Peoples Association (DPA), a Bangalore-based NGO with a vocational training program, although I had never met the other woman, who was older, perhaps in her forties. Zahra did not know either of them but we quickly started chatting after ascertaining that we were all deaf or "*deaf deaf same*," and that we all had some degree of fluency in Bangalore variety Indian Sign Language (BISL). The two women told us that they were coming from another deaf church and that they were on their way home. When they told her which church they were coming from, Zahra remarked that she had previously attended their church but that she did not think that it helped her to "*develop*." She then suggested that they switch to the True Life Bible Fellowship because it was "better for development." Then the younger woman asked Zahra questions about her job and which NGOs she had gone to for vocational training and job placement help. In the span of just a few minutes, the four of us had an intense discussion (common in deaf networks) about churches, Zahra's job and the older woman's lack of one, and the various deaf-focused NGOs in Bangalore. The conversation was really about deaf development and which Bangalore-based deaf resources could best facilitate this development. A few stops later, the two women got off the bus, and a new stream of deaf people climbed on, also heading to the multilevel marketing business meeting.

The three events that day—the Jehovah's Witness assembly, NGO meeting, and multilevel marketing recruitment session—represented three different paths toward what my deaf friends called "*deaf develop*," or "deaf development." Deaf people in Bangalore and elsewhere in India frequently discussed deaf development and deliberated about where it could be found. My deaf friends defined deaf development as the emergence of deaf-centered, and therefore sign language–centered, structures and institutions that help deaf people develop language, educational, economic, social, and moral skills for living in the world as both a member of deaf sociality and part of a larger normal world. These structures and institutions would include deaf-run and deaf-administered schools, NGOs, businesses, churches, and old-age homes. Deaf development will result in deaf people's becoming equal to normal people—although it will not result in their becoming the same. Desiring deaf development requires that people take what I call "deaf turns" and become oriented toward each other. Going forward, I treat deaf development as an analytic category and the desire for it as an ethnographic fact.

My deaf friends strongly believed that they had to actively seek deaf development on their own. This is because the needs and desires of sign language–using deaf people have largely been invisible to both the state and the public at large (comprising people who are not deaf and who do not use sign language). There is no reliable data on how many deaf people, sign language–using or not, live in India. The Indian government has not recognized Indian Sign Language (ISL), and India's landmark legislation on behalf of people with disabilities * * * does not say anything about sign language. * * * Deaf people therefore generally believe that the state has failed to provide them with deaf development and that their social, moral, and economic practices are invisible to outsiders. Thus conversations like the one that I had on the bus with Zahra and the other two deaf women take place frequently, and often with some urgency, as well.

The experience of living in India's urban centers is changing for deaf people. On the one hand, the emergence of neoliberal political economic policies means that fewer social and economic protections, social services, and public sector employment opportunities are available. On the other hand, multinational corporations can be found in information technology enabled services (ITES), hospitality, and other sectors that offer new structures of employment opportunity as well as funding for disability-focused vocational training programs and nongovernmental organizations. Vocational training centers, churches, and multilevel marketing businesses that cater specifically to deaf people offer new forms of social, educational, and economic support and new spaces for creating aspirations for deaf development. Indeed, while Bangalore exists as an exceptional case study of how India has been transforming over the last two decades, my deaf friends may also be exceptional case studies of Indians' changing relationship with the state; they depend less on the state for education, employment, and personal development and instead turn to NGOs, multinational corporations, multilevel marketing businesses, other internationally funded organizations such as churches and missionary organizations, and to each other.

* * * Deaf people circulate through structures and institutions—schools, workplaces, churches and other fellowship spaces, and multilevel marketing businesses—in search of deaf development. However, despite repeated and overlapping circulation, deaf development rarely actually takes place in these spaces. What does take place is the production of deaf selves and deaf socialities (or deaf social practices and processes). Deaf selves and socialities are produced through feelings of *"deaf deaf same."* This is a common sentiment and statement in Bangalore's deaf worlds, and it is a way of expressing deaf similitude or a shared experience of being in the world based on common sensorial experience, use of sign language, and an awareness that structural barriers exist for deaf people. Feelings of *"deaf deaf same,"* combined with circulating together through the same spaces, produce deaf turns. I argue that as deaf people move together through spaces, they also turn toward each other. * * * The concept of taking a deaf turn foregrounds acts of movement in space and in sentiment. Deaf turns result in deaf selves and deaf orientations.

* * * I examine how my deaf friends take deaf turns and produce deaf selves and deaf orientations. I argue that there is a specific practice that is required to enact these deaf orientations. This is a practice that I call "sameness work." Through sameness work, deaf people learn to adjust their expectations and negotiate class, caste, geographic, educational, religious, and gender differences in order to productively study, work, socialize, and spend time together. As part of sameness work, deaf orientations are cultivated and foregrounded.

Sameness work also manifests itself as "copying" or imitation as deafs attempt to model themselves after other successful deaf people and follow in their footsteps. While part of sameness work, "copying" also establishes deaf hierarchies in which deafs with good sign language skills, access to information, and strong deaf social networks are seen as more developed people who should be imitated. These hierarchies may not, and often do not, map neatly onto class or caste hierarchies. For example, a deaf person with deaf parents from a lower-class background may have excellent sign language skills that would enable him to cultivate a vast deaf social network. * * * Thus, although hierarchies do exist, "*deaf deaf same*" and shared desires for deaf development often privilege sameness over difference in deaf worlds.

To be sure, negotiating deaf hierarchies and engaging in sameness work can be ambivalent and fraught. Sameness work is by no means a seamless process, and it requires active *dis*orientations and *re*orientations. * * * Deaf people learn how to disorient from their families in order to take deaf turns and reorient themselves toward other deaf people. In addition, deaf sociality is not always harmonious, and deaf people must negotiate shared histories of schooling, working together, and socializing that often involve disagreement and tension. Indeed, "adjusting" and negotiating sameness and difference are very much a part of the active work * * * of becoming a deaf person oriented toward other deaf people.

*   *   *

Multiple Registers and Temporalities of Development

Deaf development * * * includes social, moral, and political economic development. Here I draw inspiration from Anand Pandian's work; * * * Pandian writes: "Development is one of the most important objects of desire, imagination, and struggle in contemporary India. What I mean by development is the promise of a gradual improvement of life, and the fulfillment of its potential for progressive growth through deliberate endeavors in transformation" (2009, 6). * * * My deaf friends' conception of deaf development includes the cultivation of specific and intertwined social, moral, and economic practices.

By social practices I mean practices such as spending time with other deaf people in both informal and formal deaf gatherings, including deaf coffee meet-ups or deaf sporting events, seeking out other deaf people with whom to ride the bus to and from school, searching for vocational training programs or workplaces where other deaf people can be found, coming early to work in order to share news and information with other deaf employees working for the same company, and privileging deaf social spaces over normal ones. Social practices also include teaching other deaf people sign language so that they can contribute to and participate in deaf sociality. They also include the social work in which deaf people engage to minimize conflict among themselves and to maintain a harmonious deaf sociality. * * * The deaf practices that I have outlined do lead to deaf people's social development or the emergence of strong deaf social worlds. As a result, deaf social worlds can become equal to normal social worlds.

Moral practices include practices such as helping other deaf people by sharing information, skills, and resources and acting as a teacher to those who are less developed. Those who are more developed are responsible to "*help support*," or help and support, those who are less developed. "*Help support*" includes practices such as bringing another deaf person to a vocational training center, a church, or a multilevel marketing business, and it can also include a gentle lecture about the importance of not quitting a job. Perhaps most important, moral practices are centered around ensuring that other deaf people are "*saved*" and not "*spoiled*." Being "*saved*" means being a member of deaf sociality and acting according to deaf social norms; it means being able to develop as a deaf person who communicates in sign language. It also includes knowing the proper way to behave, such as not gossiping or behaving promiscuously with members of the opposite sex, and paying careful attention to other deafs and normals who are trying to help. In the words of a students at a Delhi-based deaf vocational training center with deaf teachers: "When I was growing up, there was no sign language, it was a problem in school, I didn't learn anything. Nothing. The same with students here. They go to school, there is no sign language, nothing. They are spoiled. Then they come here and they learn English and sign language and it is good and they are saved. Saved." In contrast, being "*spoiled*" means going "the wrong way" and not being open to having other deaf people guide you toward deaf development. While one can "*spoil*" oneself, one needs other deaf people to be "*saved*." * * *

Economic practices revolved around the importance of finding meaningful livelihood. Many of my deaf friends wanted to be teachers in deaf schools, vocational training centers, NGOs, and churches and fellowships. They also wanted to find employment teaching sign language to normals. They felt that teaching would allow them to "*help support*" other deaf people and that they would be able to financially benefit from their deaf orientations. For many deaf people, economic development meant having jobs that helped other deaf people to develop. Economic development also meant, for many, engaging in meaningful and stable work in employment settings in which deafs and normals were equal. Many of my deaf friends told me bitter tales of feeling subservient to normal workers or being passed over for promotions and pay raises. Not unimportantly, economic development also meant having the ability to consume material possessions and experiences.

* * * Deaf young adults are finding jobs as back office data entry operators, data analysts, and graphic designers for both multinational and domestic companies. They are working as "silent brewmasters" in India's new coffee café chains, and they are deep frying chicken and taking orders at "special" Kentucky Fried Chicken outlets. Some are finding jobs as missionaries or evangelists with funding from international missionary organizations. And others are working as teachers at new NGOs, sign language teaching programs, and educational courses for deaf children and youth. Many of my deaf friends attributed these increased opportunities to the work of NGOs, which provide

vocational training and job placement support. * * * These NGOs and employment opportunities have emerged because of public-private partnerships, corporate social responsibility initiatives, and a new interest in disability because of international disability legislation.

To be sure, * * * most of my interlocutors were extremely ambivalent about these "opportunities" and doubted that they were "*for life*," an important concept for my deaf friends (and for many Indians in general) that indexed financial security and stability (see Nair 2005; Parry 2013). Despite this ambivalence, however, there was a strong sense that deaf development would take place in the future. There was a sense that things were changing, gradually, for the better. * * * My deaf friends had a strong sense that deaf development was yet to come, unlike many normals who lamented the impossibility of development. * * *

Multiple Regimes of Value

In thinking about how * * * disability and development might be different from other kinds of development based on other categories such as caste, gender, or sexuality, for example, it becomes clear that disability might productively be viewed as a source of value. With the emergence of new domestic and international disability laws and treaties, increased funding opportunities in the arena of disability and development, and the very close relationship between Indian corporate social responsibility initiatives and disability services and employment, it is possible that the category of disability offers disabled people additional rather than fewer opportunities in both India and elsewhere in the developing world. * * *

* * * I want to think about how what might be considered stigmatized could actually function as a source of value, or at the very least how it creates conditions for producing alternative regimes of value, some beneficial to deaf people and some not.

*   *   *

Deaf Studies has long been concerned with carving out an analytical and activist space for valuing deaf people, their experiences, and their languages. Along these lines, scholars have recently proposed the concept of "Deaf Gain." * * * [Accordingly], deaf people have unique perspectives and knowledges to share with the world, from their use of sign language to their social practices to their art and architecture forms. In examining how deafness is an asset, "Deaf Gain" exists as an alternative to and play on the medical term "hearing loss." * * *

While I am appreciative of these attempts to carve out a space for valuing deaf people, their experiences, and their use of sign language, I am wary of discussions about "added value" and the argument that deaf people contribute to human diversity. * * * These are the arguments made by NGO administrators and human resource managers at multinational corporations to explain why they train and hire deaf workers. Although

I am cognizant that these arguments are made by scholars and activists in a (much needed) attempt to preserve deaf bodies as deaf, especially in light of so-called advances in medical research promising to eradicate deafness, the increasing prevalence of cochlear implant technology, and the closing of deaf schools, I am concerned about how these new discourses about deafness are being harnessed for others' advantages. * * *

Deafs and Normals

While writing this book, I struggled with the appropriate terminology for writing about deaf people in India and about deaf people in general. The field of Deaf Studies has grappled with these issues extensively, most concretely in the debates around whether deaf should be written with a capital or lower case d/D. Following James Woodward (1972), most Deaf Studies scholars choose to write about Deaf people, and not deaf people, as Deaf represents a person or group of people as a member of a linguistic and cultural minority. In contrast, deaf is seen to be a medicalized condition, a disability, and/or an impairment. Most Deaf Studies works focus on a binary between Deaf people and hearing people, and there are few works that explore the tensions between deaf and Deaf as categories. This is a very specific construction of d/Deafness that has been used in the United States to demand political rights and representation (Shapiro 1994).

The deaf young adults whom I met in Bangalore, however, never wrote deaf with a capital D nor did they talk about being a linguistic or cultural minority (unless they had substantial contact with international Deaf visitors)—although they did express a strong sense of being different from those that could hear. My interlocutors also did not talk about deaf and hearing people but about deaf and normal people. Indeed, "*Deaf normal which?*" or, "Are you deaf or normal?" was the ubiquitous question that deaf people in India asked other people that they met. One was either deaf or normal. * * * I, like many Westerners, was initially uncomfortable with this terminology and at first avoided using it. For example, people often asked me if my husband or family members were deaf or normal, and I replied that they were hearing (I used the correct sign but I mouthed "hearing" instead of "normal," to blank faces). I quickly came to realize that "normal" meant normal hearing and that the use of "deaf" and "normal" served to create both categories as distinct norms. * * *

Although many readers may view the use of the word "normal" as signifying some internalized oppression or stigma on the part of my deaf friends, I argue that most of my interlocutors were unaware of the negative connotations that often accompany the word. According to the *Oxford English Dictionary*, normal means "conforming to a standard; usual, typical, or expected." It seemed to me that my deaf friends were using a definition of normal that was similar to the *Oxford English Dictionary* definition, as it is more usual and expected that people are hearing than deaf. When I asked deafs to clarify what normal meant, they told me that it meant someone who could hear. * * *

I want to note that the category of deafs included deaf people with varying sign language abilities as well as deaf people who were not (yet) signers at all. The category of normals encompassed disabled (but not deaf) people and normal people who were fluent signers. * * * There were normals who said that they "loved" deafs (although deafs did not "love" normals in return), and while some of these normals identified as being deaf or said that they had "deaf hearts," deaf people did not consider them to be deaf. * * * My deaf friends had both ambivalent and rewarding relationships with normals, and aspirations for deaf development also included aspirations for *"deaf normal equal"* (but not *"deaf normal same"*).

Exceptional Bangalore

Located in the southern state of Karnataka, Bangalore is India's third most populous city. It was once known as a sleepy tree- and bungalow-lined "garden city," a colonial outpost where British military officers and expatriates settled, and a pleasant place for Indian retirees to spend their last years. However, it has been remade as India's Silicon Valley, a cosmopolitan "technopolis" to which highly educated Indian migrants and foreign engineers gravitate for work. * * *

Reflecting broader changes in the city, the field of vocational training and the structure of employment opportunities available to deaf young adults has shifted. Previously, many deaf people were able to find comfortable and secure jobs working as welders, electricians, watch assemblers, and clerks in Bangalore's many public sector factories, but this is increasingly no longer the case. As government industries shrink or close altogether, there are fewer jobs to be found in the public sector. Deaf people are increasingly turning to NGOs for help with finding employment. In meeting and also producing this demand, Bangalore is home to more deaf-focused NGOs that provide vocational training and computer training than any other city in India. NGOs with close ties to corporations provide deaf young adults vocational training that is designed to make them productive workers in India's growing service sectors (including ITES and hospitality). In turn, corporations have funded these same vocational training programs, encouraged employees to volunteer at them as part of mandatory volunteering programs, and provided deaf people with jobs.

*   *   *

Bangalore occupied a very specific place in deaf Indians' imaginations. Deaf young adults from all over India flocked to Bangalore to seek training at one of its NGOs and to find jobs; it was considered to be a key site for seeking education and livelihood, and ultimately deaf development. Despite this influx of deaf people from elsewhere in India, there was still a sense of an intimate deaf world. As Jamie, one of my deaf friends, said, "Bangalore's deaf world is very small." What Jamie meant was that deaf people came to know each other, often quite well, because of circulating together through various spaces.

Deaf people spend Monday to Saturday together at vocational training programs and then meet again on Sunday at church or multilevel marketing recruitment meetings (or both). Trainees enrolled in vocational training programs were often hired by the same employer, and after completing their training they worked together. Many deaf people—from Bangalore and elsewhere—attended the same deaf schools as children, and they continued to study, work, and go to church together after they finished secondary school. Deafs also encountered each other on buses and trains and when walking through the city, and then ran into each other again at different deaf functions. Deaf people therefore created dense social networks while repeatedly circulating together through multiple spaces.

*   *   *

Returning to *"Deaf Deaf Same"*

One of my most vivid memories from conducting fieldwork in Bangalore is standing on a very crowded public bus heading to a deaf church on the outskirts of the city in the summer of 2007. I was traveling with two deaf young men, and we were standing toward the back of the bus. We were trying to hold onto something to secure ourselves and to sign at the same time. There was a young woman, one of many without seats, standing toward the front of the bus. She waved to the people I was with and looked at me and signed: "Are you deaf?" When I signed back that I was, she replied *"deaf deaf same"* with a broad smile. This woman turned out to be Zahra, who I introduced in the opening vignette, and this was our first encounter (we were heading to the Korean church this time).

As a deaf person, I was often told *"deaf deaf same"* by my interlocutors, and because of this sense of similitude, I felt that they were more willing to engage with me, answer my many questions, bring me home to meet their families, and be patient with my very awkward BISL. I experienced instances in which my deaf friends lectured other deafs about the importance of helping me with my research because we were all deaf and therefore they had the responsibility to help me. My deaf friends also felt a sense of responsibility for making sure that I understood what was happening in different spaces—including churches, multilevel marketing recruitment sessions, and deaf gatherings. They often asked me if I understood and offered to interpret or repeat things if I needed help.

Ultimately, I wondered too if my interlocutors felt a sense of responsibility for helping me to take a deaf turn. Like many of my deaf friends, I had been raised orally and had not learned sign language until I was in my early twenties. Unlike many of them, I was presumably a successful product of oral education and I benefited from my use of hearing aids and later on a cochlear implant (a source of much curiosity and occasional scorn). In any case, my deaf friends were unstintingly patient and compassionate with my presence and many questions, and they often told me that my research and my doctoral degree was part of overall deaf development.

I must confess that this sense of responsibility was reciprocated. I found myself acting as an advocate in certain situations. For instance, I pestered vocational training center administrators about the importance of hiring deaf teachers and utilizing sign language. With these same administrators, I advocated for deaf trainees to be able to find a wide range of jobs, beyond those at multinational corporations as back office data entry operators. I felt compelled to become such an advocate because many of my friends asked me to "*help*" them. "*Help*" is an important concept in deaf sociality and it serves to create substantial bonds between people. As I was "helped" by my deaf friends who so generously shared with me, I found myself enmeshed in deaf sociality as well. And this is why I often call my interlocutors for this research my deaf friends. I feel that I was bound to them by very real feelings of mutual bonds of affection, sentiment, and responsibility.

I was and am well aware of the power differentials that exist and the privilege that comes with being a highly educated white foreigner conducting research in India. I am grateful, though, for a shared sense of deafness that overcame barriers and helped to make this research especially rewarding and rich. This shared sense of deafness certainly overcame the communication barrier created by the crowded physical mass of people on the bus.

* * *

What would it mean for deaf turns, deaf sociality, deaf orientations, and desires for deaf development if there were fewer structural barriers? Henri Lefebvre (1991, 190) writes: "To change life ... we must first change space." While I agree with this statement, I also argue that there is something unique about deaf orientations. Changing spaces, or structures, to make them more accessible to deafs will not completely change deaf lives. The uniqueness of deaf orientations means that removing structural barriers will not result in the obliteration of deaf sociality. "*Deaf normal same*" may never be possible, although "*deaf normal equal*" may be. And the removal of structural barriers in the arenas of education, employment, and language access are essential in order for deafs to be equal to normals.

* * * There is something unique about deaf sociality, something that is more than just two or more deaf bodies together in space. It is about being intensely oriented toward other deaf people, wanting to help and support them, and desiring deaf-run institutions. Indeed, a desire for deaf development is more than just a desire for more sign language in the world, it is a desire for deaf people to be capable and confident as they both build deaf worlds and circulate through normal ones. Building deaf worlds is key here—deafs want to continue to cultivate their own social, moral, and economic practices while also being able to circulate in normal worlds. When deaf development occurs, deaf people will be confident, strong, and capable of moving successfully through both deaf and normal worlds. * * * And so, even if structural barriers were to disappear, I argue that there would still be an orientation—"*deaf deaf same*"—that is unique to deaf people. It is this orientation, and not just two bodies in space, that makes it so easy to sign "*deaf deaf same*" across a crowded bus to someone whom you have never met before.

ENGAGING THE TEXT, ENGAGING THE WORLD

- What does Friedner mean by "deaf development"? How does the desire for development express itself in India's deaf community?

- What does it mean to make a "deaf turn"? And why is this essential for creating deaf sociality and identity?

- Friedner introduces the concept of "deaf gain" in contrast to the term "hearing loss" to explore ways deafness may be viewed as a source of value, as an asset rather than a deficit. What opportunities for "deaf gain" does Friedner identify for India's deaf community?

- What is the controversy around the language used to refer to deaf people? Why does Friedner choose the language of "deaf" people and "normal" people in her writing? What do Friedner's deaf friends mean by "normal"?

- How did Friedner's own deafness and sign language use shape her ethnographic research?

15
Art and Media

Anthropologists consider a vast array of human expression and interaction when exploring the world of art. Anthropologists define **art** broadly as all the ideas, forms, techniques, and strategies that humans employ to express themselves creatively and communicate their creativity and inspiration to others. Art may include music, songs, stories, paintings, plays, design, sculpture, architecture, clothing, food, and games. Art is both created and received. Cooking and building, fashion and oratory, decorating and dressing, sewing and play all represent media through which artists and audience communicate. Through these often-dynamic encounters, art takes its shape not only in creation but also in perception.

Art in Western traditions has often been associated with notions of high culture or fine art, especially elite representations of visual and performance arts experienced in formal venues. Paintings, sculptures, operas, symphonies, ballets, and plays fit this view of **fine art**. Such art is often evaluated and portrayed in contrast to **popular art**—less refined and less sophisticated creative expressions associated with the general population—in the same way that high culture might be simplistically compared to popular culture. From an anthropological perspective, however, art is not the sole province of the elites or professional artists. Art is integral to all of human life. As such, it can be expressed through elaborate performances in specialized venues as well as through routine activities in mundane settings.

The significance of art cannot be underestimated as anthropologists consider the full expression of human life. All creativity carries rich deposits of information about culture as a system of meaning and as a system of power. In fact, the very distinction between fine art and popular art may have more to do with political choices and hierarchies of power than with an intrinsic character of the art itself. Who decides, for instance, what will be performed in an opera house or displayed in a national museum? Brent Luvaas's article, "Designer Vandalism: Indonesian

Indie Fashion and the Cultural Practice of Cut 'n' Paste," explores this question of what is legitimate art through a study of Indonesian indie fashion designers who appropriate designs from global brands, "cutting and pasting" into their own products sold in the local youth market. Can you identify other cultural dynamics of power and stratification—perhaps race, gender, class, religion, or sexuality—that might be reflected in decisions and representations of what is fine art and what is popular art?

Anthropologists' unique approach to art includes particular attention to how art is embedded in a community—how art connects to social norms and values and economic and political systems and events. Who makes art and why? What does it mean to the people who create it and to those who perceive it? As ethnographers, anthropologists of art attend not only to the form of the art itself—its designs, movements, and sounds—but also to its context. Aimee Cox's article, "The BlackLight Project and Public Scholarship," explores the ways young African American women in a Detroit homeless shelter create public performances of dance, song, and drama to raise community consciousness and inspire action. As the articles in this chapter reveal, art is embedded in everyday exchanges, social networks, business negotiations, and other struggles over profit, power, and prestige.

Placing art in context has become more complicated in recent years. Today, in an era of intensifying globalization, local art is created in a global landscape. Local art practices, objects, and events intersect with global movements of people and ideas. Art is often a key juncture through which local communities engage the global economy. As we see in both of the following articles, within this global "artscape" (Appadurai 1986), the creation of local art may provide not only a means of economic activity but also a venue to demonstrate cultural skills and values and to assert local cultural identity in the face of rapid change. As a result, contemporary anthropologists of art explore the journeys of objects across boundaries and the implications of the traffic in culture for both those who produce art and those who consume it (Marcus and Myers 1995).

Art intersects with key systems of power such as race, ethnicity, class, gender, sexuality, politics, religion, and economics. In the process, artistic expressions can unmask patterns of stratification, make the unconscious conscious, and open space for alternative visions of reality.

Designer Vandalism: Indonesian Indie Fashion and the Cultural Practice of Cut 'n' Paste

Brent Luvaas

Art, appropriation, and youth culture

Whereas Western art traditions may emphasize innovation and originality—creating something entirely new—other traditions may celebrate improvisation on already existing material. In such traditions, artistic value is created as the artist explores variations on established themes. Likewise, whereas many Western cultures may idealize the artist as an individual genius—as a cultural outsider separated from mundane daily life—other cultures may prioritize engagement with the audience and interaction with the community as the highest aspect of artistic expression. So, what is art?

In the following article, Brent Luvaas explores the dynamic world of independent Indonesian fashion designers who appropriate global brand designs to create their own. Are they artists? Are they pirates? Denby Darman, cofounder of the Indonesian independent clothing label 347, states that pirates just copy. He, on the other hand, consciously appropriates global brands to make them his own, marking them up in a way an urban gang might tag a building, to stake out a space within the dominant culture of transnational capitalism. Through this process, young people become culture producers, not just culture consumers.

Hit hard by financial crises in the 1990s, many of Indonesia's middle-class young people struggled to maintain their economic position and consumer lifestyle. They pooled resources and shared luxury goods, including computers, Internet access, and graphic design software. Eventually many decided to stop buying overpriced imported designer brand clothing and began to experiment with creating their own. Luvaas introduces Claude Levi Strauss's concept of bricolage—the assembling and reassembling of cultural components to create new formations and new meanings—to describe the process Indonesia's indie fashion designers

From Brent Luvaas. 2010. "Designer Vandalism: Indonesian Indie Fashion and the Cultural Practice of Cut 'n' Paste." *Visual Anthropology Review* 26(1): 1–16. Some of the author's notes have been omitted.

employ to refashion global brands into something meaningful in the Indonesian context. In doing so, Luvaas argues that Indonesian young people resisted the dominant global capitalist culture of consumerism and worked to renegotiate their own position and status in the global power hierarchies.

Now is the era of cut 'n' paste.

—*Dendy Darman, cofounder and owner of Unkl347*

Introduction

The Indonesian independent clothing label 347 has made a name for itself out of other people's designs, not through anything so contentious as stealing or copying, but instead through the clever—and strategic—appropriation of immediately recognizable commercial iconography. It specializes in the art of the fashion remix, producing vividly colored T-shirts, hooded sweat jackets (hoodies), and backpacks that draw their aesthetic from such international corporate giants as Pepsi, Fuji, Microsoft, and Yellow Pages, and rock 'n' roll iconography from the likes of Suede, Joy Division, The Rolling Stones, and the Velvet Underground.

One of its most famous—or perhaps infamous—designs came out a few years back when the company was still called "Eat." It featured the Nike "swoosh" logo with the Eat brand name superimposed on top of it in big, bold letters. It was a simple motif, not particularly subtle, and certainly not groundbreaking in its use of color or composition. But it attracted a lot of attention in Indonesian design circles nonetheless.

Other designers accused 347 of copying another brand's merchandise and charged them with being lazy (*malas*), or even worse, pirates (*pembajak*). But according to Dendy, the avuncular and charismatic cofounder of 347, those charges were missing the mark. This is not piracy (*pembajakan*), Dendy insisted, as we chatted over bottles of heavily sweetened ice tea in the cramped industrial warehouse in southern Bandung that served as 347's office. Indonesia has plenty of pirates, a long and sometimes sordid history of black market entrepreneurs employing the counterfeit as a path out of poverty (see Siegel 1998). The Southeast Asian island nation, after all, has a poor record of copyright enforcement, and as a consequence, the tourist districts of Kuta, Bali, and Yogyakarta, Java, are chock-full of imitation designer goods. Whole neighborhoods in Jakarta specialize in fake Louis Vuitton handbags. Pirate clothing companies, in fact, occupy similar industrial spaces just down the street from 347's office.

347, however, does not count itself among them. Dendy has nothing personal against pirates. They are just people who want to support their families, he shrugged. But they have no real critical intent behind what they do, no creative vision, or personal urgency. They imitate, or to use the Indonesian term in vogue for the practice, *nyontek*. It is a word with connotations of both copying and cheating, and it implies a lack of personal investment, a merely pragmatic incentive. 347, however, invests a great deal in what and how it appropriates. "As for us," said Dendy, leaning back in his chair and outstretching his arms for dramatic effect, "we are conscious (*sadar*) of it. And being conscious is good, you know."

347 not only chooses the designs it appropriates with careful deliberation, but it also wants its customers to realize it took the material from somewhere else. "We even go so far as to acknowledge it [in our designs] so that people know," said Dendy, adding something like visual citations to 347's work. Another one of its designs, for instance, features an almost exact copy of the album cover for "Goo" by the New York art punk band Sonic Youth. A young, modish couple in bowl cuts and sunglasses smoke cigarettes while they lounge in each other's arms. Beside the image, the original handwritten words "I stole my sister's boyfriend" have been replaced with the sardonic "I stole my Sonic Youth."

As for its controversial Nike design, 347 never intended to pass it off as its own. 347 has no interest in riding the coattails of an international sporting gear giant. Instead, the design does something else. It takes ownership over the Nike swoosh and tags it the way an urban gang might mark up an overpass or a warehouse wall. It engages in what could be called brand vandalism, or "brandalism" (Moore 2007), working to forge a public domain out of private industry. The design is a repudiation of the classic Western notion of individual authorship, a defiant assertion of the sociality of production, and a visual acknowledgment of what is already implicitly understood in Indonesia, that the culture of transnational capitalism—with its larger-than-life billboards, its circuitry of commercial images, its visual bombast of ads and icons—is the world Indonesian youth now inhabit. Designers like Dendy are tired of dwelling in other people's territory. They have marked it as their own.

This essay is about such reworking of popular representation through Indonesian indie clothing design. Based on a year of fieldwork in several outposts of the Indonesian "indie" scene, most notably Yogyakarta in Central Java and Bandung in West Java, it describes an emergent culture of Indonesian fashion centered precisely around such appropriative modes of production. I analyze Indonesian indie designers' acts of aesthetic appropriation and attempt to make sense of such practices in light of both the middle-class subject position designers occupy and the marginality they experience within an increasingly global commercial culture.

In doing so, I employ the structuralist notion of *bricolage*. * * * The types of activities Lévi-Strauss attempted to capture with the concept are becoming evermore prevalent in modern life. Computer technology and a range of readily available new media resources have made cut 'n' paste the de facto practice of creative production for youth nearly everywhere. In our culture of simulation (Baudrillard 1994; Turkle 1995), young people have become adept at reworking images, remaking other people's creative labors, and customizing culture for their own personal use. We have, as Turkle claims, become a culture of bricoleurs.

I argue in this essay, however, that bricolage, as it has often been conceptualized by social theorists, has tended to either overemphasize its resistant potential or render it mundane, denying its efficacy as a medium of change altogether. What I propose instead is a * * * conception of bricolage * * * that interprets its assemblage of diverse forms as above all an act of social positioning, not just image manipulation. Indonesian indie designers, I argue, use their designs to construct a diverse, even contradictory, set of associations and imagery that have become representative of a transnational youth culture. In the process, they position themselves as producers of that culture, active participants in an ongoing project of differentiation and distinction. To engage in bricolage, I conclude, is * * * an effort to assume an empowered position in relationship to the increasingly dominant international culture of consumption. It is, in fact, to work to reorganize the hierarchy of production, asserting one's own place within it as a producer of culture, not just another marginalized subject of the Western world's encroaching consumerist regime.

The Cut 'n' Paste Generation

"It happened at first with my friends, my buddies, and me," Aji, then 32 years old, told me, as we sat in the back of his small shop in Bandung in the spring of 2007. I had just arrived in the West Javanese city after several months researching indie music and fashion production in Yogyakarta, and I was touring the major outposts of Bandung's indie clothing network on the back of the motorbike of my self-appointed tour guide "Megadeath." Aji's shop was stop number four on a daylong introductory blitz. He went on:

> We used to skateboard together, then play in a band together. Then at some point, at the time of the monetary [crisis], I tried to make my own clothing line, just to satisfy our needs really. Just our needs as young people . . . At first it started from that. I borrowed a sewing machine from my mom, an old sewing machine. I borrowed my mom's garage too, and I started production there. It was all truly do-it-yourself (*Benar-benar do-it-yourself lah*).

It was a story I heard over and over throughout my fieldwork. In the midst of the Asian Financial Crisis of the late 1990s, young, middle-class urbanites like Aji found themselves in a difficult position. The relative economic prosperity of the late Suharto period, coupled with economic deregulation, had expanded the size and spending capacity of the Indonesian middle class (Dick 1985; Lev 1990; Robison and Goodman 1996). Many young people had gotten used to a consumerist lifestyle, to American fast-food chains and chichi coffee joints, imported media and designer fashion (Heryanto 1999; Kompas 1990, 1999; Priyono 1999). The only trouble was that they could no longer afford it.

So urban youth had to adopt other strategies for maintaining their middle-class lifestyles and differentiating themselves from the some 95 percent of the Indonesian population who were never able to afford them in the first place. They pooled their resources and shared luxury goods (Gerke 2000). They bought knockoff versions of designer brands, sought out low-cost alternatives to more upscale fare, did whatever they could to secure their tenuous position (Liechty 2003) in the shifting social landscape of the island nation. And in cities like Bandung, a number of disaffected skaters, punks, and metal-heads decided to stop buying overpriced skate and rock T-shirts from imported chains like Planet Surf and just make them for themselves (Iskandar 2006).

Aji and his friends built their own silkscreens from scrap wood and cloth, printed their designs onto low-cost, local-made T-shirts, and sometimes even sewed their own. Aji admits that their first efforts were pretty unsophisticated, mostly amateur editions of Australian and American surf brands, and copies of rock band T-shirts, but it did not take long for them to bring their wares up to market quality. After all, there were a number of factors working in their favor. As the New Order regime eased restrictions on media throughout the 1990s, allowing direct foreign investment for the first time, a flood of new visual resources entered the market, from international television networks to scores of foreign design magazines.

Furthermore, the technological tools for producing or reproducing imagery had become much more readily available to them (Heryanto 2008). A thriving black market, no doubt boosted by the ailing economy, enabled aspiring designers to pick up a pirated copy of the Adobe Creative Suite or the Corel Graphics software for a mere 7,000 *rupiah* (75 cents at the time of my research) and use their shared, discount electronics-fair PCs to cut and paste more or less any images they wanted into a pretty accurate approximation of whatever was cool at the moment. The Internet, cheap and readily available throughout urban Indonesia by the end of the 1990s (Heryanto 2008; Hill and Sen 2005), provided an ever-expanding resource bank of visual ideas and style motifs.

Aji and other kids like him took advantage of all these new media resources and started piecing together their own designs from the image reserves of international pop culture. They borrowed extensively from foreign album design and the imagery of the international punk, skate, and hardcore scenes and put their own creative stamp on reworked, deconstructed, or sometimes outright copied foreign motifs.

At first, Aji and his friends simply gave away their products to other friends. Then, as demand increased, they began selling them at concerts, in roadside stalls, or outside shopping malls to whoever would buy them. Soon, they started setting up their own shops, dubbed "distro" (short for "distribution outlets"), which featured their own and their friends' clothing lines, along with rock and skate merchandise and homemade cassettes of local bands. These distros became local outposts for international youth culture, one-stop shops for music, fashion, and information. Distros combined resources, promoted each other's products, and used the Internet to establish a nationwide network of bands and brands that became known collectively as the "youth independent" or "indie scene."

It was a network of the self-consciously "anti-mainstream" (see Thornton 1996) of "kids" who saw their own do-it-yourself (or DIY) production practices as at odds with the commercial overdrive the nation had gone into, their own system of cooperative capitalism as an alternative to the cold materialism of the deregulated market. Along with 347, Riotic, and Reverse, Aji's distro, known as "No Label Stuff" was one of the first distros in Indonesia, and it remains one of the most prominent to this day.

Today, there are hundreds of distros in cities throughout the Indonesian archipelago that follow No Label Stuff's example and sell thousands of local clothing labels, along with CDs and cassettes of local rock bands, and locally produced magazines. Distros have become a significant economic force in the island country, with single clothing lines, like 347, bringing in as much as US$75,000–100,000 per month. Television actors wear distro brands on their live appearances. Rock stars are frequently "endorsed" by local labels. And the bands whose music is sold at distros are now some of the most commercially viable in Indonesia. Distros, in other words, have helped make local products cool and are consequently working to shift middle-class patterns of consumption away from the foreign and toward the homegrown. It has become commonplace for aspiring designers with little to no formal training in design to open up their own clothing shops or distribute their work through the vast networks of the indie scene.

The "cut 'n' paste" practice of design used by distros has in effect democratized the world of Indonesian fashion, not in the sense of making all fashion equal—Indonesians still recognize a distinction between bigger indie labels and smaller indie labels, and even the biggest labels among them, like 347 and No Label Stuff, are in no position to compete directly with brands like Nike or LaCoste—but in the sense of tearing down the barriers to participation in fashion, opening it up as a contested terrain (Hall 1977), where thousands of young people from diverse backgrounds struggle to get their voices heard and their visions out there. Indie fashion has become a dynamic site for the struggle over meaning in Indonesia, and cut 'n' paste has become its principal weapon.

*   *   *

Like the bricoleurs Lévi-Strauss discusses in *The Savage Mind*, these indie designers assemble and disassemble, combine and recombine, instead of creating something wholly from scratch. They tinker with the images they locate through the World Wide Web, put a new spin on them, and remake them for a local audience.

Lévi-Strauss first coined the term *bricolage* to describe the "science of the concrete" (Lévi-Strauss 1966), whereby an individual "makes do with 'whatever is at hand'" to conduct a number of diverse tasks (Lévi-Strauss 1966:17). The bricoleur, he explains, constructs works out of available materials, whether they were intended for this purpose or not. Unlike "the engineer," who constructs from raw materials "conceived and procured for the purpose of a project" (Lévi-Strauss 1966), the bricoleur puts existing things to new purposes. The engineer creates; the bricoleur tinkers. And this is not just tinkering for the sake of tinkering. The bricoleur "speaks through the medium of things" (Lévi-Strauss 1966:21), that is, makes meaning out of assemblage.

*   *   *

At its most [ordinary], bricolage in these texts simply refers to how people put pieces of things together to form a complex whole. At its most extravagant, bricolage is no less than the dynamic sub-version of dominant forms.

*   *   *

[Anthropologist] Lila Abu-Lughod has argued that we can "use resistance as a *diagnostic* of power" (Abu-Lughod 1990:42), and perhaps the same can be said of bricolage in this case. Following the lead of Michel Foucault (1978), she suggests that the appearance of resistance itself helps shed light on where power relations lie, gives us a sense of where to look for inequalities and forms of domination. In the case of indie fashion design, finding the demarcating lines of power is fairly easy. 347 and Monik/Celtic are tiny companies by world standards, run by a bunch of skaters and surfers from a poverty-stricken industrializing nation, with no real expectations of "making it big." They are small fish in a big sea, even if in Indonesia's fashion scene they are about as big as brands can get. The source companies from which designers borrow, meanwhile, tend to be major players in the international economy, brands like Nike, Microsoft, and Volcom, media companies like Twentieth Century Fox, Sony, and Viacom. Their products are all over Indonesia, whereas 347 and Monik/Celtic, after ten or so years of relative success at home, have barely managed to begin selling their products in Singapore and Malaysia. The hundreds of other independent clothing companies in the archipelago nation are not doing nearly as well.

This is not a case of literal domination, though. These brands have little direct power over Indonesian designers. Rather, I would argue, these transnational companies compose a matrix of global brands that assert more and more dominion into the daily lives of Indonesian youth. They dominate the aesthetic landscape of Indonesia, its roadways, its malls, its billboards, its television stations, and its Internet content. They mediate their interaction with other countries and other cultures, produce the foods they eat, the music they listen to, and the clothes they wear. These brands are all around them, compose the very fabric of contemporary life. "They are who we are," Dendy told me.

Modern life has become so deeply saturated with international brands that they are integral to the very way contemporary youth conceive of themselves * * * in the sense of establishing a measure of their own deprivation, a recognition of how little they have in comparison to similarly situated youth in other places.

Iyo, Chief Executive for *Ripple Magazine*, one of the key advertising venues for Indonesian independent clothing labels, describes the position of designers like Dendy and Marin as being "in the middle" (*di tengah-tengah*). They are not the poorest of the poor by any means, but they are not the richest of the rich either. They have a relatively decent economic position by Indonesian standards and are well educated, but by world standards they are barely middle class. And these are the most successful among indie designers. The vast majority of them remain well below the poverty line by the reckoning of any industrialized nation. They may be able to afford a cell phone (or two) and a motorbike, but they still tend to live in bleak, student housing units well after graduation, many surviving on less than US$2 a day.

The young Indonesian designers I met while carrying out my fieldwork in 2006–7 do their best to live a cosmopolitan lifestyle of fast food and designer clothes, imported music and fashion, but even for Dendy and Marin their access is limited. Most young people involved in the Indonesian indie scene cannot afford cable television or subscriptions to foreign magazines. Very few have ever left the country. Many do not even own a TV, most do not own a computer, and they get most of their music through swapping MP3s and burning CDs. Most of them have to rent Internet access by the hour and share computers with friends and colleagues to keep costs down. This can make cutting 'n' pasting a painfully slow process.

Indonesian indie designers, then, are both empowered and constrained by their middle-class status. They have more money than the average Indonesian, with some degree of access to personal computers, the Internet, foreign media, and the resources of production. But they retain a marginal position in the global economy. They occupy an uncomfortable middle ground between "here" and "elsewhere," the "traditional" and the "modern," the "First" and the "Third" World. They can observe global youth cultures from afar, but they are not yet full participants within them. In other words, they have just enough to know how little they have. It is a frustrating position, Iyo explains, and it speaks volumes about why Indonesian designers do the kind of work they do.

Tributes from Afar

This uncomfortable in-betweenness is particularly evident in the work of Hamid, designer for the Yogyakarta distro and clothing label Triggers Syndicate. Hamid grew up in Pekanbaru, South Sumatra, listening to bands like Motörhead, Metallica, and Slayer. He liked the hard stuff, music with attitude and grit, theatrical atmospherics composed of power chords and screams. It is the kind of music that makes you feel powerful, he told me, in the checkerboarded storeroom of Triggers Syndicate, like you can do anything. Indonesia, he says, has yet to produce bands like that, and so Hamid has always preferred stuff from the United States and the United Kingdom, the old guard of metal, with their loud, abrasive sound and larger-than-life personae. He started growing his hair long in his early teens and joined the "headbanger army," those thousands of metal fans scattered throughout Indonesia (see Baulch 2007; Wallach 2008), and indeed the rest of the world, decked out in a common uniform of black T-shirts and faded jeans. Music was a big part of his self-concept back then. It still is.

For Hamid and his metal-fan friends, though, being a fan just was not enough. He wanted to be part of the music in a more direct way, to adopt for himself something of the kind of power such bands emitted. He wanted to be more like his idols, he told me, to "have a strong character and image" that "endures" (*tetap jalan*) and gives other people a frame of reference for understanding who he is and what he is all about. Those of his friends with enough financial resources to do so scraped together whatever instruments they could and began playing in bands. The rest of them just borrowed their instruments from those friends. That is what Hamid had to do. His parents were civil servants, middle class by local reckoning, but by no means well off. Like most kids in his position, for Hamid sharing resources was just a fact of life (Gerke 2000).

It worked out okay for him. He played with friends, practiced when he could. But he was never much of a musician. "I just didn't have any talent," he told me, remorsefully. He took up the guitar briefly, but the strings left his fingers stinging and his ego bruised. He tried singing, but could not muster up much of a voice. Eventually, he came to the conclusion that he just was not cut out to play music. It was a sad realization, he told me, but it turned out to be a blessing in disguise.

Hamid moved to Yogyakarta, Central Java, in the late 1990s to study economics at the Indonesian Islamic University. He was not all that interested in economics, but his parents, always pragmatic about such things, felt it was an appropriate course of study for someone of his social stature. He was not a great student, he admits, but university life provided plenty of opportunities to pursue other passions, most significantly music. He got involved in the local hard rock and metal scene, became friends with bands, went to countless gigs, spent his evenings hanging out at local distros.

A number of his friends at the time were beginning to get involved in clothing design, and Hamid would watch them assemble images on Corel Draw. He peered over their shoulders, trying to figure out how to do it himself, and eventually began tinkering with the program. He said to himself, "If other people can [do this] why can't I?" and explained to me that "everyone is capable [of designing] if they are willing to learn."

Over the course of several months of often frustrating late nights at his friends' boarding houses, he became quite adept at using the Corel Graphics suite, and he experimented with doing posters for his friends' bands. He went on to design album cover art, fliers, and other band merchandise, all in the tradition of heavy metal. His work featured lots of skulls and crossbones, decomposing skeletons, and coiled snakes. Putting together such pieces took up more and more of his time, until Hamid decided, finally, to drop out of school and make design his full-time occupation. When one of his friends opened Triggers Syndicate several years back and asked Hamid to come on board as the designer, Hamid jumped at the chance. It felt like he finally knew what he wanted to do with his life.

"At first, my parents questioned it all," he said, "but now they support me. I was able to show them that I could support myself." In fact, Hamid began to be able to support himself pretty well, bringing in a respectable 3 million *rupiah* a month (roughly US$312, more than the starting salary of the average civil servant). His parents saw that he was doing well and seemed happy, and eventually they even gave their consent. "They always taught me," Hamid explained, "that you can do whatever you want, so long as you're willing to accept the consequences of it." * * *

The main theme of Hamid's design, as he describes it, is "rock." All of his work "reeks of music" (*berbau musik*). It borrows from the aesthetics of hard rock and heavy metal, occasionally even snippets from his favorite songs. He has channeled his passion for heavy sounds into a visual medium and describes his work as a form of "tribute" to the rock bands that have had a significant influence over his personal aesthetic.

*　　*　　*

[A] line of clothes he has recently completed includes a series of T-shirts and jackets inspired by favorite rock songs. To compose this line, Hamid would first look for inspiration from his substantial CD, cassette, and MP3 collection; then he would select a song he liked and play it repeatedly until it triggered some sort of visual idea. He then took to the Internet to look for images that could approximately represent his vision. Yahoo proved a reliable place to look, as did Google Image, a whole set of rock T-shirt websites, some graffiti art websites, and the websites of specific companies, such as the California-based skate/punk clothing brand Atticus. When he found what he was looking for—a pointing skeletal hand, perhaps, a scantily clad pinup, or a cobra ready to strike—he would attempt to re-create the image using Corel Draw.

"Obviously, if you're talking about originality," Hamid told me, "I can't say I'm original, because I can't even draw. . . . I'm not the one who draws these things. I take pictures [from somewhere else]. But not just randomly, not just any old thing that I have no connection with. And not without changing it." This distinction is critical to Hamid. It is what separates his own appropriative practice from that of the "posers," those less-invested, would-be designers who sample haphazardly from the annals of youth culture, and "pirates" who wholesale copy the designs of major labels. It creates a more substantial link with what he is depicting and who he is. The resulting design, he explained, is more than the inspirational image. It takes on a new composition. It becomes something else.

For Hamid, then, the practice of cut 'n' paste is very much about his own relationship with that which he depicts. For one, his rock-themed design is a way to participate in a musical culture he has long been involved with as a fan and enthusiast but never able to contribute to in a more direct way. It aligns him with a musical lineage beyond the range of the archipelago, gives him an honorary place within its ranks. For another, it converts him from one of many "mere" consumers of such cultural products—the "mainstream" of consumers, as it were—into a kind of expert, a connoisseur, with knowledge and understanding beyond those other kids whom he seeks to educate about the "roots." Above all, it establishes his place as a creative contributor to this culture, helping determine how it is received, experienced, and understood locally.

As a designer, he has been able to assume a more proactive stance toward the cultural products in which he had invested so deeply. He has repositioned himself within the hierarchy of cultural production. Through his "tributes," he leaves his own mark on those images that inspired him. He becomes an active participant in those processes of cultural production on whose sidelines he used to stand.

Hamid's work is a pastiche of heavy metal and rock-themed imagery. It mimics an international repertoire of rock music tropes, assembling them together into new compositions. But it does so without any of the neutrality described by Jameson.

Bricolage like his simply cannot help but take a stand. It always positions its practitioner in some sort of relationship with that which it reproduces, whether it be sympathetic, as Hamid's design certainly is, or otherwise. In the most basic sense, bricolage involves a reconstitution of the consumer as a producer. Dendy, Marin, and Aji have placed themselves within a pantheon of internationally recognized designers by appropriating their work within their own. Hamid has aligned himself with a global heavy metal underground by placing its imagery, and lyrics, within his work.

*   *   *

Conclusion: We Are the Brands We Consume

Anthropologists have found resistance in nearly every nook and cranny of contemporary lives. * * * We have had a long and well-documented love affair with "the romance of resistance" (Abu-Lughod 1990). But despite a rather large body of critiques against the overuse of the concept, talk of resistance continues to pop up all over the place in ethnographic work. We have yet to come up with an alternative explanation sufficient for making sense of such deconstructive acts of bricolage that are becoming increasingly common in the Information Age (Castells 2000): the remixes of popular songs, the mashups and video collages that animate the Internet, the cut 'n' paste designs of Indonesian indie fashion.

There is, I would argue, an element of resistance to what distro-label designers do, sometimes explicit, sometimes more subtle, but we have to be careful about assigning resistance too liberally to youth aesthetic practice. Indie designer resistance is always an ambivalent resistance * * * (Kondo 1997). Indie designers uphold, often even glorify the source material of their designs. 347's Nike logo, for instance, both takes over the international brand and declares the brand something worth taking over. In fact, when I asked Dendy point-blank if there was an element of critique to his Nike design, he nodded, said "yeah" in a noncommittal way, then added, "But it's not that I don't like Nike. In fact, I only wear Nike. They're cool shoes."

This is not, then, the kind of conscious undermining of capitalist spectacle that the Situationists advocated (Debord 1995), nor the sort of politicized "culture jamming" or "adbusting" that has become a mainstay of urban guerilla art. In truth, the work of indie designers tends not to have a clear or consistent political agenda. It messes with other people's brands, alters, and distorts, but not so much out of spite or ideology as a sort of playful oppositionality. These designers are not trying to throw off the conceptual shackles of cultural imperialism; they are trying to assert some degree of direct control over the new commercial world they live in. Designers like Dendy and Marin are less concerned with subverting international commercial culture than working with it, or perhaps more accurately, inserting themselves into it.

Just as an emphasis on bricolage as an expression of the cultural logic of capitalism misses a great deal of its subtlety, to call such work "resistant," then, also misses the mark.

The principal motivation of designers like Dendy, Hamid, [and] Marin * * * is not so much critiquing the source material from which they borrow as with asserting a kind of ownership over it, appropriating commercial imagery in efforts to reproduce themselves as global citizens.

Sometimes the reconstituted aesthetic objects they produce take on subversive meanings. * * * Sometimes they work to reproduce or reinforce an existing meaning. * * * The most compelling feature of indie fashion bricolage, then, is not its utility as a mode of resistance, nor its complicity with the dominant culture, but the way it repositions individuals in relationship to those materials from which they sample. Bricolage is a means of taking claim of and asserting authority over cultural forms produced by other, more powerful social actors in other places and other times. It is a technology (see Boellstorff 2008; Foucault 1986) of cultural production, and what it produces is not only a new set of meanings in association with a borrowed image or idea, but also a new relationship between that image and its bricoleur. To put it in the simplest terms, bricolage is a technology by which a consumer of culture transforms herself into a producer of culture.

* * *

Techniques of bricolage may not threaten the smooth functioning of the capitalist economy, but they do challenge the power relationships operating within it. They destabilize the distinction between producer and consumer and help break down the barriers between professional and amateur, "Third" and "First" World, global and local.

ENGAGING THE TEXT, ENGAGING THE WORLD

- Describe the lifestyles of most indie fashion designers, like Hamid, despite their position in the Indonesian middle class.

- Do you consider cut 'n' paste fashion design art or piracy? What is the author's position in this debate?

- What is bricolage? Why does the author consider this an appropriate metaphor for the work of independent clothing designers in Indonesia?

- What does Luvaas mean that cut 'n' paste is a weapon young Indonesians use in the struggle over meaning in transnational capitalist culture?

- Lila Abu-Lughod argues that we can use resistance as a "diagnostic of power" to identify inequalities and forms of domination. How does Indonesian indie fashion design play this diagnostic role and help identify power, inequality, and domination?

- How do you see the bricolage work of Indonesia's indie fashion designers as a type of resistance to global consumer culture and a challenge to the power relationships operating within it?

The BlackLight Project and Public Scholarship

Aimee Cox

Anthropologist Aimee Cox began dancing when she was three years old and studied classical ballet in high school at the College Conservatory of Music at the University of Cincinnati. While at Vassar College Cox spent a semester studying with the Dance Theatre of Harlem—the world's first black ballet company—and then spent a semester at the Alvin Ailey School to pursue modern dance. Eventually Cox danced professionally with Ailey II in New York City. Reflecting on those years, Cox recalls, "through dance, through moving my body and telling stories through my body, I felt like that was a space where I had a certain type of voice and I could express myself. But I still felt limited. I was marrying modern dance and classical ballet. But I felt like I was telling the story in somebody else's language—classical ballet, for example."

That feeling began to change in graduate school as she explored the connections between anthropology and performing arts—particularly while directing a homeless shelter in southwest Detroit for young women ages 16 to 21. Art, as Cox describes it and the young women in the shelter create it, is not the art of museums, galleries, and recital halls. Rather it is art created in community and expressed through body, word and music. In this article she considers the power of performance to create a kind of arts activism. She also wrestles with the challenges for scholars who are involved in community-based projects for social change, sometimes called public or engaged scholarship.

"When I came to graduate school," Cox says, "I had this vague idea that I was interested in studying how young women, low-income young women, who are seen as the most marginal people in society, find ways to navigate social systems. How do they find ways to survive, and in some ways be successful in the ways that they define success? What are the creative ways they do that?

"The minute I came to the homeless shelter, those young women would not allow me to leave [my professional training] behind. They were dancing on their

From Aimee Cox. 2009. "The BlackLight Project and Public Scholarship: Young Black Women Perform Against and Through the Boundaries of Anthropology." *Transforming Anthropology* 17(1): 51–64.

own—not trained, they were not taking classes—they were moving their bodies, choreographing each other, making these connections across their individual stories through dance and through writing. When I saw that, I said to myself, 'I need to start dancing again. I can't act like this is not a part of me.'

"It started off for them as kind of a creative healing space. They were frustrated at the end of the day by their struggles to survive in Detroit, and they started moving and dancing. I helped turn it into an artistic medium and a community, an educative creative space where they used those art forms to connect their stories. Then they realized, 'Oh yeah! I'm not the only one that feels this way at the end of the day.' Through dance and storytelling they began to move from feeling their frustration and anger, to in-house community building, to political commentary.

"Through this kind of embodiment, something else opens up—a different space, a different way of seeing the world, a different language, and even a different sort of courage around thinking about possibilities."

There were close to one hundred young women and men assembled in the large meeting room at the Allied Media Conference (AMC) in Detroit. They were gathered in groups around the perimeter of the space based on the city and grassroots organization they were representing. Each group of four to seven teens, along with their adult mentor, was busy setting up tables with poster boards announcing their organization's name in colorful tags, CD players blasting their voices rhyming over beats and melodic tracks, MacBooks streaming YouTube images of their work, digital camcorders poised to record and handmade business cards. These high- and low-tech marketing tools were laid out with efficient precision, as if the youth had moved through this conference choreography a dozen times before. The Allied Media Conference, now in its 10th year, was established as a creative and strategic planning space to devise alternative ways to utilize media in service of social justice. *Social justice media* here are defined to include the revolutionizing of mainstream, privatized television and radio, as well as grassroots initiatives to develop publishing houses, recording studios, innovative approaches to cyberspace, and the limitless options provided through the performing arts.

I was attending the AMC with five young women from BlackLight, the project I co-founded with two of the members less than a year previously. The AMC organizers invited us to present our arts activist methodology at the youth summit portion of the conference to provide an example of a different model for raising social awareness. The bulk of the 3-hour summit was devoted to showcasing the work of youth-focused organizations through round robin interactive presentations. Half of the youth organizers facilitated ten-minute workshops for the other youth groups as they sequentially made their way to each of their posts. When the last group completed the round, the facilitators and participants switched roles and the sharing cycle repeated. Gina, Tia, Felicia,

Destiny and Kendra[1], the core members of BlackLight, planned a workshop intentionally designed to demand the full commitment of their peers. When each new collective of energized, talkative youth approached our table, the young women took turns briefly introducing the purpose of the BlackLight project ("we use artistic expression to get people to think more creatively about addressing problems in our community"), and then asked the youth to talk about the concerns they had with the local and global communities in which they live and/or identified.

We listened intently, captivated by the eloquence of young men and women from North Carolina expressing their frustration with the effects of gentrification in Durham; young men in their early twenties from a community organization in Cincinnati detailing what the city (my hometown) has been like for black youth after the "riots";[2] kids from a Brooklyn high school describing the work they are doing to connect their experiences to youth in Palestine with hip-hop acting as the global mediator and translator of their parallel life narratives; and the witty insights of young women discussing what led to their organizing efforts to increase accessibility for physically and mentally challenged girls and women in Chicago's public spaces. The BlackLight young women recorded these stories as the passionate youth spoke directly into our ipod, and then instructed the participants to use the modeling clay, markers, finger paints, butcher paper and CD player we provided at our post to document the residue from their stories. The residue, from the BlackLight perspective, is the emotional impact of living in underresourced communities that is left out in the linearity of storytelling. Residue creates the invisible fissures in low-income urban neighborhoods that often are recast in academic and policy discourse as generalized behaviors and phenomena of cultural deprivation and despair.

With these new artistic tools, the young people reconstructed the problems and reimagined potential solutions for their communities through frameworks inspired by their own creativity and the rearticulation of residue. During this part of our session, Tia and I stayed with the visiting group while the other four members of BlackLight migrated to the hallway to translate the oral narratives into movement. Working with very little time, but propelled by the words of their peers, the girls choreographed a corporeal response to the social commentaries they had just witnessed. Five minutes later, they returned to the conference room to represent the participants' stories through the perspective of their dancing bodies. Limp torsos barely suspending rigid arms in space reflected both the powerlessness and resistance in the fight for affordable, decent urban housing. Destiny and Gina made bridges with their backs that Kendra and Felicia stepped over to symbolize the effectiveness of coalition building and community support. The young men and women in our interactive audience were impressed with

---

1. All names that appear in this essay are pseudonyms.
2. On April 7, 2001, Timothy Thomas, a 19-year-old black man was fatally shot by a Cincinnati police officer. His death was the 15th fatality involving young black men under the age of 40 between 1995 and 2001. The riots or, depending on your perspective, community protests after Thomas' death lasted a little over a week.

their own powers of persuasion as they watched their perspectives replayed and projected through the dancers' bodies. Exclamations of "That's the joint!" and "What?! Do that, then!" by the intrigued participants were quickly replaced by comparisons between BlackLight's choreography and the poetic verses the young people had written on butcher paper and the abstract shapes they molded with dollar store clay. These poems, drawings, and sculptures in progress became an alternative representation of their community and personal histories, and, thus, provided new ways of seeing and imagining possibilities for action.

The youth summit at the Allied Media Conference is just one example of a venue where the social justice and cultural redefining work of young people of color is acknowledged for its impact on events in the public sphere at the level of reeducation, awareness raising, and eventual policy change. Although these youth cultural workers are practicing ethnographers and agents of social change in their neighborhoods, they are all too often visible only as social problems and threats to the safety of a public that does not always include them. * * *

In this essay, I use the resistance work of residents at the Fresh Start shelter for young women in Detroit and BlackLight, an arts-based social justice project that emerged from the shelter, as the frame to consider * * * tensions within public anthropology. I am particularly concerned with what is at stake in the processes of both defining and practicing public anthropology for minority scholars working against the traditional boundaries of the academy and the public. * * * The work of the young women of Black-Light ultimately presents one model for mobilizing publicly engaged anthropology and also calls for a reconsideration of power and its multiple, tricky manifestations in the public sphere. * * *

As an African American female anthropologist, I continue to grapple with both the ethics and professional career consequences of attempting truly collaborative research with a group of which I both consider myself a part and also understand myself to be "studying" and, therefore, separate from. I am curious about the implications of practicing public anthropology as a minority scholar under these circumstances. In large part, my concerns are responsive to the current political climate that urgently demands our academic scholarship have relevancy beyond the university campus or the limited group of colleagues that gather annually to listen to us read the analysis of our work in small conference rooms. In many ways, whether the discussion focuses on increasingly distracted students or the daily life tragedies that play out outside our office doors, down the street, around the corner, in our own neighborhoods, in our own families, the public—however you choose to define it—presents us, yet again, with the charge of accountability.

*　　*　　*

My decision to work as the director of the Fresh Start homeless shelter where I was also conducting fieldwork was, perhaps, the ultimate double transgression of anthropology's boundaries. Already a suspect insider based on my black female identity and decision to conduct research among a largely black female population, I had now put myself in the position of being identified solely as an advocate or activist. Although the word activist is an esteemed label in the community where I grew up and a moniker that recalls a history of courageous struggle in my mind, it is not a term that always aligns well with traditional definitions of legitimate scholarship.

On the other hand, in the institutional context of the Fresh Start shelter and the larger context of the grassroots and non-profit community in Detroit, the standards for my validation were negotiated along the lines of legitimate advocacy. In these nonacademic settings, the sincerity of my activism was threatened by my university affiliation. * * *

[An] overtly expressed intentional application of knowledge and scholarly expertise to improve lives and solve social predicaments is, from my perspective, public anthropology.

Public anthropology is, indeed, both intellectually curious and action oriented and, as such, erases the lines drawn between scholarship and activism, academy and community. * * * I acknowledge both my power and marginalization as a minority anthropologist. Representing largely African American low-income urban communities in my work, I have also witnessed the power and marginalization of members of these communities as they move through public spaces and assert their voices in the public sphere. * * *

The precursor to BlackLight was a dance and creative writing program led by residents of the Fresh Start homeless shelter where I held the position of Director for two and a half years. * * *

The Fresh Start Shelter

The Fresh Start shelter and transitional living program for young women was established in 1987 after a concerned group of community residents in southwest Detroit noticed girls and young women hanging out on the streets during school hours and participating in various risky behaviors, including what appeared to be street-level prostitution and drug trafficking. These concerned citizens opened Fresh Start on the day the first 16-year-old girl came knocking on the door even though, at the time, the shelter was without funding, staff or even a name. This Fresh Start origin story is told and retold at fund-raising and informational events as an example of the power of community awareness and civic participation to transform young lives. The five volunteers who ran the shelter for the first year have been described as embodying "the spirit of true grassroots advocacy." Just a little over 20 years later, the shelter can now accommodate up to 40 young women between the ages of 15 and 21 including their children. The curriculum and case management services provided in addition to room and board now include counseling; health screening; job training and educational support; parenting classes for both young women and their partners; housing assistance; and financial literacy and life skills workshops. These facility and programmatic expansions have taken

Fresh Start a long way from the original 12-bed shelter housed on the second floor of a small Episcopal church.

Fresh Start exists in the context of Detroit, a metropolis that has been called "the nation's poorest big city," "the nation's murder capital," and "the city of ruins" and that has maintained a stigmatized identity in the popular media since the riots of 1967. Detroit is also known as a "chocolate city," an overwhelmingly black city (a little over 85 percent of the metropolitan Detroit population is African American) where one out of three residents in 2005 were living below the poverty line and nearly half of all children under the age of 17 were living in homes defined as impoverished (Montemurri et al. 2005). The "hard-knock life" image of the city combined with its racialization as a black space has coalesced in a reputation that is alternately worn like a badge of honor or hidden like a mark of shame by many Detroiters depending on the circumstances and what may be gained through choosing either representation or denial. The young predominantly African American residents of Fresh Start see themselves reflected through Detroit, a geographic space that symbolizes collective black urban poverty. Like Detroit, they have been saddled with labels such as "poor," "at-risk," "high-risk," "high school dropout," and "teen mother" that do more to conceal than describe. * * *

While I was working as the shelter director and even after I resigned and played various roles from volunteer dance instructor to board member, I felt the frustration along with the staff and residents of trying to effectively operate within the shelter's visibility as a public institution and its scrutiny by the public as a solution to the social problems of youth homelessness, unemployment, and undereducation. Everyone from federal grantors and foundation officers to interns and neighborhood residents had an idea of how to "fix those troubled girls" so that they could "make up for their mistakes" or "join the rest of society." * * * Although some individuals were able to cite the potential structural issues that frame the Fresh Start residents' experiences, the final explanatory analysis they offered generally included some questioning of the young women's moral character, problematic nature, or failure to follow familial, school or other institutional rules.

*   *   *

Performing Protest: The Head Scarf Incident

* * * At Fresh Start, the mandate to help homeless and high-risk young women (who also happen to be predominantly African American) become economically and socially mobile is severely challenged by the realities of a city where unemployment and high school dropout rates are among the highest in the nation. In this context, the shelter staff often found focusing on residents' appearance and enforcing informal codes of respectability a more realizable goal than combating the city's disparities—self-improvement being more feasible than social change. Therefore, when a young woman returned to the

shelter after an 8-hour day of waiting for buses, walking down long boulevards, meeting with surly managers, and filling out outdated applications, she would be expected to objectively hear and apply codes of respectability (disguised as job readiness strategies) such as making stronger eye contact and lowering the height of her heels so that she might win a job at Forever 21, Payless Shoes, or Cinnabon.

It seemed as if the attention the shelter staff paid to the residents' personal appearance and self-presentation increased in direct proportion to the decrease in opportunities for young under-skilled women in Detroit, as well as the decrease in morale among Detroiters battling the effects of high unemployment, corruption in the local government, and a devastated reputation based on these and other persistent struggles. The sense of powerlessness among the Fresh Start staff to insure that the residents could truly succeed in this environment was manifest in the implementation of rules such as "no head scarves allowed." The headscarf rule was a policy created by the shelter staff that forbade the young women from wearing the brightly colored bandanas and silk kerchiefs they tied around their heads to maintain their hairstyles in the public and common areas of the shelter such as the activity room, lobby, and administrative areas. The residents argued that the headscarves extended the life of their relatively expensive hairstyles, and were, thus, a cost-saving strategy in line with what they were being taught in the shelter's financial literacy classes. The shelter staff, however, called the headscarves "ghetto" and claimed they mocked the environment of professionalism and productivity the shelter was trying to promote. The disagreement culminated in a protest by the residents who refused to go out on job searches or attend the mandatory educational workshop for 1 week. * * * The protest represented the residents' discomfort with the shift in the implementation of the Fresh Start program from a focus on building actual skills and knowledge to cultivating the appearance of the acquisition of skill and knowledge through the performance of respectability. * * * The young women were also protesting the representation of the black female body as a social problem through the inordinate amount of attention paid to their physical presentations and public behaviors.

*   *   *

After the controversy surrounding the head scarf incident subsided, the shelter residents who coordinated the protest formed a dance and creative writing group that provided classes and workshops for other Fresh Start residents and staff. This creative movement became the space within, yet apart from, the shelter where the residents could practice identifying themselves and articulating the intersecting forces that shape but did not wholly determine their lives—a way to both name and voice. It also became a space for the residents to relieve the toxins of stress and frustration and repair the ruptured shelter community. The practices of identifying inequities, protesting and healing through the creative arts exhibited during both the headscarf incident and the subsequent performing arts program have become the guiding principles of Black-Light's performance activism in the larger Detroit community outside of the shelter.

Blacklight: Performance Ethnography
and Anthropology of the Public

* * *

The workshop at the Allied Media Conference, although greatly condensed, incorporated all the key elements of the BlackLight working methodology: community-identified issues and concerns; uncensored space to voice these issues and concerns; creative expression as an alternate way of both articulating and hearing calls against social injustice; the body as the site of intervention and central tool of expression; translation of written and spoken words into movement; and open dialogue about new solutions to old problems. BlackLight deploys all of these elements to demonstrate the potential for performance to be "an act of intervention, method of resistance, form of criticism, and a new way of revealing agency (Denzin 2003:8)." The Fresh Start shelter and the Allied Media Conference are both private spaces with captive, primarily youth audiences. This, however, is not the case for the majority of BlackLight's work that occurs on the street and in other public spaces such as monthly community center gatherings among diverse intergenerational, often unsuspecting participants/performers. Here, BlackLight typically introduces the work by starting with a performance that includes a combination of dance and poetry. This opening performance highlights the disruption of the traditional audience/performer boundary that takes place later in the workshop when the audience becomes participants performing their response to the individual concerns they bring to the collective stage.

* * *

The creative work BlackLight brings to the community treats political acts as pedagogical and performative and as part of the radical performative social science necessary for nurturing democratic culture (Denzin 2003). This arts-based methodology opens new spaces for social citizenship as public anthropology becomes anthropology of the public. The testimonies of community members are integral to the ethnographic aspect of the BlackLight project where the stories people tell and the opinions they offer become, like interviews that take place on any other site, part of BlackLight's field notes. Transcription and analysis of the interview texts happens on site, in the moment and are collaborative processes between the BlackLight ethnographers and the community members who read themselves and each other through their performances. The public here both practices and remakes ethnography while contributing to entirely new techniques for achieving community engagement, social justice awareness and grassroots activism. The public in the BlackLight process is also participating in the construction of new spaces where they can reclaim their stake in their own communities and their rights as residents, citizens and human beings to define themselves outside of identities that have been imposed on them from sources outside of their community. Thus, the BlackLight public workshops and street performances are forums for deliberation where community members begin to consciously re-present themselves and contradict the identities constructed for them through the systems of the state. * * *

In BlackLight's street performances, young black women are present as more than vulnerable bodies in hostile spaces. On street corners and in empty lots, blighted spaces that have been the preoccupation of urban social scientists for decades, theory and practice meld in performances where cultural theorists emerge from this new public in the BlackLight audience. Tia developed an interactive street theatre activity that demonstrates the social critique that takes place in and among marginalized publics. This exercise was a riff on the concept of the ubiquitous street performances found in the subways and high-traffic blocks of major cities. In this exercise, Tia and the other young women performed one of their dance/spoken word pieces on a central street corner in Detroit. However, instead of the overturned hat usually set out in front of performers to collect money from passersby, their hat was filled with slips of paper on which were written statistics about the city, such as the decline in available jobs and number of single female-headed households, as well as headlines from local and national newspapers reporting city events from a range of perspectives. The girls previewed only the briefest part of their performance to get the attention of people on the street. In order to see the Blacklight performers complete their piece, an individual had to select a piece of paper from the hat and respond to the message it carried. The young performers saw this creative intervention as a way to engage the street corner audience in dialogue about critical issues impacting the city. In this public arena in the midst of buses flying by and pedestrians making their way home, the young women of BlackLight made room in the public discourse of the inner city to include the Detroiters most often talked about but excluded from critical engagement in these discussions. We watched as one person's rebuttal to media circulated facts quickly turned into a spontaneous, public colloquium. * * * In this simple performance act, the BlackLight artists reconstitute the public space of Detroit neighborhoods where the visual representation of the black bodies there are tethered to stigmatized identities rooted largely in this geography, while the public face of these neighborhoods concurrently is represented through the degradation of blackness, urban youth, and the poor.

*   *   *

The ability to critically deconstruct the way they have been constructed through popular media, legislative discourse, and within their own homes is the light BlackLight shines on the shadows in the corners of my own anthropological project. * * * And yet, in my desire to transcend a traditional western methodology of speaking for others, I find myself struggling with how to truly speak with the young women whose lives are embedded in and reflective of my own, yet vastly different. * * * Even with the powerful political implications of their public workshops and street theatre activities, the overtly political aspect of their work is just one part of why the young women are invested in the project. The other significant element that fuels their dedication is joy. Dancing, writing, debating, and forming new dialogical spaces within their communities makes them, on the most fundamental level, feel good. This creative activist work additionally infuses them with the confidence of knowing that what they do and say matters and impacts how others envision agency in their lives. Releasing the residue of externally imposed ways of being and recovering a sense of self is profoundly satisfying to the BlackLight young women who define themselves first and foremost as artists.

ENGAGING THE TEXT, ENGAGING THE WORLD

- Describe the ways that residents of the Fresh Start shelter use creative expression to raise awareness of key social issues.

- How do the young women in the shelter use ethnographic strategies in creating their performances?

- Describe the debate in the shelter over wearing headscarves and the conflict between the performance of respectability and the acquisition of skills and knowledge for social and economic mobility.

- Why does Cox suggest that arts activism is a particularly effective model for community organizing and raising social awareness?

- How does Cox define public anthropology?

- Public anthropology, she argues, presents anthropologists with the responsibility to be accountable. Who are anthropologists accountable to?

- Cox states that her decision to work as director of the Fresh Start shelter while conducting fieldwork created a double bind between the academy and the community. Describe why her public anthropology was a challenge in both arenas.

Glossary

agency The potential power of individuals and groups to contest cultural norms, values, mental maps of reality, symbols, institutions, and structures of power.

Anthropocene The current historical era in which human activity is reshaping the planet in permanent ways.

anthropologist's toolkit The tools needed to conduct fieldwork, including information, perspectives, strategies and even equipment.

anthropology The study of the full scope of human diversity, past and present, and the application of that knowledge to help people of different backgrounds better understand one another.

art All ideas, forms, techniques, and strategies that humans employ to express themselves creatively and to communicate their creativity and inspiration to others.

band A small kinship-based group of foragers who hunt and gather for a living over a particular territory.

biomedicine A practice, often associated with Western medicine, that seeks to apply the principles of biology and the natural sciences to the practice of diagnosing disease and promoting healing.

chiefdom An autonomous political unit composed of a number of villages or communities under the permanent control of a paramount chief.

class A system of power based on wealth, income, and status that creates an unequal distribution of a society's resources.

core countries Industrialized former colonial states that dominate the world economic system.

critical medical anthropology An approach to the study of health and illness that analyzes the impact of inequality and stratification within systems of power on individual and group health outcomes.

cultural anthropology The study of people's communities, behaviors, beliefs, and institutions, including how people make meaning as they live, work, and play together.

cultural capital The knowledge, habits, and tastes learned from parents and family that individuals can use to gain access to scarce and valuable resources in society.

cultural construction of gender The ways humans learn to behave as a man or woman and to recognize behaviors as masculine or feminine within their cultural context.

cultural relativism Understanding a group's beliefs and practices within their own cultural context, without making judgments.

culture A system of knowledge, beliefs, patterns of behavior, artifacts, and institutions that are created, learned, shared, and contested by a group of people.

disease A discrete natural entity that can be clinically identified and treated by a health professional.

economy A cultural adaptation to the environment that enables a group of humans to use the available land, resources, and labor to satisfy their needs and to thrive.

enculturation The process of learning culture.

engaged anthropology Applying the research strategies and analytical perspectives of anthropology to address concrete challenges facing local communities and the world at large.

ethnic boundary marker A practice or belief, such as food, clothing, language, shared name, or religion, used to signify who is in a group and who is not.

ethnicity A sense of historical, cultural, and sometimes ancestral connection to a group of people who are imagined to be distinct from those outside the group.

ethnocentrism The belief that one's own culture or way of life is normal and natural; using one's own culture to evaluate and judge the practices and ideals of others.

ethnographic fieldwork A primary research strategy in cultural anthropology typically involving living and interacting with a community of people over an extended period to better understand their lives.

ethnomedicine Local systems of health and healing rooted in culturally specific norms and values.

field notes The anthropologist's written observations and reflections on places, practices, events, and interviews.

fine art Creative expression and communication often associated with cultural elites.

flexible accumulation The increasingly flexible strategies that corporations use to accumulate profits in an era of globalization, enabled by innovative communication and transportation technologies.

gender The expectations of thought and behavior that each culture assigns to people of different sexes.

gender ideology A set of cultural ideas, usually stereotypical, about the essential character of different genders that functions to promote and justify gender stratification.

gender performance The way gender identity is expressed through action.

gender stereotypes Widely held preconceived notions about the attributes of, differences between, and proper roles for men and women in a culture.

gender stratification An unequal distribution of power in which gender shapes who has access to a group's resources, opportunities, rights, and privileges.

gender studies Research into masculinity and femininity as flexible, complex, and historically and culturally constructed categories.

globalization The worldwide intensification of interactions and increased movement of money, people, goods, and ideas within and across national borders.

grammar The combined set of observations about the rules governing the formation of morphemes and syntax that guide language use.

health The absence of disease and infirmity, as well as the presence of physical, mental, and social well-being.

hegemony The ability of a dominant group to create consent and agreement within a population without the use or threat of force.

identity entrepreneurs Political, military, or religious leaders who promote a worldview through the lens of ethnicity and use war, propaganda, and state power to mobilize people against those whom they perceive as a danger.

illness The individual patient's experience of being unwell.

imagined community The invented sense of connection and shared traditions that underlies identification with a particular ethnic group or nation whose members likely will never all meet.

intersectionality An analytic framework for assessing how factors such as race, gender, and class interact to shape individual life chances and societal patterns of stratification.

key informant A community member who advises the anthropologist on community issues, provides feedback, and warns against cultural miscues. Also called cultural consultant.

kinship The system of meaning and power that cultures create to determine who is related to whom and to define their mutual expectations, rights, and responsibilities.

kinship analysis A fieldwork strategy of examining interlocking relationships of power built on marriage and family ties.

language A system of communication organized by rules that uses symbols such as words, sounds, and gestures to convey information.

life chances An individual's opportunities to improve quality of life and realize life goals.

magic The use of spells, incantations, words, and actions in an attempt to compel supernatural forces to act in certain ways, whether for good or for evil.

mapping The analysis of the physical and/ or geographic space where fieldwork is being conducted.

marriage A socially recognized relationship that may involve physical and emotional intimacy as well as legal rights to property and inheritance.

mental maps of reality Cultural classifications of what kinds of people and things exist, and the assignment of meaning to those classifications.

migration The movement of people within and between countries.

mutual transformation The potential for both the anthropologist and the members of the community being studied to be transformed by the interactions of fieldwork.

nation-state A political entity, located within a geographic territory with enforced borders, where the population shares a sense of culture, ancestry, and destiny as a people.

neoliberalism An economic and political worldview that sees the free market as the main mechanism for ensuring economic growth, with a severely restricted role for government.

norms Ideas or rules about how people should behave in particular situations or toward certain other people.

nuclear family The kinship unit of mother, father, and children.

origin myths A story told about the founding and history of a particular group to reinforce a sense of common identity.

participant observation A key anthropological research strategy involving both participation in and observation of the daily life of the people being studied.

periphery countries The least developed and least powerful nations; often exploited by the core countries as sources of raw materials, cheap labor, and markets.

pilgrimage A religious journey to a sacred place as a sign of devotion and in search of transformation and enlightenment.

polyvocality The practice of using many different voices in ethnographic writing and research question development, allowing the reader to hear more directly from the people in the study.

popular art Creative expression and communication often associated with the general population.

power The ability or potential to bring about change through action or influence.

profane Anything that is considered unholy.

race A flawed system of classification, with no biological basis, that uses certain physical characteristics to divide the human population into supposedly discrete groups.

racism Individual thoughts and actions and institutional patterns and policies that create unequal access to power, privilege, resources, and opportunities based on imagined differences among groups.

reflexivity A critical self-examination of the role the anthropologist plays and an awareness that one's identity affects one's fieldwork and theoretical analyses.

religion A set of beliefs and rituals based on a unique vision of how the world ought to be, often focused on a supernatural power and lived out in community.

rite of passage A category of ritual that enacts a change of status from one life stage to another, either for an individual or for a group.

ritual An act or series of acts regularly repeated over years or generations that embody the beliefs of a group of people and create a sense of continuity and belonging.

sacred Anything that is considered holy.

sex The observable physical differences between male and female, especially biological differences related to human reproduction.

sexuality The complex range of desires, beliefs, and behaviors that are related to erotic physical contact and the cultural arena within which people debate about what kinds of physical desires and behaviors are right, appropriate, and natural.

social mobility The movement of one's class position, upward or downward, in stratified societies.

social movement Collective group actions that seek to build institutional networks to transform cultural patterns and government policies.

social network analysis A method for examining relationships in a community, often conducted by identifying whom people turn to in times of need.

sociolinguistics The study of the ways culture shapes language and language shapes culture, particularly the intersection of language with cultural categories and systems of power such as race, gender, class, and age.

state An autonomous regional structure of political, economic, and military rule with a central government authorized to make laws and use force to maintain order and defend its territory.

stratification The uneven distribution of resources and privileges among participants in a group or culture.

symbol Anything that represents something else.

syntax The specific patterns and rules for combining morphemes to construct phrases and sentences.

thick description A research strategy that combines detailed description of cultural activity with an analysis of the layers of deep cultural meaning in which those activities are embedded.

time-space compression The rapid innovation of communication and transportation technologies associated with globalization that transforms the way people think about space (distances) and time.

tribe Originally viewed as a culturally distinct, multiband population that imagined itself as one people descended from a common ancestor; currently used to describe an indigenous group with its own set of loyalties and leaders living to some extent outside the control of a centralized authoritative state.

uneven development The unequal distribution of the benefits of globalization.

values Fundamental beliefs about what is important, what makes a good life, and what is true, right, and beautiful.

References

Abdul Ghafar, Ismail. 2010. *Money, Islamic Banks and the Real Economy.* Singapore: Cengage Learning.

Abu-Lughod, Lila. 1986. *Veiled Sentiments: Honor and Poetry in a Bedouin Society.* Berkeley: University of California Press.

———. 1990. "The Romance of Resistance: Tracing Transformations of Power Through Bedouin Women." *American Ethnologist* 17(1):41–55.

ACT UP/Chicago. 1992. "AIDS Activist News (ACT UP/Chicago newsletter)." Summer: 1–12. Document housed in my personal ACT UP archive.

ACT UP/New York. 1987. Leaflet. "National AIDS Demonstration at the White House." Document housed in my personal ACT UP archive.

Adams, Kenneth Alan. 1981. "Arachnophobia: Love American Style." *Journal of Psychoanalytic Anthropology* 4(2):157–97.

Adamson, Joni, Mei Mei Evans, and Rachel Stein, eds. 2002. *The Environmental Justice Reader: Politics, Poetics, and Pedagogy.* Tucson: University of Arizona Press.

Africa News. 2002. "Lesotho: Union to fight second-hand clothing retail." May 15.

Agamben, Giorgio. 1998. *Homo Sacer: Sovereign Power and Bare Life.* Palo Alto, CA: Stanford University Press.

———2005. *State of Exception.* Translated by Kevin Attell. Chicago: University of Chicago Press.

Agency for Toxic Substances and Diseases Registry (ATSDR). 1994. "Health Consultation Final Release."

Ahearn, L. M. 2003. Writing Desire in Nepali Love Letters. *Language & Communication* 23(2), 107–22.

Ahmed, Leila. 1992. *Women and Gender in Islam.* New Haven, CT: Yale University Press.

Aitken, Hugh. 1960. *Scientific Management in Action: Taylorism at the Watertown Arsenal.* Princeton: Princeton University Press.

Alberts, Bruce, et al. 1983. *Molecular Biology of the Cell.* New York: Garland.

Alexander, M. Jacqui. 2005. *Pedagogies of Crossing: Meditations on Feminism, Sexual Politics, Memory, and the Sacred.* Durham, NC: Duke University Press.

Allan, Stuart, and Einar Thorsen, eds. 2009. *Citizen Journalism: Global Perspectives.* New York: Peter Lang.

American Lung Association. 2002. "Asthma: An Impact Assessment." September.

———. 2004. *Trends in Asthma Morbidity and Mortality.* April. New York: Epidemiology and Statistics Unit Research and Scientific Affairs.

Amin, Ash, ed. 1994. *Post-Fordism: A Reader.* Oxford: Blackwell.

Anderson, Stuart. 2013. "How Many More Deaths? The Moral Case for a Temporary Worker Program." National Foundation for American Policy Policy Brief. March.

Angel-Ajani, Asale. 2004. "Expert witness: Notes toward revisiting the politics of listening." *Anthropology and Humanism* 29:133–44.

Anderson, Benedict. 1983. *Imagined Communities: Reflections on the Origin and Spread of Nationalism.* London: Verso.

Appadurai, Arjun, ed. 1986. *The Social Life of Things: Commodities in Cultural Perspective.* Cambridge: Cambridge University Press.

Arditti, Rita, Renate Klein, and Shelley Minden. 1984. *Test-Tube Women.* London: Pandora.

Arney, William Ray and Bernard Bergen. 1984. *Medicine and the Management of Living* Chicago: University of Chicago Press.

Associated Press. 2009. "Grandma: Octuplets Mom Obsessed with Kids." MSNBC.com, January 31. Electronic document, http://www.msnbc.msn.com/id/28948599, accessed January 31, 2009.

Auerbach, Nina. 1982. *Woman and the Demon.* Cambridge, MA: Harvard University Press.

Baltz, Jay and Richard A. Cone. 1985. "What Force Is Needed to Tether a Sperm?" Abstract for Society of the Study of Reproduction.

———. 1986. "Flagellar Torque on the Head Determines the Force Needed to Tether a Sperm." Abstract for Biophysical Society.

Baltz, Jay M., David F. Katz, and Richard A. Cone. 1988. "The Mechanics of the Sperm–Egg Interaction at the Zona Pellucida." *Biophysical Journal* 54(4):643–54.

Bank for International Settlements. 2016. "About Derivatives Statistics." www.bis.org/statistics/about_derivatives_stats.htm

Bartolomé, Miguel. 2000. *El Encuentro de la Gente y los Insensatos: La Sedentarizacion de los Cazadores Ayoreo en el Chaco Paraguayo.* Asunción, Paraguay: CEADUC, 308.

Basu, Ellen Oxfeld. 1991. "Profit, Loss, Fate: The Entrepreneurial Ethic and the Practice of Gambling in an Overseas Chinese Community," *Modern China* 17(2):227–59.

Baudrillard, Jean. 1994. *Simulacra and Simulation.* Ann Arbor: University of Michigan Press.

Baulch, E. 2007. *Making Scenes: Reggae, Punk, and Death Metal in 1990s Bali.* Durham, NC: Duke University Press.

Baxstrom, Richard. 2008. *Houses in Motion: The Experience of Place and the Problem of Belief in Urban Malaysia.* Stanford, Calif.: Stanford University Press.

Been, Vicki. 1993. "What's Fairness Got to Do with It? Environmental Justice and the Siting of Locally Undesirable Land Uses." *Cornell Law Review* 78:1001–1005.

Been, Vicki, and F. Gupta. 1997. "Coming to the Nuisance or Going to the Barrio? A Longitudinal Analysis of Environmental Justice Claims." *Ecology Law Quarterly* 24:1–56.

Beeson, Mark. 2000. "Mahathir and the Markets: Globalisation and the Pursuit of Economic Autonomy in Malaysia." *Pacific Affairs* 73(3):335–51.

Beldecos, A., et al. 1988. "The Importance of Feminist Critique for Contemporary Cell Biology," *Hypatia* 3(1):61–76.

Benjamin, Walter. 1999 [1921]. "Critique of Violence." In *Selected Writings*, vol. 1. Edited by Marcus Bullock and Michael Jennings. Cambridge, MA: Harvard University Press.

Bessire, Lucas. 2014. *Behold the Black Caiman: A Chronicle of Ayoreo Life.* Chicago: University of Chicago Press.

Bigsten, A. and R. Wicks. 1996. "Used-clothes exports to the Third World: Economic considerations." *Development Policy Review* 14:379–390.

Binkin, Martin, and Mark J. Eitelberg. 1982. *Blacks and the Military.* Washington, D.C.: Brookings.

Black, Kate. 1996. *Fighting for Life: Lesbians in ACT UP.* Masters thesis, University of Kentucky.

Blackwood, Evelyn. 1995a. "Falling in Love with An-Other Lesbian: Reflections on Identity in Fieldwork." In *Taboo: Sex, Identity and Erotic Subjectivity in Anthropological Fieldwork*, edited by Don Kulick and Margaret Willson. Pp. 51–75. London: Routledge.

———. 1995b. "Senior Women, Model Mothers, and Dutiful Wives: Managing Gender Contradictions in a Minangkabau Village. In *Bewitching Women, Pious Men: Gender and Body Politics in Southeast Asia*, edited by Aihwa Ong and Michael Peletz. Pp. 124–158. Berkeley: University of California Press.

Bloemen, S. 2001. *T-shirt travels: A documentary on second-hand clothes and Third World debt in Zambia.* Video. New York: Grassroots Pictures.

Bodnar, John. 1985. *The Transplanted: A History of Immigrants in Urban America.* Bloomington: Indiana University Press.

Boellstorff, T. 2008. *Coming of Age in Second Life: An Anthropologist Explores the Virtually Human.* Princeton, NJ: Princeton University Press.

Bolin, Anne. 1994. "Transcending and Transgendering: Male-to-Female Transsexuals, Dichotomy and Diversity. In *Third Sex, Third Gender: Beyond Sexual Dimorphism in Culture and History*, edited by Gilbert Herdt. Pp. 447–485. New York: Zone Books.

Bonner, Philip. 1990. "Desirable or undesirable Basotho women? Liquor, prostitution, and the migration of Basotho women to the Rand, 1920–1945." In *Women and gender in Southern Africa to 1945*, edited by Cheryl Walker. Pp. 221–50. Cape Town: David Philip/London: James Currey.

Braverman, Harry. 1974. *Labor and Monopoly Capital.* New York: Monthly Review Press.

Bright, J. S. n.d. *Lively Love Letters.* New Delhi: Goodwill.

Brokaw, Cynthia Joanne. 1991. *The Ledgers of Merit and Demerit: Social Change and Moral Order in Late Imperial China.* Princeton, NJ: Princeton University Press.

Brown, Francis J. 1946. *Educational Opportunities for Veterans.* Washington, D.C.: Public Affairs Press, American Council on Public Affairs.

Bryers, Alex. 2014. "#Ferguson: Social Media More Spark than Solution." Politico.com, August 20. http://www.politico.com /story/2014/08/ferguson-social-media -more-spark-than-solution-110202.html, accessed October 15, 2014.

Bullard, Robert. 2000. *Dumping in Dixie: Race, Class and Environmental Quality.* 3rd edition. Boulder, CO: Westview Press.

Bullough, Bonnie, Vern Bullough, and John Elias, eds. 1997. *Gender Blending.* Amherst, NY: Prometheus.

Bunnell, Tim. 2004. *Malaysia, Modernity and the Multimedia Super Corridor: A Critical Geography of Intelligent Landscapes.* London: Routledge Curzon.

Burawoy, Michael. 1985. *The Politics of Production.* London: Verso.

Burawoy, Michael, and Janos Lukács. 1992. *The Radiant Past: Ideology and Reality in Hungary's Road to Capitalism.* Chicago: University of Chicago Press.

BusinessWorld (Philippines). 2001. "Second-hand stores may be conduits for illegal drug trading. September 7.

Butchart, Alexander. 1998. *The anatomy of power. European constructions of the African body.* London and New York: Zed Books.

Butler, Kim D. 1998. *Freedoms Given, Freedoms Won: Afro-Brazilians in Post-Abolition São Paolo and Salvador.* New Brunswick, NJ: Rutgers University Press.

Butler, Judith. 1991. "Imitation and Gender Insubordination." In *Inside/Out: Lesbian Theories, Gay Theories*, edited by Diana Fuss. Pp. 13–31. New York: Routledge.

Campbell, Nancy. 2000. *Using Women: Gender, Drug Policy, and Social Justice.* New York: Routledge.

Carrier, Joseph M. 1995. *De Los Otros: Intimacy and Homosexuality among Mexican Men.* New York: Columbia University Press.

Casper, Steven, and Bob Hancké. 1999. "Global Quality Norms within National Production Regimes: ISO 9000 Standards in the French and German Car Industries." *Organization Studies* 20(6): 961–85.

Castells, M. 2000. *The Information Age: Economy, Society, and Culture.* Malden, MA: Blackwell.

Center for Policy Alternatives. 1994. *Toxic Wastes and Race Revisited.* Washington, DC: Center for Policy Alternatives.

Chau, Adam Yuet. 2006. *Miraculous Response: Doing Popular Religion in Contemporary China.* Stanford, CA: Stanford University Press.

Chavis, Benjamin. 1993. "Foreword." In *Confronting Environmental Racism: Voices from the Grassroots*, edited by Robert Bullard. Pp. 3–5. Boston: South End.

Chin, Christine. 1998. *In Service and Servitude: Foreign Female Domestic Workers and the Malaysian "Modernity" Project.* New York: Columbia University Press.

Çizakça, Murat. 2011. *Islamic Capitalism and Finance: Origins, Evolution and the Future.* Cheltenham, U.K.: Edward Elgar.

Cole, Alan. 1998. *Mothers and Sons in Chinese Buddhism.* Stanford, CA: Stanford University Press.

Commission for Racial Justice. 1987. Toxic Wastes and Race in the United States: A

National Report on the Racial and Socio-economic Characteristics of Communities with Hazardous Waste Sites. New York: United Church of Christ.

Cornelius, Wayne A. 2001. "Death at the Border: Efficacy and Unintended Consequences of US Immigration Control Policy." *Population and Development Review* 27(4):661–685.

Cromwell, Jason. In press. *Making the Visible Invisible: Transmen and Transmasculinities.* Urbana: University of Illinois Press.

D'Emilio, John. 1992. *Making Trouble: Essays on Gay History, Politics, and the University.* New York: Routledge, Chapman and Hall.

Dalfiume, Richard M. 1969. *Desegregation of the U.S. Armed Forces: Fighting on Two Fronts, 1939–1953.* Columbia: University of Missouri Press.

Damisch, L., Stoberock, B., Mussweiler, T. 2010. "Keep Your Fingers Crossed! How Superstition Improves Performance." *Psychological Science* July; 21(7): 1014–20.

Davis, Mike. 1990. *City of Quartz.* London: Verso.

———. 1998. *Ecology of Fear: Los Angeles and the Imagination of Disaster.* New York: Vintage.

Denzin, Norman K. 2003. *Performance Ethnography: Critical Pedagogy and the Politics of Culture.* Thousand Oaks: Sage Publications.

Department of Statistics Malaysia. 2010. "Population and Housing Census." http://www.statistics.gov.my/portal/index .php?option=com_content&view= article&id=1215%3Apopulation -distribution-and-basic-demographic -characteristic-report-population-and -housing-census-malaysia-2010 -updated-2972011&catid=130%3 Apopulation-distribution-and-basic -demographic-characteristic-report -population-and-housing-census -malaysia-2010&Itemid=154&lang=en (accessed August 31, 2013).

Devor, Holly. 1989. *Gender Blending: Confronting the Limits of Duality.* Bloomington: Indiana University Press.

Dick, H. W. 1985. "The Rise of a Middle Class and the Changing Concept of Equity in Indonesia: An Interpretation." *Indonesia* 39:71–92.

Dicken, Peter. 1992. *Global Shift: The Internationalization of Economic Activity.* New York: Guilford.

Doty, Roxanne. 2011. "Bare Life: Border-Crossing Deaths and the Spaces of Moral Alibi." *Environment and Planning D: Society and Space* 29:599–612.

Dougherty, Sean Thomas. 2006. "Killing the Messenger." *Massachusetts Review* 47(4): 608–616.

Dusuki, Asyraf Wajdi. 2010. "Can Bursa Malaysia's Suq Al-Sila' (Commodity Murabahah House) Resolve the Controversy over Tawarruq?" Kuala Lampur: International Shari'ah Research Academy for Islamic Finance.

Dyakonov, Sergei. 2002. Interview transcript, archived at Russian Archives Online. http://www.russianarchives.com/rao /catalogues/trans/yfs/yanks_serg_1.html.

Eberhard, Wolfram. 1967. *Guilt and Sin in Traditional China.* Berkeley: University of California Press.

Echols, John M., and Hassan Shadily. 1989. *Kamus Indonesia Inggris: An Indonesian-English Dictionary*, 3rd ed. Jakarta: PT Gramedia.

Eggan, Ferd. 1999. Interview conducted by Deborah Gould, October 30, in Chicago, IL. Interview housed in [Gould's] personal ACT UP archive.

Ehrenreich, Barbara. 1997. *Blood Rites.* London: Virago.

Elignon, John. 2014. "Michael Brown Spent Last Weeks Grappling with Problems and Promise." *New York Times*, August 24, 2014.

Elliston, Deborah. 1995. "Erotic Anthropology: "Ritualized Homosexuality" in Melanesia and Beyond." *American Ethnologist* 22:848–867.

Ellman, Mary. 1968. *Thinking about Women.* New York: Harcourt Brace Jovanovich.

Epprecht, Marc. 2000. *"This matter of women is getting very bad": Gender, development, and politics in colonial Lesotho.* Pietermaritzburg: University of Natal Press.

Epstein, Julia, and Kristina Straub, eds. 1991. *Body/Guards: The Cultural Politics of Gender Ambiguity.* New York: Routledge.

Epstein, Steven. 1999. "Gay and Lesbian Movements in the United States: Dilemmas of Identity, Diversity and Political Strategy." In *The Global Emergence of Gay and Lesbian Politics: National Imprints of a Worldwide Movement*, edited by Barry D. Adam, Jan Willem Duyvendak, and Andre Krouwel. Philadelphia: Temple University Press.

Ericksen, Thomas Hylland. 2010. *Ethnicity and Nationalism*, 3rd ed. Boulder, CO: Pluto Press.

Esposito, John L. 1998. *Islam and Politics*. Syracuse, N.Y.: Syracuse University Press.

Evers, Hans-Dieter. 2003. "Transition Towards a Knowledge Society: Malaysia and Indonesia in Comparative Perspective." *Comparative Sociology* 2(2):355–73.

Farmer, Paul E. 2004. "An Anthropology of Structural Violence (Sidney W. Mintz Lecture for 2001)." *Current Anthropology* 45, no. 3: 305–25.

———2002. "La violence structurelle et la matérialité du social." *Lettre du Collège de France*, no. 4 (2002).

———2004. *Pathologies of Power: Health, Human Rights, and the New War on the Poor*. Reprinted with a new preface by the author. Foreword by Amartya Sen. Berkeley: University of California Press. Originally published in 2003.

Farmer, Paul E., Bruce Nizeye, Sara Stulac, and Salmaan Keshavjee. 2006. "Structural Violence and Clinical Medicine." *PLoS Medicine* 3, no. 10: e449.

Feldman, G. 2003. *U.S.–African trade profile*. Washington, DC: Office of Africa.

Fischer, Johan. 2008. *Proper Islamic Consumption: Shopping among the Malays in Modern Malaysia*. Copenhagen: NIAS.

Fleck, Ludwik. 1979. *Genesis and Development of a Scientific Fact*, edited by Thaddeus J. Trenn and Robert K. Merton. Chicago: University of Chicago Press.

Florini, Sarah. 2014. "Tweets, Tweeps, and Signifyin': Communication and Cultural Performance on "Black Twitter."" *Television and New Media* 15(3):223–237.

Fogel, Daniel, and Suzanne Etcheverry. 1994. "Reforming the Economies of Central and Eastern Europe." In *Managing in Emerging Market Economies: Cases from the Czech and Slovak Republics*, edited by Daniel Fogel, 3–33. Boulder: Westview.

Foner, Jack. 1974. *Blacks and the Military in American History: A New Perspective*. New York: Praeger.

Foucault, Michel. 1977. *Discipline and Punish: The Birth of the Prison*. New York: Pantheon.

———. 1978. *The History of Sexuality: An Introduction*. New York: Random House

———. 1986. *The History of Sexuality: The Care of the Self*. New York: Random House.

Fremson, Ruth. 2001. Allure Must Be Covered. Individuality Peeks Through. *New York Times*, November 4: 14.

Galloway, Allison. 1997. "The Process of Decomposition: A Model from the Arizona-Sonoran Desert." In *Forensic Taphonomy: The Postmortem Fate of Human Remains*. Edited by W. D. Haglund and M. H. Sorg. Pp. 139–150. Boca Raton, FL: CRC Press.

Gamson, Josh. 1989. "Silence, Death, and the Invisible Enemy: AIDS Activism and Social Movement 'Newness.'" *Social Problems* 36(4): 351–367.

Ganong, William F. 1975. *Review of Medical Physiology*, 7th ed. Los Altos, CA: Lange Medical Publications.

GAO (Government Accountability Office). 2001. "INS's Southwest Border Strategy: Resource and Impact Issues Remain after Seven Years." Report to Congressional Requesters. www.gao.gov/new.items /doI842.pdf.

Garret, Kelly R., and Paul Resnick. 2011. "Resisting Political Fragmentation on the Internet." *Daedalus* 140(4):108–120.

Garrison, Jessica, and Kimi Yoshino. 2009. "Octuplets' Mother Obsessed with Children." LA Times, January 30. Electronic document, http://latimesblogs .latimes.com/lanow/2009/01/nadya -sulemans.html, accessed April 28, 2009.

Gellner. Ernest. 1983. *Nations and Nationalism*. Ithaca, NY: Cornell University Press.

Geraldo Rivera: "Leave The Hoodie At Home". 2012. YouTube video, 3:02, from Fox News Broadcast on March 23. Posted by tpmtv. https://youtube.com/watch?v =2Yyqkcc-a8U, accessed October 15, 2014.

Gerber, David. 1986. Introduction. In *Anti-Semitism in American History*, ed. Gerber, 3–56.

Gerke, S. 2000. "Global Lifestyles under Local Conditions: The New Indonesian Middle-Class." In *Consumption in Asia: Lifestyles and Identities*. Edited by B.-H. Chua. Pp. 135–158. London: Routledge.

Glauser, Benno. 2006. "Paraguay: Pueblos indígenas aislados." *Suplemento antropológico* 41, no. 2: 192.

———2007. "Su presencia protegé el Corazon del Chaco seco." In *Pueblos indígenas en aislamiento voluntario y contacto inicial en la Amazonia y el Gran Chaco*. Edited by Alejandro Parallada. Copenhagen: International Work Group for Indigenous Affairs, 220.

Goldenberg, Suzanne. 2002. "The Woman Who Stood Up to the Taliban." *The Guardian*, January 24. Electronic document, http://222.guardian.co.uk /afghanistan/story/0,1284,63840.

Goodman, Ellen. 1987. "Whose Right to Life?" *Baltimore Sun*, November 17.

Goody, J. 2000. *The Power of the Written Tradition*. Washington: Smithsonian Institution Press.

Goose, Stephen D., and Frank Smyth. 1994. "Arming Genocide in Rwanda—The High Cost of Small Arms Transfers." *Foreign Affairs* 73 (5): 86–96.

Gordon, Milton. 1964. *Assimilation in American Life*. New York: Oxford University Press.

Gordon, S. L. 1989. "Institutional and Impulsive Orientations in Selectively Appropriating Emotions to Self." Pp. 115–136 in *The Sociology of Emotions: Original Essays and Research Papers*, edited by David D. Franks and E. Doyle McCarthy. Greenwich, CT: JAI Press.

Gould, Deborah. 2000. "Sex, Death, and the Politics of Anger: Emotions and Reason in ACT UP's Fight Against AIDS." Doctoral dissertation, University of Chicago.

Gourevitch, Philip. 1998. *We Wish to Inform You That Tomorrow We Will Be Killed with Our Families: Stories from Rwanda*. New York: Farrar, Straus, and Giroux.

Gramsci, Antonio. 1971. *Selections from the Prison Notebooks of Antonio Gramsci*. Translated by Quintin Hoare and Geoffrey N. Smith. New York: International Publishers.

Grief, Avner. 1996. "Contracting, Enforcement, and Efficiency: Economics beyond the Law." In *Annual World Bank Conference on Development Economics 1996*, edited by Michael Bruno and Boris Pleskovic. Washington, DC: World Bank.

Guardian. 2004. "Clothes line." February 25.

Guyton, Arthur C. 1984. *Physiology of the Human Body*, 6th ed. Philadelphia: Saunders College Publishing.

Haggblade, S. 1990. "The flip side of fashion: Used clothing exports to the Third World." *Journal of Development Studies* 29(3)505–521.

Hall, S. 1977. "Culture, the Media, and the 'Ideological Effect'." In *Mass Communication and Society*. Edited by C. J. M. Gurevitch and J. Woollacott. Pp. 315–348. London: Edward Arnold.

Hansen, K.T. 1994. "Dealing with used clothing: *Salaula* and the construction of identity in Zambia's Third Republic." *Public Culture* 6: 503–523.

———. 2000. *Salaula: The world of second-hand clothing and Zambia*. Chicago: University of Chicago Press.

Hansen, Valerie. 1990. *Changing Gods in Medieval China, 1127–1276*. Princeton, NJ: Princeton University Press.

Harding, Rachel E. 2003. *A Refuge in Thunder: Candomblé and Alternative Spaces of Blackness*. Bloomington, IN: Indiana University Press.

Harrison, Faye. 2005. *Resisting Racism and Xenophobia: Global Perspectives on Race, Gender, and Human Rights*. Walnut Creek, CA: AltaMira Press.

Hartman, J.F., R.B. Gwatkin, and C.F. Hutchinson. 1972. "Early Contact Interactions between Mammalian Gametes *In Vitro*." *Proceedings of the National Academy of Sciences (U.S.)* 69(10):2767–69.

Harvey, David. 1989. *The Condition of Postmodernity: An Enquiry into the Origins of Cultural Change*. Oxford: Basil Blackwell.

————. 1990. *The Condition of Postmodernity: An Enquiry into the Origins of Cultural Change.* Malden, MA: Blackwell.

Hatfield, Donald John W. 2009. *Taiwanese Pilgrimages to China: Religion, Complicity, and Community.* New York: Palgrave.

Hearn, Jonathan. 2006. *Rethinking Nationalism: A Critical Introduction.* New York: Palgrave Macmillan.

Hefner, Robert. 2010. "Religious Resurgence in Contemporary Asia: Southeast Asian Perspectives on Capitalism, the State, and the New Piety." *Journal of Asian Studies* 69(4):1031–47.

Herdt, Gilbert, ed. 1994. *Third Sex, Third Gender: Beyond Sexual Dimorphism in Culture and History.* New York: Zone Books.

Heryanto, A. 1999. "The Years of Living Luxuriously: Identity Politics of Indonesia's New Rich." In *Culture and Privilege in Capitalist Asia.* Edited by M. Pinches. Pp. 159–187. New York: Routledge.

————. 2008. "Pop Culture and Competing Identities." In *Popular Culture in Indonesia: Fluid Identities in Post-Authoritarian Politics.* Edited by A. Heryanto. Pp. 1–36. London: Routledge.

Higham, John. 1955. *Strangers in the Land.* New Brunswick: Rutgers University Press.

Hill, D. T., and K. Sen. 2005. *The Internet in Indonesia's New Democracy.* London: Routledge.

Hippler, Mike. 1985. "A Year to Celebrate: Coming Up with New Strategies for Surviving in the Age of AIDS." *New York Native.* November 18–24, pp. 30–31.

Hou, Ching-lang. 1975. *Monnaies d'offrande et la notion de trésoserie dans la religion chinoise.* Paris: Collège de France.

Hsieh, Steven, and Raven Rakia. 2014. "After #Ferguson." *Nation.* October 27, 2014.

Hubbard, Ruth. 1983. "Have Only Men Evolved?" in *Discovering Reality: Feminist Perspectives on Epistemology, Metaphysics, Methodology, and Philosophy of Science,* edited by Sandra Harding and Merrill B. Hintikka. Dordrecht: Reidel.

Hurd, Charles. 1946. *The Veterans' Program: A Complete Guide to Its Benefits, Rights, and Options.* New York: McGraw-Hill.

Indonesian National News Agency. 2002. "Second-hand clothing banned." August 23.

Institute for Southern Studies. 1992. "States with High African American and Hispanic Populations Rank Worst on Environmental Health, According to 1991–1992 Green Index Report." News release, April 18.

International Campaign to Ban Landmines (ICBL). 1999. "Rwanda." *Landmine Monitor Report 1999: Toward a Mine-Free World.* www.icbl.org/lm/1999/rwanda.html (accessed July 12, 2009).

————. 2007. "Rwanda." *Landmine Monitor Report 2007: Toward a Mine-Free World.* www.icbl.org/lm/2007/rwanda.html (accessed July 12, 2009).

International Work Group for Indigenous Affairs. 2010. "The Case of the Ayoreo: Report 4." Copenhagen: International Work Group for Indigenous Affairs.

Iqbal, Munawar, and Philip Molyneux. 2005. *Thirty Years of Islamic Banking: History, Performance, and Prospects.* Houndmills, U.K.: Palgrave Macmillan.

Irwin, Susan, and Brigitte Jordan. 1987. "Knowledge, Practice, and Power: Court Ordered Cesarean Sections." *Medical Anthropology Quarterly* 1(3):319–34.

Iskandar, G. H. 2006. "Fuck You! We're from Bandung! –MK II." In *Resistensi Gaya Hidup: Teori dan Realitas.* Edited by A. Adlin. Pp. 270–283. Bandung: Forum Studi Kebudayaan, ITB.

ISRA (International Shariah Research Academy). 2009. "Responsibility Banking." ISRA *Bulletin*, April.

Jackson, John L. 2008. *Racial Paranoia: The Unintended Consequences of Political Correctness: The New Reality of Race in America.* New York: Basic Civitas.

Jacobs, Sue-Ellen, Wesley Thomas, and Sabine Lang, eds. 1997. *Two-Spirit People: Native American Gender Identity, Sexuality, and Spirituality.* Urbana: University of Illinois Press.

Jasper, James M. 1998. "The Emotions of Protest: Affective and Reactive Emotions in and around Social Movements." *Sociological Forum* 13(3): 397–424.

Jenkins, Richard. 1996. *Social Identity*. New York: Routledge.

Jewkes, Rachel, and Naeema Abrahms. 2002. "The epidemiology of rape and sexual coercion in South Africa: An overview." *Social Science and Medicine* 55:1231–44.

Johnson, Jesse J. 1967. *Ebony Brass: An Autobiography of Negro Frustration amid Aspiration*. New York: Frederick.

Johnson, Simon, and Gary Loveman. 1995. *Starting over in Eastern Europe: Entrepreneurship and Economic Renewal*. Cambridge: Harvard Business School Press.

Jomo Kwame Sundaram. 1990–1991. "Whither Malaysia's New Economic Policy?" *Pacific Affairs* 63(4):469–99.

Jones, Reece. 2009. "Agents of Exception: Border Security and the Marginalization of Muslims in India." *Environment and Planning D: Society and Space* 27(5): 879–897.

Karabel, Jerome. 1984. "Status Group Struggle, Organizational Interests, and the Limits of Institutional Autonomy." *Theory and Society* 13:1–40.

Kessler-Harris, Alice. 1982. *Out to Work: A History of Wage-Earning Women in the United States*. New York: Oxford University Press.

Kipp, Rita Smith. 1993. *Dissociated Identities: Ethnicity, Religion, and Class in an Indonesian Society*. Ann Arbor: University of Michigan.

Klein, Naomi. 2013. "How Science Is Telling Us All to Revolt." *New Statesman*, October 29. http://www.newstatesman.com/2013/10/science-says-revolt.

———. 2008. *The Shock Doctrine: The Rise of Disaster Capitalism*. New York: Macmillan/Picador.

Knauft, B. 2001. "Critically Modern: An Introduction." In *Critically Modern: Alternatives, Alterities, Anthropologies*. Edited by B. Knauft. Bloomington: University of Indiana Press.

Kompas. 1990. "Young Professionals of Jakarta: Millions in Salary of Hard Work." In *The Politics of the Middle-Class Indonesia*. Edited by R. Tanter and K. Young. Pp. 167–174. Glen Waverly, Australia: Aristoc Press Pty.

———. 1999. "Survei Kompas tentang Kelas Menengah Jakarta." In *Kelas Menengah Bukan Ratu Adil*. Edited by Hadijaya. Pp. 271–288. Yogyakarta, Indonesia: Pt. Tiara Wacana Yogya.

Kondo, D. 1997. *About Face: Performing Race in Fashion and Theater*. New York: Routledge.

Konner, Melvin. 1987. "Childbearing and Age." *New York Times Magazine*, December 27.

Kornai, János. 1992. *The Socialist System: The Political Economy of Communism*. Princeton: Princeton University Press.

Kovid, P. n.d. *Prem Patra* [*Love Letters*]. Varanasi, India.

Koźminski, Andrzej. 1992. *Po wielkim szoku* (After the great shock). Warsaw: Panstwowe Wydawnictwo Ekonomiczne.

———. 1993. *Catching Up?: Organizational and Management Change in the Ex-Socialist Bloc*. Albany: State University of New York Press.

Kracher, Jeanne. 2000. Interview conducted by Deborah Gould, February 15, in Chicago, IL. Interview housed in [Gould's] personal ACT UP archive.

Krieger, Nancy. 2008. "Proximal, Distal, and the Politics of Causation: What's Level Got to Do with It?" *American Journal of Public Health* 98, no. 2: 221–30.

Lefebvre, Henri. 1991. *The Production of Space*. Oxford: Blackwell.

Lev, D. S. 1990. "Intermediate Classes and Change in Indonesia: Some Initial Reflections." In *The Politics of Middle-Class Indonesia*. Edited by R. Tanter and K. Young. Pp. 25–43. Glen Waverly, Australia: Aristoc Press Pty.

Lévi-Strauss, C. 1966. *The Savage Mind*. Chicago: University of Chicago Press.

Lewin, Tamar. 1987. "Courts Acting to Force Care of the Unborn." *New York Times*, November 23, A1 and B10.

Liechty, M. 2003. *Suitably Modern: Making Middle-Class Culture in a New Consumer Society*. Princeton, NJ: Princeton University Press.

Linton, Ralph. 1936. *The Study of Man*. New York: D. Appleton-Century Co.

Lister, Ruth. 2004. *Poverty*. Cambridge, UK: Polity Press.

Lo Bue, E. 2011. *Wonders of Lo: The Artistic Heritage of Mustang.* Gaithersburg, MD: Marg Publications.

Luke, A. 1988. *Literacy, Textbooks and Ideology: Postwar Literacy Instruction and the Mythology of Dick and Jane.* London: Falmer.

———. 1996. "Genres of Power? Literacy Education and the Production of Capital." In *Literacy in Society (Applied Linguistics and Language Study).* Edited by R. Hasan and G. Williams. Boston, MA: Addison-Wesley.

Lumholtz, Carl. 1990. *New Trails in Mexico: An Account of One Year's Exploration in North-western Sonora, Mexico, and South-western Arizona, 1909–1910.* Tucson: University of Arizona Press.

Lutz, Catherine. 1986. "Emotion, Thought, and Estrangement: Emotion as a Cultural Category." *Cultural Anthropology* 1:287–309.

Lyman, Rick. 1998. "Mother of the Octuplets Goes Home to Recover." *New York Times,* December 31.

Malinowski, Bronislaw. 1948. "Magic, Science, and Religion." Glencoe, IL: The Free Press.

Mamdani, Mahmood. 2001. *When Victims Become Killers: Colonialism, Nativism, and the Genocide in Rwanda.* Princeton, NJ: Princeton University Press.

Manohar. n.d. *Love Letters.* New Delhi: New Light.

Marcus, George E., and Fred R. Myers. 1995. *The Traffic in Culture: Refiguring Art and Anthropology.* Berkeley: University of California Press.

Martin, Emily. 1987. *The Women in the Body: A Cultural Analysis of Reproduction.* Boston: Beacon.

———. 1994. *Flexible Bodies.* Boston: Beacon Press.

Martinez, Daniel E., Robin C. Reineke, Raquel Rubio-Goldsmith, Bruce Anderson, Gregory Hess, and Bruce O. Park. 2013. "A Continued Humanitarian Crisis at the Border: Deceased and Missing Migrants Recorded by the Pima County Office of the Medical Examiner, 1990–2012." Tucson: Binational Migration Institute, Department of Mexican American Studies, University of Arizona. http://bmi.arizona.edu/sites/default/files/border_deaths_final_web.pdf. Accessed April 19, 2015.

Martyn, Byron Curti. 1979. "Racism in the U.S.: A History of Anti-Miscegenation Legislation and Litigation." Ph.D diss., University of Southern California.

Maurer, William. 1999. "Forget Locke? From Proprietor to Risk-Bearer in New Logics of Finance." *Public Culture* 11(2): 47–67.

McDonald, Kevin. 1993. "Why Privatization Is Not Enough." *Harvard Business Review,* May–June, 49–60.

Mead, Margaret. 1928. *Coming of Age in Samoa: A Psychological Study of Primitive Youth for Western Civilization.* New York: William Morrow.

———. 1935. *Sex and Temperament in Three Primitive Societies.* New York: William Morrow.

Meyer, Robinson. 2014. "When the World Watches the World Cup, What Does That Look Like?" *Atlantic,* July 15. http://www.theatlantic.com/technology/archive/2014/07/when-the-world-watches-the-world-cup-what-does-it0-look-like/374461/2/, accessed October 15, 2014.

Middaugh, John. 1993. Letter to Kevin Cable, the Department of Energy, Nevada, from Alaska Governor Hickel's office, February 23.

Milgram, L.B. 2004. " 'Ukay-ukay' chic: Tales of fashion and trade in second-hand clothing in the Philippine cordillera." In *Old clothes, new looks: Second-hand fashion.* Edited by A. Palmer and H. Clark. Oxford: Berg.

Miller, Jonathan, and David Pelham. 1984. *The Facts of Life.* New York: Viking.

Miller, Peter, and Nikolas Rose. 1990. "Governing Economic Life." *Economy and Society* 19: 1–31.

Milne, R. Stephen, and Diane Mauzy. 1999. *Malaysian Politics under Mahathir.* London: Routledge.

Monkkonen, Eric H. 1988. *America Becomes Urban.* Berkeley and Los Angeles: University of California Press.

Montemurri, Patricia, Kathleen Gray, and Cecil Angel. 2005. "Detroit Tops Nation in Poverty Census." *Free Press,* August 31.

Moore, Elizabeth Anne. 2007. *Unmarketable: Brandalism, Copyfighting, Mocketing, and the Erosion of Integrity*. New York: The New Press.

Moore, Jason W. 2015. *Capitalism and the Web of Life: Ecology and the Accumulation of Capital*. London: Verso.

Moreno, Caroline. 2012. "Border Crossing Deaths More Common as Illegal Immigration Declines." *Huffington Post*, August 17, 2012. www.huffingtonpost.com/2012/08/17/border-crossing-deaths-illegal-immigration_n_1783912.html. Accessed April 19, 2015.

Morgan, Lewis Henry. 1996 [1851]. *League of the Iroquois*. (Introduction by William N. Fenton). Secaucus, NJ: Carol Publishing Book.

Morris, Alan. 1999. *Bleakness and light: Inner city transition in Hillbrow, Johannesburg*. Johannesburg: University of Witwatersrand Press.

Mosch, Theodore R. 1975. *The GI Bill: A Breakthrough in Educational and Social Policy in the United States*. Hicksville, NY: Exposition.

Mountcastle, Vernon B. 1980. *Medical Physiology*, 14th ed. London: Mosby.

Movsesian, A. J. 1993. *How to Write Love Letters and Love Poems*. Bombay: Jaico.

Mullings, Leith. 2005. "Interrogating Racism: Toward an Anti-Racist Anthropology." *Annual Review of Anthropology* 34: 667–93.

Myerhoff, Barbara G. 1974. *Peyote Hunt: The Sacred Journey of the Huichol Indians*. Ithaca, NY: Cornell University Press.

Najmabadi, Afsaneh. 1998. "Feminism in an Islamic Republic." In *Islam, Gender, and Social Change*. Edited by Yvonne Haddad and John Esposito. Pp. 59–84. New York: Oxford University Press.

Nair, Janaki. 2005. *The Promise of the Metropolis: Bangalore's Twentieth Century*. New Delhi: Oxford India Paperbacks.

Nalty, Bernard C., and Morris J. MacGregor, eds. 1981. *Blacks in the Military: Essential Documents*. Wilmington, Del.: Scholarly Resources.

Nash, Gary B., Julie Roy Jeffrey, John R. Howe, Allen F. Davis, Peter J. Frederick, and Allen M. Winkler. 1986. *The American People: Creating a Nation and a Society*. New York: Harper and Row.

Nestle, Joan. 1992. "The Femme Question." In *The Persistent Desire: A Femme-Butch Reader*, edited by Joan Nestle. Pp. 138–146. Boston: Alyson Publications.

Nevins, Joseph. 2005. "A Beating Worse Than Death: Imagining and Contesting Violence in the U.S.-Mexico Borderlands." *AmeriQuests* 2(1):1–25.

Newman, Katherine. 1999. *Falling from Grace: The Experience of Downward Mobility in the Age of Affluence*. Berkeley: University of California Press.

Noor, Farish A. 2010. "On the Permanent Hajj: The *Tablighi Jama'at* in South East Asia." *South East Asia Research* 18(4): 707–34.

Norris, K.L. 2003. "The life-cycle of clothing: Recycling and the efficacy of materiality in contemporary urban India." Unpublished PhD thesis, University College London.

Oetomo, Dede. 1991. "Patterns of Bisexuality in Indonesia." In *Bisexuality and HIV/AIDS: A Global Perspective*, edited by Rob Tielman, Manuel Carballo, and Aart Hendriks. Pp. 119–126. Buffalo, NY: Prometheus Books.

Offe, Claus. 1985. *Disorganized Capitalism*. Oxford: Oxford University Press.

Omi, Michael, and Howard Winant. 1994. *Racial Formation in the United States from the 1960s to the 1990s*, 2nd edition. New York: Routledge.

Ong, Aihwa. 1999. *Flexible Citizenship: The Cultural Logics of Transnationality*. Durham, NC: Duke University Press.

———. 2006. *Neoliberalism as Exception: Mutations in Citizenship and Sovereignty*. Durham, NC: Duke University Press.

Osman, Mohamed. 2010. "The Transnational Network of Hizbut Tahrir Indonesia." *South East Asia Research* 18(4): 735–55.

Oxfeld, Ellen. 1992. "Individualism, Holism and the Market Mentality." *Cultural Anthropology* 7(3): 267–300.

Pachirat, Timothy. 2013. *Every Twelve Seconds: Industrialized Slaughter and the Politics of Sight*. New Haven: Yale University Press.

Pakistan Newswire. 2001. "SITE appreciates." November 12.

Pandian, Anand. 2009. *Crooked Stalks: Cultivating Virtue in South Asia*. Durham, NC: Duke University Press.

Papanek, Hanna. 1982. "Purdah in Pakistan: Seclusion and Modern Occupations for Women." In *Separate Worlds*. Edited by Hanna Papanek and Gail Minault. Pp. 190–216. Columbus, MO: South Asia Books.

Pariser, Eli. 2012. *The Filter Bubble: How the New Personalized Web Is Changing What We Read and How We Think*. New York: Penguin Press.

Parker, Richard. 1986. "Masculinity, Femininity and Homosexuality: On the Anthropological Interpretation of Sexual Meanings in Brazil." In *The Many Faces of Homosexuality: Anthropological Approaches to Homosexual Behavior*, edited by Evelyn Blackwood. Pp. 155–163. New York: Harrington Park Press.

Parry, Jonathan. 2013. "Company and Contract Labour in a Central Indian Steel Plant." *Economy & Society* 42 (3): 348–374.

Patten, Mary. 1998. "The Thrill Is Gone: An ACT UP Post-Mortem (Confessions of a Former AIDS Activist)." Pp. 385–406 in *The Passionate Camera*, edited by Deborah Bright. New York: Routledge.

Pepinsky, Thomas. n.d. "Islamic Finance in Multicultural Indonesia." https://cources.cit .cornell.edu/tp253/docs/islamic_banking.pdf (accessed May 21, 2012).

Petchesky, Rosalind. 1987. "Fetal Images: The Power of Visual Culture in the Politics of Reproduction." *Feminist Studies* 13(2): 263–92.

Pinnock, Barbara. 2000. *Skyline*. Johannesburg: David Philip Publishers.

Pitluck, Aaron. 2008. "Moral Behavior in Stock Markets: Islamic Finance and Socially Responsible Investment." In *Economics and Morality: Anthropological Approaches,* edited by Katherine Brown and Lynne Milgran, 233–55. Lanham, MD: AltaMira Press.

Poole, John Fitz Porter. 1996. "The Procreative and Ritual Constitution of Female, Male and Other: Androgynous Beings in the Cultural Imagination of the Bimin-Kuskumin of Papua New-Guinea." In *Gender Reversals and Gender Cultures: Anthropological and Historical Perspectives*, edited by Sabrina Ramet. Pp. 197–218. London: Routledge.

Postwar Jobs for Veterans. 1945. *Annals of the American Academy of Political and Social Science* 238 (March).

Priyono, A. E. 1999. "Konsumtivisme Kelas Menengah Perkotaan." In *Kelas Menenga Bukan Ratu Adil*. Edited by Hadijaya. Pp. 223–228. Yogyakarta, Indonesia: P.T. Tiara Wacana Yogya.

Quiroga, Selina Szkupinski. 2007. "Blood is Thicker than Water: Policing Donor Insemination and the Reproduction of Whiteness." *Hypatia* 22(2): 143–161.

Ramet, Sabrina Petra, ed. 1996. *Gender Reversals and Gender Cultures: Anthropological and Historical Perspectives*. London: Routledge.

Reineke, Robin. 2013. "Arizona: Naming the Dead from the Desert." *BBC News Magazine*, January 16. www.bbc.co.uk/news /magazine-21029783. Accessed July 7, 2013.

Roberts, Dorothy. 1997. *Killing the Black Body: Race, Reproduction, and the Meaning of Liberty*. New York: Pantheon Books.

Robinson, Kim Stanley. 2012. *2312*. New York: Orbit/Hachette.

Robison, R., and D. S. G. Goodman. 1996. "The New Rich in Asia: Economic Development, Social Status, and Political Consciousness." In *The New Rich in Asia: Mobile Phones, McDonalds, and Middle-Class Revolution*. Edited by R. Robison and D. S. G. Goodman. Pp. 1–18. London: Routledge.

Romo, Frank, and Michael Schwartz. 1993. "The Coming of Post-Industrial Society Revisited: Manufacturing and the Prospects for a Service-based Economy." In *Explorations in Economic Sociology*, edited by Richard Swedburg, pp. 335–373. New York: Russell Sage Foundation.

Roscoe, Will. 1991. *The Zuni Man-Woman*. Albuquerque: University of New Mexico Press.

Rosly, Saiful Azhar. 2005. *Critical Issues on Islamic Banking and Financial Markets: Islamic Economics, Banking and Finance,*

Investments, Takaful and Financial Planning. Kuala Lumpur: Dinamas Publishing.

Ross, Ellen, and Rayna Rapp. 1981. "Sex and Society: A Research Note from Social History and Anthropology." *Comparative Study of Society and History* 23:51–72.

Rubio-Goldsmith, Raquel, M. Melissa McCormick, Daniel Martinez, and Inez Magdalena Duarte. 2006. *The "Funnel Effect" and Recovered Bodies of Unauthorized Migrants Processed by the Pima County Office of the Medical Examiner, 1990–2005.* Report, October. Tucson: Binational Migration Institute, Mexican American Studies and Research Center, University of Arizona. www.derechoshumanosaz.net /images/pdfs/bmi%20report.pdf. Accessed March 30, 2015.

Sadiq, Jahabar. 2012. "Disquiet over BNM Request to Fund US$1b Mega Islamic Bank." *Malaysian Insider.* June 23. http:// www.themalaysianinsider.com/malaysia/ article/disquiet-over-bnm-request-to-fund-us1b-mega-islamic-bank (accessed June 28, 2012).

Samuel, G. 1993. *Civilized Shamans: Buddhism in Tibetan Societies.* Kathmandu: Mandala Book Point.

———2006. "Tibetan Medicine and Biomedicine: Epistemological Conflicts, Practical Solutions." *Asian Medicine: Tradition and Modernity* 2(1): 72–85.

Saxton, Alexander. 1971. *The Indispensable Enemy.* Berkeley and Los Angeles: University of California Press.

Schatten, Gerald and Helen Schatten. 1984. "The Energetic Egg." *Medical World News* 23, January 23: 51–53.

Schieffelin, B. B. 2000. "Introducing Kaluli Literacy: A Chronology of Influences." In *Regimes of Language: Ideologies, Polities, and Identities.* Edited by P. V. Kroskrity. Pps. 293–327. Santa Fe, NM: School of American Research.

Schoenberger, Erica. 1997. *The Cultural Crisis of the Firm.* London: Blackwell.

Scott, James C. 1985. *Weapons of the Weak: Everyday Forms of Peasant Resistance.* New Haven: Yale University Press.

———1998. *Seeing Like a State: How Certain Schemes to Improve the Human Condition Have Failed.* New Haven, CT: Yale University Press.

Shapiro, Bennett M. 1987. "The Existential Decision of a Sperm." *Cell* 49(3): 293–94.

Shamsul, Amri Baharuddin. 2001. "A History of an Identity, an Identity of a History: The Idea and Practice of 'Malayness' in Malaysia Reconsidered." *Journal of Southeast Asian Studies* 32(3): 355–66.

Shapiro, Joseph. 1994. *No Pity: People with Disabilities Forging a New Civil Rights Movement.* New York: Three Rivers Press.

Sharma, Sanjay. 2013. "Black Twitter? Racial Hashtags, Networks, and Contagion." *New Formations: A Journal of Culture/Theory/ Politics* 78(1):48–64.

Siegel, J. T. 1998. *A New Criminal Type in Jakarta: Counter-Revolution Today.* Durham, NC: Duke University Press.

Sieple, Frank. 1999. Interview conducted by Deborah Gould, July 13, in San Francisco, CA. Interview housed in [Gould's] personal ACT UP archive.

Silberman, Charles. 1985. *A Certain People: American Jews and Their Lives Today.* New York: Summit.

Silliman, Jael, Marlene Gerber Fried, Loretta Ross, and Elena R. Gutierrez. 2004. *Undivided Rights: Women of Color Organize for Reproductive Justice.* Boston, MA: South End Press.

Skinner, B.F. 1938. *Behavior of Organisms: An Experimental Analysis.* New York: D. Appleton-Century Co.

———. 1953. *Science and Human Behavior.* New York: Macmillan.

Sklare, Marshall. 1971. *America's Jews.* New York: Random House.

Smedley, Audrey. 1993. *Race in North America: Origins and Evolution of a Worldview.* Boulder, CO: Westview Press.

Smith, Aaron. 2013. "Smartphone Ownership 2013." Pew Research Center. June 5. http://www.pewinternet.org/2013/06/05/ smartphone-ownership-2013/ (accessed 10/15/2014).

Smith, Andrea. 2005. "Beyond Pro-Choice Versus Pro-Life: Women of Color and Reproductive Justice." *NWSA Journal* (Spring) 17(1):119–140.

Snellgrove, D. 1981. *Himalayan Pilgrimage.* Boston: Shambhala.

Solomon, Eldra Pearl. 1983. *Human Anatomy and Physiology*. New York: CBS College Publishing.

Sontag, Susan. 2003. *Regarding the Pain of Others*. New York: Picador.

Sowell, Thomas. 1981. *Ethnic America: A History*. New York: Basic.

Spar, Debora. 2009. "Taming the Wild West of Assisted Reproduction." Columbia Spectator Online Edition. February 26. Electronic document, http://www .columbiaspectator.com/2009/02/26 /taming-wild-west-assisted-reproduction, accessed February 27, 2009.

Spivak, Gayatri Chakravorty. 1988. "Can the Subaltern Speak?" In *Marxism and the Interpretation of Culture*. Edited by Cary Nelson and Lawrence Grossberg. Pp. 271–313. Urbana: University of Illinois Press.

Steinberg, Stephen. 1989. *The Ethnic Myth: Race, Ethnicity, and Class in America*. 2nd edition. Boston: Beacon.

Stelter, Brian. 2009. "Jon & Kate 'Are a Business at This Point,' Magazine Editor Says" May 27, 2009. Electronic document, http://mediadecoder.blogs.nytimes.com/ 2009/05/27/jon-kate-are-a-business-at -this-point-magazine-editor-says/?scp= 2&sq=Jon%20and%20Kate%20 Gosselin&st=cse, accessed June 14, 2009.

Stewart, Dianne M. 2005. *Three Eyes for the Journey: African Dimensions of the Jamaican Religious Experience*. New York: Oxford University Press.

Stewart, Kathleen. 2008. "Weak Theory in an Unfinished World." *Journal of Folklore Research* 45(1): 71–82.

Stites, Richard. 1989. *Revolutionary Dreams: Utopian Vision and Experimental Life in the Russian Revolution*. Oxford: Oxford University Press.

Straus, Scott. 2006. *The Order of Genocide: Race, Power, and War in Rwanda*. Ithaca, NY: Cornell University Press.

Street, B. V. (ed.) 2001. *Literacy and Development: Ethnographic Perspectives*. New York: Routledge.

Sunstein, Cass. 2009. *Republic.com 2.0*. Princeton: Princeton University Press.

Synott, Marcia Graham. 1986. "Anti-Semitism and American Universities: Did Quotas Follow the Jews?" In *Anti-Semitism in American History*, edited by David A. Gerber, 233–274.

Sztompka, Piotr. 1992. "Dilemmas of the Great Transition." *Sisyphus: Social Studies* 2(8):9–28.

Tadiar, Neferti Xina M. 2009. *Things Fall Away: Philippine Historical Experience and the Makings of Globalization*. Durham, N.C.: Duke University Press.

Tadikamalla, Pandu R., Dagmar Glückanford, and Stephen L. Starling. 1994. "Total Quality Management in Czechoslovakia." In *Managing in Emerging Market Economies: Cases from the Czech and Slovak Republics*, edited by Daniel Fogel, 209–24. Boulder: Westview.

Takaki, Ronald. 1989. *Strangers from a Different Shore*. Boston: Little, Brown.

Tett, Gillian. 2009. *Fool's Gold: The Inside Story of J.P Morgan and How Wall Street Corrupted Its Bold Dream and Created a Financial Catastrophe*. New York: Free Press.

Thornton, S. 1996. *Club Cultures: Music Media, and Subcultural Capital*. Hanover, NH: Wesleyan University Press.

Turkle, Sherry. 1995. *Life on the Screen: Identity in the Age of the Internet*. New York: Simon & Schuster.

Turner, Edith. 1989. "From Shamans to Healers: The Survival of an Iñupiat Eskimo Skill." *Anthropologica* 31(1):3–24.

———1996. *The Hands Feel It: Healing and Spirit Presence among a Northern Alaskan People*. Dekalb: Northern Illinois University Press.

Turner, Victor. 1969. *The Ritual Process: Structure and Anti-Structure*. Chicago: Aldine.

Tuzroyluk, Rex. 1992. The Nuclear Waste Dump at Chariot. Report to the Tikigaq Native Corporation, Point Hope, Alaska.

U.S. Bureau of the Census. 1930. *Fifteenth Census of the United States*. Vol. 2. Washington, D.C.: U.S. Government Printing Office.

———. 1940. *Sixteenth Census of the United States*. Vol. 2. Washington, D.C.: U.S. Government Printing Office.

U.S. Government. 2002. Electronic document, http://www.whitehouse.gov/news /releases/2001/11/20011117. Accessed January 10.

Udovitch, Abraham L. 1970. *Partnership and Profit in Medieval Islam.* Princeton, NJ: Princeton University Press.

United Nations. 1996. *1995 International Trade Statistics Yearbook. Vol. 2: Trade by commodity.* New York: United Nations.

———. 2003. *2001 International Trade Statistics Yearbook. Vol. 2: Trade by country.* New York: United Nations.

Ury, William, ed. 2002. *Must We Fight? From the Battlefield to the Schoolyard—A New Perspective on Violent Conflict and Its Prevention.* San Francisco: Jossey-Bass.

Van Atta, Don. 1986. "Why Is There No Taylorism in the Soviet Union?" *Comparative Politics* 18(3): 327–37.

Van de Port, Mattijs. 1998. *Gypsies, Wars, and Other Instances of the Wild: Civilization and Its Discontents in a Serbian Town.* Amsterdam: Amsterdam University Press.

Van Gennep, Arnold. (1908) 1960. *The Rites of Passage.* Reprint, Chicago: University of Chicago Press.

Vander, Arthur J., James H. Sherman, and Dorothy S. Luciano. 1980. *Human Physiology: The Mechanisms of Body Function*, 3rd ed. New York: McGraw Hill.

———. 1985. *Human Physiology: The Mechanisms of Body Function*, 4th ed. New York: McGraw Hill.

Vega, Tanzina. 2014. "Shooting Spurs Hashtag Effort on Stereotypes." *New York Times*, August 12.

Venardos, Angelo M. 2006. *Islamic Banking and Finance in South-East Asia: Its Development and Future.* Hackensack, NJ: World Scientific.

Verdery, Katherine. 1996. *What Was Socialism and What Comes Next?* Princeton: Princeton University Press.

Vyse, Stuart. 1997. *The Psychology of Superstition.* Oxford: Oxford University Press.

Waldman, Amy and David Rohde. 2005. "Fearing a Sea That Once Sustained, Then Killed." *New York Times,* January 5.

Walker, Olive. 1970. "The Windsor Hills School Story." *Integrated Education: Race and Schools* 8(3):4–9.

Wallach, J. 2008. *Modern Noise, Fluid Genres: Popular Music in Indonesia, 1997–2001.* Madison: University of Wisconsin Press.

Warde, Ibrahim. 2010. *Islamic Finance in the Global Economy.* Edinburgh: Edinburgh University Press.

Warner, Michael. 1993. "Introduction." In *Fear of a Queer Planet: Queer Politics and Social Theory.* Edited by Michael Warner, pp. vii–xxxi. Minneapolis: University of Minnesota Press.

Warsaw Voice. 2002. "Clothing—end of the lumpecs." June 14.

Washington Post. 2002. "The dumping ground." April 21.

Wasik, Bill. 2009. *And Then There's This: How Stories Live and Die in Viral Culture.* New York: Penguin.

Wassarman, Paul M. 1987. "The Biology and Chemistry of Fertilization." *Science* 235(4788):553–60.

———. 1988. "Fertilization in Mammals." *Scientific American* 259(6):78–84.

Weller, Robert P. 1994. *Resistance, Chaos and Control in China: Taiping Rebels, Taiwanese Ghosts and Tiananmen.* Seattle: University of Washington Press.

Werneck, Jurema. 2007. "Of Ialodês and Feminists: Reflections on Black Women's Political Action in Latin America and the Caribbean. *Cultural Dynamics* 19: 103.

Weston, Kath. 1993. "Lesbian/Gay Studies in the House of Anthropology." *Annual Review of Anthropology* 22:239–367.

Wiegman, Robyn. 2001. "Object Lessons: Men, Masculinity, and the Sign *Women.*" *Signs: Journal of Women in Culture and Society* 26(2): 79–105.

Wilchins, Riki Anne. 1997. *Read My Lips: Sexual Subversion and the End of Gender.* Ithaca, NY: Firebrand Books.

Willenz, June A. 1983. *Women Veterans: America's Forgotten Heroines.* New York: Continuum.

Williams, Raymond. 1977. *Marxism and Literature.* Oxford: Oxford University Press.

Wockner, Rex. 1988. "AIDS Activists Go Local after FDA." P. 13 in *Outlines.* Chicago. December.

Wojcicki, Janet Maia. 2002. " 'She drank his money': Survival sex and the problem of violence in taverns in Gauteng Province, South Africa." *Medical Anthropology Quarterly* 16: 267–93.

Wolf, Eric R. 1956. "San José: Subcultures of a Traditional Coffee Municipality." In *The People of Puerto Rico: A Study in Social Anthropology*, by Julian H. Steward et al., pt. 7, 171–264. Urbana: University of Illinois Press.

———. 1982. *Europe and the People without History*. Berkeley: University of California Press, 6–7.

———. 1990. "Distinguished Lecture: Facing Power—Old Insights, New Questions." *American Anthropologist* 92: 586–96.

———. 1997. *Europe and the People without History*. Berkeley: University of California Press.

———. 1999. *Envisioning Power: Ideologies of Dominance and Crisis*. Berkeley: University of California Press.

———. 2001. "Ethnicity and Nationhood." In *Pathways of Power: Building an Anthropology of the Modern World*. Berkeley: University of California Press.

Wong, Dorothy C. 2004. *Chinese Steles: Pre-Buddhist and Buddhist Use of a Symbolic Form*. Honolulu: University of Hawaii Press.

Woodward, James. 1972. "Implications for Sociolinguistic Research among the Dead." *Sign Language Studies* 1 (1): 1–7.

Wynn, Neil A. 1976. *The Afro-American and the Second World War*. London: Elek.

Yanagisako, Sylvia, and Carol Delaney. 1995. "Naturalizing Power." In *Naturalizing Power: Essays in Feminist Cultural Analysis*, edited by Sylvia Yanagisako and Carol Delaney. Pp. 1–22. New York: Routledge.

Yang, Mayfair Mei-hui. 2000. "Putting Global Capitalism in Its Place." *Current Anthropology* 41(4): 477–509.

Credits

Lila Abu-Lughod: "Do Muslim Women Really Need Saving? Anthropological Reflections on Cultural Relativism and Its Others," *American Anthropologist* Vol. 104, No. 3, Sep. 2002, pp. 783-790 (excerpted). Reproduced by permission of the American Anthropological Association. Not for sale or further reproduction.

Laura Ahearn: "Literacy, Power and Agency: Love Letters and Development in Nepal," *Language and Education* 18(4):305-316. Reprinted by permission of the publisher (Taylor & Francis Ltd, http://www.tandfonline .com)

Bobby Benedicto: Excerpts from *Under Bright Lights: Gay Manila and the Global Scene* (Minneapolis: University of Minnesota Press, 2014). Difference Incorporated series, edited by Roderick A. Ferguson and Grace Kyungwon Hong. Copyright © 2014 by the Regents of the University of Minnesota. Reprinted with permission.

Lucas Bessire: Excerpts from *Behold the Black Caiman: A Chronicle of Ayoreo Life* (Chicago: University of Chicago Press, 2014). Copyright © 2014 by Lucas Bessire. Reprinted by permission of University of Chicago Press.

Evelyn Blackwood: "*Tombois* in West Sumatra: Constructing Masculinity and Erotic Desire," *Cultural Anthropology* Vol. 13, No. 4, Nov. 1998, pp. 491-521 (excerpted). Reproduced by permission of the American Anthropological Association. Not for sale or further reproduction.

Laura Bohannan: "Shakespeare in the Bush," by Laura Bohannan. From *Natural History* Volume 75, September 1966, copyright © Natural History Magazine, Inc. 1966. Reprinted with permission.

Yarimar Bonilla and Jonathan Rosa: "#Ferguson: Digital Protest, Hashtag Ethnography, and the Racial Politics of Social Media in the United States," *American Ethnologist* 42(1):4-17. © 2015 by the American Anthropological Association. Reprinted by permission of John Wiley & Sons, Inc.

Philippe Bourgois: "From Jíbaro to Crack Dealer: Confronting the Restructuring of Capitalism in El Barrio", in *Articulating Hidden Histories: Exploring the Influence of Eric R. Wolf* (Berkeley: University of California Press, 1995), edited by Jane Schneider and Rayna Rapp. © 1995 by The Regents of the University of California. Reprinted with permission.

Melissa Checker: Excerpts from *Polluted Promises: Environmental Racism and the Search for Justice in a Southern Town*. Copyright © 2005 by New York University. Reprinted by permission of NYU Press.

Julie Y. Chu: "The Attraction of Numbers: Accounting for Ritual Expenditures in Fuzhou, China." *Anthropological Theory* Vol. 10, Issue 1-2, pp. 132-142. Copyright © 2010 SAGE Publications. Reprinted by permission of SAGE Publications. Ltd.

Aimee Cox: "The *BlackLight* Project and Public Scholarship: Young Black Women Perform Against and Through the Boundaries of Anthropology," *Transforming Anthropology*, Vol 17, No.1, April 2009, pp. 51-64 (excerpted). Reproduced by permission of the American Anthropological Association. Not for sale or further reproduction.

Sienna Craig: Excerpts from *Healing Elements: Efficacy and the Social Ecologies of Tibetan*

Subject Index

The selections in this reader can be used to supplement discussion of many subjects that may be covered in an introductory course.

Index

Page numbers in **boldface** refer to key concepts.

A

Abe (Aliyah Center director), 81
Abu-Lughod, Lila, 43, 49–57, 381
Afghanistan, 49–51, 52–57
Agamben, Giorgio, 10–11
agency, 54, 106, 108–9, 112, **114**, 132, 149, 228, 273, **287**, 303–4, 311, 394, 396
Agus (tomboi), 173, 174, 175, 177–78
Ahearn, Laura, 105–12
Ahmaogak, George, 28
Ahmed, Leila, 52
Aiken, Johnny, 24, 26
Aji (Indonesian designer), 378–80, 385, 386
Alexander II, Czar of Russia, 74
Alger, Horatio, 117, 121
Allen, Woody, 183
Amado, Jorge, 129
Amos (whaling captain), 20
Andaman Islands, 290
Anderson, Benedict, 145
Angola, 299
Anna (Magda A's mother), 352–54
Anthropocene, **6**, 230–35
anthropologist's toolkit, 3, 4, **70**
anthropology, **3**
  critical medical, **348**, 350
  cultural, **3–4**, 5
  engaged, **6**, 19, 31, 390
Appadurai, Arjun, 148
Areguede, 68
Argentina, 34, 295
Aristotle, 286
art, 42, 259, 260, 367, **373**, 374–76, 383–85, 387–88

Atkins, Tyler, 140
Austin, Jim, 320
Australia, 254, 290
Aziz, Zeti Akhtar, 331

B

Bahadur, Bir, 106–7, 110
Bahadur, Vajra, 110–11
Balcerowicz, Leszek, 265
Baltz, Jay M., 184*n*
bands, 58, 59, 62–64, 67, 68, **286**
Basha (Jewish immigrant), 72–75, 77, 81
Beauharnais, Josephine de, 110
Belgium, 150, 152, 153
Belgium-Luxembourg, 252
Benedicto, Bobby, 191–201
Bergerac, Cyrano de, 110
Bernard (Filipino gay man), 199
Bessire, Lucas, 43, 58–69
Bhuttan, 92
Bin Laden, Osama, 51
biomedicine, 86, **349**
Bista, Gyatso, 85–92
Bista, Tenzin, 85–89, 92–93
Blackwood, Evelyn, 168, 169–79, 190
Blair, Cherie, 50
Bochy, Bruce, 322
Boggs, Wade, 320, 325
Bohannan, Laura, 94, 95–104
Bolivia, 58, 59–61, 62, 63–64, 66
Bonilla, Yarimar, 116, 133–44
Bosco, Juan, 11
Bosnia, 50
Bourdieu, Pierre, 283–84
Bourgois, Philippe, 236, 238–49
Boutros-Ghali, Boutros, 24, 25, 31
Bowerman, Dr., 28
Braun, Eva, 107, 110

Brazil, 32, 33–34, 35, 38, 65, 116, 127, 128–33
Bright, J. S., 110
Brodkin Sacks, Karen, 116–26
Brooks, Mrs., 128
Brown, Michael, 116, 133, 134–35, 136, 138, 139–40, 141, 142
Bujang (tomboi), 173–74, 175
Bullard, Robert, 306
Burnett, Sean, 322
Burundi, 153
Bush, George H. W., 206
Bush, George W., 51
Bush, Laura, 50, 51, 52, 56
Butler, Judith, 17
Butler, Kim, 131

C

California, 67, 70, 72–82, 222, 224
Cameroon, 149
Canada, 44, 146, 158–66
Carl (Filipino gay man), 197
Carter, Kevin, 18
Casorte (Scheper-Hughes's friend), 33
Charis, Benjamin F., Jr., 311
Checker, Melissa, 287, 303–14
Chen Qiang, 339, 340, 341–43, 344, 345–46
chiefdoms, **286**
China, 84, 86, 91, 92, 119, 146, 152, 220, 260, 261, 275–80, 328, 336, 338, 339, 340, 341
Christos (Magda A's boyfriend), 356, 358
Chu, Julie, 263, 275–80
Chukwu, Iyke, 221
Chukwu, Nkem, 221

globalization, **3**, 4, 5–7, 43, 84, 267, 272, 287
  art and, 374
  economic, 250, 255, 259–60, 262–63, 275, 280–81
  fieldwork and, 24, 30–31
  kinship and, 213, 230
  religion and, 316
  sexuality and, 190–92
  uneven development and, 237
Gmelch, George, 317–25
Goldstein, Melvyn, 213, 214–20
Gonzalez, Luis, 321
Goody, Jack, 111
Gorer, Geoffrey, 289
Gosselin, Jon and Kate, 227
Gotay, Julio, 320
Gould, Deborah, 191, 202–12
grammar, **94**
Gramsci, Antonio, 114
Gran Chaco, 59–61, 62, 63, 64, 66, 67, 69
Grant, Madison, 118–19
Grant, Oscar, 134
Great Britain, 51, 64, 67, 86, 92, 93, 252
  see also England
Greece, 116
Grégoire (Rwandan boy), 150, 151, 152, 156
Grossini, Dennis, 318, 320
Guatemala, 34, 50
Guest, Kenneth J., 337–47

H
Habyarimana, Juvénal, 154
Haiti, 147, 150, 155–56
Hamid (Indonesian designer), 382–85, 386
Hansen, Karen, 237, 250–57
Haraway, Donna, 213, 230–35
Harding, Rachel, 130
Hargrove, Mike, 320
Harrison, Faye, 132
Hartman, J. F., 188
Harvey, David, 188
Harvey, David (geographer), 262
health, 189, **348**, 349, 350
  Inupiat and, 19–31
  racism and, 304–15
  Rwanda and, 147–58

Tibetan traditional medicine and, 83–93
  see also disease; illness
hegemony, **114**, 169, 179, 240, 303
Henderson, Ricky, 322
Henry VIII, King of England, 110
Hitler, Adolf, 107, 110
Holland, Al, 322
Holmes, Scott, 23
Honduras, 34
Hong Kong, 252
Howe, Art, 323

I
identity entrepreneurs, **146**
illness, 21, 89, 96, 147, 156, **348**, 349, 350, 351, 360, 361
  see also disease; health
imagined community, **145**
India, 32, 34, 35–36, 38, 53, 85, 91, 92, 93, 145, 146, 220, 254–55, 261, 312, 349–50, 361–72
Indonesia, 169–79, 253, 291, 336, 375–86
intersectionality, **236**
interviews, **70**, 79, 162, 394
Iran, 54, 332
Iraq, 145, 146
Ireland, 50, 116
Ishi (Yahi tribesman), 67
Italy, 38, 116, 299

J
Jackson, David, 313
James, William, 288
Japan, 92, 146, 252, 254, 332
J. D. (Audra Simpson's friend), 164, 165
Joanna (Edith Turner's landlady), 20
Jolie, Angelina, 224, 227
Jones, Shanequa, 305
Jordan, 252
Julio (drug dealer), 241, 242, 243, 245–46, 247–48

K
Kaleak, Jesse, 24, 26
Kee, Bob, 8–9
Kenya, 252, 299
key informants, 19, **71**, 260
Kigali, 154, 155
Killeen, Joanne, 224

King, Martin Luther, Jr., 305, 314
King, Rodney, 135
kinship, 170–71, **213**, 214–35
  ethnicity and, 145
  globalization and, 213, 230
kinship analysis, **70**
Kirschman, Gloria, 243, 245
Knauft, Bruce, 92
Koonuk, Ray, 24, 26, 28
Korea, 34
Kovid, Prakash, 109
Kracher, Jeanne, 210
Krieger, Nancy, 156
Kuwait, 336

L
Lackey, John, 318–19
Lane, Barbara, 22, 28
Lane, Jacob, 28
language, 45, 55, 56, 57, 74, 85, **94**, 95–112, 145, 152, 168, 180, 182, 228
  deaf people and, 361–72
  ethnicity and, 145, 152
  gender stereotypes and, 168, 180, 182, 186
  power and, 242
  religion and, 338–39
  sexuality and, 191
LaRosa, Mark, 322
Lefebrre, Henri, 371
Le Marcis, Frédéric, 350–60
Lenin, V. I., 268
Lesotho, 253, 352, 354
Lester, Jon, 318–19
Lethata, Todd, 350–60
Lévi Strauss, Claude, 375, 377, 380
Leyland, Jim, 323
Libya, 336
Lieberman, Carole, 225
life chances, **236**, 237, 275, 304, 309, 349, 361
Linton, Professor, 44, 46
Lin Zezu, 346
Littman, Lynne, 80
Lodge, Henry Cabot, 118
Lopez, Jennifer, 224
Lowell, Mike, 320
Lumholtz, Carl, 8
Lundquist, David, 27
Luvaas, Brent, 373–74, 375–86
Luzon, 200, 254

Tibet, 70, 89, 215, 217–18, 219
Tié (Ayorco Indian), 59, 60, 62
time-space compression, **5, 259**
Torre, Joe, 321
tribes, 44, 152, 161–63, 164, 261,
    286, 289, 291
Tristan (Filipino gay man), 197
Trobriand Islanders, 318, 321, 324
Tsing, Anna, 234
Turkey, 54
Turner, Edith, 6, 19–31
Turner, Victor, 72, 337
Tuzroyluk, Piquk, 22, 28, 30
Tuzroyluk, Rex, 21, 22, 23–24,
    28, 31
Tuzroyluk, Tuzzy, 22

U
Uganda, 252
uneven development, **5, 237**, 259,
    260, 304
United Arab Emirates, 336
United States, 6, 37–38, 40, 67,
    70, 72–82, 86, 236, 238–49,
    250, 252, 263–64, 272, 273,
    288, 299, 316, 337–47
    Chinese immigrants in, 275–76,
        277, 280, 316, 337–47
    class in, 236, 238–49

environmental racism in,
    304–14
European immigrants in, 72,
    74, 75, 116–22, 125
financial collapse in, 281–85
Mexican immigrants in, 7–18,
    238, 246, 248
Native Americans in, 146,
    158–66
other cultures as viewed in, 43,
    49–57
racism in, 115–22, 133–43
sexuality and gender identity
    in, 169, 172, 174, 178, 179,
    190, 191, 202–13, 221–30

V
values, 40, **42**, 56, 79, 91, 95, 112,
    113, 114, 145, 169, 220, 221,
    237, 268, 303, 332, 336, 348,
    349, 359, 374
van Gennep, Arnold, 337
Vietnam, 336
Virchow, Rudolf, 350
Vyse, Stuart, 324

W
Wagner, Honus, 323–24
Walker, Larry, 323

Ward, Turner, 322
Wassarman, Paul, 185–87
Waterhouse, Olivia, 14, 16
Wells, Mike, 8, 9
Wendell, Turk, 320, 322–23
Werneck, Jurema, 129–30
Werner, Brad, 233
Western Europe, 40
West Papua, 65
White, Luise, 34
Willie (drug dealer), 247–48
Wilson, Darren, 139, 142–43
Wilson, Woodrow, 118
Wojcicki, Janet Maia, 357
Wolf, Eric, 66, 113, 155
Wolf, Eric R., 238
Woodward, James, 368

Y
Yoteuoi (former *daijnal*
    "shaman"), 61–62
Yugoslavia, 145
Yul (Agus's lover), 173, 174, 177

Z
Zahra, 362–63, 364, 370
Zaire, 154
Zambia, 250–57
Zimmerman, George, 139, 141